THE
Readers Digest
READER

THE
Readers Digest
READER

SELECTED BY

Theodore Roosevelt

AND THE STAFF OF THE

Reader's Digest

Doubleday, Doran & Company, Inc.

NEW YORK   1940

PRINTED AT THE *Country Life Press*, GARDEN CITY, N. Y., U. S. A.

Contents

v

CONTENTS

CONTENTS

Introduction

By

THEODORE ROOSEVELT

IN OUR ATTIC, neatly arranged in a wooden box, are the back numbers of The Reader's Digest for a number of years.

The other day I went to the attic to look for a fishing rod. I saw the box and remembered I had wanted to look up some articles in the Digest that bore on a speech I was making. I sat down on the floor and went to work. In a short time I found that instead of merely reading the articles on my subject I was browsing at random. Before I knew it a couple of hours had passed and the light from the skylight was too dim to read more.

Probably many others have had a similar pleasure in resurrecting copies of The Reader's Digest from the shelves and watching their contents come alive again; but I am sure that some readers are too likely to go merrily on from month to month, beguiled by the contemporary and missing this other richness of enjoyment.

Enjoyment is the keynote, for what stands out in my mind as I think back over the experience is the fun I had. Another evening I sat reading back copies for hours. Every time I finished an article which was off my main course, and which I shouldn't then have taken time to read, I thought that I would read only one other—well, at least only one and the short item that followed it. Then another subject piqued my interest and lured me on.

This bothered my hard-headed Dutch common sense. I felt that I was squandering time. To break the spell I dipped into an issue ten years back. But here the interest was even greater. A forgotten world came into being—not reminiscently but with touches of unmistakable reality. I was astounded to find how much of the past decade I had actually forgotten and how much more I remembered only vaguely. Yesterday's heroes and manners, changing social complexions, penetrating vignettes that tell the story of art, of politics, of science, of business—to find these things is to have pass before one's eyes the cavalcade of American life. And as you refresh your memory you improve your present perspective. The current scene gains new significance.

If there is pleasure in rediscovering events, there is a double pleasure in re-examining ideas. It was not merely that my memory was refreshed as I browsed in these back copies of the Digest. I was myself renewed by the variety of exciting points of view I met. I understood what Justice Holmes had in mind when he pointed out that the life of the mind can be genuinely adventurous. I found ideas that were practical, and I found timeless guides for daily living. I found dreams that had been made true by effort, prophecies that were sound and penetrating, convictions that had been put to work. I had a new determination about my own life—a determination that had come from the stimulus of example.

I am sure that from now on I will be better able to enjoy not only the current issues of The Reader's Digest but also current life—because I have formed the habit of turning back to the treasure that lies in earlier issues.

THE
Readers Digest
READER

How to Keep Young Mentally

Condensed extracts from The American Magazine

MARY B. MULLETT

Alexander Graham Bell gives his rule for self-education, which, he says, is a life-long process. It applies to everyone and is the mind's "Fountain of Youth."

ALEXANDER GRAHAM BELL, the famous scientist and inventor, will be seventy-five years old in March. Yet an intimate acquaintance said, "The most remarkable thing about Doctor Bell is that he is younger, in mind, than most men of half his age. Mentally, he seems to have discovered a Fountain of Youth, which keeps him perennially alert and vigorous."

I repeated to a very able and highly educated man Doctor Bell's ideas on how to study and to learn. This man said with emphasis:

"If anyone would follow that plan consistently, he would learn more than he would get through any college education. It is the best rule for everybody, at any age, and in any walk of life, that I have ever heard."

"The education of the mind," said Doctor Bell, "is, after all, not a mere question of remembering facts which someone else gives us. The mind should conduct its own education to a larger extent. And it cannot do this unless it thinks for itself. A mind that does not reason is comparatively useless.

"I have given the subject of self-education a great deal of thought and have evolved what you might call a 'Rule of Three' in regard to it. The rule is simply this: 'Observe! Remember! Compare!'

"First, observe concrete facts; then use the memory of these facts to compare them, and to note their likenesses and differences.

"Think that over, and you will see that it is the way in which all knowledge is gained. The successful business man is the one who has observed, remembered, and compared the facts of business. All the achievements of science have come from doing these three things. The extent to which *anyone* does them will measure the extent of his education and of his ability to continue to educate himself.

"The very first essential of any real education is to observe. Without that you have no material out of which to manufacture knowledge. Remember what you have observed. Compare the facts you have observed; and you will find yourself thinking out conclusions. These conclusions are real knowledge; and they are your own.

"That was what made John Burroughs a great naturalist, Morgan a great financier, Napoleon a great general. It is the foundation of all education. And the wonderful thing about it is that gaining an education in this way is not a penance, but a delight.

"As an illustration: What is a detective story, if it is not a record of observing, remembering and comparing facts—and of then drawing conclusions? Practically all of us enjoy reading these books, because, while we read, we ourselves are all the time observing, remembering, comparing, and trying to draw the correct conclusion.

"We can pursue knowledge in just the same way, and can have even more pleasure doing it. The great advantage in pursuing knowledge is that we may capture something that will contribute to the welfare of the world.

"In any case we enrich ourselves; we open new windows through which to behold interesting things. Did you ever look up a word in the dictionary without gaining more than the one definition you were seeking? I never do. I have the same sort of an experience when I start out with a fact, or an idea.

"We cannot perform the simplest act without having some principle of science brought into play. And there is nothing of more enthralling interest than to study these simple

acts and to try to learn something from them.

"In dealing with children, the main essential is not to tell them things, but to encourage them to find out things for themselves. Ask them questions, but leave them to find out the answer. If they arrive at the wrong answer, do not tell them they are mistaken; and do not give them the right answer. Ask them other questions, which will show them their mistake, and so make them push their inquiry further.

"For example: Suppose you wanted to teach a child about moisture and condensation. You could state to him that there are minute particles of water vapor in the air exhaled from the lungs, and that this water vapor will be condensed under certain conditions. In other words you give him a general conclusion which other people have arrived at and ask him to memorize it.

"Now suppose you tell him nothing, but simply ask him to breathe into a glass tumbler. He sees the moisture on the glass. Ask him where it came from. Have him breathe against the outside of the tumbler. Have him try the experiment with a glass that is hot and with one that is ice cold. Have him try it with other surfaces. And don't do his thinking for him. Make him observe what takes place, stimulating him to remember the different results he observes, and, by comparing them, to arrive at conclusions.

"I believe that self-education is a life-long affair. It comes, naturally and inevitably, through using the mind in the three ways I have pointed out. And I may add that following this 'Rule of Three' seems to be the greatest factor in keeping the mind young and active.

There cannot be mental atrophy in any person who continues to observe, to remember what he observes, and to seek answers for his unceasing hows and whys about things."

Keeping up with the World

Excerpts from a regular department in Collier's

Freling Foster

THE Indians who sold Manhattan Island to Peter Minuit in 1626 for some firewater and $24 worth of trinkets were smart boys. They did not own it. They were Canarsies, Montauks and Rockaways from Long Island—just in town for a visit. So Peter had to buy it again from a tribe "uptown."

THE corn-husking bee is one of the major sports of the United States. The 110,000 spectators at the husking tournament on a farm near Newtown, Indiana, on November 8, 1935, have been exceeded in number by only five other crowds in the history of American sports.

EXCEPT the Capitol in Washington, the only place in the United States over which the American flag is allowed by law to fly each night in times of peace is the grave of Francis Scott Key in Maryland. The purpose is to make true always the line in his song, *The Star-Spangled Banner:* "Gave proof through the night that our flag was still there."

IN THE past five U. S. population censuses far more men than women refused to report their ages.

DURING the World War the Germans often tapped the telephone systems of the Allies and secured valuable information. But one day new and strange sounds began to come over the wires, baffling code experts and linguists until the Armistice. It was the language of a group of American Indians who had been taught to send and receive the messages.

CALIFORNIA innkeepers are circumventing the state law which prohibits the use of signs announcing alcoholic beverages for sale. The old familiar signs now read: Aloon, Avern, Peer, Puffet, Bee Garden and Ocktail Ounge.

Don't Growl—Kick

Digested from McClure's Magazine

JAMES H. COLLINS

How to complain effectively. A valuable talk on constructive criticism.

1. At times it pays to complain.
2. How not to do it.
3. Making an effective complaint.
4. The changed attitude of corporations.

A DOZEN passengers boarded a New York surface car, presenting transfers. "Not good on this side," the conductor declared to each one. "You'd ought-a got on over on the other crossing. Fare, please!"

Each passenger growled, and some of them tried to argue; but the conductor listened only in amusement. "It's a rule of the company" was his retort. In the end they all paid another fare, and as the conductor took the money, triumphantly, it was clear that this rule afforded him much diversion—he liked to watch its infallible workings.

1. One of those passengers wrote to the Public Service Commission the next day asking why a mere difference in sides of a street made transfers worthless at that crossing. The facts were set down without anger. A couple of weeks later the Commission wrote that the street-car company had modified its rule, making transfers good on both sides of that street.

Nobody knows how long people had been growling about that rule, yet doing nothing further. The Public Service Commission had never had a complaint before, and the street-car company was probably astonished to learn that its rule, made originally for some sound traffic reason, was not giving the public pleasure.

2. Talk with anybody in the management of a business that serves the public, and you will find that the average American will growl, but seldom complains when something is wrong in his daily life. He will likely argue with a ticket-seller, or a meter-reader, or a city employee. They have no authority to set things right. But he will not go to the trouble of sending an orderly complaint to officials, with names, dates, facts. Least of all does he suspect that he owes a duty to the community in such matters.

Sometimes he holds his anger long enough to write to the newspapers. He tattles to them. If something goes wrong he tells the editor about it, relieving his feelings by vague scolding. His letter gives no names, dates or facts upon which anybody

4

anxious to set matters right could act.

3. An editor could not get to sleep in his New York apartment because some fellow across the area was busy hammering at a night job of home carpentry. In desperation he telephoned to the police with very little hope of relief. To his astonishment the police were interested, and thanked him. Within a few minutes a patrolman appeared and told the disturber he was violating a city ordinance, forbidding unnecessary noise after a certain hour at night.

It really pays to stop growling, and kick!

But before kicking, get all the facts. Just assume that you were going to be called into court, and have facts upon which you can testify. Then the next best step is—forget to grow angry. Most of the irritation over such happenings comes from your own assumption that it will not be much use to complain, that corporations are soulless and greedy, public officials indifferent, that nobody will do anything about it anyway.

As affairs are run nowadays, this is a false assumption. Corporations really have souls, public officials actually try to serve, the system is much better than the average fellow knows, and somebody is probably waiting to attend him in this very matter.

Just assume that Mr. Somebody is waiting, even though you send your complaint to the company. For, tomorrow you may receive a call from him, and find him a regular human being, and you would certainly be very sorry if you had written him a pert letter, reflecting on his ability or honesty.

When you are ready to write your letter, it is good policy, if nothing else, to be courteous—even a little smooth! Say that you believe the company is trying to give good service. Say you realize that there are many chances every day for details to go wrong in a big business, and that you believe they will be glad to hear of your experience, and have an opportunity to improve the service.

A letter like that will bring better results than a sarcastic one. Ten or fifteen years ago there was real indifference in the matter of complaints on the part of many corporations. But the corporations have paid for their sins in state regulations, ill-will, hostility. Today they are anxious to be good. Indifference to complaints was largely poor organization, anyway. Now they are organized to handle trouble. The dissatisfied customer, formerly a nuisance, has been turned into an asset. When he learns how fair a corporation can be, he tells others. The corporations are not only working hard to create good-will through courteous handling of complaints but today often inform the whole public about their methods, thus forestalling unfounded complaints.

It pays to kick!

Americans suffer silently, in the belief that an individual stands no chance of being heard by a corporation.

Editors aren't the only ones who have to interest people. Preachers have to, teachers have to, salesmen have to, theatrical and moving picture managers have to, nearly everybody has to—in order to get along.

Table Manners à la Française

Excerpt from " 'Taint Right" by *Westbrook Pegler*

THE AFFECTATION of Americans at table is notorious, and they hamper themselves by rules having no basis in common sense. They are afraid to dig for the best fragments of chicken or lobster, they avoid the gravy as though it were poison, and the last spoonful of soup always goes back to the kitchen because somebody once made a law against tipping the plate. The Englishman's kit is even more complicated than ours; he can't eat berries or a dab of custard without fork and spoon, a trick which spatters dessert all over the ceiling when Americans try it.

It is the French who are the masters in these things.

When he comes to the table, the Frenchman, like the old Scotch golfer, endeavors to do what is to be done without superfluous weapons. He sits down, ties his napkin behind his ears, picks up a knife and fork and goes to work with admirable directness. He dunks his bread in the juice of the snail, he chases fragments of steak and gravy with a piece of crust, he licks his fingers, and says "Ah!" He is far too sensible ever to permit a desirable morsel to be carried back to the kitchen out of respect for a rule devised by the English whose etiquette decrees that a man at the table should never appear to be hungry. If it is too small or too liquid for a fork he will not hesitate to use his knife for a squeegee and wipe the knife on the bread.

He does not require a special niblick to blast the peas out of the mashed potatoes or a tweezer to overcome asparagus. If a slice of mushroom reposes in a difficult downhill lie on the rim of the plate he doesn't ignore it, as the American or Englishman would, but goes after it and gets it even if he has to play three strokes off the tablecloth, which some of us would consider out of bounds.

It is by no means a sordid spectacle. On the contrary, the Frenchman's enjoyment and simple skill at table are admirable, combining the greatest simplicity with the best results.

To Bore or Not To Bore

Condensed from The Atlantic Monthly

RALPH W. BERGENGREN

TAKE me away," said Thomas Carlyle at a dinner-table where one of the diners had been monologing to the extreme limit of boredom, "and put me in a room by myself and give me a pipe of tobacco!"

Many of us have felt this emotion; and some realize that we have occasioned it. The nice consideration for the happiness of others which marks a gentleman may even make him particularly susceptible to this haunting apprehension. Carlyle defined the feeling when he said, "To sit still and be pumped into is never an exhilarating process." But pumping is different. How often have I myself, my adieus seemingly done, my hat in my hand and my feet on the threshold, taken a fresh grip, hat or no hat, on the pump-handle, and set good-natured, Christian folk distressedly wondering if I would never stop! And how often have I afterward recalled something strained and morbidly intent in their expressions, a glassi-

From: *The Perfect Gentleman*, by Ralph W. Bergengren, reprinted by permission of the author and Little, Brown & Company.

ness of the staring eye and a starchiness in the smiling lip, that has made me suffer under my bed-cover and swear that next time I would depart like a sky-rocket.

The Bore Positive pumps; the Bore Negative compels pumping. Unlike Carlyle, he regards being pumped into as an exhilarating process; he sits tight and says nothing; he keeps his victim talking.

In the last analysis a bore bores because he keeps us from something more interesting than himself. Coleridge's Ancient Mariner, full of an unusual personal experience that the leisurely reader finds most horridly entertaining, bored the Wedding Guest because at that moment the wedding guest wanted to get to the wedding. But the Mariner was too engrossed in his own tale to notice this lack of interest, and so invariably is the Bore Positive: everything escapes him except his listener.

But no matter how well we know we are bored, none of us can be certain that he does not sometimes bore. On the very occasion when I have felt myself as entertaining as a three-ring circus, I may in effect have been as gay and chatty as a like number of tombstones. There are persons, for that matter, who are bored by circuses and delighted by tombstones. My mistake may have been to put all my conversational eggs in one basket—which, indeed, is a very good way to bore people.

Dynamo Doit, teaching you through his famous mail course, "How Not to Be a Bore," would probably write: "Do not try to exhaust your subject. You will only exhaust your audience. Never talk for more than three minutes on any topic. And remember that it is not so much what you say as the *way you say it* that will charm your listener. Speak plainly. Remember unless you are heard you cannot expect to interest."

The first virtue that we who do not wish to be bores must practice is abstemiousness of self. I know it is hard, but I do not mean total abstinence. A man who tried to converse without his I's would make but a blind stagger at it; he would become a Bore Negative of the most negative description. But one can at least curb the pronoun, and confine the personally conducted tour into and about Myself within reasonable limits. Let him say, "I will not talk about Myself for more than thirty minutes," then reduce it to twenty-five; then to twenty—and so on to the irreducible minimum; and he will be surprised to feel how his popularity increases with leaps and bounds at each reduction—provided, of course, that he finds anything else to talk about.

Your Complete Bore, however, is incapable of this treatment, for he does not know that he is a bore. There is, however, one infallible rule for not being a bore—or at any rate for not being much of a bore—and that is, never to make a call, or to talk to a person, for more than fifteen minutes. But to apply this rule successfully one must become adept in the Fine Art of Going Away. You get up to go. Others get up—or, if there is but one other, she. But now that everybody is up, new subjects of conversation, as if rising with the rising infection, come up also. If you bore a person sitting down and wondering when you are going to get up, you bore far worse a person standing up and wondering when you will go away. That you have in effect started to go away—and not gone away—and yet must go away some time—and may go away at any time: this consciousness, to a person standing first on one tired foot and then on the other, rapidly becomes almost, but never quite, unendurable. Reason totters, but remains on the throne. One can almost lay down a law: *Two persons who do not part with kisses should part with haste.*

But the fifteen-minute call followed by the flying exit is at best an unsatisfactory solution, it is next door to always staying at home. Better far to come out of your cave, mingle, bore as little as may be—and thank Heaven that here and there you meet one whom you feel reasonably certain that you do not bore.

The Art of Opening a Conversation

Condensed from Vanity Fair

STEPHEN LEACOCK

OPENING a conversation is really the hardest part. It may best be studied in the setting and surroundings of the Evening Reception, where people stand upright and agonize, balancing a dish of ice-cream. Here conversation reaches its highest pitch of social importance. One must talk or die. Something may be done to stave it off a little by vigorous eating. But the food at such affairs is limited. There comes a point when it is absolutely necessary to say something.

The beginning, as I say, is the hardest problem. Other communities solve it better than we do. In China, conversation between strangers after introduction is always opened by the question, "And how old are *you?*" This strikes me as singularly apt and sensible. Here is the one thing that is common ground between any two people, high or low, rich or poor—how far are *you* on your pilgrimage in life?

Compare with the Chinese method the grim, but very significant, formula that is employed in the exercise yards of our penitentiaries. "What have you brought?" asks the San Quentin or Sing Sing convict of the new arrival, meaning, "And how long is *your* sentence?" There is the same human touch about this, the same common ground of interest, as in the Chinese formula.

But in our polite society we have as yet found no better method than beginning with a sort of medical diagnosis—"How do you do?" This admits of no answer. Convention forbids us to reply in detail that we are feeling if anything slightly lower than last week, but that though our temperature has risen from ninety-one-fifty to ninety-one-seventy-five, our respiration is still normal.

Still worse is the weather as an opening topic. For it either begins and ends as abruptly as the medical diagnosis or it leads the two talkers on into a long and miserable discussion of the weather of yesterday, of the day before yesterday, of last month, of last year and the last fifty years.

9

Let one beware, however, of a conversation that begins too easily. This can be seen at any evening reception, as when the hostess introduces two people who are supposed to have some special link to unite them at once with an instantaneous snap, as when, for instance, they both come from the same town.

"Let me introduce Mr. Sedley," says the hostess. "I think you and Mr. Sedley are from the same town, Miss Smiles. Miss Smiles, Mr. Sedley."

Off they go at a gallop. "I'm so delighted to meet you," says Mr. Sedley. "It's good to hear somebody who comes from our little town." If he's a rollicking humorist, Mr. Sedley calls it his little old "burg."

"Oh, yes," answers Miss Smiles. "I'm from Winnipeg, too. I was so anxious to meet you to ask you if you knew the McGowans. They're my greatest friends at home."

"The—who?" asks Mr. Sedley.

"The McGowans—on Selkirk Avenue."

"No-o, I don't think I do. I know the Prices on Selkirk Avenue. Of course you know them."

"The Prices? No. I don't believe I do—I don't think I ever heard of the Prices. You don't mean the Pearsons? I know them very well."

"No, I don't know the Pearsons. The Prices live just near the reservoir."

"No, then I'm sure I don't know them. The Pearsons live close to the college."

"Close to the college? Is it near the William Kennedys?"

This is the way the conversation goes for ten minutes. Both Mr. Sedley and Miss Smiles are getting desperate. Their faces are fixed. Their sentences are reduced to—

"Do you know the Petersons?"

"No. Do you know the Applebys?"

"No. Do you know the Willie Johnsons?"

"No."

Then at last comes a rift in the clouds. One of them happens to mention Beverly Dixon. The other is able to cry exultingly—

"Beverly Dixon? Oh, yes, rather. At least, I don't *know* him, but I used often to hear the Applebys speak of him."

And the other exclaims with equal delight—"I don't know him very well either, but I used to hear the Willie Johnsons talk about him all the time."

They are saved. Half an hour after they are still standing there talking of Beverly Dixon.

An equally unsuccessful type of conversation, often overheard at receptions, is one in which one of the two parties to it is too surly, too stupid, or too self-important, and too rich to talk, and the other labors in vain.

Mr. Grunt, capitalist, is approached by a willowy lady.

"Oh, Mr. Grunt," she is saying, "how interesting it must be to be in your place. Our hostess was just telling me that you own practically all the shoe-making machinery factories east of Pennsylvania."

"Honk," says Mr. Grunt.

"Shoe-making machinery must be absolutely fascinating, is it not?"

"Honk," says Mr. Grunt.

"I should love so much to see one of your factories. They must be so interesting."

"Honk," says Mr. Grunt.

Then he turns and moves away. Into his little piggy eyes has come a fear that the lady is going to ask him to subscribe for something, or wants his name on a board of directors. So he leaves her. Yet if he had known it she is probably as rich as he is, or richer, and hasn't the faintest interest in his factories, and never intends to go near one. Only she is fit to move and converse in polite society and Mr. Grunt is not

To Their Inspiration

P. G. WODEHOUSE dedicates *Golf Without Tears:*
    To my dear daughter
without whose unflagging interest and constant assistance
this book would have been written in half the time

FRANCIS HACKETT dedicates *The Invisible Censor:*
    To my wife
    Signe Toksvig
whose lack of interest
in this book has been
my constant desperation

HENRY WATSON FOWLER, noted lexicographer, dedicates *Some Comparative Values:*
    To the instructress
who has been teaching me for
20 years how the ideal wife may
    be surpassed by the real

JOHANNES KEPLER, German astronomer:
    The die is cast; the book is written, to be read either now or by posterity. I care not which. It may well wait a century for a reader, since God has waited 6000 years for an observer like myself.

PIETRO MASCAGNI, famous for his *Cavalleria Rusticana*, grew weary of his critics and dedicated his opera, *The Masks*, thus:
    To myself, with distinguished esteem and unalterable satisfaction

Ex Libris: Gelett Burgess

THE errant cat, though long astray,
Comes back to home at last one day;
Ah, may this book when lent be feline
Enough to make a homeward beeline!

Beyond Man

LAFCADIO HEARN

COULD a world exist in which the nature of all the inhabitants would be so moral that the mere idea of what is immoral could not exist? Imagine a society in which the idea of dishonesty would not exist, because no person could be dishonest, a society in which the idea of unchastity could not exist, because no person could possibly be unchaste, a world in which no one could have any idea of envy, ambition or anger, because such passions could not exist, a world in which not to be loving, not to do everything which we human beings now call duty, would be impossible. Moreover, there would be no difficulty, no pain in such performance; it would be the constant and unfailing pleasure of life. Morality would have been transmuted into inherited instinct.

Can we imagine such a world? I answer that such a world actually exists. The world of insects actually furnishes examples of such a moral

Summarized from a chapter in *Books and Habits*, Dodd Mead Co., New York.

transformation and the important thing is the opinion of scientific men that humanity will at last, in the course of millions of years, reach the ethical conditions of the ants. Some of these conditions, established by scientific evidence, have startled the whole moral world, and set men thinking in entirely new directions.

These facts have been arrived at through the study of hundreds of different kinds of ants, by hundreds of scientific men. The details of the following picture are furnished by a number of the highest species of ants only; that must not be forgotten. Also, I must remind you that the morality of the ant, by the necessity of circumstance does not extend beyond the limits of its own species. Ants carry on war outside their own borders; were it not for this, we might call them morally perfect creatures.

The ant is so intelligent that we are justified in trying to describe its existence by a kind of allegorical comparison with human life. Imagine, then, a world full of women, working night and day, building, tunnelling, bridging, also engaged in agriculture, in horticulture, and in taking care of many kinds of domestic animals. (I may remark that ants have domesticated no fewer than 584 different kinds of creatures.) This world of women is scrupulously clean; busy as they are, all of them carry combs and brushes about them, and arrange themselves several times a day. In addition to this constant work, these women have to take care of myriads of children—children so delicate that the slightest change in weather may kill them. So the children have to be carried constantly from one place to another in order to keep them warm.

Though this multitude of workers are always gathering food, no one of them would eat or drink a single atom more than is necessary; and none of them would sleep for one second longer than is necessary. Now comes a surprising fact, about which more will be said later on. These women have no sex. They are women, for they sometimes actually give birth, as virgins, to children; but they are incapable of wedlock. Sex is practically suppressed.

This world of workers is protected by an army of soldiers, who help in some of the work. The soldiers are very large, very strong, and shaped so differently that they do not seem at first to belong to the same race. Now comes the second astonishing fact: these soldiers are all women, but they are sexless women. In these also sex has been suppressed.

Most of the children are born of a few special mothers—females chosen for the purpose of bearing offspring, and not allowed to do anything else. They are treated almost like empresses, being constantly fed and attended and served, and being lodged in the best possible way. Only these can eat and drink at all times—they must do so for the sake of their offspring. They are not suffered to go out, unless strongly attended, and they are not allowed to run any risk of danger or of injury. The life of the whole race circles about them.

Last of all are the males, the men. One asks why females should have been specialized into soldiers instead of men. It appears that the females have more reserve force, and all the force that might have been utilized in the giving of life has been diverted to the making of aggressive powers. The real males are very small and weak, and appear to be treated with indifference and contempt. They are suffered to become the bridegrooms of one night, after which they die very quickly. By contrast, the lives of the rest are very long, at least three or four years. But the males live only long enough to perform their solitary function.

Now comes the most astonishing fact of all: this suppression of sex is not natural—it is voluntary. It has been discovered that ants are able, by a systematic method of nourishment, to suppress or develop sex as they please. The race has decided that sex shall not be allowed to exist except in just so far as it is absolutely necessary to the existence of the race. Here is an instance of the most powerful of all passions voluntarily suppressed for the benefit of the community at large.

But that is only one fact of self-suppression, and the ant-world furnishes hundreds. To state the whole thing in the simplest possible way, the race has entirely got rid of everything that we call a selfish impulse. Even hunger and thirst allow of no selfish gratification. The entire life of the community is devoted to the common good and to mutual help and to the care of the young.

Its life is religion in the practical sense. The individual is sometimes said to be practically sacrificed for the sake of the race; but such a supposition means the highest moral altruism. Therefore thinkers have to ask, "Will man ever rise to something like the condition of ants?"

When the ancient Hebrew writer said, thousands of years ago, "Go to the ant, thou sluggard, consider her ways," he could not have imagined how good his advice would prove in the light of twentieth century science.

Grand Larceny

NEAR Steubenville, Ohio, thieves stole a mile of railroad track from a Pennsylvania Railroad spur. They ripped up the rails, cut them into small lengths and sold them as junk.—Baltimore *Sun*

H. A. FITZGERALD constructed a 158-apartment building in Chicago. While it was still unfinished, thieves entered and stole 158 bathtubs.—N. Y. *Herald Tribune*

IN MIAMI, the Homestead Machinery Company reported the theft of a 10-ton steam roller.—Baltimore *Sun*

IN LITTLE FALLS, N. Y., James Hallinan reported the theft of a granite monument weighing 1600 pounds.—Baltimore *Sun*

JOSEPH T. COUSINS of Kansas City notified the police that two men had stolen the furnace out of his house. Posing as repair men, they had gone down to the basement, dismantled the heating plant, and removed it by truck.—Baltimore *Sun*

A THIEF stole $500 worth of gold leaf from the steeple of the First Parish Church at Concord, Mass. He posed as a repair man before the church committee, and substituted cheap gold paint for the gold leaf.—N. Y. *Times*

THIEVES stole a complete house one night in Paris. They removed furniture, doors, windows and bricks, leaving nothing but the foundation.—Baltimore *Sun*

On the Length of Cleopatra's Nose

Condensed from Scribner's Magazine

BRANDER MATTHEWS

1. How spinsters aid British army.
2. Van Dyke's portraits and whale fishing.
3. Tudor architecture and turnips.
4. Nelson's victory gave us English jams.
5. The Gulf Stream and sports in England.

PASCAL calls attention to the way in which a little thing may have great consequences, saying that causes so trivial that they can scarcely be recognized, move all mankind. "The nose of Cleopatra—if it had been shorter, the history of the world would have been changed."

If Cleopatra's nose had been unduly short, she would probably not have descended the corridors of time as the heroine of the most disastrous of historic love-stories. She might not have found Mark Anthony at her feet.

If Mark Anthony had escaped the coils of this Egyptian Serpent, he might not have lost the battle of Actium; he might have been the founder of the Roman Empire. But Mark Anthony lacked the self restraint, the caution, and the astute statecraft of the Augustus who laid solid the foundations of the grandeur that was Rome. It is unlikely that he would have ruled wisely. The empire would not have been skilfully buttressed, and the barbarians would have broken in. There would have followed swift disintegration and destruction, and there would have been no lingering Decline and Fall for Gibbon to chronicle. Then we moderns would not have come into the heritage upon which our civilization is based.

If we look a little deeper, however, we are likely to conclude that Anthony's fatal weakness was in himself, in his unstable character. If he had never laid eyes on Cleopatra, the ultimate result might have been the same. There were other charmers of her time, and any one of them could have lured the unstable Roman to his allotted doom. As one writer has pointed out, the little thing which sometimes seems so significant is only what the physicians call "an exciting cause," always far less important than what they term "a predisposing condition." The last straw does not break the camel's back unless the beast is already laden to the limit of endurance. The slight pressure on the hair-trigger which fires the gun did not load the weapon or aim it.

1. But even if little things are un-

15

likely to have great consequences, results often transpire from remote causes which are not immediately apparent. I remember reading a whimsical suggestion to the effect that the stubborn resistance of the British army was due to the prevalence of spinsterhood in Great Britain. The explanation of this paradox is to be found in a sequence of causes and consequences. The British soldier is nourished on beef, and the quality of the beef is due to an abundance of clover, which needs to be fertilized by bees. But bees cannot multiply and live unless they are protected against the field-mice which destroy their broods and ravage their reserves of honey. The field-mice can be kept down if there are only cats enough to catch them, and cats are the favorites of the frequent old maids of England. These lonely virgins keep pets who prevent the mice from despoiling and destroying the bees, so clover flourishes luxuriantly and the cattle wax fat to supply the soldiers of the king with their strengthening rations.

2. Sir Martin Conway tells us that the beautiful costumes of the Cavaliers of England, as we see them in Van Dyke's portraits, owe their chief embellishment to the hardy mariners who ventured into the stormy waters near Spitsbergen. The chief use to which whale-oil was put was the manufacture of the better class of soap. Before the beginning of the English whale-fishery on the Spitsbergen coasts about 1610, there was very little good soap in Tudor days in Eng-

land. Improved laundry work followed the whale-fishery. Hence the relatively small ruffs we see in Tudor portraits and the small amount of linen displayed. Later portraits show more linen and more lace.

3. Once in a chat with Sir Martin in London we touched on this topic of the unknown origin of things well known. "Are you aware," he asked with a smile, "that the out-flowering of Tudor architecture, which is one of the glories of England, must be ascribed to the cultivation of the turnip by the Dutch?

"Well, England has a damp climate, and that makes it the best grazing country in the world—especially for sheep. But until the culture of root-crops was developed in Holland and transplanted to England, our farmers found it almost impossible to carry their sheep through the winter. This was made easy for them by the introduction of the turnip. Whereupon there was an immediate increase in sheep-raising, which ultimately gave England the immensely profitable wool trade. And the enriched Tudor merchants, like true Englishmen, spent their gains freely on their houses."

4. "Now I can tell you," I said, "how it is that Nelson's victory at Trafalgar brought about the popularity of British jams and marmalades in the United States. Nelson's defeat of the French and Spanish fleets gave England thereafter the undisputed command of the sea and cut the Continent off from the

colonies. The chief of the importations from tropical countries was sugar, and the deprivation was so keenly felt that Napoleon offered a tempting reward for a method of making sugar independent of sugar-cane. This was the origin of the beet-sugar industry, which had at first to be fostered by bounties from the government. After Waterloo, half the countries of the Continent found themselves with thousands of acres of beet-fields which would go out of cultivation if cane-sugar should be allowed to compete. To protect the farmers, some countries put a high tariff on cane sugar and paid an export bounty on beet-sugar. This bounty-fed beet-sugar was dumped on the London market. It ruined the sugar-planters of Jamaica, but it gave the British makers of preserves their chief raw material at a price which enabled them to import oranges and strawberries, and then to export to the United States their jams and marmalades."

5. Then I asked Sir Martin if he had ever considered the influence of the Gulf Stream on the field-sports of England. As the British Isles are as far north as Labrador, they would be desolate were it not for the warm Gulf Stream. Because it is nearer the Arctic, England has a longer day than France or the United States, and therefore the young men and maidens can do a day's work and still have two or three hours of daylight in which to play outdoor games.

The gentle reader is now in possession of the principles of a novel sport, and he can hunt down strange, unsuspected, and remote causes whenever he is sleepless at night or bookless on a train. The game can be played as a solitaire; or a half-dozen may take part, sitting about the wood-fire while the winter wind swirls the snow against the frosted windows.

When the Critics Crack the Quip

ONE of the briefest musical criticisms on record appeared in a Detroit paper: "An amateur string quartet played Brahms here last evening. Brahms lost."

I HAVE knocked everything except the knees of the chorus girls, and God anticipated me there.—Percy Hammond in N. Y. *Herald Tribune*

HER performance belongs rather in a sandwich than on a stage.—Robert Garland in N. Y. *World-Telegram*

A. B. WALKLEY, London critic, wrote the following review of a play called *Dreadful Night:* "Exactly."—James Aswell

The Wisdom of Laziness

Condensed from Harper's Magazine

FRED C. KELLY

1. Why women age sooner than men!
2. Lazy waiters the most satisfactory.
3. Nearly all progress due to lazy men.
4. Most great executives and writers are lazy.
5. "We comprise the hope of the race."

ONE of the lessons in Mc-Guffey's Readers that made a deep impression on me dealt with the nonconformist attitude of Lazy Ned, who deplored the time and energy which must be devoted to trudging up a hill after coasting down. Lazy Ned, it appears, was the only one of the coasting party who showed any intelligence. We have no record of what became of him in after life. But presumably he grew up to be a successful executive, or efficiency engineer, with a knack for industrial economies and labor-saving devices.

From childhood we hear our elders talk about lazy people as if laziness were ignoble, whereas the truth is that except for our lazy men there would be no progress and the lives even of energetic persons would be filled with drudgery. When a little girl helping her mother to clear away the dinner dishes sensibly carries a large tray-

load to eliminate more trips, the mother chidingly observes: "Lazy man's load!" and the child thinks she has done something wrong. After a few reprimands of that sort, she falls into the habit of squandering her energies by needless steps until by the time she is grown, she wears the world-weary expression so characteristic of housewives who imagine that laziness is a curse.

1. Most women, it may be noted, show their age sooner than men, doubtless because the average woman is less lazy than her husband and doesn't mind ten steps where one or two would be enough. She would rather be conventionally tired than intelligently lazy.

2. The lazy waiter in a restaurant is always the most satisfactory and best. He brings everything that the diner will need *the first trip* because he regards every extra step as an abomination. It is the energetic waiter who brings coffee but no sugar or spoon and doesn't object to unnecessary journeys one at a time to fetch these while the coffee grows cold.

3. Nearly all progress in human affairs must have been due to the contrivings of lazy men to save themselves steps. When our early kinfolk lived in rude caves, every time a man desired a drink of water he had to walk to the spring. Presently some lazy fellow, tiring of so many trips to quench his thirst, fashioned a rude pail in which he could bring home a day's supply all at once. But even carrying a bucket of water is not pleasant, if one is lazy enough, and the next step was doubtless to hew troughs by which water could be diverted from the spring direct to the cabin of the consumer. A later achievement of the lazy man, to avoid carrying his water up a hill, was a pump and windmill. Similarly, the first boat, consisting of a hollow log, must have been born of the desire of one of our ancestors to avoid walking around the lake or along the bank of the river.

More than 100 years ago, so the story goes, a lad, Humphrey Potter, was hired to sit alongside of a crude steam engine and let out the exhaust steam after each stroke of the driving rod. Being lazy, he found his task tiresome and rigged up some strings and latches by which the valves could be opened and shut automatically. This not only permitted him to run and play, but also immediately doubled the capacity of the engine. He had lazily discovered the principle of reciprocating valves.

More recently we have agricultural machinery *with seats*. These were not first thought of by energetic farmers who didn't mind walking all day, but by those to whom the idea of sitting down had a strong appeal. True, inventors often devise labor-saving machines that they themselves would never have occasion to use. But they do this because they know that there are always plenty of lazy men who will be interested in avoiding effort, and that money can be made by selling labor-saving devices to others. The money thus acquired enables one to live *without working so hard*. Thus it is laziness that prompts the inventive effort.

4. Frank B. Gilbreth, the great industrial engineer and student of human motions, frequently makes moving pictures of expert workmen in various trades, to determine how few movements are needed in performing a piece of work. He finds that the best worker—the one from whom the others can learn the most, is invariably a lazy man, too lazy to waste a single motion that he can avoid. The more energetic man is far less efficient, because he doesn't mind squandering his energy in unnecessary movements. At the end of the day he is fatigued out of all proportion to the work done. Most great executives are lazy. It is logical that they should be. A good executive is one who never does anything that he can get anybody else to do for him. Only years of laziness can establish in a man the habit of having others wait on him instead of doing things himself.

It is a tremendous asset to be lazy enough willingly to sit still until a bright idea comes along, instead of frittering away the golden hours in wearying routine activity. The best books are written necessarily by lazy authors. Too energetic an author pants to be up and doing and cannot content himself at a desk calmly improving his manuscript or idly waiting hours at a time for a bright phrase or a clever twist of a plot. Many of our greatest statesmen were brought up on farms and would have remained on farms if they hadn't been too lazy to face so much hard work and looked about for something easier. It is the scholars and thinkers, too lazy for much physical activity, who do most to change the thought of the world for the better.

5. Moreover, mental laziness appears to be equally advantageous. Most important rules and formulas have been arrived at by lazy men who were trying to make mental short cuts. The discoverers of the laws of gravitation must have been lazy men tired of laboriously working out the explanations for each separate bit of phenomena. Think what a job it would be to determine how long it takes an apple to fall from the top limb of a tree, or for a cat to fall from a balloon a mile high, without actually trying it, if one had no law of falling bodies! Think of the complications and wearisome annoyance we should have in ordinary daily affairs if some lazy individual had not established the general rule that two and two are invariably four!

The truth is that lazy people, both those who get things done, and those who do not, are the folk on whom progress must mainly depend. It is time that we lazy people were receiving the serious consideration that is our due. We comprise the hope of the race.

Time Makes a Word for It

Time, The Weekly Newsmagazine, insists that "there is no such thing as Time style, but only Time tempo and attitude." These are reflected in many time-chopping, space-saving devices, especially the telescoping of two or more old words to make a new one. Some of the resulting contractions are as follows: Adman, AAAdministrator, ballyhooligan, Brisbanalities, cinemansion, cinemaddict, cinemasculated, dramateurs, franchiseler, GOPossibility, intelligentsiac, newsheet, microphonies, radiorator, ransoman (Jafsie), RFChairman, sexpert (Earl Carroll), sophomoron, slimelight, socialite, tennist, and vitalics ("He spoke in vitalics"). In a moment of punning weakness, Time once referred to Mae West as "America's Sweethot."

Time-typical locutions such as "legacy-stalking," "smudge-moustached," and "bug-eyed," long regarded as extremely modern, are actually patterned upon Homer, who also had a penchant for double-barreled modifiers such as "wine-dark sea" and "far-darting Apollo." In a copy of The Iliad owned by the late Britten Haddon, co-founder of Time, all the compound epithets are underlined, and evidently furnished the literary inspiration for Time's first editors.

The Witch Panic in Salem

Condensed from The Mentor

HILDEGARDE HAWTHORNE

FEAR has probably been responsible for as many crimes as deliberate evil. A frightened man or woman is something to be afraid of; a frightened community may give way to acts that will horrify the whole world. Salem, Massachusetts, in the dreadful months of 1692–93, gave proof of this fact, and murdered 20 innocent persons before its panic was cured.

It is difficult for us today to realize the actuality of the belief in the devil and his presence in this world of ours that inspired almost everybody in the 17th century. The wisest men of that time believed absolutely in the personal activity of Satan; Blackstone, oracle of British law, on whom not only England's law but also our own is founded, declared in positive terms that witches existed, and many lawyers and ministers agreed with him.

In 1690 Cotton Mather, who was one of the most important ministers of the Puritan Church in America, published a book in which he attempted to prove the existence of witches, and cited many cases of their power and their methods. A prodigious amount of discussion followed, till the minds of the people were filled with morbid fears and suspicions. In Boston, in 1688, an old Irish crone had been hanged for witchcraft on the testimony of the four children of John Goodman, a most respected citizen, and there had been executions in Charleston, Dorchester, and Cambridge, while a certain Mary Oliver, in 1650, had actually confessed to being a witch.

In the winter of 1691, several young girls of Salem met in the home of one Samuel Parris, a minister of the Gospel, to practice palmistry and other "magic" tricks under the tuition of a West Indian slave woman, Tituba by name. Presently two of this group, the two youngest, about 10 and 11 years of age, were noticed acting queerly, and very soon two more joined them in what were described as curious antics. They would creep into holes, or under tables and chairs; they made rambling, ridiculous speeches, odd gestures, and even fell down in fits. A whisper ran through the town: "These children must be bewitched." Doctors could do nothing for them. Presently the girls spoke of being obsessed by the old slave woman to whom they had been going for magic instruction. Poor Tituba was forthwith seized, beaten, and threatened with worse unless she confessed. She admitted that she was a witch, and stated that she had signed a big red book, being urged thereto by the devil in person. In a short time all of the ten girls that had met at Mr. Parris's were affected and they began to accuse others, among them Goodwife Cory, saying that she bit, scratched, and strangled them.

The whole village was in a turmoil by this time, and the ten afflicted persons became the center of interest. Mr. Parris got testimony from the bewitched, and was eager for the punishment of the accused. A public hearing was held in April, presided over by six magistrates and several ministers of the Gospel. During the hearing, a Mrs. Proctor was "cried out of," as they put it, meaning that she was accused of being a witch. As she sank down in terror at the cries, her husband endeavored to comfort her; upon which he too was "cried out of." So these went to prison with the slave woman and Goodwife Cory, and two others. Fear was invading the hearts of the entire community—fear not alone of the witches and their evil spells, but fear of accusation, of being "cried out of." Cotton Mather got very much excited, and put all his elo-

quence and effort into the fight with the devil. Those who were accused were hustled quickly into prison. And on June 10th one Bridget Bishop, who had been accused 20 years before of being a witch, but had escaped conviction, was hanged on the testimony of a sick man. Later, dying, this man confessed that he had lied about the old lady.

Sir William Phips now became governor of the colony. He threw the accused into chains, and for a while the torments of the afflicted ceased. This seemed to be pretty fair proof against the witches, so, later in the same month, five more were hanged. Each and all protested innocence to the last. New batches were sent to prison, and the number of the afflicted persons increased. On August 19th, five more were brought to be hanged on Gallows Hill. One of these was a minister, a Mr. Burroughs. On the ladder, with the noose about his neck, he gave so serious a speech, protesting his own innocence, that tears filled the eyes of many spectators, and there were murmurs that things were going too far. His accusers, thereupon, shrieked out that they could see a squat black man standing at his elbow and dictating to him, and so fear held all sympathizers silent. Another of this batch, John Willard, had been active in running down suspected witches, when suddenly he was himself "cried out of." Giles Cory, seeing how the juries feared to give any acquittal, refused to be tried, being "a bold stout man." But his courage helped him not. He was squeezed to death in a press, a ghastly execution.

Less than a week later eight more went to their death. Accusations still poured in. Among those accused was a Mrs. Hale, wife of a minister. Minister Hale had been most eager in persecuting witches, but now that it was his wife who fell under the ban he began to see a new light. Other "very sober people" were also accused. And now some began to think, and even to say, that perhaps the devil could take on a good man's shape merely to deceive people and to bring about the destruction of those he hated for their very goodness. This idea began to prevail with many, and gradually to gain influence enough to prevent further executions.

In fact, the storm was over. The madness disappeared almost as swiftly as it had come. In the early part of 1693, many were set free, and even those that had confessed to witchcraft were released. As soon as the panic died, the afflicted ceased to be harmed. Those that had served on the juries admitted they had acted under delusion and begged forgiveness of their fellow men and of God. Those that had confessed declared the confessions had been forced from them in fear of torture and death. The bloody hands were washed; the bones of the dead were given decent burial, and Salem turned to other matters.

In order to appreciate just what this horrid chapter in human history meant, let us stop to consider that these ideas were held with just as entire a conviction as you give to the wonders of radio. The "Old Serpent" was considered to be everywhere about, driving the briskest business imaginable, bargaining for souls in every likely or unlikely spot, using strange and fearful spells to win his victims, having it in his power to offer all manner of worldly blessings in return for the article he needed to keep hell full. It is against this background of conviction and fear that the Salem delusion must be placed in order to be fairly seen.

Times Have Changed

THE following rules were in force at Mt. Holyoke College in 1837:

"No young lady shall become a member of Mt. Holyoke Seminary who cannot kindle a fire, wash potatoes, repeat the multiplication table and at least two thirds of the shorter catechism.

"Every member of the school shall walk a mile a day unless a freshet, earthquake, or some other calamity prevent.

"No young lady shall devote more than an hour a day to miscellaneous reading.

"No young lady is expected to have gentlemen acquaintances unless they are returned missionaries or agents of benevolent societies."—*School Activities*

Does It Pay to Advertise?

Extracts from The Century Magazine

WINIFRED KIRKLAND

As EVERY school-child knows, it was on October 15, 1924, that the entire population of the United States woke up, to find that during the night, mysteriously, every advertisement had been erased from everywhere. From that date to this, throughout all the United States, neither by tongue nor pen, neither by painted sign nor gesture, has anybody been able to invite anybody to buy anything. . . .

In the 30 years ensuing we have become accustomed to the new manner of existence, but reconstruction of American living and thinking was nothing short of a revolution. Keen observers noted even physical disturbances of the atmosphere. Backwoods people, whose ears were trained to a nicety in distinguishing the calls of birds and of insects, were aware of a curious sound, seeming to come out of the air—a sound like the far-away escape of steam from many engines, indefinitely prolonged. This sound was at last diagnosed as the release of energy. . . . In those earlier times magazine readers

were accustomed to follow the tail of story as it whisked around the edge of a giant tire, or wriggled through an army of men in shaving-soap. In this pursuit a great deal of attention was dissipated, and it is to the complete disappearance of the words "Continued on page 37" that our observant British critics attribute the new concentration of the American mind conspicuous during the last 30 years.

When paper could no longer be used for advertising, the oversupply in the warehouses became a menace to the fire insurance companies. American resourcefulness came to the rescue, and the present thriving trade in paper clothes dates from this period. The drop in the price of paper was accompanied by a drop in office boys. Previously whole regiments of likely lads had been employed to open the envelopes containing advertising matter and convey it to the waste-basket. A great many office boys had to go back to hoeing potatoes.

Commercial travelers had to follow the office boys, and many persons remember the congestion of trains on all lines during that time when all agents and publicity men were making their famous trek back to the farm. . . . The agricultural problem was solved as if by magic. The potentialities of the soil were now for the first time revealed to minds sharpened through the sale of safety-razors, and scoured by contact with every kind of tooth-paste. As a consequence of this redirection of intellectual energy, where there had been before 1924 only one Luther Burbank, there is now a special edition of Who's Who devoted solely to bur-bankers. . . . Master minds trained to coerce a whole continent to the purchase of a washing-powder, found it mere child's play to subdue a desert, to create and supply markets, or to wheedle a refractory Congress.

Agriculture is only one instance of the marvelous impetus given to all forms of activity by the diversion of energy from words to work. The cost of living went down three steps at a time because nobody was lured into buying anything he didn't need. The five-hour day came into being automatically, and with it the menace to communism faded away; for when everybody had time to play, nobody remembered to grumble at the Government. Now every Smith Jones on the place found he had within himself some long-neglected fad—and spare time enough to devote to it. Men who all their lives had talked tires to possible buyers now found themselves actually interested in rubber, and the interest carried some of them as far as Africa, with ultimate benefit to geography. Men who had been too busy advertising stained-glass windows to learn anything about the subject now turned unexpectedly into artists. Men who for years had been painting pictures of chefs to adorn packages of cereals discovered that they themselves had been longing to invent new receipts, and these became most accomplished cooks. Illustrators whose whole time had been given to home interiors pictured in the interests of a reading-lamp often themselves became domesticated daddies reading to little sons by library tables. The ramifications of the change spread to every department of life.

When people at last had leisure to make and do things to please themselves rather than a customer, art promptly popped into the place vacated by advertising. Every one has observed how during the last 30 years the United States has attained world leadership in all the arts and sciences. . . . The profound improvement in mentality is easily explained. An advertisement was a frank intimation that the reader was a person worthy a salesman's regard. No one is so humble as not to purr with pride when he is asked to buy something. The less money one had, the more time he spent in looking at all the fine things he was being asked to buy, until, what with making advertisements and reading them, the average citizen had very little brain for anything else. . . .

Many heads of colleges who had

formerly been compelled to do nothing but run about the country talking up their institutions and holding out their hats discovered within themselves, now that they were confined to bounds, a real flair for teaching the young. Money soon poured into college treasuries, so that now, in this year 1954, it would be hard to find a college professor who cannot buy two pairs of shoes a year and send his children to the movies once a month. Millionaires are so pleased with the boys and girls now being turned out by the colleges that a special secretary has to be employed to acknowledge gifts. Sometimes merely one manly and well-educated college senior produces such an effect on some philanthropist that a ten-thousand-dollar check is mailed to the secretary that very night.

Politics was another intellectual activity improved by not being advertised. A specific form of political manoeuvre was known as an election promise. Every candidate for office was expected to advertise his noble purposes by means of pre-election speeches and posters, but nobody dreamed of calling him to account if afterward he failed to live up to his advertisement. The reason for this was that each voter expected some day to be a candidate, and forgave as he himself hoped to be forgiven.

This happy irresponsibility was a safe enough political practice so long as we kept it at home, where everybody was used to it; but when we carried it across the water, the beans began to spill. At home there was nothing we advertised to ourselves so loudly as American ideals. We entirely forgot that show implies substance. We placarded our ideals all over Europe, and Europe stopped fighting and looked and listened. But sadly enough, the advertising and the listening were all that happened on either side of the Atlantic. It is just possible that in the light of the Europe which resulted from our not delivering the goods we might, even without the great event of October, 1924, have come to some wise conclusions about the two-edged nature of all advertising.

The Hole in the Doughnut

SO THAT'S HOW IT STARTED!

AN OLD New England sea captain, one Hanson Gregory, gave the modern American doughnut its hole. The date of the great contribution was 1847. The captain was a boy at the time. Watching his mother fry doughnuts, he noticed that the centers of the cakes always seemed doughy, and suggested eliminating this part before the cakes were cooked. Laughingly she followed the suggestion and the result was so satisfactory that she never went back to the old way. Her method was copied by others until it spread over the whole country.—Adapted from the *American Restaurant Magazine*.

The Chappell Art Sale

Condensed from Vanity Fair

GEORGE S. CHAPPELL

MANY persons, I believe, find themselves in a position similar to that occupied by myself prior to the Sale of the Chappell Collection of Art Objects, namely surrounded by various impediments of domesticity, the accretion of a lifetime. Shall I be entirely frank and say that I was stocked up with junk that I longed to get rid of? No, out of deference to the purchasers of my collection I will not go as far as that. I will simply tell the story and let my readers draw their own conclusions.

It was on a Sunday in late winter that I wandered about my modest country house and took stock of various items of its furnishing that I would gladly see no more. My wife joined in the condemnation proceedings with hearty good will. "We will sell the lot to Itzmann, who keeps the shop near the station," she said.

We tackled the furniture first, while I computed the sums I should receive and issued warnings as to being firm with the wily dealer. The process lightened my heart.

How gladly I would eliminate that morris-chair with its cushion squashed down in the centre and bulging at the edges! A tea-table, an umbrella-stand, a hat-tree with branching metal arms, a Victorian sofa, chairs with broken seats and pictures, the original excuse for which had been that they covered spots on the wallpaper, were added to the list. But it was the attic which added the greatest store of loot—small objects, old clothes, goloshes, banished books, dolls' furniture, a framed motto. Warming to our work, we resolved on a clean sweep.

On my return home the next day, I was met by astounding news. "Itzmann actually sneered at the things," said my wife, "after all our work." I was furious. "We'll give them away," I said. But would you believe it? Tony, who comes to shake the furnace, absolutely refused to have our gifts showered upon him. In a last desperate effort, I made advances to the ash-man. I can see his expression now as he said, "Say, whadder yer think I am, a moving-van?" Our belongings could not be sold, bestowed or even thrown away. And then, like a ray of a search light, came my big idea. We would have an art sale. I felt sure that, given the right setting and plenty of publicity, anything could be sold. Immediately all my objects graduated from the junk class and became certified Antiques. . . .

Here and now I wish to make a grand salaam to the Tourniquet Galleries. When I walked into their main room and saw our furniture all set around the wall on neat pedestals against rich hangings of dark red, I simply gasped. My wife said weakly, "We must be in the wrong place." "No," I said pointing to the catalogue, "this is us all right. There's the hat-tree." Yes, there it was; and there were all the old familiar pieces, but so changed, so completely metamorphosed by their surroundings that we could hardly recognize them. The larger objects occupied positions of state on raised platforms like freaks in a side-show, while the smaller ones were grouped in handsome cases, where they stood out nobly from rich velvet backgrounds.

The place was crowded. This was the first of the three days of exhibition prior to sale. Hawk-nosed dealers flitted about marking their catalogues; rapt amateurs stood entranced before the exhibits pointing out their particular qualities. The younger Tourniquet was everywhere, agreeing with every one. "Quite so, Madam, yes indeed, a very rare bit. Of course the cushions are original." I turned away, blushing. They were discussing the morris-chair. He stroked his blond moustache to cover a smile as he turned to an austere gentleman to say, "Have you seen this early travelling set? A precious thing." When I saw that he was pointing out an old shaving-brush and a half-used stick of soap that had been thrown pell-mell into a box of odds and ends, I thought it was time to leave.

We came back for the sale. The chairs were filled half an hour before the senior Tourniquet took his place in the rostrum. "You all have your catalogues," he said, "and you have likewise had opportunity to inspect this unusual collection. I may say that in my 30 years experience as a distributor of rare and beautiful *objets d'art*, it has never been my good fortune to act as agent for a more unique grouping of bibelots."

The attendant produced the first object—a pair of old goloshes; but Mr. Tourniquet went calmly on, without a quiver in his voice. "Item Number One," he read from the catalogue. "A pair of very early sabots-de-neige, American, with original clasps and fuselage. Textile upper-drapes, with gum foundations. Unrestored. Shall we start this interesting object at $20?"

A voice said loudly, "Twenty!" and the excitement was on. From then on, the afternoon was a glorious, confused dream of successful salesmanship.

In a trance, I listened to the Old Master. . . . "Now we come to Item No. 37" (enter the hat-tree). "A golden-oak vestaire-de-salon, with brass crochets. A similar piece to this is to be seen in the foyer of the Bethel Seamen's Mission, in New London, Connecticut. What do I hear to start with?" . . . A magnificent success was attained by the despised motto which we had raked out of our attic. As "a crewel-work overmantel on oyster-white buckram with hand-embroidered, floral-lettered affiche, 'Learn to Say No,' suitable for small salle-à-manger, carved American walnut encardrement simulating natural-wood forms; very rare," this work of art was knocked down to a wild-eyed lady decorator for the modest sum of $163.

Nothing was neglected. The bits of dolls' furniture were disposed of as, "Child's miniature set, consisting of commode chaise-longue and bureau-de-travail, slightly broken but no pieces missing."

Listening to Mr. Tourniquet's skillful patter, I realized the immense importance of knowing the auction language. It is a tongue apart. Each simple household object appeared as something rich and strange. There were girandolles,

compotes, torcheres, Heaven knows what! A cracked butter-dish from the Five-and-Ten became "a crystal porte-beurre, with incised pastoral decor and fine patine."

And then a rather ghastly thing happened. We were watching the sale of a horrible sofa-pillow, for which I had paid $4 and which Tourniquet was describing as "a late nineteenth century petit-point cushion top with arabesque border," when suddenly my wife succumbed to the mob psychology of the occasion. She began to bid. "$35!" she cried. For an instant, I was paralyzed by terror. I had visions of a van backing up at our house, loaded with things we had struggled to get rid of. Whipping out a silk handkerchief, I slipped it tightly over my wife's face, gathered her in my arms, and made for the door. "The lady has fainted," I explained to the crowd. . . . The relief of getting back into a comparatively empty house was indescribable. As my wife said, "It gives us so much more room to put other things in when we get them."

Intimation of Immortality

A VETERAN NURSE (quoted in *The American Magazine*): It has always seemed to me a major tragedy that so many people go through life haunted by the fear of death—only to find when it comes that it's as natural as life itself. For very few are afraid to die when they get to the very end. In all my experience only one seemed to feel any terror—a woman who had done her sister a wrong which it was too late to right.

Something strange and beautiful happens to men and women when they come to the end of the road. All fear, all horror disappears. I have often watched a look of happy wonder dawn in their eyes when they realized this was true. It is all part of the goodness of nature and, I believe, of the illimitable goodness of God.

That Tired Feeling

Condensed from The American Magazine

FRANK B. GILBRETH

IF YOU ARE "all tired out" at the end of the day, or even before, do you know why? Most of us think it is our work that has exhausted us, but in nine times out of ten this is probably not true. Very often this fatigue is caused not by the work itself but by the conditions under which the work is done.

Misfit shoes are such an important factor in causing fatigue and undermining efficiency that some big factories have found it paid to go to the expense of providing properly fitting canvas shoes for their employes. . . . The shoe should be long enough so that you can put a good-size almond in the toe. Even with the almond in the toe, you ought to be able to wear the shoe for an hour or so without real discomfort. If you cannot do this, your shoes are almost certainly too short. Wear them a year and you will pay in fatigue many times the original cost of such misfits.

An office manager was subject to daily headaches and fatigue, when in his office. A brief study disclosed the cause: His desk and chair were so placed that when he was dictating he looked out the window into the light. When engaged in other duties, he faced a gray dark wall. His eyes were constantly adjusting themselves to these extremes of light and dark. It was a simple matter to arrange his office so that he escaped both the unnecessary fatigue and the headaches.

The abuse of the eye by badly arranged lights and work probably causes us more unnecessary fatigue than any other one thing. Looking far off occasionally after confining yourself to close work, is another matter. That *rests* the eye. The eye has a lens which changes its shape, its convexity, so that you get the right focus. If, while you are reading something at a distance of 12 to 18 inches, you have to fix your eyes at frequent intervals on copy, or a chart, two feet or a yard away, this change in the shape of the lens is just as frequent. An hour or two of it may drain you of so much energy that you will be conscious of fatigue the rest of the day.

You probably have no conception of the price you pay in fatigue for letting the bright reflection from highly polished surfaces reach your eyes. The glare from the nickel on a typewriter or from an ink bottle leaves a record in fatigue. . . . We have even found that it aids production in a factory to give the nickel and other bright parts of machinery a dull black finish. . . . If you are getting enough light for your work, be sure there is no light shining into your eyes. When reading, have your book or paper placed so that no reflected light shines from the page. If your desk has a brilliant finish, cover it with green, blue or white blotting paper. Place your desk so that the light comes over your left shoulder.

Any kind of distraction, whether you are conscious of it or not, increases the fatigue of your day's work. Many of the distracting things that needlessly tire us are the result of bad habits or thoughtlessness. If you have the habit of keeping your finished and unfinished papers heaped in confusion on your desk, you are certainly adding to your fatigue. Have the tools you use—whether briefs, books, or chisels and dies—in the most handy place, arranged so that you don't have to look for them. Make a practice of getting everything in readiness for doing your work before you begin. And clean up afterward, so that you are ready for the next job. And see that you get enough fresh air and light. Avoid having your home and your work place overheated.

Much of your fatigue and annoyance in the course of a day may come from the habit of trying to carry too much in your head. If you haven't the habit of using a notebook, you are probably forgetting two or three things a day; and the failure to do them when you should gives you a sense of uneasiness and exasperation. That is another kind of distraction to be avoided.

One of the most important facts established by scientific investigation and exact records is that a little fatigue is easily overcome if proper rest is taken immediately; but twice the amount of fatigue requires more than twice the amount of rest. Four times the amount of fatigue requires, by a still greater margin, more than four times the amount of rest. In other words if, day after day, you are spending more energy than can be restored by the rest you get at night, serious consequences may follow.

Do you get up early in the morning feeling fresh and energetic? Do you feel fatigued after working two or three hours? The symptoms of fatigue are irritability, depression, inability to concentrate. Are you doing less work, or work of poorer quality, than you should? If so, why?

Whether your job is brain work or manual labor, you should have frequent intervals of rest during the day. From scientific observation, experts know almost exactly how many short rest intervals will enable a man to work year in and year out with maximum efficiency.

In your own case you may not hit the result with exactness; but if you adopt the idea of changing your position, and of allowing yourself a brief rest at frequent intervals, you will make your work more enjoyable and increase the amount you can do. . . . When you hold yourself long in one position—with your back bent over a desk, or with your arms inconveniently elevated because of the high arms on your chair—an overfatigue of tissue results. The longer you hold the position the more fatigued you get.

Especially at times of intense concentration are you subject to this kind of fatigue. Becoming interested in your work, you hold yourself as rigid as though you were spellbound. After an hour or two of it you may find yourself so fagged out that you will feel it for the rest of the day. The longer you have held yourself in one position the longer it will take to recover from the fatigue. You should teach yourself the habit of changing your position frequently without breaking in on your thought.

Intense concentration, the kind a man achieves when he is doing his best work with all his skill, is a joy. With the men who have accomplished great tasks it has amounted to a passion, a sort of creative intoxication. And I suppose the real thrill of concentration seldom or never comes to the man who has no definitely recognized purpose for which he is ready to spend himself. . . . Whatever a man's purpose, it seems to lead him to the use of his best energies if it is kept constantly before him. Have a definite program for your work.

If you realize in advance that interruptions are coming, you can be prepared for them and they will be less trying. Suppose you know that in the midst of your morning you will have to telephone to a shoe dealer, confer with an associate, and receive a caller. Set a definite time for these things, if you can: say 11 o'clock. Then you will be able to work uninterruptedly from 9 to 11; and at 11:30 or 12 you will find yourself free to concentrate on the particular task again. But don't make your program so rigid that the plan itself involves a burden.

Frozen Assets

THOUSANDS of years ago, retreating northward with the ice, the mammoths of Europe and Asia made a last stand in Siberia. Countless numbers bogged down in the soft, icy marshes, were frozen in the unthawing soil. They are occasionally discovered now, perfectly preserved for more than 10,000 years in nature's refrigerator; the hide, hair, flesh, even the remains of undigested meals in their stomachs; bunches of moss, grass, sedges and wild thyme unchewed in their mouths. Siberian farmers cut off chunks of the red flesh to feed their dogs.—*The Literary Digest*

The Lip-Lazy American

Condensed from The Century Magazine

EDWARD W. BOK

SUPPOSE a boy has the desire to make something of his life. He naturally feels that his first step to success is to excel at school. But who will teach him *how* to study? Not what to study, but how to study? And even when he does learn what to study without being told how to study it, who will teach him how to tell others intelligently what he has learned—how to tell it so that others can understand what he says? Who will teach him to open his lips when he recites? Who will teach him to enunciate clearly, to pronounce his words fully and distinctly? Who will teach him how to put the emphasis on the right word? "Oh," is the blithe answer, "the teachers teach that." The teachers? How can they teach an art in which they are never trained and are themselves almost totally deficient? How many teachers speak distinctly? And if they teach distinct pronunciation and clear enunciation, as some claim, why is it that the American is the lip-laziest person in the world?

"But do you consider that part of an education?" an educator once asked me. Are we not told that education is supposed to fit the young for life?

"Show me how to study," said a boy to his instructor, "and I'll learn whatever you put before me."

"Ah, my boy," came the enlightening answer, "that's exactly the thing for you to learn." This is the point of view held by the average instructor of our future men and women: they are told what to learn, but not how to learn it.

I attended an important educational conference in Washington, and during the four days that a friend and I listened to some thirty-odd speakers from the platform and the floor, we decided that not half a dozen could be clearly understood. Yet the speakers included some of the principal educators in the country. The hall was small, the acoustics seemed excellent, and yet here were a company of men and women engaged in the important field of education who spoke so indistinctly as to make what they said

33

inaudible to one-half of their audience. It was significant, too, that the only speaker, a woman, to whom it was a pleasure to listen for her clear enunciation, was an Englishwoman. Go to any play with an English cast of actors, observe the clear and full value which they give to each word spoken, and then listen to the lines of a play spoken by American actors. The contrast is like the force of a blow.

An interesting incident happened at the premier of a well known play. The leading part was taken by an actor notorious for "mouthing" his words, and his co-star, an actress of some repute, was equally famous for her lack of clear enunciation. The first act of the play had not proceeded for more than 15 minutes when, suddenly, in the fifth row from the front, a man of distinguished appearance, who turned out to be a well known member of the bar, arose, and in a well modulated voice said:

"Excuse me for interrupting you, Mr. ———, but I think you should know that scarcely any one in the audience, I believe, can understand what Miss ——— and you are saying. Will you not make it possible for us to enjoy the play?"

The actor flushed, and then he proceeded to give a tongue-lashing to his critic for his impertinence. The curtain was rung down, and some hundred or more of the men in the audience went out into the lobby, sought the manager of the play, and told him they all agreed with the auditor who had shown the courage to rise and speak their thoughts, and that if the lines could not be better spoken, they would demand the money for their tickets and leave the theatre. To their surprise, the manager said he heartily agreed with the patrons, and that he was on his way "back stage" so to inform the two principals of the stage; that he himself had been able to understand scarcely a word spoken.

After a few minutes, the curtain was rung up, the two principals bowed their thanks to the audience, and the first act was replayed. So carefully did the two actors speak their lines that they received an ovation, and the play became one of the successes of the season.

The rebuke should have been unnecessary. There should be more and better American schools of acting where our actors should be taught clear speaking and distinct enunciation, as is the practice in England. The stage is a powerful educational influence, and could be a great factor in its influence upon the manner in which we as a people should speak.

We fail to see the value of distinct speaking, or, if we do, we certainly take no pains to see to it that it is taught to our children. And the fault is with us who are elders. It is curious that the American man, with his perceptions always alive to assets, has not sensed the value of a trained speaking voice. There are few possessions more of an asset than the ability to speak distinctly and to know where to put the emphasis, whether a man is a salesman or an executive anxious to make his points effective in speaking to a business conference, or before a public audience. It is one of the most valuable "selling" qualities a man can possess, whether he is selling a bill of merchandise or making a point in argument. Nothing is of equal value to the lawyer impressing a jury or bench, it is the chief asset of the preacher, it is invaluable to the statesman, it is the instrument of success with the public speaker. Yet apparently we pay not the slightest attention to the almost complete absence of a study of the subject in our schools and colleges, save in two or three colleges, and permit generation after generation

to inherit our national lip-laziness. We are known in other countries for our slurring speech and carelessness of pronunciation, and yet an era of international relations faces our children for which we should equip them with all the natural qualities necessary for their greatest efficiency.

The place to begin is, naturally, in the home, but home training should be supplemented by the school and the college. "How well he speaks!" should not be the occasional surprised comment; it should be, as it can be, the nationally accepted hall-mark of the American.

Americana

Excerpts from The American Mercury

Alabama: The alert Shelby Democrat reports that rarity, the good loser—a man ignominiously defeated when he ran for sheriff:

HE GOT 55 votes out of a total of 3500, and the next day he walked down Main Street with two guns hanging from his belt.

"You were not elected and you have no right to carry guns," fellow-citizens told him.

"Listen, folks," he replied, "a man with no more friends than I've got in this country needs to carry guns."

California: Divorce news from San Francisco:

TO WHOM does the warm spot in the bed belong on a cold night—the wife who first climbed between the icy sheets or the husband who comes home later and demands the covered place as lord of the household? Superior Judge Van Nostrand has the perplexing problem to decide in the divorce suit of Mrs. Anna Weisinger of Buchanan Street, and Jack Weisinger. The testimony was that the police were called to the Weisinger home to quiet a war that started when Weisinger ordered his wife to move over and she insisted on remaining in the spot she had warmed up.

The Christmas Guest

Condensed from The Atlantic Monthly

KENNETH IRVING BROWN

THERE are times when a man yearns for his home and the companionship of his friends. I had reached such a state of mind after four months in South America in search of flora for my botanical museum. . . .

I lay back in the native dugout, lost in pleasant thoughts of home and a land where Nature was tamed. Pedro, a native Carib guide, between the lazy strokes of his paddle, had told me, in a lingo of distorted English and incomprehensible Spanish, of Cispatia, a tiny Carib town inland on the Mulatto River which he knew, of the villagers' "heart warmness," and of their isolation. If I understood him correctly, no white man had visited them for 20 years.

"And this is the day before Christmas," I mused. "We shall spend Christmas Eve at Cispatia; I shall be their Christmas guest." The thought was ironical, and I smiled bitterly.

It was approaching twilight when the village came into view. It consisted of a score of small huts with novel grass-roofs, many of them built on sticks for protection against the attack of wild animals. . . . An old man espied us and stood as if rooted to the spot, staring intently at us. Then with a wild shout, such as I have never heard, he cried: "*Hombres, hombres! Venid!*" and straightway running from the huts came men and women. They stopped abruptly when they saw us; with one accord they fell upon their knees and bowed their faces in the dust, all the while making a rhythmic moan, strangely beautiful.

I knew not what to make of this strange performance and my guide offered no information. As I stepped ashore, not a person stood, nor even peered at me through half-closed eyes; evidently that which I had taken for a moan was a prayer.

"Tell them we want to spend the night here," I said to my guide. No sooner had he spoken than they rushed toward me. In no human eye have I ever seen expressed such emotion as was written in theirs. Their eyes scanned my face with a hunger and avidity quite disconcerting. When I raised my arms to them to

36

signify that I would be their friend, they fell at my feet; they even kissed my sandals. . . . The entire performance was incomprehensible to me. Amazement at the presence of a white man hardly accounted for their apparent worship. Presently I strolled down to the bank of the stream and sat in wonder, while the shadows of twilight thickened.

I could see the *hombres* and *mujeres* in the distance. They were talking in soft tones. Suddenly one of the muchachas, young and slender, came toward me. She walked with difficulty, leaning heavily upon a staff at each step. Apparently her left side was paralyzed. Her foot dragged as a leaden weight, and her arm hung useless. No one moved among the group in the background, and yet I could see they were watching her intently. The young girl was trembling violently. I rose, wondering what was expected of me, and even as I did she stumbled. Her staff fell from her hand and she pitched forward. I caught her easily, and held her trembling body for a moment. Then, with a cry of ecstasy, the young thing leaped from my arms and flew back to the shadows. As if waiting for this moment, her friends raised their voices with hers and there arose a solemn chanting, crude, yet beautiful in its sincerity and resplendent in its recurring note of joy. I longed to know the secret of the mystery.

The muchacha's staff lay at my feet. Could it be that these poor people, hearing of our progress in medicine, believed in the white man's miraculous power to heal?

Faith is the ability to believe the incredible, I had heard it said.

I was so astounded at what had taken place, and so disconcerted by the plaintive chanting, that I hurried to the old father and made signs that I would retire. He understood and led me to the largest hut, where they had prepared a spreading of fresh palm-leaves with a blanket covering—the choicest sleeping-accommodation the camp offered, I knew—and I accepted with a gracious heart.

It was dawn when I awoke. Christmas Day—and yet how unbelievable. What was Christmas Day in a land of wilderness and black folk? What could it mean to these Carib Indians? It was with a feeling of wretchedness that I recalled past Christmases. . . .

The dream was dispelled as I became aware of the voices which had awakened me, yet they stirred something within which quieted the loneliness of my heart. There about the hut were gathered the inhabitants of the camp, with their arms laden. At sight of me they bowed themselves to the ground; then slowly one by one they came and laid their offerings at my feet. I stood as a man in a dream. At the foot of my ladder were heaped great skins of tiger and lynx, bananas, curiously carved images, and a reed basket woven in intricate design.

I did my best to express my thanks by smiles and gestures, but my confusion was turning to puzzled incredulity. I wanted to question my guide. . . . They brought me food;

and when I had eaten I sought my guide. "Pedro," I said, "we must away, at once."

He went to my host with word that we were going. The old man hurried to my side and through Pedro and pantomime begged me to stay. Then, seeing I was resolute, he motioned me to remain for a moment while he called the villagers together. Grouping themselves about me, they fell on their knees. By frantic gesticulation my host endeavored to communicate an idea to me. "Bless," said Pedro. They wanted me to bless them. I, an old, homesick, botany professor! I lifted my hands and repeated the words: "The Lord watch between me and thee, when we are absent from one another." Then, turning to my companion, I entered the dugout, and we pushed off. . . .

"Pedro, what did it all mean?"

He looked at me with eyes filled with amazement and doubt. "You know."

"I don't know; tell me." He hesitated; but at last he spoke.

"Christ come." No white man uttered such words with deeper reverence.

"Christ come!" I echoed, as I remembered their greeting and the incident of the night before.

"Yes, old miss'nary tell—Christ come. He come day 'fore Christmas; come up river at shade-time in dugout with hombre. He stay all night at Cispatia. They know at Cispatia."

I sat stunned by the thought. This then was the reason for their reception and their gifts: this the reason for the muchacha's confidence.

It was an idea which made me tremble. How inconceivable their childish faith, how perfect their adoration!

The canoe moved on. In the distance I heard music. It was the solemn chant they had sung for me when I came; they were singing it again as I left them. . . .

Pedro leaned toward me. "It is true, *no es verdad?* You are, you are —He?"

Hubbub for Posterity

BECAUSE many experts believe that modern street noises will be unknown in the cities of the future, records of typical street and sidewalk sounds were recently sealed into the cornerstone of a New York building. Recordings of honking horns, squeaking brakes, police whistles and other familiar urban noises were made on chromium-plated copper disks, coated with an imperishable tarry compound, and locked in a copper box. Included also were a phonograph and instructions for removing the tarry compound and playing the records.—*Popular Science Monthly*

The Man in the Glass Cage

Condensed from the American Magazine

DAVID GRAYSON

I REMEMBER once a man asked me what my business was, and how the truth jumped straight out of me, as truth sometimes will, before I could think:

"I am a man trying to understand."

I consider this business the most interesting in the whole world, though it never made any man rich, except in satisfaction. I have conducted this business for many years in the country, where it is possible to have some success at it. But in the City—

Let me tell now of a strange experience that came to me after I had spent several months in the City. . . . I had at first a deep interest in the people I found there, and talked often with them at street corners, or in little shops; but presently the grim-walled factories there, especially a certain Mill with tall chimneys, began to have a curious fascination for me. . . .

One day I went in to see my

From: *Adventures in Understanding*, by David Grayson, copyright, 1925, by Doubleday, Doran & Company, Inc.

friend, John Pitwell, who has much of the precious gift of old urbanity. There is a magic circle in the City. Within it everyone belongs; without it, no one belongs. Mr. Pitwell was within it. He not only knew the Mill, but was actually a director in the company that owned it. He explained that they had been having an ugly strike, and he gave me a slip of paper which, he said, would get me past the gate.

The slip took me truly into that magic place; and the very next evening, I met the Man of the Glass Cage. His name was John Doney. "You want to see how she works?" said he.

"Yes," said I, "very much. I am from the country, and it is wonderful to me."

I followed him up the iron ladder to his cage, where he relieved his "side pardner," as he called him, and sat on a stool near him. From that vantage the great dimly lighted room with its enormous clashing machinery appeared still more awe-inspiring.

John Doney showed me, with

faint evidences of pride, shouting at the top of his voice to make me hear, what this lever did; the purpose of that electric button; and how, with a motion, he could start or stop a fifty-ton crane, or turn over a red-hot ingot weighing a ton or more. But it was not what he told me, amazing as it was, that impressed me most, but what I saw as I watched him.

For I began to have the uncanny impression that he was doing these things without volition, moving instinctively, like a man in a trance. "Why," said I suddenly, "he is as automatic as the machinery down there on the floor."

I looked at his eyes and had, in a strange flash of understanding, the sense that he saw nothing at all with them. He was blind!

The immobility of his face, then, was not the serenity of understanding; it was sheer blankness. It came to me with a flash that it was not he that controlled the machinery, but the machinery that controlled him. He was as much a part of it as any lever, roller, pin, or cog. Instead of having his consciousness, his understanding, sharpened by the marvels of his nights in this place, his personality seemed literally effaced.

At the change of the shift, I went out with John Doney and sat on a stool at the night-luncheon place. I found him talkative enough, about his family, the rent he had to pay and his insurance; but when I came up to the great questions I wanted most to ask, I got answers that seemed to me curious and vague.

Finally, I plumped the problem straight at him:

"Why are you doing this work, anyway?"

He looked around at me, puzzling: "Why, I get forty a week."

"Is that all you get?" I asked.

"Yes," said he, "and it ain't really enough."

"But what do you do up there?"

"Why, you've seen it: I'm the control-operator."

"I know," I said; "but haven't you any idea of what you are doing—I mean the whole big job—when you sit up there night after night? Aren't you *interested* in it?"

He looked around at me suspiciously, half alarmed. "What do you mean; a man's got to live, ain't he? He's got to make his wages, ain't he?"

It was hopeless. And at that a wave of compassion for this man—this blind automaton!—came over me; and I thought that it would be the greatest thing in the world if I could wake him up a little, make him see what he was doing, the sheer importance and beauty of it, the bigness of it. So I said to him quietly:

"Do you know what I thought as I saw you in the glass cage? Well, I thought you were the most important man in the whole Mill. I thought you could tell me all about what was being done in the Mill, what was made there and why it was made. You controlled everything. If anything happened to you, everything would go to pieces."

He was still looking at me with an intentness I cannot describe—

but now a look of puzzled alarm came into his face. "Say—what are you drivin' at? You talk like one o' these labor agitators."

I tried further, but soon saw that I had lost out; he seemed afraid even to carry on the discussion. "I got to go back," said he gruffly. "I got wages to earn."

I walked homeward in the night with a deep sense of depression; and in the following late afternoon went again to see my friend Pitwell. He suggested that we take a turn in the Park.

"Well, Grayson," said he, "how did you like our Mill?"

"It is one of the most wonderful places," said I, "that I ever visited. But strange. Can you stand a country parable? Well, you know I keep bees. I enjoy this greatly. They have come to seem like people to me. I like to stand watching them, or, better yet, lie down close to their hives, say in May when the drones are plenty and the young queens come out for their courting —and swarms are likely. It is a fine and wonderful society they have built up—"

"It must be," said Mr. Pitwell.

"But at times," said I, "there seems something positively terrifying about it: and this is what I am getting to. The bees are more highly developed in some ways than men; and their development is much older. You know that bees have been found in fossil form in the Baltic amber, showing that millions of years ago they existed in forms practically identical with those of today. Think of it!

"Lying there by my hives in the sun, I have thought of this with a strange feeling of weariness: the endlessness of it, the ceaseless, terrifying repetition, and no change, no progress!

"Well," I continued, "I had something of the same feeling last night when I sat looking into that strange hive you call a mill. I had a curious flash of wonder if men were not drifting into a blind alley of mechanism like my bees—where they would go on repeating themselves wearily for a million years— and never come to know what it was all about, or be able to change it. Among the bee-people the organization or mechanism absolutely controls the bees: not the bees the mechanism."

"Go on, go on," said Mr. Pitwell, when I paused.

"Well," said I, "I had an amusing conversation with that Man in the Glass Cage. I felt afterward as though I had tried to argue with one of my worker bees, I seemed to make so little impression upon him."

I told Mr. Pitwell, then, as exactly as I could, what happened in the Mill. . . . "It is odd, Mr. Grayson," he remarked presently, "how little we *have* thought about the larger meanings of what we are doing." After another pause, he asked, "What did you make out of the strike? We've tried to treat our men well—we have treated them well—but they strike."

"It impressed me as curious last night," said I, "as I sat in that magic room, the sheer wonder and glory of human genius: that it could build such a marvel and set it to work for the benefit of mankind. It is greater than anything that Plato could have imagined or Napoleon brought to pass. You have built a kind of steel giant to do your work for you. It toils night and day, summer and winter; it never gets tired, it demands no vacations, it exacts no wages, it joins no union.

"And yet, as I sat there last night in that high cage, looking down upon that toiling but willing slave, I thought how it was that you, who have done all this, are quarreling over the management of it. Not long ago you actually had soldiers picketed around the Mill to prevent some of the men who are interested —the workers—from breaking up or crippling this willing slave which helps feed and clothe you all. You're wonderful when you invent and build; but how utterly you fail when it comes to controlling or using what you invent."

"It's true, Grayson, it's true. But what is there to be done about it?"

"Well," said I, "I am only a Countryman, and know very little about such things. But I had the impression powerfully last night when I was talking to the Man in the Glass Cage, that if somehow I could wake him up, and make him truly feel the wonder and importance and beauty of his job, he'd be quite a different man: happier, and a better worker.

"I had a feeling last night that if I found myself becoming just a kind of cog or pin or lever of that machinery—an automaton—like the Glass Cage Man, I'd do *anything*, even smash the machine, to prove that I was really a man."

"Well," said Mr. Pitwell, "you need not think that these problems have not bothered me." Presently he looked at me curiously, and asked: "Grayson, are you happy?"

This is a hard and sharp question to ask any man. But it is truly—as I thought afterward—the first question to put to the critic; for if the critic has not arrived at an understanding with himself (which is as near true "happiness" as any man ever gets) what right has he to criticize? I replied instantly (wondering since somewhat about it!):

"Yes, I am. Once I had a civil war going on in me; and I was unhappy. Now, I know who I am; and what I am trying to do. I know what life is for."

It is only occasionally—once or twice in a dozen years—that two men get down thus into the very roots of things.

"Well, what is life for?" asked Mr. Pitwell.

"It's to make better men, nobler men—and after that still nobler men. It's to throw all you are and everything you have into that one purpose. It's to understand the wonder and the truth of life—and then to make other people understand. It's to make of life a great adventure; an expedition, an enthusiasm. Not to blink sorrow, or evil, or ugliness; but never to fear them! If I could have made that Man in the Glass Cage see what I see and feel what I feel, his whole life would be changed."

Mr. Pitwell said nothing.

"If a city produces good and noble and beautiful human beings then it is a good city; if a mill produces good and fine men, then it is a good mill. This is true. It isn't enough to produce steel in a mill."

I have felt abashed since when I thought how I orated there; and yet, should not a man, when asked, tell what he honestly thinks true about life—the true and ultimate thing it means to him?

We walked homeward, for the most part silent; but I had the strange warm feeling that this man by my side was more my friend than ever before.

When we parted at the foot of my street, he took my arm—or just touched it—but it was enough.

"I think," said he, "you are right. It isn't enough to produce steel in a mill."

Americana

Excerpts from The American Mercury

Intellectual government in Los Angeles is progressing as shown by the Associated Press:

FOR TWO HOURS the City Council argued the question of whether dogs can read, then delayed action on the subject because no expert opinion could be found. The argument was over a proposed ordinance requiring dogs, chickens, cats, turkeys, canaries, and donkeys to be silent in the city between 10 p.m. and 6 a.m. Councilman Byron Brainard precipitated the argument with the question: "Can dogs read? How will they know when they should not bark?"

Colorado: The Colorado Springs Independent issues a statistical report on petting conditions in the Great Open Spaces:

A STORY is being told of a tourist who at nightfall found himself lost in the Garden of the Gods and finally resorted to firing a gun he was carrying, in the hope that the sound might bring aid. Imagine his surprise, following the report of the gun, to be able to count the headlights of 159 automobiles, just turned on.

District of Columbia: Results of one of the highly important investigations undertaken by bureaucrats, as reported in Uncle Sam's Diary, a magazine for federal employees:

WORK HABITS of field mice have been clocked by federal scientists; 6 a.m., reveille; breakfast hunting, until 7:30 a.m.; rest period until 11 a.m.; lunch 1 p.m.; general nosing about until 2 p.m.; dinner, 4:30 p.m.; half hour for napping, and then to bed at 5 p.m.

Why "O. Henry"?

Condensed from The Bookman

EDWARD LAROCQUE TINKER

MANY secrets lie hidden in port cities. Ships and trains are continually stranding in their streets nervous strangers fleeing from crimes committed or troubles too great to bear. Of New Orleans this is particularly true, for she is the gateway to those picturesque little Central American countries whose boundaries are a bar to the laws of extradition. Sidney Porter was one of this stream of fear ridden fugitives; and he left in that city the answer to a secret about himself which has long baffled the public.

It is now common knowledge that a Texas grand jury indicted him for alleged complicity in the embezzlement of the funds of a bank, and that he boarded a train with every intention of going to the county seat to give himself up. It is equally well known that during this journey he fell a victim to his own marvelous imagination, which tortured him with frightful pictures of disgrace, and the penitentiary. He did not have enough will power to get off at the county seat, but continued to ride until he reached New Orleans.

Here fear finally drove him to further flight and he took ship to Honduras. He was now safe from the law, but he became so homesick that he decided at last to go back and face the charges. Arrived again in New Orleans, he once more weakened; and he stayed on, always promising himself that he would start the very next day on that journey which ended so disastrously in the penitentiary.

The name "O. Henry" was suggested to him while he was in New Orleans. There used to be a very popular barroom called the Tobacco Plant Saloon. Henry, the barkeeper, was particularly clever at picking up scraps of information most useful to newspapermen. Reporters from all the different newspapers used to stop so often to see if Henry had any new tips that the place came to be considered a sort of newspaper club. It is not surprising that "Sid" Porter, himself a writer, should have gravitated to the place.

One morning when he stopped in he found Ernest Hepner, an artist for the "Times-Democrat," and Billy Ball, a young reporter, standing at the bar. Porter joined them in a drink and after some desultory talk turned to the barkeeper and said, "Oh, Henry! Set 'em up again." While they were waiting, he pulled a manuscript from his pocket and remarked, "See here, boys, here's something I've written. I don't want to sign my own name, what'll I write instead?"

Hepner said in his quiet way, "Why don't you sign it 'O. Henry'? Goodness knows you say that often enough!"

Porter laughed, and forgot about the incident—for a time. . . . Later, he was sitting inside a grimy little cube of monotonous gloom called a cell in a penitentiary. He had just finished writing the last page of one of his inimitable short stories, vivid with all the life and freedom and warmth of human comradeship for which he was aching. He was racking his brain for a name which would serve to hide his identity and, with it, his disgrace. Suddenly a picture of the cheerful barroom of the Tobacco Plant flashed into his consciousness. Porter's hand reached out to the sheet of paper before him and wrote—"O. Henry."

Let Us Prey

When Mark Twain wrote this "War Prayer," 30 years ago, he said, "It can be published after I am dead, for only dead men can tell the truth in this world and I have told the whole truth in that prayer." Here it is:

O LORD our God, help us to tear their soldiers to bloody shreds with our shells; help us to cover their smiling fields with the pale forms of their patriot dead; help us to lay waste their humble homes with a hurricane of fire; help us to wring the hearts of their unoffending widows with unavailing grief; help us to turn them out roofless with their little children to wander unfriended through wastes of their desolated land in rags and hunger and thirst, sport of the sun's flames of summer and the icy winds of winter, broken in spirit, worn with travail, imploring Thee for the refuge of the grave and denied it—for our sakes, who adore Thee, Lord, blast their hopes, blight their lives, protract their bitter pilgrimage, make heavy their steps, water their way with their tears, stain the white snow with the blood of their wounded feet! We ask of One who is the spirit of love and who is the ever-faithful refuge and friend of all that are sore beset, and seek His aid with humble and contrite hearts. Grant our prayer, O Lord, and Thine shall be the praise and honor and glory, now and ever. Amen.

—N. Y. *World-Telegram*

The May Flies' Dance of Death

Condensed from Nature Magazine

WILLIAM ATHERTON DU PUY

THIS is the season of the year when one may see that strange, joyous tragedy, the dance of death of the May flies, those dainty fairies of Nature which, at the approach of summer, come into the world for a day, frolic themselves to death in the sunshine, and are gone.

Read here their story; then go forth and, with understanding, witness one of the rare idyls of the open.

One moment an ugly creature of the mud, the next, as though by the gesture of a magic wand, the May fly is off, radiant as an oriole, with a shimmer of new-found wings, fragile as the gossamer of a spider's web, with its streaming two or three thread-like tail filaments, twice as long as its body, marking time to its fitful, up-and-down, joyous flight.

Out there in the blue, as by instinct, it finds its mate, for this is its bridal day. The two frolic together for an hour in a world that seems too gross for creatures as fine as they. Then they part, and each, ceaselessly, goes on and on until the last bit of vitality in its frail body is spent.

Then one settles, perhaps on your coat sleeve or mine. The feet with which it clings are unused little feet, for all its life it has been in the air. They are hardly able to support even its dainty weight. It wavers there for a moment and tumbles over like a bit of thistledown. Its brief span of life has come to an end. The May fly is dead.

So brief is its life that one who would make its acquaintance must hurry. The opportunity comes but once a year—in the early summer —and is not unlikely to impress itself on the individual who lives near a lake or river, for the May fly is water-born, and near borders of it is likely to be very plentiful. For one day or two or three in the year the lake dweller is likely to have the existence of the May fly impressed upon him. The street lights in his town may draw millions of them— millions that happen at that moment to be engaged in the fling that comes in that short time when they are given wings. The street lights of

Atlantic City gather, each season, a countless toll of May flies. So do those of Niagara, and Natchez on the Mississippi, and Geneva on its far-away Swiss lake, and ancient Bagdad where the Tigris flows down to the sea. Along the St. Lawrence and on the shores of the Great Lakes, May flies swarm by the million so as to produce imitation snowstorms in the summer.

A strange creature is this dainty May fly. For one thing, it eats nothing from its cradle to the moment of its death. It does not even possess a mouth with which it might eat if it felt so disposed. It comes into the world with a certain amount of vitality in its frail body, it dances gaily until that strength is gone, and dies.

Equally strange is the birth of the May fly, a birth which almost any observer may witness if he happens to be sharp-eyed by the waterside almost anywhere at just the right minute. If he watches closely, he may see many tiny creatures as big as house flies emerging from the mud at the bottom of the lake or stream. These little creatures are leaving their usual place of abode, where they have stayed close at home for two or three years, and coming to the surface—a thing they have never done before.

These are ugly little water insects with sturdy legs, an active tail used in swimming, and with gills through which they breathe as do other water creatures. But as they reach the surface of the water, a most surprising thing happens. Their skin down the back splits open, there is a wriggling within it and, quickly as a flash, there emerges, not this water creature in a new dress, but a dainty May fly, a thing as different in appearance from the water insect from which it came as a peacock is different from a rat. In a way it is more different, for but a moment ago this creature breathed water through gills like a fish, and now it breathes air and would drown if you thrust it under water.

This new-born creature stretches its gossamer wings and flutters away to a nearby twig. There, in a very few minutes, it again sheds its skin, even to the covering of its wings. It is strange in this also, the scientists say, for it is the only creature under the sun which sheds its skin after it has acquired wings. Then it flies away on its endless dance until the time of death.

Back of this brief blaze of glory in which the life of the May fly goes out there is, however, a long period of preparation. The little water insect that gave birth to the May fly has been battling for its existence two or possibly three years among the creatures that live in the mud at the bottom of the water. The original egg from which this insect came was laid by a May fly two or three seasons ago. It sank into the mud and there hatched into the larva, a crawling and wriggling creature, which kept growing and developing into higher forms.

These insects have difficulties peculiar to them as they grow. Their skins or shells will not stretch, so they grow inside those skins until they become too tight. Then they burst open, and a new and looser skin forms, which is worn until it again becomes too tight, when it likewise is burst and discarded.

It is on its day of frolic that the May fly lays its eggs. Through all the three years of its cycle this is the only day upon which this creature takes thought of its own reproduction. It is undoubtedly true that Nature transforms the mud-inhabiting grub and turns it into a creature of the air for this brief period that it may be given an opportunity to scatter its eggs far and wide.

While on the wing the May flies spread out over the surface of the water. Those of them that strike inland, that congregate about the street lamps, fail of their purpose, have lived to no avail. As their more successful fellows float up and down in the sun over the water they are directed by instinct to plant their eggs where they will have a chance to hatch out into other generations of May flies. Some of them drop their eggs and flit about a while longer until their strength is gone, and in doing so sink to drop to watery graves. Others fold their wings about them and plunge into the water, diving deep to assure their deaths. It is the way they want to die—in the performance of their duty. Their final mission is accomplished, their day of glory at an end, their dance of death completed.

Keeping up with the World

Excerpts from a regular department in Collier's

Freling Foster

EVERY EVENING during the past ten years, and until he died recently, a dog came to the entrance of Shibuya Station in Tokyo and waited in vain for hours for the return of his dead master. This devotion so touched the heart of Japan that it has not only erected a statue of him beside the spot where he waited, but it has sent statuettes to every school throughout the empire as a symbol of faithfulness.

THE STOMACH of a 40-pound dog can hold at least three times as much food as that of a 150-pound man. Hence dogs often eat more food than their masters. . . . A newly invented dog whistle is pitched so high that it is virtually inaudible to the human ear.

NATURE sometimes creates life without providing food to sustain it. The opossum has litters of 18 babies, yet only 12 of them can be reared. They are the youngsters who, in the race into the pouch, get one of the 12 nipples, which they do not relinquish for six weeks. The other third of the litter just looks on—and dies of starvation.

Like Summer's Cloud

Condensed from The Yale Review

CHARLES S. BROOKS

IT IS imperceptibly that we have changed. The cloud that rises in the summer's sky moves not on such secret silent foot.

I was thinking of this recently as I came along the street. What has become of the gas lamps? In former days a spry old fellow with a ladder and a can of guttering oil trotted past at twilight to touch the glistening rows of jets that flashed upon our porches. And once there were hitching posts along the curb and those of our richer neighbors held horses' heads on top with rings hanging through the nostrils, as if the brutes had borrowed a savage custom from the ladies of the Fiji Islands. And there were stepping-stones upon our street, so that a lady might mount to her victoria without exposure of a prudish limb. Mincing steps of stone —for the clock upon her stocking was not, as now, a public dial. Where are those ladies who took the air with colored parasols tipped across their shoulders to guard their pink complexions from a freckle? They worked in thread lace. They sewed a comforter from checkered squares of red and white. When old they wore a cap of lace and congress gaiters with cloth elastic sides.

These ladies wore gingham of a morning. They turned a cunning hand to pie, and knew a homely remedy for every ill. Those were the days when a blush mantled a lady's cheek. Her limbs moved then in the secret twilight of a petticoat —once the symbol of the sex—but now the brazen leg has issued from its home and won the vote.

Every house had a fence between it and the street; and lawns did not, as now, run unobstructed to the walk. The slamming of a gate when guests arrived was the signal to the kitchen for the tipping of the smoky kettle to the silver soup tureen. And the very tureen is gone, once the center of hospitality, with its mighty ladle and its invitation for a second helping.

Trees upon the street used to wear lattice collars to save them from the nibbling of a milkman's horse. Buggies, rattling on the cob-

49

bles, have trotted into silence, and the stamping of horses' hoofs. Leaves of our once more wooded village lay to deeper thickness in the gutter, and the smoke of these October fires still lingers in my memory to build the unsubstantial fabric of the past.

Church bells rang on Sunday morning to call us to the service, and any laggard at his window might see his neighbors trickle from their gates to join the sober current of the righteous. Are church bells gone forever? I listen vainly on a drowsy Sunday morning.

Do children still go on strange journeys, pounding at their hoops? Do they walk on stilts? Wash poles once gave but a lazy Monday to the wash, and all the week beside they stretched us into giants.

Every house had its stable with a loft for hay and its Sunday carriage covered with a cloth. And with stables gone there can be no alley in any proper sense.

What has become of the torch-light processions that were the powerful argument for votes in a great election? Their feeble glow-worm, once thought so pretty, would be lost in our brighter lights. Where are the bicycles with tinkling bells that thronged the evening pavements and sipped a nickel soda from a stool?

There is now no casual dropping-in for euchre and a dish of apples. It was seldom that we passed a solitary night—seldom that chairs were not brought out from the sitting room to reinforce the native

rockers of the porch. Rockers were then the fashion—the symbol of our softer wealth—the distinct product of America, unknown to Europe—and a lady placed a patch or button in the leisure of their soothing rhythm without thought how she might save the world. The very word, *caller*, threatens to disappear from customary speech. We have parties still, to be sure, but we dress in spangled clothes and the friendly village has departed from our streets.

Hammocks were the fashion, and often they were slung in the back yard between the apple trees. And to sit with a young lady in a hammock was an intimacy denied upon a sofa. It seemed a device for sudden lovers, and sagged in the middle to an easy familiarity that loosened the heart upon a moonlit night.

There are no boys who peddle apples in an August twilight. Popcorn has left its whistling cart for a sedentary stand. With the coming of electric lamps the match-boy—three large boxes for a nickel—has gone out. No more does the hand-organ come among us with infested monkey to soil agreeably the summer night. Hardly a rag-picker drives now his drooping horse to sing of the wares he seeks.

I remember our first apartment house—sniffed at by conservative folk used to village elbow room. Here dwelt folk of prosperous purse in a flat life of two dimensions with a neighbor perched upon their shoulders. Respectability no longer required a lilac bush and whitened stones along a carriage drive.

A horse car rattled citywards with a fare box and a driver on a padded stool. There was straw on the floor in winter and the windows rattled in the tempest of the journey. Only men of broken age signalled for the car to stop. A public boarding-house came among us to shock our stiffer crinoline. One neighbor, and then another, put in a telephone, and there was less use for gossip across the fence.

Men of business used to come home for midday dinner. We saved all broken crusts of bread for puddings to which we gave sentimental names to disguise their humble origin. Watermelons were round and had not been stretched into the likeness of a giant cucumber. Apples were not aristocrats in separate tissue wrappers, but they stewed like democrats in a common barrel. Pepper, salt, plates, and cloth stayed always on the table and were not swept to a fashionable discard between meals. It was an age of tidies—the pattern of an elk upon a chair back, cloths over the piano with long silk tassels; and a transparency of Niagara Falls that boasted of our travels to our jealous neighbors. The top of fashion was a chair that rocked on stationary runners with coils of springs that squeaked. There are now no carpets to be ripped up at cleaning time, with pads of dusty paper underneath.

For a bath we ran to the kitchen to feel the boiler behind the stove, and when it rumbled we knew that the water was ready for the tub. Coffee cups had guards for whiskers. The railway station was called a *deepot*, a veranda was a porch, an attic still a garret. Neckties came made up. Buttons, not laces, held our shoes. The cry of knives-to-grind no longer breaks upon our quiet street, umbrellas to repair, or glass-to-mend that rings a bell to the rhythm of a lazy step.

Like a cloud that moves on silent foot the city has swept upon us, and the village of my youth is gone.

Accent on Scent

IF YOU LOVE the scent of flowers, plant those which smell the sweetest near the house. Border the walk to the entrance with English lavender or old-fashioned pinks; plant clumps of phlox, climbing roses, sweet alyssum, mignonette, stock and sweet William, narcissus and hyacinth, near the living-room windows. Nicotiana, which smells sweetest at night, belongs under bedroom windows, as do lilacs. Brier and other old-fashioned roses and flowering currant blooming near the dining-room will waft their delicate perfume into the room. For your garden walks, try Francis Bacon's plan, and plant them with "burnet, wild thyme and water mints, which perfume the air most delightfully when trodden upon and crushed, so that you may have pleasure when you walk."

Paper Making 2000 Years Old

Excerpts from The Mentor

ROYAL S. KELLOGG

Papyrus, the writing-material of the ancient Egyptians—made from the rush-like plant of the sedge family (from it the word "paper" is derived), served its purpose for thousands of years, but it was not until Ts'ai Lun devised a process of maceration of wood in China about 130 A. D. that the world had real paper.

Mr. Kellogg, the author of several books on paper making, conceived the interesting idea of presenting the story of Ts'ai Lun in dramatic form. So, on the occasion of an assembly of scientists and manufacturers engaged in paper industries, Mr. Kellogg, arrayed in Chinese robes and impersonating the wise old minister of agriculture who invented paper, told the story of Ts'ai Lun, as follows:

I AM Ts'ai Lun, minister of agriculture under the Celestial Emperor Ho-Ti and made by him a marquis in the year which the Christians call 114 A. D., but which, according to the true calendar of the Flowery Kingdom, was 592 years after the death of Confucius.

During the many years of my life I brought various plants from the far places and caused them to take root, flower and fruit in the Imperial Gardens. Then the seed therefrom was carried to gardens elsewhere, sown according to my direction, and the yield thereof increased manifold.

Moreover, I taught the people to plant rice this year, beans next year and another crop the year after, because I found that the great Mother Earth does not take kindly to the same seed each year.

Thus it was that the people had more and better rice to eat and tea to drink, larger shoots of the bamboo with which to build shelter, more cotton for weaving and still finer silk when they were taught to choose and care for the worms that lived in the thickly leaved branches of the mulberry trees.

Yet was there always need for some light material, not so costly as silk, nor so cumbersome as bamboo, upon which to record the wisdom of our sages and the deeds of our great men. One day did the mighty Ho-Ti say unto me: "Ts'ai Lun, how wilt thou leave behind thee directions so that those who come after thee may learn to do these many things that thou hast discovered? What availeth all thy labors if there be no way in which thy learning may be passed on to those who follow in cycle after cycle?"

One night, when I could not sleep because of the charge laid upon me, there appeared before me the spirit of Confucius, who said: "Ts'ai Lun, go thou to the tree which feedeth the silkworm. Remove the bark in strips, leaving somewhat of bark so that the tree will not die. Then do thou separate the fibers and place them in a vessel in which there is lye leached from the ashes of wood, saving the outer bark that thou mayst make a fire under the vessel. When the fibers have been in the vessel one cycle of the moon, thou shalt put them upon a rock and beat them with a cudgel, after which thou shalt put them into a vat with much clean water and stir them until they become exceedingly fine.

"Then thou shalt make a frame of bamboo one cubit square, with a fine screen across the top made of bamboo splints tied evenly with silk. And upon this screen shalt thou place another frame like unto the first, except that it be open at one side. Then shalt thou grasp them firmly in both hands, dip evenly into the vat of fibers, lift up and shake gently to and fro that the water may run through the screen, and thou wilt find upon it a wet sheet of tangled fibers.

"Then shalt thou remove the frame and place the sheet upon a clean cloth, placing another cloth over it. Then shalt thou dip the sheets into warm water wherein the hoofs and horns of cattle have been boiled, and dry them again. And at last thou shalt rub them to a great smoothness with a polished stone.

"Then shalt thou take the sheets to the Emperor Ho-Ti and tell him thou hast made this wondrous new material upon which the deeds of mankind may be inscribed and put into the hands of all the people."

Thus spake the spirit of Confucius. And it was even so. And after I made paper from the mulberry tree, I taught my people of the Flowery Kingdom how to make even a stronger and better paper from rags of cotton and flax, and also a cheap paper from the straw of the rice plant.

And it was from rags that the craftsmen of Arabia and of Europe and of America learned to make paper, and for 1,700 years but little paper was made of aught else—*and no better paper has ever been made than was made in those days.*

The pleasantest things in the world are pleasant thoughts: and the great art of life is to have as many of them as possible.—Montaigne

Panic!

Condensed from The Scientific American

JAMES H. COLLINS

GIVEN a disaster that would suddenly start the skyscraper population of downtown New York hurrying into the streets in a blind rush like a theater panic—what would happen?

The nearest answer thus far found to that question came on the afternoon of Nov. 7, 1918. It was the day of the "false armistice." During the lunch hour a premature report that peace had been signed sent New York into the wildest carnival it has ever known. People rushed into the street, abandoning work. The shops were quickly stripped of everything that would make a noise. By some common impulse, thousands already in the city started for the downtown skyscraper section, and many more thousands outside hurried in the same direction.

Chief John Kenlon, of the New York Fire Department, responsible for the safety of the city, viewed the merry making from that standpoint. "And had New Yorkers been determined to destroy their city that day," he says, "they were

taking the most effective means of doing so."

The first thing people did to express their joy was to throw into the street tons upon tons of fluttering paper—ticker tape, torn-up telephone books and newspapers, old records, anything and everything that would swell the snowstorm of inflammable material falling upon the joy-crazed crowds below. From uptown, motor cars came until they were packed solidly along the main streets, absolutely blocked so far as their own movements were concerned, and making the streets impassable for fire apparatus. Tons upon tons of paper littering the streets, and thousands of gallons of gasoline a few inches above! And dense masses of human beings milling over the inferno that might be started any minute by a carelessly tossed match or cigarette butt!

Yet not a single fire alarm was turned in by lower Manhattan that day! Ordinarily, fires start every day in downtown New York from a dozen causes.

"I can account for it," Chief Kenlon told me, "as the intervention of an all-wise Providence—for six or seven hours that afternoon, the city was literally in the hands of God. Or mathematically, it was the thing that happens once in 10,000 times. But there was one single ray of sunshine. The people were too excited to smoke! It is a fact that when people are excited, they rarely smoke. They are too busy, too distracted. We sent firemen to hydrants with hose, and orders to stay there, as the only substitute for apparatus, but had the paper caught fire, the packed automobiles would have furnished terrible fuel, and the fire traveled beyond control."

The armistice crowd was not frightened. Instead of trampling its neighbor, it wanted to put its arms around his neck, and let him dig it in the ribs, and make as much noise as possible. But suppose the signal that set this pandemonium loose had been a catastrophe like an earthquake—what then? It need not be a destructive earthquake. One severe enough to sway the skyscrapers, and rattle down a very little of the brick, stone, and other building material, might easily have that effect.

From that viewpoint, there is no place in the world like lower New York. The most severe panic, and the greatest panic hazard is in theaters. Downtown New York, roughly below the City Hall, is the largest theater in the world, should anything throw its whole skyscraper population into a panic. People are seldom burned in modern theaters, but crushed in the aisles. If there is fire, but no panic,

seldom is anyone killed or even hurt. Downtown New York in an earthquake would be precisely the same. Few of the people in modern buildings would be hurt, if any. But if a panic occurred, the problem would be strictly one of aisles, and probably great loss of life would occur in the aisles, or streets.

Consider the mad rush, the reasonless panic, which completely overtakes the passengers of a crowded subway train in the event of an unexpected and threatening occurrence, such as the blowing out of a fuse and the burning of insulation with its attendant pungent smoke and flame. Then try to imagine the scene on every inch of downtown New York if suddenly the city was thrown into a real panic by sudden disaster, such as a violent earthquake. Six million crazed people on lower Manhattan. Self preservation the first law of nature. Each fighting for his life, with all reason completely gone. Such might well be the scene in a panic in New York.

It has been found by H. F. J. Porter, an engineer who has made many investigations, that people crowding into the interior stairway type of fire escape, even though calm and orderly, will pack so tightly that movement is impossible. In panics, they wedge tightly enough to burst away the stair railings.

Chief Kenlon holds that what would happen, in the event of a disaster, would depend entirely upon state of mind.

"Don't write me down an alarm-ist!" he says. "The chances for a great explosion, or fire, that would cause general panic in the skyscraper district are remote. In my opinion, New York is in no danger of a destructive earthquake. But let us assume that an earthquake severe enough to rock the skyscrapers and bring down tons of their wall and cornice material did occur. That would tend to create panic. New York's skyscraper population might conceivably start in alarm to reach the street. And if subways and skyscrapers were emptied of their occupants simultaneously, pedestrians in the streets would be literally 'three-deep.'

"In that event, the safest place would be the skyscrapers themselves, and the most dangerous place would be the street. People in the streets would be in peril from falling material. People in old buildings of moderate height would likewise be in danger, for if the shock were severe enough, the structures would collapse. But while the skyscrapers might sway, all earthquake experience with modern steel buildings shows that they withstand shock. There is nothing in them to collapse, except the outer walls, and practically nothing to endanger people inside. The walls might be stripped from a skyscraper, but its beams would be intact, and its floors being really arches buttressed against the steel beams, could not fall.

"So, those in skyscrapers who had presence of mind enough to stay where they were, would escape the two chief dangers of such a disaster—the danger of being hurt or killed in the street, and that of panic in the building itself."

Architects' dreams for New York are wrapped up in taller and taller buildings—tower cities a thousand feet high or more, terminating in pinnacles, and set at such distances from each other that there will be ample light and ventilation around them. It is logical to ask, "What would become of the people in such structures in case of disaster like a major earthquake?" And the answer seems to be, "The higher the buildings, the more proof they will be against such disaster, and the safer people will be in them."

THERE IS still one place in the world where the full-rigged sailing ship is doing business, and where those travelers who regret the lost romance of the days of sail may find solace. Gustaf Erikson of Finland operates three sailing ships which carry passengers to Australia around Cape Horn. One is fitted to take 80 passengers, of three classes, and in summer makes Baltic cruises, with a tug fussing along behind in case of need.

—A. J. Villiers in *National Geographic*

You

Condensed from Scribner's Magazine

EDWARD W. BOK

IF TIMID folk could only realize the potentiality that is implanted in each one of us—singly! These folk have aspirations, the urge to do. But, invariably, they are deprecatory, ever disparaging of self. They fall back upon the plaint: "I am just one man" or "one woman. What can I do?"

What was Florence Nightingale but one woman? Yet her work led straight to the Red Cross! How far would be the humane processes of healing the wounded and sorrowful all over the world today had this English nurse sat down and bemoaned the fact that she was "just one woman"?

Where would the marvellous work done by radium be today if, when bereaved, Madame Curie had folded her arms when her husband passed away and minimized herself by saying: "I am just one woman"?

Yes, but exceptional women, you say. Quite to the contrary. "I had faith: that was all," said Florence Nightingale. "I had confidence, little else," said Madame Curie, and to their work each applied her fullest aspiration and trust.

A young actress came from New York to Philadelphia one evening to appear in the chorus of a musical comedy. She was at a loss to know where to find a hotel, and made inquiry of an elderly woman. As the two walked along the street, the young chorus girl said: "Don't you think there should be some one place in a great city like this that we girls could go to?" Today, as a result of that remark and the initiative of the elder woman, the Charlotte Cushman Club in Philadelphia has a club-house for young actresses which, in a single year, accommodates over 1,200 girls employed in the different theatrical companies which visit the city. Were either of these women "exceptional"?

Was that mother "exceptional" whose six-year-old boy came home from school one day with a note from his teacher suggesting that he be taken from school as he was "too stupid to learn"? "My boy is

Reprinted from *Dollars Only*, by Edward W. Bok, copyright, 1926, by Charles Scribner's Sons.

not stupid," said the mother. "I will teach him myself." She did, and Thomas A. Edison was the result.

Another example: "I am just a home body, busy with the daily task." ... So was Abraham Lincoln's stepmother "just a home body." But she taught and inspired the son of her husband—not even of her own blood—and held a torch before him which he carried to emancipate a people. "The greatest book I ever read, you ask me?" asked Lincoln in a letter. "My mother." So was Dwight L. Moody's wife "just a home body." But she taught her husband how to write, put the love of God and of his fellow-men into his heart, and sent him forth as the greatest evangelical force of his century.

There was another wife whose husband had to leave home for an indefinite period, leaving his son in his wife's care. "I will take his father's place," she said. And she read to him of the achievements of the great men of his time and stirred his ambition. She implanted in him the highest ideals of Christianity. For years she did this; "just a home body." She produced Robert E. Lee.

We do not seem to get it into our heads that the great works of the world always begin with one person. Emerson put a sermon in a dozen words: "A great institution is but the lengthened shadow of a single man." A man disgusted with committees thus expressed a large truth: "The ideal committee consists of three, with two of the members ill." Every institution that has contributed to American progress, said Roosevelt, has been built upon the initiative and enthusiasm of an individual.

We have become obsessed in this country with the idea that we cannot work alone: only in organization. Look at these organizations, and invariably the creative part, the driving power, is traced to the individual: ofttimes, one: other times, two: rarely more. "Yes," it is agreed. "But these are greater than I am." "There are no great and small," says Emerson. "We fancy others greater than ourselves because they light the divine spark given them, and we do not. We are all children of one Father. It is because we minimize ourselves that we do not accomplish. We do not realize the power of the positions in which we are placed."

Take this example: "I am just a teacher!" Fancy! In a belittling tone this is said of the greatest post of potential influence in life today next to a mother. So said once a teacher I know. Then the vision came to her. From that day her work in her class changed: her eye took on a new radiance to her children: her voice that of the supreme confidence which God gives to us all to bring into being. She had lighted the divine spark within her. Within 18 months she was principal of the entire school. Today into hundreds of hitherto perplexed eyes of the little foreigners in her school she has put a steady light: a true Americanization, and every June she is sending out into America a line of true little Americans who, within a few years, will register the teachings of this one woman at the ballot-boxes and in the homes of our land!

"O ye of little faith." That is where the trouble lies: either we have no faith at all, or we are "of little faith." What a sentence that is which Jesus spake: "If ye have faith as a grain of mustard seed, nothing shall be impossible unto you."

I stand aghast at young men who busy themselves with introspective thoughts, full of argument of whether they can do this or that. Wasting their time. Instead of saying: "God put me here for some purpose. I am going to realize it." Once we are convinced of that

single fact: that we are put here for a purpose: that the seed of divine energy has been given us and that it is for us to cultivate it to its fullest bloom, the way will be shown us. It is our part to make the effort and to put the fullest force and integrity into that effort. It is the young man of little faith who says, "I am nothing." It is the young man of true conception who says "I am everything," and then goes to prove it.

Napoleon struck at the very foundation of all this when he said "Circumstances? I *make* circumstances." That was not the word of an egotist. It was a fact. We *all* make circumstances.

When Wives Speak Out

MRS. ABRAHAM LINCOLN: Yes, he is a great favorite everywhere. He is to be President of the United States some day; if I had not thought so, I would never have married him, for you can see that he is not pretty. But doesn't he look as if he could make a magnificent President?

MME. TOLSTOY: There is so little genuine warmth about him; his kindness does not come from the *heart*, but merely from his *principles*. His biographies will tell of how he helped the laborers to carry buckets of water, but no one will ever know that he never gave his wife a rest and never—in all these 32 years—gave his child a drink of water or spent five minutes by his bedside to give me a chance to rest a little from all my labors.

MRS. JAMES G. BLAINE: First of all, I miss Mr. Blaine. I cannot bear the orderly array of my life. I miss the envelopes in the gravy, the bespattered table linen, the uncertainty of the meals—for you know he always starts out on his constitutional when he hears them taking in dinner.

MRS. ARNOLD BENNETT: It was not the fact of having to do what Arnold wished that made me rebel, it was the dictatorial way he expressed himself. I had not foreseen that a husband who loved you could be sharp with you. It was very stupid of me.—*The Golden Book*

Do People Get on Your Nerves?

Condensed from The American Magazine

WILLIAM S. SADLER, M.D.

AMONG my patients I have found over 40 "pet peeves." One business man was upset because his partner was always saying "Listen." I set about to teach him tolerance. In my first conference with him I discovered he had a habit! In his conversation he constantly asked, "Do you understand?" I went right after him; and when he recognized an equally or more objectionable mannerism in himself developed tolerance and sympathy for his partner. He had a friendly chat with his associate and learned how his "Do you understand?" irritated *him*. He tells me they are now both trying to overcome these things, and enjoying the joke of it all immensely.

A woman allowed her room-mate to "get her goat" because she left her things strewn all over the apartment. I advised my patient to do the same thing—and to quit picking up after her room-mate. Their apartment was soon a sight; even the careless room-mate began to complain. There was a grand blow-out, and the guilty one begged her room-

mate to help her overcome her habit of untidiness. They have since come to really enjoy their efforts to master their little shortcomings.

One man's pet peeve was to blow up when his wife let him get off the trail when they were motoring. It worried her so that she all but refused to take a trip with him. I told her to do half the driving each day. When the husband began to manage the road maps, he let his wife get off the trail every now and then. I had rehearsed her so that she could blow up in great style; but I had taught her to finish each explosion of temper with a laugh. Her husband had sense enough to catch on. When he starts to blow up she now starts to laugh, and they are having real fun out of it.

You probably think it nothing unusual if you "blow up," "go to pieces," or otherwise lose control of your emotions. Yet the effects of these "emotional sprees" on the health are almost as bad as the results of an alcoholic spree. People who indulge in emotional sprees are sick—mentally sick, nervously dis-

60

ordered. *They are victims of deficient self-control.* They always have an alibi—they lay the blame for these upheavals on what someone has said or done to them. What the nervous individual fails to recognize is that he is, after all, responsible for a breakdown in nervous morale which, he must realize, was largely determined by the way in which he *reacted* to the sayings and doings of other people.

The trouble with most nervous people—and nervous people are always emotional—is that they are bestowing too much thought upon themselves. They waste on themselves what the world so much needs—love, pity, sympathy. In other words, they are self-centered, self-absorbed, and introspective. They are wonderfully helped by anything that makes them get their minds off themselves.

The point for them to remember is that *no matter where the blame rests, if you allow other people to get on your nerves, you are allowing their habits to tyrannize over you.* No matter how reprehensible their practices you just cannot afford to let them make you miserable. You can't control habits of the rest of the world, therefore you must, in self-protection, learn to react with less vehemence. *You must continue to live in this world as it is. You cannot possibly regulate and control the habits and practices of all those with whom you come in contact.*

I wish all married couples would take each other less seriously in little things. Every doctor meets constantly this thing of married folks irritating each other. We must not be so foolish as to let little things upset the home. I have seen an otherwise happy home spoiled more than once over just trifles.

Now suppose *you* are one of these high-strung, inordinately sensitive souls, and somebody is always getting on your nerves. You are certainly doomed to lifelong suffering unless you acquire some degree of emotional control. I have just talked to a newly married woman who got sick and went to bed the other day because her husband read his paper during breakfast, and hardly spoke to her. I advised her to try the plan of a nurse I knew who, when her husband read the paper at breakfast, excused herself and returned with her sewing. He took the hint and stopped reading at the breakfast table.

In the case of one confirmed hysteric we made a list of 32 pet peeves that got on her nerves. We arranged them in order of their gravity, starting out with the smallest ones. They were each written on a piece of paper, along with specific instructions for the nurse to carry out. They tackled a new trouble every other day. The patient has now gone through 25 peeves on this list, and has made good.

You see, it is just like developing weak muscles into strong muscles; it requires exercise. Thinking and wishing and willing alone never get us anywhere; we have got to get right down to brass tacks and actually *do* the very thing we are afraid of or that we dislike.

Every time fathers and mothers fail to teach their sons and daughters self-control when they are young, especially if they are nervous children, then, later on in life, husband or wife, or someone else, will have to do the teaching; but the lessons are much easier to learn when young!

While we cannot escape from our emotions, *we can learn to control and manipulate them*. You can form dislikes without indulging in excessive hates. You can experience indignation without indulging in violent outbursts of anger. In other words, you can learn to become temperate in your emotional life, and that is simply another way of saying that you can acquire self-control. A perfectly sane business man will go home at night and rave like a semi-insane man just because dinner is late or some little thing doesn't suit him. He spoils his own digestion by such emotional blow-outs, and also upsets the digestion of the whole family.

This whole nervous battle is in reality a character struggle. We are all engaged in it. The normal, average person wages the battle without much ado; but the victim of spoiled nerves, the neurotic individual, makes a great hullabaloo out of this normal fight of life.

The economical method of attaining self-control is to *prevent exhausting and weakening reactions to undesirable impulses*. You must form the habit of killing undesirable impulses as they arise in the mind. You must go right back in your mind, dig up the soil, plant the seed, and cultivate a new habit of thinking; really, actually, and honestly change your desires, change your viewpoint, make up your mind on this one thing and bring yourself where you can say: "*I will not wish to do it*, and therefore I will not." This is what we mean by "nipping impulses in the bud."

True self-control, then, consists in changing the mind, in mastering the art of making up the mind, in controlling desire at its fountainhead, in preventing the full birth, growth, and expression of an undesirable wish.

The mastery of nerves requires the acquirement of self-control, and this is done not only by thinking but by *acting*.

When the Job Gets the Man

I OFTEN TELL my people that I don't want any fellow who has a job working for me; what I want is a fellow whom a job has. I want the job to get the fellow and not the fellow to get the job. And I want that job to get hold of this young man so hard that no matter where he is the job has got him for keeps. I want that job to have him in its clutches when he goes to bed at night, and in the morning I want that same job to be sitting on the foot of his bed telling him it's time to get up and go to work. And when a job gets a fellow that way he'll amount to something.—Charles F. Kettering, Vice-President, General Motors Corporation.

The Plight of the Genteel

Condensed from Harper's Magazine

KATHARINE FULLERTON GEROULD

I WONDER if we Americans are not seeing a social revolution in our own time. There are no middle-classes any more: only rich and poor. For our plutocracy is imposing a social standard that takes count only of purchasable things. Possessions are, more and more, the sole basis for social distinction.

I can think of nothing my husband and I have which the electrician or the carpenter would like to have—unless, possibly, the faculty privilege of applying for tickets to the Yale game. What, indeed, have we that they could envy us for? Travel, the opera, books, pictures? We do not have them because they cost too much; they do not have them because they do not want them. They want expensive cars and clothes; the best cuts of meat, and radio sets, and electric refrigerators. A comfortable life to them does not mean privacy-ensuring space, or intellectual progress, or aesthetic satisfaction; it means physical comfort and the ability to purchase costly objects. The man who can afford motor cars and fur coats and diamond rings is the rich man. The man who cannot afford them is poor. The standard is very simple, and takes no account of anything between the two.

The plight of the genteel is, actually, prospective extinction. "Genteel" here indicates that class of gently bred people whose incomes, though slender, were compatible with a way of life which to them was both socially and personally necessary. This meant, usually, a house which might be shabby in spots, but where were books, and light, and space, and quiet; where hospitality could be unostentatiously offered. It meant a home which was neither so tiny nor so unattractive that every member of the family had to seek all his pleasures outside it. And, by the exercise of daily frugality, it meant always enough money for school and college bills, and perhaps sometimes for a trip to Europe. Such "gentility" was possible only in a world which agreed that these things were necessities to a large class.

Once, the things the genteel renounced were things which they could do without and which no one despised them for not having. In foregoing luxury they did not forego dignity. It seems to me that this state has passed. The man who cannot afford purchasable things is considered poor, no matter what intangible goods he may possess.

From the point of view of the race, is the elimination of the genteel unimportant? The swashbuckling biographies of men who sprang from obscurity to national prominence tend to dim an important fact: that the vast majority of our more useful and distinguished citizens were born of the class we have been describing. They inherited certain tastes and ideals that prompted their limited expenditures; but not being poor, they did not have to spend all on bare subsistence. They were familiar with frugality, and honest toil, able to do without luxuries, but unable to do without decency.

These households are having very few children today. Those who maintain that birth-control is encouraged only by people who are too selfish to make sacrifices forget that Americans have worked towards an ideal of romantic marriage—the mate comes first. Many a woman would take chances of ill health or domestic routine, yet is unwilling to see her husband fail under mental and financial strain. Many a man refuses, for his wife, the straitened and difficult years. The genteel were always the people who should have had children, because they had traditions best calculated to make good citizens. They had sifted out the essentials. But the class is being eliminated, turned into the frankly poor; it is too sensitive, too conscientious to be prolific.

The poverty of the genteel class is real. When you cannot afford your proper mode of existence, you are poor. We can afford subsistence, yes; but few of the amenities of life. I do not consider myself poor because I cannot afford a motor car; it is not, to me, a necessity. But Europe has been, for years, a necessity both to my husband and to me. It is now an unthinkable indulgence. We have less and less, each year, of the advantages we have preferred to the rich man's toys: less leisure and privacy; less domestic service, fewer books, and duller holidays.

Childless, we could afford more; but every impulse of my being opposes that. We can manage, by sacrifice, to give our children a good chance of health and a reasonable education. It is more difficult, in these days, to teach them to put civilization above success; that personalities are more than palaces. It grows harder, all the time, to make them see that it is more important to have a home which you might like to stay in than to have an automobile in which to get away from home.

The solution is not easy to find. I fear that the genteel must make up their minds to poverty. We who care about things of the mind and spirit must refuse to let the standards of the majority be ours; must, with a certain bravado, if necessary, spend our tiny surplus for things despised by both Labor and Capital. We must strike against the physical laziness of our generation: make our legs walk, and our hands toil, and bluff ourselves into believing that this is no hardship.

In meeting simplicity half way and embracing it on both cheeks, shall we accomplish the survival of our class? Only if we manage to make the community feel that our class has an importance of its own. The present plight of the genteel is due to two facts: the increased cost of living, and the increased indifference, in the heart of the American people, to the kind of thing the genteel desired.

We cannot endure as a class, in large numbers, the strain of perpetual living beyond our incomes, of never having a margin. Such a strain is too disintegrating. A large part of our plight is that the public, seeing no need of the genteel class, will not help it to live. We cannot save on schooling. "Health" is a much more expensive business than it used to be. My husband and I discovered a few years ago that milk—mere milk—cost one-tenth of his yearly salary. I submit that no reasonable budget can be made when the single item of milk absorbs one-tenth of one's salary.

No: society at large will not help us, for at present it respects only the people who can afford anything they want. Nothing in America so arouses suspicion as inability to make money. Whatever a man's occupation, people feel that if he were any good he would be rich.

No one save a Communist or a Socialist resents the man of wealth who is also a man of taste, or spiritual and mental balance. Personally, I do not even resent the rich vulgarian. What one resents is the state of mind that considers wealth in itself significant, that measures a man by his purchasing power rather than by what he actually purchases. All of us have known rich people who were delightful, as all of us have known rich people one would do anything to avoid passing an hour with. For the sake of civilization, that honest discrimination against the millionaire who happens to be stupid or vulgar or vicious, ought to be cherished and perpetuated. Somewhere in the republic other than financial ratings should prevail. The class known as the genteel was the chief preserver of such desirable discriminations. A pity to grind it down below the subsistence-level!

GENERAL U. S. GRANT had no memory for music. On one occasion he remarked to a friend sitting next to him at a concert: "Why, I only know two tunes. One is 'Yankee Doodle' and the other isn't."

The Intolerable City

Condensed from Harper's Magazine

LEWIS MUMFORD

WHY is it that people think that life is far more attractive in a large city? The New York Housing Commission recently reported that only one-third the population of New York City had an income sufficient to enable the family to live in decent modern quarters. But what about the fortunate minority?

Mr. Brown, for example, works in splendid offices, but under artificial light; and in spite of the system of ventilation, the middle of the afternoon finds him dull. The subway ride does not help his appetite; nor the thick fumes of gasoline when he walks out upon the street. Eventually he sits at dinner and looks out on an air-shaft. There is no hint of sunset or moonlight, no variation from season to season; only the smells from other kitchens creep through the windows. Mr. Brown pays so much for his four cubicles that, probably, there are no children. The Browns hope some day to have either a baby or a cheap car: it is hard to decide which, but the car would make it possible to get out into God's country on Sunday.

This pursuit of God's country would make the angels weep: a ride along a dusty, straight concrete road, breathing the exhaust of the car ahead, furnishing dust and exhaust for the car behind; long hours wasted at ferry-houses, bridges, and similar bottlenecks.

After dinner neither Mr. Brown nor his wife is in condition to listen to great music or attend the theater. The price of seats is high; and the prospect of another hour in the subway kills most of the impinging joys. But oh, yes, they have the movies, the same movies that come to Peoria; and the radio, which works no better than, if as well as, in the villages. Brown grumbles; but he is only beginning to doubt. By adding to the city's population, he raises the value of its real estate; and so he increases rents; and so he makes parks and playgrounds and decent homes more difficult to obtain; and so he increases his own difficulties and burdens; and his flat gets smaller, his streets bleaker, and

66

his annual tribute to the deities who build roads and subways and bridges and tunnels becomes more immense.

The city is no place for children. The schools are too crowded for proper education. Play is almost out of the question. And so much money is spent in the detection of criminals, in the treatment of disease, in the building of refuges for the mentally unstable and, above all, in the labyrinth of sewers and subways, that there is relatively little left for the more fruitful processes of living and learning.

So note the paradox. As a city increases in "population and wealth" it becomes less able to afford the things that make life gracious, interesting, and amusing. The difficulties of mere physical existence are so terrific that a major part of a city's money and energy, which should be spent on making life itself better, is devoted to the disheartening task of keeping "things" from getting worse.

Is the suburb a "solution"? The sort of life the suburb aims at is of course only partial: the suburbanite loses many of the cultural advantages of a complete city; but even its limited effort to obtain two essential things—a decent home for children and a comely setting for life—is ephemeral. The suburb is not a solution—merely a halting place. So long as the big city continues to grow, the suburb cannot remain suburban. Its gardens, its quiet streets, the countryside around it—all are doomed. Sooner or later the suburb will be swallowed up in the maw of the great city.

The evils of cities are not accidental defects. They will not be wiped out by a little adroit street widening; and the technicians who devote themselves to easing the burdens of congestion are the first to admit that their remedies are not permanent. The reason is plain: the cost of each new transit line, each marvelous double-decked avenue, must fall back eventually on the land; and in order to meet the taxes of our monster skyscrapers, still greater monsters must be erected. New transit lines, or thoroughfares, would not be tolerated, on business principles, if they did not promise an increase of population within a single congested area. A vicious circle!

Physically, there is perhaps no limit to the heightening and extension of New York and Chicago; the real limitations on city development are not physical but social. Would a 200-story building make life one whit more tolerable? So the question is: How are we to obtain the physical foundations of a good life in our cities?

The garden city now has distinguished adherents in every country. They believe that the congested city is wasteful, obsolete; that it arose out of industrial conditions not in full force today. During the railroad era urban growth took place linearly, along the tracks. But modern motor transportation makes it possible to serve a whole area instead of simply those "points on the line." This works toward decentralization and regional development.

Giant power and industry planning are the two forces capable of turning motor transportation into socially constructive ends. Whereas for a century we have lived where industrial and commercial opportunities seemed greatest, we can now reverse the process, and deliberately plant our industries and our communities in regions where the human opportunities for living are best. Mr. Ford's attempt to restore smaller factory units in the open country is significant. Once the desire for better living conditions is effectively expressed, there is nothing in modern industry to hinder the building of new garden cities. Every day new factories are founded; every day new houses are built. It needs only social foresight and financial co-ordination to connect them.

How would these new communities differ from existing cities? First, they would be established in relation to the best water and power resources, and in country districts where land values are low. They would be surrounded by a permanent belt of agricultural land, to provide green vegetables, and to preserve open spaces. Second, provisions for all necessary public institutions for a community of a given size, say 10,000 or 50,000, would be made from the beginning. Land needed for shops would be allocated. The residential parts of the city would be planned for quiet, safety, and beauty. In general no houses higher than three stories, or offices higher than five, would be allowed. If expansion caused the city to fill its sites, another city would be founded, similarly restricted, similarly surrounded by a rural belt. The provision of gardens and playgrounds would likewise be made on the initial plan; and since the population would be definitely limited, their adequacy would be permanently insured. The time now wasted in subway travel would, since the area of the city is limited, be available for sport, rest, education, or entertainment.

I am not dealing with an imaginary town: I am just translating the realities of English garden cities.

Here then is the choice—between the "mechanical extension" of existing urban areas, and growth by the foundation of new communities, fully equipped for working, learning, and living. Sooner or later, we shall find out that, in Professor Geddes's tart phrase, metropolitan growth means "more and more of worse and worse." When the super-city crumbles in our imagination, nothing will keep us from achieving solid human communities in fact. They existed once. They will exist again.

America never lost a war or won a conference.—Will Rogers

Seeing Ourselves in Our Dogs

Condensed from The Century Magazine

FRED C. KELLY

A DOG is probably never more human than when he insists on keeping other dogs from using what he himself does not want. How often we all do that very thing! Even marriages have resulted from the desire to keep a supposed prize from another. After my sweet-natured Airedale, Jimmy, has exhausted the possibilities of a soup-bone he is deeply distressed to see the bone exciting the interest of a visiting brother. How human! Jimmy is scarcely able to eat if other dogs are fed near-by, so busy is he casting covetous glances at their plates. He is more interested in their food than in his own and is unhappy so long as another dog has a morsel left. Here perhaps is the animal origin of the human disposition not to be content with what we have, even when it is enough, but to worry about what the neighbors are doing. Old Badger has a slightly different philosophy from Jimmy's. He eats contentedly

enough and minds his own business so long as there is food on his own plate. But being a rapid eater, he is usually through ahead of other dogs. The instant his own supply is exhausted, he begins to growl, obviously irritated because others still have food when he has not. Many of us are secretly like that, I fear, though less honest about it.

Dogs of course have a decidedly noticeable trait of jealousy. Booth Tarkington once told me a story of two dogs, one his own and another belonging to Harry Leon Wilson. The two men and their dogs had been living together in Europe. Tarkington and Wilson made a trip to the United States, bringing along Wilson's dog, but leaving the Tarkington dog behind. The two dogs had always been great friends. But when the two men returned, having the Wilson dog with them, Tarkington's dog seemed to realize that his one-time playmate had enjoyed a long trip with his master while he himself had been compelled to remain in a lonely kennel. He turned on the Wilson dog in jealous rage, and they were friends no longer.

One trait which I am sure most dogs possess more than their owners realize is a sense of embarrassment. I recall walking with old Badger one day when he started to chase what he thought was a rabbit but which proved to be only a piece of paper moved by the wind. When he discovered his error he immediately stopped short and looked around with a silly expression to see if I had noticed him. When I laughed at him he went slinking away, a picture of mortification. In this connection George John Romanes tells of a terrier that used to be fond of catching flies on a window-pane, and if ridiculed when unsuccessful was evidently much annoyed. "On one occasion," says Mr. Romanes, "to see what he would do, I purposely laughed immoderately every time he failed. It so happened that he did so several times in succession and eventually became so distressed that he positively *pretended* to catch the fly, going through all the appropriate actions with his lips and tongue, and afterwards rubbing the ground as if to kill the victim; he then looked up at me with a triumphant air of success. So well was the whole process simulated that I should have been quite deceived, had I not seen that the fly was still upon the window. Accordingly I drew his attention to this fact, as well as to the absence of anything upon the floor; and when he saw that his hypocrisy had been detected he slunk away under some furniture, evidently much ashamed of himself."

Badger has long had an absurd habit, or one might almost call it a fetish, which I have never been able to explain except that the old rascal has a streak of get-even spirit. If I go away and leave him alone in the house, he is certain to go from one bedroom to another, jump up on each bed, and rumple it up. He never under any circumstances jumps on a bed if there is any one in the house, but the moment he is alone he seems to waste no time in carrying out this secret project. He is not prompted by a desire to lie on the bed, because he never remains longer than necessary to place the bed in a state of general disorder. It cannot be that he is doing it to try to find me, thinking I may still be in bed, because he has seen me go out of the front door. Can it be that he does it as a means of revenge for being left alone? He realizes each time that he is doing wrong and will later be scolded. Yet so great is his desire to commit this offense that he would rather do it even though he must spend the rest of the day with a guilty conscience. Usually when I return from a brief absence, Badger comes bounding to the door in hilarious fashion to greet me. If he fails to do so I know that he has been alone in the house and is ashamed of having been up to his old tricks. I call him, and with great reluctance he finally comes, tail down, utterly dejected. It has been impossible to break up his habit of tearing up beds. I never caught him in the act until one time when he and I occupied a small cabin in the Maine woods. I was in the habit of going to a near-by cabin for meals and would leave Badger in our cabin alone. Almost invariably when I returned the bed would be in a state of disorder. One day I went out, and then tiptoed back to where I could peek in the window. Immediately Badger jumped on the bed and began to rumple it up. He happened to glance toward the window and saw me. Without waiting for a word his whole appearance changed to a shame-faced air that I have come to think of as his bedroom look, and he went slinking away. But as always under such circumstances he watched my face for a sign of forgiveness and at the first suggestion of a smile came bounding at me like a happy child. He has become acquainted with the joy of "making up."

Dogs like humans dislike to admit they are getting old or for any reason cannot do everything that they ever could. Badger, aged 15 at this writing, now prefers to lie quietly and sleep most of the time. But if he sees me playing with a younger dog, he is certain to make a great show of romping about, evidently to make me think that he is still just as spry as ever.

Dogs and folks share a broad-minded willingness to tolerate insults from those that they know they can whip. I once saw James J. Corbett smilingly permit an undersized man to call him names.

I have often noticed that dogs practice a form of deceit in a spirit of politeness. My little Welsh terrier, Megan, seems to think my feelings might be hurt if she were to refuse food I offer her. When she has had enough she takes the food eagerly and dashes away as if to eat it in leisurely fashion in some favorite nook. But what she does is to drop it where she thinks I will not see it, hoping evidently that I will suppose she has eaten it.

How often I have wished I might do the same thing, especially when a charming hostess implores me to have a second helping of soggy pie prepared with her own fair hands! What a convenience it would be if I could run gaily with my plate out into the back yard and secrete it behind a bush!

Crumb Complex

WHICH KIND of person are you: a crumber or a brusher? Between courses, do you automatically brush them away? Or surreptitiously nibble them? Doubtless some professor of psychology can place the crumbers and brushers each in their respective categories. Meantime, look around the table at your next dinner party and see for yourself who are what.—*House and Garden*

Are You a Crape-Hanger?

Condensed from the Woman's Home Companion

MARY B. MULLETT, In Collaboration with DR. F. E. WILLIAMS

THERE are just as many crape-hangers among the rich as among the poor. It isn't a question of how many troubles we have, or how few pleasures. It is a question of which one we *think* most about.

We know perfectly well that our friends don't want to hear about our trials, whatever these trials are; yet we have to overcome that mysterious and powerful impulse to talk about them.

"Why do we have this impulse?" I asked Dr. Williams.

"Fundamentally," he replied, "it is nothing more or less than a *bid for attention*. And the people in whom the impulse is strongest are the ones who in early childhood did not get the attention, or the kind of attention, they craved.

"Let's start with this fact: There is in every human being an instinctive craving for the approval of other human beings. We want them to notice us; to like and to admire us. In other words, we want to feel and to have them feel that we are making good. Even a little child has this strong desire.

"But suppose a mother is careless and indifferent. She may be always so busy that she pushes the child aside, when it wants to show her what it has been doing. She tells it to quit bothering her. Or perhaps it is the father who is indifferent, or cold, or irritated by the child's attempts to gain his attention. The craving for approval which is in the child as it is in us all is baffled and defeated.

"Now for the crape-hanging! One of the first things a child learns is that if it cries it gets attention. As it grows older it is constantly learning more lessons along that line. For instance, if it tumbles down or pinches its fingers or bumps its nose it is instantly the object of solicitous care. Mother picks it up, pities it, kisses the spot to make it well.

"A child discovers over and over again that to be hurt or sick or in trouble of any kind brings attention! It is almost a sure-fire means of making oneself the center of interest.

"Moreover, children see how the same thing works with older peo-

72

ple. They see their mother being pitied and waited on when she has a bad headache. They observe her carrying some particularly appetizing food to a sick neighbor. If their father is ill the whole household revolves around him.

"They learn that *any* kind of hard luck serves to focus attention on the victim of the misfortune.

"There probably isn't a single day in the life of the average child when it doesn't learn these lessons in the efficacy of *trouble* as a means of gaining attention; and attention of a peculiarly gratifying kind. If the child feels that it isn't making good, that it is failing to win the approval it craves, what could be more natural than that it should resort to this means of attracting notice?

"The crape-hanger impulse starts in childhood as an instinctive *bid for attention*. And that is exactly what it is in the grown person who is always complaining, always talking about his or her troubles: a bid for attention.

"The impulse can be overcome. The best way to deal with it is to begin by understanding what it is. Realize that it is simply a bid for attention. When you parade your troubles you are exactly like the beggar on the streets. He parades his deformity, his blindness, his poverty, in an attempt to gain your sympathy and your alms.

"The woman who is always talking about her troubles is doing the same thing. She makes her appeal by telling you about her nervous breakdowns, her sorrows, her self-denials, her worries, her anxieties.

When she catches herself doing this, let her picture herself as nothing but a beggar shaking a tin cup to attract the notice of passers-by. That will give her a salutary shock.

"The next thing for her to remember is that her crape-hanging is simply a subterfuge; an attempt to wheedle us into giving her the notice she doesn't win legitimately.

"I have seen people completely cured of their crape-hanging tendencies, their habit of complaining; and I think it always happens in one of two ways. If they really were failing, the cure comes by finding some work, or some effort, in which they did make good, and knew that they were making good. If they were people who were not failing, but who only thought they were, they were cured by finding out their mistake; by learning to believe that, in their own way, they were making some worth-while contribution to life.

"There is a deep satisfaction, contentment, almost complacence, in doing a thing well, no matter how small. It is a powerful antidote for self-pity. There must be some things you can do well. Get busy with those things! It will strike at the very root of the complaining habit; for that root is the old childish feeling that we have somehow failed to *earn* attention and so must make another kind of bid for it.

"And of course there is the obvious advice to devote your own attention to the pleasant things of life, instead of to the unpleasant ones."

I asked Dr. Williams how parents can keep a child from developing the habit of complaining.

"In the first place," he replied, "don't set the example! Don't be a crape-hanger yourself. Talk as little as possible, especially before children, of your own troubles. At least, don't talk of them complainingly. Do it constructively.

"By that I mean that you can discuss a trouble as something to be remedied, a difficulty to be overcome, a lesson to be learned. Take the attitude of 'Well, here's this! Let's see what we can do about it!' To take that attitude is one way of preparing a child to meet the emergencies which will come to it later on.

"Remember that children resort to complaints as a means of drawing attention to themselves. Don't force them to do this. Notice their good behavior. Don't pay too much at-

tention to their misbehavior. Don't exaggerate the importance of any little hurt, like a pinched finger. Be sympathetic, of course; but don't make a mountain out of every little molehill.

"Try to have children feel that they are making good in some way. They are sure to be and to do *something* which you can commend. Show them that you notice whatever they do well; and encourage them to try to do other things. Keep a sensible balance between praise and criticism. Don't give them too much of either. Make them have enough of the confidence in themselves which gives them the courage to go on.

"We ought to go more slowly and quietly; not get so excited over their small failures and successes. Keep yourself and them on an even keel; I think that is the secret of the whole matter."

This Age of Ingenuity

A SIREN which will shriek for six hours and can be heard for five miles is being installed on trucks to frighten off hijackers. It can be silenced by an intricate combination of locks and buttons known only to the driver, and goes off if the truck is tampered with in any way. The equipment, leased to users by the Brooklyn Burglar Alarm Co., can also be installed in passenger cars.—*Fortune*

GAS for cooking, heating, lighting, and power for farm equipment is supplied by a compact gas generator using anything that burns—corncobs, leaves, straw, paper, refuse. Two tons of farm waste will yield enough gas to last an average family nearly three months.
—*Architectural Record*

MANY hospital-born babies will in future have their names "sunburned" on their backs at birth with the rays of a quartz lamp, thus removing any possibility of going to the wrong parents. The name lasts six months.—Louisville *Courier-Journal*

The Discovery of Anesthesia

Condensed from Hygeia

HUGH H. YOUNG

IN comparison with surgical anesthesia, all other contributions to medical science are trivial. Before anesthesia, surgery was a horror! Surgical operations were dreadful ordeals, a hell to the patients, a purgatory to the surgeons. The frightful shrieks from the hospital operating rooms filled those waiting their turns in the wards with terror.

The awful experiences of operative surgery and the attendant high mortality caused the best minds in medicine to avoid operations. Indeed, for centuries many major operations in Europe were left to itinerant quacks, and in England the barber surgeons did the work while the medical profession stood by and vainly tried to assuage the anguish of the patient.

Since the beginning of medical history our records show that the never despairing hope of physicians was to conquer pain and thus be allowed to carry out surgical procedures with tranquil thoroughness rather than in a mad rush against pain and death.

"Sacred, profane and mythological literature abound in incident, fact and fancy showing that since earliest times man has sought to assuage pain by some means of dulling consciousness," says Gwathmey. "In these attempts many methods and diverse agents have been employed. The inhalation of fumes from various substances, weird incantations, the external and internal application of drugs and many strange concoctions, pressure on important nerves and blood vessels, magnetism and mesmerism, etc., have played their part in the evolution of anesthesia."

Mandragora was used by both Greeks and Romans for hundreds of years to produce sleep, and Asiatics employed hashish to dull consciousness of pain. Later, opium and hemlock were used.

It was not until the early chemical discoveries of hydrogen, nitrogen, oxygen and nitrous oxide in the latter part of the 18th century that the way was found for a scientific anesthesia. Sir Humphrey Davy said, in 1800, "Since nitrous oxide is capable of destroying pain it may be used in surgical operations," and 25 years later Hickman anesthetized rabbits with nitrous oxide and carried out many operations on them successfully without a struggle. However, these demonstrations were unheeded, and the surgical theater continued to be a torture chamber.

But nitrous oxide and sulphuric ether, neglected by the medical profession, were seized on by the populace, who found in them a pleasant means of becoming exhilarated. Itinerant lecturers on the marvels of chemistry roamed over the country and popularized their meetings by giving young people ether to breathe, while the audiences roared with laughter over their unconscious antics on the stage.

Knowledge of these drugs reached even to the distant rural hamlets. In one of these, Jefferson, Ga., many miles from a railroad, Crawford W. Long was practicing medicine. Fresh from the University of Pennsylvania, he knew of the exhilarating properties of these drugs and frequently furnished ether to young men who met at his office for an "ether frolic" in the winter of 1841–42. But let him tell his story:

"They were so much pleased with its effects that they afterwards frequently used it and induced others to do the same, and the practice soon became quite fashionable in the county.

"On numerous occasions I inhaled ether for its exhilarating properties, and would frequently, at some short time subsequent to its inhalation, discover bruised or painful spots on my person, which I had no recollection of causing and which I felt satisfied were received while under the influence of ether. I noticed that my friends, while etherized, received falls and blows that I believed were sufficient to produce pain on a person not in a state of anesthesia. On questioning them they uniformly assured me that they did not feel the least pain from these accidents. Observing these facts, I was led to believe that anesthesia was produced by the inhalation of ether, and that its use would be applicable in surgical operations.

"The first patient to whom I administered ether in a surgical operation was James M. Venable. It was given to Mr. Venable on a towel, and when fully under its influence I extirpated a tumor on his neck. The patient continued to inhale ether during the time of the operation, and, when informed that it was over, seemed incredulous until the tumor was shown him. He gave no evidence of suffering during the operation, and assured me, after it was over, that he did not experience the least degree of pain from its performance. This operation was performed on Mar. 30, 1842."

Here, then, was the first successful attempt to render a patient insensible to pain during a surgical operation! Long did not rush into print, but like a painstaking scientist quietly continued his work, removing another tumor on the same patient a few weeks later, and then amputating a toe under complete ether anesthesia in July. His meager practice furnished him only a few surgical cases each year. He continued to operate under ether, while he bided his time, waiting for a major operation before publishing his claims to a discovery that he well realized would revolutionize surgery.

In 1896, I chanced to meet Mrs. Fanny Long Taylor, who amazed me by saying that her father was the discoverer of surgical anesthesia. I had heard only of Morton, in whose honor, as the discoverer of anesthesia, a great celebration was in preparation in Boston. I was thrilled when she said she could put Dr. Long's documentary proof in my hands, and a few days later I went through his time-stained papers, case histories, account books, affidavits from patients, attendants, physicians in his town and elsewhere in Georgia, and from professors of the University of Georgia, all of which furnished overwhelming proof of the originality of his discovery.

Jackson and Morton united in claiming the discovery in 1846, Morton admitting that he got the idea from Jackson. Wells then came forth with his claim of having used nitrous oxide in 1844. Morton and Jackson subsequently fell out, and Dr. Jackson, hearing of Long's claims, visited him in Georgia to investigate them, and then generously wrote a long letter to the Boston Medical and Surgical Journal setting forth in detail the genuineness of Dr. Long's claims.

The next years witnessed a sad spectacle of litigation and controversy between the rival New England claimants for a bonus from Congress for the discovery of anesthesia. In this Dr. Long took no part, but a presentation of his documents by Senator Dawson of Georgia promptly killed the bill to give Morton $100,000.

That the general usage of ether in surgery came after the surgeons of the Massachusetts General Hospital had operated on persons anesthetized by Morton in October, 1846, no one will gainsay. But in this epoch-making discovery there is surely glory enough for all. No true friend of Long would try to belittle the great achievements of Morton and his surgical co-workers in Boston from which world-wide recognition of the possibility of surgical anesthesia came.

AT THE BOTTOM of his shaft the Mexican miner has a shrine of the Blessed Virgin, dressed usually in overalls with a miner's hat cocked over her head. Here, when he goes to work, he prays for a day free from accident; and, before leaving, many a peon prays again, this time that the high-grade ore he has stolen and secreted about himself will not be discovered.

—John van Steen Tolman in *Travel*

The Habit of Going to the Devil

Excerpts from The Atlantic Monthly

ARCHER BUTLER HULBERT

1827 A glance at our country and its present moral condition fills the mind with alarming apprehensions. The moral desolation and flood tides of wickedness threaten to sweep away not only the blessings of religion but the boasted freedom of our republican institutions as well. Every candid person must admit that if ignorance, licentiousness, and a disregard of all moral laws prevail in our communities, then demagogues and spendthrifts will sit in 1828 the halls of legislation; ambition, self-aggrandizement and love of power will supplant patriotism, public spirit, and attention to the best interests of the nation. Due to the lack of moral restraint, the very freedom which we enjoy hastens this degrading process. Today no virtuous public sentiment frowns down upon the criminal to shame him into secrecy. Let another half century pass in our present indifference and inactivity, and existing evils will have attained a strength to be overpowered.

It is clear that instead of the masses of our people improving they are sadly deteriorating. 1843 Murders, robberies, rapes, suicides, and perjuries are as common as marriages and deaths. Killings appear to have become contagious; no day passes without an attempt somewhere in our country. Lawlessness has so increased that the expense of watching our army of criminals, of tracking and arresting them, and of maintaining them in prison (together with the huge cost of their felonies) is immeasurable.

The wave affects not only the lower class. In a court in Pennsylvania John Doe recently pled guilty to the charge of bigamy. As he rose to be sentenced by the judge he interrupted that official's verdict by handing him a pardon from the governor of that state! And our irreligious clergy! What can 1828 be done for the conversion of the many ministers of the Word who preach error for truth, because they themselves have never known salvation? What will become of churches under such leadership? In ten or twelve counties in Indiana a number of 1843 churches recently voted not to co-operate with any missionary, or temperance societies, or Sunday School associations, since in their present form they are not warranted by the teachings of God's Word.

And what of our youth! Today, where one child hails the Sabbath 1829 with delight, as the day for Bible Study, one hundred young immortals are growing up in ignorance and sin. The lamentable extent of dishonesty, fraud, and other wickedness among our boys and girls shocks the nation. The army of youthful criminals from the slums is augmented by children abandoned by the shiftless of the working classes, by families wrecked by living beyond their means, and by wayward unfortunates from reputable families. Large numbers of these 1830 youngsters belong to organized gangs of thieves and cutthroats, and are in the regular employ of old criminals who teach them the tricks of the trade. Many such have no homes; some cannot even return to the gang's headquarters unless the day's profit amounts to a stipulated sum. 1831 Half the number of persons actually convicted of crime are youths who have not reached the age of discretion. Of 256 convicts in the Massachusetts State Prison, 45 were thieves at 16 years of age; and 127 had, at that age, become habitual drinkers. Youthful

gambling, accompanied with most degrading language, as in the game of shooting craps, begins al- 1833 most in infancy. A gentleman passing along the streets of Boston recently overheard a gang of boys shooting craps. The language issuing from their young lips might well have come from Hell, and even there would almost have shocked the Satanic proprietor himself. And even amid more refined surroundings our 1828 young people are everything but seriously minded today. At——University the few students who profess religion stand, as it were, alone; to attempt to stem the torrent of vice and immorality there would be considered a freakish innovation.

A disregard for all laws, and feverish and foolish efforts to check crime by profuse legislation, 1843 are common. A man in Baltimore was recently arrested for fast driving. This is as it should be. Disastrous consequences of fast driving frequently follow carelessness in observing the traffic ordinances provided against such offenses. Equal heedlessness is shown in our halls of legislation. With us nothing is fixed or permanent. There is a constant hankering for new laws, or for tinkering up old ones. We run on from change to change in a restless round of experiment. This restlessness shows 1857 itself in extravagance in dress. Silk stockings, curiously wrought with quirks and clocks about the ankles, and interwoven with gold or silver threads, are all the rage. Persons with the smallest of incomes do not stick to have two or three pairs of silk stockings. Time was when one could have clothed himself from head to toe for what one pair of these silk stockings costs.

War has affected the world's nerves. The military events of the earlier years of this century 1830 were so extraordinary that it is charitable to forgive those who wish to tell or write about their experiences. We rejoice that this is true. Let the tale be told as often and as vividly as possible! Let it be repeated until everyone shall be impressed with its horrors! Let those who delight in the "pomp, pride, and circumstance of glorious war" explain fully the fascination which lures them on to fill the world with tears—that we may candidly judge of war's value, and compare it with the sacrifices paid for it.

Keeping up with the World

Excerpts from a regular department in Collier's

Freling Foster

IN ALEPPO, Syria, sheep are the favorite household pets. Nearly every family owns one and dyes it several bright colors. It may have green ears, an orange muzzle, a red tail and a blue-striped body. Every afternoon the streets are a riot of color as these little "muttons" are taken for their walk.

THE royal palace in Gwalior, India, contains a miniature train made of silver and operated by electricity, which travels slowly around the Maharajah's great dining table during meals with its trucks loaded with wines, condiments and fruit. Removing and replacing a dish automatically stops and starts the train.

OF ALL the people in the world today, not more than one-third eat with a knife and fork. Another third use chopsticks. And the final third still eat with their fingers.

NOT so many years ago, many of the small circuses that traveled about the United States not only made each ticket seller pay up to $35 a week for his job—because short-changing was so profitable —but they even sold the pocket-picking privilege for the season to the highest-bidding gang.

IN MANY PARTS of this country during the middle of the last century, both men and women indicated their attitude toward matrimony as well as their marital status by the way they wore a ring. When on the first finger it meant they wanted to be married, on the second that they were engaged, on the third that they were married and on the fourth that they wished to remain single.

The Havoc Wrought by Professor Bell

Condensed from Vanity Fair

DEEMS TAYLOR

THE morning's interruptions have finally been disposed of, and you are ready at last for a good long stretch of what Wells would describe as some "hard, clear, merciless thinking" on that Big Work. Just as the thinking has begun to be hard without being clear, the doorbell rings. With a muttered, "Excuse me, posterity!" you rush to the front door. Outside stands a woman, engrossed in The Story of Philosophy. You wait. She turns a page. Finally you say, "Well?" She looks up.

"Who is this?" You give your name. "Wait a minute," she says. Whereupon she returns to her book. You wait. After a considerable interval a Business Man saunters up to your door with a companion. You can tell that he is a Business Man because he is in Conference with the other man—that is, both are smoking expensive cigars and comparing golf scores. As they reach your door, the woman says, "Here you are, Mr. Gulp."

"All right," says Mr. Gulp, and continues the description of how he got out of that trap on the 14th. Finally he says, "Excuse me a minute, Jim," and turns your way. "Yes?" he says testily, "who are you?" You tell him who you are.

"Are you the Little Giant Posthole Corporation?" Meekly you admit that you are not. "Isn't this 1327 Dienerstrasse?" No, you assure him, this is 1463 Rue de Rivoli. "Hell, that's the wrong number!" he shouts angrily. "Go away."

Now this is a supposititious anecdote. People do not send their secretaries to ring your doorbell and ask who you are, and then insult you because you aren't the person they hoped you were. However, if you will revise the anecdote to the extent of changing the doorbell to a telephone bell, you will find that it coincides fairly closely with your own daily experience.

In short, we have not many telephone manners and what we have are unspeakable. When the instrument first came into use the excitement of hearing a human voice come over a wire was so unusual that what the voice said was of little

81

consequence—just as the enthralling thing about the first moving pictures was the fact that they moved. But nowadays, when the bell tinkles, I do not start up, thinking "Oh, goody! When I put my ear to that little black dingus I am going to hear the voice of somebody who may be 50 miles away! How wonderful science is!" Not at all. A telephone conversation is just a conversation.

Consequently, you would think that the usages that govern other conversations would prevail. They do not. The foundation of good manners is considerateness; but most people, I find, unleash their inhibitions the moment they lift a telephone receiver, comporting themselves as boorishly and irritatingly as possible on all occasions.

Consider, for example, what havoc Professor Bell's invention has wrought with the dinner invitation. In the olden times—say about ten years ago—your prospective hostess, rendered desperate by five successive turndowns, sat down and wrote you a formal polite note. In due time you received this summons, and having decided that death at the heels of wild horses would be slightly preferable to one of Mrs. M.'s dinners, you wrote an equally polite note of regret that you would be unable to accept Mrs. M.'s kind invitation. And that was that.

Today, however, hostesses are imbued with the go-getter spirit, and thanks to the telephone, like the Royal Northwest Mounted Police they generally get their man.

Mrs. M. now calls you up. "What are you doing on the eighth?" Incautiously you reply, "Nothing." "That's lovely!" she exclaims. "I want you for dinner that night."

With enormous presence of mind you say, "On the seventh?" "No, the eighth." "Oh, I'm so sorry! I thought you said the seventh. I'm sailing for Europe on the eighth." "What a shame," she rejoins. "However, I haven't asked any of the others yet. We'll make it the seventh."

And there you are, trapped. Later you telephone and say that you just remember that you had accepted an invitation from the Delphiniums for the seventh; but it transpires that the Delphiniums are coming to Mrs. M.'s. And so you have no further recourse except to telegraph on the afternoon of the seventh that you have just broken your leg. Whereupon, of course, Mrs. M. telephones you on the morning of the eighth, in your absence, to inquire after the state of your leg. How much pleasanter things were in the old days, when the simple fact that you didn't feel like going somewhere was sufficient reason for not going!

Telephone bad manners are so ingrained in most of us that we don't even know they are *bad* manners; reading about them will do no good. Direct action is the only remedy left. Wherefore I propose a league whose members shall be pledged to deal appropriately with the more familiar telephone nuisances. Let me cite a few specimens, with suitable antidotes.

The most frequent, of course, is "Who is this?" My practice, which has proved satisfactory, is to reply, "This is Catherine of Russia. Whom did you wish?"

Next comes the Business Man's call, already outlined. As soon as the secretary has said, "Wait a minute, please; Mr. Whoozis wishes to speak to you," the best plan is to wait ten seconds and then hang up. I find that a repetition of this ceremony is usually sufficient to cause a blinding light to dawn upon Mr. Whoozis. On the third call he will probably be at the telephone.

A difficult problem is the friend who calls you just at dinner time. He or she generally remarks, "I hope I didn't call you away from dinner." The best method is to say, heartily, "Yes, but don't you mind a bit. The telephone is right here at the table. Just go ahead." Thereafter speak as one whose mouth is full, being careful to be completely unintelligible. This method is generally efficacious after three minutes.

Another type greets you coyly with, "Do you know who this is?" In this case, just say, "And I don't give a damn," and hang up.

The person who humorously pretends to be someone else is dangerous to deal with. It is well to exercise caution. Unexpected people do call up sometimes, and are likely to become annoyed when mention of their names is greeted with, "Ho! ho! Bernard M. Baruch. That's a hot one!"

The last of the more common types of nuisance is the idiot who doesn't bother to inquire after your identity, and plunges into a conversation before making sure that he has the right number. One afternoon I was dragged from profound meditation by a voice saying, "This is the Sacred Heart Convent. If that milk isn't here by four we'll get another milkman." And slam! went the receiver. In this instance, the breach of etiquette carried its own punishment—as indeed it does in nearly all similar cases.

A friend, to cite a further example, once answered a telephone call, to hear someone say, "This is Mrs. Blank and I'm having a few people in after the theater this evening."

"Yes?" said my friend eagerly, thinking that at last his social gifts were about to receive proper recognition.

"—And I want you to send over a supper for ten—simple; nothing heavy. I want about 50 sandwiches, and ices of some sort; and a salad, and some claret punch. And send silver and linen, and three very good waiters. Do you understand?"

Under the circumstances, what would you have done? He murmured, "Yes, ma'am," and dazedly hung up. I have often wondered what the guests thought and what she said.

My Gardens

Condensed from Personality

EDWARD W. BOK

A DUTCHMAN loves three things: First, his flowers. He must have flowers near him; else he is not content. Second, bells. A carillon must be in the belfry of his church or in the tower of the municipal building. Third, his tobacco. A Dutchman takes to his cigar or pipe from earliest boyhood.

It was only natural that I should have imbibed these triple interests. The American, I felt, needed to know his flowers better, and I might help. Outside the fence of our home place at Merion, Pa., there was a grass sward, some six feet wide, and it occurred to me that this would be ideal for spring bulbs. I ordered from a Dutch grower 22,000 croci and 5000 daffodils, and the following spring I had a wonderful display. The purple, white and yellow of the croci vied with the yellow of the daffodils. They were far from the house, and my friends felt sure there would be pilfering. So I devised a sign, placing the responsibility for the flowers on the public.

This was it: THESE FLOWERS ARE UNDER THE PROTECTION OF THE PUBLIC.

The public came and stopped. The sentiment of the sign worked! It constituted every adult a policeman, and now and then when a child steps forth to pick one of the flowers the hand of an adult invariably reaches to the child and stops it. Each spring scores drive by the place, and on Sundays a line of automobiles forms to look at the display.

After each spring's display of these bulbs, I was regretful that there was nothing else to continue to show until the idea struck me to have our road lined on both sides with dogwood trees. My neighbors liked the idea, and it was not long before there was a succession of dogwoods that make our road a veritable dogwood lane—the most beautiful of all roads in our vicinity with a mantle of white on both sides of the road.

I had a neighbor whose house faced on the other road. He was captivated with the dogwood display, and I suggested that he line his road with the pink horse-chestnut, so as to have something different. He planted 100 trees and each year, as they have grown, the display has become more and more beautiful until now it has become marked.

Once while in France I saw a railroad station fairly embowered with flowers, learning afterward that it was known as the "station of flowers." I felt that this might well be done with our station. So I consulted the railroad officials, finding them very much surprised that I was willing not only to plant, but to maintain a station filled with flowering shrubs. I planted some 50 of five different varieties of Japanese flowering fruit-trees—cherry, plum, crab-apple and the white and pink peach—so that I should have a succession of bloom lasting some two or three weeks. I used new soil, with the result that the trees grew prodigiously, and the display is one of the sights of the Main Line.

On each side of Merion Station there was an uninteresting bank of dirt, which I wanted to cover with roses. When I explained my plan to the President of the Pennsylvania Railroad, he seemed rather unresponsive. But the next day he called at my home.

"Well," he said, "you must have thought that I was unappreciative yesterday. But the shock of a member of the public walking into my office and offering to do something for the Railroad was too great. It tightened my vocal cords so that I couldn't speak. We are not accustomed to that, you know. But I want to thank you now most heartily and to say that the banks are absolutely at your disposal."

Now, after six years, it is a customary sight to see men busy talking on the observation platform of a Western express suddenly stop, point to the rose banks, and comment on the bloom. For it is estimated that the thousands of rose-plants have a bloom each summer of over half a million roses at one time and present a veritable blanket of pink bloom.

More than that. The unique display found its way into the newspapers. This comment attracted the attention of a director of the New Haven Railroad, and the following spring there were at the approaches to the stations at Rye and New Rochelle and likewise at Providence, similar rose displays. The official of a Western railroad saw the planting, and he tried the idea also, with equal success. Only last summer an English railroad official passed Merion on a train when the roses were in full bloom, gasped in astonishment, took the idea back to England and today several stations on his road are abloom with roses.

As the roses were freely accessible to the public, I put the same sign here as I did on our place. Not a single rose has ever been taken. I have learned a curious point here: plant a few flowers and the public is tempted. Plant a mass and the public desire is lost.

I had now purchased a camp in Camden, Maine. The drive from the road to the camp was a third of a mile long, and I decided that here was a place for mass-planting. I decided that here should be ferns, growing wild in adjacent fields. I planted a border 25 feet deep on each side of the road to the camp, transplanting some 200,000 ferns. I now sprinkled through the ferns several hundred Lilium Canadense, which grows wild in Maine fields, the blue lupine and the wild black-eyed Susan. And there they are today: a beautiful border of ferns on both sides of the drive, with no suggestion whatever that they were planted. A famous landscape-artist paid the greatest possible compliment to my gardening. He commented on the beauty of the ferns, but was amazed to learn that it was not a natural border.

My success at the camp made me wish for a place where I could indulge in mass-planting to a larger extent. I purchased 14½ acres, at the highest point in Florida, and decided to transform this into a sanctuary. Hundreds of thousands of trees and shrubs were used until now the ground is scarcely visible, transforming the once sand-bare spot into a natural sanctuary.

I decided that I would go a step further here and express the second of the Dutchman's fondnesses. The half of the mountain I had purchased was now completely planted. I purchased the other adjoining half of the mountain, and decided upon the erection of a carillon tower on the summit. The tower is to be 200 feet high, 50 feet square at the base and 40 feet at the top, built of Georgia pink marble at the top and base and coquina stone used in the center. When complete I believe it will be the most beautiful structure of its kind in America. There will be 61 bells in the tower, and the plan is to play these each day at sunset for 15 minutes and on Sundays for half an hour at high noon. A moat of water surrounds the tower, a grove of 200 large live-oak trees was transplanted here last spring, so that when the bells are ready to be rung a year hence its environment will have been established, and a scene of surpassing beauty will await the visitor, with a tower reflected in a lake some 150 feet long, made purposely in front of the tower.

This sanctuary and tower are located at Mountain Lake, Florida.

And this is the story of my gardens, small and large. At least, I have, in a sense, carried out my grandmother's injunction to her children and now transmitted to her grandchildren: "Make you the world a bit better or more beautiful because you have lived in it."

LOPE DE VEGA, Spanish dramatist, soldier, great lover, had attained a ripe wisdom when he wrote: "With a few flowers in my garden, half a dozen pictures and some books, I live without envy."— *House & Garden*

A Sabbatical Year for Marriage

Condensed from Harper's Magazine

SAMUEL HOPKINS ADAMS

MY MODEST suggestion is merely a palliative, a preservative. It is the simple, old, and well-tested expedient of a vacation at stated intervals, such as all colleges and many progressive business institutions now include in their regime, a sort of sabbatical year or month or fortnight. Conceive of a state of society wherein the marriage agreement should contain without public scandal, a clause to this effect: "In and after the second year of the joint life of the contracting parties, they shall, circumstances permitting, separate for a period of not less than . . . weeks nor more than . . . months, during which time each shall honestly endeavor to reconstitute his or her own individuality."

Timorously, I venture the theory that 90 per cent of the trouble with matrimony lies in its being too close a corporation. Certainly it is the closest corporation known to society, modern or ancient. In none other do I discover any such undertaking as is tacitly read into the compact by so many love-blinded absolutists, to wit: "I hereby agree to live with this man (or woman) day in and day out, to share his quarters, his meals, his amusements, his vacations, his goings-out and his comings-in, world-without-let-up, Amen."

This mutual slavery would seem to derive from a belief that by the sacrifice of two individualities a joint-personality can be achieved, a theory more in consonance with medieval alchemy than with modern habit. Small wonder that so many marriages fail to survive the deadly compression. I once heard a famous bishop say, "A divorce usually represents a marriage that has been smothered to death."

There is important social and psychological significance to the fact that 50 years ago the house commonly boasted two or more floors, plus a garret, plus a cellar, not to mention the yard. This meant for the housewife the blessed possibility of privacy, of escape, if you will. Today, married life, particularly in the early and vitally important period of adjustment, is lived on a single floor. A "flat" is a term of sinister suggestiveness. The companion adjectives, "stale and unprofitable," are all too likely to occur in time to the pent-in partners.

No other partnerships, in business or in the professions, are ever maintained upon such unrelentingly close terms. Imagine two business associates agreeing that they would breakfast and dine together daily, spend their evenings in common, take their vacations at the same time and place. How long would that association last?

I once knew in Caracas two Englishmen who operated an asphalt lake back from the coast, where for months on end they had no associates but themselves. Knowing that distaste which such enforced companionship sometimes breeds, particularly in the tropics, I was surprised to find in the partners an attitude of almost boyish camaraderie, eventually explained by one of them. Each had built for himself a cottage, at the far ends of the property. There he slept and ate. Once a day they met in the office, to discuss and plan. Twice a week and on special holidays they invited each other to dine. In nearly four years they had never had a quarrel. That is, I believe, a record for marooned whites in the Caribbean wilds.

Why not give to marriage a set vacation once in so often? The ever-startled moralist will scent depravity. The more timid among womankind, a rapidly vanishing tribe, may suspect the siren presence of the hetaira, the Other Woman, lurking somewhere in the background. But these are merely vestigial survivals of the ancient and puritanical conviction of sin in the other fellow, on the theory that the logical alternative to monotony is infidelity. There is nothing repugnant to morality in this proposal; and it might well keep life from wearing threadbare.

Who shall say that the motivating influence behind the Crusades was not the salutary feeling that it was a good thing for families to be separated for a time and thus learn the better to appreciate each other? Certainly these and similar pilgrimages occurred at suspiciously frequent intervals, and the leaders had small difficulty in recruiting sufficient forces from all ranks of society. Alas that these quests have passed!

The modern pilgrimage is to a sanitarium. Often it serves the suggested purpose of the Crusades, although that purpose is carefully concealed from the pilgrims. Twenty years ago the pioneer in this field told me of his big idea: "I am going to build a retreat for husbands and wives. I shall call it a sanitarium. They'll flock to it, and it will save homes by the thousands." Other "rest cures" of the same kind have sprung up. The desideratum is to separate temporarily two people who have rubbed raw upon each other, and give them time to reconstitute their own threatened personalities. A distinguished neurologist, who boasted that he had prevented the breaking up of more households than any other man in America by prescribing the "rest cure," added a word of wisdom: "People will not understand that habitude may become the worst of corrosives."

There was never yet a combination of personalities so perfect but that, sooner or later, it needed a change of air to keep it fresh and sweet. Stevenson has observed that the marriages of seafaring men are usually the most lasting, attributing it to the enforced separation. One of the most successful menages that I know has for 17 out of 20 years of its existence divided once annually. It was agreed in the third year of their union that at least three weeks out of every year should be spent apart. Of those people I heard an old lady say with wonder, "Their marriage is like a house through which a spring wind is always blowing."

There was the case of Mr. and Mrs. A., young married people who settled in a city, and proceeded to live a life "world-forgetting, by the world forgot." For nearly five years, evening after evening, their silhouettes could be seen on the drawn shades of their library, as they sat together and presumably contented. An idyll of the busy city. Then they woke up. They found themselves drained of novelty, of emotion, of interest. All the glow had been rubbed from life by the long-maintained closeness of that contact. They have never got it back. Both are decorous members of a conventional circle. There will be no divorce. There will be nothing but a sterile existence, "stretching long and straight and dusty to the grave," in a vista of blank and hopeless boredom.

For the sabbatical vacation no claim is advanced other than that it might give marriage in general a better chance of survival. Granted that it would definitely end a number of unions. Darby would never come back from that fishing trip, or Joan would next be heard of from a round-the-world-in-two-years tour; these are the fragile combinations. We may fairly ask whether they were worth preserving in any case. Would not an equal or greater number of imperilled but still salvable unions be saved? The leave-of-absence would keep a happy fellowship keen and vivified; it might well, by affording surcease of friction, render a maladjusted combination endurable, and so durable. At worst, if the temporary separation becomes permanent, it is better that a marriage end by a clean severance than be slowly stifled to death through years of intolerable contact . . . Why not let in a breath of fresh air?

A CAT-POST operated in Berlin had in 1879 thirty tomcats in the service. It worked on the principle of the carrier pigeon: You got the cats used to one place as a home, and then they would take letters back there from a distance of three or four kilometers.
                                                                —*The Seven Seas*

When We Had 87 Varieties of Time

Condensed from Business

GEORGE W. GRAY

MASSACHUSETTS AVENUE almost exactly bisects Washington, D. C. When it reaches the north-western suburbs, however, it curves unexpectedly to the north, describing a bend of more than a quarter of a mile before it resumes its straight-line course. Unknown to most people, this sweeping curve is part of a great national public service that affects and controls the daily habits of millions of people.

The bend of the avenue is the arc of a large circle, and in the center of the circle is an underground vault. To safeguard the contents of this vault, Congress passed a special act forever prohibiting the building of any public thoroughfare within a radius of 1000 feet of it.

Why? The answer is—time. That vault is the clock room of the Naval Observatory, and its precious contents, so carefully guarded, are three solemn-faced clocks. The elaborate measures of protection are to protect the delicate works of these clocks from the jars and vibrations of traffic. The clocks themselves are housed within sealed glass cases, in a brick-walled vault where every precaution is taken to keep temperature, pressure, and moisture uniform.

To most of us, correct time is something taken for granted; there are so many easy ways of checking the accuracy of your watch. But accuracy is not accidental. It depends upon that vaulted clock room in the center of the naval observatory's circle. Daily, at noon, naval-observatory time is transmitted all over the North American continent by wire, and is heard in thousands of telegraph offices, telephone exchanges, railroad offices and government bureaus. At the same instant it is flashed by radio from powerful Navy wireless stations at Arlington, Annapolis, Key West, and San Diego. These radio signals are powerful, and have been heard in the Indian Ocean and in Australia.

Captain E. T. Pollock, superintendent of the observatory, explained to me why the Navy undertook this large and expensive responsibility of determining correct time and of broadcasting it to the ends of the earth.

"The Navy needed accurate time for itself, as an aid to navigation, and apparently we needed it more than did anyone else. At all events, nobody else undertook the job, and so we were driven to it. This was away back in 1831, and we have been at it ever since."

When the Navy first went into the business of determining time, there was, indeed, little demand for this queer commodity. Railroads were in their infancy—the needs of train-dispatching had not yet arisen. There were, of course, no telegraph or telephone wires; industries were small and mostly agricultural; and hours were reckoned from sun-up to sundown. Almost everywhere, time was regarded as a purely local affair, and many persons set their watches and clocks by the noon shadow on the sun dial. Exact time on a general scale was unknown, and, therefore, not missed. If a stagecoach managed to keep within an hour of its schedule, passengers were satisfied.

Meanwhile, American ships were being built and sent to sea. Every ship needed a chronometer and, in order to insure its accuracy, each chronometer needed to be rated. To mariners exact time was a prime necessity, a matter of safety in navigation, often a matter of life or death.

"But all timepieces," Captain Pollock explained, "are subject to error under changing conditions of temperature, weather and travel. If the variation is known and is con-

stant, a chronometer may be 'rated,' and its error allowed for, and thus fairly accurate timekeeping is assured. It was to rate the Navy chronometers that a small 30-inch telescope was set up in Washington in 1831. By sighting the transit of stars with this glass it was possible to determine exact time, and thus to test the accuracy of chronometers. Today the observatory represents an investment of more than a million dollars—72 acres of land, 54 buildings, and much equipment."

It is difficult to visualize, now, the confusion of time reckoning that prevailed over the United States in the years before 1883. One of the railroad guides published in 1881 lists 87 places in the United States and Canada in each of which the time differed from that of Washington and of all the others; and each of these 87 varieties of time was the established standard for the operation of trains on one or more roads.

Trains operating between New York and Boston were scheduled, at one end of the short run on New York time, at the other end on Boston time, and at certain intermediate points on Hartford time. In many instances the local standards varied so slightly as to serve no purpose but to add to the general confusion. Thus, Albany time differed by only one minute from New York time, and Montreal only an additional minute from Albany. Yet no city displayed a willingness to yield even a single minute.

But this confusion now has disappeared—thanks mainly to the railroads. In 1883 the railroad managers agreed to adopt the "hour-zone system" for all trains, and on November 18 of that year the new time system went into effect, substituting for more than 80 varieties of time a simple arrangement of four continental standards—Eastern, Central, Mountain, and Pacific.

Don't imagine, however, that the time zones are four uniform strips of the United States. The division lines that separate the zones bend and zig-zag, in some instances following state boundaries, and in other instances intersecting states. The zone divisions are fixed by the Department of Commerce to meet local preferences, and they involve some curious anomalies. El Paso, on the Texas border, is farther west than is Denver, but because Texas is in the Central Zone and Colorado is in the Mountain Zone, it is legally noon in El Paso when it is only 11 A.M. in Denver.

It would seem, then, that standard time is somewhat artificial. "Yes," Captain Pollock agrees, "and it is necessarily so. The chaos that existed before the adoption of the hour-zone system was a natural reflection of the fact that true time varies for every step you take east or west on the surface of the globe. When it is true noon at Philadelphia, it is really 11:59 o'clock 13 miles west of Philadelphia, and 11:58 26 miles west, and so on. If every farm, village, and city lived to itself, and had no outside intercourse, each community might observe its own local time without inconvenience or confusion. But in our interdependent life, with so many human activities conditional on a common measurement of time, the zone system is the only practicable arrangement.

Standard time is now in effect in all except a few sparsely settled and undeveloped regions. The whole circumference of the earth has been divided into 24 zones, each of 15 degrees width in longitude and one hour's difference in time. The meridian of Greenwich determines the time of the initial zone, and is the zone meridian in reckoning standard time the world over. Our eastern standard noon is exactly five hours later than Greenwich noon.

The international date line is determined by the 180th meridian, which is in the Pacific Ocean exactly half way around the world from Greenwich. Ships at sea change their date on crossing the international date line. To the traveler from the Orient eastward it is always a queer sensation to see the calendar jump backward.

Standard time *is* artificial, but like standard coinage and other commodities of civilization, it is a world-wide convenience.

A NEW YORK newspaper photographer, covering an important story deep in New Jersey for his paper, hired an automobile hearse to speed him back to Manhattan, developing his plates inside it on the way so that they were all ready when he reached his office just before press time.—Neal O'Hara in N. Y. *Post*

The Dreams That Come True

Condensed from Personality

HELEN KELLER

MANY people marvel when I tell them that I am happy. They imagine that my limitations weigh heavily upon my spirit and chain me to the rock of despair. Yet, it seems to me, happiness has very little to do with the senses. If we make up our minds that this is a drab and purposeless universe, it will be that, and nothing else. On the other hand, if we believe that the world is ours, and that the sun and the moon hang in the sky for our delight, there will be joy because the Artist in our souls glorifies creation. Surely, it gives dignity to life to believe that we are born into this world for noble ends, and that we have a destiny beyond this physical life.

"But don't you get tired," some will say, "of the sameness of objects you touch when you can't see the play of light and shadow upon them? Aren't the days all alike to you?"

Never! My days are all different, and no hour is quite like another.

Through my sense of touch I am keenly alive to all changes and movements of the atmosphere, and I am sure the days vary for me as much as for those who observe the skies—often not caring about their beauty, but only to see if it will rain. There are days when the sun pours into my study, and I feel all of life's joys crowded into each beam. There are rainy days when a sort of shade clings about me and the smell of the moist earth rises everywhere. There are really "dark" days when I feel the ten windows in my study shudder and sob with the winter blast. And there are drowsy summer days when the languid breeze tempts me to go out to my little screened tent, stretch out and dream with the irises and bee-haunted pinks.

There are also hours of breathless haste to catch up with the letters that cover my desk, and endlessly varied hours spent with the thinkers and poets. How can there be a dull moment when my books are all about me?

There is meaning in all the vibrations which find their way to me through the channels of touch.

There are footsteps passing and re-passing, and the sudden bark of my beautiful Great Dane. Every now and then huge trucks filled with building material rumble by, and instantly I feel astir with the fierce, splendid, never-resting activity of New York. Some time ago I had a breathless moment when 20 air-planes rushed by on their way to the Lindbergh parade, and several of them came so near the house I distinctly perceived the roar of the motor through the walls of my study. What a crowd of thoughts that vibration started! The daunt-less youth who took a dream, and carried it on dewy wings into the shining east, his plane swaying with the winds and curving with the clouds! My spirit seemed to stand still as I imagined him leaping into the void, with a million white-faced deaths blowing across his path. All this I felt as the planes sped to do him honor.

I have other sensations which bring me warm, human contacts with the outer world. The sense of smell is most precious and impor-tant in my every day world. The atmosphere is charged with count-less odors, from which I learn much about places and objects. I recog-nize many flowers by their grace-ful shapes and fragrance, and it is amazing how many kinds of sweet-ness there are in leaves, fruits, and seeds! Even the same plant gives forth a different scent in sunshine and rainy weather. There are ten-der odors like the lilac. The honey-suckle seems to lavish its fragrance with something like affection. The odor of the lily is a precious sensa-tion, but how shy and elusive! And there are other odors for which I have not found anything like a satisfactory vocabulary. Smell is like a friend who gossips with me about little things. It tells me when it rains, when the grass is cut, when automobiles pass in the street, what new houses are going up—and when it is mealtime.

I should like the city pretty well if it were not for my exacting touch and odor perception. But the avalanche of noises and the turmoil of New York weary me, and the heavy smells of the crowded shops and sultry streets and air congested with gasoline oppress me. Give me a summer day in the country, when all out-of-doors breathes an irre-sistible invitation to be young again, to run away like a boy with a circus.

Are you amazed, O reader, that I should sympathize with the boy's enthusiasm for the circus? Well, I have a perennial desire myself to get under the circus tent, and be a part of the riotous pageant. I re-member when I was not quite seven years old, my teacher took me to the circus. It was the greatest ob-ject-lesson of my childhood. My vocabulary was very limited. Miss Sullivan had been teaching me only two months; but I understood that I was to touch tall, large, strong animals.

The first thing of which I was conscious when we finally got in-side the tent was a strange, terrify-ing smell. I clutched Miss Sullivan's skirt, and for a moment my impulse to run away was stronger than my curiosity. But, her hand on one side and the big hand of the circus man on the other side reassured me. They gave me a bag of peanuts and took me at once to see the elephant. I felt his huge forelegs, and the circus man lifted me up on his shoulder, so that I could touch the creature's head and fan-like ears. I was told to give him some peanuts, and perhaps he would let me touch his "long nose." I was amazed, and a little angry; for I liked peanuts, and had intended to eat some myself. But some one gave me another bag of peanuts, and I was allowed to feel my benefactress's beautiful, slim body. She was a trapeze performer, and wore only pink tights. She laughed with pretty confusion at my scrutiny, and kissed me.

I also made the acquaintance of the Arabian marvels and their gorgeous riders, and felt the splendid chariots. The camel was made to kneel, and let me climb up on his queer, humpy back. But oh, the smell of him!

It is a far cry from the horse and buggy in which we went to the circus to the swift automobile in which I ride today. But it illustrates the magical changes I have witnessed in the past 40 years, and the stored up interest of my experiences.

St. Paul says, "When I am weak, then am I strong"—which is an exceedingly comforting thought to those who are physically damaged. The explanation undoubtedly is that limitations drive one inward for diversion, with the result that one's own thoughts become absorbingly interesting. It is a miracle how an incident of no particular value comes out of the mental crucible beautiful and precious. Little by little the transformation and classification of ideas take place in the brain, where are registered the beings and the events which give delight to circumscribed lives. Stored in the memory, they furnish plentiful entertainment for solitary hours; and that is why I never feel "deaf blind." I left that horrible abyss of hopelessness long, long ago.

My life has been happy because I have had wonderful friends and plenty of interesting work to do. I seldom think about my limitations, and they never make me sad. Perhaps there is just a touch of yearning at times; but it is vague, like a breeze among flowers. The wind passes, and the flowers are content.

Perhaps it would be a good idea, fantastic as it sounds, to muffle every telephone, stop every motor and halt all activity for an hour some day, to give people a chance to ponder for a few minutes on what it is all about, why they are living and what they really want.—James Truslow Adams, historian and author

The Middle-Class Smell

Condensed from Harper's Magazine

PHILIP CURTISS

DOLLY is a member of the gallant and direct younger generation. A staggering proof of this was furnished the other day by the way in which she characterized the Bishems.

Now, the Bishem family consists of a well-to-do mother and two middle-aged daughters, all very nice women, all very kind and thoughtful women, all women highly punctilious in social relations. Their voices are low and their English is perfect. Their attitude toward the world seems fair and flexible. There is, in short, no single quality on which you could lay your finger as a personal handicap.

"I went in to call on the Bishems, today," she remarked, "and you know—I can't understand it, but their house never seems to lose a faint middle-class smell."

For the moment it might seem as if I were playing directly into the hands of the advertising pages, but Dolly did not mean that, although she would certainly have said it if she had. It was not a question of hygiene or ventilation. Least of all was it a question of social standing.

Nor was the Bishems' aura something resident in their house as a dwelling, for they had merely rented the latter for the summer. It was something in their make-up and character that they carried about with them and implanted indelibly in their personal surroundings. Whether they had lived in a New York apartment or in a Venetian *pension*, it would still have been there. When I was a small boy I used to play in a big Victorian house where someone used to smoke medicated cigarettes for asthma, and I always supposed that the queer atmosphere in that house came from that cause. Now I know that cigarettes had nothing to do with it. That house had nothing more nor less than the middle-class smell.

Dolly's careless frankness had uncovered, I think, a great unexplored region of human experience. Smells in a house, in a coat, in a man's pipe, in a woman's kitchen are not a mere matter of drains or improper usage. They are a keen mark of character and personality and in making that statement I am merely saying what any dog has known these million years. Everyone has a smell of some kind or, rather, leaves one behind him. Is there anyone who has never gone into a certain room or opened a certain box of relics and become instantly conscious of a father, a mother, or a sister departed years before? Whenever I enter the peculiar atmosphere of cigars smoked in a bedroom, I can visualize my grandfather who died when I was less than seven.

We notice a smell to the degree with which we are in tune with its background or causes. I, for example, can never smell sailors' oilskin without a sensation just short of pure ecstasy; but for another the smell might bring nausea. As for the individuality of the matter, why is it that one man gives his pipe no noticeable scent, while another has only to smoke a pipe a short time to make it smell worse than the average navvy's? Any true smoker will tell you that the strength of the tobacco has nothing to do with it. It is, as I say, a sheer matter of character.

What a complete world the human race has denied to itself when it has disclaimed the fifth and most accurate of its senses. Of the four principal words used to indicate smells—smell, odor, scent, and aroma—only the last two are in polite standing, and of these the first is used chiefly for flowers and the last for boiling coffee.

The lower animals have not been so foolish. Problems that mystify us must be apparent to them at a whiff. One day I noticed that a board was loose on the front fence. I got a hammer, fixed the fence and returned through the kitchen to the spot where I had been sitting. Fully 20 minutes later my dog came back from some business of his own, jogging as he always does on purely routine matters. He passed six feet from the spot where I had nailed the fence, and instantly his attitude became electric. He went to the proper board to verify his notes, then headed—not for where I was sitting, but for the kitchen, where I had first gone.

Here, of course, the dog was making the same mistake that we make—using one sense to the exclusion of all others, but even so he was working on a surer basis than a human, for if I had tried to hide he could have found me, whereas by sight alone I could have mystified him all afternoon. No matter what I had done in the past 20 minutes, he had one fact to which he could have sworn absolutely in court.

What new worlds would be open to literature if readers and writers had accustomed themselves to think in terms of smells. If Pliny had told us exactly what the court of the Cæsars smelled like in the first Christian century how perfectly could we visualize the streets of Rome! Sinclair Lewis, to my mind, has gone farther in this direction than any other writer. It is seven years since I read *Main Street* but to this day I can remember his description of a drowsing little Ohio town: "It was full of old red brick houses and smelled constantly of rotten apples."

With most modern writers, however, smells are mentioned to express only an extreme of taste or distaste—honey-suckle or garbage. They follow the precedent of ages, while the true graphic force of the fifth sense will be reached only when smells of all kinds are catalogued not as pleasant or unpleasant but as things purely definitive in themselves, like blue or green, like heat or cold.

We are all familiar, of course, with the old farmhouse smells, so many and so complicated as to defy enumeration: the smell of the milk room, of the meal room, of a cold upper hall paved with oil-cloth, of sheets warmed with a soapstone, of a candle blown out without snuffing. A very modern country house always smells like the first-cabin corridor of an ocean steamer—that smell caused by endless coats of white paint on metal pipes.

Subconsciously, I believe, all smells are still regarded as sensory swear words. While a gentleman may, to be sure, have a nose, yet on the whole no gentleman is supposed to do very much smelling. If the adults of the party make free with their descriptions of the smell of sawdust or pine needles, what may the children do when we get to a soap works? Like many a race of persons or ideas, the race of smells has suffered cruelly on account of its lowest members.

Yet if the true mission of literature is not to convey facts but to start the reader off on his own trains of reverie, what could do it more perfectly than a deft catalog of scents, odors, aromas, and smells? Because some persons have had unhappy experiences, we are taught to shudder at train smoke; yet to me the smell of train smoke through a fog is as lyric as the bass of a tug-boat whistle. The smell of leather is wine to a horseman, and if I were a champion golfer with triumphs behind me I am certain that I should love even the smell of a locker room. In short, leaving aside the hideous odors that no one wants anyway, and the prim, permissible little "scents" that have been killed by sentimental repetition, why should we deny ourselves all the crowded thousands of commonplace, homely, suggestive odors that, in their variety, make up the aromatic kaleidoscope of our lives?

Only 100 Years Ago

THERE was not a public library in the United States.
Almost all furniture was imported from England.
An old copper mine in Connecticut was used as a prison.
There was only one hat factory and it made cocked hats.
Every gentleman wore a queue and powdered his hair.
Crockery plates were objected to because they dulled the knives.

—Quoted in *National Glass Budget*

The World of the Dog

Condensed from the Scientific American

C. J. WARDEN

ALMOST everyone has wondered what sort of world his favorite dog, or other familiar pet, lives in. Naturalists and philosophers have indulged in endless speculation regarding the matter, and numerous attempts have been made to draw realistic pictures of how the world must seem to infra-human forms.

What do we know concerning the ability of the dog to see, hear, smell, and in other ways sense the objects which constitute its everyday world? What evidence of intelligence does the dog exhibit in fitting into the somewhat arbitrary scheme of man's life? To what extent, if at all, does the dog understand human language?

In the first place, we must recognize the fact that different breeds of dogs differ markedly in capacities. Certain breeds, for example, are superior to others in visual, auditory, or olfactory capacity, and most certainly in general intelligence. Not only so, but individuals within any one breed differ in these respects much more widely than is commonly supposed.

In discussing the world of the dog we may well begin with the sense of smell, for the common assumption is quite true that the dog lives predominantly in a world of odorous objects. More tests have been made on olfactory sensitivity than upon any other of the senses. Many of these tests have been made in the open and deal with the practical use of the sense of smell in trailing.

There is nothing mysterious in the unusual ability of the dog to trail game, or man himself as in the case of the bloodhound. The organ of smell is highly developed, as are also the olfactory lobes of the brain. Naturally the animal makes use of the more highly developed sensory mechanism and thus comes by force of habit to make exceedingly fine discriminations.

The dog follows the trail to leeward when the wind is blowing. Trails a few hours old are not easily followed since the odorous substance left by the foot of the animal tends to dissipate in the air. The crossing of trails often causes confusion, although the trail can usually be picked up again quite readily. It has long been known that a dog cannot trail a man by smell through the snow if the man's boots are carefully encased in paper while the man is walking along.

In general it may be said that whereas man hardly notices the odor of an object unless it is markedly pleasant or unpleasant, the dog lives and moves and has his being in a world of smelly objects.

It is now definitely known that the dog does not see very well, probably possesses no color vision, and hence sees everything as some shade of grey. The retina of the eye is poorly developed, the fovea which man uses in fine visual work being absent and numerous opaque fibers showing through as blind areas. The dog is somewhat inferior to man in distinguishing between the intensity of two lights, and very much inferior in the matter of discriminating between objects of different sizes and shapes. The dog is extremely far-sighted and apparently uses vision mainly in making gross reactions to distant, moving objects.

Sight thus plays a secondary rôle in the adjustment of the animal to the external world, whereas it is of primary importance in the space-world of man.

The auditory capacity of the dog appears to be quite similar to that of man insofar as ordinary sounds are concerned. The dog can usually hear well enough the sounds that his master can hear, including of course those constituting human speech. And here, the question arises as to what use the dog can make of the spoken language of man.

The most outstanding instance of such ability so far noted is that of the German shepherd male, Fellow, whose ability along this line was recently subjected to critical tests in the animal laboratory at Columbia.

Mr. Herbert, owner of Fellow, has talked to the dog for several years as one talks to a child during the earlier months of taking on language. The dog is now able to perform scores of requests when given in a purely hit or miss order with his master quite out of sight behind a screen, or in another room. He can also do very well at retrieving a particular object upon request when required to go into another room and pick it out from among three objects placed in a row. Such a task is really more difficult than it may seem, especially when done under test conditions which differ from those under which the animal has been trained.

As is well known, the supposedly mathematical stunts performed on the stage by dogs, horses and other animals involve nothing more than a highly developed ability to react to minute gestures, or changes in facial expression, often unconsciously exhibited by the trainer. The feat of Fellow went far beyond anything of this sort.

That the dog can make use of human speech-sounds need not mean that he can understand language in the sense in which an adult human being does. Nevertheless it can, at any rate, be said that the dog can come to associate human speech-sounds with definite objects and modes of response, and hence that the language of his master enters in an important manner into his world.

Comparison of the intelligence of a dog with that of other animals is difficult with our present limited knowledge. At the present time no really adequate laboratory for testing animals exists anywhere, except, perhaps, that of Pavlov in Russia. Wealthy dog-lovers appear to be mainly sentimentalists who content themselves by declaiming on the loyalty of the dog to the man without feeling called upon to shoulder the task of establishing research laboratories in which the dog's world might be competently investigated. The animal psychologist is amused at times by the naïveté of the dog lover who seriously asks for a scientific opinion as to the intelligence of his pet after a few minutes' exhibition of simple tricks which a child might easily teach the dumbest mongrel.

Such tests as the psychologists have made, in spite of the lack of adequate laboratory facilities, suggest that the dog is probably one of the most intelligent of the higher mammals. Even an ordinary dog can solve problems requiring the successive operation of several simple mechanical devices, or finding the shortest way through a complicated maze to secure food. There is some evidence for supposing that the dog is far superior to the cat in intelligence, and not far below the raccoon and the monkey. By intelligence we mean the ability of the animal to adjust himself to a changing environment.

In comparing the world of dog and man, the most important difference, aside from the obvious point of general intelligence level, would seem to be that the dog's world presents a continuum of odorous objects, indistinctly seen and colorless, while the world of man is a panorama of colorful objects, more clearly outlined, but, for the most part, altogether odorless. The fact that the dog is extremely far-sighted should warn us against punishing him for mistakes he cannot help. Perhaps the dog makes more use of hearing than of sight, and if so would differ in this respect also from his master.

The Talk of the Town

Excerpt from The New Yorker

A MOVIE GENTLEMAN, one of those known to live in a welter of highly histrionic domesticity, came East for a quick visit recently and got on the phone at once to exchange affectionate words with the loved one back home. After about eighteen dollars' worth of endearments at night rates, the connection suddenly went bad. All he got over the wire was a dim, scratchy jumble and he was shouting frantically to his darling to speak louder when a voice cut in closer at hand. It was the operator. "She says she loves you, too," the operator explained.

How I Made a Crime Wave

Condensed from The Bookman

LINCOLN STEFFENS

EVERY now and then there occurs the phenomenon called a crime wave. New York has such waves periodically; other cities have them; and they sweep over the public and nearly drown the lawyers, judges, preachers and other leading citizens who feel that they must explain and cure these extraordinary outbreaks of lawlessness. Their diagnoses and their remedies are always the same: the disease is lawlessness; the cure is more law, more arrests, swifter trials and harsher penalties. The sociologists and other scientists go deeper into the wave; the trouble with them is they do not come up. I enjoy crime waves.

I made one once; I was a reporter on the New York *Evening Post*. Jacob A. Riis helped; he was a reporter on the *Evening Sun*. Many other reporters joined in the uplift of that rising tide of crime, but it was my creation, that wave, and Theodore Roosevelt stopped it. He was the President of the Police Board. But even he had to get Riis

From: *The Autobiography of Lincoln Steffens*, copyright, 1931, by Harcourt, Brace and Company, Inc.

and me to stop the wave. I feel, therefore, that I know something the wise men do not know about crime waves, and so get a certain sense of happy superiority out of reading editorials, sermons, and speeches on my specialty. It was this way:

The basement of the old police headquarters was a cool place in summer, and detectives, prisoners and we reporters used to sit together down there and gossip or doze or play cards. Good stories of the underworld were told—true stories. One day in this way I heard a particularly good story about two New York burglars who, by posing as care-takers of a certain house, got the policeman on that beat to help them load some valuable furniture from the sidewalk, where they had carried it, into a wagon. The policeman had even put the parlor clock in by himself. Because the victim of that robbery was the family of a well-known Wall Street broker, I wrote a news story about it, though I did not give away the source of my information. Since only The *Post* had the story, the morning newspapers printed the "beat" and Riis was asked by his editor why he did not have it. In the course of his irritated reply he said that he could get all he wanted of that sort of stuff and his editor answered:

"All right, get it, then."

That afternoon Riis reported a burglary which I knew nothing about, and it was my turn to be called down. My editor wanted to know why I was beaten.

"I thought you didn't want crimes in The *Post*."

"No, but a big burglary like that——"

All right; I called my assistant, and told him we must get some crimes. We spent the day button-holing detectives. I sat an hour in the basement in vain. Nothing but old stories. My assistant saved the day by learning of the robbery of a Fifth Avenue Club. That was a beat on Riis, but Riis had two robberies that were beats on me. By that time the other evening papers were having some thefts of their own. The poker club reporters were loafers only by choice. They could get news when they had to, and being awakened by the scrap between Riis and me, they went to work, a combine. They were soon beating me, as Riis was. I was sorry I had started it. I picked up some crimes, but Riis had two or three a day and the combine had at least one a day. The morning papers not only rewrote ours, they had crimes of their own, which they grouped to show that there was a crime wave.

It was indeed one of the worst crime waves I ever witnessed, and the explanations were embarrassing to the Reform Police Board which my paper and my friends were supporting in their difficult reform work. The opposition papers, Tammany and the unreformed police officers rejoiced in the outbreak of crime, which showed that the reformed police, and especially the new detective service, could not deal with the criminals. The outbreak of crimes all over the city so alarmed Roosevelt that he was almost persuaded that the opposition was right in its criticism. He called a secret meeting of the Police Board and was making one of his picturesque harangues, when Commissioner Parker interrupted him.

"Mr. President, you can stop this crime wave whenever you want to."

"I! How?"

"Call off your friends Riis and Steffens. They started it and—they're sick of it. They'll be glad to quit if you'll ask them to."

Roosevelt was perplexed, as Parker meant him to be.

"I don't understand," he said.

Parker explained that when the crime wave was running high he inquired into it, not as the editorial writers did: he asked for the police records of crimes and arrests. These showed no increase at all; on the contrary, the total crimes showed a diminution and the arrests an increase. It was only the newspaper reports of crimes that had increased; there was a wave of publicity only. He turned therefore to the newspaper boys and asked them about it. The poker combine explained that they were getting their stories by hard detective work, which they disliked; but that they had to keep it up as long as Riis and I kept it up. And, in their opinion, we got our dope from some inside office detective, who was squealing.

T. R. adjourned the meeting, sent for Riis and me—and *bang:* "What's this I hear? You two and this crime wave? Getting us into trouble?"

"And you laugh!" he blazed at me. I couldn't help smiling. But Riis looked serious, he saved us.

Riis told him about it: how I got him called down by printing a beat, and he had to get even. And did. "I beat the pot out of you," he boasted to me, his pride reviving. "And I can go right on doing it. I can get half-a-dozen crimes a day if I must, or a dozen. I can get all there are every day.

"But," he turned to T. R., "I don't want to. So I'll tell you where my leak is and you can close it up."

And Riis, the honest, told us how the reports of all robberies were sent by the precincts in to the heads of inspection districts and were then compiled in a completed list which was filed in a certain pigeon-hole in the outer office of the chief inspector. Not he, Riis, but his boy, Max, had observed this one day long ago, and had reported it to Riis, who resisted temptation to some extent.

"I told Max never to pry into that pigeon-hole—except in emergencies. And we never did till you" —he turned on me—"got so smart. Mr. President, that file should be kept in the inside office."

And this was the way in which Riis had been getting information about crimes reported to the police but not reported to the newspapers —the crimes which none of the rest of us could learn of except by hard detective work.

Thus the crime wave was ended. T. R. took pleasure in telling Parker that he had deleted not only the wave, but the source of the wave, which was in Parker's department. He would not say what it was. Parker had to resolve that mystery by learning from the chief of detectives that the President had ordered the daily crime file removed from the public to his inner office.

What's New in College Courses

THE University of New Hampshire offers a course on weather forecasting, in which students are taught to forecast the weather at least 12 hours in advance. It is felt that there is a real field for meteorologists with commercial aviation firms.—N. Y. *Times*

A COURSE for those interested in adventure and scientific methods of exploring is given at the University of Michigan. The first summer work was done in the Yukon, the students traveling slowly across the uncharted wilds, mapping the land, studying plant and animal life, and carefully estimating natural resources and geological conditions.—N. Y. *Herald Tribune*

We All Need Praise

Condensed from Liberty

PRINCESS ALEXANDRA KROPOTKIN

Most of us need praise—need it badly.

Probably if parents administered it oftener, if bosses were more lavish with encouragement, the psychoanalysts would get a rest from the overwhelming rush of patients suffering from inferiority complexes.

Fame and wealth may outrun us from start to finish, yet we cannot help expecting just a little human recognition for our efforts. We must bask in the warmth of approval now and then; otherwise the health of our self-respect becomes seriously endangered.

It is perhaps in the home that the value of praise is less appreciated than elsewhere. Not everyone realizes that praise is the handiest fire extinguisher to have around, and that no household can be safe without it. As a rule, husbands are blinder to this than wives. A recent survey of rural life in this country uncovered one general complaint made by women living on farms. The wife of one prosperous Ohio farmer wrote to a friend:

Maybe when I'm deaf and blind and a hundred years old I'll get used to having everything I do taken for granted. As it is, life comes pretty dull and hard when you don't hear a word of thanks for all your efforts to keep things nice and bright. It isn't easy to keep on doing your best when you're never told whether your cooking is good or not. Sometimes I feel like copying the woman who served her menfolk cattle fodder one day for dinner, after waiting 20 years for a word of praise. "I've never heard aught to make me think you'd know the difference," she said when they declared she must be crazy.

Farmers—and city husbands too—might well take note of a good old custom which prevailed at the house of the nobility in Russia, where the chef was always summoned to the dining room after a good dinner, complimented, and introduced to the guests. The guest of honor usually made a point of begging the cook to disclose the secret of some particular dish.

Not a little jealousy has its foundation in hearing another praised for something we do equally well. Take the point of personal appearance. It is a curious thing how many men, who never fail to observe the looks of other women, let their own wives go year after year without a word of attention. Thereby is sown the seed for much suspicion.

But, like pastry, praise can be served too lavishly, to the damage of the consumer. A young bride of my acquaintance determined to enroll herself in the list of those who help their husbands to success by faith and encouragement. He was a hard working young man in the advertising business, efficient but no whirlwind. Mrs. Wife proceeded to "yes" him so diligently that she soon had him thinking of himself as a regular little Napoleon. He was all for instructing the boss. But the boss saw otherwise, and finally had to fire him.

Years ago, before children were allowed to have personalities, *Punch* ridiculed the habit, then prevalent, of always thwarting them. A picture showed a young mother reclining gracefully with a novel, and calling to the nursemaid, "Go see what Tommy is doing and tell him he mustn't." A fundamental part of the curriculum of "don't" lay in the idea that children never should be praised, never encouraged, only goaded to achievement by ridicule and fear. That idea has vanished almost completely today.

On this subject I was privileged to talk recently with Dr. Ira S. Wile of New York, whose wide experience, both as education commissioner for that city and as an expert dealing with hundreds of difficult children, has brought him to realize the need of praise as a practical doctor's prescription. Dr. Wile mentioned one particularly interesting illustration.

"It was a case of twins," he said; "two boys. One seemed particularly bright; the other was considered mentally inferior. The father asked me to find the reason.

"When I managed to gain the child's confidence he told me the story I expected to hear—the story children almost invariably tell in such cases.

" 'Why don't people like me,' he asked, 'the same as they like my brother? When he does anything they smile. When I do anything they scowl. I can't ever seem to do anything as good as he does.'

"I separated those boys as much as possible," said Dr. Wile. "I had them placed in different classes in school. I told their parents to stop using comparisons as a goad upon the backward one, and to praise him for his own little accomplishments. When I had him standing on his own feet he soon made headway. He had just been withering in his brother's shadow.

"In other cases brought to me I find it necessary to counteract a parental tendency toward overpraise. Too much praise may turn a child into a snob, a prig, or a bully. When such children are brought to me I have to trim their sails, deflate them. Usually it is the parents who really need deflating."

Today nearly every big business

organization builds on the foundation of encouragement given by the head of the firm to the workers. The system pays. Ten years ago this was not the case.

One New Year's Day a millionaire of my acquaintance, whose pride it was never to offer a tip for any service, faced an unforgettable tragedy. His chief accountant committed suicide. The books were found to be in perfect order, the affairs of the dead man—a modest bachelor—were prosperous and calm. The only letter left by the accountant was a brief note to his millionaire employer. It read: "In 30 years I have never had one word of encouragement. I'm fed up."

It requires experience, an attentive eye, and real knowledge of human nature to know just what to praise in another person and to choose just the right moment for doing it. Serious study is necessary and application. Flash criticism is much easier than intelligent praise; and, unlike flattery, real praise is much more than an indolent short cut to friendliness.

One of the world's greatest dressmakers, a Frenchwoman with an exceptionally fine knowledge of human character, built up her great reputation and following on her ability to grasp the most praiseworthy point in her clients' appearance. She always emphasized that point and encouraged its development. Even with her most unprepossessing "cases" she managed to pick out what was worth displaying, instead of glossing over bad features.

I was present once when a very stout and ungainly matron came to Mme. P—— to be redecorated.

"I'm afraid I'm a terrible figure to dress," she stammered.

Mme. P—— looked her over carefully, then gave the slightest of shrugs. Throwing out her hands in a charming little gesture, she said, "But madame knows how to laugh. Madame can make others gay."

The matron's fat, kindly face beamed. As she drew herself up, one felt that even with her figure the great couturière would succeed.

The wisest man I ever knew said once, "If people did no more than they had to, life would come to a standstill tomorrow." The bit over and above what we are obliged to perform counts most of all. Duty alone will never inspire that last, extra grind. Only devotion backed by self-respect can win it. And such devotion comes only to those whose judgments are just, yet whose praise is willing, quick, and generous.

Boiled Camel

VISITORS at the gigantic goodwill feast recently held for Arabian chiefs at Amman were regaled with one of Arabia's most highly prized dishes, boiled camel. Each camel is stuffed with three sheep, which have been stuffed with eight chickens stuffed with eggs and nuts. The meat is served with boiled rice.—N. Y. *Times*

George Washington——Business Man

Condensed from Nation's Business

PROFESSOR ALBERT BUSHNELL HART

GEORGE WASHINGTON, of course, was a land-owner. That is, his prime business was to run landed estates. Altogether he had 9000 acres of land, pretty much in one body along the Potomac including Mount Vernon. It was a declining business when he inherited it, and his responsibility was to make it pay if he could.

He was the first Virginian to see that the land was played out from raising tobacco crops. So he turned to the culture of wheat. He built a mill and sent his wheat into the market under his own brand. According to the custom of the time he put up a distillery in order to make a different disposition of a part of his product. He sought diversification in agriculture. He raised blooded stock of a superior kind. The King of Spain made him a present of a very valuable jack, and he raised mules and apparently raised them to advantage.

Furthermore, Washington was a natural accountant, and the proof of this is in his diaries and account books. He kept his records in a clear, legible hand. He kept them according to the customs of the times. That is, he recorded whatever went on. His diaries have been published in four volumes but they tell you nothing of what Washington thought; merely what he did.

He was an analytic book-keeper, and I suspect one of the first in America. Hence we find his accounts very carefully subdivided. We find an account for each plantation, a general account, how much he gained out of wheat, how much from tobacco, how many slaves he had, and so on.

Washington loved to keep books. One of his biographers has calculated his losses in gaming. He lost 75 pounds in a year, and he kept the account and added it up. But the biographer fails to notice that on the other side of the page Washington put down his winnings. His winnings were 70 pounds. That is, he was five pounds to the good, because, after all, he had had the fun of it and the fun must have been worth at least ten pounds.

Washington imported the best

agricultural implements that he could hear of. He introduced seeds, he planted cuttings, he raised trees and shrubs. He was a creative farmer. At least he made a living out of the farm, and left it much more valuable than he found it.

Again, he was a surveyor by profession. He loved to handle the surveying instruments. He loved the exactness of the science. He loved to get things right. Furthermore, he was a traveler and explorer. He visited all the states there were at that time in an attempt to make himself familiar with them. I do not know of any American of his time who traveled so widely. He had been up on the Mohawk. He had been out on the Western rivers. He was much interested in the scenery that he saw in various parts of the country.

Everybody is aware that Washington laid out the District of Columbia. He selected the ten-mile square, and he had it surveyed. What is more, he invested his own capital in real estate there, and built some brick houses, intending them to serve as residences for Congressmen.

Even more important, Washington was the first man who understood and appreciated the significance of the West. When in 1754 he was sent out as the messenger of the Virginia government, under directions from England, to warn the French to keep out of the valley of the Ohio, he wrote an account of his journey in his Journal, which is one of the most fascinating books of travel ever written by

an American. We know that it was actually read by the King of England. It made Washington, next to Franklin, the most famous literary man in America for the time being.

He was the first reclamation engineer in the history of the English colonies. He took hold of the problem of the great Dismal Swamp. A company was formed; he was its executive. He reclaimed something like half the swamp which presumably has remained good land to this day. What is more, he made a handsome profit, for himself and the stockholders. He had no instruction in engineering, but simply took advantage of whatever opportunities came his way.

He was the first man who attempted to "realize" in the West. He went out there early. He received certain soldiers' bounty rights. He bought up the bounties of others. Hence he has been accused of robbing the other soldiers, because he bought their claims when nobody else would.

Washington located on the north side of the Ohio River a very considerable tract of land. He said somewhere that "it is not to be supposed that those who were first upon the ground were inattentive to the advantages of the situation." That is, he took good land where he could get it. He had a running fight all his life, however, to maintain his titles.

Washington was a builder of canals; and the canal was the first engineering effort to create long arteries of communication which would bind different parts of the Union together. It is curious that to Washington is due the first suggestion of canals penetrating into the mountains, through the valleys of the Potomac and the James. Both of those lines were eventually built. Of course, he knew that there must be some wagon transit across the mountains, and he made a rough survey of the route. Washington went over a considerable part of the tract that was later followed by the first line of the Baltimore & Ohio Railroad. Throughout his public life he believed intensely in the development of the West, and of the canals as a means of reaching it.

What is more, it is established by the best historical evidence that the first man to conceive of an Erie Canal was George Washington. He was the first man to envisage a continuous water route from the ocean to the Great Lakes by way of Otsego Lake and Lake Ontario. That was the original Erie Canal. Furthermore, he foresaw exactly what has been in the mind of another engineer-statesman of our own time, the President-elect; namely, the possibility of linking the Great Lakes with the Mississippi tributaries, particularly the Ohio, by a system of canals. In 1783 he wrote about it like a prophet. Some of those canals were built, and there is now a project, as everybody knows, for a great system of internal waterways in that region. But Washington was the first business man to see that possibility.

Beyond that, Washington was a financier, a fact that has been clouded and obscured. We are in the habit of thinking of Washington as a frontiersman, then as an elegant young man in Virginia, then as a tough soldier. But he was also a stockholder in the Bank of England. After the Revolution that bank set a splendid example to all banks. It paid for the stock and it paid dividends in full. The mere detail that Washington had been the principal agent in depriving England of her fairest group of colonies and her greatest opportunity for expansion did not stand in the minds of honest and foresighted bankers. Washington's knowledge of finance was of tremendous service to his country when he helped to create the financial institutions which in the early days of the Republic were indispensable for its continuance.

Washington made one of the most remarkable wills of all time. Without legal advice he created what I suppose to have been one of the first trusts for wills established in America. He appointed a board of executors and, after certain specific bequests, divided the remainder into 23 shares: money, as it came in, was to be distributed in twenty-thirds.

Washington was a great employer of labor. At one time he suggested making the purchase "of a cargo of Germans." That did not mean they were to be slaves. It meant that the Germans were to come over on the ordinary seven-year contract. There were many such cases. Oliver Wendell Holmes was the direct descendant of a Scotchman who was sold for seven years, and whose name was not Holmes at all. It was McComb. McComb wrote home at times and that is why the name Holmes stuck to him.

The point is that many indentured men and women became leaders. Washington held both indentured servants and slaves, and in his will he set the slaves free. He said he had not done it before because there were so many intermarriages between his slaves and those of Mrs. Custis that it would have been a difficult matter. What is more, he established a fund for the support of those who had been in his service for many years, so that the old slaves would not be left in want. It was nearly 40 years before the last of them died off. Out of all the southern planters of that period who objected to the principle of human slavery, George Washington and John Randolph were the only ones who actually freed their slaves.

Washington was greatly interested in education. The proof lies in the fact that he was a college president. That is, he was nominally—chancellor of William and Mary College for years. He sent his own nephews to various colleges, and was much interested in Yale, Princeton, and Harvard. He himself was a self-educated man. He had a good library, though we do not know how much of it he read.

In conclusion, it may be said of Washington that he set an example of skill, inflexible honesty, and sound accounting to the whole nation, and he enforced it so far as was humanly possible upon the government on which he set his stamp.

Only 100 Years Ago

Virginia contained a fifth of the whole population of the country.

A man who jeered at the preacher or criticized a sermon was fined.

Two stagecoaches bore all the travel between New York and Boston.

A day laborer considered himself well paid with two shillings a day.

The whipping post and pillory were still standing in Boston and New York.

Buttons were scarce and expensive, and the trousers were fastened with pegs or lace.

Leather breeches, a checked shirt, a red flannel jacket and a cocked hat formed the dress of the real artisan.

Beef, pork, salt fish, potatoes and hominy were the staple diet all the year around.

—Quoted in *National Glass Budget*

Atrocity Charges in the Civil War

Condensed from The World Tomorrow

LAURA A. WHITE

IT is of great interest to compare American newspapers for the Civil War period with the atrocity stories which we heard daily from 1914 to 1918. Only the substitution of "Hun" for "rebel" or "Yankee" is necessary to make them sound familiar.

It was inevitable, doubtless, that in the South, where the desire for separation must be strengthened and where the invading armies soon appeared, that war psychology should manifest itself at once in all its virulence. The venom of the Charleston *Mercury*, prophet of secession for many years, causes no surprise; but the Charleston *Courier*, which had long championed the Union cause, now preached the gospel of hate with all the zeal of a recent convert. In these and other Southern newspapers, stories of atrocities committed by Federal troops were published and republished, their credibility vouched for by editors or their correspondents. Writing of "Federal villainies in Maryland," the *Courier's* correspondent says, "One single fact will

serve as a specimen. A party of Sickle's 'dead rabbits' who had been turned loose upon the unfortunate populace in lower Maryland burned the homestead of a wealthy citizen, turned his family out into the fields, and carried off one of the young ladies to their den, where she was outraged by nine of the devils."

Tales of attacks upon women were numerous, and form the background for the South's reaction to "Beast Butler's" famous order to the women of New Orleans. This act, said Yancey in the Confederate Congress, was only equaled by the record of the invasion of Virginia, where "in numerous instances, daughters have been foully dishonored in the presence of their aged parents, by commissioned officers of the United States army, and more than once the broken-hearted father shot to death for attempting to save the honor of his family."

There were other charges, now all sounding equally familiar, such as the defiling of public buildings, the firing at long range on women and children at Fredericksburg, and the wanton despoiling of churches. After the evacuation of Newbern, the Raleigh *Journal* published the story of how the Yankees had desecrated the graveyards, and exposed and mutilated the bodies.

The atrocities of course were declared to be sanctioned by officers and government, in many cases originating with them. "Our enemy," said the Charleston *Courier*, "has inscribed destruction upon his banner. He has instructed his soldiers to steal, desolate, destroy and murder, making these huge crimes as much their duty as the work of fighting." "How long," cries the Richmond *Whig*, "must our wives and daughters endure the outrages of brutes gathered from the sinks of Northern and European civilization?"

The Federal army was "as villainous as the worst pirates who ever infested the sea." "Look at the horde of ruffians, and say what jail has been robbed to bring together these hireling assassins." "They combine all the vices of savages," said Barnwell Rhett, "with the intelligence of the civilized man. [They are] brutal fanatics . . . a nation of criminals."

Northern leaders were described with similar invective. Salacious stories about Federal generals were repeated with relish. To find commanders, said the Richmond *Whig* in 1864, Lincoln must have robbed the grog shops and gambling hells; strike off from the roll of Yankee officers the disreputable characters, drunkards, miscegenators, *et cetera*

and there would not be enough left to command a single corps. "Butler the Beast, Grant the Butcher, Sherman the Brute—what a precious trio, what heaven-defying, monstrous specimens of humanity!" exclaimed the Atlanta *Intelligencer*. Lincoln himself was called "the Baboon President," "a low-bred obscene clown."

The Northerners made repayment with interest. The Southern troops were cowards, convicts, white trash. The New York *Evening Post* said in 1861, "Conduct which would disgrace any tribe of savages is imputed to them, such as firing upon hospitals, deliberately shooting down women in attendance upon the sick, and bayonetting poor mutilated creatures." Tales of Southern ferocity became a commonplace; prisoners were murdered; the fingers of the dead were cut off to secure the rings; many of the dead had their eyes picked out; their skulls and bones were "cut and carved into drinking cups; and the women of the region, equally ignorant and cruel, wear them and gloat over them with glee."

Probably no publication was so effective in spreading propaganda as *Harper's Weekly* because in this magazine the misdeeds of the enemy were presented in vivid drawings. In September, 1862, for example, a guerilla raid was pictured, with houses burned, men strung up and women attacked—all there in lurid detail. Here is a typical summary of charges:

"The cruel and incredible bar-

barities of the rebels every day accumulate in horror. They cut off the heads of our dead at Manassas; they boiled the bodies to get the bones more readily; they buried our brave brothers with their faces down; they swung their heads as trophies upon their homeward march through East Tennessee; they drew Kenly and his heroic troop of Marylanders with a white flag, then unrolled the black and massacred them. . . . Dishonor and infamy of every kind; ferocity which Feejees could not emulate; superstition, ignorance, and bestiality. . . ."

For vivid characterization of the leaders in the struggle the palm seems to go to the South. Yet the New York *Times* referred to General Magruder as "the whiskey-headed, blustering, profane fop and bully." The Boston *Transcript* described how General Lee had with his own hand flogged a slave girl and put brine on her bleeding wounds.

As such atrocity stories spread throughout the North and South, the cry rose in both sections for a policy of retaliation. Each side conceded that the worse deeds of the enemy could not be imitated by civilized people, but insisted fiercely upon a "just retaliation." "Considering the horrible atrocities of the rebels in the prosecution of this war," said the New York *World*, "it is a piece of bare-faced and brazen effrontery in them to appeal to the usages of civilized warfare." Meanwhile Southern spirit was kindled to white heat by the Emancipation Proclamation and the use of Negro troops.

All who are concerned with minimizing the chances of war for the next generation must be interested in the fact that in this "brothers' war," even as in the World War, no atrocity was too horrible to be given credence by the press on both sides. When, sometime ago, the revelation was made of the concoction in England, for American consumption, of the report of the boiling of their dead by the Germans, many expressed the hope that in another war the propaganda would at least be less crass. If the men of the next generation know as little of the true situation in 1917 as we know of the credulities of 1862, what is that hope but the imagining of a vain thing?

—and You Won't Feel the Cold

PEOPLE who are too sensitive to the cold of winter can protect themselves by cultivating immunity, according to the *Journal of the American Medical Association*. The treatment is simple: The patient immerses a hand in water chilled to 50° Fahrenheit one or two minutes a day for from three to four weeks. This gives systemic or general desensitization.

Teaching Your Child Religion

Condensed from the World's Work

HARRY EMERSON FOSDICK

THE religious training of a child inevitably begins in the home the day the child is born. A child reared in fear under parents who rely on fright to achieve good order will be predisposed to be afraid of any God in whom he may believe. Another child, reared in an atmosphere of trust, will find the love of God a congenial idea.

Whether a child shall grow up to regard life with suspicion or with confidence, to be deceitful or straightforward, contentious and grasping or coöperative and loyal —these and other basic characteristics are early determined by the treatment he receives, and obviously they enter into the essential quality of his spiritual life in general and of his religion in particular. When parents, therefore, say that they are not teaching religion to their children, they are deceiving themselves. They cannot help teaching religion.

A further truth becomes evident as the growing child passes out of infancy into youth: Religion is imitated rather than learned. In the long run no teaching of religion in a home matters except that which expresses the way of living that the home practices. In a family where generosity reigns, where differences between Jew and Gentile, Protestant and Catholic, white and colored, rich and poor, learned and ignorant are lines across which appreciation and good will run freely, alike in word and action, religious teaching will be the elucidation of a kind of life visible to the child's eyes. It will be readily assimilated, and it will sink deep.

This same truth holds about the more intimate matter of teaching children to pray. Of course, the real way is not to teach them to pray at all, but to pray with them. Parents should also see that prayer soon becomes a matter from which they should keep hands off, trusting that the child will know by observation the value of prayer to people whom he himself has loved and admired.

Religion is something that only secondarily can be taught. It must primarily be absorbed. Only when religious teaching is an outward explanation of what is first of all an inward and experienced way of living, does it carry through.

After these two initial stages have been passed, in which the child's basic emotional reactions have been set and his family's religion or irreligion absorbed, there is sure to come the period of conscious questioning. Many parents are upset and distressed by this. They have taken it for granted that they had the right to hand on to the child their own religion. It is often difficult to persuade them that the rise of impatient and even distracted questioning is a sign of intellectual life, and that it is so much to be expected that the psychologists can fix the average age when this condition should occur—at about 18 years in boys and 15 years in girls.

Robert Browning, as he himself says, was "passionately religious" when he was a boy, and he certainly was nobly and undiscourageably religious when he was a man, but in between came the upset when he questioned everything and called himself an atheist. This must have been a very disturbing phase for Browning's parents. But Browning was finding that in religion supremely Goethe's words hold true: "What you have inherited from your fathers you must earn for yourself before you can really call it yours."

The attitudes of parents toward this fact are interestingly diverse. Some are so much impressed by it that they feel all definite teaching of religion to their children to be impertinent intrusion; and they try to keep the child's mind neutral until, coming of age, he can choose for himself. The attempt is uniformly unsuccessful. The child's mind never stays neutral. From primitive and inescapable questions, such as who made the world or what happens when our friends die, to curiosity about habits of worship, the child's mind is bound to take a religious bent one way or another. Parents cannot put off their responsibility in this matter.

Some parents go to the opposite extreme. They endeavor so to indoctrinate the child's mind with their own conceptions of religion that he never can escape them. Often fear is powerfully employed in this class of teaching, and I find grown people still laboring under an ingrained dread of thinking for themselves. In this way children are taught to associate doubt with sin, questioning with treachery against God, and so the child's mind is bound hand and foot to start with, forestalling the first motions in the direction of religious independence.

Wise parents will, I think, adopt neither the policy of neutrality nor that of dogmatic dragooning. Two major considerations will, instead, control their method.

First, they will take it for granted that the child's religion must be his own; that he will in all probability come to the time when he will question what he has been taught, will rethink it, will alike retain, reject, and adjust it, and that no parent should wish him not to. In view of this, the parent will desire above all else to teach the child from the beginning as little as possible that he will need to unlearn.

The way parents lie to their children in matters of religion is to me a constant and shocking astonishment. Here is a mother who tells me that in answer to her four-year-old's question as to where God is she has said, "In heaven"; and in reply to the further inquiry as to where heaven is she has said, "In the sky." This mother has now waked up to the fact that these heedless answers were downright falsehoods. She did not believe what she said. And she did not, apparently, comprehend that teaching the child an idea of God set in such an incredible framework of imagination was the surest way to have that child say some day that she did not believe in God.

The New Testament says that God is love; that where love is, God is also, dwelling in those who are lovers of their fellows; that God is spirit, surrounding and interpenetrating us so that he lives in us and we live in him. Some parents seem to think such an idea of God too rarefied to be taught to children. Upon the contrary, it is adults who commonly are too crass to understand it, while children can grasp it more easily than they can any other. Most parents condescend to their children when they talk about religion. They never need to.

The second item in a wise parent's program logically follows: When questions begin to come the parent will deal with them honestly. If he knows the answer, he will give it as he sees it. If he does not know the answer, he will say so. In any case he will scrupulously tell the truth. This advice may seem superfluous. The fact is, however, that many parents shamelessly tell falsehoods about all the deepest matters of life, from camouflaging the facts about sex to doling out sophistries about the Bible. An honest agnostic who takes his son into his confidence, talks over with him the solemn problem of life as if they two were intellectual comrades facing an elemental mystery and trying together to see some sense in it, will have a much better spiritual result than a believer who dodges the real questions, assumes certainty he does not feel, gives answers he himself does not understand, and in general pretends.

We have been dealing with the religious training of children within the home, but it is an unhappy home that must solve the problem without the coöperation of the church. Religion is both individual and social. It is an inward, mystical experience, but if it is wholesome it overflows in coöperative fellowship. No man can be completely religious all alone.

The tendency in many American homes today is to neglect those factors in religious training for which the church chiefly stands. In doing so they overlook an educational factor which psychologists are constantly emphasizing. Children learn by doing. Telling a little child a truth is the worst way to teach it to him. Let the child, if possible, do something that involves the lesson; let him act as though it were true. To tell a child that he should be courteous is to begin at the wrong end. Teach him to say "Thank you," to lift his hat, to rise when a lady enters. Train him, that is, in the concrete ritual practices of courtesy, and so, say the psychologists, the doing of the courteous acts will beget the courteous spirit.

The popular undervaluing of outward religious acts is thus thoroughly bad psychology. Granted that ritual in any realm from courtesy to worship can become formal, empty, and stiff. Nevertheless, with all its dangers it is an absolute necessity. We cannot neglect all formal expressions of courtesy and still retain courtesy itself, nor can we train children in the spirit of religion if the appropriate activities of worship and devotion are forgotten.

This truth especially applies to the rearing of a child. Let him be trained as early as possible not only in ethical behavior but symbolic behavior, such as bowing in thanks before meals, kneeling at family prayers, joining in the worship of the church.

To be sure, all this can quite easily be made dry as dust. Some churches and some ministers are murderers, not makers, of beauty in worship, and render repellent what should attract the soul toward God. Happy the homes where, as in some families I know, being made to stay home from church is one of the most dreaded punishments in the parents' entire arsenal.

When London Was One Vast Cathedral

WHEN the carriage of the King and Queen had swept past on its way to St. Paul's, I turned from the window, thinking the great moment of the Jubilee was over. The service at St. Paul's was beginning to come in over the radio—the pealing of the bells, the blasts of the trumpets as the King and Queen entered the Cathedral, and one by one we rose to our feet for "God Save the King." Just then I caught a glimpse through the window of the crowds in the street below. They, too, stood still: the whole of London had frozen into immobility, for the service at St. Paul's was being broadcast at every street corner throughout the city. Millions of people were taking part in the same service that only a few were actually witnessing.

I rushed into the street. Along Pall Mall and Saint James's people still remained in their places in the stands; others stood in groups in the streets joining in the hymns that were at that moment being sung at St. Paul's. People even dropped to their knees and joined in the prayers, and everyone was bareheaded. This was the most thrilling scene of all.—John McMullin in *Vogue*

The Amazing Persecution of Dr. Dix

Condensed from The New Yorker

HERBERT ASBURY

ON A morning in February 1880, the Rev. Dr. Morgan Dix, rector of old Trinity Church, answered the door-bell of the rectory at No. 27 West 25th Street, and stepped across the threshold into one of the most exraordinary series of persecutions that have ever perplexed the New York police. His visitor was a clerical gentleman, who said that he was prepared to quote favorable terms for the care and training of the three little girls whom, according to a letter ostensibly from Dr. Dix, the rector wished to place in a select academy. The bewildered clergyman explained that a mistake had been made; but scarcely had the clerical gentleman departed than another arrived. Thereafter they came in droves, more than a score calling before nightfall.

Mingled with them were many representatives of Bible societies, publishing houses, and all sorts of

From: *All Around the Town,* by Herbert Asbury, reprinted by permission of Alfred A. Knopf, Inc.

manufacturing establishments, all of which had received letters saying that Dr. Dix wished to inspect samples before purchasing large quantities of supplies for various charitable organizations under his control. The postman was meanwhile delivering huge sacks of letters from firms which had not sent salesmen. Next day the procession of callers continued, and the mail was augmented by grave communications from leading Episcopal bishops and clergymen throughout the East, who had received curt notes, to which the signature of the rector had been forged, reprimanding them for not having answered Dr. Dix's letters. Several of the divines hinted that perhaps the distinguished rector of Trinity should consult a physician.

On Feb. 21, 1880, Dr. Dix received a letter stating that Washington's Birthday would be a memorable occasion for the rector, as numerous old-clothes women would call to negotiate for the purchase of Mrs. Dix's entire wardrobe. The next morning a fat woman appeared at the door, demanding that the clothing be produced. Within a few moments, another woman, with a sack slung over her shoulder, rushed through the gate and elbowed the first caller away from the door. The rector retreated, and the women settled down on the stoop to wait, convinced that Dr. Dix merely wanted to haggle. By noon the lawn of the rectory was filled with the excited clamor of 28 old-clothes women. Several neighbors who attempted to enter the rectory and console the distressed clergyman were set upon by the women, who insisted upon bargaining for the clothing upon their backs. Dr. Dix finally called the police, who drove the women from the yard.

Scarcely had the clatter of their carts died away than a carriage raced through 25th Street and drew up in front of the rectory. One of the city's leading physicians dashed into the house, only to emerge a few moments later very indignant. He had received an urgent call that Dr. Dix had gone into an epileptic fit and was dying. Similar messages had been left at the offices of some 30 other doctors, and it was after midnight when the last of them had come and gone. Dr. Dix slept fitfully that night, and before breakfast was awakened by a half-dozen shoemakers who had been notified to call at the rectory and measure some children for shoes, and before lunch at least 50 men and

women who had advertised for work appeared. They had received notes advising them that jobs were to be had from Dr. Dix. About dusk a score of the most prominent clergymen of New York presented themselves at the rectory, having received invitations, to which the rector's name had been forged, to dine with Dr. and Mrs. Dix and meet the Bishops of York and Exeter.

Next morning the leading department stores received curt letters, also supposedly signed by Dr. Dix, saying that the rector had turned their impertinent communications over to his lawyer for immediate legal action. Since no such communications, of course, had ever been written to Dr. Dix, officials of these firms hurriedly sent emissaries to the rectory to assure the clergyman of their undying respect. Dr. Dix next received a letter signed "Gentleman Joe," which said that the annoyances would cease if the rector would pay him $1000. Dr. Dix was instructed, if he was willing to make the payment, to publish in the *Herald* two days later a personal saying, "Gentleman Joe: All right." The police now began to grapple with the problem. Upon their advice Dr. Dix inserted the advertisement as directed, but Gentleman Joe paid no attention to it.

Shortly afterward, a lawyer came to the rectory with a letter to which Mrs. Dix's name had been forged, and which said that she wished to consult him about a divorce. Twenty other lawyers, bearing exactly similar missives, called during the day, as well as an agent for a steamship line, with two tickets to Havana, and a score of persons who, having advertised for lost property, had been notified that their belongings were being held for them at the rectory. During the next three days at least a hundred persons appeared in response to summonses of various sorts, and about a week later an indignant stranger forced his way into the rectory, accused the astonished Dr. Dix of being too friendly with his wife, and threatened to cane the clergyman unless he immediately made a public apology. Next day the rector received a letter from Gentleman Joe saying that he had thoroughly enjoyed his visit, and boasting of his ability as an actor.

The police made extraordinary efforts to capture Dr. Dix's persecutor, assigning every detective on the force to the case. Gentleman Joe had gone to the expense of procuring stationery engraved with "Trinity Parsonage, 27 West 25 Street," but the printer could not be found; and the police also failed when detectives were stationed at mail boxes throughout the city to open the receptacles, whenever a letter was mailed, and compare the handwriting with that known to be Gentleman Joe's. But it was not until a clergyman of another denomination happened to see a former Trinity Sunday-school teacher on the street and mentioned the fact to Dr. Dix, that the police finally pounced on the rascal's trail. This man, Edward E. F. Williamson, had been expelled from Trinity when, having been unmasked as a person of low character, he scorned reformation and boasted of his amorous experiences in Turkey. Believing that spite might lie behind the persecution, the police began a search for Williamson. He was finally traced to Baltimore, where he was arrested.

Williamson admitted that he had annoyed Dr. Dix, but maintained that he had been impelled solely by a craving for amusement. Williamson was tried on a charge of blackmail, was convicted and sentenced to Sing Sing, where he died.

The police discovered that after his expulsion from Trinity, Gentleman Joe had gone to England, where he served a term in Newgate Prison for tormenting a Hebrew gentleman in London, in much the same fashion as he later persecuted Dr. Dix. Upon his release in 1875, he came back to the United States and lived in Pittsburgh for several years, swindling a few jewelry firms out of small amounts. The police regarded him as a very mysterious person, and suspected that he was the ne'er-do-well son of an English family, and received remittances from his relatives. Apparently he had devoted his life to the commission of small crimes, not for the purpose of gain, but simply to amuse himself.

The Tree as an Invention

Condensed from The Atlantic Monthly

CHARLES D. STEWART

IN any tree, however alive, the substance composing trunk and branch—the solid part of the tree—is inert and lifeless matter. The heartwood of a tree is dead in every sense. Its tubes no longer convey sap upward. From the heartwood outward to a point very near the surface we find the water-conveying structure consisting of long tubes; and these tubes are mere conduits, inert and lifeless. At first, when they were being built, there were live cells working inside of them, little bags of protoplasm; but, once they were completed, the live tenants disappeared.

The only part of a tree that is really alive is a thin sheath of cells at the surface of the wood called the cambium layer. It is this live part that keeps building and making the tree larger.

If we cut through a tree, we can count the rings of its annual growth. A cut across a tree near the ground may show 300 annual rings, while cuts at higher points will disclose but 100, or 50, or 40. The rings become fewer and fewer.

If we take a particular ring and follow it up we find that it grows smaller and smaller till it diminishes, a ring near the center of the stump coming to an end at no great distance from the ground. And each of these rings, according as it is the 40th or 100th from the center, will show the height as well as the thickness that the tree has attained in that number of years. Just as a tree grows smaller upward, so likewise do these inner sheaths of annual growth. All the successive surfaces of the tree are enclosed here.

Thus we see that a tree is really a sheath of life spread over the dead trees of other years. Generation stands within generation, successively wrapped about. The outer life of cambium and leaf and bud uses this trellis to go up and reach out sunward and skyward. Instead of throwing its old skeleton aside each year and starting anew, it clings to its dead bones, profits by their stature, and makes tubes in them to provide a supply of water for a larger growth. When we compare this way of growth with other methods, both animal and vegetable, it must strike us as a most interesting invention.

As the inner or lifeless part of a tree is incapable of growth, a nail driven into a young tree at any particular height will remain at that distance from the ground throughout the life of the tree. And a branch coming out at any point will not be carried upward as time goes on.

A tree, like other forms of life, is engaged in the constant circulation of fluid through its tissues. Life processes, animal or vegetable, can go on only so long as each individual cell is surrounded by a fluid containing nutriment. To meet this demand and to provide for a large amount of evaporation, a tree passes up a great deal of water. A fairly large beech tree will use about 65 gallons of water on a dry, hot day, and a large oak will require much more. Even a sunflower will use two pounds. And this water, in the larger species of trees, will have to be lifted 200 and even 300 feet.

Anyone familiar with pressures in a water tower must be interested in asking, How is this done? In the present stage of man's knowledge of physics, we do not know.

The lamp-wick principle, capillary attraction, will not go far in raising water. Water rises in a capillary or fine tube to a height in proportion to the fineness of the tube; and the viscosity of water is such that if the tube is very fine it will not rise at all. Capillary attraction would not raise water to the top of even a moderate-sized tree.

Root pressure or osmosis, a sort of powerful absorption due to unbalanced chemical pressure, has been considered. By cutting off a plant near the ground and fastening a glass tube upright on the stem, it is possible to ascertain the height to which its sap will rise by the pressure from below. Under favorable conditions a grapevine will exert a pressure sufficient to raise a column 36.5 feet, while a birch has tested as high as 84.7 feet. This might seem a promising line of inquiry except that root pressure takes place only in early spring, and especially in the morning. It has been found that when the tree is evaporating the greatest quantities of water, on dry, hot days of summer, there is no root pressure whatever.

It has been proved that the rise of water in the tubes of a tree is caused by a pull from above. A branch, if cut from a growing plant, with its end inserted in an air-tight manner in a glass tube, will draw a supply of water from the tube with such force as to pull a column of mercury up after it. But here again a difficulty intervenes in the solution of the problem.

A suction pump at its best will lift water but 33 feet. The pump, by the lift of its piston, removes air pressure from the upper surface and tends to create a vacuum, in consequence of which the water is pushed up the pipe from below by the weight of the atmosphere, a pressure of 15 pounds to the square inch at sea level. No invention can be made which will pull more than the laws of physics will enable it to do. And 33 feet falls far short of reaching the top of a sequoia.

But water has *got* to go up those tubes to the top of a tree. It will and does. Hence, scientists began to consider whether water in thin columns, as in these fine tubes, has not an actual coherence, a tensile strength, sufficient to stand a strong pull. Possibly, after all, water may be drawn up from the top as if it were a rope. Strange to say, experimentation has gone quite far in proving this to be the case. But there is a difficulty.

The rise of water to the top of a tree is dependent upon evaporation, which makes room for the continual upflow, and gives rise to the strong absorptive pull, or osmosis. This being true, if a plant or a branch is placed in an atmosphere so saturated with moisture that evaporation is impossible, it will be unable to keep the water flowing up its stem. Yet experiment has shown that the intake persists, though it is slowed up, even when the leaves are entirely submerged in water. So the rise of the water still remains a mystery.

A tree manufactures its food direct from earth and air, a thing the animal cannot do; and though it has no lungs, nor anything corresponding to such a device, it feeds life's constant fires by taking in oxygen night and day. And how can a tree breathe without lungs? Another mystery!

It is when we consider the tree as a plant made to conquer difficulty, a sea creature living on land, that we see its lofty waterworks in their full significance. The tree was a very bold and original idea in nature; and the steps leading up to it were four. First in the order of development came the primitive water plants, the thallophytes, floating freely about or living in the saturated soil along the shore. And in those days there were no other kinds of vegetation. Second came the amphibious plants, such as the mosses; third the woody plants beginning with the ferns; and fourth the most modern woody and two-sexed plants of this highly mechanized vegetable age.

In the mosses we see vegetation crawling on its belly up towards the dry land. Stealthily and cautiously it draws away from the water's edge, lying low. It must not venture far, for it has no true roots; and it cannot raise its head out of the moisture. At first it was but a thin sheath of cells, lying flat on the mud; then it became several layers thick, the moisture being passed from cells below to those above by absorption.

Finally, the great idea came to pass in the form of a fern. Here was a vegetable mechanism with true, running roots, which the moss has not; and it possessed a woody stem provided with tubes for conducting water. With the invention of the fern, piping the water upward, while the roots struck down to bring it from below, nothing more was necessary to the making of the tree. It only remained for the stock company of cells to go ahead and, in modern parlance, construct a "bigger and better" plant.

Water is the food and life of the tree cells. Every cell had to be immersed in water. And that is just what came to pass. Every cell in the top of a tree continues to be immersed in the life-giving water. Between a cell in the sea and one in the topmost twig there is no essential difference in situation. And the reason is that everything is done to control evaporation and hold it within bounds. Every leaf is coated with a preparation that most effectually seals it. Air can enter and water escape only through microscopic openings called stomates on the under sides of the leaves; and every stomate is capable of being opened or closed according to conditions. The whole trunk and every limb of the tree are jacketed in the protective, suberized bark. There is nothing more waterproof than bark, more stubbornly impermeable. It is because cork is so waterproof that it makes stoppers for bottles and gaskets for engines. It is because it is so impermeable that it is ground up to make linoleum. A tree, from head to foot, is armored against evaporation. Consequently its cells, though they hang in the very eye of the sun, are in water as wet as that which surrounds them in the sea.

It is when I look at a tree from this point of view that I feel like pinning—or nailing—a medal on its chest. If a man is the height of achievement in the animal world, so is a tree in the vegetable. A bronze tablet really ought to be hung on a tree here and there to memorialize scientific facts. The inscription could be a very simple one, as, for instance:

HERE STANDS
THE KING OF VEGETABLES
A SEA CELL THAT BECAME
AMBITIOUS

Extra-Curricular

FOR A PREMIUM ranging from 50 cents for freshmen to 35 cents for seniors, the Students' Protective Insurance Company, formed last year by students of Providence College, Rhode Island, sells "exam insurance." The company provides each policyholder with a special syllabus of "hot tips" on a course; if the student fails to make a passing grade it pays the additional examination fees to the college: $2 for the first try, $5 each for the next two. The plan is being adopted by students at Boston College, Columbia University, Princeton, and the University of California.

STUDENTS of Denver University have evolved a new method of earning money for their college expenses: party driving. "Party drivers" guarantee sober driving for other students on parties. Of late, police starting to arrest drivers of cars filled with shouting, singing students have been checked by the explanation: "I'm a party driver."—UP

Must Our Children Start Where We Did?

Condensed from Harper's Magazine

EMILY NEWELL BLAIR

THERE is in America a widespread dogma that only those who begin with nothing can, or do, exercise the virtues of hard work or self-denial. There is felt to be a special virtue in the necessity of getting money for oneself.

Several ideas are back of this "start at scratch and win your own way" standard. There is the egotistical one, "What was good enough for me is good enough for my boy." There is that of simple logic, "I started with nothing and made good; therefore, if he starts with nothing he will make good." And there is the one springing from a father's vanity, "So long as I have all the money in my own hands I shall remain the important member of my family, the big man in the community." And there is what may be the most powerful idea of all: that the making and ownership of money are the chief tests of worth. If a man's place in the community is due solely to the amount of money he has made, naturally he will want to emphasize the im-

portance and value of money, as this will emphasize his own importance. How do it better than to deny it to the younger generation, make them get it for themselves, keep them envying those that already have it? Nothing would so lessen its importance and his own as to treat it casually as a means rather than an end.

It is true that the need to meet expenses is an incentive to some men; but it is equally true that to others it is a terrible handicap, preventing the entire absorption in their task which is necessary for their success. Still others require a sense of mental peace, a sense of security, before they can do their best. There are other incentives to work than the necessity of providing necessities. Men continually strive to take something and make of it something more. Why, then, may they not start with something and make out of it something else? Why not begin with money and make out of it a profession, a success, a career? The career will call for work, energy, ability, and self-control in quite as large proportions as though one had started at scratch.

"Would you then advocate," I can hear many a father ask scornfully, "that we settle money on our children when they marry?"

I know the very question calls to mind profligacy and social degeneration. Yet why not? A son is brought up with the best possible education, denied no opportunity of travel and preparation. Why, then, suddenly at the age of 21 or 22, deny him the most precious gift of all—opportunity to use his years of young enthusiasm, great ambitions, and abundant energies in the work he wants to do? Many of us must spend these years in making money, in the hope that later we may have the time to exercise our talents—only, alas, to find that by the time we have the money there is neither energy nor the ability left for the ambitions. With us, with so many, there is no choice. But what a waste for those who might start with something to be held back as we are, making believe they start with nothing and duplicating our efforts, because their fathers think there is more virtue in making money than in doing work you want to do! One father said to me, "If what my son wants is to play the violin, then he shall do it if only to compensate for the 30 years I've spent in a drug store every day of which I longed to be a soldier."

And after all it is only make-believe, this enforced starting with nothing. However much the wealthy parent may try, he cannot create artificially the conditions that exist when a son actually starts with nothing. There is a world of difference between the necessity that springs from knowing one can never have anything he does not earn and the compulsion that comes from a parent's refusing or postponing assistance. In one case it is sink or swim. In the other, there is actually no possibility of sinking. And all the pretense does is to rob the child of the compensations of starting with something.

The wise parent knows this, and so seeks to get for his boy by some other means the sort of advantage that comes from "starting with nothing." The best way to do this is to stimulate his son to want something which his wealth may help him to achieve but which it cannot achieve alone. It may be success in another business, or in a profession, or in some art, or in scholarship. There is a very real opportunity for starting with money and turning it into taste, knowledge, action, beauty, happiness, or power.

Any of these substitutes can develop in the child the same courage, self-control, determination, sportsmanship, industry, and economy as are supposed to be developed in the journey from poverty to fortune. But the finding of these substitutes requires imagination, and—alas for the child—it is so much easier for the parent to demand an imitation of his own experience!

A rich mother once told me of her plan with her daughters: "It seemed ridiculous to set them such daily tasks as making beds and darning their own stockings, once they had learned how, with servants standing by. So I set about trying to find tasks for them that grew logically out of their money. Each girl when she was 14 was given a budget to do over her room. She had to study decoration long enough to learn to do it right, to buy the furniture proper to the room. I let each one buy one good picture a year from an unknown artist, and this led to a study of art. Each one has a garden of her own, and each a responsibility for buying the new books on certain subjects. There never has been any sense of compulsion because they see what they do is a logical result of their fortune."

I know a millionaire whose one son was recently married. The son lives in a tiny apartment, and his wife, a charming college graduate who does her own work and makes her own clothes, cannot afford to entertain her friends or indulge her taste for the studies she enjoyed before her marriage. The father is delighted to find her so "sensible." Yet could anything be more senseless? While the father's fortune piles up, his only son, living little better than a peasant, is setting out to make his own millions. This is all right if that is what he wants. But what his wife wants, I happen to know, is a family, and space to house them, plenty of ground in which they may play, a good servant, leisure to keep up her music and read, time to play a little golf. By the time she is 50 it will be too late to get these things. What good

will a palace do her then when her children have left her? It is when children are young and their habits and ideas of life are being formed that a mother wants dignity and ease and comfort in her home.

Suppose a father, instead of forcing his son to walk in his footsteps, said to him, "Here, take this stock and use the dividends to pay for a servant. Have as large a family as you wish, without worry. I want my grandchildren to have a healthy, rested mother, informed, active, a mother of whom they can always be proud and who will have much to give them. My life is lived and I want you to begin where I've ended."

The theory that one must make money to appreciate its value is a theory divorced from experience. Anyone who has compared the lavishness of the new rich in large cities with the careful expenditure of those who inherit large houses, established social positions, and an unearned income, knows that the fear of losing money, and the possession of tastes dependent on it for satisfaction, furnish a greater appreciation of its value than the earning of it.

Not long ago the papers heralded the fact that an heiress to millions would do her own housework. What virtue is there in that, when she might be preparing herself for the responsibility of that great fortune? The present English ruling family could teach the American billionaire a lot about bringing up his children to meet great responsibilities.

If fathers can start with nothing and end with ten million, can they not use it to get the next generation beyond the starting point, so that instead of doing a sort of merry-go-round here in America, each generation may develop a pattern of living more satisfying than that of their fathers? If each generation began a little earlier to consider the quality and enjoyment of life, might we not be able to put more of beauty into the technic of living, and even, perhaps, achieve a higher national standard of culture and taste?

How much of our standardization, our lack of originality or appreciation of beauty, our poverty of interests, I wonder, may be charged to the fact that all the years of youth must be spent in slaving to become able to gratify tastes or express real desires? Surely, the excuse for wealth is that it frees some men from the necessity of struggle for a livelihood, so that they may spend their time and energy making something more of life than a mere struggle for physical survival. This is how aristocracies are made, aristocracies of character and breeding. A family tree may live for generations, growing ever stronger and more beautiful.

It is not enough to begin with nothing and end with something. This something should be made to go on to something else—a more stable, a more beautiful mode of living for each generation.

A Chinese Rejection Slip

ILLUSTRIOUS BROTHER OF THE SUN AND MOON:

Behold thy servant prostrate before thy feet! I kowtow to thee and beg that of thy graciousness thou mayest grant that I may speak and live. Thine honored manuscript has deigned to cast the light of its august countenance upon me. With raptures I have perused it. By the bones of mine ancestors! Never have I encountered such wit, such pathos, such lofty thought. With fear and trembling I return the writing. Were I to publish the treasure thou hast sent me, the Emperor would order that it be made a standard of excellence and that none be published except such that equaled it. Knowing literature as I do, and that it would be impossible in ten thousand years to equal what thou hast done, I send thy writing back by guarded servants.

Ten thousand times I crave thy pardon.

Behold! My head is at thy feet and I am but dust.

Thy servant's servant,

WANG CHIN, Editor

What It Means to Marry a Catholic

Condensed from The Forum

BY ONE WHO DID

IF THE Catholic rule forbidding the marriage of a Catholic with a non-Catholic could be enforced, many tragedies would be averted. But every year thousands of Catholics apply for and receive a dispensation from the law and enter into the marriage contract with those whose conception of marriage is totally different from theirs.

Before my marriage to a Catholic I noted the beautiful features of Catholic worship, and sincerely believed that I had "become" a Catholic. But now, after years of earnest attempt, I realize the difficulty of accepting religion entirely on authority.

In the first place, the Catholic conception of marriage is that one marries primarily to beget children. The happiness of husband and wife may follow as a hoped-for result, but this is secondary to having children—many children. This theory I did not dispute before marriage. I loved children and wanted many.

But the physical and financial strain of family life cannot be correctly estimated until one has mothered a child or two. Under certain conditions, a large family becomes impossible. Then the Romanist command looms up. "No sin is worse than birth control!" The fact that many Catholics do practice birth control does not alter the grave situation. Among my acquaintances there are many, I am convinced, whose lives are continuously perturbed by the thought that they are "living in mortal sin." Satisfying family life is hard to attain under these conditions.

Since a genuine Catholic marriage is primarily for procreation, it is well to understand what is implied by the pledge required of non-Catholics to bring up their children in the orthodox faith. Most persons who sign this pledge probably foresee in it nothing more than sending their children to Mass and seeing that they abstain from meat on Fridays and fast days. But in nine cases out of ten it means sending the children to a parochial school.

The profound sincerity of the

130

Catholic clergy in believing "Catholic education" to be the ultimate redemption of the world is, I think, not fully realized. It is because every Catholic leader believes so thoroughly that salvation is only possible through the Roman Catholic Church that such zealous efforts are made to draw every child of Catholic parents into the school. This applies particularly to the children of mixed marriages. Catholic zealots feel that a child whose misfortune it is to live under the influence of a non-Catholic father or mother must be watched and kept within the fold. To go against what the Catholic group considers right brings the severest criticism and ostracism. There may even be a threat of refusal of absolution after confession. That is the most terrific blow that can be dealt anyone who accepts the Pope as "Christ's Vicar on earth" and the priest as his "representative."

The non-Catholic parent, therefore, must yield if there is to be anything like peace in the family. I had made up my mind not to send my four children to a parochial school, but when the situation actually confronted me, it was impossible to hold to my determination. My principal reason for not wanting to send my children to a church school was that I did not want class consciousness forced upon them. I dislike to have my children's relationships limited to any *one* class of people. I should not favor sending them to a fashionable private school, for the same reason.

It had always been my hope that my sons and daughters would be friendly with all classes—with rich and poor, with Jews, gentiles, and atheists. Instead, I now listen to arguments about the superiority of Catholic schools over all others and to stories of street squabbles between parochial and public school children. Not that the Sisters and Brothers mean to encourage unfriendliness. But their constant remarks on Catholic preëminence cannot but have their effect on impressionable children. I had hoped to "condition" in my family a spirit of friendliness toward all classes of people. Instead my children are being led, through no fault of their own, into intolerance of all whose beliefs are not identical with theirs.

That the economic burden imposed by the parochial school is greater than the Catholic population can safely carry, I have also learned by observation and bitter experience. To contribute according to one's means to the support of the pastors is one of the six chief commandments of the Church, a violation of which constitutes a "mortal sin"—enough to deprive one of all hope of heaven. The parochial school is one of the legitimate expenses of the pastor; and the interpretation of "according to one's means" shows a lack of proportion on the part of the clergy. In most parishes it is a practice to publish at regular intervals the exact amount each member of the congregation has given to the support of church and school. Disgrace befalls a person whose name appears on the monthly list with a contribution considered too small.

In our own case, though our income is far above that of the average Catholic family, the monthly payment toward our parish school always comes first with my husband —as it does with thousands of others —and as a result we have little left for anything beyond bare necessities. I plod along at dishwashing, cooking, cleaning, and mending, and by evening am too tired and perturbed to sit down and read with my children, or to play games with them in the home which I had always meant to make for them the most attractive place on earth.

These sacrifices, heavy as they are, I would cheerfully make if I could believe that my children were getting a sound education. But my opinion—based on observation in many parts of the country—is that the methods of teaching in the average Catholic school are inferior to those used in the average public school.

Our public schools, with all their defects, have made progress in the past decade or two. The very essence of the new pedagogy is that a child should be induced to think independently and to act in real situations. Observation, thought, and appropriate action are more to be desired than mere accumulated facts.

This attitude of independent thought is incompatible with parochial school methods. They do not even try to achieve it. For example, history as taught in Catholic schools seems to be an effort to impress children with the glorious part Catholics have played in world achievements. Moreover, children must spend precious hours droning answers to the catechism which they cannot comprehend. My nine-year-old daughter came home weeping because she had been required to kneel on the floor for half an hour in punishment for not knowing the answer to "How may the first commandment be broken?" Realizing her distress, I helped her learn the answer. It is: "The first commandment may be broken by giving to a creature the honor which belongs to God alone; by false worship; and by attributing to a creature perfection which belongs to God alone."

This is something of what it means to carry out one's pledge to bring up a child in the Roman faith. It is not easy to meet the obligations involved in marrying a husband or wife who adheres to that religion of another age.

"AFTER-DINNER" speeches in Japan come before the meal. The custom not only relieves the speaker's nervous tension but also limits the length of the speech, as the serving of the meal interrupts a long-winded orator.

Confessions of a Sun Worshiper

Condensed from The Nation

STUART CHASE

SOME people collect postage stamps, others, old masters. I collect ultra-violet rays, preferably non-synthetic. In the city where I was reared, the institution I regard more sentimentally than any other is the L Street Bathhouse in South Boston. Here on a warm spring day more than a score of years ago, I made my début into the society of sun worshipers. Passing through the old warren of a bathhouse with its tier on tier of lockers, one emerged upon a strip of sandy beach, perhaps a hundred yards wide, flanked by high board fences that ran far into the water. Along the east fence, for the sun was in the west, lay and squatted and dozed a hundred naked men, nine out of ten of them colored like South Sea Islanders—and it was only early May. Naked they did not seem, but clothed in the most just and timeless covering of *homo sapiens*. But how naked I felt, creeping out to lie among them, a pale white wraith in a field of bronzes. Thereupon I resolved to clothe myself aright, and from that day to this the resolution has been kept.

I came again and again to L Street. Slowly the stark white gave way to ever-deepening shades of brown. Slowly I learned the laws and dogmas of my cult. The high priest was a man named Richards. He wore a circular hat fashioned out of newspaper and nothing else. He was a teacher of music and would spend long hours enlarging on the monopolies, cabals, and high crimes of the House of Ricordi. He spoke with circumstantial precision, but without bitterness—for who lying in the sun can be bitter?—and about him sprawled a professor of English at Harvard, a policeman from Dorchester, a banker, a night-worker in a powerhouse, a famous criminal lawyer, an advertising man, a locomotive engineer, and a notorious gunman.

Interminable, drowsy conversations were always in process. We talked of law, science, government, women, crime, sports, history, races—without passion, with a detached philosophy which held, I am convinced, an authentic wisdom. The sun nourished that wisdom, that all-pervading tolerance. Beating down upon us, it ironed out the taut impetuosities, the nervous, hasty judgments, the bile and the bitterness of men who walk the streets of modern cities in their clothes.

Our rules were few but strict. One never stood in a brother's sunlight. One never yelled, threw sand, or broke into conversation violently. It was mandatory to "take the water" at least once, whatever the time of year. Practical jokes of all kinds excluded one from the fellowship. As why should they not? An utterly relaxed body is in no psychological condition for practical jokes.

All winter long we came when the days were bright. If the sky was clear, the wind not too sharp, it was amazing how warm one could keep in a sheltered corner. Our color ebbed a little, but never really left us. Red copper gave way to pale mahogany. On Christmas day the hardiest of us had a swimming race, with shivering reporters in attendance, who served it up with all the regularity of the annual groundhog story. We were the L Street Brownies, half man, half walrus.

Nobody had ever heard of ultraviolet in those days. Few of us arrived because of a doctor's orders—though there were doctors among us. But by and large we *knew*, with a profundity which mocks science, that what we were doing was good for our bodies and good for our souls.

I could not explain it then, and I cannot explain it now. I have known hundreds of men and women who have loved to bathe, to lie on summer sands, to feel the sun striking into their marrows, but who have been utterly untouched by that deeper call which binds them eternally to Helios. In a way it is like a drug; a sunless month, and the world goes askew. But contrary to the laws of drugs the after-effects are never painful. (No accredited sun worshiper is silly enough to burn his skin; he knows to the minute when he has had enough.) No, the after-effects are a sense of well-being, of calmed nerves, of inner vitality.

It takes time, patience, understanding, and perhaps above all, personal freedom to become a regular communicant. How shall a shop or office worker join when his nine-to-five schedule imprisons his body while the sun is at its best? We L streeters were, relatively speaking, free men. Some of us shifted our jobs, or indeed gave them up altogether, if they interfered with our devotions. Freedom, a head not readily overheated, a pagan regard for the comeliness and wellbeing of one's body, a ruminative turn of mind, a sound belief in the important function of laziness in life, a hatred of the round, silly face of a clock, an understanding of the irrelevancy of clothes—who shall say of what strange and primitive juices, what fantastic combination of electrons, the true sun worshiper is made?

L Street, I have not trod your sacred portals for many years, but your lessons have never been forgotten. I have bowed my body to the sun halfway around the world, in season and out, legally and illegally, whenever opportunity offered. And in what strange corners have I not met my brothers, practicing their devotions before scientific sanction was ever heard of. We are an old battalion. We have stripped in the teeth of all the *mores* and all the constables. We have kept on dune and ledge, and trafficked not with hospital and clinic.

Once I saw a million brothers, yea, and sisters, too. I witnessed the incredible spectacle of fifty thousand brown bodies in one work-day noon on the Moscow River—some in bathing suits, some in trunks, perhaps the majority as God made them. What were systems of government in the face of this fact? These people were my people, and I cared not how deplorable their civil institutions.

A whole city throwing its clothes into the air! America, we shall undress and bronze you yet! Shall we? The prescriptions are going out by the thousands from the highest medical authorities, but if it is the natural sunlight you desire, in quantities greater than that provided by a bathing suit, try and secure it. It has taken me a dozen years of skilled investigation to learn how to secure my share, nor am I always successful.

I have been associated with many reform movements in my life, and it is with considerable astonishment that I find one actually gaining ground. Two years ago a man was arrested at a Florida beach for appearing in trunks. A hasty signal from a brother was all that kept me from sharing his cell. This year, if you please, the municipality has provided two solariums, male and female, where one may spend the day without a stitch.

Most of this sun-worship I believe is profoundly good. Is it only a temporary craze? Will America strip by the million in the next few years, only to be back in its shroud in a decade? I neither know nor greatly care. If the republic wants to go native and can hold to it with any fidelity, it will probably do more than any other conceivable action to balance the inhibitions and pathological cripplings induced by the machine age and the monstrous cities in which we live. If it but wants a new fad to play with and presently to toss aside, I know where to find sheltered spots where comes the sun and the wind and men come not.

Design Your Living

WORRY is a thin stream of fear trickling through the mind. If encouraged, it cuts a channel into which all other thoughts are drained.—Arthur Somers Roche

The Bequests of Eccentrics

Condensed from Plain Talk

JOSEPH PERCIVAL POLLARD

You must have a genius for charity as well as for anything else.—THOREAU.

ONE day along toward the end of the 19th century an elderly English woman fairly well equipped with treasure dusted off an idle quill and sat down to sign her will. A smile of satisfaction appeared on her face as she reflected that she was doing her bit to make mankind more happy. Calling two servants to witness, she gave the quill a flourish on the dotted line, put the document carefully away, and proceeded to water the pansies.

When she died, her counselor read the will to a few hopeful relatives: "It is my express will that the produce of all my real and personal estate shall be applied to the printing, publishing and propagation of the sacred writings of the late Joanna Southcott."

And who, gasped the relatives, was this creature to whose scribblings was now dedicated every penny of the property? A demented religious fanatic, dead these 50 years! An old maid who when she was 60 years old proclaimed to the world that she was about to give birth to a second Messiah, and named the exact date. A woman who wrote and published many incoherent religious ravings, among them *Prophecies Announcing the Birth of the Prince of Peace*, and who died a raving idiot about the time she was to be delivered. That was Joanna Southcott. But when the relatives contested the will, the High Court of Chancery held that the gift of the old lady was for a valid charitable purpose.

This little episode gives one a rough idea of the freak causes considered worthy of being aided by various wills. Sealed with a red wafer and spread upon the record of courts of probate throughout the world are words that express the hot urge of a weird idea. The particular weird idea that happens to be near and dear to the heart of the particular will-maker is frequently the weed that sprouts from the seed of his own experience. The man who in 1626 left a considerable part of his fortune to be used for the ransom of captives held by pirates had a vivid recollection of the time he was forced to become the guest of the bad boys of the Caribbees.

The legal conception of charity is very broad. It includes not only gifts for the relief of poverty and ill-health, but for the promotion of education and religion and all manner of general public undertakings. Consequently there is great leeway for legal lunacy on the part of the will-makers.

A prominent citizen of a small New England town set aside a fund for the employment of a person to go about the church during the sermon keeping people awake and chasing dogs out of the edifice.

Sometimes the field of beneficiaries is made so narrow that the money might as well be thrown into the sea. A case of this nature came to light some years ago in Bridgeport, Connecticut, where a considerable sum was willed for the relief of "worthy, deserving, poor, white, American, Protestant, Democratic widows and orphans residing in the town of A."

Many gifts for the relief of poverty show wealth of imaginative power on the part of the giver. Some years ago an old traveling salesman of Virginia donated a fund to be used in establishing a Travelers' Rest, but not without adding a small condition: "Let care be taken that women and men lodge not near together." A Vermonter flavored his generosity with the requirement that the silver coins he was casting away be dropped upon his tombstone and then picked up by the poor of the village. A skeptical Englishman gave a sum to the poor of the parish, who were to come to the church at the beginning of prayers, and "If they can, let them sing the 15th Psalm. But for God's sake, let them be no drunkards or common swearers."

Animal lovers are represented by the southern lady who gave a sizeable fund "to be used for the support of our dog Dick; for him to be kept in comfort, that is, being well fed, have a bed by the fire and treated well every day."

An Ohio animal-fancier recently laid out quite a sum for a cat-infirmary, to be equipped with sporting-grounds and well stocked with rats. Another man created a trust fund to feed sparrows.

A glance through many of these curious wills reveals that the lavish dispenser can be as emphatic in his dislikes as in his likes. Take the case of the New Jerseyite whose entire estate consisted of ten dollars, but who cut his wife off with one of them. Or the harassed head of a London family who bequeathed his wife "one shilling for picking my pockets of 60 guineas." Or the son of Lady Montague, who wrote, "To Lord A. I give nothing, because I know he'll bestow it on the poor."

Gifts for the public improvement may be grouped under two heads: (1) gifts that in their tangible results manage to keep the donor himself pretty well out of the picture; (2) gifts whose main function is to glorify the donor. Among the notable examples of the first class is the unique bequest of Mr. Sanborn of Medford, Massachusetts, that his skin be made into drumheads and given to the leader of the local drum corps, on condition that on Bunker Hill at sunrise of June 15th of each year he should beat on the drum the tune of "Yankee Doodle." Pope's Universal prayer was to be inscribed on one drumhead, and the Declaration of Independence on the other. Further:

The remainder of my body to be composed for a fertilizer to contribute to the growth of an American elm, to be planted in some rural thoroughfare, that the weary wayfarer may rest, and innocent children play beneath its umbrageous branches rendered luxuriant by my remains.

As to the cast-an-eye-on-me philanthropies, we find that these frequently go beyond the mere requiring of the name of the donor to be posted on the library or museum or gate-post or whatever it is. There is the case of the man who donated a fund to the city of Detroit to erect a fountain in a public park with a life-sized statue of himself rampant thereon.

Going one step farther we find the many donations in which the public plays no part at all but are made to glorify entirely the memory of the donor. A French disciple of Savarin actually directed that a new cooking-recipe be pasted on his tomb every day; and a resident of Easton, Pennsylvania, created a cemetery fund for the purchase of a burial plot 100 feet square, on which was to be erected a granite monument and fence to cost between $50,000 and $60,000. There was also to be formed a military cornet band to march to the cemetery on the anniversaries of his death, on holidays, and on "other proper occasions," and to play appropriate music. The court, however, did not agree with the deceased that the instrumental music was a dandy idea, deeming him to be sufficiently ennobled by the granite.

Such are the many atrocities committed under the widespread auspices of Charity. Would it not be well for judges to put the judicial torch to all testaments dedicating the income of estates to objects of no utility, public or private, whose only purpose is to perpetuate at great cost and in an absurd manner the idiosyncrasies of an eccentric testator?

Contents Noted

AN OLD WOMAN at the Ulster frontier was asked if she had anything to declare. No, nothing at all. But what was in the bottle? Oh, only holy water, holy water from Lourdes. The customs officer pulled the cork. "Whisky it is," said he.

"Glory be to God!" cried the offender. "A miracle!"

—*The Countryman*

Answer Yes or No

Condensed from The North American Review

JOHN HOLLEY CLARK, JR.

THERE are time-honored methods by which a lawyer tries to confuse or discredit a witness. They were succinctly stated 1900 years ago by the Dean of Roman Law, M. Fabius Quintillian: "If the witness is timid he may be frightened; if foolish, misled; if irascible, provoked; if vain, flattered; if prolix, drawn from the point; if, on the contrary, a witness is sensible and self-possessed he may be hastily dismissed as malicious and obstinate or he may be put out of countenance by a jest."

For thousands of years the lawyers have been "practising" this art of cross examination. They have written books about it. They gleefully recall instances where witnesses were confounded. They pride themselves on winning cases—whether with or against the evidence.

It all seems a delightful game as you read of it, and practise it. It is big-game hunting! Man hunting!

I thought well of it, had some scalps at my belt, and was an enthusiast on the warpath until recently—when I had to be a witness myself. After a vigorous—even brutal—cross examination, it occurred to me that perhaps too little attention had been paid to the instruction of the cross examinee.

All laymen are in imminent danger of cross examination. They ought to know what to do about it. The best thing is to remember Professor Quintillian. First of all, do not be timid or you will be frightened. Nervousness is hard to control, but it can be concealed. I have seen perfectly truthful witnesses give every appearance of lying. They move uneasily in the witness chair. They put hand to mouth. They let their eye wander. They are the picture of the caged animal. Such an appearance is fresh meat to the cross examiner. He will take it for granted you are lying and subject you to what Wellman calls "the particular form of torture in store for the perjurer."

Witnesses should not answer yes or no to a question which cannot be answered yes or no. No witness is required to do that. The reason cross examiners try to pin witnesses down is to avoid explanations. For, as Wellman says, "If you allow the witness a chance to give his reasons or explanations, you may be sure they will be damaging to you, not to him."

The witness' defense against this is to control himself. No matter how simple the question he is asked to answer "yes or no," if it cannot be so answered he should say so and keep on saying so until allowed to explain. Beside the classical question, "Have you stopped beating your wife?" there are many others which cannot be answered by yes or no. A witness often is badgered to answer yes or no until he gives in. He thinks if he maintains that he cannot answer yes or no he will seem to be evasive.

It is better to appear evasive than to fall into a trap. You can always fall back on the effective retort of Henry Ward Beecher when his cross examiner in the Tilton case asked him why he was so evasive. "Because I am afraid of you," said Beecher simply.

Always remember that the jury is watching the duel. They know when you are being badgered. Also remember that after the cross examination is finished, your own counsel can take you in hand on redirect and let you explain your evasions, your inconsistencies and all your lapses.

The second maxim, don't be foolish, explains itself. Don't be irascible, is the third maxim. "Hold your temper while you lead the witness to lose his," is the Golden Rule of cross examiners. It is even more important for witnesses. If you get angry you will say things you don't mean—or don't want known.

The fourth maxim is, don't be vain. The smoothest trick of the examiner is to get you to admit you are quite a remarkable person. Then he traps you into showing that you are not. A doctor, for instance, was called in a railroad accident case. The lawyer flattered him. He had of course read Smith on this, Jones on that, Gervais on the other and so on through a long list of authorities that never existed. The doctor fell. He had read them all. But toward the end he got suspicious. Finally he was asked about Hall on Neurosis, a bona fide authority. "There is no such book," said he. He was ruined.

I have seen vast numbers of witnesses taken in by such obvious soft soap as "You have quite a remarkable memory, Mr. Jones"; "You are a very expert accountant, Mr. Brown"; "You have made a deep study of this subject, Mr. Smith?" etc., etc. Every time the cross examiner gets oily, look out. Always remember he is your enemy. If he puffs you up it is only to explode you.

And finally don't be prolix. Don't try to explain everything. It makes you appear nervous. If you are allowed to explain, either the cross examiner is asleep at the switch or he thinks that you will explain yourself into difficulties.

It is my experience that the

ordinary man is a match for the ordinary lawyer. Even the best of lawyers have been put to rout by honest witnesses. One instance of this was the doctor who had tried to qualify as an expert on a certain disease. The cross examiner asked him to answer yes or no whether he was not a "neurologist pure and simple." Quickly he answered "Moderately pure and absolutely simple." The laugh saved him.

Wellman gives an instance of another sort. He knew his witness had once been in an insane asylum on Ward's Island. Sneeringly he asked, "You were once on Ward's Island, weren't you?" He was quite put to rout by his reply: "I was sent there because I was insane; you see my wife was very ill with locomotor ataxia. She had been ill a year. I was her only nurse. I tended her day and night. We loved each other dearly. I was greatly worried over her long illness and frightful suffering. The result was I worried too deeply; she had been very good to me. I overstrained myself; my mind gave way. But I am better now, thank you."

So witnesses sometimes have their innings. Quintillian says "All questions ought to be extremely circumspect because a witness often utters sharp repartees in answer to the advocate and is thus regarded with a highly favorable feeling by the audience in general."

Every real opportunity to confound the examiner should be taken advantage of. But don't be anxious for it. Many witnesses, by trying to get the best of the cross examiner, give an impression of forwardness and smartness that hurts their testimony. Don't be so anxious to score a hit that the jury may think you are trying to examine the attorney.

To most witnesses the supreme delight of laying the cross examiner flat is not granted.

The best they can do is remember the five don'ts. Don't be nervous, don't be foolish, don't be irascible, don't be vain, don't be prolix. Tell the truth and shame the devil—of a lawyer.

Table Talk

HAVE YOU EVER wondered what becomes of those cakes you see in advertisements? They're eaten. At General Foods they keep eight cooks and an office staff of 40 just thinking up and testing recipes. A good day's average is four cakes, several batches of cookies and three or four molds of jello. Testing time comes about four every afternoon, when the stenographers, clerks and editors are gravely called in and each given a sample. It's all a part of the day's work. Most highly valued are the opinions of those who aren't too used to restaurant cooking. If the head-nodding is unanimous, the recipe is accepted.—*Life*

Where Logic Reigns Supreme

Condensed from The Bookman

JANET RANKIN AIKEN

Our language, in nearly every detail, is illogical. In this lies a charm.

Imagine two human beings in the extremity of despair. One says, "I cannot but die." The other says, "I can but die." If words mean anything, one should die and the other live. But both die.

What difference can you discern between *ravel* and *unravel?* Or between "I wonder if she's there" and "I wonder if she's not there?" Or between "a matter of the first importance" and "a matter of the last importance?" Logically, by all rules of speech, these pairs should be contraries; in fact, they come to the same thing.

Let us consider other departments where logic reigns supreme. Do we have, as consistency would dictate, *myself, herself, ourselves, hisself, theirselves?* Or, what would be equally logical, *himself, themselves, yourself, meself, and usselves?* No, we must needs employ now a possessive, now an objective, pronoun. Consistency is nowhere.

English has *may* and *might, shall* and *should.* To be consistent it should also have *mote* and *must, owe* and *ought.*

When it comes to singular and plural, our language's notion of logic is hazy indeed. *Many a man* is undoubtedly as plural in intent as *many men.* Yet the former takes the singular *lives,* the second the plural *live.* A *domino* is a mask, but *dominoes* is (are?) a game. *Vapor* is steam, but the *vapors* was (were?) a fashionable malady of the 18th Century. *Vesper* is evening, but *vespers* is (are?) evening service. Do you use *this* or *these* with the singular words *odds, politics, news, pains* (i.e., taking pains), *wages, means, tidings?*

But the big story has been reserved to the end. There is one field wherein English beats the world, past and present, near and far, in this matter of illogic. That is spelling.

Do you know that there are over 20 ways to spell a sound which has no alphabetic symbol of its own in English, but which we call the *sh*-sound? Then let me marshal for

142

your inspection the words *she* (sh), *sugar* (s), *chande*-lier (ch), *nation* (ti), *schist* (sch), *barouche* (che), *tension* (si), *fuchsia* (chs), *session* (ssi), *fashion* (shi), *ocean* (ce), *omniscience* (sci), *vitiate* (t), *officiate* (c), *social* (ci), and *nausea* (se). Now add to these *righteous* (teo), *latch* (tch), *anxious* (xio), *inflexion* (xi), and *nature* (tu), where the sounds in parentheses each represent two sounds, one of which is *sh*, and we have a total of 21 orthographic representations for this single sound. Could inconsistency farther go?

The answer is *yes*. For one vowel, the medial sound in *cake*, is found spelled in over 25 different ways. With little study I have found 26, and a thorough research would probably add to the list.

Would you care to hear it? Then consider *pale* (a-e), *paler* (a), *pail* (ai), *play* (ay), *gauge* (au-e), *campaign* (aig), *champagne* (ag-e), *straight* (aigh), *freight* (eigh), *vein* (ei), *they* (ey), *reign* (eig), *steak* (ea), *fête* (ê), *coupé* (é), *ballet* (et), *demesne* (es-e), *prayer* (aye), *praise* (ai-e), *parfait* (ait), *mêlée* (ée), *métier* (er), and add to the list of the British pronunciations of *gaol* (ao), *eh* (eh), *dahlia* (ah), and *half-penny* (alf).

English has some 44 sounds, 24 consonantal and 20 vocalic. To represent these 44 sounds in spelling, English has well over 400 separate orthographic combinations, making an average of 10 possible spellings per sound! What can you do with a language like that!

Mencken on Mistering

H. L. MENCKEN says that only an American would think of referring to his wife as Mrs. So-and-so, when speaking to an equal. In England she would be *my wife*, and to a friend, she would be *Gertrude*, even though a duchess. *Mrs.* is reserved for social inferiors. Mencken's chief concern, however, is our excessive *mistering* among men. Over here we usually make a direct leap from *Mr.* to *Charlie*.

"Both, under ordinary circumstances, are silly," says Mencken. "*Mr.* belongs rightly to strangers and superiors, and by a chilly extension, to certain inferiors; and *Charlie* belongs to intimates. Correct address for equals is the simple surname. Go to dinner in an Englishman's house (or in his club, for that matter) and you are *Snodgrass* to him thereafter, and he is *Smithers* to you. The moment he restores you to *Mistership* it is a delicate sign that you have offended. There are exceptions in the cases of men of great age or great distinction, but they are not many. We use as many *Misters* in a week as the English use in a year."—*The William Feather Magazine*

Taming of the Shrews

Condensed from The Mentor

FAIRFAX DOWNEY

A SHOUTING, jeering crowd jostles through the principal street of a pleasant English village in the year 1655. They make a procession at the heels of two figures, one, an officer, leading the other by a chain. The prisoner, by her clothes, is a woman—not much can be seen of her head, for it is enclosed by an iron harness. Though the crowd hoots and reviles her and she is renowned for her sharp and ready tongue, she utters no word.

The chain by which she is led is attached to an iron collar around her neck. From this a hinged crosspiece curves vertically up over the middle of her face, passing over her head and locking to the collar at the nape of her neck. Her nose protrudes through an opening in this iron strip and from its interior surface an iron tongue juts out and has been forced into her mouth. It holds her tongue so that she cannot possibly speak. She is most effectively muzzled.

Such was the brank, the gossip's bridle, the scold's helm. In its mildest form it was cruel; in its most severe it was torture. The gagging tongue was not always smooth and flat but might be pointed and sharp-edged or spiked like the *poire d'angoise*—the pear of agony which expanded on springs when thrust into the mouths of the prisoners in France.

Branks were in wide use in England—50 of them survive as museum pieces. Freedom of speech was considered decidedly not feminine. And it was often kept in mind that the "curste queane" might be a witch whom prompt treatment with the brank would prevent from muttering some malevolent incantation wreaking any amount of evil on the community.

The brank was employed in England as late as 1824. The mere display of it was enough to subdue an unquiet woman in 1858. While it was used in France it never crossed the Atlantic. In the Colonies the authorities favored a simpler device to cause "termagants" to hold their tongues—a

144

cleft stick. There are many historical references to this punishment being imposed for "swearinge railinge and revilinge."

Men did not escape the brank and the stick as a punishment for lying, blasphemy and slander. The latest victims of the cleft stick were talkative school children, who, on into the past century, paid sorely for noise in class.

Still it was the ducking stool which was regarded as the shrew-tamer par excellence. Benjamin West hymned the ducking stool in 1780, suggesting that one immersion might fail to do the trick:

If so, my friend, pray let her take
A second turn into the lake,
And, rather than your patience lose,
Thrice and again repeat the dose.
No brawling wives, no furious
    wenches,
No fire so hot but water quenches.

The ducking stools sometimes were decorated with carvings of devils seizing on scolds or of men and women bickering, which last recalls an instance of poetic justice when a quarrelsome married couple were ducked back to back.

The ducking stool was imported to America and used without stint, along with the tumbrel, which was a ducking stool mobile on wheels, so that if the regular ducking pool dried up the implement could be moved elsewhere without delay. The dame with the turbulent tongue, rich or poor, married or single, was haled off to the pond, bound in the seat on the end of the seesaw-like plank and submerged for a half-minute or so.

A companion piece to the ducking stool was the cucking stool. This was landbound and was simply a chair in which scolds were tied up for 24 hours usually and left to the mercy of the gibes of the mob.

Scolds were also restrained in bilboes, an iron bar to which the feet were shackled. Goody Gregory of Springfield was confined to the stocks in 1640 for telling a neighbor, "Before God I could break thy head." In the stang or skimmington riding, members of a community went to the homes of nagging women and mimicked them. Scolds and slander stirrers were not infrequently flogged, in Boston being dragged to the whipping post in a cage. One poor creature was thus condemned for exercising the gift of prophecy. Another Boston woman was condemned to stand for half an hour with her breast marked, "Public Destroyer of Peace." Excommunication was the penalty imposed on shrews by the ecclesiastical courts of London in the 17th century. It is of actual record that in 1614 a woman was thus punished for "misbehavying her tonge toward her mother-in-law."

Neither Church nor State spared their severities for more than 300 years. All manner of chastisements failing, man finally gave up his attempts to dull the keen edge of that sharpest of all weapons—a woman's tongue.

The Size of Living Things

Excerpts from The Atlantic Monthly

JULIAN S. HUXLEY

SIZE, which we are so apt to take for granted in ourselves and in the organisms about us, is one of the most serious problems with which evolving life has had to cope.

The largest organisms are vegetables, the big trees of California, with a weight of nearly 1000 tons. The largest animals are whales, some of which considerably exceed 100 tons in weight. They are not only the largest existing animals, but by far the largest which have ever existed, for the monstrous reptiles of the secondary period, which are often supposed to hold the palm for size, could none of them have exceeded about 50 tons.

The largest invertebrates are to be found among the mollusks; some of the giant squids weigh two or three tons. The runner-up among the invertebrates is, strangely enough, a certain huge jellyfish with a disk over seven feet across and 18 inches thick and great bulky tentacles five feet long hanging down below. One of these weighs as much as a good-sized horse. What we might call the most successful of all invertebrates, the ants, never reach more than one gram in weight. The largest ant colonies known possess a million or so inhabitants. This whole population would weigh about as much as one large man. Indeed, the small size of most insects is at first hearing barely credible. If you bought an ounce of fleas, you would have the pleasure of receiving over 80,000 of them!

Nature seems to have found it unprofitable to construct a vertebrate out of less than several hundred million cells. Within the groups there is great variation. It is a surprise, for instance, to find a frog that weighs as much as a fox terrier. It is a still greater surprise to know that there exist fully formed adult insects—a beetle or two, and several wasplike creatures—of smaller bulk than the human ovum and yet with compound eyes, a nice nervous system, three pairs of jaws and three pairs of legs, veined wings, striped muscles, and the rest! It is rather un-

146

expected that the smallest adult vertebrate is not a fish, but a frog; and it is most unexpected to find that the largest elephant would have ample clearance top and bottom inside a large whale's skin.

The great bulk of land vertebrates range from ten grams to 100 kilograms in weight. Why is this narrow range so popular?

A disadvantage in being *very* small is that you are not big enough to be out of reach of annoyance by the mere inorganic molecules of the environment. The molecules of a fluid like water are rushing about in all directions. They run against any object in the water, and bounce off again. When the surface of the object is big enough for there to be thousands of such collisions every second, the laws of probability will see to it that the number of bumps on one side will be closely equal to that on the other; the steady average resulting we call fluid pressure. But when the diameter of the object falls to about one thousandth of a millimeter, it may easily happen that one side receives a rain of bumps while the other is spared. The result is that the smallest organisms are kept in a constant St. Vitus's dance, christened Brownian movement after its discoverer.

It is impossible, however, simply to magnify an object without changing its shape—if you do so, without meaning to, you have changed all its properties. For the surface increases as the square of the diameter, the volume as its cube. And so the amount of surface relative to bulk must diminish with size. A big African elephant is one million times as heavy as a small mouse. But the amount of surface for each gram of elephant is only one-hundredth of what it is in the mouse.

The most familiar effect of this surface-volume relation is on the rate of falling. The greater the amount of surface exposed relative to weight, the greater the resistance of the air. If a mouse is dropped down the shaft of a coal mine, the acceleration due to gravity soon comes up against the retardation due to air resistance, and after 100 feet or so a steady rate is reached, which permits it to reach the bottom dazed but unhurt, however deep the shaft. A cat, on the other hand, is killed; a man is not only killed, but horribly mangled; and if a pit pony falls over, the speed at the bottom is so appalling that the body makes a hole in the ground, and is so thoroughly smashed that nothing remains save a few fragments of the bones and a splash on the walls.

Relative surface is also important for temperature regulation in warm-blooded animals; for the escape of heat must be proportional to the surface, through which it leaks away. As heat is derived from the combustion of the food, a mouse must eat much more in proportion to its weight than a man to make up for its unavoidable extra heat loss. The reason that children need proportionately more food than grownups is not only due to the fact that they are growing, but also to the fact that their heat loss is relatively greater. A baby of a year loses more than twice as much heat for each pound of its weight than does a 12-stone man. For this reason, it is doubtful whether the attempt should be made to harden children by letting them go about with bare legs in winter; their heat requirements are greater than their parents', not less.

The big animal inevitably fails to be a mere scale enlargement of its smaller relative. Everyone knows the small-eyed look of an elephant or of a whale. To obtain a good image, an eye has to be a certain absolute size; and once this size is reached, any advantage due to further enlargement is more than counterbalanced by the difficulties of construction, just as very little advantage is to be gained in photography by making a camera over full plate size.

We come back to the advantages and disadvantages of size. At the outset, it is not until living units are quit of the frenzy of Brownian movement that they themselves become capable of regulated locomotion. The first step in size is to become so much bigger than ordinary molecules that you can forget about them.

But even then you are microscopic. Only by joining together tens or hundreds of thousands of cells can you make headway against such brute forces as currents. Size also brings speed and power, and this is an advantage in exploring the environment.

When we get to whole grams, however, winged life at least has the world before it. Many migratory birds that regularly travel thousands of miles weigh less than ten grams. Swimming soon follows suit; think of the migration of tiny eels across the Atlantic, or of baby salmon down great rivers.

Before a real brain can be constructed, the animal must consist of tens of thousands of cells. The intelligence of a rat would be impossible without brain cells enough to outweigh the whole body of a bee, while the brain of a human being outweighs the very great majority of existing whole animals.

Man, in fact, is a very large organism. During his individual existence he multiplies his original weight a thousand million, and comes to contain about a hundred million million cells. He is a little more than halfway up the size scale of mammals, and nearly two-thirds up that of the vertebrates.

WHEN he knew the end was inevitable, Justice Holmes made a characteristic gesture. His friend, Professor Felix Frankfurter, stood by his bedside, concern written in his face. Nurses and physicians hovered about. Deliberately the great jurist lifted his hand, placed the thumb against his nose and solemnly wagged four fingers. It was his last gesture.—N. Y. *World-Telegram*

Does It Ever Rain Fishes?

Condensed from The Scientific Monthly

DR. E. W. GUDGER

BARON MUNCHAUSEN, the prince of tellers of "big stories," never told of a rain of fishes. But a certain John Kendrick Bangs, feeling that this was an oversight, wrote such an account for him under the subhead "Recent Adventures." Bangs says that his narrator-hero when a boy secured a large quantity of gunpowder and planted it in a fishpond. When this was touched off the whole pond was blown high in air and after some days the contents of the pond, containing many fishes, rained down on the astonished people.

Now the interesting thing is that an imagined rain of fishes is not necessary, for there is a multitude of true accounts of such rains. Having a penchant for the unusual in natural history, for many years I collected and filed away accounts of rains of fishes. When I came to publish them I found I had 48 accounts ranging from A. D. 300 to 1901, and in space from America (eight accounts), Great Britain (ten), Germany (eight), France and Greece (one each), through India (ten), Ceylon (three), Malaysia (two) and the South Seas (one).

The publication of this article aroused much interest and letters came in calling my attention to overlooked references and giving personal experience. These accounts I brought together in another article. There were 26 of them, but I think that three are duplicates and that I have established only 23 new falls.

There are thus put on record about 71 accounts (more or less well authenticated) of rains of fishes. These accounts in range of time and space make for sure testimony as to the actuality of the occurrence of this phenomenon. I have personally never been so fortunate as to experience or even witness such a rain, but I cannot disregard the evidence recorded by scientific men.

Since the publication of my previous articles there have come to me two accounts of falls of fishes which are so well authenticated that it seems worth while to put them on record. The first, a personal experience, was related to me by Mr. Richard Hoadley Tingley, of Port Chester, New York, whom I have known personally for a number of years. This fall occurred on May 15, 1900, on the outskirts of Providence, Rhode Island. A severe thunder-storm with a high wind brought a heavy downpour of rain and with it living squirming perch and bull-pouts, from two to four and a half inches long, which fell on yards and streets—covering about a quarter of an acre. Mr. Tingley says that he was out in the storm and was pelted not only with raindrops but with fish as well. The boys collected these fishes by the pailful and sold them, while a reporter on the Providence *Journal* gathered a bucketful of them and these were displayed in various shop windows on one of the principal business streets of the city.

In July, 1928, I heard of a fall of fishes near Tarboro in my native state of North Carolina. I have spent some time in getting the particulars, and even more effort in getting corroboratory evidence; and I am persuaded that full credence is to be given to the account and to my informants. Here follows the story of this fall of fishes as communicated to me.

On May 18, 1928, a rain of fishes fell on the farm of Mr. S. N. Clark. This farm is operated by Mr. W. L. Doughtie, and from him and his wife I have gotten the following details. A heavy downpour of rain came on this day. There was very little wind but there were fishes, hundreds of them. No one was out in the rain, but immediately after the shower the children went out and began wading about in the puddles where they found many little fishes, some of them alive and swimming. The fish were pretty uniform in size, about one and a half to two inches long. Mr. Doughtie estimates that there were several hundreds of these little fishes scattered over two or three acres of ground. This spot is some three quarters of a mile from the nearest water course, which is not known to contain any number of fishes.

Now for the explanation of these and all other rains of fishes. High winds, particularly whirlwinds, pick up water, fishes and all, and carry them inland where, when the velocity of the air and clouds becomes relatively lowered, the fishes fall to earth. Can anyone who has seen a waterspout doubt that it could pick up and carry off fishes? No one, I believe, who has experienced or even seen the prodigious effects and carrying power of a land tornado can have any doubt of the ability of a waterspout, a water tornado, to bring about a "Rain of Fishes."

The Magic Wand Eternal

ROMAIN ROLLAND

IT is impossible to imagine what Jean-Christophe made of a simple piece of wood, a broken bough found alongside a hedge. It was a magic wand. If it were long and thin, it became a lance, or perhaps a sword; to brandish it aloft was enough to cause armies to spring from the earth. Jean-Christophe was their general, marching in front of them, setting them an example, and leading them to the assault of a hillock. If the branch were flexible, it changed into a whip. Jean-Christophe mounted on horseback and leaped precipices. Sometimes his mount would slip, and the horseman would find himself at the bottom of the ditch, sorrily looking at his dirty hands and barked knees. If the wand were lithe, then Jean-Christophe would make himself the conductor of an orchestra: he would be both conductor and orchestra; he conducted and he sang; and then he would salute the bushes, with their little green heads stirring in the wind.

From Jean-Christophe. Copyright Henry Holt and Company.

He was also a magician. He walked with great strides through the fields, looking at the sky and waving his arms. He commanded the clouds. He wished them to go to the right, but they went to the left. Then he would abuse them, and repeat his command. He would watch them out of the corner of his eye, and his heart would beat as he looked to see if there were not at least a little one which would obey him. But they went on calmly moving to the left. Then he would stamp his foot, and threaten them with his stick, and angrily order them to go to the left; and this time, in truth, they obeyed him. He was happy and proud of his power. He would touch the flowers and bid them change into golden carriages, as he had been told they did in the stories; and, although it never happened, he was quite convinced that it would happen if only he had patience. He would look for a grasshopper to turn into a hare; he would gently lay his stick on its back, and speak a rune. The insect would escape: he would bar its way. A few moments later he

151

would be lying on his belly near to it, looking at it. Then he would have forgotten that he was a magician, and just amuse himself with turning the poor beast on its back, while he laughed aloud at its contortions.

It occurred to him also to tie a piece of string to his magic wand, and gravely cast it into the river, and wait for a fish to come and bite. He knew perfectly well that fish do not usually bite at a piece of string without bait or hook; but he thought that for once in a way, and for him, they might make an exception to their rule; and in his inexhaustible confidence, he carried it so far as to fish in the street with a whip through the grating of a sewer. He would draw up the whip from time to time excitedly, pretending that the cord of it was more heavy, and that he had caught a treasure, as in a story that his grandfather had told him.

He used to sit on a heap of loose stones or a milestone, or some high seat, uncomfortable and peculiar; and he used to wag his little legs, and hum to himself, and dream. Or sometimes he used to lie on his back and watch the clouds go by; they looked like oxen, and giants, and hats, and old ladies, and immense landscapes. He used to talk to them in a low voice, or be absorbed in a little cloud which a great one

was on the point of devouring. He was afraid of those which were very black, almost blue, and of those which went very fast. It seemed to him that they played an enormous part in life, and he was surprised that neither his grandfather nor his mother paid any attention to them. They were terrible beings if they wished to do harm. Fortunately, they used to go by, kindly enough, a little grotesque, and they did not stop. The boy used in the end to turn giddy with watching them too long, and he used to fidget with his legs and arms, as though he were on the point of falling from the sky. His eyelids then would wink, and sleep would overcome him. Silence. . . . The leaves murmur gently and tremble in the sun; a faint mist passes through the air; the uncertain flies hover, booming like an organ; the grasshoppers, drunk with the summer, chirp eagerly and hurriedly; all is silent. . . . Under the vault of the trees the cry of the green woodpecker has magic sounds. Far away on the plain a peasant's voice harangues his oxen; the shoes of a horse ring out on the white road. Jean-Christophe's eyes close. Near him an ant passes along a dead branch across a furrow. He loses consciousness. . . . Ages have passed. He wakes. The ant has not yet crossed the twig.

How The News Grew

Condensed from The New Freeman

J. B. S. HARDMAN

THOSE who watched the Communist demonstration in Union Square on March 6, may be interested in knowing how the events of that day were recorded in the *Rote Fahne,* the official daily of the Communist Party of Germany. The number of participants in the demonstration, properly speaking—in the open-air mass meeting, held under a police permit—was estimated by the New York *Times* as consisting of 2000 Communist "shock troops," and of another 35,000 onlookers attracted to Union Square by the police-made publicity. The *Herald Tribune* set the total at 40,000, with an allotment of active Communist demonstrators similar to that of the New York *Times*. The *World* estimate agrees with that of the *Times*. The *Daily Worker,* official organ of the Communist Party in New York, probably proceeding from the generally correct premise that bourgeois papers are wont to tell only a part of the truth, adds up these three estimates in order to get at the whole truth. By this device, arithmetically invulnerable, the Communist organ arrives at a truly grand total of 110,000 (35,-000 + 40,000 + 35,000 = 110,000), and to "make it unanimous" all the 110,000 are classed as unemployed workers who have accepted the Communist leadership. However, the *Rote Fahne* goes *ein klein bisschen* further. The report in that paper, published under the heading: *"Never Before Has New York Lived Through Such Battle,"* reads in part as follows:

NEW YORK, March 7. The day of March 6, in the United States has exceeded the most daring expectations. The dollar press is scared stiff: "Never before have such things happened in America."

About half a million workers participated in the demonstration in New York. Over 120,000 workers marched in close ranks. Hundreds of thousands filled Union Square. An hour before the time set for the demonstration the gigantic Square was occupied by 100,000 demonstrators, as estimated by the bourgeois press. The words of the Communist speakers were met with enthusiastic approval and drowned in the tones of the *Internationale* sung by hundreds of thousands.

After the mass meeting, the masses

of workers in powerfully closed ranks marched, completely unmindful of the ban of the police authorities, toward the City Hall. The front ranks of the police cadres were broken at once. Undaunted, the masses rolled forward and onward.

In front of the City Hall the demonstrators were met by an army of 25,000 police, in full fighting military array. The demonstrators would not budge. As the police opened fire from machine-guns in the streets and from the roofs, an embittered man-to-man fight ensued and lasted late into the evening. The New York Police Commissioner, personally in charge of the massacre, was surrounded by the demonstrators and beaten till he bled. With great difficulty a shock regiment of police saved him. The bourgeois press asserts: "Never before has New York lived through such a battle."

This reportorial chef-d'oeuvre of the central organ of the German Communist Party is topped by an editorial summary of the American revolution:

The events of March 6, in the United States, are the most colossal revelation of the day. For the first time, in the land of as yet powerful dollar-capitalism, there echoed the onward march of the millions organized under Communist leadership. If it were still necessary to demonstrate the unavoidable, rapid-tempo breakdown of American capitalism, it was March 6 that led the grave-diggers of capitalism, the American proletarian masses, in hundreds of thousands, into the streets, to declare revolutionary war on the dominant class.

The European bourgeoisie, paling with fear in face of demonstrating masses, have been overcome with panicky terror when faced with these revelations from America. The international proletariat, on the other hand, draws new confidence and gains new strength for its own struggle from the heroic advance of the American working class. Therein lies the enormous international significance of American events.

. . . For the first time in its history our young American fraternal party has succeeded in attracting hundreds of thousands of workers to its banners. American Communists have mobilized over one million workers under the Party's economic and political slogans and forged them into a tremendous revolutionary front. The Communist Party of the United States has thus become the acknowledged leader of the broad masses of the American proletariat.

The mass-party of Communism in the United States has an enrolled membership of fewer than 6000. There were 60,000 members ten years ago, but that was before the party had gained recognition as "the fighting leader of the revolutionary American proletariat."

Now that we know, via Berlin, what happened in New York, the people of Berlin ought to be advised of what happened in Berlin on that memorable March 6. There are two sources of information, both equally as reliable, I should say, as is the *Rote Fahne*. The *Daily Worker*, of Union Square, New York, printed on March 7:

Today's unemployment demonstrations were held everywhere in Berlin, with violent collisions in many places where the jobless assembled repeatedly in spite of the prohibition of all street gatherings by the "Socialist" police chief, Zoergiebel. There was furious police-clubbing in all sections . . . At this moment, 5:30, violent collisions are going on . . . Clubbing is ineffective and the workers are fighting back. The police have just fired several volleys. But the workers have reassembled and the demonstrations are continuing . . . (Later) Despite all the force used, the Communists occupied and held Buelow Square, in the face of repeated police charges. . . . Severe fighting continued late into the night in Berlin. . . .

The *Daily Worker* and the *Rote Fahne* are quits, and nothing is lost. Everybody is happy. What a pity that New Yorkers go to watch performances. Cabled reports are infinitely more colorful. Berliners, too, would have been better off had they confined their curiosity to reading accounts from New York of doings *Unter Den Linden*. But what *do* Berliners say of the revolution of March 6 in Berlin? Well, they envy New York. To quote

Gegen den Strom, a weekly publication of leading German communists, the original founders of the German party, now, however, at odds with the official party:

After the memorable defeats of May 1, of August 1, of February 1, comes the defeat of March 6. Of course even this defeat is being belied into a victory by the official party press . . . With the exception of the partial successes in the United States of America, this latest international "day of struggle" has met with an even more negligible response than did the earlier calls of the Communist International, "for a day of great international struggle. . . ."

The friends of the Communist International need not lose heart at the failure of the "great day." Failures are never final in social movements. However, someone *in the part-pub-fin-dep*, if that is the proper designation for the Department for Financing Party Publicity, ought to suggest the observance of the old Russian advice: Bluff, but moderately.

Keeping up with the World

Excerpts from a regular department in Collier's
Freling Foster

ONE OF the oldest legends in the Christian world concerns the constant quivering of aspen leaves, even in apparently still air. A large number of persons believe the aspen tree supplied the wood for the Cross and has never ceased to tremble for the part it played in the crucifixion.

ONLY the Japanese cultivate the unique art of growing dwarfed trees in pots for room decoration. Sometimes these little trees, even after hundreds of years, are less than two feet in height, yet their proportions of stem, branch and leaf are preserved with fidelity. Pots containing groups of six or eight fine ones, suggesting a forest, have been sold for thousands of dollars.

Audubon—Failure and Success

Condensed from The New York Times Magazine

AMY MacMASTER

JOHN James Fougere Audubon, the world-famous American woodsman and ornithologist, was born in 1785, the son of a French sea captain. "The Birds of America," the basis for his fame, is no mere book of birds, but a set of about 500 large and scientifically accurate paintings of birds drawn and colored direct from nature—one of the treasures of ornithology.

In gathering the material for these paintings in the undeveloped America of 100 years ago, when methods of travel were scarcely out of the primitive stage; in the 12-year task of reproducing and privately publishing reproductions of these pictures, when every engraving plate had to be etched and each lithograph colored by hand; and, finally, in the personal sale of these reproductions at $1000 a set, thus actually in the course of publication accumulating the $100,000 that the work cost—in these, Audubon accomplished three extraordinary feats.

And this happened in spite of the fact that up to his 34th year Audubon had been a total failure in every business venture to which he put his hand, condemned by everybody who knew him, except his wife, as an indolent good-for-nothing.

He was born in the seaport town of Les Cayes, Haiti, and his earliest recollections were of lying among flowers, watching the movements of a mocking bird. A large part of his youth was spent in France. Daily he would make excursions to the woods, setting out with a haversack full of eatables and coming back with it filled with birds' nests, eggs, moss, curious stones, and whatever else took his fancy. Presently he began to make drawings of birds and soon had more than 200 finished. For a short time he studied under the artist David, and it is probable that that was the only instruction in drawing he ever received.

In his late teens he was sent to America to look after the family property in Mill Grove, near Philadelphia. There he lived on the rent paid by a tenant and gave his time

156

to hunting, fishing, skating, swimming, dancing and drawing. Then he married the daughter of a neighbor and for 12 years strove to make a living as a merchant. He became a traveling dealer in general merchandise to frontier emigrants; then traded in pork, lard and flour; later he had a general store, and finally he ran a steam saw and grist mill. In these ventures he lost nearly everything he possessed. Everybody except his wife despaired of him.

At the age of 34 he determined to devote himself entirely to his art. He became an itinerant portrait painter and so paid his rambling way over the East and Middle West while working at the huge self-imposed task of painting all varieties of American birds. He hunted and drew animals as well as birds. In his diary an entry indicates the care he put into drawing a snake. It says: "The heat of the weather was so great that I could only devote 16 hours to the drawing."

Skill in graphic art became his legal tender. He obtained passage on a Mississippi steamer by sketching the captain and his wife; he acquired two pairs of shoes by painting the portrait of a shoemaker and his wife; he paid his rent with portraits of the landlady and her child. At one period he earned money by painting life-like portraits of dead persons, becoming so popular at this that a certain clergyman had the body of his child exhumed in order that Audubon could paint her portrait.

His merriment and impulsiveness, his kindness and his readiness for whatever adventure turned up, made him welcome among simple folk. In winter quarters with the Indians he played the violin and flute while the young braves danced, the squaws laughed, and the older men "smoked their pipes with such serenity as only Indians can."

In his rambles in isolated places he "picked up friendships" again and again with men who had fled from the "fees, lawyers and taxes" of populated places. He had a camera-keen eye for the peculiarities of men and animals. His first aim in painting was always fidelity; his second, artistic beauty.

Great good fortune attended his choice of a wife. She not only encouraged him in his ambitions, but took a position as governess in order to support herself and the two sons. Later, she started a school and was so successful that she soon was receiving an income of $3000 a year—and this, we must remember, was in the 1820's.

Unable to find a publisher in this country for his work, Audubon sailed for England. In Liverpool he gained a host of friends and advisers. In Edinburgh he became a sensation and was fêted and lauded. His wolfskin coat, his long hair and eagle eyes made him a striking figure. He wrote to his wife that he thought his hair was doing as much for him as his paintings.

But if his appearance amazed people, his paintings took them by storm. His prestige mounted, and when he started to solicit subscriptions for the "Birds of America" he met with a ready response from wealthy men and public institutions. The King of England became a subscriber at the regular price, $1000 a set, "not as kings generally do, but as a gentleman," and he gave Audubon permission to publish the work as under the King's personal patronage. The King of France, too, became a subscriber.

According to his own records, Audubon sold 165 complete sets of the original edition of the "Birds of America"—82 in the United States and 83 in England, Scotland and France. Ninety of the existing sets are now in the great libraries and scientific museums of the world. About 30 are privately owned. The work today is worth $6000 or more a set. A New York bookseller last year listed one at $12,500.

Two years after his return to America, Audubon bought a permanent home, Minniesland, a 30-acre estate in the wilderness along the Hudson at what is now 155th to 158th Street, New York. At that time it was "far from the crazy city." In this home, still standing,

Audubon entertained his many friends. One of them, Samuel Morse, experimented with his telegraphic invention here, stretching wires across the Hudson from New Jersey. The first telegraphic message ever sent from Philadelphia to New York was received in Morse's room on the northwest corner of this Audubon house.

In 1843, when 58 years old, Audubon made an eight months' journey to the Northwest to gather additional material for his book "Viparious Quadrupeds of North America." One of his sons accompanied him. Later years he spent at Minniesland, with his family, grieving over his failing eyesight and impatient over his enforced inactivity. He died in 1851 and was buried in Trinity Cemetery, on Washington Heights, near his home.

Today thousands of Audubon societies carry on his work. Through the association motto, "For the protection of North American birds and their eggs from wanton and indiscriminate destruction," Audubon's name has become a world-wide symbol for the sentiment that lay close to his heart.

THE Big Eye, the new 200-inch telescope being built by the California Institute of Technology, is 640,000 times as farsighted as your own two eyes. To appreciate its vision, imagine that you are standing in New York looking at a sign across the street. With the Big Eye you could see that same sign clear across the continent from San Francisco. Astronomers expect the telescope will reveal 100,000,000 *new* universes, most of them galaxies of suns, each as potent as our own.—Frank J. Taylor in *The American Magazine*

The Last March

Condensed from The Golden Book

EXCERPTS FROM THE DIARY OF CAPTAIN R. F. SCOTT

*I*N *November, 1911, Scott began his sledge journey to the South Pole. Before him lay a journey of some 1600 miles of icy desolation —800 miles to the pole, and back. Supporting parties, with crude motor sledges and dog teams, went ahead. Scott and the main party followed with pony-drawn sledges carrying food and equipment. The motor sledges soon broke down. The ponies suffered greatly from the weather and were at length shot and fed to the dogs. These, and men themselves pulling sledges, continued with loads for the depots which had to be established along the entire route against the return journey.*

At the foot of the glacier the dog teams were sent back, and three sledge parties of men toiled up alone. At the top one sledge, with the weakest men, was sent back; and halfway from there to the pole a second party was turned home. Scott went on with his four hardiest companions: Captain Oates, Lieutenant Bowers, Dr. Wilson, and Petty Officer Evans.

They reached the pole January 18th only to find that Amundsen had beaten them. Bitterly disappointed, they began the dangerous homeward journey. "We have turned our back now on the goal of our ambition," says the diary, "and must face 800 miles of solid dragging—and goodbye to most of the day-dreams!"

Saturday, January 27. The forenoon march was over the belt of storm-tossed sastrugi (waves of crusted snow); it looked like a rough sea. Wilson and I pulled in front on ski, the remainder on foot. It was very tricky work following the track. . . .

Our sleeping bags are slowly but surely getting wetter, and we are slowly getting more hungry, and it would be an advantage to have a little more food, especially for lunch. If we get to the next depot in a few marches (it is now less than 60 miles and we have a full week's food) we ought to be able to open out a little, but we can't look for a real feed till we get to

159

the pony food depot. A long way to go, and, by Jove, this is tremendous labor. . . .

Thursday, February 1. Heavy collar work most of the day. Did 8 miles, 4¾ hours. Working on past 8 P.M. we just fetched a lunch cairn of December 29, when we were only a week out from the depot. It ought to be easy to get in with a margin, having 8 days' food in hand (full feeding). Evans' fingers now very bad, two nails coming off, blisters burst. . . .

Saturday, February 17. A very terrible day. Evans looked a little better after a good sleep, and declared, as he always did, that he was quite well. He started in his place on the traces, but half an hour later worked his ski shoes adrift, and had to leave the sledge. The surface was awful. We stopped after about one hour, and Evans came up again, but very slowly. Half an hour later he dropped out again on the same plea. Abreast the Monument Rock we stopped, and seeing Evans a long way astern, I camped for lunch. After lunch, and Evans still not appearing, we looked out, to see him still afar off. By this time we were alarmed, and all four started back on ski. I was first to reach the poor man and shocked at his appearance; he was on his knees with clothing disarranged, hands uncovered and frostbitten, and a wild look in his eyes. Asked what was the matter, he replied with a slow speech that he didn't know, but thought he must have fainted. We got him on his feet, but after two or three steps he sank down again. He showed every sign of complete collapse. Wilson, Bowers, and I went back for the sledge, while Oates remained with him. When we returned he was practically unconscious, and when we got him into the tent quite comatose. He died quietly at 12:30 A.M.

Sunday, February 18. At Shambles Camp. We gave ourselves 5 hours' sleep at the lower glacier depot after the horrible night, and came on at about 3 today to this camp. Here, with plenty of horsemeat, we have had a fine supper, to be followed by others such, and so continue a more plentiful era if we can keep good marches up. New life seems to come with greater food almost immediately. . . .

Monday, February 19. We have struggled out 4.6 miles in a short day over a really terrible surface. It is perhaps premature to be anxious about covering distance. In all other respects things are improving. We have our sleeping bags spread on the sledge and they are drying, but, above all, we have our full measure of food again. Tonight we had a sort of stew fry of pemmican and horseflesh, and voted it the best hoosh we had ever had on a sledge journey. . . .

Wednesday, February 22. There is little doubt that we are in for a rotten critical time going home. Shortly after starting today the wind grew very fresh from the S. E. with strong surface drift. We lost the faint track immediately. Lunch came without sight of the cairn we had hoped to pass. In the afternoon, Bowers, being sure we were too far to the west, steered out. Result, we have passed another pony camp without seeing it. It is a satisfaction to note that such untoward events fail to damp the spirit of the party. Tonight we had a pony hoosh so excellent and filling that one feels really strong and vigorous again. . . .

Sunday, February 26. Very cold nights now and cold feet starting march, as day footgear doesn't dry at all. We are doing well on our food, but we ought to have yet more. I hope the next depot, now only 50 miles, will find us with enough surplus to open out.

Tuesday, February 28. Thermometer went below –40 degrees last night; it was desperately cold for us, but we had a fair night. I decided to slightly increase food; the effect is undoubtedly good.

Friday, March 2. Misfortunes rarely come singly. We marched to the (Middle Barrier) depot fairly easily yesterday afternoon, and since that have suffered three distinct blows which have placed us in a bad position. First, we found a shortage of oil; with most rigid economy it can scarce carry us to the next depot on this surface (71 miles away). Second, Titus Oates disclosed his feet, the toes showing very bad indeed, evidently bitten by the late temperatures. The third blow came in the night, when the wind brought dark overcast weather. It fell below –40 degrees in the night, and this morning it took 1½ hours to get our footgear

on, but we got away before eight. The surface was simply awful and we have done only 5½ miles. We are in a *very* queer street since there is no doubt we cannot do the extra marches and feel the cold horribly.

Saturday, March 3. This morning the outlook is blacker than ever. The surface grew awful beyond words. God help us, we can't keep up this pulling, that is certain. Amongst ourselves we are unendingly cheerful, but what each man feels in his heart I can only guess. Pulling on footgear in the morning is getting slower and slower, therefore every day more dangerous.

Monday, March 5. Regret to say going from bad to worse. We got a slant of wind yesterday afternoon, and going on 5 hours we converted our wretched morning run of 3½ miles into something over 9. We went to bed on a cup of cocoa and pemmican solid with the chill off. The result is telling on all, but mainly on Oates, whose feet are most wretched.

Tuesday, March 6. The sun is shining now and the wind gone. Poor Oates is unable to pull, sits on the sledge when we are track-searching—he is wonderfully plucky, as his feet must be giving him great pain. He makes no complaint, but his spirits only come up in spurts now.

Wednesday, March 7. A little worse I fear. One of Oates' feet *very* bad this morning; he is wonderfully brave. We still talk of what we will do together at home. . . .

Thursday, March 8. Worse and worse in the morning; poor Oates' left foot can never last out, and time over footgear something awful. We did 4½ miles this morning and are now 8½ miles from the depot—a ridiculously small distance to feel in difficulties, yet on this surface we know we cannot equal half our old marches.

Saturday, March 10. Things steadily downhill. Oates' foot worse. He has rare pluck and must know that he can never get through. He asked Wilson if he had a chance this morning, and of course Bill had to say he didn't know. In point of fact he has none.

Sunday, March 11. Titus Oates is very near the end, one feels. What he or we will do, God only knows. We discussed the matter after breakfast; he is a brave, fine fellow and understands the situation, but he practically asked for advice. Nothing could be said but to urge him to march as long as he could. One satisfactory result to the discussion; I practically ordered Wilson to hand over the means of ending our troubles to us, so that any one of us may know how to do so. We have 30 opium tabloids apiece and he is left with a tube of morphine.

Monday, March 12. We did 6.9 miles yesterday, under our necessary average. Things are much the same, Oates not pulling much, hands and feet pretty useless. . . .

Friday, March 16 or 17. Lost track of dates. Tragedy all along the line. At lunch, the day before yesterday, poor Titus Oates said he couldn't go on; he proposed we should leave him in his sleeping bag. That we could not do, and induced him to come on, on the afternoon march. In spite of its awful nature for him he struggled on and we made a few miles. At night he was worse and we knew the end had come.

Should this be found I want these facts recorded. Oates' last thoughts were of his mother. He did not—would not—give up hope to the very end. He was a brave soul. This was the end. He slept through the night before last, hoping not to wake; but he woke in the morning —yesterday. It was blowing a blizzard. He said, "I am just going outside and may be some time." He went out into the blizzard and we have not seen him since. . . .

We are all cold on the march now, and at all times except meals. Yesterday we had to lay up for a blizzard and today we move dreadfully slowly. . . .

Sunday, March 18. My right foot has gone, nearly all the toes. Bowers takes first place in condition, but there is not much to choose after all.

Monday, March 19. We camped with difficulty last night, and were dreadfully cold till after our supper of cold pemmican and biscuit and a half a pannikin of cocoa cooked over the spirit. Then, contrary to expectation, we got warm and all slept well. Today we started in the usual dragging manner. Sledge dreadfully heavy. We have two days' food but barely a day's fuel. All our feet are getting bad—

Wilson's best, my right foot worse, left all right. . . .

Wednesday, March 21. Got within 11 miles of depot Monday night; had to lay up all yesterday in severe blizzard. Today forlorn hope.

Thursday, March 22 and 23. Blizzard bad as ever—no fuel and only one or two of food left—must be near the end. Have decided it shall be natural—we shall march for the depot with or without our effects and die in our tracks.

Thursday, March 29. Since the 21st we have had a continuous gale. We had fuel to make two cups of tea apiece and bare food for two days on the 20th. Every day we have been ready to start for our depot 11 miles away, but outside the door of the tent it remains a scene of whirling drift. I do not think we can hope for any better things now. The end cannot be far.

It seems a pity, but I do not think I can write more.

R. Scott.

For God's sake look after our people.

* * *

(Wilson and Bowers were found in the attitude of sleep, their sleeping bags closed over their heads as they would naturally close them. Scott died later. He had thrown back the flaps of his sleeping bag and opened his coat. The little wallet containing the three notebooks was under his shoulders and his arm flung across Wilson. So they were found eight months later.)

Sales Parrots

THE Willmark Service System, which shows retailers how to sell more goods, recently had their incognito investigators buy things from 1000 different clerks, to see how good they were at "suggestive selling"—influencing customers to spend more than they intended to. More than 300 of them stuck to such clichés as "And what else?" and "Will that be all?" Nearly 150 did make specific suggestions, but they were pretty feeble: "Got plenty of handkerchieves?" "Any coffee, sugar, salt or butter today?" "You wouldn't be interested in any lace collars, would you?" or "Would you be interested in a flashlight?" Some let slip such things as "Here's a cheaper hat that looks twice as good as your old one," and "Do you use an astringent? You're inclined to be oily around the nose, you know."

Willmark believes that suggestive selling, done right, can work wonders. "We have a new model shoe that will look perfect on a small foot like yours" was a line recommended for a shoe store. A midwest drug chain found that only 3.8 percent of their luncheon customers were responding to "Would you care for any dessert?" They switched to "Will you have apple pie à la mode? It's special today," and 22.5 percent bought. A word-picture of a specific food is much more likely to arouse appetite than the vague, colorless term, "dessert."

Can One Influence an Unborn Child?

Condensed from The Parents' Magazine

DR. THOMAS D. WOOD and ZILPHA CARRUTHERS

"FLESH of my flesh and blood of my blood" men and women have said of their children since time began. And yet it is a fundamentally mistaken idea.

Every human being has within him two essential materials; first, the kind of life-stuff called "body cells" which go to make up the various members and organs of the human body; and second, the kind of life-stuff called "germ cells," which have nothing to do with making the body and whose sole function is to pass on the family and racial life stream from one generation to the next. Thus, not even out of his parents' flesh and blood, but out of their hereditary germ cells the baby comes.

Every father ought to understand this fact, because it will increase his realization of his importance to his children. No mother can any longer think of herself as overwhelmed by the task of "making" her child; she is the trustee of something far finer than she could possibly make single-handed. This means that while the mother can no longer hope to produce a preacher by reading sermons, she need no longer fear that if frightened by a mouse or what not she will deposit a "birthmark" in the shape of a mouse upon the child.

By the time the baby sees the light of day he has already been influenced by three different prenatal currents. He has received from the family germ cell his racial characteristics, such as the general body type, the form of face and head, and capacities or aptitudes for certain mental and temperamental developments. He has, in the second place, been affected by the physical characteristics transmitted by both his parents to these germ cells to which his parents' bodies are hosts. The germ cells are not easily affected by any of the ordinary ups and downs of the parents' well-being. But long continued abuse of the human body may injure them. The germ cells may be poisoned by alcohol, phosphorus, lead, and

164

certain chemicals, or by the toxins of certain diseases—most serious of all by syphilis. The influence of nutrition upon the germ cells is probably greater than has been realized until very lately. It is thus essential that every man, as well as every woman, who hopes to see his family line continue strong and healthy, should do his part to preserve his racial inheritance conveyed by the germ cells.

In both these types of influence the parents have an equal share because they act upon the single germ cell itself and not upon the child who has already begun a new life out of the union of two cells, one of which comes from each parent. From that point on whatever good comes to the child is its mother's gift, for at the moment of conception the influences that can touch the cells while independent have completed their work and all other gates of gifts, save the mother's, are closed.

And yet there is no other phase of human life in relation to which so many fallacies have existed and still persist. It is true that the mother can influence the well-being of her unborn child, but it has taken humanity multitudes of generations to find out how and why.

There is just one channel through which the mother can reach the child, and that is through her blood. Science has never discovered any nervous connection, for nature has surrounded the child with a protective mechanism which is as perfect and complete as anything in life. The mother's whole task is one of nurture and nutrition. Her duty is to supply the child with food and to carry off waste products. Both of these come and go through the blood. Through this channel, too, in spite of its protective mechanism, the unborn child may actually be poisoned by certain chemicals, including alcohol, lead and others, and by the toxins of certain diseases.

But the cases in which such poisoning occurs are proportionately exceedingly few; the great source of maternal influence is through nutrition. Most mothers have been told by physicians that they must eat plenty of vegetables and milk, and that they must guard their diet. But not all of them know that, since there is no nervous connection whatever, it is practically their only way of meeting their responsibilities. For there is nothing but the two blood streams and even these do not actually meet, as they are carried along in systems of tubes.

The mother's job begins and ends with safeguarding her own and the child's nutrition. And yet credulence in so-called "maternal impressions" is so much a part of folk-belief that it is hard to cast it entirely aside. A graduate student in a great university reported that she had known a case in which a mother, frightened by a circus elephant, gave birth shortly after to a child with a long trunk-like nose; and another, in which a little girl was born with her right hand gone at the wrist five months after her mother's brother had lost his right hand at that point.

These are typical of the sort of "true stories" we still hear. But science proves such things cannot be done. Peculiarities of structure occur so early in prenatal life that the mother could not influence them, for she doesn't know anything about what is happening. And, since there is no nervous connection there is no conceivable way for such impressions to reach the child anyway. The greatest specialists of today agree with the observation made more than a half century ago by Darwin's father, who was an exceptionally observant and shrewd physician. He was in the habit of asking the women in his hospital to record before the baby's birth any experience of their own which might influence the child. As a result of hundreds of these records he reported, "Absolutely not one case (of maternal impressions) came right."

"But," someone says, "how explain the case of the mother who studied counterpoint while her baby was on the way and whose son grew up to be a talented musician; or of the mother who took up Italian, and whose child early developed an astonishing skill at languages?"

Science would explain these and similar cases not by mysterious "psychic" maternal impressions, but by two very well known influences—heredity and environment. The son of a woman who studied the technique of music not only received an hereditary musical endowment from the same ancestral source from which his mother received hers, but grew up in an atmosphere of musical culture, his every aptitude encouraged and trained. And so with the linguistic prodigy.

But though the mother has no more chance of telepathy with her child than have "his uncles and his cousins and his aunts," it is not true to say that her emotions cannot affect her child in any way. Any grief or worry or fright sufficient to affect her own health will react on her child, just as any other detrimental influence will react upon it, through her blood.

To sum up then: In the mother's care lies the preservation of something greater than herself. Hers is the last and greatest of the three sources of the gifts of life—from the racial inheritance, from the influence of both parents upon the germ cells, and finally from the mother's care, which should be as sane, and thoughtful, and happy before the child is born as after.

A WOMAN with her hair combed up always looks as if she were going some place, either to the opera or the shower bath—depending on the woman.—Orson Welles in *Vogue*

Battling a Sea Monster

Condensed from The Golden Book

VICTOR HUGO

GILLIATT wandered among the smaller rocks where the *Durande*, ten weeks before, had first struck upon the sunken reef. For two months he had lived almost entirely upon crabs. This time, however, the crabs were wanting. The tempest had driven them into their solitary retreats, and they had not yet mustered up courage to venture abroad.

As Gilliatt was trying to make up his mind to be content with sea-urchins, a little clattering noise at his feet aroused his attention. A large crab, startled by his approach, had just dropped into a pool.

He chased the crab along the base of the rock; but the crab moved fast, and suddenly disappeared. It had buried itself in some crevice under the rock. As he suspected, there was an opening in which the creature had evidently taken refuge. It was more than a crevice; it was a kind of porch.

The water beneath it was not deep, and the bottom, covered with large pebbles, was plainly visible. Holding his knife between his teeth, Gilliatt descended, by the aid of his feet and hands, from the upper part of the escarpment, and leaped into the water. It reached almost to his shoulders.

He made his way through the porch, and found himself in a blind passage, with a roof shaped like a rude arch over his head. The crab was nowhere visible.

He noticed, above the level of the water, and within reach of his hand, a horizontal fissure. It seemed to him probable that the crab had taken refuge there, and he plunged his hand in as far as he was able, and groped in that dusky aperture.

Suddenly he felt himself seized by the arm. A strange, indescribable horror thrilled him.

Some living thing, thin, rough, flat, cold, and slimy, had twisted itself round his naked arm, in the dark depth below. Its pressure was like a tightening cord, its steady persistence like that of a screw. In another instant the same mysterious spiral form had wound around his wrist and elbow, and had reached

167

his shoulder. A sharp point penetrated beneath the armpit.

Gilliatt recoiled, but he had scarcely power to move! He was, as it were, nailed to the place. He made a desperate effort to withdraw his arm; but he only succeeded in disturbing his persecutor, which wound itself tighter. It was supple as leather, strong as steel, cold as night.

A second form, sharp, elongated, and narrow, issued from the crevice like a tongue out of monstrous jaws.

It seemed to lick his naked body; then suddenly stretching out, it become longer and thinner, as it crept over his skin, and wound itself around him. At the same time a terrible sensation of pain, utterly unlike any he had ever known, made all his muscles contract.

A third long undulating shape issued from the hole in the rock, seemed to feel its way around his body to lash itself around his ribs like a cord, and fix itself there.

Intense agony is dumb. Gilliatt uttered no cry. There was sufficient light for him to see the repulsive forms which had wound themselves about him.

A fourth ligature—but this one swift as an arrow—darted towards his stomach, and wound about him.

It was impossible to sever or tear away the slimy bands which were twisted tightly around his body, and which were adhering to it at a number of points. Each of these points was the focus of frightful and singular pangs. It seemed as if innumerable small mouths were devouring him at the same time.

A fifth long, slimy, ribbon-shaped strip issued from the hole. It passed over the others, and wound itself tightly around his chest. The compression increased his sufferings. He could scarcely breathe.

Suddenly a large round, flattened, glutinous mass issued from beneath the crevice. It was the center; the five thongs were attached to it like spokes to the hub of a wheel. On the opposite side of this disgusting monster appeared the beginning of three other similar tentacles, the ends of which remained under the rock. In the middle of this slimy mass were two eyes.

These eyes were fixed on Gilliatt.

He recognized the Devil-Fish.

It is difficult for those who have not seen it to believe in the existence of the devil-fish. Compared with this creature, the ancient hydras are insignificant.

The devil-fish has no muscular organization, no menacing cry, no breast-plate, no horn, no dart, no claw, no tail with which to hold or bruise; no cutting fins, or wings with nails, no prickles, no sword, no electric discharge, no poison, no claws, no beak, no jaws. Yet he is of all creatures most formidably armed.

This frightful monster which is so often encountered amid the rocks in the open sea, is of grayish color, about five feet long, and about the thickness of a man's arm. It is ragged in outline, and in shape strongly resembles a closed umbrella, without a handle. This irregular mass advances slowly towards you. Suddenly it opens, and eight radii issue abruptly from around a face with two eyes. These radii are alive; their undulation is like lambent flames.

Its folds strangle; its contact paralyzes. It has the aspect of gangrened or scabrous flesh. It is a monstrous embodiment of disease.

Underneath each of the eight antennae are two rows of suckers, decreasing in size, the largest ones near the head, the smallest at the extremities. Each row contains 25 of these. There are, therefore, 50 suckers to each feeler, and the creature possesses 400 in all. These small tubes are capable of piercing to a depth of more than an inch.

It is with the sucking apparatus that it attacks. The victim is oppressed by a vacuum drawing at numberless points; it is not a clawing or a biting, but an indescribable scarification. A tearing of the flesh is terrible, but less terrible than a sucking of the blood.

Such was the creature in whose power Gilliatt had fallen.

Of the eight arms of the devilfish, three adhered to the rock, while five encircled Gilliatt. In this way, clinging to the granite on one side, and to its human prey on the other, it chained him to the rock. Two hundred and fifty suckers were upon him, tormenting him with agony and loathing.

As we have said, it is impossible to tear one's self from the clutches of the devil-fish. The attempt only results in a firmer grasp . . . Gilliatt had but one resource—his open knife was in his left hand.

The antennae of the devil-fish cannot be cut; it is a leathery substance upon which a knife makes no impression; it slips under the blade; to sever it would be to wound severely the victim's own flesh.

The creature is formidable, but there is a way of resisting it. The fishermen of Sark know it. Porpoises know it, too; they have a way of biting the cuttle-fish which decapitates it. In fact, its only vulnerable part is its head. Gilliatt was not ignorant of this fact.

He had never seen a devil-fish of this size. His first encounter was with one of the largest species. Any other man would have been overwhelmed with terror.

With the devil-fish, as with a furious bull, there is a certain instant in the conflict which must be seized. It is the instant when the bull lowers his neck; it is the instant when the devil-fish advances its head. The movement is rapid. One who loses that moment is irrevocably doomed.

Gilliatt looked at the monster, which seemed to return the look.

Suddenly it loosened from the rock its sixth antenna, and darting it at him, seized him by the arm. At the same moment, it advanced its head with a quick movement. In one second more its mouth would have fastened on his breast.

He avoided the antenna, and at the very instant the monster darted forward, he struck it with his knife. There were two convulsive movements in opposite directions—that of the devil-fish, and that of its prey. The movements were as rapid as lightning.

Gilliatt had plunged the blade of his knife into the flat, slimy substance, and with a rapid movement, like the flourish of a whiplash in the air, had described a circle round the two eyes, and wrenched off the head as a man would draw a tooth.

The struggle was ended. The slimy bands relaxed. The air-pump being broken, the vacuum was destroyed. The 400 suckers, deprived of their sustaining power, dropped at once from the man and the rock. The mass sank to the bottom of the water.

Breathless with the struggle, Gilliatt could dimly discern on the stones at his feet two shapeless, slimy heaps, the head on one side, the rest of the monster on the other. Nevertheless, fearing a convulsive return of the death agony, he recoiled to be out of reach of the dread tentacles. But the monster was dead.

Grounds for Divorce

"WHILE he never actually struck me," explained Mrs. Sarah Sanders, suing Edward Sanders for divorce, "he would go around slamming his fist against doors and saying: 'I wish it was you.'"
—*Time*

WILLIAM WILSON divorced his wife because she took his false teeth and held them for $2 ransom.—*Time*

CHARGING that he hurled a prickly cactus plant at her while she was in a stooping position, Mrs. John B. Crane of Cambridge, Mass., won an uncontested divorce from her husband, a Harvard University instructor.—*Newsweek*

TESTIFYING that her husband had knocked her out by hitting her on the head with a live chicken and then, finding that the impact had killed the chicken, revived her and ordered her to cook it, Mrs. Viola Beck sued for divorce.—*Time*

ADA LEONARD, strip-tease dancer, filed suit to divorce her husband because, her attorney explained, "She resents the fact that her husband doesn't resent the fact that she is doing this kind of work. Is that clear?"—*Newsweek*

SAMUEL HOFFENSTEIN, scenarist and poet, of Hollywood, was divorced by his wife, who objected to jingles he dedicated to her:

> When you're away, I'm restless, lonely,
> Wretched, bored, dejected;
> But here's the rub, my darling dear,
> I feel the same when you are here.
> —*Newsweek*

In Defense of Shyness

Condensed from Vanity Fair

HAROLD NICOLSON

IT IS surely discreditable, under the age of 30, not to be shy. Self assurance in the young betokens a lack of sensibility: the boy or girl who is not shy at 22 will at 42 be a bore.

No, let us educate the younger generation to be shy in and out of season: to edge behind the furniture: to say spasmodic and ill-digested things: to twist their feet round the protective feet of sofas: to feel that their hands belong to someone else—that they are objects, which they long to put down on some table away from themselves.

For shyness is the protective fluid within which our personalities are able to develop into natural shapes. Without this fluid the character becomes merely standardized or imitative: it is within the tender velvet sheath of shyness that the full flower of idiosyncrasy is nurtured: it is from this sheath alone that it can eventually unfurl itself, colored and undamaged. Let the shy understand, therefore, that their disability is not merely an incon-

From *Some People*, by Harold Nicolson, reprinted by permission of Houghton Mifflin Company, Publishers.

venience but also a privilege.

I do not think that shyness can be kept within bounds by any ethical arguments. I used to tell myself, for instance, at those moments outside the doorways of the great when shyness becomes a laughing monster with its fangs already gaping at one's heart—I used to tell myself that I was as good, as powerful, as rich, as beautiful as any of those I was about to meet. This was not a good system. It made me pert. I would bounce into the room gaily, as if I were the Marquis de Soveral; be somewhat impudent to my hostess, cut my host dead, show undue familiarity towards the distinguished author, and fling myself into an armchair. The chair would recede at this impact and upset a little table on which were displayed a bottle of smelling salts, a little silver cart from Rome, a Persian pen-box, and a bowl of anemones. These objects would rattle loudly to the floor, and with them would tumble my assertiveness.

Such deductive systems invariably fail. Fatal also is the reverse process of behaving like the worm one feels. "Remember," I have said to myself on giving my hat and coat to the footman, "remember that you are a worm upon this earth. These people have only asked you because they met your aunt at St. Jean de Luz. They do not wish to see you, still less do they wish to hear you speak. You may say good evening to your hostess, and then you must retreat behind the sofa. If addressed, you will reply with modesty and politeness. If not addressed, you will not speak at all." Things do not work out that way. The place behind the sofa is occupied by an easel: and then one falls over the dog. No—shyness must be controlled by more scientific methods.

In the first place, you must diagnose the type of shyness from which you suffer. There are two main divisions of the disease, the physical and the mental type. The physical type are shy about their limbs—their arms and legs make jerky movements which cause breakages and embarrassment. The mental type are shy about what they say or where they look. It is the latter who are most to be pitied. For whereas the physical sufferer can generally, by using great circumspection, avoid the worst consequences of his affliction, the mental type is not released until he finds him- or herself alone again in the motor, homeward bound. It is upon the latter type that I desire to concentrate.

The first rule is to make it perfectly clear to one's parents before arriving at the party that one is to remain unnoticed. One's mother should not be allowed to make gestures at us—down the table—of encouragement and love. One's father should be forbidden to confide to the hostess that this is the first time that you have worn an evening suit or a low necked dress—should be forbidden to cast sly paternal glances at one, or to observe whether one does, or does not, enjoy oneself. One must be left alone with one's shyness.

The second rule is to determine from the outset that one does not desire to shine either socially or intellectually. Nor should one attempt to appear older than one actually is. These things do not carry conviction. You will find yourself, if you give way to these ambitions, slipping into phrases which are not your own phrases and of which, once they have escaped the barrier of your lips, you will feel ashamed. You may be calling, for instance, upon the wife of a neighbor: you will find her sitting on the veranda in a green deck chair: if you are wise, you will have the modesty to say merely "How are you, Mrs. Simpson?" But if you are unwise, and wish to appear at your ease, you will exclaim "Please don't get up!" Having said this, you will reflect that Mrs. Simpson had no idea of getting out of her deck chair for such a worm as you. Do not, therefore, adopt or even adapt the phrases of your elders. Above all do not break into conversations. It may well be that the Primavera is a picture painted, not by Cimabue, but by Botticelli.

But it is not for you, when others attribute the painting to an earlier artist, either to interfere or to correct. A slight pursing of the lips is all that you may allow yourself. The only justification for being shy is to be shy to all the people all the time. You must avoid being pert to governesses and polite to bishops. But if you are always shy, people will end by imagining that you have a modest nature: and that, since it will flatter their own self-esteem, will make you extremely popular. Only when you have become popular can you afford to be interesting, intelligent, or impressive. It is a great mistake to endeavor to awaken admiration before you have stilled envy, and it is only when people have started by ignoring the young that they end by liking the young. It may be a comfort to you therefore to consider that it is an excellent thing, at first, to be regarded as being of no importance.

There are certain more practical hints which I should wish to furnish to the youthful shy. It is essential, for instance, to have quite clear in your mind what are to be the opening words which you will address to your hostess. Unless you have prepared these words, other words may come skipping into their place, and instead of saying "How are you, Mrs. Simpson? It was too kind of you to let me come," you will say, "Your butler has got the largest carbuncle I have ever seen."

Then there is that business about saying goodbye. I became quite good at what we might call "set" goodbyes, the ones, that is, for which I was prepared in advance. It was the unexpected greetings and farewells that I failed, for so long, to manage. The meeting with one's schoolmaster in Regent Street. The few minutes' conversation—the terror of how to get away. One cannot swing around on those occasions and walk off briskly in the opposite direction. The dodge is to begin to move while still speaking. "Well, don't forget to ring me up," one says—walking backwards and away from the man, "Central 4689," one shouts at a receding figure.

Perhaps shyness is a purely Anglo-Saxon failing. I doubt whether even the tenderest of the Roman poets, whether Virgil even was shy. Horace, as we know, was one large lump of bounce. Nor was Dante shy—disagreeable was Dante, but never shy. Yes, I think shyness is an Anglo-Saxon quality. And as such it should be honored as a bond between the English-speaking nations.

Echoes of Will Rogers

"WHEN I DIE," Will Rogers once said, "my epitaph, or whatever you call those signs on gravestones, is going to read: 'I joke about every prominent man of my time, but I never met a man I didn't like.' I am proud of that. I can hardly wait to die so it can be carved, and when you come around to my grave you'll probably find me sitting there proudly reading it."—N. Y. *Herald Tribune*

Night by a Jungle Lagoon

Condensed from Nature Magazine

TOM GILL

PEDRO's wrinkled face smiled. "After all, it is only at night when the jungle speaks. In two short months here in our Mexican forests, you think, perhaps, you have learned something of the way of the wild things. But it is not really so. For only at night, *señor*, the bitter fight for life begins. Then the jungle things awaken and come forth."

My old Mexican guide was right. Two months knocking about through the mahogany forests of southern Mexico had certainly not rewarded me with much knowledge of the abundant wild life that I knew must exist there. I waited for old Pedro to speak again.

"Always the eyes of the children of the jungle are upon us—they follow us and signal about us, and know our coming and going. Yes, even the Caribe Indians know we are here. And I think, if they wished it, we should not see tomorrow's dawn."

Now, I had already heard of the Caribe Indian and his playful way with blow-gun and poisoned arrow.

Farther to the south, where they are unfriendly, white men had lost their lives, but here they were thought a peaceful people.

"Sometimes when we are caught out at night," Pedro's soft, lisping Spanish went on, "sometimes we hear the jungle awaken. The bats, and the great moths and puma, the big cat, watch us. But soon we light a campfire, and everything moves back."

My curiosity was so aroused by this talk that the following sunset I took leave of Pedro and his comfortable campfire, to spend the night on the banks of a lagoon.

Already night had fallen. Behind me loomed the jungle, black and impenetrable. The vampire bats were out. Back and forth before me, three of them kept me eerie company for an hour, flying so close that I could dimly trace their evil, hairy faces, and distinctly feel the rush of wind beneath their wings. Curious fellows. More than once they hung motionless, so close I could have struck them with my hat, peering at me.

174

Far out in the lagoon I heard the muffled ripple of moving water. I could see nothing, and flashed on my flashlight, playing it back and forth over the smooth water of the lagoon. At last I held it steady where two dull red eyes glowed like garnets in the darkness. The alligator, that old killer of the jungle, was abroad.

Held by the spell of the flashlight, he came almost to the bank of the lagoon, and there beneath my feet he waited, with upturned wicked, bloodshot eyes. Soon from the left, out of the darkness, came another cautious ripple, and farther on still another. And before half an hour had passed 12 pairs of ruby eyes were ranged down there before me, all looking hungrily, expectantly up into the flashlight. Above them, attracted by the illumination, great giant moths were fluttering on soft, brilliantly-colored wings just over the water's edge.

I thought of the Indian legend that tells how the souls of good children, in dying, are sometimes favored by the gods, and pass into these moth bodies, abiding there until they are born again.

Tired at last of that solemn scrutiny of steady eyes, I chose a large stone and dropped it carefully on the nose of the biggest alligator. Followed an indignant snort, a mad lashing of the water beneath, and a sudden extinction of all those pairs of eyes. Once more I was surrounded by silence and jungle blackness.

Just at midnight rose the sound of a jaguar. Now it is one thing to hear the midnight rumble of a jaguar when you are lying in the comparative security of a campfire's glow, but it was somewhat different perched upon the edge of an alligator-infested lagoon. From the crackling and trampling, it sounded unmistakably as if he were working my way. With cocked automatic in my right hand, I flashed a stream of light down into the tangled mass of bamboo and palms.

The rest is a confused memory —a snarl of surprise, a mottled, sinewy form not ten feet away, and the flash of my automatic as twice I fired wildly. I must have missed by yards. The shots shattered the peace of the surrounding jungle. Parrakeets chattered and swore, while from afar off a band of monkeys shrieked and howled. It was hours before quiet returned to the jungle.

Just as dawn was painting its first silver over jungle and lagoon, and I had almost given up hope of seeing more—just then my long vigil was rewarded by something I would have journeyed many miles to see.

Beyond the rising mists I first noticed a clump of palms shaking in a way no movement of wind could have accounted for. Then I saw two dark arms push the palms aside, and a moment later the almost naked figure of an Indian had moved silently down to the water's edge. In his left hand he grasped a bow and several arrows. His long black hair fell below his shoulders. I knew then that I was looking upon one of that little known, mysterious Caribe tribe, those furtive, almost legendary people so few travelers ever see. For no other Indian of southern Mexico allows his hair to grow long and to hang loosely about his shoulders. No other Indian wears only a band of stringy burlap-like bark about his waist.

Noiselessly the Caribe crept to a point of land not far from where three mallard ducks were swimming lazily about. He had laid aside his bow and arrow and held some large object about the size and shape of a pumpkin, but darker in color. Slowly he slipped into the water. As it reached his shoulders he put over his head that hollow spherical object, then let himself sink until only that strange headdress was visible above the surface. It bobbed and moved and stopped and moved again, as naturally as any light object might be blown about by some soft morning breeze, but always with a kind of menacing certainty it approached nearer and nearer its quarry. Once a duck turned as if to paddle away, but apparently changing its mind, resumed feeding. The hidden Caribe was only a few feet away, and I found myself straining forward to catch the end.

The end came quickly. The unseen hunter was floating quietly now, directly among the feeding ducks. A hush, almost of expectancy, had fallen. Suddenly a frightened squawk broke the morning silence.

With a terrified flapping of wings one duck arose and sped back into the jungle. The other two were nowhere to be seen! Beneath that quietly floating object, two dark hands were grasping the ducks that only a moment before had been feeding in such complete security. In another moment my Caribe had thrown off his camouflage and gained the farther bank, where he stood glistening and streaming with water, holding in either hand the prizes of his hunt. Silently he turned back into the jungle and was gone.

Hungry and weary, an hour later, I was telling Pedro my story. He listened without comment, but as I finished he said quietly, "Give thanks to the Mother of God, *señor*, that the Caribe did not see you. They do not greatly like to be spied upon, those jungle people."

Amends to the Camel

Condensed from Asia

RODNEY GILBERT

For more than ten years I have never looked a camel in the eye without feeling under obligation to expiate in public print a crime that I perpetrated years ago when I said, as every one else seems to have said before me, that the camel was an ill-tempered, evil-smelling, stupid anachronism. Recently in an encyclopedia I came upon an even more abusive attack upon the beast's character.

A big proportion of all that has been written about camels has been about the Arabian camel, the tall, one-humped beast that sheikhs ride. My particular friend is the two-humped, long-haired, short-legged Bactrian camel, bred and used throughout Mongolia, northern Tibet and Central Asia generally. No Occidental with any common sense ever gets into a situation where familiarity with the Bactrian camel is possible. I, however, used to enjoy notoriety in the Far East for getting into just the situations sensible persons kept out of. In the fall of 1918 I was commissioned to advance into western China and Turkistan, to explain the war and victory to certain Mahommedan potentates. At the town of Ningsia my camel expert deserted me, and it became my duty to groom and feed my two querulously talkative animals. I started off into the uninhabited Ala-shan, and the dreary desert beyond, sometimes leading my beasts, sometimes riding them, pitching my tent each morning in a gale with the thermometer 30 degrees below zero, collecting dry dung for my fire by the light of the morning star, cooking mutton stew and tea, packing and unpacking the patient but obviously lonely and bewildered camels.

Then I fell in with a string of 1000 camels and 80 men going my way and my troubles were over; but for the rest of the winter I kept on learning more and more about camels. I learned that the greatest obstacle to sympathetic understanding with the camel is his nose rope, made fast to a wooden pin through his nostrils. A heavy handed person can give this rope a jerk that is extremely painful. The result is that when anyone approaches a camel with outstretched hand, he throws his head as high as he can, edges clumsily away and screams his protest. If you can take the leading rope without exciting any such demonstration, you may be sure you have won the camel's confidence. It requires infinite patience, but once your mount does have such confidence, he regards you as a friend, and will even lower his head and gurgle affectionately as a hint that he would enjoy having his ears scratched.

Orientals almost never pet domestic animals. The camel driver takes excellent care of his beasts, but he has no desire for their affection and therefore does not get it. Consequently, the attentions that my two beasts bestowed on me never failed to astonish the men of the wilderness. If we met other caravans and camped with them, the strangers would invariably be told of my trick camels. I would be asked to walk off and call them, have them put their heads down to be scratched, talk to them and have them reply with unearthly squeaks, stroll about so that they would follow and frisk around me like a couple of playful puppies.

One was a female, and if I did not send her about her business, she would follow me into the heart of the camp, stand behind me and make little chirping noises above my head, and then, if I stood still, she would put her muzzle on my shoulder, close her eyes in content-ment and drool green saliva down the front of my sheepskin coat. This was the final act in my performance, which never failed to elicit exclamations.

Once for six weeks I was separated from my two devoted beasts. When finally I entered the compound where they had been kept for me by a Chinese friend, they were on the farther side, eating from a pile of hay. They heard the squeak of the hinge, looked to see who had entered and then, with shrill cries of delight, came charging for me at a terrific pace. My Chinese friend was terrified and bolted. They brought up in front of me almost on their haunches, raising their heads high above mine, and spat their rank-smelling cuds into the air. It was a physically unpleasant yet gratifying demonstration, and brought me much advertising among the whole colony of animal dealers, who were loath to believe that a camel had any affection for any one.

That camels can be not only affectionate but solicitous for a rider's welfare I learned on another occasion. Near the Tibetan frontier I had contracted flu, and although the attack did not last more than five days, I continued to have fever for many days afterward. Deciding to work it off, I set out for the town of Dangar on the back of my young female camel. We had not done a mile before I was thoroughly tired and had developed a backache so severe that it was actually nauseating. I squirmed about, trying all sorts of positions, and my mount looked around frequently to see what was the matter. Finally, when I had fallen forward over the hump, she stopped and took a good look at me, made some sort of remark in her throat and very carefully sank to the ground.

It was as plain a suggestion to get off and rest as a human being could have made, and I took it. Now, being young, this animal was often foolish. She usually refused to kneel at all. When I wanted to mount her I always tried to have someone hold her head until I was firmly seated, because otherwise she would be up with a leap, and she left me many times sprawling on the ground. On this occasion, however, she not only knelt but stayed down, inspecting me once in a while with her big, birdlike eyes. When I came to get painfully on again she turned her head and watched me, waiting until I was securely in my place, and then very slowly got up in the three successive upheavals customary with a camel under a heavy pack. If she had done so with any speed I should not have had the strength to hold on. My young lady, however, managed the business as if she were an equilibrist with a bucket of water on her back which she was not to spill, and this performance we went through not once but a dozen times that day. I have told this story often, and have never failed to contrast it with the behavior of the noble horse, because a horse will always take advantage of a rider that he thinks has anything the matter with him.

One of the most attractive features of camels is their conversational ability. They comment on everything that goes on around them, and they make a wider variety of noises than any other domesticated beast. They grumble when they are loaded and scream when they think they are about to suffer indignity; but, when you come to understand their language, you discover that they can ask very politely for their food, thank you when you have attended to their wants, express pleasure at seeing you and almost inquire into the state of your health.

I hope I have established that the camel has unsuspected charms. But one must sample them while muscles are resilient, and circulation still so vigorous that one can freeze solid by night and thaw out by day for weeks on end. In other words, intimacy with the camel in the deserts of Asia must be a prerogative of youth. To those who enjoy mummifying desert heat and paralyzing desert cold, I recommend the much-abused camel as a gentle, loyal and affectionate friend.

What War Does to the Minds of Children

Condensed from The World Tomorrow

S. RALPH HARLOW

IN A course at Smith College, in which we discuss international and race relations, I asked some 200 students to write a statement covering their childhood memories of the World War. Answers were required for such questions as the following: What did you believe the cause of the war to be? What actual experience of the war did you have yourself? What was your attitude toward Germans and things German? What are the outstanding memories of those years of war?

The students were from ten to seventeen years of age when the Versailles Treaty was signed. The papers were written the first week the class met, before the students had time to become influenced by discussions or by their outside reading on the war and its causes.

Two dominant traits appear in practically all of the 200 papers: first, an intense and growing hatred of the enemy; second, highly emotional moments in which a desire to share in the "glory" was uppermost. A few quotations—typical and in no way exceptional—will reveal what was in the child-mind better than any comments.

"I had visions of millions and millions of giant ogres, with stiff blond beards and pointed teeth and spiked helmets, dragging women by the hair, leaving rack and ruin, and rows on rows of bloody corpses." . . . "We hated the Germans with an intensity that is hard to realize in a child. I remember breaking into bits a lovely china doll, the most beautiful in my doll family, because I read on the back 'Made in Germany.'" This incident is related again and again.

The following quotation is typical, the young woman coming from a home of unusual culture. "I was just past seven when the war broke out. My clearest memory is of the hatred of Germans which increased in my father and mother as time went by. I was told that the German officers cut off the hands of all the babies when they entered a Belgian or French town." The granddaughter of America's most famous evangelist, and herself the daughter of a

Christian leader, writes: "My hatred was kindled to the highest pitch. I hated the Germans and amused myself by thinking up the worst tortures for them; I hated Wilson for keeping us out of the war and hated myself though less keenly for being too young to take a 'spectacular' part."

There is marked indication that mothers more than fathers spread the contagion of hatred. "From the very beginning mother hated the Germans and would not permit anything 'Made in Germany' to remain in the house. I remember how daddy used to get provoked at her for being so vehement on· that subject."

There are scores of reports of German children being tormented, driven from the school and the neighborhood; of German teachers being dropped, and German nurses sent away after years of faithful service.

Some of my students belonged to this persecuted class and their memories are poignant. Here is one: "There could have been no family more American than ours, but we bore a German name. How I suffered! I was continually asked, 'Was your grandfather born in Germany?' And my truthfully affirmative reply damned me. Even the teachers 'picked on me' in school and I was shoved to the end of the line by my schoolmates, no 'American' being willing to walk behind me. A very bad self-depreciation resulted that brought an unhappiness from which I have suffered for the past six years."

Of intolerance there is no end of examples. "We were studying European geography that year and the geography book contained a picture of the Kaiser. I took my pencil and blacked out the picture and the word 'Germany,' and wrote 'hateful' all over the pages dealing with Germany and Austria. From the school songbook I scratched out all the hymns and songs with German names." Another student writes: "I jumped for joy when mother threw in the fire all our German books. 'Just think,' she said to me, 'of the hours I spent studying the language of those horrible Huns.' There could be nothing good about them; they were beasts, fiends, all of them—men, women and children."

As to the causes underlying the war, there is only abysmal ignorance and prejudice among the average college students today. The majority of the children believed that the war was fought to "pay Germany back" for the "sinking of the Lusitania" and her barbarous treatment of Belgium.

The daughter of an American missionary in India throws this light on a child's reactions to the facts of war: "As a youngster I saw something of the tragedy behind it all such as few American girls were able to see. I watched regiment after regiment of broken, wounded German men march through the streets of Ahmadnagar to the wire-entanglements of their prison. I saw many of them that looked just like daddy, or Uncle Fred, or Tom, and not at all like the cruel and terrible Huns that we had been told about."

Emotionalism and desire for a share in the glory dominated many of the children's mental attitudes. One writes: "I liked the festive side of the war, the excitement, the flags, the parades, and the dramatic appeals to patriotism, I liked to think that I belonged to the most wonderful country in the world and to the superior race." Much regret is expressed that they were "too young to really have any share in making history."

There is an astonishing and predominating fear revealed that their own fathers or brothers will have to go, and the confession that in the household this dread was shared by many in the family circle. They wanted the enemy killed and beaten but they did not want their own loved ones to share the risks involved. Rhymes attacking the Kaiser and Germans in general were sung with great delight by all. The influence of moving picture propaganda was tremendous. I can cite but one typical statement, though more than a score of papers contained similar ones: "I first realized the atrocity of war when I saw 'Hearts of Gold.' I saw little, fat, innocent babies being massa-cred by the Germans, villages pillaged, unburied dead lying about in the fields, and blood, blood, blood, everywhere. After that I was afraid to sleep alone, and the horror of my thoughts drove me frantic at times. I began to loathe and hate the Germans with all my soul, and I tried to picture all sorts of terrible ways to avenge those babies who had their hands cut off."

Typical of the treatment of other children is the following: "We forced a little girl of German parentage to spit again and again on a picture of a German officer we found in her home. We made her salute the American flag ten times in succession, and then get down and kiss the ground at our feet, because we were superior American beings."

The reports of the armistice celebrations can be summed up in one word, "delirium"; children going mad with emotional excitement, burning images of the Kaiser, yelling songs of patriotism and revenge.

Here, briefly, are some of the psychological experiences which we must expect in children when a nation goes to war. They should be weighed in the balance when we face the war problem.

THE AUTOMATIQUE, a Viennese cafeteria service, was recently introduced in the United States. You sit at table and watch everything on the menu pass by on a belt, and help yourself to what you want. Payment is determined by the color of the plates you have used.
—*Business Week*

Romance in a Realist World

Condensed from Harper's Magazine

AVIS CARLSON

THIS is an unromantic age. Realism, placing the emphasis on facts, is dominant. The intellectual leaders of the time are the scientist and the realistic writer, and the chief business of the rest of us is therefore to face facts and to accept whatever view of life they seem to present.

There have been many definitions of romanticism. Most of them connect it with escape, with the human desire to "get into the land where I am not." Escape! To get out of the dreary or, at best, commonplace here and now; to transcend the baseness and cruelty inhering in what we know as facts; to have play for the untamed center of the being, which can never be reconciled to its bondage —that is the romantic impulse.

If, as we are so frequently told, we are just now both unromantic and deeply thirsty for romance, the reason is not far to seek: one by one all the old well-worn avenues of escape—wonder, adventure, religion, and love—have been closed or greatly narrowed.

That the door of wonder is all but closed is proved by the passing of our taste for myth. As soon as one is taught to think of thunder in terms of air expansion, the myth of Thor's hammer becomes merely an idle fancy. When a flower becomes a fusion of chemical elements, the breathless mood of contemplation is lost. The love of adventure cannot be satisfied now by packing up and proceeding to an entirely new mode of existence. The frontier is gone. We can and do move about incessantly, but in Maine and California the billboards, hot-dog stands, prohibition jokes, and apartment house-rules are much the same. Religion, once the Great Romance and the warmest of all escapes from an austere here and now, has in our day become a strenuous business of seeking truth, of building one's own religious system. That program means not release from facts but a new prodding into the stern work of facing them. And romantic love, the fourth of the great avenues of escape, is losing much of its mystical value. I am

183

not so foolish as to maintain that there is any less falling in love than formerly. But young people in love now poke fun at themselves and are cynical about the emotion that is overwhelming them.

And yet—and yet, reality is no easier to face than it has always been. Life is no prettier or softer, facts no easier to endure. Indeed, since we were never so tightly bottled up and never so thoroughly impressed with our gnatlike insignificance in the general scheme of things, our position is actually harder. The terrific conflict between the relentless force of the age pushing us into the realistic attitude and our aversion for facts is, I think, at the heart of much of the modern unrest and weariness.

The salvation of the individual depends upon working out a romantic escape that does not involve denial of facts. To ignore them is the height of stupidity. To submit to them wholly is death to romance. Somewhere between those attitudes is the one for the modern romantic, who is rebelling not not against facts but against their arrogant claim to be sovereign in the whole of life.

Facts belong to the external world, which is none of man's creating. There he can't blink them and he daren't disobey them. But in the imaginative world facts have no authority. Romance most certainly belongs to that world. The modern who feels that he cannot do without it must above everything else insist upon freedom of the imagination. The romantic of

today will not, for instance, deny himself the romance of love simply because he realizes that love rests on the substratum of biologic fact. He knows that the human imagination has built on that fact a poetry which is distinct from fact and not accountable to it.

It is much the same with adventure. An aviator does not attempt an ocean flight without taking into careful consideration all the facts he can get at. But the facts do not constitute his adventure. That is born of his imagination. And if his imagination is dulled, he may as well drive his car through a familiar country lane for all the adventure he will get out of flying the ocean.

Someone objects, "But how does it apply to me?" In this way: while opportunities for translating the adventurous type of romantic escape into the world of fact are nowadays limited, adventure itself is untouched, except as the imagination has been blunted. I used sometimes to ask freshmen students in composition to tell of an adventure they had had. Always when the assignment was given, the young people looked first blank and then angry. They had never had any adventure. The more they thought of the matter the more indignant with me they became. Their themes were sure to describe either an automobile smash or a hold-up that never happened. But always one or two of the class would respond. The incidents described may have been nothing much in themselves, but they had been enough to stimulate the imaginative activity that is the essence of adventure. The duller the imagination the stronger the jolt of event required to create adventure.

Romance can be achieved by redeeming the commonplace imaginatively. For that there are a hundred methods, most of them open to anyone whose sensitivity has not been jaded by noise and hurry, bootleg and piffle. I have space here for only the merest hint about two of them.

I know a woman who has managed to keep a sense of romance through ten years of heavy responsibility and a particularly galling type of poverty. She has done it by deliberately cultivating mental interests. Every fall she chooses a new field of study. She hasn't a chance for physical adventure, but this other type, which is just as real and more lasting, is no farther away than the public library. Mental adventure has hitherto been the special possession of scholars. It need not be.

The same is true of the aesthetic activity. No artist, whether musician, dancer, or painter, ever found life dull. He may have found it ugly or hateful, but not simply boring. The tendency for people in general, however, has been to leave the aesthetic activity to artists. A worse mistake was never made.

Several times a year I have to drive through a section of Kansas that grows an admirable brand of hard wheat but is lamentably deficient in the more obvious forms of natural beauty. That trip used to be a weariness of the flesh to me till I heard an intelligent woman talk enthusiastically of the beauties of just such a landscape. I determined to find them, and every minute of my next trip was a vivid pleasure. The difference? On those first trips I had lazily accepted sights that I could not possibly miss. When I began really to use my eyes I was thrilled by color and line I had never seen, by tall purple grasses, by a symphony of browns, by the thick brooding quietness. The uplift and sense of power I got were of the essence of romance.

Out of such experiences comes a passionate rebellion against a realism which seeks to make us walk sedately in a world where nothing but facts and common sense matters. Science may feed us, and the realistic temper may toughen our minds. But if we are born with a hankering for hyacinths we are likely sometimes to sicken on bread.

An ELECTRIC FAN in a cabinet equipped with bottles of a special type will waft your choice of aromas about the room—anything from a deodorant to a favorite perfume. Available also is a balsam odor, said to be good for hay fever; and an ozone odor as an antidote for cooking and smoking fumes.—*Review of Reviews*

The Man Behind "The Arabian Nights"

Condensed from The Elks Magazine

GEORGE CREEL

ALTHOUGH everybody loves "The Arabian Nights," the man behind the book remains in shadow. Yet Richard Francis Burton, hawk-faced Irishman with eyes of flame, had a life more packed with color than any of the tales spun by the fair Scheherazade for her peevish sultan. Of the choice brotherhood of master adventurers, a fit mate for Marco Polo or Pizarro, Burton knew 29 languages as though they were his own, and an equal number of dialects; no *maître d'armes* in all Europe could stand against him with a rapier; a soldier and poet, he was also a famous geographer. The stories that make up "The Arabian Nights," as a matter of fact, were mere by-products of dangerous journeys that carried Burton deep into the Dark Continent, for he told them first to earn hospitality or save his life while penetrating the hidden mysteries of Somaliland. Wild Bedouins, barbarous Somalis, mutinous bearers, were won to friendship as the bearded giant regaled them with the exploits of Haroun-al-Raschid and the rest.

There must have been a gypsy dash in Burton's blood, for not only did he love wandering, but he had the swart coloring that enabled him to pass as Pathan, Persian or Arab. As a youngster in the Bombay army, it was his delight to strap on the pack of a native peddler and spend weeks in the bazaars, chatting with the men, making eyes at the girls and soaking up the knowledge that was to make him the greatest Orientalist of all time.

He was the first white man to enter the holy city of Mecca, where death would have been the penalty for discovery. Disguised as an Afghan—the Haji Abdullah—the young Irishman sailed up the Red Sea with a horde of pilgrims, made the tedious camel ride through mountain passes, bawled his prayers before the tomb of Mahomet at Medina, in Mecca made the dreary round of shrines, jostled by sweating thousands—yet never was there a suspicion that the turban of the pious Haji Abdullah concealed an accursed Frank. Burton's Arabic, Persian, Hindustani and Turkish were without fault, he made no mistake in the complicated Mahometan ritual, and such was his familiarity with the Koran that even learned elders called upon him to settle religious disputes.

Fired by this tremendous experience, Burton dreamed of exploration that would open up the recesses of Africa, ending the ignorance of 2000 years, and in 1854 he set out to enter Somaliland. He went as an Arab merchant, and there were four months during which the world gave him up as dead. A nightmare journey it must have been, of hunger and thirst, strange fevers and the menace of savage tribes. Ten days he spent in forbidden Harrar, a town with a language all its own and a sultan who had sworn that no white man should ever put foot inside the walls. But Burton laughed behind his great beard and rode forth with the same lordly air that had marked his entry. The return journey came close to being fatal, yet he staggered forward when his bearers died and camels dropped in their tracks.

On a second Somali expedition he received a javelin thrust through the jaw, but after an ill-fated attempt to win glory in the Crimea, he turned again to Africa, determined to find the sources of the Nile—an age-old quest in which Egyptians, Greeks and Romans had failed. Henry M. Stanley, following a blazed trail 15 years after Burton, was to spend $130,000 on a single expedition, but all the Royal Geographic Society allowed Burton was $5000. On June 14, 1857,

the shabby little expedition set out from Zanzibar and, while Captain John H. Speke marched at his side, Burton's broad shoulders bore the full responsibility. His was the endless task of bartering with tribal chieftains, and heartening the wretched bearers as they staggered through swamps and jungles. Mysterious maladies afflicted the two white men—sudden attacks of numbness almost paralytic in character, and spells of blindness. Nine months the caravan marched and suffered, but the end was ample compensation, for through the crystalline light of a spring morning, Burton looked down upon the cool waters of Lake Tanganyika and thrilled to the knowledge that he was the first European to reach its shore. For 30 days he sailed the lake in hollowed tree trunks for boats, buffeted by hurricanes and menaced by cannibal tribes. The survey proved that the Nile's sources were yet to be found, and Burton, eager to write down all that he had learned, turned the balance of the journey over to Speke, though personally superintending every detail. Why should the thought of treachery occur to him?

Six weeks passed and Speke returned, drunk with excitement, telling of a great sea that he had seen—a sea that he called Victoria Nyanza in honor of England's queen. Burton planned to confirm the report, but circumstances forbade. It was doubtul if enough of his money—he had spent $7000 of his private funds—remained to carry him back to the coast. Once again in Zanzibar, almost two years after their departure, Burton suffered a return of fever. Speke did not stay to tend him, but hurried back to England and not only announced himself as discoverer of the Nile's source, but took all the credit of the expedition, thrilling the public with lurid accounts of adventure.

What with paralysis, blindness and fever, Burton was near to death, and Speke's conduct pushed him nearer to the grave. It was not to be the end, however; and there came a time when Speke was called upon to face the benefactor that he had betrayed. At the encounter, the younger man, paling, turned and walked away. Later a messenger brought word of Speke's death. According to report he had gone hunting and lost his life through a gun's accidental discharge.

After visiting Brigham Young in Utah, and panning gold in California, Burton accepted the post of consul at Fernando Po, fever-ravaged island off Africa's west coast. Between times he explored the mysterious Cameroons.

Eventually England gave Burton the consulate at Damascus, and once again he was in a land that he knew and loved. He found time to explore the whole of unknown Syria, visiting ancient cities, determining the source of rivers and laying the foundations for geographers who were to follow him and claim full credit. Time after time he risked his life in Bedouin country. Rarely had he been more happy, yet all the while a storm was brewing.

Mrs. Burton, as it happened, was a religious fanatic, and no sooner was her husband installed in Damascus than she set about her self-appointed task of Christianizing all Islam. Slowly at first, but more and more swiftly, the ridiculous business rushed to its inevitable conclusion. The outraged Moslems turned away from Burton, who had been welcomed as their blood brother, and when resentment reached the point of an attempted assassination, the British government recalled him peremptorily.

Crushed and impoverished, life seemed to be at an end for the unhappy man, but an outcry from the press and public forced the government to give him another consulate. The Foreign Office buried him in Trieste. Even so, adventure still beckoned to Richard Burton. Ismail, Khedive of Egypt, conceived the idea that there were gold and jewels to be found in the land of Midian, and induced Burton to secure a leave of absence for the exploration. Once more in turban and flowing robes, he gave seven months to the work, scouring mountains and plain and bringing away great quantities of gold and silver ore and lumps of turquoise. He felt he had found a treasure house. Ill-fated man! Scarce had he returned to Cairo in triumph than Ismail was deposed, and Tewfik had neither money nor inclination for any Midian venture.

Back to Trieste Burton shambled. In the twilight of life, broken and needy, he turned to literature with a last desperate rush of energy. Always from his youth he had written tirelessly, book after book. Not one of them had made him money, and in despair he decided upon the completion of "The Arabian Nights," a work that had occupied his interest for more than 30 years.

It was on the pilgrimage to Mecca that Burton first heard the tales. They were, it is true, by no means new to Europe, but earlier translations were either abridgments, careful paraphrases or prodigies of expurgation. What Burton did was to give not only the whole treasury of Moslem folk lore, but a literal translation, together with copious annotations made possible by his extensive knowledge.

On publication, a roar of shocked protest went up, even though Burton had limited circulation to a comparatively small list of selected subscribers, but it was drowned out by the chorus of praise from the scholars of the world.

The indomitable man at once began the translation of a volume of Arabic couplets, "The Scented Garden," into which he meant to pour all his poetry and knowledge of the Orient. It was a race with death, and when he passed away on October 20, 1890, the last pages had just fallen from his hands. On the very night of her husband's burial, Mrs. Burton read the manuscript and horror possessed her. Burton himself had told a friend "The Arabian Nights" was a baby tale compared to this, but there was beauty in the verses, high spiritual values as well as Eastern sensualities, and accompanying notes embodied 30 years of research. But all Mrs. Burton saw was the "indecency," and she set a match to the pages and watched them burn. And so not even death could protect poor "Dick" Burton from the mischances that cursed his life. When he died with a smile of hope on his lips, his nearest and dearest destroyed the work that would have meant laurel on his tomb.

Keeping up with the World

Excerpts from a regular department in Collier's

Freling Foster

FINLAND is believed to be the only country that has abolished all unnecessary street noises. The law has silenced motor horns, streetcar bells, traffic whistles, hand organs and the cries of hucksters, newsboys and sidewalk orators; and a Sabbatarian calm prevails every day, even in the heart of Helsingfors.

IN JAPAN undressing in public is quite permissible. Passengers on railway trains frequently step into the aisles and change all their clothing.

Treasure Hunting

Condensed from The Yale Review

SAMUEL SCOVILLE, JR.

WHEN I have caught my first trout of the year and found my first bird's nest, then I feel that spring has indeed arrived.

To me a nest is always full of revealments of the personality of the birds who made it. There are also little mysteries about certain nests that even the most expert ornithologists have not yet fathomed. Why do crested flycatchers have to have a cast-off snake skin in their nests before they will lay in them? Why does a chipping sparrow use a hair mattress and a wren a feather bed? How do chimney swifts glue together their crescent-shaped nests, made of tiny twigs broken from the tops of dead trees while in full flight, in which they raise their broods in the dark? Why do long-billed marsh wrens build a number of dummy nests around the one which they finally use? There are a thousand other delightful oddities on the part of our little brothers of the air.

The month of May found me in the Barrens in southern New Jersey, where one day I wandered

along a brook which flowed between high banks of snowy sand. In midsummer along its slopes grow colonies of the rare threadleaved sundew, those carnivorous plants whose pink flowers flaunt above traps and gins made of long sticky hairs baited with drops of honey. Let an unwary insect alight to taste their sweetness and at once it is enmeshed by the hairs, which fold around it. These pink blossoms flaunting above the long line of dead and dying prisoners always make me think of that attractive lady mentioned in Proverbs— "whose house goes down to the chambers of death."

Farther along the stream I sat down upon a smooth carpet of pine needles to read. One never obtains the full flavor of a book until it is read in some hidden place with the perfume of flowers and the song of birds in the air. Then, as I sat there reading, leaning against the trunk of a pitch-pine, a little grating noise on the bank caught my ear, and I saw moving towards me across the snowy sand a Prince of the Barrens, a five-foot blacksnake.

With head up, his smooth body

flowed across the stones with a certain infernal dignity, and his tongue played around his grim mouth like a forked black flame.

I sat perfectly still, and he came on and on, his head held fully a foot above the ground, and slithered across first one of my legs and then the other. As he moved he turned his head from side to side, evidently on the alert, and once his flat, lidless, glittering eyes looked squarely into mine, yet he evidently did not recognize me as any living thing. I could see his lead-blue belly, the gunmetal black of his smooth scales, his milk-white chin and throat. When he had crossed my legs I stirred slightly. At the first movement he flashed across the sand like the flick of a whiplash and disappeared.

Earlier in the month four of us had made a "century run," during the bird migration, which involves the identifying of 100 different kinds of birds between dawn and dark. While on this run we skirted the famous Charlestown Woods outside of Haddonfield. From the depths of the woods we heard a frantic cawing of crows so fierce and prolonged that we were sure that those sky pirates were on the trail of an owl. So we plunged into the woods and soon saw a burly, round-headed bird flap through the air pursued by crows—it was a great-horned owl, seeking refuge in some thick tree.

As we came back to our trail, there was a quick scurrying in the underbrush as if some large animal had been disturbed, and out into the open flapped the black body of a turkey vulture. We realized that she must have been nesting nearby, but although we searched the woods carefully we found no trace of her nest.

A week or so later, early in June, we went back to the woods to make another search. We reached the spot where the vulture had flown up and hunted here and there for her nest. Ordinarily a vulture chooses a hollow log or a cave for a nesting place, but as there was none of these in the offing we knew that somewhere on the bare ground the grim bird's eggs awaited our finding. It seemed incredible that eggs so large could escape our search. Yet we quartered back and forth covering every foot of likely ground, and still there was no sign of any nest. At last, when we were almost ready to give up, one of the searchers discovered the eggs beneath the trunk of a dead Spanish oak raised by its branches some two feet from the ground. They were blotched with black, tobacco-brown, and pale gray, and were the size of a turkey's egg, and rested directly on the dry leaves without any semblance of a nest though the ground showed plainly the prints made by the heavy body of the brooding bird.

All about us were thickets of laurel, sweet pepper bush, and white azalea. As we stooped to examine the eggs, there came a sharp hiss above, and we looked up to see a great, dingy black bird with naked red head and malevolent eyes regarding us from a dead tree not

30 feet away. When we shouted at her, the mother vulture flapped heavily away only to drop down silently from mid-sky later and hiss threateningly at us from various trees near her eggs.

A friend of mine once found a vulture's nest in a hollow log. The ornithologist who crawls into a hollow log or a cave where a turkey vulture is nesting is taking great chances, for the bird's method of defense in such circumstances is to disgorge over the intruder all the carrion she may have eaten that day.

On the way back to the train we walked through a suburb in which there was a playground where a dozen children were disporting themselves on swings and slides under a few discouraged looking maples—about the last place in which one would expect to find any bird nesting. Yet as we approached the place, a humming-bird darted like a bullet from one of the trees to attack a passing grackle. In an instant the tiny, swift bird had reached her opponent, 20 times her size, and prodded him repeatedly with her long needle-like bill. The grackle made no attempt to defend himself but squawked with pain and flew away at full speed. The humming-bird gave him one final jab and buzzed back to the tree. We could see by her white throat that she was a female; her nest, looking like a tiny lichen-covered knot, was saddled to a limb about 15 feet from the ground. When the children had left the place, we took turns in climbing the tree and admiring the daintiest and smallest bird's nest to be found in our Eastern States. It was made of seed husks and plant down bound around with a tiny balloon of spider webs, and so thickly thatched on the outside with lichens that it seemed to be part of the bough to which it was fastened. Inside were two tiny white eggs. The opening of the nest was no larger than a 25 cent piece.

The finding of a humming-bird's nest is always an event. The nest is so difficult to see, and such an exquisite little jewel casket when found, that the discovery of one always gives me the feeling that I have suddenly stumbled upon a hidden treasure.

We reached our homes late that night tired and hungry, but thrilled with the recollections of the record day when we discovered sets of the largest and smallest birds' eggs to be found in this part of the United States.

Table Talk

A SOUTHERN WOMAN told us something only insiders know about selling live crawfish. Shaking a can she showed how quickly they became enraged and struck out with their claws. "See how they swell up?" she said. "We don't make much money selling a bucket of them when they're quiet. We do better when we shake them up and make them fighting mad. Then a few fill a bucket."

—*Food Industries*

Calling on a Cloud

Condensed from The Sportsman Pilot

DON ROSE

SOME years ago I was among those present on Pitcairn Field, near Philadelphia, when a pilot with nothing better to do caught sight of a storm cloud high in the sky and wondered what it would be like to fly in it. It was an ugly cloud, though deceitfully decorated at the edges with gold from the setting sun. Its shapes and shadows shifted as we watched, with some internal agony of unrest. Yet its changes were slow and majestic, so that it seemed legitimate to suppose that a fast airplane might fly safely among them.

The pilot, no doubt, should have known better. Since then he has flown far and often with the air mail and learned a decent respect for wind and weather. But on that summer's evening he could not resist the impulse to climb 5000 feet or so and poke his nose into a thunder cloud.

We watched him go up until he looked about as impressive as a horsefly trying to find an opening in the hide of the world's biggest elephant. We saw him turn head-on toward the cliff of cloud and vanish into it. And a few minutes later we saw him thrown out on his ear, upside down and in a general condition of aeronautical disorganization. He fell about two thousand feet before he collected his controls and found out which way was up, and landed later in a perceptibly chastened mood.

The moral of this tale is that those who go cloud-chasing should remember that there are clouds and clouds. Those that are on the point of falling apart with lashing rain had best be left alone. The gods of storm are no fit playmates for innocent pilots. The giant power of lightning and hurricane is likely to get rough with the best of airplanes.

But among the sporting experiences of the sky the exploration of suitable cloud country is too much neglected by those in search of beauty, thrill and novelty. They can find Fairyland there, a place that was far beyond reach of reality until the world put wings on machinery.

193

I am, of course, not suggesting that there is any special fun in flying through a fog, which is exactly the nature of the normal cloud from the inside. Such flying soon wipes the determined smile of pleased interest from the pale face of the passenger, and gives him an uncanny sensation of going nowhere in a foolish hurry.

The clouds that are worth visiting are those that lie sometimes around a summer sky in settled weather, drifting along like fantastic ships on an invisible sea. They are on their way to make trouble somewhere, but in the meantime they are quiet and approachable. There is sunshine all about them and they are shaped sharply and clearly.

On an August afternoon I noticed a dozen of them drifting calmly along the horizon, floating on the hazy heat of a true summer day. So did Harold Pitcairn, a real sportsman among pilots. It was his idea that we should pick out a cloud and pay it a visit. We selected one that was flat as a floor beneath, but was piled sky-high in shapes of sheer fantasy.

It took twenty minutes to fly from a dusty airport to the front doors of Fairyland. Down below lay a landscape of green and misty blue. But the cliffs of cloud seemed solid and loomed dangerously at our side as we raced along in their shadow. Nowhere else in the air was I ever so much aware of the breathless speed at which the airplane travels. Nothing but spaces covered and schedules kept will tell the ordinary air traveler that his chariot is eating up a mile every thirty seconds. So a genuine thrill awaits the excursionist to the cloud country. There is no peril in missing a corner of a cloud at 100 miles an hour, but the sensation of speed is real. It would not do to fly casually through the Ausable Chasm or down Park Avenue in New York City, but there is a comparable excitement in scooting at full speed through the canyons of a thunder cloud. And to make matters more interesting my intrepid pilot turned suddenly sideways and headed full-tilt for a snow-white wall that looked substantial enough to discourage an avalanche.

We hit it head-on and it didn't hurt. In a split second we were in the middle of nowhere, wrapped around in wet smoke, tearing the stuffing out of the cloud and tossing the pieces into the slip-stream.

What lies in the heart of a thunder cloud is nothing to be told with words. An incredible and magical landscape is hidden there, snow-white in the full sun and tinted with cool color in the shadows. There are smooth places that seem to invite a landing and hillsides tumbled in fantastic disorder; there are sheer cliffs with caves cut deep into their sides; there are towers thrust high into the sky and snowy peaks too steep to be compared to mountains. The core of the cloud is like a giant's totem-pole, curiously and playfully carved in patterns beyond the imagination of architecture. And here and there the cloud floor thins to nothing, and far below is the patterned earth —a world that is easily forgotten in the mood and magic of this Fairyland of the sky.

Yet there is nothing there except an illusion fashioned of water and hot weather. It will be gone by nightfall, for it is moving slowly to join the other heaps of cloud. Somewhere they will come together and be smashed to pieces by wind and lightning. A sudden upheaval in the central column of the cloud suggests as much, so a prudent pilot decides to go home, satisfied with the discovery that amusement and adventure are not far away for those who fly with imagination. Cloud-flying is fascinating fun and its pleasures are still unspoiled by competition and crowding. A man in a plane can have a cloud to himself, and the exclusive enjoyment of its brief beauties. Or he can thrill his friends by showing them something that no human eye had seen before men learned to fly. The place is on none of the airways and is served by no transport schedules, but it is close at hand for those who will take the trouble to visit it by air.

Why Not Adopt More Generally?

AGAINST THE opposition of practically every newspaper and politician in the state, Senator George Norris persuaded Nebraska to adopt a one-house (unicameral) legislature. The benefits he explains thus:

"The outstanding evil of the bicameral system is that it enables politicians to escape responsibility for their official acts. Each house is able to pass the buck to the other, while a conference committee, acting behind closed doors and without any record being made of their votes, really does the dirty work. The most important decisions often are made by five or six men not elected for that particular purpose and whose names usually go unnoticed by the public."

Nebraska's new laws will be made by 43 legislators. They meet every two years, unless called by the governor or themselves to special sessions. However frequently they assemble, they draw only $872.90 a year, reducing the total legislative salary bill about 30 percent, not counting the savings in salaries for clerks, pages, doorkeepers, etc., of a discontinued chamber.

The new unicameral legislators are elected on non-partisan ballots, since party circles for voting straight tickets were taken off Nebraska's ballot two years ago. Each legislator is selected on his own platform.

Nebraska revived the whole unicameral movement. More than half the states have now introduced measures for one-house legislatures, and New York and New Jersey have special commissions studying the subject.—Adapted from *Time* and *The Literary Digest*

On Being Deaf

Condensed from The American Mercury

WARREN M. SMALTZ

How does it feel to be deaf?" new acquaintances often ask me. I have a ready reply. "Oh, quite exhilarating," I tell them.

They laugh feebly, supposing I am trying to be funny. But though they can see only pathos in deafness, my reply is reasonably sincere; for I have discovered to my own satisfaction that silence is not a total calamity and that it tends, moreover, to lead into diverting situations.

Of course, my deafness carries with it certain definite disadvantages. For one thing, my choice of possible occupations is seriously circumscribed. My opportunities for preferment are fewer. I find it harder to strike up satisfying intimacies and friendships; and there is a profound sense of loss in being unable to hear any form of melody.

There are other disabilities, but in spite of them I laugh at silence. Or, more accurately, I find myself precipitated repeatedly into situations that compel my risibilities.

To illustrate, I was a visitor, alone, in a mid-Western city some years ago, and a Sunday afternoon found me strolling the sidewalks, and wondering dismally how to pass a dull day. Arrived at a street intersection, I was about to cross over when a tap on my shoulder made me turn about to confront a policeman. He said something or other, which as nearly as I could judge was a casual remark. So I nodded my head in friendly agreement and smiled pleasantly, exactly as if I understood him. Then I started again to cross the street.

This time a more emphatic tap halted me. He spoke again, but still I failed to comprehend. However, I knew my little pantomime well: I nodded and smiled even more engagingly than before, and essayed once more to cross the street. With disconcerting quickness I was firmly grasped and whisked in a patrol wagon to a police station. It developed that I had obstinately persisted in an attempt to commit a traffic violation.

"Do you know that you must obey the lights here, sir?" the officer had inquired, very civilly. To which I had nodded affirmatively, and attempted to proceed. "Here you! Do you think you can get away with that?" he had next demanded, bristling.

Again I had nodded, with extra emphasis, and had smiled upon him in a way which he misinterpreted. As I stepped off the curb for the third time, my arrest followed.

The joke was undoubtedly on me, and we all enjoyed a satisfying laugh. A plain clothes man off duty suggested a café, and my problem of how to pass a dull afternoon was solved.

Perhaps you wonder why, when the officer first addressed me, I did not tell him at once that I was deaf, and thus avoid the ensuing complications. That was because of a peculiar psychology. The deaf man's affliction is a very real thing, but it is mercifully concealed from the casual gaze. That in itself is a vast comfort and he tries diligently to improve upon it.

Therein lies the motive which impels the deaf to grasp at so illusive an art as lip-reading. The accomplished lip-reader whose proficiency is not due to a considerable amount of residual hearing is merely an amazingly good guesser. The fundamental fact is that he can hope at most to seize upon two or three basic words in a spoken sentence. The rest he must supply himself as best he can, by intuition, or by sheer good luck.

The luck is not always good, however. During an interview, a newspaper reporter asked me one question in particular that will linger long in memory. "Do you drink?" he inquired blandly. "Life," I answered impressively, "would be intolerable to a deaf man without it."

I was stunned when this conversation appeared in the paper. As a lip-reader I had innocently supposed that he had asked me merely, "Do you *read?*"

So far as visible movement of the lips is concerned, there is not a particle of difference between the words *drink* and *read* when casually uttered, although they sound so dissimilar to the ear. But what is more to the point, the number of such words in the language is truly confounding.

The general public knows surprisingly little about the deaf. Consider the ingenuity with which deaf-mutes habitually surmount the ordinary obstacles in their daily existence. I am often questioned about so simple a matter as the door bell: I open my door in answer to a ring, and am confronted by a stranger. He presents a vacuum cleaner, or a clothes brush, and discourses fluently.

I interrupt to tell him that I am totally deaf and cannot hear a word. He is nonplussed. Suspiciously he eyes me from head to foot. "Say, if you are deaf, then how did you hear me ring your door bell?" he demands triumphantly.

I close the door upon him and laugh softly. The answer is, of course, that I did not hear the bell. I have contrived a little arrangement of my own. When my bell button is pushed it lights a number of incandescent bulbs distributed at strategic places throughout the house, and their flash is infallibly visible. There are other arrangements that are equally adequate, such as the dropping of a weight upon the floor, or the waving of a bright-colored cloth.

An understandable curiosity requires that something should be said about the little understood sign language. I have met deaf travelers from Russia, from Turkey and from China, and although they did not know a syllable of English, and I was likewise ignorant of their national tongues, yet we conversed together with satisfying ease. This was possible because the sign language is ideographic; its facile gestures do not represent words but mental images or pictures. Some of the signs are pure pantomime. Expertly used, the language conveys meaning with the vividness of the motion picture.

Educators of the deaf have united to oppose the extension of the language, believing that it is detrimental to the acquisition of good English, and nowhere is it now formally taught. In spite of this it is used the world over, wherever genuinely deaf people congregate.

It is difficult for the person with normal hearing to realize that the deaf cannot hear their own voices. In the stress of great mental excitement they are apt to produce strange throaty sounds without being at all aware of the fact. A little company of mutes was once assembled in a hotel bedroom, conversing animatedly in the sign language. Meanwhile, a strange bedlam of noises issued from their throats.

Outside in the hallway a colored porter happened to be passing and he paused in surprise before their door. There were gruesome grunts, weird whistles, and ghoulish moans such as he had never dreamed existed, and he screwed up his courage to investigate.

Gently he rapped upon the door. There was no response and the unearthly sounds continued undiminished. He knocked a second time with more insistence, and still the medley assailed his ears through the unopened door. Abruptly the true explanation of the phenomenon dawned upon him, so he thought. He dashed down the stairs and into the lobby, and breathlessly confronted a startled clerk.

"Oh Lawd, Lawd!" he gasped with starting eyes. "Ghosts!"

A NEW development of infrared photography brings out clearly the words on valuable papers that have been so completely blackened by fire that the human eye can distinguish neither writing nor printing on them.—N. Y. *Herald Tribune*

Pitchmen

Condensed from Nation's Business

EARL CHAPIN MAY

A FEW months ago in my home town, Rochelle, Ill., an oratorical gentleman stood in the rear end of a motor car and sold $100 worth of razor blades in three hours. He performed this miracle of merchandising in spite of the fact that at least six stores within two blocks were selling very good razor blades. He was a persuasive gentleman. Among his many cash customers was Colonel Kepner, our auctioneer. Three times in the course of that demonstration of salesmanship Colonel Kepner purchased razor blades. Colonel Kepner makes a good living by selling, in the open, oratorically. The conquest of Colonel Kepner completed the miracle performed by the visiting pitchman, one of a hundred thousand merchandisers who travel this fair land of ours.

Properly speaking, a pitchman is one who sells his own merchandise, which he owns by right of personal manufacture or cash purchase, to cash customers whom he finds on the streets. He is a pitchman because he pitches his tent, metaphorically, wherever he finds an opportunity and folds it and steals away when lack of business or the law's unfriendliness urges him to seek another temporary abiding place. He is an Arab among merchandisers. His stock in trade is his "joint." If he is numbered among the humbler members of his fraternity and "makes his pitch" with his "joint" in a satchel or "keister" mounted on a folding tripod or "tripes" he is a "low pitchman." If he works from a motor car he is a "high pitchman," member of the upper class.

Most of these free lance traveling merchants are legitimate; that is, their wares are nearly as good as they are said to be. It is true that the fountain pen you may purchase from pitchmen at a county fair for from 25 to 50 cents cost the pitchmen ten cents or so. It is also true that in his selling demonstration he jabs his pen point into a block of wood, just to show the pen point's permanency—only the block of wood is peculiarly nonresisting. It is also true that the imported pearls he offers to you at two dollars per

199

string cost him, wholesale, only $1.56 per dozen strings. But he must operate on a wide margin to cover his uncertain overhead.

But the crooked "jam sale" is not legitimate. The jam artist starts his pitch by selling a few articles to assistants known as shillabers. Then, perhaps, he sells some watches. Each watch is a "lumpy" —it looks like something of value but is pure shoddy. He hands these out at two dollars each, with the promise to refund the money if the customer is dissatisfied. Then he disappears suddenly, while the suckers sneak away to avoid their neighbor's merriment.

These jam sales make it hard for straight-shooting pitchmen, those who repeat in trade territory annually. Hence they have two national organizations, the National Pitchmen's and Salesmen's Protective Organization, with lodges in various cities and headquarters in Los Angeles, and a similar organization with headquarters in Cincinnati, both working to discourage jam sales, and "open" towns which have been closed to pitchmen. In theory these two organizations are the clearing houses for trade information. In reality much of such information comes by word of mouth or by communications to the *Billboard* which carries a department known as "Pipes for Pitchmen" which is edited by Gasoline Bill Baker. Through the *Billboard* the boys get much guidance. G. T. Hylan sends a postcard to Baker "infoing" him that there is a big tobacco crop around Wilming-

ton, N. C., and that nearby towns are "tip top now." W. P. Darker "pipes" that he met 37 of the boys working on Maxwell Street, Chicago, and that all were doing well.

The med shows still cater to the populace. Some are on trucks and carry a small vaudeville company which entertains the customers before the lecturer pitches on the healing qualities of the roots, barks and herbs gathered by wise though untutored savages. But the rank and file of the pitchmen's army works from tripes and keisters on the streets, selling small merchandise purchased from supply houses. There is no credit in the pitchmen's business. Pitchmen buy and sell for cash.

Fountain pens are their favorites largely because they are handled easily and there seems to be a certain mystery about a fountain pen. The buyers do not know what is inside of it and manufacturers warn them not to investigate. Other specialties are potato and apple peelers; "white-stones"—glass diamonds backed with mercury; Chinese lily bulbs; "wipes" or handkerchiefs; "shivs" or knives; "leather" or billfolds.

Pitchmen, with their tripes and keisters and their adventurous, itinerant merchandising, are fattening the bank rolls of our generals of industry. Their turnovers run into millions of dollars annually. The business regularly supports many factories of respectable magnitude, and many other factories have turned to pitchmen to dispose of articles after other outlets were "dead" for them. Among my pitchmen friends is a millionaire who sold his system of shorthand in that way until he got into larger merchandising.

The mammoth toy industry has never ignored the gentlemen of the tripes and keister. More than one now popular dancing doll or similar novelty is in the stores because manufacturers first quoted attractive sales prices to pitchmen.

Sometimes a manufacturer moves a sticking article by advertising for pitchmen as demonstrators, or actually goes out into the highways and byways and gathers them into store aisles or display windows. Such recruits are usually paid a salary plus a bonus.

One of these old timers joined me in visiting a very high pitch in New York this year. It was a medical or health culture pitch with gold letters on the front windows. But the ladies and gentlemen who were pitching called themselves "demonstrators," much to the old timer's disgust. He clings to his sidewalk pitch.

Each successful pitchman has personality. To the attention-arresting value of this personality he adds oratory plus a demonstration of the appliance or book he sells. He trades on human curiosity

and on that type of mob psychology which causes some to pause because others pause. And he "closes" or "turns the joint"—turns from oratory to cash collecting—instinctively.

My own impression, after many years of acquaintance, is that pitchmen are misguided selling geniuses. Some 90 percent of pitchmen die in want. They would end their days in prosperity if they would only stay with established houses.

But they cannot conquer their excess of individuality. They are too proud of being on their own. In storm and stress, across the continent, they flivver after the salesman's dollar. If they run out of gas they wait until another pitchman comes along, borrow a "five-spot"—and start again.

I discussed this with Dad Wicks one day. Dad has been pitching for half a century.

"I'm as good as I was when I was a kid," he proudly replied to my pessimism. "Pitchmen have put over the old dime bank, the Pigs in Clover and many another specialty that has stuck in the factories because stores would not take up with them. Some day I'll get hold of a specialty that'll make *me* a captain of industry."

You have to hand it to pitchmen for their incurable optimism.

AN ELECTRIC GLOVE, insulated to the wearer's hand, provides police with an effective means of subduing criminals who resist arrest. A small battery and spark coil, carried on the hip, produce high voltage; and a touch with the glove itself paralyzes temporarily but, unlike the policeman's club, leaves no after effects.

—*Popular Science Monthly*

For Ignoble Pacifism

Condensed from Harper's Magazine

GERALD W. JOHNSON

WHEN the late unpleasantness broke out in Europe, I toured France as a member of Pershing's personally-conducted party. I admit I didn't win the War. I merely attended it. All that I saw was the "lighter side."

Still, I have a fairly intimate knowledge of the humorous incidents that characterize an active campaign. I have experienced the delights of marching under a full pack with flu shaking my bones. I know what a merry jest it is to have your fingers frost-bitten until the flesh comes sloughing off, and how it feels to go three months without a bath, while *pediculus vestimenti* thrives and increases marvelously. I know how laughable it is to have shells land close enough to jar the ground under your feet, and I know the pleasure of having to be servile to a brutal officer whom I would kick down the steps if he tried to enter my house in time of peace. I have seen burial parties and hospital trains. Perhaps I am little more than a pseudo-

veteran. But I do know something about war, and I do not like it.

Yet when anyone accuses me of being a pacifist, I deny the soft impeachment. The existing pacifist organizations are far too noble for me. If I could find a downright ignoble one I might join it.

Mind you, I have no objection to fighting. I know by experience that a first-class fist-and-skull argument frequently can

Cleanse the stuff'd bosom of that
    perilous stuff
Which weighs upon the heart.

But what has modern war to do with fighting? Although I know hundreds of veterans, I have never yet encountered one who had stood up to a German, man to man. Pumping the bolt of a Springfield rifle with nothing for a target but some distant whiffs of dust, or feeding shells into a 75, hour after hour, with only a set of coördinates for guidance is not the sort of fighting that is good for a man. A warm appreciation of the value of belligerence is not at all inconsistent with pacifism, as regards organized warfare.

The people who form pacifist organizations are stuffed with high moral principles, and it is precisely on high moral principles that all major wars are fought. As regards the late War, it is pretty generally understood now that everybody was right; and all that is needed to close the incident is for a new Pish-Tush to skip off the stage singing,

And we are right, I think you'll say,
To argue in this kind of way.
   And I am right,
   And you are right,
And all is right—too-looral-lay!

Yet the dead remain dead, and the fact that the War was fought on the highest principles doesn't alter the fact that it cost enormously more than it was worth.

I believe my objection to war is deeper rooted than that of most of the bishops and ladies who direct our pacifist organizations. After all, ignoble principles are not easily controverted.

Suppose governments threw moral principles overboard altogether and never waged a war save on plainly ignoble motives—what would happen? Why it is clear that nobody would ever fight anybody else who could fight back; for if you pick an opponent who can fight, under modern conditions no one can hope to win a tithe of what the fight will cost him.

To illustrate, let us suppose that we fell into an argument with Japan over the possession of some such scrap of the earth's surface

as the Island of Yap. As long as statesmen were governed by the ignoble sentiment of Safety First there could be no question of war. Everyone would have in mind the fact that the price of a couple of broadsides from the battle fleet would be more than the whole place is worth. But who can imagine that they would be so guided? As soon as the crisis became acute the question of relative values would be abandoned to give place to the high moral principle of protection of the nation's dignity, which cannot, of course, be measured in money. And we should be betrayed into the imbecility of fighting a war over Yap.

Pacifism, thoroughly sound and sensible if based upon ignoble sentiments, becomes a flat denial of plain facts once it becomes involved with high moral principles. To repudiate wars against strong enemies on the ground that it is idiotic to fight a strong nation is thoroughly sensible, if unromantic. But to repudiate war in general on the ground that it is always wasteful is simply silly. In all the world there exists no great nation that has not been built up by wars which brought in more than they cost and, therefore, were paying investments. The United States, to be specific, has fought 103 wars. The vast majority of these, so far from being silly and wasteful, were highly profitable, since they secured from the Indians our continental domain, which is worth infinitely more than all they cost. To deny that we, like other world powers, have profited exceedingly by war is to deny the plain fact.

I like to toy with the idea of a pacifist organization got up by no idealist, but by a lewd fellow of the baser sort. It would have for its first objective the absolute prohibition of war under any circumstances against people who can fight. It would have for its second objective the absolute prohibition of conscription. This would compel the government to offer soldiers in the ranks a reward somewhat commensurate with the risk they run. (If the Government planned a campaign against Mexico, for instance, it could undoubtedly raise half a million men by offering every survivor 100 acres of Mexican land after the conquest.) Nobody would be compelled, then, to take part in a conquest unless he felt like gambling his life against the stakes offered. Finally, this organization would strive to fix the penalty of death for any statesman who, whether by error or by design, entered into a war which after five years from the date of the beginning of hostilities was still unprofitable.

This scheme, I assert without fear of successful contradiction, is ignoble in every detail. There is not a moral principle in it anywhere. But the way it would head off wars cannot, in my opinion, be approached by any of the methods proposed by any of the existing pacifist organizations.

Conquest based on sound economic considerations never has been restrained. Probably it never will be even in the future. But if we had to pay an army adequately for its services, we would go into a country frankly as conquerors who were after the money, and not as agents of the higher civilization intent on inculcating high moral principles in the backward people with the aid of shrapnel, poison gas, and machine guns. Doubtless it is a quaint and old-fashioned prejudice that makes the ignoble pacifists object to their country's lying like Munchausen whenever it goes forth to war; but the fact remains that they do object.

The present opposition to all wars whatever is not getting very far; but I believe that immense numbers of people could be interested in a pacifism that set some limits to its nobility. No war at all may be the ideal. But as a practical program why should we not, to begin with, demand fewer wars and franker ones, smaller and sounder wars, murder for profit, not for pleasure? For surely it is better to be a hijacker than a sadist.

For the sake of peace and quiet in your home when Junior practices his music, a silent piano and a silent violin have been invented. The playing is audible only to the instructor and his pupil, through earphones.—W. E. Farbstein

Sermon in Skulls

Condensed from The Virginia Quarterly

J. C. FURNAS

ABOUT a century and a half ago a Viennese physician named Gall gave an odd party in the back-kitchen of his respectable house. He invited as his guests all the coachmen, footmen, lady's maids and cooks in the neighborhood who could get leave for the evening. Food and drink were plentiful and, as their embarrassment wore off, their earnest host began to ask them personal questions about one another. Was this man particularly quarrelsome? Was that one particularly timid? As soon as he had arrived at a fair notion of the varying degrees of pugnacity among his guests, he made them line up on opposite sides of the room, fighters on one side, milksops on the other. Then he solemnly produced a set of formidable instruments and measured their skulls. When he finally retired to his library, he had overwhelming evidence that the heads of pugnacious people are markedly wide between the ears.

Dr. Gall was engaged in found-

ing the science of phrenology. All that remains of it now is the mumbled patter of an occasional cheap-jack charlatan with a colored chart of the head displayed outside a shabby room and a standard charge of 50 cents for "readings." Dead as it is, it did not die in vain. Having been a serious popular infection, it prepared the way for similar seizures to follow.

At the height of its glory—say in 1840—phrenology was a fascinating and imposing theory to the effect that you could tell what went on inside a living head by inspecting the outside of it. It combined a fortunate superficiality and an extreme simplicity with the impressive thunder of a scientific-sounding vocabulary which reverberated to great effect in the popular fancy. Briefly, it taught that each function of the brain could be definitely localized in a specific region of its surface, and that the comparative size and development of these regions indicated the character of the person who lived inside. Dissection was fortunately unnecessary, since the skull always adapted its shape to fit the brain it contained. The various functions had grand names such as Amativeness, Self-Esteem, Benevolence, Destructiveness, Philoprogenitiveness, the sum of them amounting to the whole human personality.

The whole thing stood and fell on whether or not any such exact localization was possible. The opponents of phrenology flatly denied it. Yet, with the reservation that a diseased condition might cause abnormal activity in an organ, the phrenologists made out a fair case for their premises, certainly too good a case for any layman to dispute.

The United States, of course, became a happy hunting-ground for the phrenologist as soon as Americans were aware of the birth of this new science. Spurzheim, the Apostle Paul of the movement, who took Gall's theories to the world at large, not without distortion, brought phrenology to Boston in the early '30s. From this intellectual center it spread as rapidly as newspapers and primitive railways could carry it.

During a visit to Charlestown prison, Dr. Spurzheim expressed surprise that one prisoner in the large and gratifying collection should ever have committed a crime. His skull, he pointed out, was strikingly non-criminal. The whole thing might have passed for commendable frankness on the phrenologist's part if, shortly afterward, the man had not been released on new evidence which proved his innocence beyond cavil.

Mr. O. S. Fowler, practical phrenologist, was waited upon by a committee of New Jersey clergymen with an anonymous skull for his description of its former tenant's disposition. He shook his head over it in grief at so much depravity and pronounced it to have belonged to "a thief who would murder for money; . . . seductive if not licentious; . . . completely destitute of moral principle; . . . makes pretentions to religion." Miraculous, said the wondering clergymen; it was the skull of a young hired man who had murdered his employers in Morristown and made off with their valuables. He had needed money in order to marry a rustic sweetheart, and, during his trial, had given agonized accounts of the religious struggles he had gone through while planning the deed.

After Spurzheim's death, Mr. George Combe was the Number One phrenologist of the world. In criminology Mr. Combe was a veritable John crying in the wilderness. He told his audiences that criminals (most of whom phrenology found to be deficient in moral organs and over-developed in animal organs) "are incapable of resisting temptation to crime presented by ordinary society—that they are moral patients and should not be punished but restrained." This was an amazing doctrine to most of his hearers. He was unmistakably denying that criminals are morally responsible for their anti-social behavior. He was presenting the criminal to society as a pathological case, perhaps incurable, but certainly exempt from reprobation. It is hardly necessary to point out that such doctrines dig broad foundations for that modern criminology which, in the persons of literary wardens and humanitarian societies, holds the criminal to be primarily a sick man.

Yet the closest parallels between our times and the hey-day of phrenology do not appear until our modern psychology comes up for measurement. There is the case of a gentleman who came to L. N. Fowler with a miserable soreness in the back and crown of his head, after conventional physicians had given him up to his inexplicable sufferings. Mr. Fowler inspected him, ascertained that he was married, and then took his patient's breath by informing him that he undoubtedly owed his pains to being jealous of his wife. The patient admitted in amazement that his jealousy of his wife was without foundation, after Mr. Fowler had told him that it was only his own unsatisfied Amativeness which produced that jealousy. This explanation sent the victim of bad judgment away satisfied. It verges miraculously near modern psychology.

The parallel runs still farther afield. All those classifications and aptitudes which modern education seeks to discover through intelligence tests or through allowing the child to regulate its own curriculum were to be discovered directly by the practice of phrenology. No longer would the deviltries of a small boy in school be attributed to natural perversity.

The size of his organ of Destructiveness would make it evident that he needed the privilege of sawing wood in the school-cellar for three hours a day. No longer would potential engineers be crammed with the classics or educated for law. And the business firms who employ psychiatrists in their personnel staffs had their long-past prototype in a London manufacturer who selected his workmen on phrenological considerations.

Mr. Combe's farewell gesture to the United States was a ponderous lecture on all the ways of turning the new knowledge to account. What potentialities existed in education, criminology, business and personal problems, has already been touched on. Of the field of politics he had much to say. "Some persons," he said, "appear to conceive liberty to consist in the privilege of unlimited exercise of the animal propensities. The head of Liberty is the very personification of this idea. She is a female figure with a villainously small, low and retreating forehead, deficient moral organs. . . . Liberty, as I should draw her, would possess large moral and intellectual organs. I should arrange her hair in simple elegance, and imprint serene enjoyment, benignity, and wisdom on her brow. Such alone is the liberty after which you should aspire." After which sermon in skulls, he turned to the practical application of phrenology to politics.

And phrenology was an unerring method of probing the inmost nature of the gentlemen who offered themselves for public office. Each candidate's character was writ large on his cranium. Once it was decided what qualities were desirable in a president or a town-marshal, the electorate had merely to go out and find a man to match a formula, and the testimony of the skilled phrenologist would be the criterion of selection.

No one has yet bothered to apply the findings of analytical psychology to politics, so that here one parallel extends beyond the other. Everywhere else—in education, criminology, sociology, personal relations—"bumpology" made straight the way for these modern notions which apply the implications of science to personalities.

It is disquieting to observe that the reaction of one's lay ancestors toward the superficial analysis and pretentious jargon of phrenology is so nearly the same as their descendants' attitude toward a different set of hypotheses. It makes one suspect that the world is prone to hanker after any hypothesis which makes it possible to deny free will for oneself and pigeonhole one's fellow-men. What is more, the public appears to be incapable of reserving judgment. It accepts the new revelation today and puts it to work tomorrow—phrenology or psycho-analysis.

Presently perhaps, if endocrinology develops its apparent promise, glands will have replaced bumps and complexes alike in popular favor. Intelligence tests will give way to analyses of blood and basal metabolism, and criminals and school children will be regarded as chemical formulæ in want of efficient balance, rather than as emotional tangles in need of unravelling. Yet even in the height of his glory, someone should whisper in the endocrinologist's ear that he would not be such an eminent social force if the intellectual public did not, now and again, mistake its need to believe for the scientific demonstration that it cannot understand or assay. Bumps yesterday—complexes today—perhaps glands tomorrow. *Plus ça change, plus c'est la même chose.*

Keeping up with the World

Excerpts from a regular department in Collier's

Freling Foster

ONE OF Europe's latest automobile developments is a luminous motorcar which is coated with phosphorescent paint and can be seen at night for half a mile. . . . A new Yankee invention is a radio alarm system for houses that, when turned on at night, creates a sensitive electrical zone around the exterior of the dwelling, several feet deep. When an intruder steps into this "field," the alarm sounds and floodlights brightly illuminate the walls and yards. Users fearing that their power lines may be cut can connect the device to a storage battery.

Spring Lamb

Condensed from Harper's Magazine

VIRGINIA BLACK

E HAD had no early rains and the weather was cold and frosty. Our ewes were old, but we had not had money enough to replace them. We had thought that with luck they might bring us another lamb crop in the spring. And our luck had been no rain and, therefore, no feed.

Jim rode the range every day, looking for the ewes that had fallen down and were too weak to get up. He would carry them in across his saddle and put them in the sheds and feed them the precious hay that we had bought at $30 a ton—on borrowed money. Every morning and every night it was necessary to lift them one by one and hold them on their legs while they obediently answered the calls of nature. "They're not worth the trouble," I raged, staring at their meek silly faces. "I don't believe they'll ever have lambs."

"Maybe not," Jim said wearily, "but I can't just let the old girls die. I'll save a certain percentage."

By lambing time we had about 150 of these hospital cases, and then the worst possible thing happened—a cold, heavy storm. Icy winds tore over the hills, and rain fell in merciless sheets, beating the dry earth to mud. Weather like that at lambing time!

When the rain began Jim stood at the kitchen window and watched the pepperwoods on the hill lashing about in the gale. He said, "Not one lamb could live through this. We'll have to bring in the sheep and lamb in the sheds."

"But we haven't enough feed."

Jim sighed. "I guess I'd better go down to the First National right now and see if I can borrow another thousand for hay and grain." He started out with all four chains on the little roadster, and I saw the wind tear the battered old top off the car just as it reached the corner of the field. He got back late that night, stiff with wet and cold. But he had the thousand and the feed had been ordered.

The drive next morning proved to be a very slow one. The sheep stood together in the timber and refused to leave this scant shelter to come out into the storm. We could not let the dogs force them because the ewes were so heavy with lamb. Some of the lambs had already begun to come and these had to be left behind with their mothers to be brought in separately.

We finally got a large bunch into the corrals and began at once the task of sorting and segregating in the chilling rain and slush. I think I have never seen sheep so soaked and wretched. The ewes kept falling down in the mire and would lie there helpless, kicking feebly like overturned beetles.

We had to separate immediately the ewes about to lamb so that Jim might give them special attention. Also many of them, weak from exposure and starvation, had been unable to bring forth their lambs and were carrying them dead. I knew that Jim would be up all night operating on these poor things and that I should have to stand by, faint with disgust, but prompt to supply forceps and douches of warm lysol.

Over the din of the milling sheep in the corrals came a sudden loud panic of bleating. I saw Jim kneel in a corner of the corral, frantically pulling at a pile of ewes heaped there.

"They're dead," he gasped. "Dead, and it's my fault. I let the dogs crowd them. And they got piled in this corner. Smothered. Thirty or forty of them." Those limp bodies were still warm, but nothing could make them breathe again. We had bought them when sheep were high—$15 a head. Of course at present they were not worth $3 in the market. But to us they were still $15 a head.

All that night, all the next day, all the next night we worked with the ewes in the stinking sheds. Our backs ached, our eyes burned, and our feet were numb. No stops for sleep or fresh clothes. No real meals; just coffee and hasty sandwiches. We had whiskey there, too, but that was not for us. That was for the lambs that we brought in half drowned from the hills. We had them all about the stove in the stifling heat of a special little shed we called the "orphanage." Beside the whiskey on the shelf were cases of canned milk, also for the lambs. Feeding and reviving these exhausted babies was my especial job.

First I gave each one a hot bath in a tub. Then I rolled him up in feed sacks, and gave him a little whiskey and hot water. If he was still alive when I next got around to him he got a drink of warm milk from a bottle. My chief remembrance of that mad winter is the suffocating, sickening odor of the lambing sheds, and the rows of supine indifferent lambs in their sacks about the stove.

I had to revive each lamb before his mother completely forgot him, which she would surely do if she did not get him back in an hour or so. It was a happy moment when I could bring one of the little beasts on his feet and see him shake himself, instead of falling down, and carry him into the pen of unattached mothers to be claimed.

Then would follow a discouraging proceeding. The ewes would heartlessly butt him over, and I would watch that tiny strength knocked right out of him. With amazing fortitude he would struggle to his feet each time and bleat for his mother. If she finally noticed his presence, smelled him suspiciously to identify him, and then tenderly allowed him to claim his dinner, I decided that there was no lovelier sight in the world.

She wouldn't have known him unless she could smell him, and because of that fact adoptions can be brought about. I find a ewe standing over her still-born lamb, anxiously and stupidly expecting some miracle to bring it back to life. I become that miracle. I put the lamb on a feed sack and drag it at the end of a long rope into the shed, slowly, so that the ewe may follow. In the shed Jim skins the lamb, and drapes the dead lamb's hide over an orphan lamb, tying it with cord across his little chest and under his belly. He looks ridiculous. We place him near the ewe and retreat to a distance to see if it will "take." She bleats uneasily, smells him worriedly. The scent of blood alarms her, but there is that undeniable odor of her child. Bewildered, she

walks away. He trots hopefully after. She noses him again and at last grudgingly allows him to nuzzle under her flank.

Every day the loose hide stretches a bit. You can cut away some parts of it, but never the tail. You long to tear off the whole thing. But it must stay on a while longer—the ewe is still uneasy. A week is none too long. By that time the old smell has become so mingled with the new that the anxious old mother is completely befooled. That is, almost always. Sometimes, on the contrary, when you have turned the pair out on the range together she will desert him after all, and days later you will find his lank corpse on the hillside.

At the end of six weeks lambing was over. A long, hard six weeks. The last straw of alfalfa had been fed. The last carcass had been decently buried. The last doddering old ewe and wobbly lamb had filed out through the corral gates onto the range that now showed a promising green. Too few, those wobbly lambs. Too many, those buried carcasses. But we had done all we could. And what we had done would mean, at least, enough money to pay off those notes at the bank.

Patter

EMILY POST, on the etiquette of eating corn on the cob, says: Attack it with as little ferocity as possible.

As the income-tax bureau sees us: America, land of untold wealth!

A woman's promise to be on time carries a lot of wait.

Three Days to See

Condensed from The Atlantic Monthly

HELEN KELLER

I HAVE often thought it would be a blessing if each human being were stricken blind and deaf for a few days at some time during his early adult life. Darkness would make him more appreciative of sight; silence would teach him the joys of sound.

Now and then I have tested my seeing friends to discover what they see. Recently I asked a friend, who had just returned from a long walk in the woods, what she had observed. "Nothing in particular," she replied.

How was it possible, I asked myself, to walk for an hour through the woods and see nothing worthy of note? I who cannot see find hundreds of things to interest me through mere touch. I feel the delicate symmetry of a leaf. I pass my hands lovingly about the smooth skin of a silver birch, or the rough, shaggy bark of a pine. In spring I touch the branches of trees hopefully in search of a bud, the first sign of awakening Nature after her winter's sleep. Occasionally, if I am very fortunate, I place my hand gently on a small tree and feel the happy quiver of a bird in full song.

At times my heart cries out with longing to see all these things. If I can get so much pleasure from mere touch, how much more beauty must be revealed by sight. And I have imagined what I should most like to see if I were given the use of my eyes, say, for just three days.

I should divide the period into three parts. On the first day, I should want to see the people whose kindness and companionship have made my life worth living. I do not know what it is to see into the heart of a friend through that "window of the soul," the eye. I can only "see" through my finger tips the outline of a face. I can detect laughter, sorrow, and many other obvious emotions. I know my friends from the feel of their faces.

How much easier, how much more satisfying it is for you who can see to grasp quickly the essential qualities of another person by watching the subtleties of expression, the quiver of a muscle, the

212

flutter of a hand. But does it ever occur to you to use your sight to see into the inner nature of a friend? Do not most of you seeing people grasp casually the outward features of a face and let it go at that?

For instance, can you describe accurately the faces of five good friends? As an experiment, I have questioned husbands about the color of their wives' eyes, and often they express embarrassed confusion and admit that they do not know.

Oh, the things that I should see if I had the power of sight for just three days!

The first day would be a busy one. I should call to me all my dear friends and look long into their faces, imprinting upon my mind the outward evidences of the beauty that is within them. I should let my eyes rest, too, on the face of a baby, so that I could catch a vision of the eager, innocent beauty which precedes the individual's consciousness of the conflicts which life develops. I should like to see the books which have been read to me, and which have revealed to me the deepest channels of human life. And I should like to look into the loyal, trusting eyes of my dogs, the little Scottie and the stalwart Great Dane.

In the afternoon I should take a long walk in the woods and intoxicate my eyes on the beauties of the world of Nature. And I should pray for the glory of a colorful sunset. That night, I think, I should not be able to sleep.

The next day I should arise with the dawn and see the thrilling miracle by which night is transformed into day. I should behold with awe the magnificent panorama of light with which the sun awakens the sleeping earth.

This day I should devote to a hasty glimpse of the world, past and present. I should want to see the pageant of man's progress, and so I should go to the museums. There my eyes would see the condensed history of the earth—animals and the races of men pictured in their native environment; gigantic carcasses of dinosaurs and mastodons which roamed the earth before man appeared, with his tiny stature and powerful brain, to conquer the animal kingdom.

My next stop would be the Museum of Art. I know well through my hands the sculptured gods and goddesses of the ancient Nile-land. I have felt copies of Parthenon friezes, and I have sensed the rhythmic beauty of charging Athenian warriors. The gnarled, bearded features of Homer are dear to me, for he, too, knew blindness.

So on this, my second day, I should try to probe into the soul of man through his art. The things I knew through touch I should now see. More splendid still, the whole magnificent world of painting would be opened to me. I should be able to get only a superficial impression. Artists tell me that for a deep and true appreciation of art one must educate the eye. One must learn through experience to weigh the merits of line, of composition, of form and color. If I had eyes, how happily would I embark on so fascinating a study!

The evening of my second day I should spend at a theater or at the movies. How I should like to see the fascinating figure of Hamlet, or the gusty Falstaff amid colorful Elizabethan trappings! I cannot enjoy the beauty of rhythmic movement except in a sphere restricted to the touch of my hands. I can vision only dimly the grace of a Pavlowa, although I know something of the delight of rhythm, for often I can sense the beat of music as it vibrates through the floor. I can well imagine that cadenced motion must be one of the most pleasing sights in the world. I have been able to gather something of this by tracing with my fingers the lines in sculptured marble; if this static grace can be so lovely, how much more acute must be the thrill of seeing grace in motion.

The following morning, I should again greet the dawn, anxious to discover new delights, new revelations of beauty. Today, this third day, I shall spend in the workaday world, amid the haunts of men going about the business of life. The city becomes my destination.

First, I stand at a busy corner, merely looking at people, trying by sight of them to understand something of their daily lives. I see smiles, and I am happy. I see serious determination, and I am proud. I see suffering, and I am compassionate.

I stroll down Fifth Avenue. I throw my eyes out of focus, so that I see no particular object but only a seething kaleidoscope of color. I am certain that the colors of women's dresses moving in a throng must be a gorgeous spectacle of which I should never tire. But perhaps if I had sight I should be like most other women—too interested in styles to give much attention to the splendor of color in the mass.

From Fifth Avenue I make a tour of the city—to the slums, to factories, to parks where children play. I take a stay-at-home trip abroad by visiting the foreign quarters. Always my eyes are open wide to all the sights of both happiness and misery so that I may probe deep and add to my understanding of how people work and live.

My third day of sight is drawing to an end. Perhaps there are many serious pursuits to which I should devote the few remaining hours, but I am afraid that on the evening of that last day I should again run away to the theater, to a hilariously funny play, so that I might appreciate the overtones of comedy in the human spirit.

At midnight permanent night would close in on me again. Naturally in those three short days I should not have seen all I wanted to see. Only when darkness had again descended upon me should I realize how much I had left unseen.

Perhaps this short outline does not agree with the program you might set for yourself if you knew that you were about to be stricken blind. I am, however, sure that if you faced that fate you would use your eyes as never before. Everything you saw would become dear to you. Your eyes would touch and embrace every object that came within your range of vision. Then, at last, you would really see, and a new world of beauty would open itself before you.

I who am blind can give one hint to those who see: Use your eyes as if tomorrow you would be stricken blind. And the same method can be applied to the other senses. Hear the music of voices, the song of a bird, the mighty strains of an orchestra, as if you would be stricken deaf tomorrow. Touch each object as if tomorrow your tactile sense would fail. Smell the perfume of flowers, taste with relish each morsel, as if tomorrow you could never smell and taste again. Make the most of every sense; glory in all the facets of pleasure and beauty which the world reveals to you through the several means of contact which Nature provides. But of all the senses, I am sure that sight must be the most delightful.

A Flower a Day

IMAGINATION IN BUSINESS

SEEING possibilities the florists were overlooking, Gurney Chrysler, a young advertising woman in New York, rented a loft in an old building in the heart of the flower market. She sent out notices to the effect that she would send a flower a day (10 cents a day for one flower and 15 cents a day for two), or a bouquet a day to persons who would contract with her and pay her by the week or month. In no time she had 1000 customers. Harriet Thorndyke, in *The Family Circle*, tells how every morning at 4:30 Miss Chrysler goes to the market, buys her flowers, and with helpers sets to work making boutonnieres. At 8, boys from a messenger service swarm in and take the packages. Then Miss Chrysler starts in on table decorations, baskets for hospitals, etc. She will send you a different flower for every day in the week if you want. Some want tulips on Monday, a gardenia on Tuesday, a red carnation on Wednesday, and so on. She also transmits heart throbs of every kind—flirtations and courtships and reconciliations, according to Princess Kropotkin in *Liberty*. One young man spotted a blonde in the office window opposite his; he called up Gurney Chrysler at once. She managed to get the girl's name and sent flowers every day. Recently she sent flowers to their baby's christening.

Minnesota's Mysterious Norsemen

Condensed from Science News Letter

EMILY DAVIS

SCHOOL CHILDREN may soon find that they have a brand new chapter of American history to learn—a chapter in the 14th century, sandwiched in between Leif Ericsson sailing to Vinland in 1000 A.D. and Columbus' voyage. It is a tale of exploration in America so unbelievable that scientists have scarcely dared to think it could be proved true.

The story concerns a band of Goths and Norsemen sailing to America in 1355 and pushing their way deep into the wilderness, as far as Minnesota. The rune stone telling about this 14th century expedition was unearthed at Kensington, Minn., 35 years ago by Olof Ohman, a farmer. The flat slab, found under the roots of an aspen, had curious marks cut into it. It gained such fame that it was displayed in the Kensington bank window.

It was a slab of dark colored rock 31 inches long, with an inscription in runic alphabet characters on one flat side and along one edge. A professor of Scandinavian languages read off part of the writing, and,

thinking in terms of 11th century Viking expeditions, pointed out that such writing was not the form then used. European scholars, too, promptly called the stone a clumsy fraud. Mr. Ohman took it back and threw it down for a doorstep in front of his granary. There it lay, face down, for nine years.

Then Hjalmar R. Holand, seeking data for a history of Norwegian immigration, heard so many stories about the Kensington rune stone that he asked for the granary doorstep. On one edge of it he found the date 1362. No wonder the runic alphabet characters were not in proper 11th century style, thought Mr. Holand. But—would they prove authentic 14th century letters? He investigated and his translation, which is regularly accepted, is as follows:

(We are) 8 Goths (Swedes) and 22 Norwegians on (an) exploration-journey from Vinland over the West We had camp by 2 skerries (i.e., by a lake wherein are two place-rocks) one days-journey from

216

this stone We were (out) and fished one day After we came home (we) found 10 (of our) men red with blood and dead Ave Maria Save (us) from evil (We) have 10 of our party by the sea to look after our ships (or ship) 14 days-journey from this island Year 1362.

Eagerly Mr. Holand searched Scandinavian literature for a Norse adventure to fit this story. He found one. "A Norse expedition was actually sent to American waters by the King of Norway and Sweden in 1355," he writes. "This expedition appears to have returned in 1364."

To many critics, one of the stumbling blocks in accepting the Kensington rune stone as authentic has been the mixed personnel of the group described in the inscription. Goths and Norsemen in one party would be absurd they declared. But an "absurd" crew of Goths and Norwegians sailed together on that unique expedition of 1355, Mr. Holand found. A king named Magnus, who ruled Norway and Sweden jointly at that time, sent Paul Knutson with a party made up of men from both countries on a missionary expedition to re-convert a colony in Western Greenland. The language on the Kensington stone, a mixture of Swedish, Norwegian, English, and a Latin phrase, is about what would be expected of such a group, Mr. Holand argues.

But how did it happen that a religious crusade to Greenland should be massacred in Minnesota? Not finding the colonists in Greenland —Mr. Holand theorizes—Knutson trailed them first to Vinland, then north around the coast into Hudson Bay to the Nelson River. There the expedition left its ships and ventured into the wilderness in canoes and on foot. And 1000 miles from the ships came the massacre by the Indians.

Another "discrepancy" was the statement about the camp being 14 days-journey from the ships. But a days-journey was a phrase used by Scandinavian sailors in the Middle Ages as a definite unit of distance, equal to about 75 miles. The Kensington stone lay just about 14 days-journey from Hudson Bay, in sailors' terms.

The age of the aspen beneath which the stone was found in 1898 has been fixed at not less than 70 years. The first pioneers came to settle Minnesota about 1850. This would apparently rule out the possibility of a fake.

To clinch this fantastic tale of medieval adventure in America, no less than four old axes have been unearthed in western Minnesota. These also were branded "impossible." But a tour of European museums convinced Mr. Holand that the Minnesota axes are authentic weapons lost by Knutson's crew. All are of medieval types and all are Scandinavian.

My Mixed Marriage

Condensed from The Atlantic Monthly

GEORGE E. SOKOLSKY

RECENTLY I heard a clergyman and a rabbi debate on the everlasting subject of intermarriage—miscegenation, the elect like to call it. The clergyman was for it, the rabbi against it.

It was impossible for me not to be facetious. "What," I asked, "do these gentlemen, who have married their own kind, really know about intermarriage? Do they know the unspoken thoughts of those who have crossed national and racial and even color barriers? Do they appreciate the problem of the child?"

Well might I ask such questions, for mine is the most mixed of marriages. My wife is Chinese. My own people are Polish Jews. My wife was born in a British colony and educated in England; her cultural heritage is British. I was brought up on the East Side of New York, and educated in New York's public school system until I went to Columbia University.

We met in Shanghai, and three years later we were married. Three years we debated the question of mixed marriages. Three years we argued our prospects of success. We had nothing in common except an affection for and a faith in each other. Could such a marriage succeed?

Everyone said it must fail. Shall I ever forget how a kindly friend sat before me for hours recounting the probabilities of failure? "If you do not succeed in life," he said, "your friends will say that it is your Chinese wife who keeps you down. And you may come to believe it. If you succeed, you may not be willing to admit that a Chinese wife helped you."

Then we were married—she, Chinese, Christian, British; I, Polish, Jewish, American.

Ten years have now passed, and we have both reached the same conclusion: that marriage is essentially a matter of readjustment—the more sensitive the individuals, the more delicate the readjustments. The elements which make for success or failure in a mixed marriage are primarily those which determine the fate of other unions. Poverty, irascibility, injustice, brutality, deceit—

218

these make for failure in any marriage. The "mixed" characteristic plays no part here.

Of course in a mixed marriage there are special stresses. Most marriages between a Chinese and a "white" woman have been unsuccessful because the problem is seriously complicated by the intricacies of the Chinese family system. The wife finds that she has to adjust herself to her husband's relatives, to his mother in particular. If she lives with the family—the usual practice in China—she faces problems of differing customs and habits, to which she may never adapt herself. If her husband was married in childhood, as often happens, and he has failed to tell her about it, she soon discovers that his people look upon her as a concubine, and treat her according to that status. If she lives a Western life, she is often too expensive. If the father is paying the bills of the entire family, as Chinese fathers not infrequently do, she becomes an occasion for bickering between father and son.

Environmental differences do make adjustments more difficult in mixed marriages. But failure comes more often from deceit and ignorance than from any inability of races to blend. American girls who marry Chinese students often imagine that their husbands are wealthy. One Chinese boy, when he was a student in this country, gave the impression that he was a prince, and the American girl who married him was shocked to discover in Shanghai that he was only another young man looking for a job. Deception, poverty, and disappointment wrecked that marriage, but in such cases it is not the mixture, it is the lies, that make for failure.

In a mixed marriage there cannot be the usual traditions. You start out by trying carefully to make up your mind just how much you can take over of your partner's attitude toward life. There may be such fundamental questions to decide as that of table manners, the precedence of husband or wife, the handling of family money, the attitude toward relatives and friends. Chinese friendship goes deep, and the Western husband may not understand his wife's expenditure of money to help old friends in need. He may apply the rule of "every man for himself," while she applies the social concept of group responsibility. Such differences in tradition must be met and solved.

But the most pressing problem in every intermarriage is the child. Not only does he face the possibility of a confused home training, a drawing hither and thither in education and religion, but he encounters a sentimental prejudice among other children, and even adults, which may develop in him a racial inferiority complex so deep as to ruin his personality. His greatest danger comes during puberty when he may grow to hate his parents for having involved him in confusion, and, later, his first love affair may leave him with psychological scars that never heal.

As we faced this problem, we

were well aware, even before the child came to us, that the task of bringing him up would involve a large measure of character building. We should have to instill in him a sense of personal pride so that he might withstand the buffets of a prejudiced world.

We felt that our boy would have a more even chance in life if he were to develop artistic traits. In the rough competition of business or politics, his racial origin would surely prove an impediment. In the arts, nothing really matters but ability. Who cares that Fritz Kreisler is an Austrian, or that Paul Robeson is a Negro? In the arts there is genuine democracy.

Yet no parent can say to his child, "My boy, go forth and practice the arts." The hidden qualities of genius, the lust for music, for color, for words—these must dawn within the consciousness of each individual. What fathers and mothers *can* do, however, is to be vigilant, providing the child with an atmosphere and environment to stimulate whatever talents he may possess.

The first duty of the parents is to make the child realize from infancy that there is nothing extraordinary about him. The recipe is the whole truth. Over a period of years, commencing with the time when the child begins to ask questions, when he notices the difference between blond hair and black, patiently, carefully, the story of his racial origin should be unfolded to him—not nationalistically, not as a problem, but as a story in which

he is an incidental character. The heroine of such a tale should be his mother. That attitude will strengthen his faith in her and in himself. He will feel that it is quite all right to have come out of her race. It will not matter what others say—he will know better.

As the child grows older he cannot help noticing that in many respects he is not like other children. Then it is that sympathy and understanding on the part of parents must play the rôle of corrective. He must not be coddled because he is different. He must learn that all human beings face special problems. Some are too rich, others too poor. Some are too beautiful, others too ugly. Some are lazy, others are nervous. Each person must carry his burden so that it does not become an impediment. Above all, one must not make the burden the principal concern in life, so that nothing matters but to carry it.

This explanation must come to the child at an early age, before some unsympathetic nurse or some ridiculous relative spoils the picture. With our boy, I find it easy to point out that a friend of his is very good-looking but has no money. "That is too bad," I say. "Maybe he won't be able to go to a good school. Well, you don't always have everything. For instance, there is the little girl in the next block who has two fathers, one in New York and the other in Baltimore. She likes her father in Baltimore better because he was her first father. But he went away, and her mother got her another. Well, you can't always arrange these things. Still, you're pretty lucky. You can go to a good school, and you have both your father and mother. But you will not always have everything you want, and maybe there will be some trouble for *you* some day. You have to be a pretty good fellow to stand up under trouble. Good fellows shake off troubles."

If there is a genuine religious difference between the partners of a mixed marriage, their children are pretty certain to grow up in an unhappy environment. In our case, we have decided to tell the boy that he is a Jew, but to make no fuss about it. Jews who "pass" to some more popular religious group do not solve any problems by mere dissembling. The easiest way to avoid the suspicion of imposture is to stand up as you are. If, later in life, the child of a mixed religious marriage wants to choose for himself, that is another matter, but the lot of an Episcopal Cohen is too trying to wish on any child.

I have tried to deal with intermarriage unemotionally. There have been tragic failures; there have been outstanding successes. A young lady once asked my advice. She wanted a page out of my experience. I could only tell her what I have written here. Then I added:

"If you were to marry the boy who sat next to you at college, you might be happy, and then again you might be the one who, out of every six or seven, is divorced. If you marry this man (an East Asian) because of novelty, it will wear off. If you love him and he loves you, then allow yourself a sure interval before you have a child. If, after that interval, you still love each other, go ahead and rear a family."

But would that advice not also apply to marriages which do not involve racial, cultural, or religious differences?

"Music Hath Power . . ."

THE MOST appreciative musical audience I ever encountered in America," declares José Iturbi, "was in a Connecticut lunch-wagon where I had stopped for coffee. There was a good deal of clatter until the Sunday evening symphonic program went on the air. Then the counterman stopped washing dishes—and listened; the man next to me set his cup down very carefully, the waitress stopped stacking dishes—and listened. By that time the place was comparatively quiet, but the counterman scowled at four hamburgers sizzling on the griddle and carefully removed them. This gave the waitress an idea: she went to the end of the lunch-wagon and took down a duck that was roasting noisily on a spit. Then the silence was complete. The incident was a more profound tribute to the power of good music than the applause of many a more cosmopolitan group of music lovers."—*Musical Digest*

The World's Most Famous Oration

Excerpt from The Golden Book

CHRISTOPHER MORLEY

Address to an Employer Upon Demanding a Raise

AS PLANNED	AS DELIVERED
I THINK you will admit, sir, that the quality of my work during the last two years has been such that my services could not easily be replaced. I speak more in pain than in anger when I say that it has been a matter of profound surprise to me to note that you have not seen fit to acknowledge my value to the firm in some substantial way. I think I may say that I have been patient. I have continued my efforts with unremitting zeal, and I think I may flatter myself that my endeavors have not been without result. I have here, carefully tabulated, a memorandum of the increased profits in my department during the last twelve months, due in great part to my careful management. I am sorry to have to force you into a decision, but I think I owe it to myself to say candidly that unless you see the matter in the same way that I do I shall feel obliged to deprive the firm of my services.	IF YOU are not too busy, sir, there is one other matter—in fact, the truth of the matter in fact is exactly—well, sir, I was precisely wondering whether—of course I know this is a bad time—indeed I have been very pleased to see business picking up a bit lately, and I am sure my own department has been—but to tell you the truth, sir, I have been wondering—of course it is just as you think best and I wouldn't think of insisting, but after all, perhaps I have made a mistake in mentioning it, but I was thinking that possibly you might bear in mind the idea of a possible future raise in salary at some future time.

From *Pipefuls*, by Christopher Morley, courtesy of J. B. Lippincott Company.

Our Pernicious Virtues

Condensed from Harper's Magazine

I. A. R. WYLIE

IF CIVILIZATION is to survive, our old-time virtues must be brought up to date. It was these virtues, rather than our wickedness, which landed us into the slaughter of the War. If we had not been brave, faithful, patriotic, and unselfish we should never have fought at all. And our next display of high-powered old-time virtue may finish civilization altogether.

Patriotism is not, as sentimentalists like to assert, one of the profoundest of man's noblest instincts. It is not an instinct at all. Before the 17th century hardly anybody had heard of it. Men, before the time of Queen Elizabeth, fought for kings, factions, loot, and very occasionally for principles. Even so the actual fighters were regarded as rabble, and it is significant that not until the 19th century when patriotism had become a mania did it occur to anyone to erect monuments to them.

The idea of patriotism served, at first, a useful and even noble purpose. It brought men together. It established their unity and common responsibility. It enlarged the loyalty to the family and the faction and fired the ideal with new enthusiasm. It was a stepping-stone. If we had gone on from there all might have been well with us. But, as usual, having discovered a virtue, we proceeded to embalm it. We nailed patriotism to the masthead and anybody who refused to stand permanently at the salute was a scoundrel.

A hundred years ago the range of patriotism's destructive capacities was limited. The worst that one virtuously patriotic people could do to another was to defeat and decimate it. Now it is possible to wipe out a whole civilization. And the worst of this virtue is that everyone enjoys it. Patriotism provides a vent for a schoolboy passion for killing things and smashing windows. It justifies our otherwise unjustifiable conceit. (Even if a man is bow-legged, knock-kneed, and weak in the head, he can still feel superior as an Englishman, an American, a Frenchman, or whatever, by accident, he happens to be.) An honest patriot today may feel extremely virtuous, but he is none the less an anachronism wandering about a powder-magazine with a torchlight.

Physical courage and patriotism are closely allied virtues. One might say that the latter is the best-known excuse for a display of the former, so that they should be deflated together.

I have never understood why physical courage should be so valued and rewarded in our modern life. It is as common to the human race as the sex impulse, and I am convinced that what we call cowardice is merely a symptom of indigestion or malnutrition and has as much to do with character as a cold in the head. I see, therefore, no more sense in shooting wretched soldiers for lack of courage than for pinning medals on the bosoms of the more fortunate whose glands happen to be functioning nicely at the right moment. Even in war physical courage is outmoded. The next great victory will be won not by brave men with bayonets, but by some bespectacled gentleman who will have the promptitude to press an electric button and reduce a nation to the ashheap.

When saber-toothed tigers ravaged the forests physical courage was a utilitarian quality without which men could not survive. There are no saber-toothed tigers on our streets today—if motorists are excepted; and the actual calls upon the individual's physical courage are so rare that the average man goes through life without knowing whether he is brave or not. For the exceptional man who cannot rest till he finds out, there are still records to be broken and, eventually, one of them will make a trial flight to the moon. Whether these exceptions add greatly to the sum of our knowledge and happiness need not be discussed. The point is that we have enough of these men for all useful purposes without forced cultivation. It might be fairly added that a great number serve no useful purpose at all. Like gangsters, they are simply exhibitionists. If we could get it clear in our minds that physical courage is much more commonplace than physical cleanliness and, in modern life, much less necessary, we should regard such people as we would regard a man who insists on cleaning his teeth at the dinner-table—as being offensively ostentatious.

This is not to underestimate or disparage a quality that has conquered our world for us. But that conquest has been made. Now we have to go on to the much more difficult conquest of ourselves. And we need other weapons—intellectual and moral heroism. The curse of our deification of physical courage is that a display of it, in the individual or in a nation, can disguise a total bankruptcy in the essential virtues. If we had any sense of what really mattered we should regard the soldier as a self-confessed failure and a martial nation as a nation of failures. For both are shirking the real business of life, which is to live and make life possible. Modern Germany, led by

Hitler, deifies the fighter not because she is a nation of heroes but because she is a nation of potential suicides who have broken under moral and emotional pressure and who know no way out save through destruction.

The ideal which we must recognize if we are to escape from the morass into which our old-time heroes have led us is the moral hero—the intellectual and spiritual adventurer. Unfortunately, as a race, we are out-of-date. We may pride ourselves on our airplanes and radios, but in character we are wandering somewhere in the Dark Ages, and though we pay lip-service to moral and intellectual courage, we cling secretly to our old gods. They demand less of us.

Another of our highly prized virtues is fidelity. We are immensely pleased with ourselves when we are faithful.

Like most of our popular virtues, fidelity had an early utilitarian origin. The family and the tribe if they were to survive had to hold together. To the feudal lord, who depended for his life upon bullying or bribing sufficient numbers of vassals to serve under his banner, the idea of fidelity was a veritable godsend. Bribery and fear were, after all, unsatisfactory because there was always a chance that someone else could bribe higher and threaten worse. But fidelity, once beaten into the vassals' wooden heads, was bribe- and threat-proof. From such beginnings the blight of a thoroughly third-rate virtue spread over men's thought, and to this very day

an English Tory will boast that he is a Tory because his father was one, an American Republican is a Republican because he always was a Republican.

We have, in fact, accepted fidelity as a virtue in itself without considering why and to what we are being faithful. Yet life moves us relentlessly on. Its basic principle is one of continuous change and it is faithful to nothing. We ourselves are not physically the same people from one day to another. So that our determination to stay fixed in our loves, opinions, and faiths is a defiance of life.

It is one thing to hold on, even at great cost, to what we honestly love and reasonably believe in. But there is no "virtue" in acceding to accepted standards in doing what we want to do. What we usually mean by fidelity is holding on to someone we have ceased to love, a religion we have outgrown, a political principle we have never reasoned about at all, and our country —right or wrong. We have got to learn a new fidelity: unfaithfulness to what was once right and has become wrong, fidelity to ourselves as we are today and may be tomorrow.

It is not a question of an irresponsible giving way to every stray impulse, but of the sober acceptance of change as the law of life and of getting into step with the law. It is the reduction of fidelity as a virtue in itself to the place of a vicious and obstinate hindrance from which we have suffered long enough.

Charity, another of the old virtues, is usually looked upon as a short cut to heaven. But too often it is a road paved with human misery, a disguise for the injustice that we mete out to our fellowmen.

To be fair, it must be said that we are slowly bringing ourselves to face the truth. The poor are beginning to refuse charity as an outrage. The rich are recognizing that they can no longer use charity as an atonement or as a means of stimulating a pleasant emotion in themselves. In the present crisis the so-called dole in England is a blundering but definite acceptance of a new principle. And, incidentally, it has saved England from a revolution.

We need justice. We need toleration, honesty, and moral courage. These are modern virtues without which we cannot hope to control the forces science has let loose amongst us. With them we could reshape our world in splendor. But recent events have revealed all too clearly that in finance, in politics, in our courts of justice, in our international relationships, these virtues are so rudimentary in their development that to speak of them savors of cynicism. Our leaders speak of them, but their conduct renders them meaningless.

Can we discard our childish values? Can we acquire virtues and ideals that accord with our material stature? Can we grow up? Above all—can we grow up in time? On the answer to that question hangs mankind's future.

Imagination on a Lark

GELETT BURGESS, author of the famous "Purple Cow" verse, has spent seven years perfecting his Mechanical Moron, a complicated machine made of knitting needles, orange sticks, paper clips, pillboxes, pins, toothpicks and matches, and run by an electric motor which causes the odd miscellany to jump about in an awe-inspiring fashion. Christened "A Woman Talking," it is guaranteed efficiently to produce nothing—hour after hour.—*American Weekly*

To ENABLE people to fulfill their frequently expressed desire to kick themselves, Commissioner Tom Haywood of New Bern, North Carolina, built a kicking machine. Placed in front of his home, it was used by many passers-by.—*The Express Messenger*

A ONE-EYED New Yorker of independent mind has a set of glass eyes of progressive degrees of bloodshotness. When he attends one of Manhattan's gayer parties, he discreetly changes his glass eye at fitting intervals to match the increasing redness of his real eye. The 13th eye has, instead of a clear blue iris, an unfurled American flag.

The Leper Mass

Condensed from The Commonweal

CHARLES J. DUTTON

VIGNETTES OF HISTORY

VEILED by swirling fog, the monastery walls sprawl their irregular outline down to the curving banks of the river. When the monks first came into England, they had been told to seek the low marshy places, "where pestilence and disease abound," in order that they might be always aware of the uncertainty of life, by having ever before their eyes the sight of death. The cemetery below the church shows how well this advice had been observed.

The village lies close to the river's edge. Between the houses, low one-story wooden structures with thatched roofs, run narrow lanes filled with holes and ankle-deep with mud. Swine root in the heaps of rubbish. Over the village hangs silence, broken suddenly by a faint clang, as the monastery gate is closed.

From within the monastery has come a procession of slowly moving figures. It is past midnight and the people of the village are not stirring from their darkened houses. The monks do not have far to go.

The village is small, the houses few.

Before one of these the marching figures pause. A hand reaches forth in the darkness and knocks three times upon the wooden door. There is the sound of someone slowly fumbling with a latch, and then the door is swung open. As the damp mist pours into the house, the priests enter, one bearing aloft a crucifix. There is but one room, small and unkempt. Rushes cover the clay floor; and because they have not been changed for months, all manner of filth and refuse mingle with the rotting covering.

Pressed against the side of the house stands a man staring dumbly, with frightened eyes, at the monks. Crouched down upon the matted straw bed, with three half-naked and dirty children beside her, a bedraggled woman sways back and forth. Her gaze is fixed upon the glittering cross. Both of them know why the monks have come. They have dreaded their advent.

Weeks before, the man noticed the faint swelling in his limbs, the suspicious thickening of his skin. It was then that fear crept over him. One day there had come the order that he must receive the medical examination for leprosy. Crude and unscientific, it was long and complicated, taking several days. Finally a messenger came to his humble dwelling and gave the verdict. He was a leper.

Henceforth in the midst of all things which live, he would be as one dead. Forbidden to stir from his house, he was required to wait until the religious authorities could arrange his removal. They had come at last. Come to take him to the church. There the Leper Mass would be said. When it was over, he no longer would have wife or child. All civil rights would be gone. By this ceremony he would become separated forever from the world and its activities.

Kindly but firm are the words of the priest. The leper is to remember that his affliction comes from God and he must resign himself to the Will of his Maker. He is reminded that this world will pass and he can look forward to an eternity of happiness. There follows a prayer, and above the kneeling man come falling drops of holy water. Silence for a moment. Then the leper is told to rise and follow them to the church. With the priest bearing the crucifix leading the way, and the monks singing, "Free me, oh Lord," they go out into the swirling fog. Far behind walks the leper, and many yards in the rear come his wife and children, now separated forever from his side.

The doors of the silent houses have opened and the people too are on their way to the church, for the entire village has been commanded to observe the celebration of the Mass. Through the monastery gate they pass. Then, with cross riding high ahead, they enter the church. There the leper is to hear read over him the service for the dead.

Before him is stretched a black mortuary cloth, supported by four upright stakes. In token of his submission he kneels beneath the black cloth, as one, when life is over, lies under it cold in death. The special garb distinctive of all lepers is thrown over him. Again the priest sprinkles him with holy water, and then drops earth upon him, as a symbol of burial. The burial service is read, prayers are chanted.

The service ends, and they leave the church. Again the glittering cross is lifted high, as they walk a few hundred yards over the wet ground to a silent, desolate field. There are graves here, graves on every side. And at the feet of the leper a narrow shallow pit can be seen.

It is lonesome here, and very still. Around them lie the dead, and for a moment not a sound is heard. Then comes the voice of the priest, slow, grave, reverent. And as he speaks the leper falls upon his knees. The priest points out the yawning grave, the wet heaped-up soil by its side. He reminds the leper that this pit is a symbol of the fate which overtakes all men. A few words of comfort, then a long list of prohibitions are given. The leper is forbidden to enter any public place, a church, mill, inn or home. He must not wash himself in any public fountain or running stream, nor must he ever pass through the narrow streets of the towns and villages.

A large wooden rattle has been placed in his hand. He is told that he must never be without this rattle. Whenever he sees someone in the distance approaching, this instrument must be sounded, as a warning that a leper is nearby. A small wooden bucket attached to a long stave is the next gift. Whenever he wishes food or wine this bucket on the extended stave must be presented for the food to be dropped within.

They turn to leave him now. It may be he will enter one of the many leper houses of the church. Perhaps he will live in a cave or small hut in the forest. It matters little. For him this world has vanished. In the midst of men and women he, a living man, has been pronounced dead.

As the priest and monks retrace their steps toward the monastery, there float back the chanted words, "Dwell in peace, God be with you." Their voices die away. The cross glistens faintly through the mist, then vanishes. The peasants slink quietly back to their homes, their hearts fearful, lest the same plight be theirs.

He is left alone. In one hand he holds the long stave, the other clutches the wooden rattle. Around him are the graves of the dead. At his feet is his own grave. On every side is silence and the white mist. The village is close at hand, but the thick fog blots it from his sight. Even the monastery walls are hidden. The world has vanished; ahead lie loneliness, perhaps long years of sorrow and pain, and at the end a horrible death. . . .

What this man thought as he stood there, we can never know. For though this happened thousands of times, it all took place long ago. The year was about 1200, when the lepers in England were a third of the population. So very many were there, and the Leper Mass was so common, that no one ever paused to question how the leper himself felt—assisting at his own burial service, left alone by an open grave. And seven hundred years were to pass, before science would even hint that it had cured its first leper.

Patter

The children always know when there is company downstairs—they can hear mother laughing at father's jokes.

Never run after a street car or a woman—another will be along any minute.

A Florida newspaper has changed its column headings, Births, Marriages, and Deaths, to Yells, Bells, and Knells. Which brings to mind the usage of some other papers: Hatched, Matched, and Snatched.

The Evolution of Eyes

Condensed from The American Scholar

THOMAS HALL SHASTID

AGES AGO, when earth had cooled and life had begun to appear in its tepid waters, one of the first things developed was eyes. Even the ameba, the lowliest of all known animals, of which countless trillions exist today precisely as they were when life originated on this planet, may be said to possess eyes. Or rather, the ameba's body is all eye—every portion of the ameba can perceive light. But while in the process of evolution some eyes, like this generalized light-sense of the ameba, have stood quite still, others, like the literally superhuman eyes of birds, have moved forward incredible distances.

When we come to the insects we find that they have two kinds of eyes: simple and compound. If one looks at a common house-fly one can see that its head consists almost entirely of two large, dark-brown lobes, the compound eyes, each made up of more than 4000 eye-units. From each compound eye a mosaic picture—of more than 4000 minute picture-fragments—is conveyed to the fly's central nervous system. The fly also has three single eyes, situated, in the form of a triangle with its sharpest point downward, in the space above and between the two compound eyes.

The compound eyes of the fly are used for distance, i.e. three to four yards, and the single eyes for near vision, from one to two inches. Some insects have only compound eyes, some only single, but most of them have both. None of these insect eyes have any movement—the eyes are set on the fly's head as solid as so many jewels in a watch.

Leaving the insects, the fishes are the first of the great backboned class of animals. In fishes, Nature produced the first true focusing arrangements and muscles with which to move eyes in their sockets. But fish are color-blind. Tell this to a fisherman with his brightly colored flies and he will laugh derisively, but it is a demonstrable fact. Fish can distinguish between different colors, but do not see them as colors—only as various shades of gray, precisely as a color-blind person would. Fish have also a very restricted visual field, seeing

230

scarcely anything below the level of the head.

The reptilia added little to eyes. In general snakes have very poor sight. Most of them see only objects in motion and are nearly deaf too, so that their knowledge of the world reaches them largely by way of the little forked tongue, probably the most wonderful tactile organ in existence. This feels myriads of vibrations in the atmosphere which, to our coarse sense of touch, are non-existent.

Birds' eyes are the most remarkable of all earthly eyes, being often both telescopic and microscopic. In birds the visual acuteness is almost incredible, in some instances 100 times as great as that in men. A bit of grain that human eyes can barely see at a distance of one yard, a bird can see distinctly at a distance of 100 yards. This remarkable sight is almost a necessity because the sense of smell in birds is exceedingly poor. Even vultures, contrary to popular superstition, do not smell their food even though it be carrion, but see it.

Mammals may be classified as non-primates and primates, the primates including monkeys, apes, and men. In nearly all the non-primates the eyes are not set out on the front of the face but at the side of the head. Scarcely any of the non-primates have any overlapping of the visual fields of the two eyes and those which do have some overlapping have no true stereoscopic vision—vision with depth and relief to it. Hares and rabbits actually have the fields overlapping behind their heads (behind, because these animals are not hunters, but hunted), yet they have no stereoscopic vision.

A very great difference exists among mammals in the shape of the pupil when in contracted condition. The domestic cat has a narrow vertical pupil, which it needs for the purpose of hunting its prey up and down trees. (This is not true of all the cat family; lions and all the larger *felidae* have round pupils.) The horse has pupils which are wide horizontally in order that the animal, when grazing, can see sidewise, both to right and to left, over a wide expanse of ground. A horse's eyes, also, are placed prominently up and out on the corners of its head so that it can aim a kick at a wolf—the horse's natural enemy —without turning the head.

All eyes that shine in the dark do so by virtue of a concave reflector behind the retina. The purpose is to enable the animal to see better in the dark. The little light that is stirring in the outer world enters the pupil, passes through the transparent retina which utilizes this light for vision, and on to the reflector, which sends it back to the same object from which it came. Here it is joined to the fresh, original light from the object, and the same process is repeated. Thus the carnivora and some other animals, whose vision is very much poorer than ours by day, see much better at night. And that is why primitive man lived in great terror of the dark. He was eater by day, eaten at night.

All the primates have strong focusing muscles. In all the monkeys and apes the eyes, just as in men, can both be converged on the same point, and stereoscopic vision thus obtained—but not very long maintained. Only in man, of all the mammals, does there seem to be a continuous binocular and stereoscopic vision. Even in the human child, however, the eyes do not as a rule move in perfect unison with each other till about three months after birth, because stereoscopic vision, in the history of life, is an extremely recent appearance. This explains the ready loss-of-binocularity (cross eyes) in many persons as the result of eye-strain.

Whenever our eyes are in motion they are stone blind, excepting only when they move without changing the point at which they look. Anyone can easily convince himself of the truth of this statement. Let him stand before a mirror and look at the image of one of his eyes. Let him look first at the right side of that eye, then at the left side of the same eye, and then back again. Never, so long as he lives, will he see his eye in motion. The reason is that, just so soon as an eye begins to move, it is blind. We are never conscious of the blind interval, partly because the picture which is last seen before the eye begins moving persists in the sight-center of the brain and thus laps a little over the interval during which the retina is blind. But the chief fact is that the retina, by means of its motion blindness, gets minute intervals of rest with

very great frequency all through our waking hours. In this way, too, the blurry and therefore useless pictures which we should receive if the eyes saw while in motion are avoided.

One peculiar thing about man's eyes, dominancy and serviency, is not found in the eyes of animals. In all mammals the eyes are *two* little cameras, each producing a tiny picture, but in the brain of man only one composite or stereoscopic picture is seen. The unique feature about the vision of a man is that the two eyes do not contribute equally to the formation of this single picture. In a right-handed person the right eye contributes practically all of the picture, in a left-handed person the left eye. In other words the right eye is almost invariably the window the brain looks through, with the left eye merely adding a little accessory information. When the right eye is closed, the left eye promptly extends its visual fields to the normal limits of the right. To test whether or not you have dominancy and serviency in your eyes, look at a tiny spot in the wall at a distance of a few feet. Next, while still looking at the spot, take a finger-ring and hold it where you will be looking through it. Then close your left eye, and see if you still see the spot through the ring. If you are right-handed, you will. Next close your right eye and look at the spot with your left and you will see it outside the ring. If you are left-handed, the result will be reversed.

Dominancy and serviency in eyes, like right-handedness and left-handedness, have come into the world very late. In no animal, so far as I have been able to learn, is there any such thing as handedness or eye-dominancy. This peculiar state of affairs is producing a condition which will eventually result in consequences of vast importance. As one result, I believe that in the course of countless ages man's two eyes will come closer and closer together, the bridge of the nose will diminish and sink, and finally at the spot where the bridge of the nose now appears there will stand one large, cyclopean eye. This single, central eye will regain stereoscopic vision just as many birds have stereoscopic vision in each eye now. Although the field of view will then be narrower than now, the eye will probably be both microscopic and telescopic; and, finally, most important of all, it will probably be able to perceive as light many forms of energy which now produce in human eyes no sort or kind of perception.

When the Critics Crack the Quip

EVERY LITTLE CRITIC HAS A MEANIE OF HIS OWN

WHEN Mr. Wilbur calls his play *Halfway to Hell*, he underestimates the distance.—Brooks Atkinson (N. Y. *Times*)

Katharine Hepburn [in *The Lake*] runs the gamut of emotions from A to B.—Dorothy Parker (*While Rome Burns*)

Tank-town performance of *Uncle Tom's Cabin*—The dogs were poorly supported by the cast.—Don Herold

King Lear—He played the King as though someone had led the ace.—Eugene Field (*Boston Globe*)

Tyrone Power as Cassius in *Julius Caesar*—A set of vocal chords wrapped up in a toga.—John Mason Brown (*Stage*)

Excuse me for mentioning it, but a play called *Are You Decent?* opened last night.—John Mason Brown (N. Y. *Post*)

If Booth Had Missed missed so completely that even the ushers failed to show up on the third night.—George Jean Nathan (*Judge*)

Perfectly Scandalous was one of those plays in which all of the actors, unfortunately, enunciated very clearly.—Robert Benchley (*The New Yorker*)

I've seen French *Camilles*, English *Camilles*, and German *Camilles*, but I never knew until I saw Miss LeGallienne's that what *Camille* died of was not tuberculosis but catarrh.—George Jean Nathan (*Judge*)

Entire review of *Tonight or Never:* Very well then, I say Never. —George Jean Nathan (*Judge*)

All Sweet Things

Condensed from The Atlantic Monthly

M. BEATRICE BLANKENSHIP

A FEW YEARS AGO I was facing one of the most difficult complications of a never-too-sweet existence. Every path I tried seemed to be unmistakably marked, "No Exit." Driving home from the city late one afternoon with my small children, I was wearily pondering my problems once more, going over and over what could be done.

Just ahead of us lay a curve in the road where four people had recently been killed. I only needed to step a little harder on the accelerator and keep my hand steady on the wheel, and before any of us had time to be afraid we should all have escaped from the weariness and futility of which life seemed to be composed. There was a black flash before my eyes, I stepped on the brake instead of the accelerator, and came around the curve at my usual cautious speed. . . . In less than three months the complications had resolved themselves and were succeeded by two of the happiest years of my life.

I think that I was held back by reluctance to acknowledge once and for all that I was defeated. And while I was confusedly thinking that, we rounded the curve and came out facing the somber beauty of the afterglow over a purple winter sea.

I have always especially loved the time when the sky burns dark orange on the horizon, the ocean shades from ice-green to darkest purple, and the little waves near the shore are for the moment as rigid as if carved out of lapis lazuli. But the utter beauty and peace of that evening sea brought tears to my eyes. I realized then, as at intervals I have ever since, that, no matter what life does to you, there is still a refuge from which you cannot be torn. The "sweet things" are still free, and there is no one of us, no matter how lonely and poor, who cannot have his share by just looking around him.

I have known physical suffering and sorrow and I have lived through both, saying to myself, "I need only live one second at a time. I don't even have to live a whole minute now—let alone hours, or months, or years—just this one second." And gradually I could turn my attention from myself to the "sweet things" that were unmarred by my grief and pain, till by degrees life was bearable again and more than bearable. The law of compensation holds good if you but give it time to operate. No matter what is taken from you—sight, hearing, the person whom you most love—something will be given you in its place, and though it may not be the thing you would have chosen, it will still piece out the pattern of your life. For if there is one merciful thing about life it is that things change. If joy goes and sorrow comes, why, sorrow goes and peace comes—and peace is sweeter, more lasting, than joy.

I am trying to point out that life does not depend for its value on the conditions surrounding it. There is a spirit that accepts whatever conditions come to it and either moulds them to its own ends or, if this be impossible, ignores them and lives on, turning its interest into channel after channel and once and for all refusing to be balked by the merely objective. This spirit realizes that objective values are about equal—that is to say, you can derive only so much enjoyment from food, no matter whether it be chicken *à la king* at the new Waldorf or a sandwich in the automat, or even a bowl of soup on a rainy night in a bread line. The same, of course, holds for clothing, or indeed for any external. What is of vital importance is the subjective—the capacity for enjoyment—and this can be and often is enlarged as objective advantages disappear. Certainly it is well recognized that the blind man has a keener appreciation of beautiful sound than I have, simply because he no longer enjoys the advantage of vision. It is just this capacity for enjoyment which is so intimately ours that life cannot deprive us of it except with our own consent. Nor can life destroy our self-respect any more than it can deprive us of our capacity for enjoyment; so long as we respect ourselves, life is worth making the most of.

Certainly the unnecessary and unjust suffering in the world is hard to bear, and yet, "we are kept keen on the grindstone of pain." It is obvious that most of us require the "sting that bids nor sit nor stand, but go" if we are to do anything at all or to develop mentally. Since human development absolutely requires some form of pain and hardship, where are we going to draw the line between what is necessary for development and what is so overwhelming as to justify refusal to bear it?

One writer has said that she cannot understand how parents who have lost a dearly beloved healthy child can look around at the cripples, the deficient, and the unwanted children who survive and still believe in a divine Providence. I have lost such a child—the youngest, our only girl, a baby of three who, running to meet me, was struck down by a car and died in my arms on the way to the hospital.

The hardest thing about such a loss is, not the agony of separation, not the knowledge that never again in this world shall I feel her tiny trusting hand in mine or hear her say confidently, "Oo won't let it hurt me, will oo, Mommie?"—not even the memory of that last afternoon when I washed her face and hands and sent her happily off to the playground. The thing that is with me night and day is the uncertainty whether all the lovely potentialities that were hers have been completely erased.

But in spite of a sorrow which for me has changed the face of the world, I can still realize how much has been left, and I am occasionally struck by the fact that everyday life seems somehow to have taken on a deeper meaning. I am often surprised to find how interesting and sometimes how lovely are the little things of every day. ˙

For everyday beauty I have the poinsettias against my neighbor's house, the purple on the neck of my own gray pigeon, the exquisite exactness with which the feathers of the white pigeons overlap, the humming bird, a gold and green song in the hibiscus, and the eloquent liquid eyes of Fluffy, our absurdly sentimental mid-Victorian dog.

Behind and around and over these, there is the beauty of the "sweet things," of day and night, of dawn and sunset. More particularly there is the beauty of the stars, which I never seemed really to see until night after night I searched them for an answer to the question, "Has she indeed perished like the grass, which today is and tomorrow is cast into the oven?" Though there came no answer from their vast and silent spaces, there was help in their solemn beauty and in the realization that they have seen countless thousands undergo my sorrow. I learned too that, lonely as one's individual grief must be, it still brings one into kinship with those who have lived and suffered before and those who will live and suffer after. This feeling of beauty and this close kinship with humanity are mine as long as I choose to keep the vision of them. And while I have them I can say: "There's night and day, brother, both sweet things; sun, moon, and stars, brother, all sweet things; there's likewise a wind on the heath. Life is very sweet, brother. Who would wish to die?"

Rise of American Civilization

1929—Marathon dancers.
1930—Tom Thumb golf.
1931—Tree sitters.
1933—Jigsaw puzzles.
1934—Hog-calling contests.
1935—"Scratch out the top name and send a dime."
—*Denver Rocky Mt. News*

The World's Most Efficient Pump

Condensed from Scientific American

G. A. SKINNER

THERE IS no man-made pump that compares in efficiency with the human heart. It is able to run a hundred years and more without the loss of even a few minutes for repairs; it tolerates for days at a time an enormous overload; it keeps on going though accelerated to three or four times its normal speed, if its valves leak, it increases its efforts to compensate for the leaks, and still does good work. It is a double force pump—not very large, about the size of its owner's fist—built of very powerful muscle, with the most remarkable control system known.

Even this efficient machine needs care, for the causes operating to induce heart trouble are many. First, probably, among them is inflammatory rheumatism, quite frequent in youth. This is very likely to leave the heart damaged, although the patient seems completely recovered and may even indulge in quite heavy athletics for some years. But trouble develops in the thirties, as a rule, and in the fifties or earlier the person with this sort of heart breaks down.

Then there is the rapid pace of present-day life, to which may be ascribed much of the increase in the death rate from heart disease of recent years. Hearts today are as good as those of yesterday, except for the changed conditions under which they are forced to labor. Years of constant tension develop "blood pressure," increasing materially the work on the heart. In time permanent damage is done which, if nothing more, restricts considerably the physical activities of the possessor.

Certain methods of exercise use up the reserve of the heart with undue rapidity. One of the most serious is the common custom, indulged in by many men who spend most of their time at desks, of trying to get a month's exercise, very strenuously, in a single day. Especially dangerous is it for such a man on a fishing or hunting trip to go into competition with guides and others who are physically active much of the time. His pride insists that he keep up with them and he does—but often at the cost of a serious heart strain. Youth withstands much more of this sort of strain than middle or late life, as the elastic limit of the circulatory system is then much higher.

The same sort of strain takes place in comparatively young men who, splendidly trained athletes in college, have then let all training go. In the course of ten years or so they acquire a fine income, a family, and probably 30 or 40 pounds of surplus weight. They decide that something must be done. If exercise is taken in moderation and gradually increased as the body becomes accustomed to it, the results usually will be excellent. Often, however, the same vigor is used right at the start that was the habit of college days, and trouble is almost certain.

In order to remain at the greatest efficiency, the heart, like all other muscles, should be used not only reasonably but regularly. Otherwise, the reserve built up in active days is gradually lost, and the heart gets "soft," unable to withstand sudden or prolonged strains. If, however, the individual takes a fair amount of exercise daily he is always in training and the heart will withstand astonishing loads, even in late life. It is this type of man who can play tennis in the late sixties, apparently without harm.

There is no set time that a man becomes old, but long observation has set 50 as the age to commence to slow down in every way, particularly in strenuous physical exertions. A man may boast that he is as good as he was at 25 but, he is

not, no matter how much he may feel that way.

If a man suddenly becomes aware that there is something wrong with him, and that his "pump" is not as good as it was, he should not become panicky. He may yet make a fair comeback, even though the valves of the heart may be leaking from a former trouble, the nervous control out of order, and the heart missing like a car with one or two spark plugs shorted, the speed 50 or even 100 percent too fast for a time.

Given half a chance this heart of ours will do unbelievable things. Much can be done, best under the direction of a physician, to keep a damaged heart working. In general, moderation in all life functions is highly desirable for all who are in middle life, and absolutely essential after there is circulatory damage. There should be absolute avoidance of sudden strains of all kinds, mental and physical. Taking time is a great safety element, as it permits adjustment to loads that could not otherwise be accommodated.

Pain about the heart is not frequent, but when it comes it is a serious warning and should be investigated immediately.

WHAT can be done when the heart ceases to beat? Until recently the only answer was the injection of a powerful stimulant into the heart itself. The heart, however, not infrequently failed to respond. A new answer is in the invention of Dr. Albert S. Hyman, heart specialist of Beth David Hospital of New York, and of C. Henry Hyman, electrical research engineer. The essential feature of the "Hyman Otor," as it is called, is a hollow steel needle, through which a carefully insulated wire runs to the open point. Both the needle itself and its central wire are connected to the terminals of a light, spring-driven generator, provided with a current-interrupting device.

This mechanism can be adjusted to give electrical impulses with the frequency of the heart-beat from infancy to old age. The needle, inserted into the right auricle of the heart, "cranks" the heart engine with its rhythmical current, stimulating the heart's own "generator" to act in step with its electrical generator until normal action is resumed. Usually this occurs quickly.—*Popular Science.*

This Age of Ingenuity

A TIRE approaching the non-skid qualities so long sought by manufacturers is now on the market. Instead of a complex pattern on the tread, it has thin, longitudinal fins, about a sixteenth of an inch apart. Tests show that the bending and twisting of these fins, under the weight of the car, result in a stronger grip on the surface of the road.—*Forbes* and *Scientific American*

THE machine age is displacing the garbage pail with an electrical garbage man which works right in the kitchen. It is a grinder, driven by an electric motor, which can be installed under the kitchen sink. Waste, placed inside, is shredded by knives and reduced to a fine pulp which is flushed away by water into the sewage stream.—*Christian Science Monitor*

A NEW rail-highway motor truck recently made a run from Akron to Cleveland over Baltimore & Ohio railroad tracks, turned off the rails at West Third Street, and proceeded to its destination. The truck has combination wheels which carry special truck tires beside steel flanged railway wheels. It is driven onto the rails at any crossing. The rubber tires are then deflated, so that the truck settles down with its steel wheels on the tracks. The front wheels are locked when the truck is on the tracks and the driver has no steering to do. When it arrives at its rail terminus, all four of the tires are inflated simultaneously from the engine by the same air-system that is used for brake operation.—*Scientific American*

The Miracles of Lourdes

Condensed from Fortune

IN AUGUST, 1926, Mme. Augustine Augault went from Craon, France, to the Roman Catholic shrine at Lourdes. She was small and worn. She would have weighed only 75 pounds except for a swelling that bulged under her coat. This, her doctor certified, was a fibroid tumor of the uterus, which weighed 25 pounds. She was being fed by means of injections. Three surgeons had refused to take the responsibility of operating, so she had come to Lourdes.

She was carried on a stretcher in the procession of the Blessed Sacrament. There were many other invalids, women with open sores and men wrapped like mummies riding in wheel chairs. Those who were able kneeled, and from the pavements below the high, white church there rose a long-drawn chant. Some of the voices were thin and breathless, others were hysterical. After she had received the Sacrament, Mme. Augault said she felt very well. Next day 30 doctors, Catholics and non-Catholics from various parts of the world, came and examined her. The swelling had disappeared. It had

not changed, they agreed, into another form. There had been no discharge. The doctors said the growth must have been "annihilated." The only evidence that it had ever existed was a slight enlargement of the uterus which soon vanished. Such wonders are frequently reported from Lourdes: the instantaneous growth of good tissue, the swift knitting of broken bones, the immediate disappearance of sores, tuberculosis, blindness, paralysis, deafness.

In Lourdes, Catholicism has a shrine of international repute. Perhaps because newspapermen are chary of reputed miracles, Lourdes seldom reaches the headlines. But each year this pocket of the Pyrenees is visited by no less than a million persons. Ninety-nine percent of the pilgrims seek spiritual, not physical aid. One percent of the pilgrims (10,000) are seriously crippled or ill, and of these about 150, or 1.5 percent of the total number of invalids, profess themselves to be cured. And each year about ten of these cures, or .1 percent of the total number of invalids, are certified by the medical bureau

240

and called miraculous by the authorities of the Diocese. These ten certified cures are so-called *incurable* cases. Usually they seem to exhibit the instantaneous growth or change of organic matter. They seem, in short, to be miracles—"exceptions to the order of nature as known in our common experience." The percentage of miracles is small, but in the matter of miracles percentages have no significance. If one miracle occurs, it is as remarkable as a hundred.

There are annual organized pilgrimages to the damp grotto of Lourdes from every corner of the earth. Beginning March 15, when the snow is not yet off the lower hills, the hotel registers of the town carry the unpronounceable names of central Europe and the Near East. June and July bring hordes of Italians, Spaniards, Belgians, and Americans—the lame, the blind, the unhappy, and the merely inquisitive. In the midsummer heat the undemonstrative faithful of England tramp the streets and then, for five hot days in August, the hotels and hospitals are jammed with the National French Pilgrimage, 100,000 of the devout. The Irish follow, and until October 15, when the season closes, fatherly missionaries play escort to silent companies of Chinese, Japanese, Malaysians, Siamese.

Pilgrims arriving at Lourdes are met by volunteer workers. The miracles have drawn hundreds of penitent volunteers to aid the pilgrims under the direction of two French Catholic societies. These societies include princes and barons, school-teachers and bookkeepers. The men act as *brancardiers* (stretcher bearers) and the women as nurses, dishwashers, cooks. These volunteers make it possible for thousands of the needy to visit Lourdes at a minimum of expense.

The special trains begin to roll in at four in the morning. Healthy visitors go to the hotels. The helpless are carried in trucks and motor buses to the hospitals. Patients are segregated by sex but not by disease. No contagious cases come to Lourdes, but the possibilities of infection are limitless. Into the same dormitories (where windows are closed in the Gallic fashion) go paralytics, consumptives, lepers, syphilitics. Patients with wasted bodies and crooked spines and sightless eyes lie next to patients with gangrenous wounds, yellow crusted sores, cancerous skins. Yet the local doctors say that no infection has ever spread at Lourdes and an English nurse writes: "At Lourdes it is a joy to flout the microbe. No critic has ever proved a single case of disease contracted by contact with the sick at Lourdes."

At 7:00 a.m. the trek to the Grotto begins. Each *malade* is assigned a *brancardier* with a bath chair or stretcher on wheels. Before the Grotto the pilgrims halt for hours, praying, saying their beads, fixing their eyes on the marble Lady of Lourdes for such long times that it is no wonder the statue is often said to smile or nod. At 10:00 a.m. the baths are opened and the sick are bathed. There are three of these baths—one for men, two for women—and each bath is capable of holding three persons at a time. The sick are stripped, wrapped in towels, and quickly immersed. The water is not changed during the day and it is black by nightfall.

The Mother Church at Rome has adopted no official attitude toward the miraculous reports from Lourdes and other Catholic shrines. It does, however, recognize the existence of miracles and has "commended" the occurrances at Lourdes as manifestations of the Virgin's power. Priests at the shrine ask the pilgrims not to expect physical miracles but to pray for spiritual grace, but despite this all the conversation at Lourdes is of miracles.

In 1887 the Bureau des Constatations Médicale was organized at Lourdes to examine and certify reported cures. The bureau is under the authority of its president (today the ex-army surgeon Auguste Vallet) appointed by the Bishop. On his staff are ten or twelve doctors who volunteer their services. The personnel changes and more than 1000 medical men of all creeds, all countries, take part in these examinations every year. The doctors are always in attendance near the Grotto. A "cured" patient is hurried away from the instantly gathered crowd and rushed to this office to be examined, X-rayed, tested. The record and history of his case from his local doctor must be presented and studied for comparison with his existing condition. This rule, the skeptic is quick to argue, still leaves a loophole. The local doctor might "fake" the record, certifying a disease that did not exist. On the other hand, it is difficult to believe that *all* the local doctors involved have been charlatans.

The doctors' bureau at Lourdes may make one of four decisions: (1) the patient is hysterical, there is no cure; (2) the case is not completely cured but an "interesting amelioration" has taken place; (3) the case, which was (under certain natural conditions) curable, has been cured; (4) the case, which was *incurable*, has been supernaturally cured. In the event of this last and most important decision the *miraculé* must return after a year's time to be reëxamined. Then, if he has suffered no relapse, his cure will be "certified" by the doctors' bureau, pronounced a miracle by the Bishop of the Diocese.

Mlle. Elisabeth Delot went to Lourdes in 1926 certified as having cancer of the stomach which had completely blocked the pylorus and produced secondary growths on the liver. X-rays had been taken and surgeons had pronounced it an inoperable case. In the water at Lourdes Mlle. Delot had a moment of excruciating pain and then felt suddenly eased. Her subsequent examination revealed not cancerous growths but healthy tissue.

Gabriel Gargam went to Lourdes in 1901, certified as having been paralyzed from the waist down after a railway wreck. He was receiving an annual injury pension of

3000 francs a year from the railway. His trouble was compression of the spinal cord by a displaced vertebra. During the procession of the Blessed Sacrament he tried to rise, fell back, then rose and walked a few steps. Within 24 hours he was walking almost normally. He returns to Lourdes each year as a *brancardier*. His vertebra is still out of place.

Other often cited cases are those of Pierre de Rudder, cured of a compound fracture of the tibia by the instantaneous creation of three centimeters of bone; Marie Lemarchand, cured of tubercular sores on face and leg. She was examined both *before and after* her immersion by Dr. d'Hombres, who declared the repulsive sores to have completely disappeared in a few minutes. John Traynor (English war hero) was reported instantaneously cured of a head wound, paralysis of the legs, and epilepsy. Although he now drives a coal truck, the Ministry of Pensions has refused to recognize his claim of cure and continues to pay him a 100 percent pension.

The list of cures grows longer each year. Documentation grows more involved but no more convincing to the skeptics. "One wooden leg," wrote Anatole France, "is worth all the discarded crutches at Lourdes." And lawyers point out that witnesses are incapable of reporting what they have seen and heard and felt.

The official answers to criticism may be summed up by a quotation from a speech by the presiding doctor, Auguste Ballet. "The cures of Lourdes are in some sense a suspension of the laws of nature, by a principle or agency which has control over these laws. The author of the laws of nature is God. Logic, therefore, forces us to admit that the cures of Lourdes are brought about by a direct intervention of God." Father John LaFarge, cultivated U. S. churchman, editor of the Catholic weekly *America*, and member of a family noted in American arts, has remarked apropos of Lourdes: "For those who believe in God no explanation is necessary. For those who do not believe in God no explanation is possible."

The Fair and Warmer Sexes

THE NOTED German hygienist, Dr. Ernst Friedberger, placed thermometers and other precision instruments beneath the clothing of men and women, and so measured the temperature and humidity next to their skins. He found that the temperature next to a woman's skin is as much as ten degrees lower than next to a man's, and that the humidity is from a third to a half less.

"The average modern man," he concludes, "spends most of his life, winter and summer, in the debilitating climate of the tropics. Only his face and hands are allowed to stick out into healthier surroundings. The average woman, on the other hand, lives in a climate like the cool, dry air of the Alps."—*Popular Science*

The Sea Serpent's Own Story

From The New York Times

FROM the Sea Serpent's middle eye a tear ran down his off foreleg and he brushed it away gently with his right dorsal fin. "So you do believe in me?" he asked.

"Certainly," said the newspaper man. "Why shouldn't I?"

The Loch Ness-Tampico Monster shook his head. "The incorrigible skepticism of the Human race," he said. "Think of what Christopher Columbus endured before he met Ferdinand and Isabella. Think of what they did to Robert Fulton until he succeeded in sailing his steamboat up the Hudson. Think of Galileo. Think of Anne Nichols until she found somebody to finance *Abie's Irish Rose*. When I first bobbed up in the Scottish lake, it was the same old harsh, unbelieving world that I had met so many times before. The more conservative London newspapers referred to me editorially as extravagant nonsense. Try to think of even nonsense being extravagant in Scotland. You *do* believe in me honestly?"

The reporter took out a cigarette and lit it in the blue flame issuing from his companion's nostrils.

"My dear Lusus Naturae," he said, "nowadays everything is credible. I have written millions of words about new scientific discoveries that would make the hair stand on end. I have written about infinite space curling up into a strictly finite rubber ball. I have written about electrons which are at the same time particles like caviar and waves like ginger ale. I have described a universe a billion years old composed of rocks five billion years old. I am familiar with quantums which can go from 34th Street to 36th Street without passing 35th Street. I know all about time which moves backward. After Professor Eddington and Professor Shapley, do you imagine it puzzles me to have you show up simultaneously in Scotland, Cherbourg, Yucatan, the Shannon River and Bering Strait? Almost any day I expect you to be reported from the Volga River. To what do we owe your latest reappearance on so many fronts at once?"

The Sea Serpent stared straight ahead of him, her or it.

"Do you know," he said, "I almost didn't show up at all. I had, to put it quite plainly, grown sick of the same weary round. To what purpose this recurrent parade in the public eye—in 1817, and in 1839, and in 1859, and in 1875, and in 1897, and so on? Like a tiresome Business Cycle."

"Why, sure," said the reporter. "There was a picture of you in the New York *Times* the other day as seen by a navigating officer in the Caribbean, all dips and curves. You looked exactly like the monthly carloadings from December, 1928, to February, 1934, inclusive. But pardon me, you were saying."

"I was saying," said the Sea Serpent, "that I grew tired of it all. People were fast ceasing to believe in me and I was beginning to lose credence in myself. After all, my time was past. I belonged in the ooze of the Eocene, not in the full blaze of 20th century civilization. And then all at once it came to me how foolish I was.

"I remember the moment distinctly," continued the Monster. "I was then swimming off Tasmania, Gilbraltar, the south shore of Lake Erie and within sight of the bathers on Waikiki Beach. The thought came to me suddenly that I was not obsolete even if I was very old. I saw men reviving so many customs, practices and beliefs from the past—all the way back from the centuries, from the jungle, from the primeval slime. Here was somebody trying to get back to Robespierre. Here was somebody else trying to get back to the Roman Empire. Here was somebody else getting back to the ethics of the primitive Teutonic forests. And on every hand were clubbings and shootings and hangings and decapitations. Children were being taught to laugh at notions like human brotherhood and human freedom, and instead were drilled in gas masks and hand grenades. So I looked around and said to myself, 'Heck,' I said to myself, 'I am not out of date after all. I belong. I fit in. With so many monstrous things about, why not a Sea Monster?' And here I am."

"How about your plans for the Summer?" asked the reporter.

"Oh, I suppose the usual thing," said the Monster. "Atlantic City, Cape of Good Hope, Spitzbergen, Puget Sound, Valparaiso and Casco Bay. You newspapers ought to make the cable companies give you a flat rate on me."

FOR THOSE tired of trying to use paper towels as washcloths there are lozenges, easily carried in the purse or pocket, that expand into sponges when dropped in water. Ten cost 60¢.—*Tide*

The Plumbers of Paris

Condensed from Esquire

JOSEPH SCHRANK

SOME PEOPLE don't know when they're well off. Charlie Harris had the nicest studio in that part of Paris. And mind you, he had a *tub*. He was one of the few. But Charlie wanted a shower bath.

On the corner was an establishment marked *M. Pettit & Fils, Plombiers*. He found M. Pettit having an *apéritif* at a café close by, and explained what he wanted while M. Pettit listened very sympathetically. "Can you do it?" Charlie concluded.

"As to that—certainly," replied M. Pettit. "You understand, monsieur, it is my *métier*. But permit me to inquire why you should wish to go to all the trouble of installing a private shower bath?"

"Why?" said Charlie, slightly staggered. "Well—I just want one, you see."

"You say you have a tub, monsieur?"

"Yes, monsieur."

"Why not just use the tub then, monsieur?"

"I do use the tub but I want a shower too," said Charlie, gritting his teeth slightly.

M. Pettit shook his head slowly. "Very well, then. I will come to your home, let us say—next Thursday—at eleven?"

"Can't you make it any sooner than that?" asked Charlie.

"Impossible, monsieur. You understand I must prepare."

Prepare what, Charlie wondered. But all he said was, "How long will the job take?"

"Ah," said M. Pettit, "that is impossible to say now. It is too soon. But—er—you are certain that even though you possess a tub you wish this shower bath also, monsieur?"

"Positive, monsieur!" said Charlie, his blood pressure undergoing a distinct rise.

"Very well, then. Thursday at eleven."

Thursday came, and Charlie welcomed M. Pettit at the studio. "Now about the shower—" he began.

"Monsieur has been long in Paris?" asked M. Pettit.

"About three years."

"Ah!" M. Pettit looked pleased. "It is charming, Paris—is it not? It must be a wonderful experience for a foreigner to come to our beautiful Paris to live."

M. Pettit's manners made it impossible to interrupt a long discourse on Paris, French food, wine, women, and culture. Not till nearly lunch time did he "permit himself to view" the bathroom. There a dark cloud settled on his brow. "It is very complicated," he said.

"How much will it cost?" asked Charlie.

Again the cloud settled on M. Pettit's brow. He shrugged his shoulders. "It will depend on many things, monsieur," he replied, "upon the quality of the fixtures, upon the amount of pressure you desire—oh, many things! And also upon how long it will take."

"How long *will* it take?" asked Charlie.

"Ah—that. It is impossible to say. A few days."

"Couldn't you send more than one man?"

"Naturally," said M. Pettit. "We never send one man alone. It would not be very pleasant for him to work. After all, a man must have someone to talk to, isn't it so, monsieur?"

About ten days later, three workmen with rosy morning faces appeared at the studio. "We are the men of M. Pettit," declaimed one. "You are the monsieur who has commanded the shower bath?"

"Yes," said Charlie.

The workmen smiled and entered. They were in high good spirits. They looked around the studio and chattered and laughed gaily. Suddenly, without any warning, they fell to with tremendous energy and began to tear down part of the bathroom wall. Charlie rushed over to remove an expensive tapestry from the wall, and then fled to a café. He got back a few minutes before eleven. A hole yawned in the wall. It looked like progress. At eleven sharp the men dropped their tools, lit cigarettes and started to leave.

"Where are you going?" asked Charlie.

"It is eleven o'clock," replied the foreman. "We are going for wine." As they passed out, the foreman turned back. "Pardon me, monsieur, the men would like to know why, since you have a tub, you desire also a shower."

"Tell the men," replied Charlie frigidly, "that I desire a shower because I desire a shower."

"Yes, monsieur," said the foreman. He looked at Charlie a little anxiously. After that the workingmen treated Charlie very carefully—like a potentially dangerous lunatic.

After that first morning, it seemed to Charlie that nothing happened for days. The three plumbers arrived every morning at eight-thirty, knocked off at eleven for wine, knocked off again for lunch (two hours), and stopped at six. They held long conversations, turned off the water for long periods, and looked at his English books curiously. Sometimes Charlie heard them arguing for hours about a detail of plumbing technique. On such occasions they dropped their tools and gave themselves up heart and soul to the discussion.

Charlie told his troubles to a friend who was a seasoned resident. "Why, don't you see?" said the friend. "It's simple. They hurry to break your wall down so you can't change your mind about having the job done. Then they take their time."

After a week of this, when Charlie was becoming pretty desperate, he came in one afternoon and found two big pipes sticking up through the studio floor outside the bathroom wall.

"What's this?" he demanded.

"You desire, monsieur?" asked the foreman politely.

"I desire to know what these pipes are doing sticking up in the room this way."

"These are the pipes for the shower bath," replied the foreman proudly.

"Yes, but they aren't going to remain in the room this way, are they?"

"But why not?" asked the foreman, rather amazed.

"Why not! It looks terrible. It spoils the whole room!"

The workmen looked at one another in surprise. One of them said weakly, incredulously, "You don't like the pipes, monsieur?"

"Like the pipes!" Charlie raged. "Sure I like the pipes. I love the pipes!"

"Thank you very much, monsieur," said the foreman, relieved. He patted the pipes affectionately.

"But," continued Charlie, "I want them concealed in the wall. Understand?"

"Concealed in the wall!" The workers were horrified. "But—but, monsieur, if they are concealed in the wall no one will know they are there. No one will *see* them!"

"That's right," said Charlie, "no one will ever see them if they are in the wall. That's right." He began to laugh a little wildly, and went out.

When the job was finished, two iron pipes graced his living-room wall.

One Sunday afternoon some time later the doorbell rang. Charlie opened the door and found the foreman of the plumbers, with a man and a woman dressed in their Sunday best. They wore expectant expressions.

"Pardon this intrusion," said the plumber, "would monsieur permit me to show my friends the work we have done in your studio—the shower bath and the pipes?"

Patter

A woman looks on a secret in two ways: Either it is not worth keeping, or it is too good to be kept.

In America there are two classes of travel—first class and with children.—Robert Benchley

Are you worried or single?—Ed Wynn

And they were married and lived happily even after.—*Church World*

The Tough Days of Baseball

Condensed from Liberty

JOHN J. McGRAW

I was brought up in a fighting baseball school. A school that had for its creed a "win by any means" spirit, an earnest conviction that a ball game—any ball game —was something to fight for. Many of our stunts would be considered unethical today, but they won ten pennants and three world's championships for the Giants under my direction, and before that made the Baltimore Orioles, especially during 1894, '95 and '96, the outstanding club of baseball history.

I recall a typical "fight" episode of the old days with the Orioles. A runner on first started to steal second. But first of all he spiked our first baseman on the foot. Our man retaliated by trying to trip him. He got away, but at second Heinie Reitz tried to block him off while Hughey Jennings covered the bag to take the throw and tag him out. The runner evaded Reitz and jumped feet first at Jennings to drive him away from the bag. Jennings dodged the flying spikes and threw himself bodily at the runner, knocking the breath out of him. In the meantime the batter hit our catcher over the hands with his bat

so he couldn't throw, and our catcher trod on the umpire's feet with his spikes and shoved his big mitt in his face so he couldn't see the play. But the funniest part was the umpire's decision: he punched the catcher in the ribs, called it a foul ball, and sent the runner back to first.

On that old Baltimore club we used to keep a row of files hanging on the wall back of a bench just outside the visiting players' dressing rooms, and as the visiting team came out to start its practice we'd be sitting there sharpening up our spikes. It was done for psychological effect, but to make it good we'd go tearing into a bag with flying spikes as though with murderous intent. As a result many a game was won before the first ball was pitched.

While playing third base for the Orioles I evolved the little trick of hooking my hand inside the belt of a base runner on third when a fly was hit to the outfield. In this way I could prevent him from getting a quick start in an attempt to score after the catch. A lot of runners were thrown out due to the time thus lost. As there was only one umpire in those days and he had to watch the play in the outfield, it was easy to get away with the trick. But one day Pete Browning of Pittsburgh put one over on me. I had hooked my hand inside his belt, but as soon as the catch was made Pete broke for the plate—and left me standing there with his un-buckled belt dangling from my hand.

I have been called "the Stormy Petrel of Baseball"—and I guess I deserve the appellation. But fre-quently I managed to change the entire aspect of a baseball game and arouse the flagging spirits of my players by this very "McGraw rowdyism."

The Giants were playing in Cin-cinnati. It was a terrifically hot day, and both teams were playing as though their only thought was to get it over with. It didn't matter to the Cincinnati club, but we needed the game; we were fighting for the pennant. To make matters worse, Bill Byron, the umpire, was having a bad day. His decisions were equally bad for both teams, but I decided to act as if he was giving us the worst of it. So I ran in from the coaching line to object, and kept it up though I seemed to be getting nowhere. Along about the sixth inning one of our players was called out at the plate on a close decision. I rushed in and gave Byron an extra-violent argument. Finally he ordered me out of the game. I refused to leave. Then he pulled out his watch. "I'll give you just two minutes—" he started to

say when I grabbed the watch out of his hand and bounced it off the home plate. The works flew in all directions. Byron was speechless. I left the game—to the hoots and jeers of the crowd—but my players went back with a different spirit and won. The next day when By-ron came onto the field, I presented him with a beautiful gold watch. His had been a cheap watch any-way. Byron was pleased; he didn't even report the incident to league headquarters.

George Stallings used these fight-ing tactics in 1914—and he drove the Boston Braves, that had only one .300 hitter and a terrible out-field, from last place on Fourth of July to a world's championship in October. Then, the day of the opening game of the world's series in Philadelphia, he saw to it that all his players were sitting in chairs directly in front of the telephone booths at the Aldine Hotel. He came stalking in, apparently as mad as a hornet, and went into a tele-phone booth, leaving the door ajar. They heard him call the playing field of the Athletics and ask, "Is that Connie Mack?" Then he said, "Well, I just called up to tell you that you ought to be thrown out of baseball for even making the sug-gestion that you did to me." He apparently listened a while. Then— "All right, all right! My players will fight it out with yours—and you'd better tell that Sunday-school bunch of yours to keep out of our way if they don't want to go to the hospital. That's all, you big boob." News of the quarrel even got into the newspapers. It stirred Philadelphia from one end to the other. The Braves went into the world's series with a fighting spirit that couldn't be denied and won the championship in four consecutive games. But Stallings had had his hand on the telephone receiver hook all the time; he had been talking into a dead wire.

Connie Mack, Stallings' unsuspecting victim that day in Philadelphia, was himself one of the trickiest catchers the game has ever known. In the days when a foul tip caught directly off the bat was out instead of being called a strike, he used to make a sound like a foul tip —striking the edge of his mitt sharply with the fingers of his bare hand as the batter swung at the ball. It fooled both the batter and the umpire. Connie got away with this repeatedly before it was discovered; then in 1895 came the rule that the batter was out on a caught foul only when the ball went at least ten feet in the air or ten feet away from the plate.

It was by playing on baseball superstitions that I gained my first pennant for the Giants, in 1902. In mid-season the team went into a batting slump, losing game after game. Then one day Frank Bowerman came into the clubhouse with a smile on his face. "Saw a load of empty barrels on my way back to the park today, boys," he announced. "Watch me pickle that old apple this afternoon!" And he did—four hits out of five times at bat. That gave me an idea. The next day three or four more players came in to tell about seeing a load of empty barrels. They too got out of their batting slump. Finally all the players had seen those empty barrels and opposing pitchers were being driven to the showers every day. Billy Gilbert, our second baseman, began to get suspicious. He had seen the barrels several times but the horses were always the same. "Sure," I agreed, "I hired that teamster by the week, to meet you fellows coming in. You don't think I could afford to have him change horses every day, do you?" The players had a good laugh—but I had broken their batting slump by taking advantage of the ball players' pet superstition.

In the fall of 1908 we were thundering down the stretch neck and neck with the Cubs. We had a series to play with the Phillies, who were going nowhere, and counted the games as good as won. But a pesky young left-hander, Coveleski, made his big league début against us and beat us three games with a sensational pitching performance that brought him the name of "Giant Killer." Any one of those games would have given us the pennant.

That winter I got some inside dope on Coveleski: I was told to imitate a snare drum whenever he worked against us. It seemed that when he was a coal miner, Covey had joined the local band. His girl, who was a nut on music, made him do it. He didn't know anything about music but they let him play the snare drum at the annual concert, where they wanted to make a big showing. Covey mixed his signals and thought that the cue for a solo from the fiddle was for him. He came in strong and broke up the concert. His girl threw him over, and the snare-drum thing had been a sore spot with him ever since.

The first game against Covey in the spring, I tried my snare-drum imitation. As he wound up for the first ball, I suddenly shouted, "Ta-rat-a-tat-tat! Ta-rat-a-tat-tat!" Coveleski hesitated and looked my way. I made motions as though I were beating a drum and shouted some more. The crowd must have thought I was crazy, but that first pitch hit the dirt in front of the plate. We scored three runs the first inning. Next inning every player on the bench was beating an imaginary drum and shouting "Rat-a-tat-tat!" In the fourth inning, the Phillies had to take Coveleski out—and the Giant Killer who had beaten us out of a pennant never won another game against the Giants. Later he was traded to Cincinnati, and we snare-drummed him out of every ball game he started against us. Finally Cincinnati sent him back to the minors.

Long before that, way back in 1894, Jennings, Keeler and I used to sit up nights figuring out schemes to win games. Then we'd try them out in practice till we got them letter-perfect. The hit-and-run play was our first big success of this sort. We tried it at the opening of the 1894 season, against the famous old New York Giants. I led off in the Baltimore batting order and got a base on balls. Keeler batted next.

At once I made a bluff to steal second, while Keeler watched the second baseman and shortstop to see which one made a move to cover second on the threatened steal. This would tell Keeler where to hit the ball when I really started for second. Keeler had a wonderful batting eye: he could place the ball wherever he wanted to. So he'd slap it through the spot vacated by the infielder who covered, while I raced on to third and he got a base hit. The Giants never suspected it had been prearranged. Thanks to this hit-and-run play, we won the next three games against a team supposed to outclass the league.

Next we figured on the possibility of scoring a runner from third on a sacrifice bunt by having the runner dash for the plate with the pitcher's first motion. We found that it was humanly impossible for any infielder to stop the runner from scoring so long as he started with the pitch and the batter bunted the ball on the ground anywhere in fair territory. So the squeeze play was born. That season of 1894 we stole the pennant by stealing bases.

In 1911 we did it again—stealing more bases than any other big league club had since 1903. I believe the effort to hold our runners on the bases, and worrying about what we would do next, reduced the efficiency of opposing pitchers at least one-third. It worried the Athletics, too, in the world's series that same year. After we had beaten them in the opening game in New York, and then gone to Philadelphia to play the next game, I was surprised at the wet condition of the base lines. A bystander told me it hadn't rained for a week. Then I knew that the base lines had been "doped" —wet down purposely to slow up our base runners. Another little artifice that we had carried to a high state of perfection with the old Baltimore Orioles, though for an opposite purpose.

In those days we mixed the soil of the infield with a kind of clay which, when wet and then rolled, was almost as hard as concrete and gave us a fast track for our base-running and bunting. In addition the ground outside the first- and third-base lines was built up slightly to keep well-placed bunts from rolling foul, while toward first base we created a distinct down grade to aid us in beating out our bunts. Another trick was to soap the soil around the pitcher's box, so that when the pitcher picked up some to dry his perspiring hands, it made his pitching hand so slippery he couldn't control the ball. Our own pitchers knew where the unadulterated earth was, or carried some private stock in a hip pocket.

Possibly the "inside game" that we used to play was too subtle for a crowd that takes more pleasure in seeing the ball whaled out of the lot. Maybe the "rough-house" tactics that we formerly employed have been outmoded by an advancing, gentler civilization. "In the old days," as Fred Clarke of the Pirates said, "there never was any friendly chatting on the field, as is a commonplace today. We were enemies and never forgot it. If we jumped into an opposing player covering a base and knocked him flat, no apologies were offered, none were expected. Today base runners actually apologize after colliding with a baseman! That's polite—but it isn't baseball as we used to play it."

Coal Mines Afire

IN SIBERIA and North Caucasia, USSR mining engineers are burning coal mines underground for their gas content. Suggested by the famous British chemist, Sir William Ramsey, before the turn of the century as the most economical way to use coal deposits of the lower grades, the scheme has been little used elsewhere in the world.

Sir William argued logically that for many purposes it was wasteful to dig mines and extensive cross shafts, send men down to dig out the coal, ship it hundreds and thousands of miles and finally burn it to make coal gas for illumination, cooking and power. He recommended setting a coal deposit on fire and then by controlled draft and flues leading the coal gas to the surface. According to Russian tests the labor spent on the gas is only from one tenth to one sixth of that needed in mining. Moreover, it is possible to obtain gas from very narrow sheets of buried coal which would be unprofitable to mine in the ordinary way.—
Science-Supplement

Mary White

A famous little classic from the Emporia Gazette

WILLIAM ALLEN WHITE

One of America's best known and best loved editors, William Allen White, wrote for his Emporia Gazette the following tribute to his daughter on the day of her funeral

THE PRESS REPORTS carrying the news of Mary White's death declared that it was the result of a fall from a horse. How she would have hooted at that! She never fell from a horse in her life. Horses have fallen on her and with her—"I'm always trying to hold 'em in my lap," she used to say. She could ride anything that had four legs and hair. Her death resulted not from a fall, but from a fractured skull, and the blow came from the limb of an overhanging tree.

The last hour of her life was typical of its happiness. She came home from school, and felt that a ride would refresh her. She climbed into khakis, chattering to her mother, and hurried to get her horse and be out. As she rode through the town on an easy gallop she kept waving at passers-by. She knew everyone. For a decade the little figure with the long pigtail and the red hair-ribbon has been familiar in Emporia. She passed the Kerrs, and waved at them; passed another friend farther on, and waved at her. As she turned into Merchant Street the horse swung into a lope. She passed a school boy friend and she waved at him, but with her bridle hand; the horse veered quickly, plunged into the parking where the low-hanging limb faced her, and, while she still looked back waving, the blow came. But she did not fall from the horse; she slipped off, staggered and fell in a faint. She never recovered consciousness.

But she did not fall from the horse, neither was she riding fast. A year ago she used to go like the wind; but that habit was broken, and she used the horse to get fresh, hard exercise. Need for that has kept the dauntless little brown-clad figure on the country roads of this community; it built into a strong, muscular body what had been a frail and sickly frame. But the riding gave her more than a body; it released a gay and hardy soul. She was the happiest thing in the world. And she was happy because she was enlarging her horizon.

254

She came to know all sorts and conditions of men; Charley O'Brien, the traffic cop; and all the girls, black and white, above the track and below the track, were among her acquaintances. She brought home riotous stories of her adventures. She loved to rollick; persiflage was her natural expression at home; her humor was a continual bubble of joy. She was mischievous without malice, as full of faults as an old shoe. No angel was Mary White, but an easy girl to live with, for she never nursed a grouch five minutes in her life.

With all her eagerness for the out-of-doors, she loved books. On her table when she left her room were a book by Conrad, one by Galsworthy, and a Kipling. She read Mark Twain, Dickens and Kipling before she was ten. Within the last two years she had begun to draw. She began as most children do by scribbling in her schoolbooks, funny pictures. She took a course—rather casually, naturally, for she was, after all, a child with no strong purposes—and she tasted success by having her pictures accepted by the high school Annual. But her delight when asked to do cartoons for the Normal Annual was too beautiful for words. The drawings accepted, her pride—always repressed by a sense of the ridiculous—was a gorgeous thing to see. In her glory, she almost forgot her horse—but never her car.

She used the car as a jitney bus. It was her social life. She never had a "party" in all her nearly 17 years—wouldn't have one; but she never drove a block in the car in her life that she didn't fill it with pick-ups! Everybody rode with Mary White—white and black, old and young. She liked nothing better than to fill the car full of long-legged high school boys and an occasional girl, and parade the town. She never had a "date," nor went to a dance, except once with her brother, Bill, and the "boy proposition" didn't interest her—yet. But great spring-breaking carloads of "kids" gave her great pleasure. Her zests were keen.

The poor she had always with her, and was glad of it. The last engagement she tried to make was to take the poor folks at the county home out for a car ride. And the last endeavor of her life was to try to get a rest room for colored girls in the high school. She found one girl reading in the toilet, because there was no better place for a colored girl to loaf, and it inflamed her sense of injustice and she became a nagging harpie to those who, she thought, could remedy the evil.

She hungered and thirsted for righteousness; and was the most impious creature in the world. She joined the church because she felt the church was an agency for helping people, and she wanted to help. She never wanted help for herself. Clothes meant little to her; she never wore a jewel and never asked for anything but a wristwatch. She refused to have her hair up, though she was nearly 17. Above every other passion of her life was her passion not to grow up, to be a child. The tomboy in her seemed to loathe to be put away forever in skirts. She was a Peter Pan, who refused to grow up.

Her funeral was as she would have wished it; no singing, no flowers save the big bunch of red roses from her Brother Bill's Harvard classmen—Heavens, how proud that would have made her! and the red roses from the *Gazette* force—in vases at her head and feet. A short prayer, Paul's beautiful essay on "Love" from First Corinthians, some remarks about her democratic spirit by her friend, the pastor (which she would have deprecated if she could), a prayer, and opening the service, the slow, poignant movement from Beethoven's Moonlight Sonata, which she loved, and closing the service the joyously melancholy first movement of Tschaikowski's Pathetic Symphony, which she liked on the phonograph; then the Lord's Prayer by her friends.

That was all.

It would have made her smile to know that Charley O'Brien, the traffic cop, had been transferred to the corner near the church to direct her friends who came to bid her goodby.

A rift in the gray clouds threw a shaft of sunlight upon her coffin as her energetic little body sank to its last sleep. But the soul of her, the glowing, fervent soul of her, surely was flaming in eager joy upon some other dawn.

What's New in College Courses

THE MOVIES find a place in the curriculum at the University of Illinois. Students attend movies and write comparisons with dramas, novels, biographies or histories on which the pictures were based. At New York University, another motion-picture course studies the sociological rather than the literary aspects of the movies.

—N. Y. *Times*

To BUTLER UNIVERSITY, in Indianapolis, goes the credit for having inaugurated a course in the proper use of leisure time. The course deals exclusively in preparing working men and women to develop cultural and profitable avocations. Public speaking, music, reading, and cultivation of trees, flowers and shrubs are among the subjects offered.—*Herald Tribune*

THE University of Michigan is one of the numerous colleges now offering courses in radio broadcasting. Under the tutelage of broadcasters from Detroit stations, more than 100 students prepare, direct and present daily programs, and study all phases of the business from the sale of commercial programs to station financing. The fact that the national radio chains will employ only university graduates as broadcasters has increased interest in the course.

—*The Journal of Education*

A Very Private Utopia

Condensed from The Nation

STUART CHASE

MODERN CIVILIZATION has nourished a great array of critics. Most of them tell us eloquently what they are against, but only rarely do they tell us what they are for. They are indefatigable in pointing out the shortcomings of society, but they are vague as to available substitutes. From all directions we hear the challenge that *homo sapiens* is only half alive. What does he look like when he *is* alive?

Perhaps by delimiting the kind of life one personally would like to live, it will be possible to remove the impersonal chill which too often hangs about Utopias. I note, then, that I am alive, by and large, under the following conditions:

On encountering a vivid awareness of health.

In pursuing creative work, intellectual or manual. There are definite time limits to both.

Dining well, in comfortable places.

Being looked up to and praised —but the butter must not be spread too thick.

Being with my friends.

Looking at beautiful scenery, beautiful things.

Reading great books, or new and stimulating ideas.

Swimming, dancing, playing tennis, mountain climbing. Watching good sport at not too frequent intervals.

Daydreaming.

Making love spontaneously.

Collecting things. For me, certain sorts of information.

The sensation of being some paces in front of the wolf.

Home life—in fits and starts.

Kindly casual contacts with strangers.

Keen discussion.

A good fight, not necessarily sanguinary, in what seems a decent cause.

The sense of being in bodily danger.

These things seem to mean the good life for me, though to hold that the list is applicable to all is of course ridiculous. What kind of community would I build to increase my living hours? I think that

I would be more alive in a community that deliberately fostered the things on my list; of which good health is probably the most important factor. Fortunately the laws of health are beginning to be understood.

Secondly, I would like to live in a community where beauty abounded; where cities were nobly planned, industrial areas segregated; where great stretches of forest, lake, and mountain were close at hand; where houses and their furnishings were spare and fine and colorful, and there was not a single billboard in a day's march. Cities and houses have been so built.

Thirdly, I would like to live, and to have my neighbors live, free from the fear of want. Such communities have been, but not many of them. Denmark is not far from it today.

Fourthly, I would like to live in a community where I could do the kind of work that is the most fun. In exchange for the fun, the giving of an hour or two a day to the necessary manual work of the world would seem the merest justice. Furthermore, by contrast, it would heighten my fun.

I would like to dress as I pleased, or indeed not to dress at all when the sun was high and the water blue. I should like to experiment with colors and combinations of dress now forbidden. I should like to be able to dance and sing more, play games more, let myself go more. I should like to travel more, visit lost cities and climb in the Andes. It does not do to turn one's

back for long on the bright face of danger.

I should like to be a more compelling and less self-conscious lover, but just how a community would proceed to organize great lovers frankly escapes me.

I would like to live in a world where many good books were being published; where good music and plays were just around the corner—without too much standing in line; where arts and crafts were indigenous rather than imitative; and especially, where good conversation abounded. Of all the joys which life has to offer none, for me, can exceed that of keen talk; and nothing is rarer in America today.

Finally, I would like to live where one could take pride in community achievements, match one's art and craftsmanship and sport against a neighbor group; where one could contribute in person to the local theater, the local schools; help to plan a beautiful region and see that plan grow—and so take root in one's own soil, a part of the earth as well as a dreamer in the clouds.

Such a Utopia may be cold to you, but it is not cold to me. How would you change it? Religion, you say, is necessary. Good. Let us have a church with a great nave and a great organ and the sound of vespers across the evening fields. You dislike my games and want other games. Again good. The more games the better so long as we play them ourselves. Add what you please, so long as it does not quench the life of many to make the lives of a few burn with spurious brightness.

My outline of the good life is crude enough, but it can be used as a searchlight. Swing it where you will. Does this institution, that person, fit in with such a community? The Olympic games would, professional baseball would not; the Lincoln Memorial would, Park Avenue would not.

Would such a Utopia make you more *alive?* It could not abolish pain, failure in achievement or in love, or even envy—they must remain as long as we are human beings. But it might tend to lessen the surplus of pain and confusion caused by stupidity. It might prepare the way for a maximum of living and a minimum of existing— the life more abundant.

Foot Twisting and Faith Healing

Condensed from an editorial in Hygeia

THE HISTORY of healing is full of records of manipulations and devices to reinforce the power of suggestion. For example, there was Emile Coué who caused patients to say to themselves, "Every day in every way I am getting better and better," as they manipulated a knotted string. There was Albert Abrams who used a weird machine and depended on dials to cause the patient to think something was being accomplished. There was Fitzgerald who put wire rings around the toes and fingers to distract the attention from pains elsewhere.

The newest development is Mahlon Locke of Canada who offers to heal arthritis by twisting the bones of the feet.

Enough has been learned about the mechanism of the bones and joints, the nerves and blood vessels, to make it quite certain that no twisting of the foot will adequately control any type of arthritis involving the joints and bringing about permanent disability. Patients with chronic rheumatic disorders are constantly seeking quick cures, and natural remissions in the disease make them particularly liable to become victims of queer methods. The few who seem to be benefited are loud in their praise. Those who fail to be benefited save their faces by keeping quiet.

Thus Mahlon Locke and his technic are not new in the history of charlatanism. Such apostles of healing come and go. They leave behind them a trail of devastated humanity which has given them money that might have been used in securing such relief as competent physical therapy and scientific medicine have to offer.

(Hygeia, November, '34)

Would You Join a Mob of Lynchers?

Condensed from Popular Science Monthly

PRESCOTT LECKY

AT THE University of Iowa, a student recently burst into a psychology classroom. Dramatically he gave details of a local kidnaping and cold-blooded murder. The criminal had been caught, had confessed, and a mob was forming to lynch him. At the height of the excitement, 200 students answered the questions: How many would go and help the lynchers? How many would go along as spectators? How many would stay away?

The student who brought the news acted so realistically that virtually the entire class was deceived in this staged test of mob psychology. The results picture what the average citizen is likely to do if he finds himself near a forming mob: if guilt is certain, 64 out of 200 people will take an active part. Sixty will go along as spectators. Only 76 will remain away. Thus, out of 200 people of better than average education, more than 120 will rush out to join or watch the mob. Why will they act as they do?

You can't measure susceptibility to mob spirit in terms of education or intelligence. In highly cultured communities as well as in backward ones, mass violence appears. A few years ago in a town in Texas having two colleges, 27 churches and 12 city parks, citizens for 14 hours were raging savages who battled Texas Rangers and National Guardsmen and finally burned a man alive.

Three times, the mob charged the courthouse where a negro prisoner had been placed in a steel vault for safekeeping. Then a woman hurled a rock through a window. Two 17-year-old boys poured gasoline through the opening and a man tossed in a lighted match. In five minutes, the building was a mass of roaring flames. Howling outside, the mob cut the fire hose and the prisoner was burned alive in the vault. Hardly had the embers begun to cool when men with acetylene torches cut into the vault to obtain the body. Placing it on a truck, 2000 men, women and children paraded the streets for an hour, then hanged the body, piled boxes beneath, and applied a match.

"Texans," said the Houston *Post*, editorially, "will share the astonishment of the outside world at this exhibition of lawlessness. It defies apology—almost defies explanation." Yet this barbarous spectacle might happen in almost any community. More than 5000 people, many of them later proved innocent, have been lynched in the United States since 1882.

Virtually every case of mob violence grows out of the same thing: a crime so revolting that it stamps the criminal as devoid of human feeling, and makes him appear a fiend. In the Texas case, the prisoner had confessed to attacking an elderly woman. In other instances, mob murders grew out of such depraved crimes as burning a whole family alive, beating out the brains of a defenseless old man, murdering a nine-year-old child. Contrary to general opinion, less than one out of five of those lynched have been accused of sex crimes.

The feeling that it is dealing with something beyond the pale of humanity, with a devil in the form of a man, accounts for the excesses of the mob. There is no feeling of guilt, no remorse at killing a human being. Members of mobs see themselves as heroes ridding the world of something that has no right to live; mob murder is a moral crusade. A few months ago, when Californians lynched the kidnapers of Brooke Hart, before they dragged the two prisoners from their cells to be stripped and hanged, members of the mob knelt in silent prayer.

In time of war, a similar attitude prevails. Moral scruples against killing fellow men are stilled by the feeling that the enemy is a devil capable of any atrocity. Remember stories of how the Germans were cutting off the hands of Belgian babies and boiling up the bodies of slain soldiers to obtain fat for soap making? So in a mob. The crimes of which the victim is accused are repeated over and over until all compassion disappears and no extreme of punishment seems too great.

In one case, leaders of a mob were preparing to hang a man when someone began reciting the awful details of the crime of which he was accused. Repeated over and over, they had a hypnotic effect upon the crowd, driving it to a frenzy. Chaining the prisoner to a stump, the mob poured gasoline over a pile of faggots and turned him into a writhing human torch. As soon as the embers cooled, they rushed in like madmen, hacking the stump and breaking up the chain to obtain souvenirs of the fiendish act.

Why does an individual do things in the mob he never could do alone? Recent tests at an American university show we are three times as likely to accept suggestions without criticism in a mob as in normal life. Thus, members of an excited crowd cease to think as individuals, but are swept along, acting on one suggestion after another without reflection, and in the end are carried farther than they intend.

A Missouri mob snatched the murderer of a 20-year-old schoolteacher from the sheriff and started to hang him from a tree. Then someone shouted: "Let's hang him in the school yard!" Immediately the crowd took up the cry and surged in that direction. At the schoolhouse, someone else yelled: "Let's put him on the roof and fire the building!" Almost automatically, men rushed for ladders, dragged the victim to the roof, and handcuffed him to the peak. Then they poured gasoline around him and touched it off with a match. While hundreds of men, women and children cheered, the fire ate through the roof and plunged the flaming body onto the desks below.

Mere suggestion, accepted without question, has almost unbelievable power over individuals. A few months ago, for example, an eastern chemistry professor tried an experiment. He held up a vial labeled "Violet Perfume" and asked his students to raise their hands as soon as they could detect the odor. Fifteen seconds after he had removed the cork every hand in the front row was up and in less than a minute three-fourths of the class signaled they could smell the perfume. The bottle contained nothing but water.

A doctor reports an even stranger incident. A man and his wife were bitten by a pet dog. The man was sure that he was going to develop hydrophobia; the woman was sure she wasn't. In three days, the man was sick in bed, his throat muscles were becoming taut and he complained of difficulty in swallowing. His wife was up and well. At the end of five days, the man reported all the symptoms of hydrophobia and when a week had gone by the physician saw he was actually on the verge of dying from a disease he didn't have. Finally, on the eighth day, the doctor convinced him that nobody with hydrophobia ever lived more than six days. He jumped out of bed and soon was as well as before the dog bit him.

This element of suggestibility explains the abnormal action of the individual in a mob—a formless group of excited people in a suggestible frame of mind, a leader who makes suggestions and directs the pent-up violence toward a given purpose. Almost always, somewhere along the way, there is a psychological moment when the action of the mob hangs in balance.

During the Siege of Paris, in the Franco-Prussian War, a famous instance of this occurred. Storming the Louvre, where the government was sitting, a mob demanded the immediate execution of a marshal of the army who, they said, had been caught copying fortification plans to sell to the enemy. Because similar plans could be bought in almost any bookstore, the charges were absurd. But the orator who saved the prisoner's life made no attempt to reason with the mob.

"Fellow citizens," he declared, "you have done a great, patriotic deed. Your work is over. Let the government conclude your investigation. Justice—pitiless justice—shall be done. In the meantime we will keep the prisoner in custody." The mob cheered, dispersed, and in half an hour the marshal was able to return safely home.

A twist of a different kind marked a lynching in Indiana a couple of years ago. One night, more than a thousand people collected about the jail where three murderers were awaiting trial. Leading citizens made impassioned pleas for law observance. A show of hands indicated that a majority of the crowd favored letting the law take its course. At that moment, the aged father of one of the victims came from the jail where he had been conferring with the

sheriff. As he emerged, those nearby surged toward him. He lost his footing and fell. Immediately, word ran through the crowd that he had collapsed from the shocking details of the crime he had heard inside. Like a match producing an explosion, the idea touched off the mob. In a fury it lynched two of the slayers and was ready to hang the third before state troopers could get the situation under control.

Such is the way something like hypnotism occurs in a crowd. Research has shown that a person with an alert mind is more likely to be suggestible than one with a slow, dull brain; and only by avoiding crowds which may become violent can most of us be sure we will not join mob action.

"There Must Be Some Mistake"

A FEW minutes after the elegant new $6,000,000 Pittsburgh post office was opened to the public, customers began complaining that there was no letter drop. Dismayed Postmaster Turner got in touch with the architects, who shamefacedly confessed they had actually forgotten all about that important item.—N. Y. *Herald Tribune*

DEAN ALFRED J. PEARSON and 42 graduates of Drake University's Class of '35 marched around the campus carrying an ivy chain in traditional farewell ceremonies. A short time later they made the painful discovery that it had been a *poison ivy* chain.—N. Y. *Times*

THE Coöperative Bank of Newburyport, Mass., spent $500 in renovating a vacant house. Then they discovered that the house didn't belong to them—theirs was two doors away.—N. Y. *World-Telegram*

WHEN a British film studio was annoyed by airplanes passing overhead, the officials had a huge sign painted on the roof—FILM STUDIO—QUIET, PLEASE. It was a sad error. The pilots only dropped down closer, in order to satisfy their curiosity as to what the sign said.—N. Y. *Herald Tribune*

Sleep

Condensed from Fortune

IN TWO YEARS, 1930–32, sales of a single sleep-inducing drug, phenobarbital, rose in this country from 25,000 to 45,000 pounds a year—enough to provide most of the population of the U. S. with a night's rest. The depression, it seems, left a nation tossing on its beds, yearning for some medicine to soothe the fear and anxiety which banish sleep.

As late as 1927 most physicians hadn't the remotest idea how sleep functioned, and until Zalmon G. Simmons, a mattress maker who himself suffered from insomnia, began his investigations, nobody knew just how people *normally* slept. There is the story of Dr. Erich Guttmann, who was studying a group of manic-depressive patients, and who found that they constantly tossed and turned in their sleep. So he wrote his classic article, describing the tortured sleep of the insane. Men of good conscience and sound mind, he assumed, slept motionless as logs— and so thought the medical profession. How far wrong that belief

was appears from the experiments in sleep motility which Dr. Harry M. Johnson of Ohio State University was even then making for Mattress-maker Simmons, who hoped to find out what kind of mattresses really *were* designed for sound sleep.

Dr. Johnson rigged up a bed with an automatic recording machine mechanically connected with the springs to chart every move the sleeper made in a night's rest. A concealed motion-picture camera, also wired to the springs, photographed the sleeper in each of his changing positions. The experiments lasted six years, and gave Dr. Johnson some 2,500,000 measurements of the movements of his 160 subjects and about 20,000 photographs of the strange postures they assumed in their sleep.

A normal sleeper, as Dr. Johnson had suspected, never slept long in the same position. During an eight-hour night, the average sleeper changed his posture 35 times, rarely held one pose longer than five or ten minutes. This nocturnal wan-

264

derlust Dr. Johnson named "motility," and he found that it always accompanied healthy sleep. Reason: the muscular arrangement of the human body is so complex that the sleeper rarely succeeds in resting all his muscles at once. As the muscles in one position grow tired, the sleeper moves, and allows these muscles their turn to relax. Complete relaxation, with the body limp all over as in a swoon, was so rare that Dr. Johnson found hardly a single instance of it.

There is a normal motility curve for each sleeper, varying with the individual; some stir only 20 times a night, some as many as 60 times. If the sleeper turns more than his allotted number of times in a night (from pain or excitement, hunger or surfeit, fever or constipation) he gets insufficient rest. But if he turns too seldom (from weariness or stupor or maladjusted beds and covers) he gets only partial rest, wakes stiff and sore. The sleep of children is violent and often disturbed; old people sleep more quietly than children, though with frequent interruptions. Manual laborers rest for longer intervals than brain workers; women rest 30 per cent longer than men. Dr. Johnson also found that narrow beds interfered with the sleeper's freedom of movement; that people who slept together in double beds would probably interfere with each other's movements; and that for good sleep a bed should be neither too soft nor too hard. These findings became the basis for Simmons' "Vitalizing Rest" campaign of 1931.

But the experiments left unanswered many questions which perplexed the medical profession, and a Georgia physician, Dr. Glenville Giddings, carried on where Dr. Johnson left off. In the mountains near Atlanta, at the site of the Tallulah Falls Industrial School, he began to study the sleep of children. Twelve girls and 12 boys, under the care of two nurses, have been sleeping nightly for Dr. Giddings ever since. From 170,000 hours of spying on sleep, Dr. Giddings concludes that most popular notions of the effects of various habits and therapies on sleep are pure superstition. These things, he found, make children more restless at night: hot weather, heavy meals before bedtime, emotional disturbances (including toys at Christmas), physical pain. These things have little or no effect on motility: hard exercise before retiring, warm baths, cold baths, intensive study in the evening, almost all hot and cold beverages. One thing seems to quiet the children and improve their rest: warm milk. Dr. Giddings also made the interesting discovery, during an epidemic, that he could predict the onset of a disease several days in advance by the increased restlessness of his children. But as to the heart of sleep—its physiological cause and function—these experiments gave no final answer.

There is seldom a sleeper so sound that he fails, when one position tires him, to assume another. Moreover, he guards each movement so that he will not fall out of bed. If he grows hot, he throws off the covers; if he grows cold, he draws them tighter, but always leaves cunning passages between covers and bed for ventilation. These are intelligent responses; and if in sleep neither physical nor mental activity is suspended, wherein does sleep differ from waking?

Says Dr. Giddings: "An observer cannot tell accurately whether a person is awake or asleep at any given instant . . . such terms as 'asleep' and 'awake' are unsatisfactory from a scientific standpoint." Which means that sleep, as we are accustomed to think of it, may not exist at all. Sleep may be simply a cutting off of all but the most immediate part of our attention to the world around us, a flight from reality whereby mind and body willingly suspend their functions in order to gather strength to face the world once more.

From hospital and university laboratories we learn that when you fall asleep certain specific things happen. You fall into a state of comparative unconsciousness. Your eyeballs roll upward and outward; the pupils contract. Your reflex muscular responses (such as the famous knee jerk) diminish or disappear. You breathe more in your chest, thoracically, less in your belly, abdominally. Your blood pressure falls, your heart beats more slowly. Some of your bodily secretions diminish, such as the urine, and mucus from the glands of the nose. Your blood becomes less alkaline. These are phenomena that accompany the process of building up tissue; they are the charging of the battery of the human vehicle, so that it may once more discharge. But none of the investigations have been able to say conclusively what induces sleep. Why, promptly after 16 wakeful hours, does a man have the impulse to sleep? Fatigue doesn't bring on sleep, for abnormal fatigue produces abnormal motility.

This much is agreed on by most students: that sleep is an impulse which comes regularly to normal human beings. It may be nothing more than a powerful habit, to which the bodily organs are accustomed by years of practice. At a specific point in the day, the individual comes to expect sleep: his blood content is changed, his squandering of energy falters; even the tear glands cease to secrete water, his eyes become hot and dry. (Thus the myth of the sandman: for when the tear glands no longer lubricate your eyes, you want to close them; and when you close them, you are likely to sleep.) Among animals and savages the sleep mechanism may function quite differently. It may bring rest through many brief naps during quiet moments of the day and night, or it may come as an impulse that follows meals. For most men, however, sleep functions best as a regular habit. If its regularity is interfered with too often, confusion and insomnia may result.

Men cannot do without sleep. The longest period of authentic wakefulness on record is 231 hours —not quite 10 days—lately achieved under laboratory conditions. Many a legend of prolonged, total insomnia has crept into newspapers; none has ever been verified. But dogs deprived of sleep will die of exhaustion. And men who sincerely believe they have not slept will usually prove to have caught scattered and prolonged naps without knowing it. Even those prodigies of vigilance (John Wesley, Edison, Bonaparte) who were content with a few hours of sleep at night caught many naps at odd hours during the day. Wesley slept in his saddle, Edison in his laboratory, Bonaparte nodded between battles. Such people sleep lightly, like animals, but probably their total slumber falls only an hour or two short of a normal eight hours' rest.

Insomnia may arise from many causes, but it is never a disease in itself. Pain may prevent sleep, emotional disturbances may make it difficult. What most insomniacs suffer from is not sleeplessness itself, but the fear of sleeplessness. Their rest becomes impaired through illness or worry or irregularity; they find sleep difficult; and the fear of insomnia disturbs their rest long after the condition which caused it has gone away.

Prolonged wakefulness, unless it is carried to such an extreme that exhaustion and death follow, has no permanently harmful effect on the body. You cannot "make up for lost sleep," as laymen like to think, by sleeping longer when you finally get to bed; even after three or four days without rest, a single night's sleep will restore you so far as you can be restored. Your efficiency may be slightly impaired for as long as two weeks afterward, but no longer. And more sleep than usual will not reduce that impairment. Your deepest, most refreshing sleep comes within the first two hours or so after you retire. From that time on until you wake up in the morning, you are getting steadily smaller returns in rest from the hours you lie in bed. Sleep is fluid as a pool of water; the mind sinks and rises, drifts and hovers in it, often near the surface.

Recent research has taught us much, and it may in time be possible to provide mankind with a new kind of sleep: conditioned sleep, scientifically controlled to give the deepest rest within the shortest space of time.

Patter

A bald-headed man has less hair to comb, but more face to wash.

One might with justice speak of life in Hollywood as mere sexistence.

The moon affects the tide and the untied.

He is a gentleman farmer—the only thing he raises is his hat.

Too many parents are not on spanking terms with their children.

What Every Woman Almost Knows

Condensed from Liberty

KATHLEEN NORRIS

WHEN her two oldest sons and her two oldest daughters were scrubbed and brushed for church, my mother always gave us parting instructions: "Don't lose your handkerchiefs, come straight home, and let Joe or Fred sit in the aisle seat!" No girl could have the aisle seat. It was for the men. If not the brothers, the papas got it.

"Don't be strong-minded, darlings, whatever you are!" my mother would say in dismayed contemplation of the brazen females who were beginning to fight for their rights. Be weak-minded, be tearful, be helpless and dependent, said the mothers of that day.

The boys escaped on Saturdays into worlds of delicious adventure; the girls stayed home. The boys followed circuses, camped on beaches, climbed trees; we could weed the garden, cook, and write up our diaries. And we were the advanced and fortunate girls of the 'nineties, our mothers reminded us. In their own days, girls had practiced scales for hours, had put up fruit and ironed papa's shirts, had sewed miles and miles of seams.

This glimpse of yesterday's helpless girls is a preamble to my comment on the fact that there are no women geniuses. No woman ever painted a great picture. No woman ever composed an even average opera. No woman ever wrote any considerable musical composition of any sort. No woman ever wrote an immortal book, play, poem. No woman ever made any important contribution to science, unless it was very recently, and then in conjunction with a husband similarly interested.

Those who point out these facts tell us that the old plea of her subjection to male domination does not wholly account for woman's ineffectualness. But I think they underestimate the accumulating weight of injustices down through the ages. To be enslaved, ignored, punished, unrewarded, scorned, belittled even for a few days, has a fearful effect on a child. Thus treated, it may never rise to normal free development again. Why is this not true in a much wider and deeper sense of the sex that under all tribal laws and in all civilizations has been stamped as inferior?

Forty years ago half the English novels dealt with the strange law of primogeniture. Sisters were born—three, seven, ten of them—to be increasingly reproached and scorned; if milord's family was to continue to possess the great fortune, there must be a boy! One may easily gather that the courage, individuality, talents of the girls were not likely to flourish in that atmosphere.

In a great part of southern Europe today no woman may control her own property, although she be an heiress and her husband a beggar; no woman has legal claim on her child; no woman may bring a lawsuit under any condition, or cast a vote concerning property even though she owns it. In Europe today there are nations whose men strike, beat, abuse their women as a matter of course. There are nations whose men ride placidly on donkey back, the women, carrying heavy loads on their heads, and often further burdened by approaching motherhood, plodding wearily behind. In several states women are supposedly disgraced by child-bearing; they must creep away to barns and hedges, must be purified by religious rites afterward. In several South American countries, a young wife is not allowed to speak in public for the first year.

These instances are not from the Orient; they are actual conditions controlling women of Christian nations. Centuries of this sort of thing, and much worse, have not tended to develop initiative, courage, originality, independence in the female. More than half the women of the world today are still living under the old restrictions of the Middle Ages and the harem.

Women who have achieved fame have almost without exception been women whose lives, morals, and policies men heartily disapproved. From the history-making immoralities of Cleopatra, Mary Stuart, Elizabeth, Catherine of Russia, George Eliot, and George Sand, down to the more moderate acts of Christina of Sweden, Anne of England, Mme. de Sévigné, Mme. de Maintenon, Mme. de Staël, Isabella of Spain, Napoleon's Josephine, and Maria Theresa of Austria, their stories are stories of long wars against ministers, critics, moralists, conventions. As for Joan of Arc, leading men, judged by men, burned alive by men, raised by men to sainthood, now a fresh generation of men is attempting to prove that she was not a woman at all.

One reason women gave the other sex the lead is physiological. For the greater part of their lives the women of yesterday were ill. Not only were they subject to the physical tides that are matched by definite mental and spiritual reactions, but the conditions in which they lived, the burdens of child-bearing before the young body had reached maturity and before anesthetics and sanitary care had made it comparatively safe, had the effect of still further crippling the sex that was already crippled by laws and customs.

Given this much start, the exultant male naturally came to his own conclusions about a "weaker sex." But as a matter of simple biological truth women never have been the weaker sex; women never stayed out of wars, feuds and vendettas, crusades and piracy and inquisitions, because they had not *strength* to face them! They kept away because they saw from the very beginning how stupid, wasteful, expensive and ridiculous all these things were; and today men—because of woman's guidance—are beginning to see them that way, too.

Let us take count of those fields where women *have* shown themselves great. They have been great actresses, great singers and dancers; above all, they have been great rulers. Under Catherine of Russia, Anne, Elizabeth, Victoria, nations have had their most prosperous days. Industry and husbandry, clinics and hospitals, shelters and schools all flourished under women rulers. Florence Nightingale did no more for today's soldiers than Elizabeth Fry did for the prisoners of all time, and Elizabeth Barrett for the children that might have been in our mines and are not there. Asking themselves surprisedly, "Why are men fools?" women were awakening even in the era of these women. Mary Shelley, Frances Willard, Emmeline Pankhurst, Sarah Hale, Harriet Stowe—the story of their varied lives says but

one thing: "Why?" Why slums and hunger and wars and prisons and slavery and drink?

Most men never picture a world free from wars, poverty, slums, sweatshops, hunger, and politics. But until these are gone, no woman will go in seriously for art. What men call masterpieces are not always important to women. To women who love children first of all, pictures, music, books, religious and national quarrels—all the things of which men have made the world —are less important than the humble creation of comfort where want and suffering have been, the putting of food before the hungry, the sheltering of a child's head under a shawl. Men like music, bands, uniforms, flags, phrases like "debt of honor" for gambling bills. Women are more practical. Mere pictures do not satisfy them in a world so bitterly in need of real food, shelter, nursing, cooking.

These things are woman's present form of self-expression. They seem urgent, all-absorbing to her. Women applaud Amelia Earhart and Edna Millay, but their passionate admiration is reserved for Jane Addams and Catherine Booth. Our sex need not reproach itself if for those biological moments that are the next few centuries it finds something else with which to occupy its recently enfranchised powers.

So, if there are no women geniuses, it is because we are not ready to compete just yet. But women are advancing toward the point where they will capture that last citadel. Meanwhile it is good to be old enough to contrast the position of the sex thirty-five years ago with that of the sex today. It is good to remember oneself as an office clerk in 1900, dragging long skirts in muddy streets, choked with a high stock, born in a time when there were no votes, no gyms, no health, no sensible clothing for women, when her salary was one-third of a man's, and a brother had to take her to the office in the morning and call for her at night lest she be attacked by wandering swains.

Give us another hundred years, gentlemen. Give us a little more time to clean the house and fill the lamps. Help us to outlaw war, prostitution, drunkenness, illness, poverty, dirt, crime, slums. You'll see!

They Have a Club for It

FIVE YEARS AGO, in penance for a printed reference to his wife's mother as "the standing army," Gene Howe, editor of the Amarillo, Texas, News-Globe, induced local mothers-in-law to form a club, taking as their creed "the elimination of unjust criticism." March 5th was set aside for the annual celebration of Mother-in-Law Day, when "good" mothers-in-law—those receiving "certificates of goodness" from their children's spouse—reap their rewards. Stores offer them free merchandise, luncheons are given in their honor. High spot of the 1938 celebration was a 12-mile parade which included 32 Navajo Indian mothers-in-law; the "most mother-in-law" enthroned with her 17 in-laws; a battleship float carrying 600 mothers-in-law; and a ball-and-chain gang of fathers-in-law. Among the guests were Mrs. Roosevelt, and the Governors of Texas, Kansas, New Mexico, Oklahoma and Colorado.

The World's Worst Railroad Wrecks

Condensed from Railroad Stories

H. T. WILKINS and J. F. BYRNE

WHEN at Lagny, France, on Christmas Eve in 1933, the Paris–Strasbourg Express crashed at a mile a minute into the rear of another passenger train, killing 200 and injuring 300, American newspapers headlined it as the world's greatest rail wreck. Apparently they had little or nothing on file about two more frightful catastrophes that occurred during the War. One was so terrible that its story was suppressed at first. It is told here in detail for probably the first time in America.

But Lagny was bad enough. The fast express from Paris to Strasbourg was an hour late out of Paris that Christmas Eve. A heavy, frosty fog hung over the country, but Engineer Lucien Daudigny was wheeling his engine at a terrific speed. He was hitting off a mile every 55 seconds and did not slow a whit as he approached Lagny, 15 miles east of Paris, as both he and Fireman Henri Carpentier peered vainly out into the thick mist. Suddenly the rear lights of a passenger train—the Paris–Nancy Express—jumped out of the murk, no more than 100 feet ahead. A second later the crash.

All the cars of the Paris–Nancy Express, standing on the main line, were wooden. They were crowded with townspeople and school children going home for the Christmas holiday. The engine of the Strasbourg Express plowed through the last three cars and stopped in the middle of the fourth. By 3 a. m. more than 150 bodies had been recovered, all of them from the Nancy train. Since the Strasbourg Express was of all-steel cars, few passengers on it were even injured. And, though their locomotive had plowed through half a train, the engine crew escaped. In the horrible wreckage were scattered Christmas gifts, cards and school reports. On one report was the notation: "Quick, intelligent; the future holds much in store for him. . . ."

The final responsibility for that wreck must be laid to carelessness, for the speed recorder on Daudigny's locomotive showed he was

272

traveling at more than 65 m.p.h. when the accident happened—and in a fog in which he could see no signals.

Carelessness, also, was the cause of the even greater disaster at Gretna Green in Scotland, where, on May 22, 1915, five trains were scrambled up in one blazing tangle. Very early on that spring morning, the night trick towerman, having put two freight trains on the sidings at the Gretna Green junction, accepted the Beattock–Carlisle local. But he knew that the London–Glasgow sleeping car express, pulled by two engines, was due behind the local, so he switched the local from the down main line to the up main line, and left a clear track for the express.

About this time, however, the night shift towerman was going off duty. He was getting ready to hand over the job to the day man when a special train loaded with Scotch troops was offered to him. In his hurry to vacate his post, he accepted it on the up main, forgetting the local train already there, squarely in the troop train's path.

But this was not all. His bell rang asking him to accept the London–Glasgow express. He did so, and set the signal to clear for that train. The first reminder of his terrible mistake was a deafening crash as the troop train, running more than 60 miles an hour, sailed head-on into the local passenger. Instantly realizing what had happened, the stunned towerman kept his head enough to think of the Glasgow Express. He was too late.

As he frantically threw the signal to danger, the engines were passing the signal posts.

Meanwhile, those who escaped in the first collision were already trying to get the dead and dying out of the wreckage. They never knew what hit them. Tearing around the curve at full speed, the express train thundered into the already wrecked local, killing both rescuers and rescued, and scattering the two freight trains on the sidings. The leading engine of the express leaped into the air when it hit, and curiously neither fireman nor engineer was killed. The second engine, however, was crushed to pieces and the crew with it.

Immediately fire broke out in the wooden sleeping cars whose gas lighting equipment was smashed. The doors were wedged tight, and those passengers who were not killed outright were burned in the flames that enveloped all five trains. In all at least 227 persons were killed and 250 injured.

Of course there was an investigation. The night shift towerman was brought to trial for manslaughter, and a more piteous trial never took place. The man already had taken more punishment from his conscience than any court could have dealt him. He pleaded guilty and was sentenced to imprisonment.

That was the second greatest of the world's rail disasters. But the most horrible of them all occurred in the winter of 1917 which was, at best, a gloomy one for the Allied forces. Although America had entered the War that spring, the

French army was desperate. General Nivelle's offensive in the Champagne had met with overwhelming defeat. There followed a mutiny in the French army affecting, according to a recent dispatch to the New York *Times*, "115 units . . . in which . . . one mutineer out of every five was chosen by lot for execution. . . ." Then, to cap it all, came the rail disaster at Modane. So terrible was that wreck that the desperate French Government suppressed all news of it. Had the facts become widely known, they might easily have been the signal for a greater revolt within the French ranks, as the French officials realized all too well. Only today has the inside story of this appalling wreck become known, let alone printed, in the United States and Canada.

It happened on the night of December 12, 1917. About 1200 soldiers were waiting at the little station at Modane, on the Franco-Italian frontier. They were going home on Christmas leave after the bloody battle of the Piave. The next stage of their journey lay through a precipitous mountain gorge along the side of which crawled the railroad. The soldiers jammed the train, yelling out of the windows, impatient to start. But the driver stepped down from his cab, excitedly gesticulating.

"The train is too heavy," he called to a group of bedizened brass hats. "It is dangerous to start. It is devilish steep ahead, with curves and a sharp grade. I will not go! It is impossible!"

"What, impossible?" snorted the blue uniforms and gold-braid. "You are a coward, my man, not a Frenchman!"

The French writer, Henri Barbusse, tells how the engineer doggedly warned the military autocrats that the overloaded train would take a header down an Alpine grade and get out of control. But the officials stuck to their orders. When the engineer refused to open the throttle, they told him to start or be put under arrest and shot at sunrise. With a look of despair and anger, he climbed back on his footplate.

The train jolted out of the little station. Very soon events proved the justice of his warning. The brakes ran hot—they screamed—sparks flew from the flanges of the wheels. But the brakes would not hold! The weight of the overloaded cars pressed behind. Engine and train tore down a dizzy slope winding along the precipitous banks of a boulder-strewn mountain torrent. The brakes now were looser than old shoes. The engineer shut off steam after vainly trying to reverse the engine, but the doomed train screamed on over the roadbed. Gusts of black smoke poured from under the cars. The friction had set them on fire!

Straight down on the station of St. Michel rushed this comet of flame and fury. The terrified soldiers smashed bleeding fists against doors shut by the pressure of the wind. Some jumped out into the night and the abyss. Few escaped. Mangled corpses strewed the line.

Then came a sharp curve where the line crossed a wooden bridge. Like a shell from a gun the doomed locomotive flashed ahead, and was hurled to one side as it took the curve. The cars piled up in a heap to the parapet of the bridge. A burst of flame in the night, and at least 400 men were burned to cinders.

Reports say that, in all, between 500 and 600 soldiers lost their lives in that terrible half hour. About 250 were injured. The most trustworthy figures available place the dead at 543, the injured at 243, although it is still maintained by some that more than 1000 men went to death in the accident.

Thus occurred the world's three greatest rail disasters: Modane, Gretna Green and Lagny. And the whole world hopes they will continue to be the three greatest—each, certainly, having taught its own terrible lesson in safety.

What's New in College Courses

IN LOUISIANA, Dillard University (for Negroes) requires a course in homemaking before graduation. Sixty-two young men share with the coeds in studying the planning of homes, selection of food and clothing, and the care of children.—*Religious Digest*

THE University of Miami maintains a classroom on the floor of the Gulf Stream for its students in zoology, who don the type of diving helmet William Beebe used in his submarine explorations.
—*Friends Intelligencer*

OVER 1500 people have earned credits toward a degree at New York University by studying what is perhaps the most fascinating subject in the world—themselves. In a course on personality improvement, they watch motion pictures of themselves and listen to phonograph records of their own voices, to discover unpleasant mannerisms. They take a dozen different tests—of initiative, thoroughness, concentration, observation, adaptability, knowledge, leadership, powers of expression, organizing ability and the impression they make upon others. On the basis of the results, as analyzed with the aid of psychologists, they plot their own "profiles," noting their strong and weak points.—N. Y. *Times*

THE University of Iowa, Vassar and Syracuse University are among the numerous colleges that now offer courses in marriage. Premarital problems and adjustments in married life are discussed in these courses, as well as the psychological and physiological aspects of reproduction, child development and care.
—N. Y. *Herald Tribune*

SOUTHEASTERN Oklahoma State Teachers' College has established a course of instruction in minor household repairs. It includes adjustment of electrical devices, correction of wiring disorders, and mending leaks in water pipes in emergency.—Baltimore *Sun*

Why Do We Buy?

Condensed from Review of Reviews

DONALD A. LAIRD

THE average person actually *needs* very little. But he *wants* a great many things, and wants them more intensely than he does the few simple essentials of life. The interesting thing is that the average person does not understand what he wants. The impulses which force him to seek this or that spring from his unconscious. His apparent reasons are often only excuses and "rationalizations." Thus a man may want to buy his wife every luxury, not so much for the great affection which he rationalizes for her as for the lurking unconscious feeling that he is not quite man enough to keep her love otherwise. A father takes out an endowment policy to assure his children a college education, not because it will be good for them, as he rationalizes it, but because he fears that he himself is not quite as proficient as men with a better education.

Fully 90 percent of the things people want to have and to do, report psychoanalysts, are because of unconscious promptings of this sort. They have compared our wants to an iceberg which is mostly below the surface. These unconscious promptings which guide us may be divided into four main motives.

First, is the *desire to be more masculine*. Strangely enough, this craving is stronger in women than in men. It is responsible for mannish attire, the boyish bob, the boyish figure, the smoking of cigarettes by women, and the preference of office work to house work. The highest flattery that can be given to a woman when she is deciding on an investment is to say: "You are reasoning this through better than most men do."

Men, too, desire to be more masculine than they think they are. So they join gymnastics classes, and buy worthless concoctions to restore vitality. They dread baldness because that makes their head resemble a baby's. They keep their collar closed in hot weather, unless there are at least a few black hairs that will show on their chest. Their coats must have padding in the shoulders to give them a masculine breadth. They drive hard bargains, not so much to save money as to prove themselves better men than their opponents.

Second, is the *desire to be more adequate.* The average customer wants power, lots of it, to let him forget his weaknesses. He may buy expensive things, not merely to impress his friends, but, strangely, to impress the salesperson. This is the cause of much returned merchandise, which averages around 15 percent of total retail sales. The average person has in his unconscious the impression that he may not be quite so bright, or so strong, or so rich, or so beautiful, or so good a conversationalist as other persons. He feels inwardly inadequate. So he may buy a larger car than he can afford, or a more expensive radio.

The poet who wrote that in spring "a young man's fancy lightly turns to thoughts of love," must have lived alone in the woods the rest of the year. For it is not merely in the springtime, and not merely young men. Everyone, all the time, has the unconscious regions of his mind taken up with the *desire for romance.* Waking or dreaming, that thought permeates the human mind.

This assumes serious significance for business. The young woman never quite loses the idea that she must get herself a husband. She wants a lipstick that makes her kissable. She does not want a dress because it is a bargain, but because the saleslady said it made her look alluring. She is a booster for the family to buy anything that will make the front of the house and the living rooms attractive to her boy acquaintances.

After she is 35 she desires to keep young and attractive. She becomes a beauty-parlor and beauty-preparation fiend. She begins to realize that her big job now is holding her husband. A table toaster which will make his morning toast just as he likes it is something she wants for this reason. She sends in coupons for cookbooks, recalling that the way to a man's heart is through his stomach.

She would like her husband to take her on a week-end trip—he seems more romantic when dressed up and away from home. Secretly she hopes he will take out more insurance, for she realizes that it would be difficult for her to remarry. She wants him to get an oil burner, for when she tends the furnace it makes her look tired and haggard. She wants to be noticed by men, perhaps even more than when she was younger.

Adam is not much different from Eve. At 20, when he bought that automobile, it was not because he "needed it for transportation," but because the slant of the windshield was admired by all the girls. Later he joined the country club because, as he said, it would be a good way to make contacts for business. But he spent most of his time contacting on the ladies' cocktail terrace.

The concealed power of this desire for romance is illustrated by the increased sales when some of the little five-cent reprints of classics, issued by E. Haldeman-Julius, were retitled. *Fleece of Gold* sold 6000 a year, but when the title was changed to *Quest for a Blonde Mistress* the sales jumped to 50,000. *None Beneath the King* sold 6000 a year with that title, but when titled *None Beneath the King Shall Enjoy This Woman* it went to 34,000.

The fourth powerful unconscious desire we recognize as the horror of death, or the *desire for life*. We notice it in the middle-aged man who leaves behind the reckless driving habits of his youth. He rationalizes that gasoline consumption and wear and tear are least at low speeds; but his real reason is fear of accident and death.

It is after 35 that people begin to take their little aches and pains more seriously. Now we can understand how there are so many big pharmaceutical companies, why patent-medicine frauds can prosper, why sunlamps and vitamin foods are in demand. People at this age join health clubs, and choose their meals more to help their health. They will buy rowing machines if the salesman casually mentions the increased death rate among the overweight. They want safety-glass and skid-proof tires on their automobiles, and become interested when the safety devices are pointed out on an electric washer. They read newspaper accounts of someone of advanced age who has just celebrated another birthday, noting particularly to what the old person attributes his great durability in this vale of tears.

Those, in brief, are the basic and unconscious motives which mind analysis has discovered. They are the forces which lead mankind to action.

The desire to be more masculine.
The desire to be more adequate.
The desire for romance.
The desire for life.

Understanding these unconscious motives has revolutionized the relief of mental disorders, has altered modern education, has solved unhappy marriages, has helped physicians to treat patients who are sick more from these unconscious sources than from germs or disordered organs. In business, too, these fundamentals may alter the advertising and selling of merchandise and services. Understand these motives, and you are well on the road to knowing why most things other than strict necessities are bought.

Americana

Excerpt from The American Mercury

Illinois: It is now morally safe to see the world via the Navy:

RECRUITING OFFICER Karl K. Jones ruled Walter K. Elger would have to put some clothes on a nude lady tattooed on his forearm before he could join the Navy. Regulations, Officer Jones explained, forbade the enlistment of persons who had offensive matter engraved on their epidermis.

Behind the Tambourine

Condensed from The North American Review

MARQUIS JAMES

A GIRL in the street jingling a tambourine, a young man on your doorstep collecting old newspapers and clothing, and at Christmas-tide those freehand representations of Santa Claus with pot and bell: by these outward signs—and by them only—do most of us know the Salvation Army. But behind the girl with a tambourine stand colleagues the world over—in leper camps, in remote criminal settlements including that of French Guiana, in the steaming jungles of India, the yellow plains of northern China, the heart of Africa. In 86 countries and colonies the Army repeats, in 80 tongues, its maxim that "a man may be down but he's never out." Tangible wealth and property are things the Army cares least about, yet in the United States alone its holdings are valued at $40,000,000. To such estate has grown within living memory an institution whose pioneers were stoned in London streets and imprisoned in London jails. Success crowned their efforts because they held to their goal of grappling with the substance of human misfortune rather than the shadow of it; and moreover because the spirit of the Army represents now what it represented 60 years ago, the translation into organization of one of the 19th century's most remarkable romances: the little-known love story of Catherine and William Booth.

In the springtime of 1852 these two met at a tea party. The host, an altruistically inclined London boot manufacturer named Rabbits, had heard young William Booth preach in a Reform Chapel of the Methodist Church. Booth's unschooled eloquence, his tremendous earnestness, so swayed Mr. Rabbits that he sought out William and learned his story. Son of a congenital failure and remarkable liar, who fed his starved brood on tales of a vanished prosperity always about to be redeemed, William knew disillusionment early in life and made the intimate acquaintance of poverty in the manufacturing town of Nottingham. At 16 the boy began to preach in the streets.

279

In a year he was the head of a nameless little band which included such personages as Besom Jack, the wife-beater, whom young Booth had prevailed upon to modify his ideas of the marriage relationship. At 19 William entered the service of a pawn-broker in London and on Sundays would put a Bible in his pocket and head for the slums.

At Mr. Rabbits' tea party, William recited a soggy American poem, *The Grog-Seller's Dream.* The tall young speaker was not quite 23 and carelessly attired. But in a moment the hearers had forgotten that. They were conscious only of the arresting eyes, the flexible lines of a strong, thin face dominated by a "Wellington" nose—inherited from his mother who was probably Jewish—an orator's voice, untrained, not always grammatical but always commanding.

The sentiments of the poem were accorded a mixed reception, but the speaker left his impress—and on none so strongly as on Catherine Mumford, a comely oval-faced girl with dimples. William escorted her home and knew he was in love.

The Reformed Methodists now established William as a lay preacher. He was surprisingly successful, lionized at tea parties and worshiped by the poor. Then the church sought to prepare its recruit for higher stations with a period of polishing at a theological college. Catherine Mumford had a hand in this, for as William's wooing proceeded she undertook to shape the destinies of her suitor. Booth had

personality and a militant imagination, but Catherine was his superior in intellectual force. William could not stick the tedium of the classroom. Thumbing a Latin grammar was not his way of preparing to alleviate suffering in the world, which to him went hand-in-hand with the extinction of sin. So he chucked the classes, swept Catherine to the altar, declined a soft church post in London and with his bride took to the road as an evangelist under the sponsorship of the Methodist New Connexion, latest of the liberal church movements.

For two years they tramped the face of England, living like gypsies, often penniless, often hungry because of private generosities, but radiantly joyful in a love that had realized ten-fold every anticipation of courtship. It was a love which, like William Booth's theory of religion, declined to scorn the flesh. "How very much I should like to see you today, to hold you in my arms and look at you and cover you with warm and earnest kisses." In a lodging house in Halifax Catherine brought their first-born into the world and caught up with her husband at his next stop.

The tour came to an end when the New Connexion terminated Booth's evangelistic work. Conservatives were alarmed at his furious methods. The journeyman accepted a year's rest in the pastorate of a grimy little factory town where their second child was born. In 1861 Booth served notice on the annual Conference at Liverpool that he would withdraw from the New Connexion if his demands for a renewal of evangelism were not met. The Conference offered a compromise. Booth hesitated, turned to the visitors' gallery and questioned his wife with a glance. Catherine rose in her place and in a voice that made the rafters ring shouted, "Never!" Amid cries of "Order! Order!" William Booth waved his hat in the direction of the door and passed out, to embrace Catherine at the foot of the gallery stair.

Together they confronted the world, without a church behind them, without a settled plan, and with hardly a shilling in their pockets. To London they carried their four babies, William plunging into the slums while Catherine, the shrewd and capable manager, established herself in the drawing-rooms of the West End where a woman preacher was an oddity and hostesses were out to greet their guests with the newest thing under the sun. The wife's heart was in her husband's work which she felt she could further best by earning enough to keep the family together. When William's health broke under the strain she took his place in the field.

Three years of flailing efforts found the two evangelists with little to show in the way of achievement, no following worthy of a name, and family life a desperate improvisation. Yet the Booths repeatedly declined attractive offers from the churches. William was convinced that these institutions were incapable of coping with the peculiar problems of England's poor. He saw drink-sodden, vice-ridden millions sinking deeper into the sloughs of hopelessness as the churches inspired in them feelings of derision rather than reverence. Defeat upon defeat, effort upon effort splintering in futility, only seemed to confirm the faith of William and Catherine Booth in their ability ultimately to triumph where others had failed. Failure to them meant only squaring off for a fresh start.

One such start was made in 1864 when Booth and a little knot of followers took their stand on Mile End Waste, a dismal stretch of derelict land near Whitechapel. Their singing drew a crowd from the Vine and Blind Beggar public houses. Booth's rugged eloquence held that crowd as he brandished his umbrella and flayed Demon Rum. Though catcalls drowned his voice Booth spoke on. Mud, garbage, stones flew through the air. William and his band held their ground, dodging and fending off missiles as best they could. Finally they retreated, the tall leader still waving his umbrella and crying out things that were unheard.

Next night he was back, only to be routed again. The night after that he returned—with the same result. In this cause or that, courage is a quality that challenges admiration. A few who had flung mud at earlier meetings began to range themselves beside the preacher. Among these was an ex-pugilist who, despite William's order to turn the other cheek, remembered enough of his old profession to diminish the enthusiasm of some of the disturbers. Owners of contiguous pubs, finding that this scarecrow preacher was emptying their places, hired thugs to annoy the meetings. To meet this opposition an organization imperceptibly formed itself which Booth called the Christian Mission. Thus on Mile End Waste the Salvation Army came into being, though it was not so named until 15 years later. The Mission attained to the dignity of a tent, then an abandoned warehouse for its services.

The spiritual reservoir upon which the embattled leader drew for inspiration was the home Catherine made for him—and into which during these early days of the Army the eighth and last child was born. A visitor to this domicile said it reminded her of a railway station because it was so busy and so wanting in confusion, a condition largely due to the administrative ability of the mother. But father contributed to the prevailing spirit of cheerfulness; in Booth's home a hearty laugh was reckoned as half a prayer.

By now Booth had struck his stride. He fought the devil with the devil's weapons. Giving his followers bright uniforms and banners, drums, trumpets and tambourines, he bade them play and sing gay tunes. The "barracks" of his Army were by design actual rivals of the public houses—warm, well-lighted, cheerful places where piety was crammed down no man's

throat. Recruits flowed to the leader's standard, and when they joined the Army they knew its terms. "Garibaldi," writes St. John Ervine, "offered his Thousand wounds and death; and got his Thousand. Booth offered half-educated or illiterate workmen and servant girls calumny and hunger and pain and persecution and a strict obedience to their general's commands; and he got an army that went across the world."

The conquest of England was the first objective. Evangelical parties were pushed out over the roads that Catherine and William Booth knew so well. These activities spurred an opposition led, from different motives, by the churches and the liquor interests. The Army's processions were the targets for garbage and dead cats. Meetings were systematically broken up. A great outcry went up from the pious when Booth discontinued the Sacrament of the Lord's Supper because he found that even the odor of wine was a peril to converts snatched from alcoholism. The Church of England was so misled by the tide of current libel as to pronounce formally certain night services of the Army a danger to morals of young girls.

In one year 669 Salvationists, including 251 women, were knocked down and beaten, 56 buildings of the Army stormed and damaged, 86 Salvationists imprisoned. The police usually sided with the heterogeneous opposition. The Army thrived on these attacks. The devotion of Booth's followers was such that the Commanding General issued a general order against starvation when he found Salvationists contributing their infinitesimal salaries to further the Army's war chest.

The Booths were now in a position to give full reign to their flair for the audacious. Their crusade against white slavery had enlisted the aid of W. T. Stead, editor of the *Pall Mall Gazette*. Bramwell Booth, the oldest son, and Stead made a plan to buy a girl simply to demonstrate that this could be done. In the Army's ranks was Rebecca Jarrett who had once made her living at that sort of thing. She attended to the arrangements whereby a girl was taken to a bawdy house, drugged and sold to Stead. When the editor exposed the transaction in his paper, he was arrested along with Bramwell Booth and Mrs. Jarrett, on the strength of their own admissions. Although they had actually rescued the girl from a life of immorality, technically these three had broken the law in so doing. A court freed Bramwell, but Stead and Mrs. Jarrett went to jail. Such daring gestures made countless new friends for the Army.

In 1886 William Booth came to the United States, where six years before George Scott Railson had landed at the head of an "expeditionary force" of seven "Hallelujah lasses" who dropped on their knees outside the immigration office in New York and claimed another continent for Christ. Booth was now 57, and conscious of his power. Yet the fountain of his inspiration was still Catherine. "Send me love letters," he wrote, "and particulars about yourself. What you do and what time you retire and whether you read in bed. Indeed anything about yourself, your dear self."

Always with one of his wife's letters in his pocket the leader toured America. He captured the imagination of the public, and when he departed the future of the Army here was assured.

Mrs. Booth was frail in health, all her life having suffered from an affliction of the spine. When the pain in her body was more than she could stand, she was prevailed upon to consult an eminent physician. Without comment she heard his verdict. She had cancer and could not live long. At a window William awaited the return of the cab to their home and ran out to help her up the steps. Smiling through her tears she told him of her doom. William tried to speak but no words came.

A few weeks before her death Catherine removed her wedding ring and slipped it on her husband's finger. To the Army she dictated a message. "My Dear Children and Friends: I have loved you much, and have helped you little. Fight on. I will meet you in Heaven." A countless multitude gathered to see "the Mother of the Salvation Army" laid to rest in Abney Park Cemetery. Though bowed with sorrow William could not let pass this opportunity to exhort sinners to seek the throne of grace. He spoke in the name of Catherine. "She was good, a thorough hater of sham, hypocrisies and make-believes. She was love, her whole soul full of tender, deep compassion. She was a warrior. She said not to others, 'Go,' but, 'Here, let me go.' "

After Catherine's death William became a wanderer, visiting the ever-expanding chain of Army outposts in the far quarters of the earth. His children and grandchildren were in the ranks and in high stations of command. The General had many of the qualities of a despot, and these irked particularly the second son, Ballington, who eventually seceded from the Army and started the rival Volunteers of America in the United States. Promptly the General-in-Chief directed that he be carried as a "deserter" on the Army rosters.

Upon the founder's death, in 1912, Bramwell Booth succeeded his father. Six years ago another schism in the family came to light in a contest which resulted in the deposition of the aged and infirm Bramwell from command. Evangeline, the youngest child but one, had built in America an Army organization that overshadowed in prestige and power the London headquarters. Her name was offered for the succession and only after a spirited contest, sharply

dividing the Booth family, did her supporters admit defeat. But last autumn when Eva, as she is called in the home circle, was finally elevated to the supreme command, there was a public reconciliation with Bramwell's widow and daughter. It was genuine, for the Booths do not do such things for show.

William Booth himself lived to see the institution that he had brought into being by flourishing an umbrella and dodging garbage on Mile End Waste become one without a peer in the world. He saw it acquire banks, insurance companies, publishing houses, factories, farms and hospitals. He saw the recruits he took from public houses and brothels replaced by graduates of Army cadet schools. The old man who had limped home cut and bleeding from the manhandling of mobs while the police looked idly on lived to exchange quips with jovial King Edward, to dine in the White House and be called into consultation by the heads of governments throughout Europe. In his last public appearance, on May 12, 1912, the patriarch told an audience filling vast Albert Hall that 200,000 homeless men slept that night under roofs of the Salvation Army. And only Queen Victoria's funeral drew a throng larger than that which saw this Christian soldier borne to rest beside his Catherine.

The Three Greatest Men in History

By

H. G. WELLS

SOME thirteen years ago I was asked to name the Six Greatest Men in the World. I did so. Rashly. I have been confronted with my former answer and asked if I still adhere to it. Not altogether. Three of my Great Names stand as they stood then—but three I must admit seem to have lost emphasis. The fact is that there are not Six Greatest Names to be cited. That six begged the question. There are more or fewer. There are many—or there are only three.

When I was asked which single individual has left the most permanent impression on the world, the manner of the questioner almost carried the implication that it was Jesus of Nazareth. I agreed. He is I think a quite cardinal figure in human history and it will be long before western men decide—if ever they do decide—to abandon his life as the turning point in their reckoning of time. I am speaking of him, of course, as a man. The historian must treat him as a man, just as the painter must paint him as a man. We do not know as much about him as we would like to know; but the four Gospels,

though sometimes contradictory, agree in giving us a picture of a very definite personality; they carry a conviction of reality. To assume that he never lived, that the accounts of his life are inventions, is more difficult and raises far more problems for the historian than to accept the essential elements of the Gospel stories as fact.

Of course the reader and I live in countries where to millions of persons, Jesus is more than a man. But the historian must disregard that fact. He must adhere to the evidence that would pass unchallenged if his book were to be read in every nation under the sun. Now, it is interesting and significant that a historian, without any theological bias whatever, should find that he cannot portray the progress of humanity honestly without giving a foremost place to a penniless teacher from Nazareth. The old Roman historians ignored Jesus entirely; he left no impress on the historical records of his time. Yet, more than 1900 years later, a historian like myself, who does not even call himself a Christian, finds the picture centering irresistibly

285

around the life and character of this most significant man.

We still catch something of the magnetism that induced men who had seen him only once to leave their business and follow him. He filled them with love and courage. He spoke with a knowledge and authority that baffled the wise. But other teachers have done all this. These talents alone would not have given him the permanent place of power which he occupies; that place is his by virtue of the new and simple and profound ideas which he released—the profound importance of the individual under the Fatherhood of God and the conception of the Kingdom of Heaven.

It is one of the most revolutionary changes of outlook that has ever stirred and changed human thought. No age has even yet understood fully the tremendous challenge it carries to the established institutions and subjugations of mankind. But the world began to be a different world from the day that doctrine was preached and every step toward wider understanding and tolerance and good will is a step in the direction of that universal brotherhood Christ proclaimed.

The historian's test of an individual's greatness is "What did he leave to grow? Did he start men to thinking along fresh lines with a vigor that persisted after him?" By this test Jesus stands first.

As with Jesus, so with Buddha, whom I would put very near in importance to Christ. You see clearly a man, simple, devout, lonely, battling for light—a vivid human personality, not a myth. Beneath a mass of miraculous fable I feel that there also was a man. He, too, gave a message to mankind universal in its character. Many of our best modern ideas are in closest harmony with it. All the miseries and discontents of life are due, he taught, to selfishness. Selfishness takes three forms—one, the desire to satisfy the senses; another, the craving for immortality; and the third is the desire for prosperity, worldliness. Before a man can become serene he must cease to live for his senses or himself. Then he merges into a greater being. Buddha in different language called men to self-forgetfulness five hundred years before Christ. In some ways he was nearer to us and our needs. He was more lucid upon our individual importance in service than Christ and less ambiguous upon the question of personal immortality.

Next, I would write the name of Aristotle who is as cardinal in the story of the human intelligence as Christ and Buddha in the story of the human will. Aristotle began a great new thing in the world—the classifying and analyzing of information. He was the father of the scientific synthesis. There had been thinkers in the world before but he taught men to think together. He was the tutor of Alexander the Great, whose support made it possible for him to organize study on a scale and in a manner never before attempted. At one time he had a thousand men, scattered throughout Asia and Greece, collecting material for his natural history. Political as well as natural science began with him. His students made an analysis of 158 political constitutions. Aristotle's insistence on facts and their rigid analysis, the determination to look the truth in the face, was a vast new step in human progress.

These are three great names. I could write down twenty or thirty names and vacillate between them for the next three places. Plato? Mahomet? Confucius? I turn over names like Robert Owen, the real founder of modern Socialism. I can even weigh my pet aversion, Karl Marx, for a place. He made the world think of economic realities even if he made it think a little askew. Then what of those great astronomers who broke the crystal globe in which man's imagination had been confined and let it out into limitless space?

Then in that original selection of mine I find that my own particular weakness for Roger Bacon crept in. He voiced a passionate insistence upon the need for experiment and of collecting knowledge. He predicted, more than six hundred years ago, the advent of ships and trains that would be mechanically propelled; he also prophesied flying machines. He, too, set men to thinking along new, fresh lines and left an influence that has lived for the benefit of all generations. But when I come to put him beside Christ, Buddha and Aristotle —it won't do.

Do you want an American in the list? Lincoln, better than any other, seemed to me to embody the essential characteristics of America. He stood for equality of opportunity, for the right and the chance of the child of the humblest home to reach the highest place. His simplicity, his humor, his patience, his deep-abiding optimism, based on the conviction that right would prevail—all these seemed to typify the best that America had to give mankind. But, against those three who are enduring symbols of brotherhood and individual divinity, of service in self-forgetfulness and of the intellectual synthesis of mankind, what was rugged Abraham Lincoln? Do you really want an American in the list yet? America is still young.

I think I will leave it at three.

Table Talk

A YOUNG AMERICAN found himself seated next to the eminent Chinese, Wellington Koo, at a diplomatic banquet. Completely at a loss as to what to say to a Chinese, this young man, with a touch of genius such as may be detected only in real *faux pas* makers, said, "Likee soupee?" Mr. Koo smiled and nodded. Several moments later, when called upon to say a few words, he delivered a brilliant talk in flawless English, sat down while the applause was still resounding, turned to the young man and said, "Likee speechee?"—*Scholastic*

The Virtues of an Old People

Condensed from Asia

LIN YUTANG

THE CHINESE are hard-boiled. There is no nonsense about them: they do not live in order to die, as the Christians pretend to; nor do they seek for a Utopia on earth, as do many seers of the West. Their virtues are the virtues of an old people, who have seen much of life and are prepared to accept it for what it is worth, but who insist, nevertheless, that it shall be lived decently and happily within one's lot. Of the noble virtues of the West, of ambition, zeal for reform, public spirit, sense for adventure and heroic courage, they are devoid. They cannot be interested in climbing Mont Blanc or in exploring the North Pole. But they are tremendously interested in this commonplace world, and they have patience, industry, regard for duty, good sense, humor, tolerance, a peaceable temper and other qualities that make their matter-of-fact existence enjoyable to them.

Chief of these qualities are tolerance and a peaceable temper, which are the mark of a mellow culture and which seem to be lacking in modern Europe. It would seem at times that Europe is suffering from hot-headed youthfulness and that, after another century of scientific progress, Europeans will perhaps learn to be a little less brilliant and a little more mature, less self-assertive and more tolerant. For tolerance will be direly needed when science has knit the world together.

The Chinese are the world's worst fighters because they are an intelligent race, nurtured by Taoistic cynicism and the Confucian emphasis on harmony as the ideal. They do not fight, because they are the most calculating and self-interested people. An average Chinese child knows what the European gray-haired statesmen do not know, that by fighting one gets maimed or killed, whether it be an individual or a nation. Chinese parties to a dispute are therefore the easiest to bring to their senses. Also, being imbued with the spirit of Taoism, the Chinese do not, when advantage comes, take all of it. It is merely a matter of culture, or what we call *"hanyang."* If the Frenchman had been a little imbued with the spirit of Taoism at the moment of his victory in 1918, his head would rest more easily on its pillow today. But France was young, and Germany would certainly have done the same, and no one realizes how silly it is for two nations like France and Germany each to try to keep the other permanently under its iron heel. Clemenceau had not read Lao Tzu. Nor has Hitler. So let them fight, while the Taoist watches and smiles.

Chinese pacifism is a matter of temperament as well as understanding of life. Chinese boys fight much less in the street than do Western boys. As a people we fight much less than we ought to, despite the interminable civil wars. Put the American people under the same misrule as that endured by the Chinese in the past 20 years, and there would have been 30 revolutions, not three. Chinese soldiers do not relish a good fight; they are merely poor people who do not know how to make a living otherwise. In any Chinese campaign one does not "see fighting"; one merely hears it. For both in private quarrels and in civil warfare the noise makes the essence of the battle. As a rule the superior army awes the inferior enemy into defeat; and the defeated general, according to the Chinese idea of fair play, is then given $100,000 for traveling expenses and sent on a "tour of industrial investigation to Europe," with the full knowledge that in another

war his services may be needed. With the next turn of events you will probably find the victor and the vanquished riding in the same car. That is the beauty of Chinese *hanyang*. Meanwhile the people have nothing to do with it. They hate war and will always hate war. Good people never fight in China.

Besides the peaceable temper that at times looks perilously like cowardice there are other characteristics—patience and indifference, for example—which paralyze the Chinese people for organized action. Capacity for putting up with insults has been deliberately inculcated as a cardinal virtue by Confucian ethics. The training school for developing patience is, however, initially the big family, where a closed door is an offense and there is little elbow room for individuals. One learns from early childhood the need for mutual toleration and adjustments in human relationships.

The Chinese people, unique in their patience, are still more justly famous for their indifference. There is a significant contrast between the parting instructions of Tom's mother to her son in *Tom Brown's School Days* to hold his head high and "answer straight" and the traditional parting instruction of the Chinese mother that her son should "not meddle with public affairs." The Chinese take to indifference as Englishmen take to umbrellas, because the political weather always looks a little ominous for the individual who ventures too far out alone. One can be public-spirited when there is a guarantee of personal rights; but when there is no such guarantee, indifference is the best safeguard. Chinese youths are as public-spirited as foreign youths, but somewhere between their 25th and their 30th year they all "become wise" and acquire this mellowing indifference to public affairs, or "idle affairs," as we call them. Some "become wise" by native intelligence and others by getting their fingers burned. When two of our most daring journalists got shot by a Manchurian war lord in Peiping, in 1926, without even a trial, the other journalists learned the virtue of indifference in no time and "became wise." Chinese bandits, who do not depend upon legal protection, do not develop this indifference but are the most chivalrous and public-spirited class we know in China.

Travelers in China, especially those who go through seldom-visited parts inland, are equally amazed at the low standard of living of the Chinese masses and at their cheerfulness. A lot of the so-called "misery" is such, not to the Chinese themselves, but to those Westerners who cannot conceive of any man's being happy unless he is living in an overheated apartment and owns a radio. The standard that measures a man's happiness by the number of buttons he presses a day is a false standard. Were it not, there should have been no happy person in the world before 1850. Chinese people, however, are perhaps more contented than Western people, class for class, when living under the same conditions; for, as

a Chinese scholar has put it, "a well-filled stomach is indeed a great thing: all the rest are life's luxuries." Contentment is part of the counsel for moderation, of that human wisdom which says, "When good fortune comes, do not enjoy all of it."

Toward the achievement of happiness the Chinese have bent their highest efforts, and, like the utilitarians they are, they have always been more interested in this most tricky problem of life than in the problem of progress. Their approach to it differs from the Western. The Chinese make a negative approach to happiness through their philosophy of contentment. The question is always reduced in the last analysis to the question of a man's wants. A Chinese gentleman wants a number of things, but he does not insist on having them if they are out of his reach. He wants at least a pair of clean shirts, but if he is too poor to have more than one shirt, he won't mind. He wants some tall old trees in his neighborhood, but if he can't have them, he will get just as much happiness from a date tree in his yard. He wants lots and lots of children and a wife who personally prepares his favorite dishes; and, if he is wealthy, then an excellent cook, and a pretty maid servant in red pajamas to tend the incense while he is reading or painting. He wants some good friends and a woman who understands, preferably his wife; but if not, then one of the sing-song girls. If he is not born with such "voluptuous luck," he won't be sorry about that either.

He wants leisure, and leisure he can have in China. He wants a secluded hut, if he can't have an entire pleasure garden. But if he can't have that, and must live in the city, he won't be sorry. He would have, in any case, a cage bird and a few pot flowers and the moon; for he can always have the moon.

A strong determination to get the best out of life, a keen desire to enjoy what one has and no regrets if one fails: this is the secret of the Chinese genius for contentment.

Breaking Up Housekeeping

WHEN a New York family had to vacate their apartment just off Fifth Avenue because the building was to be torn down, it occurred to them they could render some assistance to the wrecking company by giving a Demolition Party the night before their departure. Their landlord readily consented, stipulating only that no glass be knocked out of windows over the street. All valuable furniture, books, and draperies were moved to the new apartment; a few rugged tables and chairs were left for the party.

Invitations were sent out in the form of membership cards in the Housewreckers' Union, and guests were asked to bring their own weapons and tools. A few did, feeling very self-conscious as they crossed Fifth Avenue in evening clothes and carrying crowbars. Most of the guests did not take the request seriously, but the hosts had provided abundant tools.

The result was an eye-opener to any psychologist. Nice, gentle, well-mannered people went berserk at the sight of sheer plaster walls, and sank axes in them to the hilt. The daughter of a nationally known banker organized a crew of four, one to hold a huge cold chisel, the other three to swing sledge hammers on it in rhythm. In no time the cold chisel shot through the floor into the apartment below. Bows and arrows being available, targets were drawn on once-beautiful walls, and chunks of plaster were shot out with infinite relish. The guests became positively ferocious as they wandered around, swinging hammers on glass doorknobs, pulling down fireplace chimneys, feeling the savage joy of swinging an axe into a polished mahogany door, when all their life they had been trained not to do just that. A broker thrust a screwdriver behind a light socket to pry it off, and with a shower of sparks all the lights went out. It was no brake on the party—guests sped out for candles and returned to demolish in a softer light. Too, the candles made good targets for the arrows; and the chandeliers crashed satisfyingly.

The only casualty was a dignified matron who cut her finger. She found that frequent insertions in the punch bowl stopped the bleeding.

Victorians Had a Word for It

Condensed from Scribner's Magazine

HELEN VAN PELT WILSON

THE VICTORIANS had a word for it. They called it— charm. Every thoughtful mother of the 1890's religiously cultivated it in her daughter, to fit her for marriage and children. To the Victorians there was no beating about the bush on this subject at least: old maids were old maids, not bachelor girls, and they bore like a brand the stigma of failure in the competition for a man.

Today, after a period of feminism in which the all-important consideration was not charm but brains, femininity is again the keynote of women's education. The Mae West figure, flower-decked hat, and sweeping train are but signs of the times. The biological function is highly respected. Statistical surveys among college girls reveal that almost 85 per cent set marriage as their goal, desiring only those careers compatible with marriage.

Charm is easy to recognize, hard to analyze, but still possible to teach to those who seem to lack it because, like a mosaic, it is made up of many small things. Girls who are really hopeless cases are rare.

Charm has at least two definite aspects—attractive appearance and pleasant personality, but especially the latter. When Sir James Barrie wrote, "If you have it, you don't need to have anything else—and if you haven't it, it doesn't much matter what else you have," he did not add that almost all children have natural charm until it is buried or distorted by education. As a mother I consider it my duty to bring the spark to a blaze and relight it if it goes out.

In developing its outer aspect, good looks, I know that I can almost proceed by rule as did my friend Marguerite Harris. She emerged from college, brainy, awkward, homely, and panicky in the presence of men. She literally achieved charm by intelligent study, in three years of transforming herself into a woman of Italian distinction. Her ugliness had style. Women noticed her and men passed by more obviously pretty girls to converse with her. "I knew what I wanted," she explained, "and I went after it. The result's coming this evening." He was a handsome young surgeon, undoubtedly a fair reward!

She started with a thorough going over at a beauty salon. A good dancing teacher taught her grace and relaxation—how to sit, stand and shake hands, things all of us can learn from books and magazine articles if we really are serious about it. Her doctor prescribed diet and exercise to make her gain weight. She achieved style through study of fashion magazines. Her improved appearance naturally brought self-assurance and poise, and with her mind thus freed of her unattractiveness, she concerned herself with other ideas, gradually learning the tricks of revealing her charm. Yet there wasn't a thing Marguerite Harris did for herself at 25 which her mother could not have accomplished more easily for her in her early teens.

These are the points I know I must develop in my daughter: first —good posture. A Worth model will look like a dress from a basement rack if her shoulders droop or her abdomen protrudes. And I cannot wait until she is 18 to think about the way she carries herself! Bones are well set by that time and habits hard to change.

I must see that she develops correct habits of eating. I have memories of Great-aunt Deborah, who weighed a good 200 pounds and loved her pie for breakfast. A trained appetite, that is, liking what is proper for you, is the only sure basis for a good figure—unless some undiagnosed illness exists such as a lazy thyroid. A doctor's advice must be sought when stubborn overweight persists.

I shall certainly teach the art of makeup, and of hairdressing and of everything that stresses personal daintiness and neatness—the essentials of that good grooming which make pleasing the appearance of even the plainest child. When she has done her best, however, I shall warningly add, "Forget it." Girls who make a cult of beauty lose that naturalness which is essential to charm. But no matter how she turns out, I want my child to feel she is attractive. The self-effacing girl never gets anywhere, while the one who may be homely but is not oppressed by the fact is taken by men at her own valuation.

Other attributes than beauty add to charm. I am striving to develop a low, well-modulated voice, as pleasing as it is rare. I shall see, too, that my daughter has some small talk but not so small no one wants to hear it. A knowledge of current events will give her something to say to people of all types and protect her from the necessity of gossip. A fair game of tennis or golf, the ability to ride and swim—not brilliantly but well enough so that fear will not be gnawing at her vitals—and a mastery of dancing are likewise important. The last is especially vital. There is nothing more damning to a girl's reputation at 15 than a boy's simple comment, "She has lead feet."

Lastly, I shall break the news to

my daughter very early that this is a man's world, made for them, and run by them. Women who early recognize this fact and gracefully accept it save themselves a lot of trouble and get places in the end.

Furthermore, my daughter must realize that marriage and children will limit any other special type of development, and yet without them she cannot expect happiness. She may as well know at the outset of her study of writing or painting or business that if at 20 she and her husband start out with equal ability and equipment he will always be about a decade ahead because, even under the most efficient management, childbearing and the care of the home are a strain. Yet this fact of a man's superior opportunity won't be a bit bad once she gets used to it.

And while this is sinking in, I shall make my daughter aware that the majority of men prefer women beautiful but not obviously too bright. The brilliant girl draws but few men, the attractive but unoppressively intelligent one brings along the pack. I want her to have the opportunity to select from the valuable minority who drift in with the majority.

I shall also impress my child with the fact that there is a time to curb a sense of humor. Man is undeniably vain and can seldom bear the joke's being on him. One of the cleverest young women I know now threads her way alone. As one ex-suitor said to her, "Ellen, you just better look out or you'll laugh your way out of your last chance for a good provider." And she did.

This same vanity in men is useful to women. The "A-1 incense burner" seldom wastes her sweetness on the desert air, though this does not mean that man sits spellbound while woman hands out compliments with a shovel. I want my daughter both subtle and sincere, realizing that in almost everyone there is something to be interested in and to admire. After all, the essence of charm is ability to attract because we ourselves are attracted.

A daughter's adjustment to life and to man lies with her mother. We cannot from a plain product develop a Helen of Troy but with patience and intelligence we can make every girl reasonably charming and so able to cope happily with life in this man-directed world. Doubtless when we consider what we want our daughters to be our own deficiencies will appear only too clear, and we can also learn, paraphrasing to ourselves Josh Billings' advice, "Train up a girl in the way she should go and walk there yourself once in a while."

THE LATEST THING in mouse traps: a metal-lined tube with plug-in attachment, which electrocutes the mouse when he nuzzles a piece of cheese.—*Literary Digest*

—And Sudden Death

By

J. C. FURNAS

Like the gruesome spectacle of a bad automobile accident itself, the realistic details of this article will nauseate some readers. Those who find themselves thus affected at the outset are cautioned against reading the article in its entirety, since there is no letdown in the author's outspoken treatment of sickening facts.

PUBLICIZING the total of motoring injuries—almost a million last year, with 36,000 deaths—never gets to first base in jarring the motorist into a realization of the appalling risks of motoring. He does not translate dry statistics into a reality of blood and agony.

Figures exclude the pain and horror of savage mutilation—which means they leave out the point. They need to be brought closer home. A passing look at a bad smash or the news that a fellow you had lunch with last week is in a hospital with a broken back will make any driver but a born fool slow down at least temporarily. But what is needed is a vivid and *sustained* realization that every time you step on the throttle, death gets in beside you, hopefully waiting for his chance. That single horrible accident you may have witnessed is no isolated horror. That sort of thing happens every hour of the day, everywhere in the United

States. If you really felt *that*, perhaps the stickful of type in Monday's paper recording that a total of 29 local citizens were killed in week-end crashes would rate something more than a perfunctory tut-tut as you turn back to the sports page.

An enterprising judge now and again sentences reckless drivers to tour the accident end of a city morgue. But even a mangled body on a slab, waxily portraying the consequences of bad motoring judgment, isn't a patch on the scene of the accident itself. No artist working on a safety poster would dare depict that in full detail.

That picture would have to include motion-picture and sound effects, too—the flopping, pointless efforts of the injured to stand up; the queer, grunting noises; the steady, panting groaning of a human being with pain creeping up on him as the shock wears off. It should portray the slack expression on the face of a man, drugged with shock, staring at the Z-twist in his broken leg, the insane crumpled ef-

Copyright, 1935, by Simon & Schuster, Inc.

295

fect of a child's body after its bones are crushed inward, a realistic portrait of an hysterical woman with her screaming mouth opening a hole in the bloody drip that fills her eyes and runs off her chin. Minor details would include the raw ends of bones protruding through flesh in compound fractures, and the dark red, oozing surfaces where clothes and skin were flayed off at once.

Those are all standard, everyday sequels to the modern passion for going places in a hurry and taking a chance or two by the way. If ghosts could be put to a useful purpose, every bad stretch of road in the United States would greet the oncoming motorist with groans and screams and the educational spectacle of ten or a dozen corpses, all sizes, sexes and ages, lying horribly still on the bloody grass.

Last year a state trooper of my acquaintance stopped a big red Hispano for speeding. Papa was obviously a responsible person, obviously set for a pleasant week-end with his family—so the officer cut into papa's well-bred expostulations: "I'll let you off this time, but if you keep on this way, you won't last long. Get going—but take it easier." Later a passing motorist hailed the trooper and asked if the red Hispano had got a ticket. "No," said the trooper, "I hated to spoil their party." "Too bad you didn't," said the motorist, "I saw you stop them—and then I passed that car again 50 miles up the line. It still makes me feel sick at my stomach. The car was all folded up like an accordion—the color was about all there was left. They were all dead but one of the kids—and he wasn't going to live to the hospital."

Maybe it will make you sick at your stomach, too. But unless you're a heavy-footed incurable, a good look at the picture the artist wouldn't dare paint, a first-hand acquaintance with the results of mixing gasoline with speed and bad judgment, ought to be well worth your while. I can't help it if the facts are revolting. If you have the nerve to drive fast and take chances, you ought to have the nerve to take the appropriate cure. You can't ride an ambulance or watch the doctor working on the victim in the hospital, but you can read.

The automobile is treacherous, just as a cat is. It is tragically difficult to realize that it can become the deadliest missile. As enthusiasts tell you, it makes 65 feel like nothing at all. But 65 an hour is 100 feet a second, a speed which puts a viciously unjustified responsibility on brakes and human reflexes, and can instantly turn this docile luxury into a mad bull elephant.

Collision, turnover or sideswipe, each type of accident produces either a shattering dead stop or a crashing change of direction—and, since the occupant—meaning you—continues in the old direction at the original speed, every surface and angle of the car's interior immediately becomes a battering, tearing projectile, aimed squarely at you—inescapable. There is no bracing yourself against these imperative laws of momentum.

It's like going over Niagara Falls in a steel barrel full of railroad spikes. The best thing that can happen to you—and one of the rarer things—is to be thrown out as the doors spring open, so you have only the ground to reckon with. True, you strike with as much force as if you had been thrown from the *Twentieth Century* at top speed. But at least you are spared the lethal array of gleaming metal knobs and edges and glass inside the car.

Anything can happen in that split second of crash, even those lucky escapes you hear about. People have dived through windshields and come out with only superficial scratches. They have run cars together head on, reducing both to twisted junk, and been found unhurt and arguing bitterly two minutes afterward. But death was there just the same—he was only exercising his privilege of being erratic. This spring a wrecking crew pried the door off a car which had been overturned down an embankment an out stepped the driver with only a scratch on his cheek. But his mother was still inside, a splinter of wood from the top driven four inches into her brain as a result of son's taking a greasy curve a little too fast. No blood—no horribly twisted bones—just a gray-haired corpse still clutching her pocketbook in her lap as she had clutched it when she felt the car leave the road.

On that same curve a month later, a light touring car crashed a tree. In the middle of the front seat they found a nine-months-old baby surrounded by broken glass and yet absolutely unhurt. A fine practical joke on death—but spoiled by the baby's parents, still sitting on each side of him, instantly killed by shattering their skulls on the dashboard.

If you customarily pass without clear vision a long way ahead, make sure that every member of the party carries identification papers— it's difficult to identify a body with its whole face bashed in or torn off. The driver is death's favorite target. If the steering wheel holds together it ruptures his liver or spleen so he bleeds to death internally. Or, if the steering wheel breaks off, the matter is settled instantly by the steering column's plunging through his abdomen.

By no means do all head-on collisions occur on curves. The modern death-trap is likely to be a straight stretch with three lanes of traffic—like the notorious Astor Flats on the Albany Post Road where there have been as many as 27 fatalities in one summer month. This sudden vision of broad, straight road tempts many an ordinarily sensible driver into passing the man ahead. Simultaneously a driver coming the other way swings out at high speed. At the last moment each tries to get into line again, but the gaps are closed. As the cars in line are forced into the ditch to capsize or crash fences, the passers meet, almost head on, in a swirling, grinding smash that sends them caroming obliquely into the others.

A trooper described such an accident—five cars in one mess, seven killed on the spot, two dead on the way to the hospital, two more dead in the long run. He remembered it far more vividly than he wanted to —the quick way the doctor turned away from a dead man to check up on a woman with a broken back; the three bodies out of one car so soaked with oil from the crankcase that they looked like wet brown cigars and not human at all; a man, walking around and babbling to himself, oblivious of the dead and dying, even oblivious of the dagger-like sliver of steel that stuck out of his streaming wrist; a pretty girl with her forehead laid open, trying hopelessly to crawl out of a ditch in spite of her smashed hip. A first-class massacre of that sort is only a question of scale and numbers— seven corpses are no deader than one. Each shattered man, woman or child who went to make up the 36,000 corpses chalked up last year had to die a personal death.

A car careening and rolling down a bank, battering and smashing its occupants every inch of the way, can wrap itself so thoroughly around a tree that front and rear bumpers interlock, requiring an acetylene torch to cut them apart. In a recent case of that sort they found the old lady, who had been sitting in back, lying across the lap of her daughter, who was in front, each soaked in her own and the other's blood indistinguishably, each so shattered and broken that there was no point whatever in an autopsy to determine whether it was broken neck or ruptured heart that caused death.

Overturning cars specialize in certain injuries. Cracked pelvis, for instance, guaranteeing agonizing months in bed, motionless, perhaps crippled for life—broken spine resulting from sheer sidewise twist— the minor details of smashed knees and splintered shoulder blades caused by crashing into the side of the car as she goes over with the swirl of an insane roller coaster— and the lethal consequences of broken ribs, which puncture hearts and lungs with their raw ends. The consequent internal hemorrhage is no less dangerous because it is the pleural instead of the abdominal cavity that is filling with blood.

Flying glass—safety glass is by no means universal yet—contributes much more than its share to the spectacular side of accidents. It doesn't merely cut—the fragments are driven in as if a cannon loaded with broken bottles had been fired in your face, and a sliver in the eye, traveling with such force, means certain blindness. A leg or arm stuck through the windshield will cut clean to the bone through vein, artery and muscle like a piece of beef under the butcher's knife, and it takes little time to lose a fatal amount of blood under such circumstances. Even safety glass may not be wholly safe when the car crashes something at high speed. You hear picturesque tales of how a flying human body will make a neat hole in the stuff with its head— the shoulders stick—the glass holds —and the raw, keen edge of the hole decapitates the body as neatly as a guillotine.

Or, to continue with the decapitation motif, going off the road into a post-and-rail fence can put you beyond worrying about other injuries immediately when a rail comes through the windshield and tears off your head with its splintery end—not as neat a job but thoroughly efficient. Bodies are often found with their shoes off and their feet all broken out of shape. The shoes are back on the floor of the car, empty and with their laces still neatly tied. That is the kind of impact produced by modern speeds.

But all that is routine in every American community. To be remembered individually by doctors and policemen, you have to do something as grotesque as the lady who burst the windshield with her head, splashing splinters all over the other occupants of the car, and then, as the car rolled over, rolled with it down the edge of the windshield frame and cut her throat from ear to ear. Or park on the pavement too near a curve at night and stand in front of the tail light as you take off the spare tire—which will immortalize you in somebody's memory as the fellow who was mashed three feet broad and two inches thick by the impact of a heavy duty truck against the rear of his own car. Or be as original as the pair of youths who were thrown out of an open roadster this spring—thrown clear—but each broke a windshield post with his head in passing and the whole top of each skull, down to the eyebrows, was missing. Or snap off a

nine-inch tree and get yourself impaled by a ragged branch.

None of all that is scare-fiction; it is just the horrible raw material of the year's statistics as seen in the ordinary course of duty by policemen and doctors, picked at random. The surprising thing is that there is so little dissimilarity in the stories they tell.

It's hard to find a surviving accident victim who can bear to talk. After you come to, the gnawing, searing pain throughout your body is accounted for by learning that you have both collarbones smashed, both shoulder blades splintered, your right arm broken in three places and three ribs cracked, with every chance of bad internal ruptures. But the pain can't distract you, as the shock begins to wear off, from realizing that you are probably on your way out. You can't forget that, not even when they shift you from the ground to the stretcher and your broken ribs bite into your lungs and the sharp ends of your collarbones slide over to stab deep into each side of your screaming throat. When you've stopped screaming, it all comes back—you're dying and you hate yourself for it. That isn't fiction either. It's what it actually feels like to be one of that 36,000.

And every time you pass on a blind curve, every time you hit it up on a slippery road, every time you step on it harder than your reflexes will safely take, every time you drive with your reactions slowed down by a drink or two, every time you follow the man ahead too closely, you're gambling a few seconds against this kind of blood and agony and sudden death.

Take a look at yourself as the man in the white jacket shakes his head over you, tells the boys with the stretcher not to bother and turns away to somebody else who isn't quite dead yet. And then take it easy.

Customer's Complaint

Excerpt from The Contributors' Club in The Atlantic Monthly

IT IS GETTING so that I cannot buy anything any more. This is due chiefly to the new advertising which assumes that the customer's sales resistance weakens as his embarrassment grows.

Once upon a time, things that you bought in a store were proffered with a kind of homely honesty. "Gents' Pants," an aisle sign would say, or "Extra Heavy Corsets." But now the goods of the world are beshrouded in such coyness and whimsy, such smirkings and oglings, as may well make a strong man blench. Alexander Woollcott has called attention, with a shudder, to those two breakfast foods for children known as *Beckus Puddy* and *Lishus*, but I am here referring to an even more afflicting noxiousness: that new merchandising technique which is responsible, for instance, for a species of women's underwear called Scandalettes.

I should not, of course, have said "underwear." The feminine form is now encased in foundation garments, and, unless my ad reading deceives me, the fashionable male is sheathing his lower torso in Short-Eez.

Sometimes, as in a nightmare, I am obsessed by the fear that one day my wife may twist an ankle and I may have to do her shopping for her. It would never have fazed me a whit to chaffer with a saleslady about corsets or drawers, but I am certain that never could I stammer out a request for a set of Snugglies. And it may be that I am exceptionally queasy, but I have a very odd feeling in my stomach at the thought of entering a perfume store and asking for a phial of My Night of Ecstasy.

It almost seems to me that there is a kind of austere beauty in those plain old unornamented words like "pants" and "suspenders" and "hair oil," which are now vanishing from the world in a vapor of evasion.

I have a plan. When next I enter a department store, and the floorwalker comes fluttering around me, I intend to say in a rumbling basso:

"A pair of long flannel underdrawers, sir, and a pound of Drayman's Plug."

I suppose it will kill him.

Chief Justice

Condensed from The New Yorker

HENRY F. PRINGLE

EVEN a member of the United States Senate looks with awe upon the office of Chief Justice, and with sound reason. The great powers of the Supreme Court mean that the Chief Justice is the highest judicial officer in the world. On the ground of rarity, too, his position is impressive. President Roosevelt is the 32nd occupant of the White House, but Charles Evans Hughes is only the 11th jurist to preside over the Supreme Court. At 73, with his luxuriant gray whiskers and pink cheeks, he is poetically and pictorially perfect in his job. For nearly six years now, Chief Justice Hughes has looked benignly down, a Judicial Jehovah, from the bench in the ancient and mellow courtroom at the Capitol. The Court has received unprecedented public attention during the Roosevelt administration. It must ultimately pass on the legality of all New Deal legislation, and every farmer, every merchant on sightseeing trips to the Capital, knows that no small part of his destiny lies in the hands of these nine impressive jurists. So the tourists throng to sessions of the Court, gaze respectfully at Chief Justice Hughes and carry home word that he is one of the best sights in Washington—comparable to the Washington Monument and the Lincoln Memorial.

Yet the office of Chief Justice is not mentioned in the Constitution, nor are the powers of the Supreme Court more than generally defined. In 1803, however, the Court made itself final arbiter on the constitutionality of acts of Congress, and today is, in addition, the tribunal of last appeal on laws enacted by the states, insofar as they endanger the basic rights of the people. Judicial review of legislation may well prove our most important contribution to the science of government. How this works was dramatically demonstrated last May when the Court unanimously declared the NRA unconstitutional. As soon as Chief Justice Hughes had finished reading the opinion, there *was* no NRA, in law or in fact.

Although a warm and amiable

individual, Mr. Hughes is shy. He has no taste for the bluff, hearty—and yet superficial—contacts which politicians maintain. At no time has he had more than a few close friends. Work has dominated his life, and his accomplishments are due to a driving energy and a facile mind. He has never labored as hard as during the years since 1930 when, at 68, he ascended the bench the second time. The pressure upon the Chief Justice is enormous; he is the presiding officer and, in a sense, general manager of the Court. He can delegate relatively few of his duties and so finds it necessary to live by a Spartan schedule, to which the entire routine of the Hughes household is geared.

The social life of Chief Justice and Mrs. Hughes, because of the burdens of his position, is severely limited. They go out or entertain on Saturday nights only and are dated up months ahead. "I'm to see you at a dinner in May," Mrs. Hughes was informed by a friend last January.

The days of the old Supreme Court room are numbered—the Court will probably have moved to its magnificent marble mausoleum across the Capitol plaza by fall. But the ritual which now marks the Court will be adhered to. By law, the Supreme Court convenes the first Monday in October and usually sits five days a week until the last Monday in May or the first in June, with a fortnight's recess several times a year so that the Justices can catch up in studying cases already heard. The Justices arrive at the Capitol between 11:30 and 12 o'clock and go directly to the robing room, across the corridor from the courtroom. There everything is arranged in strict order of precedence—the Chief Justice's judicial gown is in the first case, that of Associate Justice Cardozo, the newest member, in the farthest. Each robe bears the initial of its owner, but there are "spares" on hand should a jurist slip on his brief walk and tear his own. The robes are of silk and cost about $100 each, paid by the Justices themselves.

At 11 o'clock, spectators begin to arrive, although there is space for only a few score. The seats are pews, as in a church. Subdued lighting, and voices hushed even when the bench is deserted heighten the ecclesiastical atmosphere.

At 12, Frank Key Green, Marshal of the Supreme Court, enters the robing room and the Justices prepare to start the single-file procession across the hall, between velvet-covered ropes. The Chief Justice nearly always spots some acquaintance in the watching crowd and smiles a greeting.

Court Crier Thomas E. Waggaman raps sharply with a gavel. Everybody rises. Mr. Waggaman begins to intone in a voice which is a blend of train-announcer and Episcopal bishop:

"The Honorable, the Chief Justice, and the Associate Justices of the Supreme Court of the United States."

The hush is now profound. Silken robes rustle like old ladies' petticoats. The Justices move to their places on the bench. As they reach them, but before they sit down, the Crier again raises his voice:

"Oyez! Oyez!! Oyez!!! All persons having business before the Honorable the Supreme Court of the United States are admonished to draw near and give their attention for the Court is now sitting. God save the United States and this Honorable Court."

The Clerk calls the first case and an attorney walks up to the lectern and arranges his papers. Each side gets an hour to present its case, but this is divided if more than one lawyer is appearing. Pleading before the Supreme Court is always an ordeal. The Chief and each Associate Justice hurl questions at any time; many a carefully planned argument has thus been torn to shreds at the start. Chief Justice Hughes is nearly always gracious; the thing that annoys him most is having some windbag make an oration instead of keeping to the issue. He is perfectly ruthless in holding attorneys to their time allowance and cuts them off in the middle of a sentence if they exceed it.

Ten cases are scheduled for each day's session. This does not mean that arguments will be heard in all —some are promptly thrown out for technical reasons. The Court Clerk puts a list of the day's cases in front of each Justice. He also drafts for each a brief abstract of the previous day's proceedings. Discreetly placed under the bench are nine china cuspidors. None of the Justices uses snuff, although that delicacy is still placed, free of charge, in the Senate Chamber by a benevolent Uncle Sam.

Green-covered tables and chairs for about 20 lawyers are in front of the bench. On the tables are old-fashioned quill pens. These pens furnish mild entertainment to the Court and its attendants. They are provided only for atmosphere— they scratch pretty badly—and lawyers are constantly slipping them quietly in their pockets as souvenirs. Wholesale purchases are necessary because of the degree to which they vanish daily.

Promptly at two o'clock, whether some lawyer is speaking or not, the Chief Justice orders a half-hour's recess for lunch. The Justices eat together in the robing room; food is sent from the Senate restaurant. At two-thirty Court convenes; two hours later, to the minute, it rises for the day. This rule is inflexible. Four hours of close listening is enough. The work in open court is only a fraction of the labor; no fewer than 931 cases were disposed of at the last session of the Court.

Saturday is Conference Day, and the Justices meet in secret, behind double doors, in a room on the cellar level of the Capitol. Here is where the vital deliberations take place, and where the Chief Justice, because he directs the proceedings, has a special opportunity for leadership.

On Friday, Mr. Hughes sends to each associate a list of the cases, already heard in court, to be discussed on Saturday. No member is certain he will not be asked to write an opinion; thus it is incumbent upon him to do his homework thoroughly before he attends. The Chief Justice opens the discussion by giving his views. The other members give theirs, and sometimes the debate grows very warm indeed and judicial calm surrenders to angry shouting. When the vote is taken, the newest Associate Justice is called upon first, on the theory that he thus cannot be influenced by his seniors. If the Chief Justice agrees with the majority, he assigns the writing of the opinion; if not, the senior majority member does so.

One prerogative of the Chief Justice is that he can reserve for himself the writing of any opinion. Chief Justice Hughes has written most of the New Deal opinions. He reads his own opinions on Mondays—Decision Day—at an appalling speed and in a clear, somewhat harsh voice. All opinions are printed before they are delivered. Curiously enough, the work is not done by the Government Printing Office, but by Pearson's, a small Washington job plant, where elaborate precautions are taken to preserve secrecy. In important cases, such as the gold clause ones, opinions are cut into sections so that no one typesetter has more than a few lines. A leak from the printers has never occurred.

In an age of publicity, the Supreme Court of the United States is probably the only organization in this country without a press agent. A few copies of its decisions are provided, but never enough for the correspondents. No transcript is kept of proceedings; unless some attorney provides a stenographer, legal learning and occasional wit are lost forever. Yet the suspicion is inescapable that these nine eminent jurists have vastly enjoyed the spotlight which has beaten upon them during the past year as on the one hand they supported the President's monetary policy, while on the other they plucked the final tail feathers from the NRA Blue Eagle. Veteran attendants admit that the Justices seem more affable when the courtroom is crowded. Indeed, there is a well-authenticated report that one of the objections to the new Supreme Court Building is that it is off the beaten track. "Everyone," complained an Associate Justice, "will forget about us."

That danger is remote.

Grounds for Divorce

JUDGES of the Paris Divorce Court got a new one to figure out when a woman sued her husband for damages because she had had six children.—*N. Y. Herald Tribune*

"*Am I Losing My Mind?*"

By

LOUIS E. BISCH, M.D.

Aм I losing my mind, Doctor?" That question has been put to me as a psychiatrist so many times it seems like a million. The general practitioner, too, knows how common is this haunting dread of insanity, knows indeed that a surprising proportion of persons harbor a sneaking suspicion at one time or another that they are heading for a mental disorder, if not the asylum.

Allow me, however, to be reassuring forthwith. The very fact that you *fear* you are losing your mind is the best possible proof that you are *not*. The possessor of a psychosis (the medical term for insanity) practically never is aware that his mind is upset.

The very essence of a psychosis is the "delusion." The characteristics of an insane delusion are: first, that the patient adopts a wholly false premise of some kind; second, that his reasoning and consequently his conclusions are illogical; third, that he tenaciously clings to what he holds to be true no matter how

From *Be Glad You're Neurotic*, by Louis E. Bisch, M.D., published by Whittlesey House.

much proof is brought to bear in an attempt to establish the falsity of his far-fetched and altogether absurd ideas. The psychotic is convinced that *you* are in error; only *he* understands. If anyone is insane it is you, not he.

Now then, the person who *worries* about losing his mind presents quite an opposite picture. He *knows* something is wrong with him. Because of one or more neurotic symptoms from which he is suffering, he is continually obsessed with the thought that he is different from others. But his premises are sound as well as his reasoning and conclusions. The link between himself and the world in general is never lost and he keeps on trying to strengthen it; the psychotic, contrariwise, has broken that link and lives in a mental world altogether distinct, peculiar and apart.

The out-and-out neurotic, of course, also may suffer from ideas that are absurd, ideas that the layman calls "imaginary." But no matter how ridiculous on the surface such neurotic imaginings may seem, the possessor of them, unlike the psychotic, is forever attempting to

305

conquer them and change them so that he may think, feel and act like other people.

A psychotic patient under my care believed all the bones in his body to be broken. Even when stood upon his feet he still held to his delusion. Another claimed that people were "working wireless" on him and this man, mind you, had formerly been a radio engineer. A third said, "My blood is dried up. That's why I feel so weak." When he was pricked with a needle and actually saw his own blood flow, he still stuck to his delusional idea.

Following are ten symptoms commonly met with that make people afraid they will lose their minds. Note how essentially different they are in content from psychotic delusions. An otherwise perfectly normal person may be troubled by one or more of these; but he should realize that the manifestation is merely an individual difference to be looked upon as a normal deviation within the normal. If several such symptoms exist, especially for several years, the condition would technically be called neurotic. But a neurosis, even in the most severe case, does *not* lead to insanity.

1. Loss of Memory—For this physical causes exist, or mental, or both. The usual physical causes are late hours, insufficient sleep, too little exercise and fresh air, too much alcohol or tobacco, sluggish intestinal elimination. Correct your faults in any of these respects and at once your memory improves.

Regarding mental causes it should be pointed out that the ability to remember depends primarily upon three factors: the recency of the stimulus; the intensity of the stimulus; the repetition of the stimulus. In other words, we are able to remember most readily an experience that occurred only a short while ago, or that was unusual or dramatic, or that occurred several times instead of once. Think of your poor memory in this light and it will explain a lot. It ought to allay your apprehensions.

As regards the relationship between failing memory and the psychosis, this occurs only after a psychosis has been existent in a full-fledged way for years, in the terminal stages of "deterioration."

2. Inability to Concentrate—This usually is an accompaniment of unretentive memory. What has already been said about the latter applies in every detail to the former.

3. Inferiority Convictions—Those who do not succeed the way they would wish in business, social affairs or in their love-life and so become discouraged, timid and self-conscious, should seek the "why" of such a condition—for the cause can always be discovered. It may date from childhood, having been caused by a domineering father, mother, or teacher. It may be linked with "guilt" feelings, which will be discussed presently. The individual often can trace the development of inferiority himself if he takes the trouble to think back carefully. If he fails after repeated trials it simply means that the causes are deeply

rooted in the unconscious mind and the services of a psychiatrist are required to assist him to find them.

Sometimes a maladjustment of the so-called glands of internal secretion (endocrine glands) is the sole cause of convictions of inferiority. Especially important here is a deficiency of the adrenal (or suprarenal) glands, which have so aptly been named the "fighting glands" of the body.

At any rate, inferiority, no matter what its origin, is the very antithesis of the mental attitude of the average psychotic. If anything, the psychotic suffers from too much ego, not too little.

4. Guilt—A feeling of guilt is the first cousin to ideas of inferiority, if not their mother. What I mean is that an individual is often made to feel guilty, then he becomes convinced that he is not as moral or as competent as others and consequently he feels inferior. All this is common sense and not at all psychotic.

Unfortunately, "don't" still is the usual cudgel word by which parents coerce their children, while punishment and making children feel ashamed, the child seldom fully understanding why, still remain the usual ways of rearing them. Which conviction of wrong-doing is, to be sure, often aided by the intimidation and fear that school and religious teachers instill into the immature and developing mind. No one, therefore, can possibly escape some measure of guilt feelings.

In addition, there are few individuals living (adult or child) who have not or do not accuse themselves of harboring sex thoughts or of having given way to practices at some time during their lives which they either have been taught or have heard are wrong. Yet the greatest harm from secret sex acts is mental, in that it produces so much unwarranted feeling of guilt. Furthermore, despite popular opinion to the contrary, onanism never has led to insanity.

5. Suicidal Impulse—Suffice it to say that when "things get a bit too thick" and the outlook appears hopeless, the thought of ending it all is a perfectly intelligent reaction. So also is it an intelligent reaction to realize one's responsibilities and to convince oneself that events somehow have a way of straightening themselves out. There are a few who do not, during the course of a lifetime, think about self-destruction. Strong guilt feelings often are a motivation. Of course, only the fool gives way. If the impulse persists, a psychiatrist had better be consulted; but it is not, in any case, a sign of insanity.

6. Worry—We worry because our minds are confused and doubtful, because we are not able to think clearly and to see a way out of something that threatens. The psychotic cannot be said to worry because he cannot be said to be confused and doubtful in the sense that I have outlined. He is too sure of his own thinking. Worry can deplete the organic brain system and lead to a nervous breakdown (a severe neurosis). It is often reported that So-and-So became insane be-

cause of worry. Investigation of such cases always reveals that worry is a sort of camouflage masking other facts. In short, it is normal to worry. How could an intelligent person be absolutely free from it these days?

7. Unreality Feelings—When the environment, including people and things, begins to "feel" unreal (as though objects did not exist or as though they were seen through a mist) you should ask yourself what it is from which you are trying to escape. Search deeply into your thought storehouse, although this may not be necessary because the reason for "flight" may be known to you. Typical, among common causes, are disappointment in a beloved one, or inability to get a job. The mind, playing the rôle of protector, attempts to blot out an offending factor by making the whole world seem not to exist as it really is.

Feelings of unreality are technically called "escape mechanisms," as is the fear of insanity itself. But, mind you, the artificial world of phantasy that the psychotic sets up for himself appears decidedly *real* to him.

8. Insomnia—Inability to fall asleep, or becoming fully awake during the night and then not being able to sleep again, is torturing and weakening but it cannot, of and by itself, produce a psychosis. Physical factors, as noted under "Loss of Memory," may be to blame, or disturbances in the emotional life. Insomnia is a result rather than a cause and it is always curable.

9. Depression—There are those who take life more seriously than others, also those who "get the blues" readily when disappointed. Women are more disposed to depression than men and their physiological cycle may be responsible. Nor should it be forgotten that everyone is more or less subject to ups and downs and that this follows a fairly regular rhythmic curve.

Depression, however, is not "melancholia." The latter, a psychosis, presents quite a different clinical picture, its victims worrying absurdly about some negligible transgression of the past, for which they are convinced they can never be forgiven. When despondency becomes psychotic it is extremely marked, of long duration and shows delusions in addition.

10. Insanity in the Family— Should you happen to find a case of psychosis somewhere in your family tree, whether near or remote, that fact in itself is nothing whatever to be alarmed about. A psychosis is not scientifically considered hereditary. It does not follow the laws of inheritance set down by Gregor Mendel in 1865, and this is the ultimate test.

To sum it all up, as I stated in the beginning, if you fear you are losing your mind it proves that you are not in any such danger at all. To be afraid of anything really shows a desire to avoid it. Far from wishing to avoid insanity, the victim of a real psychosis welcomes it as a complete escape from reality.

You Won't Be Snubbed

By

HENRY MORTON ROBINSON

AROUND ME, a bright-muffled throng of winter-sports enthusiasts loafed in the white Adirondack sunshine. Lean ski jumpers puffed at blunt brown pipes; bobsledders tossed challenges and snowballs at each other; wind-burned débutantes, whose color was at least half their own, basked in deck chairs. The thin northern air crackled with frost and gaiety; everyone was having fun.

That is, everyone but me. The deck chair beside me was vacant, yet no one sat down in it. For years, no one ever *did* sit down by me voluntarily. For some reason I had always been unable to draw other human beings into warm personal contacts.

But the whole picture changed on that snow-brilliant day when David Jessup sat down in the deck chair beside me. I had particularly observed this man; it was a joy to watch him approach a stranger and melt the icy cellophane that most human beings come wrapped in. I saw him do it dozens of times, so gently and so *right* that even the chilliest glaze of hostility was quickly transformed into a lubricating warmth between two human beings. I envied him his easy approach to others, yet I would have gone to my grave (so stern were the proprieties of my New England upbringing) before speaking to him or any stranger first.

But evidently my high-fenced reserve was no barrier to Jessup, for he turned his friendly gray eyes on me, and smiled with genuine good nature. There were no inanities about the weather, no self-conscious preliminaries. Like a man imparting news of interest to an old friend, he said without tension or embarrassment: "I saw you watching that bronzed chap mending his snowshoes. He's the Rhodes Scholar from New York. He stroked the Cornell crew last year and was president of the debating club besides. Don't you think he's a splendid type to represent American youth at Oxford?"

Jessup's opening remarks led us at once into a discussion of Cecil Rhodes' dream of cementing Anglo-American friendship. From that take-off, our talk continued through many fields of common interest and special information. When we stopped an hour later we were friends. It was something of a miracle, and I asked Jessup point-blank how he did it.

"Your happy knack of speaking to strangers—how do you manage it? Personally, I'm limited in my human acquaintance, which is confined to a small circle of friends, all of the same type. All my life I've wanted to mingle with strangers who could widen my interests and quicken my sense of being alive, yet I've always hung back, afraid of a rebuff. How does one overcome this fear of being snubbed?"

Jessup waved his hand inclusively at the throng around us. "My fear of being snubbed," he said, "completely disappears when I remember that the dearest friends I have were once strangers. So when I see a young woman arranging a cluster of holly boughs, or a group of men tinkering with a bobsled, they needn't belong to my private collection of acquaintances before I speak to them. If I speak, perhaps they *will* belong to that collection, and I shall be the richer for knowing them."

"But," I persisted, "how about being misunderstood?"

"If you approach your fellow man with honest sympathy and a desire to be humanly friendly," said Jessup, "he is not likely to misread your motive. I have met men of the most formidable self-importance, and found them all responsive, eager to visit with me.

Rarely have I encountered even the slightest hint of a snub. No, my friend, you mustn't let fear be the basis of your seclusion. The new, the unusual, is no more dangerous than the familiar, and it has the advantage of being decidedly more exciting."

Subsequent experiences with David Jessup proved how right he was. Wherever he went, he would enter into conversation with all manner of people, and was forever turning up strange new types and odd, stimulating information. On one of our trips together we passed a granite quarry in which a number of men were walking about on tiptoe, carrying red flags and acting like advance messengers of doom. Instead of hurrying past, Jessup spoke to one of the flagcarriers, and in a few moments the man was telling us a hair-curling story. It seems that many years ago, engineers had drilled 50 holes in this quarry, packed the holes with dynamite, then wired them up for a blast. But some of the wiring was defective, and as a result only half of the dynamite exploded! For 20 years workmen could not be persuaded to go near the quarry; it had to be abandoned, and was now being reopened by men who received double pay because of the attendant danger.

Another time, on the shore of a beautiful lake in a state park, Jessup noticed a man making sketches. Skillfully engaging the man in conversation, Jessup discovered that he was a marine horticulturist with a new idea called "pond-scaping."

"On the lakes surrounding the ancient Aztec capital," said the sketcher, "were many floating islands covered with feathery trees and rare flowers. I believe that I have rediscovered how such islands can be constructed and kept in motion, and am now making some sketches to interest the park commission in my idea."

On the way home I remarked, "That was one of the most interesting things that ever happened to me. Both the man and his drawings were fascinating."

Jessup agreed, then added slyly: "And you wouldn't have met him in a thousand years if you had waited for an introduction, would you?"

"Don't rub it in, please. I've always known that I was missing a great deal, but I never knew how to get people started."

"To talk to a stranger," advised Jessup, "begin with a remark that penetrates to the core of his interest. Usually it will be something that applies to his work. Inane general remarks or fussy little questions only irk the busy man. One must be genuinely interested in what the stranger is doing, make an intelligent comment, then wait for him to respond. And he *will* respond, for the simple reason that most human beings are overjoyed when another person shows interest in their work. Take that floating-garden chap for instance: if we had seemed bored he wouldn't even have begun to talk, for no man likes to expose his treasures to the indifferent. But when he saw that we were really deriving pleasure from his conversation, he tried to reward our interest and prolong our pleasure. Why should he do this? Simply because no one has ever yet discovered a keener happiness than giving pleasure to others."

I was always expecting Jessup to be snubbed, but the snub never came. Once while touring with him, a trio of noisy roughs boarded our bus and began to annoy the passengers with a display of downright coarseness. Dignified, serious, Jessup got up and went back to them. "Here," thought I, "my friend is riding for a fall." But I was wrong. What Jessup said to those fellows I never knew, but within five minutes he had engaged the three of them in an earnest discussion of labor conditions throughout the country and their own chances of employment.

I've seen Jessup address women bred in the strictest code of convention, and often wondered how he avoided being cut by them. He explained it in this way: "If in speaking to a woman you reveal that you are primarily interested in her personally or as a member of the opposite sex, she will instantly resent it, as she has every right to do. In effect, you are insulting her by the assumption that her attention may be so cheaply won. But speak to her as one human being to another, as one interested in the same scenery, the same music, or the same social problems, and she will extend her ready fellowship. Both men and women love to use their minds, and women especially regard it as a distinct compliment to be met on the intellectual plane that both sexes hold in common."

Since knowing David Jessup, the stranger at my elbow has become the most interesting and approachable thing in life. No longer do I ride for hours in cold dumbness beside him rather than risk one tentative remark. For I have grown to believe that he is just as eager to know me—to know why I wear ear muffs and smoke a calabash pipe —as I am to know similar things about him. And I have finally learned that if I approach him unaffectedly, without a false sense of toploftiness on the one hand, or advantage-grabbing on the other, there is no danger of my being snubbed.

For ultimately we are not so different from one another. Training and tradition may have cast us in dissimilar molds, but the basic stuff of our humanity is pathetically the same. It is this realization that now makes every stranger accessible to me. He may be a barber or a banknote-engraver, but it is almost certain that he can tell me something that will heighten my mental stature or increase my spiritual gauge. I may like him or I may not; if he bores me, I can be off. But the thing that constantly surprises me is the scarcity of people who are really boresome or offensive. By far the larger part of our human race is composed of unexpectedly interesting and friendly members, all pitifully eager to know each other. And I have yet to see the man or woman who did not become more attractive and more *alive* for laying aside their too-prized reserve and mingling on equal terms with other members of our common, struggling, hungering human family.

Table Talk

A TRAVELER in a Southern wayside restaurant once threw the help into confusion by asking for coffee without cream. The Negro waiter went to the kitchen and was gone an unconscionable period. When he returned he approached the traveler timidly.

"I'm sorry, suh," he said, "we can't let you have coffee without cream. But we *can* let you have it without milk."

"FOUR AND TWENTY blackbirds baked in a pie," is no idle invention of Mother Goose. A certain Robert May, whose book, *The Accomplished Cook*, was published in the 17th century, amused himself and his masters by devising large pies containing live frogs and birds: "When lifting first the lid off one pye, out skip some frogs, which make the ladies to skip and shreek: next after the other pye, when out come the birds, who by natural instinct flying into the lights will put out the candles, so that what with the flying birds and the skipping frogs, the one above, the other beneath, will cause much delight and pleasure to the whole company."

—*The Gourmet's Almanac*

Trial by Newspaper

Condensed from Scribner's Magazine

PAUL HUTCHINSON

SEVERAL YEARS AGO Maureen Watkins, then a sob-sister on the Chicago *Tribune*, wrote a play giving a detailed account of a criminal trial in that city. While it was advertised as a burlesque of criminal trials, it was difficult to point out where accurate reporting ended and burlesque began.

The scenes at which audiences laughed most uproariously were almost literal transcripts of what continually goes on in news-worthy criminal trials. From the frenzied competition among the police to be photographed with the beautiful defendant at the time of her arrest ("And be sure you get the name spelled right!"), through the hair-pulling jealousies between the several lady killers in the county jail over the size of their respective newspaper scrapbooks, down to the climactic courtroom scenes—cameramen shooting from the floor at the defendant's crossed legs as she sat in the witness chair, and after the acquittal photographing her with her arms around the neck of judge and jury foreman—the play was a factual presentation.

This sort of thing undoubtedly does more to put criminal justice in the United States into contempt than all other influences put together. But all this ballyhoo, all the destructive effect of the handling of crime news by the press could be stopped at once without passing a single law—*if the courts really want it done.*

Let us begin when the crime has been committed. All the criminal has to do, we are told, is to read the papers to learn precisely where the police net is being spread to catch him and how, therefore, to escape it. Very often this is true. But who gives the reporters their information as to what the police are doing? The police themselves; they come hot-foot with every development, all on the understanding that the papers shall give credit to Captain Doyle of the 12th Precinct and Detective Sergeant Pestalozzi, who are running the criminal to earth. The reporter who fails to give them the publicity they are after might as well turn to the reporting of hotel arrivals or ship news.

When the arrest is made the prosecuting attorney meets the press daily. He begins with an announcement that the wretch now in jail is unquestionably the guilty party, and details are added to persuade the public that it knows exactly how the crime was committed. The next day there is promise of an impending confession, which, when it comes, is given to the papers in full. (Later the confession may not even be introduced at the trial; if introduced, the chances are better than even that it will be thrown out.)

Then follow, during the weeks before the trial, announcements of sinister facts discovered in the past life of the defendant and of the thwarting of plans made by the defense to tamper with the jury. After the trial starts, there is a daily demonstration of the failure of the defense to establish its case, and a summary of the devastating points scored by the prosecution. The printing of columns of this sort of thing makes the prospect for even-handed justice considerably less than zero. But where does the public suppose the newspaper gets it? And would there be hell to pay if a paper should refuse to play ball with the district attorney's office!

The defense lawyer also has his press conferences, asserting that his client's confession has been extracted by third-degree methods; that he has an unbreakable alibi; almost every day yields another "surprise" witness. Even more important is the attempt to get special reporters assigned to the defendant's side of the case—for the more successful the defense counsel is in reducing public opinion to blubbering sentimentalism, the more roseate his prospects.

And the judges? Well, judges differ. But there are few who do not have a vivid sense of the personal advantage to be gained from presiding at extensively reported trials. Hence, at every step in this anti-social process the press is bedeviled *by officers of law and courts* to do precisely what it does.

They do these things better in England. This is not to say that there is no vulgarity, no sensationalism, in the treatment of English crime news. There is plenty; the public taste is continually debauched by crime stories with as much gory detail, with as much "glorifying" of the criminal, as any printed in this country. But there is no trying of cases in advance in the newspapers. And there is no making the judicial process an adjunct in a feverish race for personal publicity.

When Secretary Stimson addressed the Attorney General's conference a few years ago he told this story: A sensational murder was committed in England as a party of American lawyers was leaving New York to hold joint sessions with the British bar. The criminal had been apprehended and indicted by the time the Americans docked at Southampton on a Saturday. The trial was held the following Monday and Tuesday. Conviction came Tuesday afternoon. The appeal was heard by the Lord Chief Justice, and sentence confirmed, on Thursday. As the group started home at the end of the week, the guilty man was hanged.

The point which Mr. Stimson made was not that speed is desirable in itself, but that it does make judicial hippodroming impossible. "So far as I can remember," he stated, "there was absolutely no indication of drama attempted. No sentimental life histories were published. No prison matrons were photographed with their arms around the prisoner."

There were a number of other things which did not appear in the English papers. During the time the police were hunting for that criminal, the press was not filled with theories as to how the crime had been committed, and—unless the London Commissioner of Police asked for such publication—nothing was said as to whom the police suspected. After the arrest, nothing was reported about it except the facts recorded on the official charge sheet. Up to the very end of the trial, nothing was said about the character of the accused or his previous record. All the methods by which the American press might take such a case and submerge the public mind in slobbering sentimentality or prejudice were out.

An English editor can be sent to jail for doing almost anything in reporting a criminal trial that an American editor might do as a matter of course. A few years ago, when a man named Mahon was

awaiting trial for the murder of a Miss Kaye, the Manchester *Guardian,* the London *Evening Standard* and the London *Daily Express* stated that Mahon had been living under an assumed name, had given Miss Kaye presents which implied a coming marriage, and so on. All of these statements were true, and the inference which the papers were discreetly suggesting was also true. But the statements were printed before Mahon had been tried, when their printing might conceivably have prejudiced the public mind against him. It cost the *Guardian* and the *Express* £300 apiece, and the *Standard* £1000, with a warning from the Lord Chief Justice that if the offense were repeated there would be a jail sentence. The *Standard's* extra fine resulted from its printing an advance interview with an important witness.

When a man named Rouse was arrested for murder—simulating accidental death by setting fire to a motorcar in which the victim's body had been placed—the London *Evening Star* drew another fine from the Lord Chief Justice for having put out street posters with the headline: "Another Blazing Car Murder." Since Rouse had not yet been convicted, Lord Hewart held it contempt of court to refer to the case as a "murder."

In another case a newspaper was fined because a reporter, in quoting from a letter used as evidence, quoted the entire letter, while only a part was actually introduced into the record of the trial.

When a member of the Totten-
ham Hotspur football team was arrested on a minor charge, only two
London papers took a chance—and
that after the case had been concluded!—on mentioning the fact
that the man accused played on
that famous professional eleven.
Imagine the American press, if a
member of the New York Giants
fell afoul of the courts, suppressing
reference to that fact lest the case
be prejudiced!

Examples such as these mean that
the courts will not tolerate "Trial
by Newspaper," or unfairness to
accused persons. Much of the English press, and a considerable part
of the bar, would be only too glad
to give English trials the same ballyhoo treatment that has wrought
such havoc in this country. But
they dare not!—not because of any
specific law but because an English
judge will, by citing for contempt,
make short work of the newspaper
or lawyer whose activities tend in
the slightest degree to bring the

proceedings in his court into disre-
pute!

Judges in America are in complete control of their own courts.
They have certain precedents for
contempt of court fairly well established. But such a means of
keeping the judicial process from
public scorn is still waiting to be
used over here. The first judges
who resorted to this method for
cleaning up criminal proceedings
would bring down on themselves
the loud indignation of all the interests which think they are making money or gaining prestige under
present conditions. But as the public came to understand what was
involved, it would approve.

So it's up to the judges. Without
any new legislation, but with a genuine determination to protect the
dignity and impartiality of every
trial over which they preside, the
men on the bench can impose regulations of adequate effectiveness on
papers, police, lawyers and prosecuting officers, *if they so desire*.

Honorable Mention

PEOPLE WITH A PURPOSE

WHEN a radio broadcast offer of an "odd" shoe brought in five
calls in 15 minutes, Mrs. N. M. Windsor, president of the Child
Conservation Conference in St. Louis, knew that their "Odd Shoe
Exchange" was filling a definite need. The shoe was one of a pair
bought by the Conference for a one-legged boy; it was used by
another cripple who wore a specially-built shoe on one foot, a
normal shoe on the other. The Exchange collects the extra shoes
from cripples who can use only one, but must buy a pair, and
redistributes them to other cripples who can wear the odd one. So
many requests from cripples thus afflicted have come in that the
Exchange has been unable to keep up with the demand.

One-Man Power

By

CHANNING POLLOCK

BASIL KING and I were sitting together in a restaurant when a woman at the next table said to her companion, "It's a disgraceful state of affairs, but what can one man do?"

The author of *The Conquest of Fear* looked at me and asked, "Shall we tell her that everything of importance in the world was begun by one man—or one woman?"

Wandering about Europe, in 1907, I was appalled at the filth of the tenements. They were bad enough in New York—but in Paris, and Berlin, and especially Naples! "Dreadful," our Italian guide shrugged, "but what can you do?" In London, a little old-maid schoolteacher had asked herself that question, and answered it. Octavia Hill's great interest was giving instruction in sewing to groups of poor women. Shocked by the squalor of their deplorable homes, she managed to lease three dwellings with borrowed money and to convert them into pioneer "model tenements." Later she opened what perhaps was the first public playground for children. By 1902,

when my Neapolitan guide was inquiring, "What can one person do?" Miss Hill and her sister Miranda had 1268 families under their wings. News of their success spread. Landlords across the Channel, hearing that there were no vacancies or repair bills in Octavia Hill's tenements, began likewise to construct modern, sanitary, fireproof buildings. Government officials saw that these produced a more contented citizenry. When Mussolini came into power, he decreed no slums in Italy. Two years ago, in Naples, I hunted in vain for the slums I had seen in 1902. The movement gains ground constantly. In America, we are just beginning the job that the penniless and obscure Hill girls took on in London three quarters of a century ago, and that has swept away rookeries from Moscow to Cape Town.

Of political abuses, most of us say, "There's always been graft, and there always will be. What can *I* do?" Yet an underpaid cartoonist, the son of a German bandsman, started the avalanche that buried the Tweed Ring—the greediest

317

bunch of grafters that ever looted New York. The Tweed Ring had the support of the biggest financiers; it controlled the legislature, the courts, and the newspapers; and its "take" was some $200,000,000 in 30 months. Thomas Nast began attacking Boss Tweed with sensational cartoons in *Harper's Weekly*. George Jones, as editor of the New York *Times,* joined in the battle. Both men were vilified, threatened with imprisonment and death, but they kept on until the city was aroused. Then huge bribes were offered them. Jones refused $5,-000,000.

"You could go to Europe and live like a prince," Tweed's emissary said.

"Yes," answered Jones, "but I should know I was a rascal."

Tweed ended in prison, and the grafters were driven out. If grafters don't *stay* out, the fault is that of the decent citizen who feels there is nothing he can do about it. I know a chap who, with his wife and daughter, last year traveled 150 miles to his home in a hotly contested district and sat five hours in a polling place which the local machine had packed with its henchmen. "What good can *you* do?" friends asked, but the man stuck, and his wife and daughter stuck, and the honest element carried that district *by two votes.*

In the 18th century prisons everywhere were "pestiferous dens, overcrowded, dark, foully dirty." And in the English borough of Bedford, there was a high sheriff, named John Howard, who was

shocked by the conditions he found in the local jail. He began a one-man crusade that within a year brought the passage of an act providing the first substantial reforms in the penal system. These reforms he carried through a large part of Europe, and when he died, the work was taken up by Elizabeth Fry, the wife of a London merchant, who made her influence felt to the four corners of the earth. Thus, the entire foundation for enlightenment in dealing with criminals was laid by a former grocer's apprentice and by a young matron who, at twenty, "amid increasing family cares," began "paying some attention to the poor and neglected of her neighborhood."

Just over 30, and recently presented at Court, Florence Nightingale followed the British Army to the Crimea, where three nations were fighting Russia, and practically no provision had been made for the wounded. You can almost hear her dancing friends asking what one woman could do. Within a few months of her arrival at Scutari, the death rate in Crimean hospitals had dropped to two in a hundred—from forty-two. This one woman, with the help of others who rallied around her, revolutionized nursing and sanitation, not only in the Crimea, but universally. Every injured soldier, in every war since the Crimean, owes much to this girl who felt that she could do something more useful than entertain her father's guests.

Our own Clara Barton was a schoolteacher whose ill health compelled her to give up her classes. During the Civil War, Miss Barton advertised in the Worcester (Mass.) *Spy* that she would distribute personally any supplies or money sent her for the soldiers. And that was the beginning of the American Red Cross. In similarly small ways, someone who had faith in one-man power started almost every great institution and accomplished reform we accept as commonplace today.

That graphic play, *Dead End*, a Broadway success this season, ironically shows society, through its police, ridding itself of one gangster even while, in the same block, it is manufacturing scores of others. Most of our gunmen are bred in the slums; sent to "reformatories," they are often only hardened in crime. This is a big problem; what can one man do?

Ernest K. Coulter, Clerk of New York's first Juvenile Court, believed that what young delinquents needed was *guiding friendship*. In 1904, he suggested to the Men's Club of the Central Presbyterian Church that each of the members take a personal interest in one boy who had been arraigned in the court. Out of that came the Big Brother Movement, which has given individual guidance to more than 16,000 boys, of whom only three or four percent ever reappear in court. The movement has spread widely; there are Jewish Big Brothers now, and Catholic Big Brothers, and French and English and German Big Brothers.

Louis Braille, blind from the age of three, taught himself to read by touching raised letters. What a blessing, thought this lad, if *all* the blind could read! By the time he was 25, he had perfected his system of raised type for the blind, and was teaching it in Paris. The Braille System has since spread throughout the world.

Booker T. Washington was a house-servant with an elementary education, who walked and "hitched" 500 miles to reach the school for Negroes at Hampton, Virginia. Later he started Tuskegee Institute in a shanty at Tuskegee, Alabama, and in spite of bitter opposition, even from his own race, he soon had 1700 enrolled students and an educational plant of 32 buildings. Tuskegee since has trained thousands of Negroes to be skilled workmen and better citizens.

Ralph Waldo Trine wrote me once: "Courage has magic in it." When, in 1776, David Hartley rose in an intolerant and hostile House of Commons to move that "the slave trade is contrary to the laws of God and the rights of men"—and was hooted outside the doors after his motion failed—could he have foreseen that this courageous stand of his was to be the beginning of the end of all slavery?

The contagion of such courage is often amazing. One man or woman raises a banner, and thousands enlist. Little movements, started locally, become world-wide. That is why I believe that even the "insurmountable obstacles" which afflict our civilization, like the conquest of war and poverty and ignorance, will be surmounted in time, thanks to one lifted voice that becomes first a clamor and then an irresistible power. Looking back over the way humanity has come within a scant three or four thousand years—led by average men, ordinary men, men of exactly your kind and mine—I thrill at the words of him who said, "One with God is a majority."

Americans Have a Club for It

S.P.E.B.S.Q.S.A., INC.

THE Society for the Preservation and Encouragement of Barber Shop Quartet Singing in America, Inc., started casually only a short time ago by O. C. Cash in Tulsa, Oklahoma, now flourishes from New York to Hollywood, from Texas to Canada. As tax attorney for three oil companies, his life harried by government regulations at every turn, Cash felt he must find a hobby as an antidote. Remembering the unfettered days of his youth, he hit on the idea of old-fashioned close harmony and asked a dozen men to join him. Three times the number came, and as news of the society spread, requests for other chapters poured in from all over the country. Celebrities and unknowns, rich men and poor have been drawn together in one of the most democratic organizations America has ever had. The original Tulsa chapter has among its active members wealthy oil executives, plumbers, lawyers, clerks, bankers; in an Arkansas chapter, two reliefers were in the quartet a banker took in his limousine for a personal appearance still talked of in Fort Worth. Bing Crosby heads the Hollywood chapter and serves on the society's national advisory board, as does Dr. Sigmund Spaeth; Owen D. Young, Jim Farley, Senator Champ Clark and many other senators and governors are among the society's long list of notables. At the first national convention in June, Cash was elected to the society's highest office: Permanent Assistant Third Vice-President.

Anywhere from 150 to 300 men attend meetings of the S.P.E.B.S.Q.S.A. They are divided into sections of leads, tenors, baritones, and basses for a giant quartet; later there are regular and impromptu quartets in barber shop harmony. The keynote of the whole movement is struck in the society's theme song:

> The old songs, the old songs,
> The good old songs for me;
> I like to hear those minor chords
> In good close harmony.

To Live Happily Even After

By

OLIVER M. BUTTERFIELD

EARLY in my experience as a minister I discovered that, in spite of romance and good intentions, many couples who come to the marriage altar are matrimonial illiterates. When you consider that we leave the highly difficult adjustments of marriage so largely to chance, the marvel is that our divorce rate is only 16 percent. An appalling number of husbands and wives are not really married but simply undivorced: they live in a sort of purgatory. Habits, responsibility to children, convention, opportunism hold them together, rather than the growing love that might have been their bond, had it not been for ignorance, immaturity, various missteps, and the wrong attitude toward their venture at the start.

To meet this situation there is growing up a group of marriage doctors—counselors skilled in the art of human relations, rendering professional service in the problems of family life. Today, after 18 years in the ministry, I am spending full time as a consultant in such mat-

ters. Remedial work is regrettably necessary, but what is most acutely needed is to see that young couples are acquainted with the realities of marriage before the ceremony is permitted.

Years ago I began to feel that I was prostituting my sacred office as a minister when I officiated at the marriage of couples manifestly uninformed. I decided to assume responsibility where before I had been hardly more than a phonograph turned on at the desired moment.

After years of experience and of observing the success of other men who have undertaken the same work, I am convinced that any pastor who fails to bring together for a frank conference every couple he unites in marriage risks making the service a mockery. I knew one minister who was so busy making blind marriages—over 500 a year—that he wouldn't play golf lest he miss an afternoon crop of hasty ceremonies. There is another who has carefully prepared over 700 pairs for marriage and, to his knowledge, only three have been lost to divorce.

So I made it an iron-clad rule to have a full and frank conversation with the high contracting parties. I found that, far from resenting this conversation, young people are eager for it. They welcome a chance to talk with someone whose interest is genuine but impersonal; and to bring before each other questions that are uppermost in their thoughts but, out of timidity or haste, often left unexpressed.

Here they are, starting off together on a union which they believe will last forever. Naturally, they are full of hope—but vaguely they know that the course of their married life may encounter hardships. Needless to say, they want guidance, not pedagogy. Usually my talks take place in my study. Occasionally couples who have announced their engagement are invited in for dinner, or perhaps my wife and I take them on a picnic, to provide the friendly, relaxed setting that is so important. Given an opportunity and a setting, couples are as determined as you to uncover the possible difficulties that are usually hidden under the romantic rubbish of popular fiction.

I begin by asking how long they have been acquainted and how long engaged. I know how soon hasty decisions are regretted. Some states require three days' notice before a marriage license is issued. A careful check in California showed that one year 2700 couples applied for licenses and never came back. What I want most to know, however, is how far ahead and how realistically the pair have thought about matrimony. Happy marriages are rarely the product of chance: they are architectural in that they are intelligently and deliberately planned. Have the affianced pair spent entire days together and found how they fit each other's nerves under trying and prosaic conditions as well as in romantic moments? Have they been together enough to quarrel, to learn frankly to adjust their disputes, and to become the better comrades for having had them? Does the young man's driving terrify the girl? Does the girl bore him by telling at length about her dreams? Is the match likely to produce a golf widow or a bridge widower? In the matters which make up the routine of married life, are they good companions or total strangers?

Many couples think they are in love when actually they are not even acquainted. Marriage is a process of constantly adjusting two egos, and they cannot know too well in advance what occasions for conflict and irritation may arise. Unless they have been "keeping company" under a wide range of circumstances that reveal the habits and attitudes of each to the other, a couple is marrying blind-folded; once the bandage is off, the trouble is likely to follow.

I ask, *What will your living arrangements be?* People often romantically suppose that love will continue to be love, whether in an attic or a mansion, alone or among in-laws. If they tend cavalierly to assume that the setting is unimportant, it may be wise to suggest a furnished room in some part of the city away from relatives. Marriage is a private affair and it is the exceptional pair who can carry it on under the surveillance of in-laws or under arrangements not congenial to both man and wife. The woman may want to live in the city, the man in the country. That is not my business, but they must be made aware in advance of the disciplined effort often required by living arrangements.

Then I come to the problem of money. Is the husband employed? Will the wife work outside the home? Has the family budget been discussed and agreed upon? You would be astonished at the number who have never given a practical thought to this all-important problem. Yet, whether their income is to be large or small, the vital thing is that there be from the start complete honesty and agreement about budgeting. After marriage, money problems should be reserved for a monthly council. If, as sometimes happens, the woman earns more than the man, the dangers to peace and to the male ego should be frankly recognized. The handling of the budget must be a joint affair, by which I mean joint control of a common fund, each shareholder with one vote. Out of this fund not only the wife but also the husband should have an allowance. This planned management of finances may well prevent the husband from becoming a financial dictator—or, on the other hand, an unwitting debtor, since the council may serve as a clearing house for troubles over charge accounts.

To be really a safeguard, planning must go far enough to settle upon amounts for entertainment. There needs to be a slush fund as well as a sinking fund. Many homes in both the large- and small-income classes are wrecked by problems arising out of a careless or thoughtless handling of incidental expenses, which could not occur if couples understood in advance the importance of honesty and fellowship in finances.

I even ask about insurance and I advise that both husband and wife carry at least a small amount—as a warranty that they have thought concretely about the future, that they are sufficiently aware of uncertainties to attempt some provision against them. In the partnership which successful marriage requires, the wife should share by paying a small amount of her allowance toward this attempted provision.

If there were no other reason for discussing insurance, it gives me an opportunity to bring up the question of health, and to urge a thorough medical examination for both. There are a pitiable number of cases on record where physical deficiencies or slight sexual malformations have gone undetected before marriage with disastrous results afterward—results that a minor operation or some medical attention could have obviated. Each party to a union has the right to knowledge about the health and physical makeup of himself and his mate. Such knowledge may make the difference between happiness and life-long misery.

Once an athlete and his fiancée came to me. She was in good health, but some months before an abcessed lung had been removed. Should she marry under the circumstances? A careful check showed that childbearing might prove fatal, and I consented to the marriage only on the ground that they plan with their physician to avoid the risk. Without that arrangement marriage could have been a tragic mistake. While this is an extreme instance, it illustrates that an unexpected warning may emerge from competent physical examination. It is possible to find, and in many cases correct, causes leading to serious physical maladjustments, to frigidity, to sterility, to chronic irritations and to mental pains and fears.

By asking, *What have you read or with whom have you discussed the sexual aspects of marriage?* I find how this most delicate and crucial matter of all may be approached. Many couples lack even the vocabulary to secure information they need and desire. Sentimental reticence must be replaced by an ability to discuss objectively and with detachment attitudes and practices of married life. There is no way in which this ability can be better acquired than through a book of sound learning and good taste. I keep on hand several of these books in addition to a supply of my own booklet, *Marriage and Sexual Harmony*. I try to fit the book suggested to the intellectual background of the couple. Of all that are available the three that seem to me most satisfactory for general reading are: *The Sex Technique of Marriage*, by Isabel E. Hutton; *The Sexual Side of Marriage*, by Max Exner; *The Sex Factor in Marriage*, by Helena Wright.

Properly entered into, nothing in marriage will contribute more to the growth of love and spiritual oneness than sex fellowship. Intuitively man and woman realize this fact. Often, though, the man is not sensibly guided by his knowledge. Some marriages are ruined by the lasting effects of the husband's ineptitude at the outset. Sexually aggressive by nature, it is hard for him to understand that a wife may not have any particular desire for sex expression until she has been specially prepared for it by loving words and an atmosphere of tenderness. If certain facts are known about the physical and emotional nature of each sex, no problems need develop out of the early days of marriage, and no young man need give offense or cause permanent emotional damage. Good books provide the facts and a healthy mental attitude. If they do not solve the difficulties, they at least give men and women a talking basis for their problems and enable them to discuss these problems intelligently with some wise counselor.

Sex is but one of the many satisfactions in married life, but unless this relationship is right, nothing else can be right. After a good deal of experience helping couples overcome sexual difficulties, and after many conferences with medical specialists, I am convinced that there are very few cases where marriage needs to fail because of sexual incompatibility. The human body is far more adjustable than the human mind when once the latter has been twisted through unfortunate experiences. I have helped couples find sexual satisfaction after years of blundering and that is why I try to start young people off right, so that they may not decide after a few months that they are hopelessly "mismated" and allow ignorance to break up what might otherwise have been a successful marriage.

As other matters must be thoughtfully planned, so it should be with children. I presume most couples intend to have children, but I inquire if they have discussed together what they think would be an ideal family, and whether they are agreed on the proper methods of spacing their children. How many they wish is none of my business but I am concerned to know whether they have reached an understanding. If they show need of help at this point I offer them such information as may be suitable both in the way of books and lists of recommended physicians with offices in their communities. There are problems concerning the best time of year to plan for babies. There are other questions—of necessary income, the most suitable living quarters—so that childbearing cannot be left wholly to

chance any more than any other phase of marriage if a couple is to find real happiness.

Too often the basic causes of unhappiness and tension seem unimportant to youth. Take the matter of religion. The other night I was a guest in a home where the wife was a very religious woman. Her husband was a talkative atheist who delighted to lambaste religion and clergymen. Obviously a home where disagreement was the husband's pastime could not have much peace. It is best therefore to talk frankly about religious attitudes because they can assume dangerous proportions. It is not necessary that couples *agree*, but it is very important that they *understand* each other. Unless they can reach a basis of tolerance on religious questions before marriage the chance of their doing so afterward is very slight.

No one must suppose that I assume a didactic attitude. The aim is not to lay down rules or make rigid prescriptions. The aim is to encourage young people to use the knowledge they have and to acquire more, to think about and anticipate the course of their life. It is through such planning that they avoid most of the pitfalls of the romanticists and achieve the richness of fellowship and security every couple wants. By forethought and careful counseling many more couples can be helped to discover that married happiness is not an automatic miracle but a practical achievement, something that can be won by love and patience and preserved by common sense.

Watch Your Wires

Condensed from The Family Circle

PAUL W. KEARNEY

IN MY HOME I have introduced an idea in the laundry which is a downright nuisance. Yet its principles should be applied in every home. Three wooden steps lead down to this laundry from the kitchen, and I insisted that all the electrical switches for that room be placed in the wall about five feet above the topmost step. This means that the laundress has to walk across the room whenever she wants to turn the lights on or off. But it means also that whenever she touches an electrical switch she stands on a dry wooden step which properly insulates her and thus contributes to the prolongation of her useful existence.

Insurance experience shows that most electrical fatalities in the home involve the dangerous combination of moisture with electricity; hence the danger points are the laundry, the kitchen and the bath. In the last, indeed, 50 percent of all the serious accidents occur. In Philadelphia, for example, a broker came home with a kink in his neck and decided that his electric vibrator and a good hot bath would help

him. So, getting into the tub of water, he applied the vibrator—and was electrocuted.

Down in Chattanooga the wife of a college president had an impending cold, and she, too, resorted to a hot bath. The house being chilly, she connected an electric heater (that round, portable type) and placed it nearby. Soon the direct rays on her bare flesh became uncomfortably hot, so she reached out to turn the heater around. When they found her she was stone dead from electrocution.

Once in Toledo a mother started to give her baby a bath, using a small immersion heater to warm the water in the small metal tub. But she put the infant into the tub without removing the heater. And because there was some flaw in the appliance, enough electrical charge had been built up in the water to kill the child.

The fundamental point is that moisture stimulates the flow of electric current, rendering even nonconductors susceptible to the charge. A dry board is a good insulator; it will protect you, say, in the act of changing fuses if you should make the common error of doing that with the current on. But a damp board will not.

By the same token, a healthy individual may usually take a shock through the dry hand from an ordinary 110-volt house current with no ill effects. But if that hand be wet—say from perspiration—the results are likely to be serious. Hence, brass sockets should be ruled out of every kitchen, laundry and bath, and porcelain ones substituted. All metal pull chains on fixtures should be supplemented by an extra length of string so that a damp hand cannot touch the chain itself. And there should be an ironclad rule in every home *never to touch an electrical appliance while standing in water, on a damp floor, or while any portion of the hands or feet are wet.*

Last fall in Newton, Mass., a high school lad hurt his thigh in a football game, and when he went to sleep that night he put an electric heat pad on it. The heat made him perspire, the perspiration soaked through the pad, and in the morning they found him dead from electrocution. Good pads are usually equipped with a rubber case to be slipped over them, but this is often mislaid.

A second rule to apply in every household is: *never handle two electrical fixtures at the same time.* Don't pull on a light with one hand while holding an electric iron in the other—don't attempt to manipulate a toaster and a percolator simultaneously. The classic case in point is the woman who was operating a vacuum cleaner when the telephone rang. Holding the sweeper in one hand, she took the receiver off the hook with the other and suffered a fatal shock. It is beside the point that the cleaner had a defect; frayed insulation on inside wiring, loose sockets, and so on are common to appliances in long use and are prolific causes of leakage which allows some current to flow into the metal parts of the machine. Under that contingency, holding a live appliance in each hand simply means that your body merges two separate circuits into one.

I've seen otherwise sensible people try to make amateur repairs with the current on. Once I was visiting a house where one of these handy men went to work on a radio set which was plugged into the house current. He not only melted the tip off his screw driver but blew out the works so completely that the electric company had to come to restore service! Another bit of insanity is trying to remove the butt of a broken light bulb from the socket with pliers, scissors or some other metal tool.

Defective appliances contribute largely to electrical accidents. Use of a run-down appliance without overhaul, or even occasional inspection by somebody qualified to find hidden flaws, invites certain trouble. This applies especially to extension cords, in connection with the fire hazard, for no other article of electrical equipment receives such abuse.

Never run extension cords under

rugs; they become worn too quickly. Do not place cords in door jams; squeezing breaks the protective covering. Cords should never be run over radiators or steam pipes. Do not disconnect appliances by pulling the cord; this loosens the connections and is a frequent cause of trouble.

Always buy extension cord which bears the approved label of the Underwriters Laboratories. Its wires will be encased in durable rubber tubing underneath the outside fabric to guard against the risks of broken wires or punctured insulation. Shoddy, bargain-price cord will sooner or later bring grief. A harrowing incident occurred in Cleveland when an infant, creeping around the floor, sucked on one of these cheap cords. When the saliva soaked through to the unprotected wires, the shock sent the child to the hospital.

Such accidents, to be sure, don't occur so often. But no matter how seldom they occur, statistics are cold comfort to the victim. So *don't take chances.*

Americana

Excerpts from The American Mercury

New York: Social note from the halls of higher learning in Syracuse, as chronicled by the Associated Press:

SYRACUSE UNIVERSITY co-eds in McCarthy Cottage are charging fees for good-night kisses as a means of raising house funds. Escorts must drop a coin in a silver bowl for every kiss. Special weekend rates are in vogue and the whole thing is on a cash basis; no credit.

North Carolina: The swarm of prospective jobholders becomes almost embarrassing, according to the Waxhaw Enterprise:

THE EDITOR and the rest of the Waxhaw delegation had a very enjoyable trip to the Democratic convention in Raleigh. The only drawback was the number of candidates there. A delegate put his hand out of the car to signal for a turn and 15 men shook hands with him before he could draw it back.

Oklahoma: A native son introduces a new note in boosterism, according to the Associated Press:

THE Oklahoma City Chamber of Commerce is considering Roscoe E. Dickson's plan to stimulate civic pride. At an unannounced time each day, Dickson suggests, all fire sirens should howl simultaneously. Thereupon every citizen should turn to the person next to him, shake hands vigorously, and exclaim: "We're living in the finest city in the United States!"

Farewell, My Lovely!

Condensed from The New Yorker

LEE STROUT WHITE

I SEE by the new Sears Roebuck catalogue that it is still possible to buy an axle for a 1909 Model T Ford, but I am not deceived. The great days have faded, the end is in sight. The last Model T was built in 1927, and the car is passing from what scholars call the American scene—an understatement, because to a few million people who grew up with it, the old Ford practically *was* the American scene.

It was the miracle God had wrought. Mechanically uncanny, it was like nothing that had ever come to the world before. As a vehicle, it was hard-working, commonplace, heroic; and it often seemed to transmit these qualities to those who rode in it.

The Model T was distinguished from all other cars by the fact that its transmission was of a type known as planetary—which was half metaphysics, half sheer friction. Engineers accepted the word "planetary" in its technical sense, but I was always conscious that it

From *Farewell to Model T*, by Lee Strout White, published by G. B. Putnam's Sons.

also meant "wandering," "erratic." Because of the peculiar nature of this planetary element, there was always, in Model T, a certain dull rapport between engine and wheels, and even when the car was in neutral, it trembled with a deep imperative and tended to inch forward. There was never a moment when the bands were not faintly edging the machine on.

In its palmy days the Model T could take off faster than anything on the road. The reason was simple. To get under way, you simply hooked the third finger of the right hand around a lever on the steering column, pulled down hard, and shoved your left foot forcibly against the low-speed pedal. These were simple, positive motions; the car responded by lunging forward with a roar. After a few seconds of this turmoil, you took your toe off the pedal, eased up a mite on the throttle, and the car, possessed of only two forward speeds, catapulted directly into high with a series of jerks and was off on its glorious errand. The abruptness of this departure was never equaled in other cars of the period.

The driver of the old Model T was a man enthroned. The car, with top up, stood seven feet high. The driver sat on top of the gas tank, and when he wanted gasoline, he alighted, along with everything else in the front seat. The seat was pulled off, the metal cap unscrewed, and a wooden stick thrust down to sound the liquid in the well. Refueling was more of a social function then—the driver had to unbend, whether he wanted to or not. Directly in front of the driver was the windshield—high, uncompromisingly erect. Nobody talked about air resistance, and the four cylinders pushed the car through the atmosphere with a simple disregard of physical law.

There was this about a Model T: the purchaser never regarded his purchase as a complete, finished product. When you bought a Ford, you had a start—a vibrant, spirited framework to which could be screwed a limitless assortment of decorative and functional hardware. A flourishing industry grew up out of correcting Model T's rare deficiencies and combating its fascinating diseases. You bought a radiator compound to stop leaks, a clamp-on dash light, a sun visor, and a fan-belt guide to keep the belt from slipping off the pulley. You bought a patching outfit, with a nutmeg grater to roughen the tube before the goo was spread on. Everybody was capable of putting on a patch, expected to have to, and did have to. Some people

bought rubber pedal pads, to fit over the standard metal pedals. Persons of a suspicious turn of mind bought a rear-view mirror; but most Model T owners weren't worried by what was coming from behind because they would soon enough see it out in front. They rode in a state of cheerful catalepsy.

After the car was about a year old, steps were taken to check the alarming disintegration. A set of anti-rattlers was a popular panacea. You hooked them onto the gas and spark rods, the brake pull rod, and the steering-rod connections. One agreeable quality of the old Fords was that they had no bumpers, and their fenders softened and wilted with the years and permitted the driver to squeeze in and out of tight places.

During my association with Model T's, self-starters were not a prevalent accessory. Your car came equipped with a crank, and the first thing you learned was how to Get Results. The trick was to leave the ignition switch off, proceed to the animal's head, pull the choke (a little wire protruding through the radiator), and give the crank two or three nonchalant upward lifts. Then, whistling as though thinking about something else, you would saunter back to the driver's cabin, turn the ignition on, return to the crank, and this time, catching it on the down stroke, give it a quick spin with plenty of That. The engine almost always responded—first with a few scattered explosions, then with a tumultuous gunfire, which you checked by racing to the driver's seat and retarding the throttle. Often, if the emergency brake hadn't been pulled all the way back, the car advanced on you the instant the first explosion occurred and you would hold it back by leaning your weight against it. I can still feel my old Ford nuzzling me at the curb, as though looking for an apple in my pocket.

Quite a large mutinous clique among Ford owners went over to a foot accelerator (you could buy one and screw it to the floor board), but there was a certain madness in these people, because the Model T, just as she stood, had a choice of three foot pedals to push, and there were plenty of moments when both feet were occupied in the routine performance of duty and when the only way to speed up the engine was with the hand throttle. Most everybody used the reverse pedal quite as much as the regular foot brake—it distributed the wear over the bands and wore them all down evenly. That was the big trick, to wear all the bands down evenly, so that the final chattering would be total and the whole unit scream for renewal.

The lore and legend that governed the Ford were boundless. Owners had their own theories about everything; they discussed mutual problems in that wise, infinitely resourceful way old women discuss rheumatism. Exact knowledge was scarce, and often proved less effective than superstition. Dropping a camphor ball into the gas tank was a popular expedient;

it seemed to have a tonic effect on both man and machine. The Ford driver flew blind: the dashboard of the early models was bare save for an ignition key. He didn't know the temperature of his engine, the speed of his car, the amount of his fuel or the pressure of his oil (the old Ford lubricated itself by what was amiably described as the "splash system"). He learned not through instruments but through sudden developments. The timer was one of the vital organs about which there was ample doctrine. Some people, when things went wrong, just clenched their teeth and gave the timer a smart crack with a wrench. Others opened it up and blew on it. There was a school that held that the timer needed large amounts of oil; they fixed it by frequent baptism. And there was a school that was positive it was meant to run dry as a bone; they were continually taking it off and wiping it. I have had a timer apart on a sick Ford many times, but I never really knew what I was up to—I was just showing off before God. I remember once spitting into one; not in anger, but in a spirit of research. You see, the Model T driver moved in the realm of metaphysics.

One reason the Ford anatomy was never reduced to an exact science was that, having "fixed" it, the owner couldn't honestly claim he had brought about the cure. There were too many authenticated cases of Fords fixing themselves—restored naturally to health after a short rest. Farmers soon discovered this, and it fitted nicely with their draft-horse philosophy: "Let 'er cool off and she'll snap into it again."

A Ford owner had Number One Bearing constantly in mind. This bearing, being at the front end of the motor, was the one that always burned out, because the oil didn't reach it when the car was climbing hills. (That's what I was always told, anyway.) That bearing was like a weak heart—you could hear it start knocking, and that was when you stopped and let her cool off. Try as you would to keep the oil supply right, in the end Number One always went out. "Number One Bearing burned out on me and I had to have her replaced,"

you would say, wisely; and your companions always had a lot to tell about how to protect and pamper Number One to keep her alive.

Springtime in the heyday of the Model T was a delirious season. Owning a car was still a major excitement, roads were wonderful and bad. The days were golden, the nights were dim and strange. I still recall with trembling those loud, nocturnal crises when you drew up to a signpost and raced the engine so the lights would be bright enough to read destinations by. I have never been really planetary since. I suppose it's time to say good-bye. Farewell, my lovely!

Keeping up with the World

Excerpts from a regular department in Collier's

Freling Foster

SCULPTORS occasionally make portrait busts with removable "hair." One interesting example is the head of Plautilla in the Louvre, Paris, which has a separate wig that can be changed from time to time to keep the lady in fashion.

SEVERAL YEARS AGO, Ecuador wanted to perpetuate the memory of its poet Olmeda by a statue. As made-to-order statues were found to be expensive, it was decided to buy a discarded one. So the junk yards of London were searched and a secondhand statue of Lord Byron was found and purchased. Today it stands in Guayaquil with "Olmeda" engraved on its base.

A MAN can be perfect—physically and mentally—yet be rejected for enlistment in the army of the United States, when his face is characterized by "extreme ugliness."

THE MOST FAMOUS catacombs in existence are those under Rome and its suburbs. There are more than 500 miles of these underground passageways—one upon another and sometimes seven levels deep—containing a total of about 6,000,000 tombs.

NOSE RUBBING is more widely used by mankind as a greeting than are handshaking and kissing, combined.

The Woman Who Never Gives Up

Condensed from The Forum

JEROME BEATTY

A GREAT minister who planned to preach on Unselfishness could do no better than to use as a text the life of Lillian D. Wald, a woman with a backbone of tempered steel and the courage of all the lions in Africa. Other noble men and women have devoted their lives to those who suffer from hunger, illness and injustice, but few have won as many battles.

While her fame is great among social workers, the average person is less familiar with her name than with the institutions she created—the Henry Street Settlement in New York, the Visiting Nurse Service, which she founded 43 years ago, and the Federal Children's Bureau, which she conceived and helped persuade President Taft to inaugurate. She originated public health nursing services in schools, in isolated sections, and for policyholders of life insurance companies. She has been called "the greatest single contributor to the public health of America."

Once someone thought it would be a stimulating idea to tell how many lives had been saved by Lillian Wald, directly and indirectly, and how many hungry and sick the world over had been cared for through her influence. The figures included hundreds of thousands of underprivileged in Russia, South Africa and China. But they were never issued. "Miss Wald would be furious," said an executive.

Lillian Wald is 69 years old and lives in a little white house in Connecticut. She rejects indignantly any suggestion that she has "retired." She is far from New York, Albany and Washington, her favorite battlegrounds, but for a few hours every day she sees visitors, dictates letters and telegrams, and uses the long distance telephone, still working for her cause. That's the life she loves.

For four years she has been an invalid, confined with cardiac trouble so serious that she walks with difficulty. Almost her only moments of relaxation are when children come from nearby homes and she has a grand time watching them play with the elevator she has installed for easy passage between the first and second floors.

Lillian Wald was properly educated in Miss Crittenden's English And French Boarding And Day School For Young Ladies And Little Girls. Influenced by relatives who were physicians, she went to New York to become a nurse—in those days a strange profession for cultured girls to adopt. After three years of training she and another nurse were asked to go to the East Side to talk to mothers on the care of the sick. They agreed, with no suspicion of the almost unbelievable misery and filth and disease they were to find.

One day Miss Wald was telling a group how to make beds. A child came, pleading for help, and led her to a foul tenement where in two rooms nine pitifully undernourished persons lived, most of them sleeping on the floor and in no need of lessons in bed making. The head of the family was a cripple who was out exposing his deformities as he begged for pennies. On the one bed, suffering from a hemorrhage, lay a woman who had not been touched for two days.

A self-respecting scrubwoman might have fled, nauseated, but 26-year-old Lillian Wald pitched in, bathed the woman, sent for a doctor, cleaned up the miserable rooms. Hours later she left, shaken by what she had seen. She and her friend, she declared, would promptly take care of cases like that. "Once people know of these frightful conditions," she thought, "they will contribute money to alleviate them

and laws will be passed so such things cannot occur."

Lillian Wald had not learned that hearts as big as hers were hard to find, and she was dumbfounded that people were lukewarm, even when she told of such cases as the mother and baby who died of infection because the midwife left in the midst of the delivery, upon discovering that the 21-year-old husband had only a dollar; and of the three children with typhoid fever, who lay in a room where a tired mother was "doing a wash" and who had no pillows to lie upon because they had been sold to buy food; and how the untutored mother, after the nurse had bathed and fed the children and through her quick skill turned them back from death, kissed the nurse's hand and cried, "Oh, God, is that what I should have been doing for my babies?"

"People like that," folks assured her, "*have* to suffer. Nobody's ever been able to do anything about it. You might as well give up."

Lillian Wald never gives up. Instead she found a powerful ally in the late Jacob H. Schiff, and with his contributions, added to those sent regularly by her sympathetic mother, she established in 1893 in Henry Street the first Visiting Nurse Service in the world.

Jane Addams had founded Hull House in Chicago four years before. The social settlement movement was spreading, but it was concerned primarily with furnishing recreation and education and relieving poverty. Charity clinics and religious bodies nursed only a few of the poor. Lillian Wald's idea was to help the sick of every creed and color. Nobody had thought of that before and although there was no precedent to help, neither was there red tape to hinder.

The Visiting Nurse Service grew rapidly. At the end of ten years figures were gathered to check the efficiency of Miss Wald's nurses on pneumonia cases, which test nursing ability to the utmost. In one year her group had cared for 3535 cases, in homes, with a mortality rate of 8.05 percent. In the same period, the rate in four large New York hospitals was 31.2 percent.

The Henry Street service today has 265 nurses who make 550,000 visits a year in New York City. They never refuse to respond to a call. For 38 years Miss Wald had a telephone beside her bed and all night calls went direct to her. She found that patients wanted to pay something, but that nearly half of them were too poor. Those who can afford it pay from five cents a call to $1.15.

When the subject of her own salary came up years ago, she said, "If I have executive ability, it is God-given and comes without effort and that I will throw into the pot. I am a nurse and to the end will accept only the same salary as is paid to the others." Recently members of the Henry Street board made up a fund to support her as she grew older. Wisely they tied it up so she couldn't give it all away.

Visiting nurse services now are found throughout the world, many, even in China and Japan, conducted by former associates of Miss Wald. Secretly she likes to think she helped a little in the miracle of the Dionne quintuplets, for the late wife of Dr. Allan R. Dafoe was a Henry Street nurse and recently the doctor told Miss Wald, "All I know about nursing I learned from my wife."

Throughout her life, Lillian Wald has just been doing what had to be done, while others stood by and worried and wondered. Doing what had to be done, it was inevitable that Miss Wald should extend her activities beyond nursing and settlement work. Soon she learned that nearly every reform is opposed by selfish interests, and she rolled up her sleeves and fought. She had the faculty of making true friends in every stratum of society and when she went out for help to influence legislation, saloonkeepers joined bankers to help her.

Beginning with laws to clean the streets and remove the garbage, she moved to Albany as a leader in the war on sweatshops and bad housing, and to Washington to help improve the conditions of immigrants and attack child labor. Every move to help the underprivileged gained her quick support. She helped organize exploited women into unions and fed them when they were on strike. Once when she was with a wealthy friend who disapproved of her labor activities they saw a striker throw a stone through a window. "That's what you're encouraging," he reproved. "I don't like force," she said, "nor unrighteous strikes, but I have observed that about the only difference between people in trouble is that sophisticated ones engage lawyers, primitive ones throw stones."

Her darkest moment came when the United States was rushing into war. Miss Wald, the friend of all races, was one of the women who led 1200 of their sisters in a parade on Fifth Avenue as a protest against war. She organized meetings, argued in Washington, fought furiously—and lost.

Small-minded women might have sulked, but Lillian Wald pitched in to protect her boys as best she could. Many of them she had helped to bring into the world. Her leading worker, with salary paid by the Henry Street Settlement, became chairman of the Draft Board so the Draft would be administered justly. Many of her nurses were among the first to go, leaving her staff depleted. Still the women and children at home must be helped. Money for Henry Street was hard to get. One of her most generous contributors, because of Miss Wald's "unpatriotic conduct," refused to give one cent more. Others, smugly viewing her as a Red, rejected with caustic reproof her appeals for money.

The war ended, her nurses and most of her boys came home. The House on Henry Street operated efficiently again. Then came a broadside from the Daughters of the American Revolution, black-listing Lillian Wald as a dangerous radical. To be called a radical disturbed her not at all. But she was terribly hurt because such a body of women, who, she believed, ought to be supporting her every step, should deliberately try to cripple her work.

Hearts were heavy in Henry Street; friends feared the blacklist would affect contributors. Their fears were foolish. Letters and telegrams expressing confidence poured in upon her. Contributions increased. So great had been their accomplishments that Lillian Wald and Henry Street were not checked even for a moment.

Today she is as attractive, as quick-witted and as dramatic a storyteller as in the days when influential families sought her as a dinner guest, though—because of her effective methods of obtaining contributions—wealthy men good-humoredly groaned, "It costs $5000 to sit next to Lillian Wald at dinner."

A few months ago she wrote an article about the Visiting Nurses and nearly 10,000 impoverished persons wrote her, telling pitiful tales of uncared-for sick, and asking how nursing could be obtained. Miss Wald replied to every letter.

Peace, meaning rest and quiet, Lillian Wald has brought to thousands—but, because of her great, unselfish heart, never to herself. And she and the world are happier so.

Wreck and Rescue

Condensed from The Atlantic Monthly

CAPTAIN GARLAND ROTCH

This saga of the sea, written by a 25-year-old boy to his mother, was discovered by Kathleen Norris, the novelist, who considers it as thrilling as Conrad's Nigger of the Narcissus *and other immortal pages about storms and the sea.*

ON BOARD SWEDISH BARK *Tana* BOUND FOR NEW ORLEANS

DEAR MOTHER:—
I suppose you know by now that the *Admiral Clark* foundered nine days ago in a hurricane off the coast of Cuba. To the best of my knowledge, there were but six of us saved.

When I came on deck at four that Wednesday morning, I found the wind blowing fresh from the northeast. By seven it was so strong that I called the Captain. There were none of the usual signs of the approach of a hurricane, yet by 10:30 it was evident we were running into one. By noon there was a heavy sea, but we had a good dinner and everyone felt confident. At one, the Skipper asked me to get some oil on the water, as the seas were starting to roll dangerously across the decks. It gave good results, and I am convinced was all that kept the *Clark* afloat as long as she was.

By three, the hurricane was at its height. The wind was terrific; you couldn't face it and breathe. To move without holding onto something was impossible: the wind hauled at you like a thousand demons trying to drag you overboard. You could not see a hundred feet for the spray which whipped from the crests of the waves and hurled through the air with the speed of bullets. Its force was such that it appeared to be lying in a sort of strata in the air. The seas towered over the little *Clark* like huge overhanging cliffs of water that would cave down and overwhelm her, and I would hold my breath, but she would slide out from under just in time. It was wonderful to watch her. The waves would make a clean sweep over the decks, hiding the entire forward end of the ship, then the bow would clear itself and the stern would submerge.

Going aft over the top of the house, Johnson, the second mate, and I passed the galley skylight. We looked down and what do you think we saw? The colored steward and the three colored cooks all on top of the stove, with life preservers on, praying as hard as they could. The galley was half full of water and everything was

337

adrift except the stove—pots and pans, tables, bits of wood and other débris. We hauled the blacks out and put them in the wheelhouse.

At four we were in the center of the hurricane, the most dreaded part. The sea was a confused mountainous mass of jumbled water; the waves seemed to come from everywhere and the poor little *Clark* was under water all the time. She had no chance, though she struggled manfully. As we entered the other side of the storm, it seemed as if every wind in creation was blowing against us; instead of a regular sea the waves came from four or five directions at once. It made even the stoutest hearts sink. But when we gathered for a supper of canned salmon and crackers, the only conversation was a few jokes about happenings of the day; no one spoke about the outlook.

At nine a sea stove in the door to the sailors' messroom and water ran through it in streams down to the engine room. I took two men forward to get a spare door, which we had to bring along the booms as the deck was continually swept by heavy seas. We were about halfway back when it was blown from our hands, and one of the men was knocked to the deck and washed overboard. The other man and I were washed off twice; the third time I was washed right around the stern of the ship, and had to climb back up on the other side. The sailor I never saw again.

There was now six feet of water in the engine room, washing from side to side with the roll of the ship.

As I got there, I saw one of the engineers dive down to get at one of the pumps, which had broken down. It was a sight I shall never forget. The heavy cranks and rods of the engines were churning and splashing the water; pieces of refuse would float into the engines and be smashed to bits and thrown about. The noise was deafening. At 10:30 the water reached the dynamos and the lights all went out. The engineers could do nothing more, and came out on deck, leaving the engines running. Soon a boiler plug blew out and the steam was shut off.

The Old Man was pretty badly broken up, but game to the core. He and I went into the chart room; I lighted my pipe and he a cigarette. Then he said, "This is hell, Rotch, isn't it? Just as we start to get out of the gale, the ship goes down." I said "Yeah," just as unconcernedly as I could. It was funny, I didn't feel the least bit worried.

The *Clark* was settling fast by the stern now, and everyone knew it was all over. A heavy sea swept the whole after-house and took both boats. Everyone but the officers had life belts—ours were stored aft and were under water, so our only chance was to catch some bit of floating wreckage. The Skipper ordered all hands forward; and all of a sudden we felt her start to go down under our feet. A big sea swept over us; when it had passed, the ship was almost vertical. I saw them starting to jump over the side. I kicked off my boots and jumped too.

When I reached the surface, the first thing I saw was something dark, and reaching out I put my hand on a raft used when we painted the side of the ship. Johnson came up close beside me and we both climbed on. Then I turned to have a last look at the *Clark*. She was standing on end, perfectly upright, her bow about 30 feet out of the water. She seemed to hang there a minute or two, then, with a sort of sigh, made by the air rushing out of her, she very slowly sank out of sight. Mother, it was a weird sight, and it hurt. She was a good little boat, and I had had some good times on her. We had a fine crowd of men; those that went, went as a sailor should go. There was no excitement.

I turned around to see who else was on the raft. They proved to be the third assistant engineer and an oiler. We heard someone shouting, and Johnson and I swam out and picked up the colored steward, who was just about all in. Soon there was another call, and we swam out again and picked up a sailor. Though we kept a sharp lookout, we could see or hear no one else. Wind and sea were drifting us fast from the scene of the wreck.

To appreciate our position you must picture our raft, which was nine feet long by four feet wide. Not as wide as your bed and only three feet longer, with six men on it. Nothing to eat, nothing to drink. None of us had shoes, except the sailor; most of us were clad in shirts and trousers. The raft was only four inches out of water, and we were never dry at any time. We had to hang on tight to keep from being washed off. There was no sleep for anyone that night.

When Thursday morning broke it was still blowing pretty hard and a high sea was running, but we were glad to feel the sun's warmth. All we did that day was hang on and keep the raft from turning over. A good many sharks swam past. They did not stop, and it was easy to guess where they were going and the awful end the poor fellows floating around in life belts met.

That night we were so exhausted we caught cat naps even with the water washing over us all the time. At daybreak Friday we started to keep a good lookout for ships. I caught myself brooding over our outlook and, knowing that would soon raise cain with our spirits, I decided to try to give everyone something to do. We took the cover off the life belt the sailor had on and made a woefully small sail, and tore some strips from the raft to make a mast. The blocks of cork in the belt we used for paddles to steer by.

I figured we were about 250 miles off the Mexican coast, and a light breeze might blow us there, if we could last that long. Saturday at daybreak we saw a large steamer heading close to us—but she passed about half a mile away without seeing us, though we whistled and hollered and waved a shirt all the time.

The pangs of hunger and thirst were beginning to make themselves felt now; our bodies were lame from sleeping on bare boards, and salt-water sores were coming out all over our bodies. I had read somewhere that the pores of the skin would absorb water into the system, and we kept our bodies wet all the time—I think this is the only thing that saved our lives. If a man's clothing started to dry, someone would sprinkle him. Our lips began to crack and our mouths were nothing but yellow rings.

That day we had a small rain squall, and we all opened our mouths to catch what we could; and spread out the sailor's oilskin and caught a mouthful apiece. It was dirty and oily, but it did taste good. That was all the nourishment we had all the time we were on the raft, though the waters were alive with fish and we tried to catch them with our hands.

By Monday we were suffering a great deal from thirst and heat. Hunger had ceased to bother us after the first two days—they say it ceases when thirst sets in. The nights were the worst of all. There was just room for four men to lie down at a time; the other two had to sit way at the end. If one turned over, all had to turn; and if anyone did any restless tossing in his sleep, overboard he would go. Water washed over us all the time, and those on the weather side had water splashing in their faces. Though the night air and the water were warm, the drying effect made it very cold to the body.

Tuesday morning I happened to look astern and saw a great big shark following us. When it reached the end of the raft it curved in so close the oiler could have touched it with his paddle. With a cry of terror, he rushed for the other side of the raft, and I jumped to the opposite side just in time to prevent its overturning and putting us all in the water at the mercy of the shark. It swam around for about half an hour before going away, and you may be sure we kept very quiet; I could feel funny little chills going up and down my spine.

That afternoon was very hot, and thirst started to tell severely. Our mouths and tongues were so swollen we could scarcely talk. I caught the oiler dipping his fingers in the water and sucking them. As drinking salt water was liable to drive him insane and jeopardize the lives of everyone, I had said I would throw overboard the first man I caught doing it. So when I jumped up, the oiler went down on his knees and whimpered like a dog for another chance. I told him he had one more; then he would go overboard. I didn't see him do it again. Evening brought cooler weather, but it was plain that the end of another day would see some changes on the raft—

Wednesday morning we saw a sailing ship heading to pass not far from us. My, how we worked with those small cork paddles, which in our exhausted condition seemed to weigh a ton. The ship passed about two miles from us and continued on her way. They had not seen us. Mother, I shall never forget the hopeless feeling that came over me. We just lay down in a heap, except the steward, who continued to wave a shirt. Then suddenly I saw her start to haul up one side of her mainsail, and knew she was going to turn around. We started to paddle again, and it was soon apparent they were heading straight for us. When she was close they asked us who we were, and I tried to tell them, but my mouth and throat were too swollen. They threw us a line and put a ladder over the side. Two of the men had to be hoisted up; the rest of us climbed.

Just as I reached the top, I gave out and would have fallen back if two men hadn't caught me. It was funny; I was conscious, but I couldn't walk. They helped us to a cabin, where they gave us a small glass of water to wash our mouths with; then a small cup of coffee and a small square of bread and butter.

You should have seen the way Johnson looked, and I guess I was as bad—he was covered with crude oil and looked like a black man. His head was blistered from the sun. He was covered with sores. He was so thin I could count every rib, and where his stomach should have been there was only a hollow.

Last night we had our first meal. Before that they would only give us bread and either coffee or water every hour or so.

Well, mother, luck does not seem to run my way. I have nothing in the world but a shirt and a pair of trousers; even the chronometer is gone. I don't know what I shall do when I arrive in New Orleans. I took in six inches in my belt the six and a half days we were on the raft.

Lovingly,
GARLAND

This Age of Ingenuity

A NEW glass-walled factory at Corning, N. Y., is to make spun-glass wool, which has now been brought to such a state of perfection that it can compete with other textiles.

Glass wool can be spun on standard textile looms, and the resulting fabrics are fireproof. In the glass houses of the future, the housewife may wear a glass dress, have glass curtains, walk on glass rugs, and sleep on glass mattresses.—*Literary Digest*

A NEW metal awning is made of narrow sheets of thin material hinged together on their long horizontal edges. When it is closed the sections fold together at the top of the window. Aluminum, copper, and rustless steel are used, sometimes painted in solid colors or stripes. The under side is usually finished in aluminum paint in order to reflect the maximum of light into a room. The fixtures are of rustless bronze. The great advantage of metal awnings is their long life, coupled with the fact that they may be left up all the year round without damage.

—Walter Rendell Storey in N. Y. *Times Magazine*

Happiness as Deep as Tears

By

GAIL CAREY

You shall have wisdom great as life can give,
You shall have happiness as deep as tears.
—HERBERT J. HALL

YOUR BABY never can be normal. His trouble is called Mongolism."*
"Never can be normal! . . . Mongolism! . . . Hopeless idiocy . . . That I can never, never face."

We have faced it, my husband and I, as honestly and as sanely as we could; and from hopeless and utter despair we have won through to happiness. To happiness not of the carefree sort; but to the happiness which comes when a sorrow has been met squarely and a problem solved in what seems the wisest way.

We were married with every confidence that our union would produce only perfect children. None of our relatives had children who were subnormal mentally, and we inferred that anyone who did had a "taint" or a "bad strain" somewhere in the family.

*Mongolism, or Mongolianism, is a congenital malformation, usually accompanied by imbecility, in which the child has slanting eyes like a Mongolian's. Except for this resemblance, the disease has absolutely no connection with the Mongolian race.

Our daughter, Helen, came when we had been married two years, and were in our middle twenties. She was perfect, just as we had known she would be. She grew as she should, and behaved as she should, and we were, no doubt, complacent, conceited parents.

When Helen was five years old, we decided that she needed a companion—and so a year later came our little son, David. He was a funny little mite, rather more like a Chinese doll than an American baby; for his eyes were tipped in the Mongolian way, and a slight attack of jaundice gave him an even more oriental appearance. But we were blissfully happy, and entirely unsuspicious that he was anything but perfect. Mongolian idiocy can be diagnosed at birth, but whether it was recognized in our baby we do not know. In any case, we were not told—and when, after a few months, our son did not begin to do the things that other babies of his age were doing, our friends constantly reassured us, "Oh, my baby didn't sit up until she was a year old." Or, "Mine didn't walk until he was two years old, and look at him now!"

Oh, kind and cheering friends, you did help us through those first two years, and what you said kept us hopeful. But if only we could have known the truth in the beginning, we would have been spared an agony of alternate hope and discouragement. If only doctors would realize that, since the blow must come sooner or later, the sooner it is given, the earlier and better will be the adjustment!

Before we knew the real trouble, a physician had recommended thyroid treatment. The tablets increased David's energy tremendously, but helped his intellect not at all. "Have his metabolism done," said another physician. "Then you can tell just how much thyroid he needs—perhaps he is not getting enough."

We arrived at the hospital for the test full of hope and confidence that all would now be well. How wonderful to be living in a modern age when so much is known about the ductless glands! But, the physician in charge gave our baby a quick glance, and then the blow fell.

Clearly, simply, and compassionately the situation was explained. We were told that David would, in all probability, never attain a mental age of more than seven years, that he would therefore never be able to look after himself, nor lead a normal life.

However long I may live, or however much sorrow may come my way, I know that there will never be a day so dark as that one. For three long hours I stayed in the laboratory while the metabolism was being done. Meanwhile the thought of Helen penetrated the fog in my brain. What of *her* future? An idiot brother! No one would want her for friend, no man would want her for his wife. Oh, if only there were some way that it need never be known!

At last the metabolism was done, and we were started on the long drive home, my little Mongoloid baby and I. My mind was chaos. I drove faster and faster. Then came the craziest of all ideas—an immediate solution. I remembered a railroad bridge high above the tracks, not far from our home. It was at the top of a steep hill, just around a blind and dangerous curve. At this speed, it was practically certain death for both of us, and it would look like an unpremeditated accident. Would that not make everything right? Certainly my baby would be better off dead, and at that moment I had no very great desire to live myself. My secret would go with me. I need never tell Helen. I would do it—I must—

I started up the hill with my foot pressed hard on the accelerator. We made the corner and then—! There in front of us stood a small car, parked directly on the bridge, and at the railing peering down onto the tracks below were three small children with their mother—looking for choo-choos!

All thought of destruction left my mind at once. I concentrated on righting the car and getting safely past that group on the bridge. It was terribly close, but we made it. I brought the car to a stop several hundred feet away and turned to see if the children were safe. They were still gazing over the bridge, unconscious of their narrow escape; unconscious, too, that they had just saved two lives.

For the next few days my husband and I were a pathetic pair. Each of us tried to keep a stiff upper lip before the other, consoling, encouraging, trying to go on about our life as if nothing had happened. When death comes, all of us are given at least a few days to adjust ourselves to the tragedy. But, in our case, one of the horrors that loomed large in our minds was that other people must know, and that perhaps they would not allow their children to come to play with Helen. We had done nothing for which we were to blame, and yet there was a peculiar sense of shame in our hearts, as if we were social lepers.

People will advertise with pride their physical infirmities; but in the face of a mental ill, there is an awed, mysterious hush. Perhaps it is a relic of the dark ages when people so affected were thought to be possessed of a demon. We were guilty of it, too, for a few days, until we began to think for ourselves.

We consulted a physician outstanding for his work in habit-training of little children, and a further blow fell. "I should advise you strongly to place your baby in an institution, as soon as possible!"

For two hours he talked to us, and for the benefit of other parents in our situation, I give in brief what he said.

First of all, he succeeded in convincing us that we were in no way at fault. "This may strike anywhere, in any family," he said. "Almost never is there more than one in a family, and parents in good health can go on having children with every confidence that the others will be perfectly normal. This is not an hereditary disease. It is an accident, something which happens before the baby is born to cause arrested development. At present no treatment is of much avail.

"If you had no other child, you might manage to keep your little Mongoloid at home, and train him yourself—but even then I should not advise it. As it is, your daughter would be made to suffer because she would not have a normal home with a mother to give her the attention she needs, and because she would have to bear the jeers of other children. Then in the end, when you have exhausted strength and money to no avail, the time will come when you and your husband will be unable to care for him longer. All of us must die, and your son may outlive you both. Then his sister will be called upon to sacrifice her life for him. She may do it willingly, but it should not be asked of her."

"But we have little money," we said, "and special schools are a great expense. Where can we find a school within our means?"

His answer came promptly. "Place him in a state institution."

"Never!" we exclaimed. "We do not want charity, and our baby must be where he will have the best of love and care."

"Then one of our state schools is the place where you will find what you wish. You will not be receiving charity; for you will pay according to your income. His care will be of the best because an institution of this kind is under constant observation from many sources. He will have the training best adapted to his needs, and will be with the type of children whom he can most enjoy. And whatever happens to you, he will be kept there as long as he lives. You will never have the haunting fear that you may die and leave him alone and uncared for."

Our first visit to that state institution which has become home, and school, and life complete for our son, was a revelation to us. The doctor had not misled us. In all my visits—and they now number several hundred—I have never known a single employe to show anything but cheerfulness and willingness to go to any amount of trouble to make patients comfortable.

"How do you manage to find teachers so young and charming, and so intelligent?" we asked the superintendent.

"Well," he said, "it isn't always easy to find the right teachers; yet when they do come, they generally stay. To you, these children seem unattractive, perhaps even repulsive, but after you have visited a few times, you will come to love them

as we do; for they are sweet, and unselfish, appreciative of attention and love. Unlike normal children, there is almost no quarreling, and when they play in a group, each is ready to take his turn, to share his toy, and to help his neighbor. This is perhaps why our staff is contented here; for as one knows each child better, the external ugliness disappears, and one sees only the beauty and innocence which lies underneath."

And we have found it so. How could we fail to see beauty in the way each child tries to help the little blind boy who is a part of the group, showing him his place at table, tying his bib, placing his hand upon knife, fork, etc., and giving him all the small attentions which a normal child would be too thoughtless to show?

Leaving David at the school was terribly hard, of course; but we tried to remind ourselves that we were glad because it was for his happiness. Each week we visit, and find him happy, healthy, busy every minute. He is always glad to see us, but is perfectly willing to have us leave without him, waving from the window with a happy smile.

Of course we have been desperately lonely at times. But we have lived through such days, and we have found that the best solution is work, and more work. We play hard, too, and each of us has hobbies to ride.

After all—agony can be made to count for something. We have learned that the small annoyances of life can be so easily disregarded;

they are as nothing beside the greater sorrow which we have had to meet.

And so the happiness which we never expected to see again has come after all; for we have found peace, which is a happiness more full of meaning than we have ever known before, a happiness "as deep as tears."

The Bicycle Comes Back

John E. Lodge in Popular Science Monthly

THE BICYCLE is back. Last year, factories in the United States turned out 750,000 machines, nearly equaling the peak production of the gay nineties. In 1933 a survey by department stores showed bicycles fourth on the list of things youngsters wanted for Christmas. In 1935 they stood first.

Four million Americans now pedal along the highways, and there are hundreds of cycling clubs. A "bicycle breakfast" was staged not long ago in New York, a horde of riders gathering in Central Park, to pedal in parade formation down Fifth Avenue to a restaurant. Special "bicycle trains" are being run by railroads to carry enthusiasts and their wheels to scenic spots for one-day outings.

There are bikes with three-speed gear shifts, automobile-type steering wheels, comfortable rubber-cushioned chairlike seats. There are tandem machines, three-seaters, six-seaters, and one "centipede bike" carrying 10 riders. A special racing bicycle is made of aluminum alloy and, completely equipped, weighs only 13 pounds. For use on tours, there is a collapsible trailer which can be extended into a six-foot bunk.

The bicycle is bringing new sports, bicycle polo having appeared in many parts of the country, and also a combination of cycling and archery, popular among movie stars, a game in which teams of two contestants each, riding tandem machines, circle a fixed target. Cycle racing, once a major sport, is also coming back. Last year there were races in 20 cities.

Cycle paths are being established in city parks. Recently, 165,000 fans in Chicago signed petitions, and as a result 100 miles of cycle trails are under way. Detroit has "handlebar paths" in several parks, as have Washington, D. C., Oklahoma City, and New York City. Cyclists are now permitted at certain hours on Atlantic City's boardwalk. Cycling organizations are urging the construction of special paths along the shoulders of roads.

About 1932, agents for Hollywood movie stars began to run out of ideas for publicity. Someone conceived of photographing the stars riding bicycles. Then some of them adopted the bike as a pleasant form of exercise, others as an easy way to pedal off a few pounds. But the majority continued to ride because cycling was fun. What started as a publicity stunt turned into a craze which has swept the country.

Heaven Doesn't Matter

Condensed from The North American Review

CHANNING POLLOCK

WHEN the celebrated critic, Matthew Arnold, died, someone remarked, "Poor Matthew; he won't like God." If this wit had said, "He won't like heaven," more of us might have understood. I've never been able to get excited about heaven myself.

There are many conceptions, of course, ranging from streets of gold down—or up—to the Buddhist state of forgetfulness. I shouldn't care for gold streets, and there's little I want to forget. Nirvana would make a greater appeal to me if it were a place of more vivid remembrance, where you could look at the stars and the sea with ten times the thrill they gave you on earth. I'm afraid the Mohammedan houris would bore me to tears.

The truth is less that I don't believe in any of these heavens than that I don't care whether they exist or not. To me, the question isn't important—I'm too much concerned with what I do while I live. The only heaven that really interests me is the heaven that could be made right here.

Ralph W. Sockman recently preached on what he called "the slot-machine attitude toward God." We put in a prayer or a decent act, he said, and expect to take out a prosperous business or an eternity of bliss. In one of my earlier plays, I opined that, "we are not punished for our sins, but by them." It is equally true that we are not rewarded for our good deeds, but by them. There is a singing ecstasy in good work. There must be an even greater and more immediate recompense for good deeds. The happiest men I know are the most occupied and the most useful.

Some of the most disagreeable people I know are quite sure of going to heaven. However, their presence won't help much. Father Duffy once told me of a nun who said that, after 40 years among saints, she knew why Christ wanted to live among sinners.

Most people who expect to survive expect to survive pretty completely. Any survival that diminishes the ego wouldn't be survival at all to them. But suppose their neuritis survives, too? Of course, it wouldn't; but shall we be ourselves without our neuritis? Shall we recognize dear old Aunt Jane in a state of perfection, or love her as much as we did when we could laugh at her little human failings? Shall we like her, or ourselves, as disembodied spirits? I've never thought of myself as a materialist, but the things I've enjoyed all seem to have required body and mind—a poem of Shelley's, first sight of the Grand Canyon, sunset from the roof of a hotel in Biskra, the smell of corn bread after a long walk in the autumn woods, even rubbing Aunt Jane's poor aching arm, and seeing her smile as she sank into slumber.

In the resurrection, there is to be no marriage nor giving in marriage —and that's a big drawback, too. Personally, I can't conceive a heaven without it. My own ego is so inextricably blended with that of my wife, and my own happiness has been so long part of hers. Nor would it help much to be vaguely associated with her in spirit. Married life is made up of so many physical and mental contacts, of so many shared fears and hopes, sorrows and joys, pains and comfortings that both of us, and millions of other wives and husbands, couldn't help missing terribly in any conceivable resort of souls.

Singularly enough, it is that very prospect of reunion after death that has given immortality its allure. "When you lose your loved ones," Basil King used to say to me, "you'll feel differently about all this." Perhaps he was right; I never lost a loved one, nor do I ever expect to do so. My profoundest conviction is that nothing loved is ever lost. (Like most of my profound convictions, this was Emerson's, too.) My father died when I was 14, and thus achieved what seems to me the truest immortality. If he had lived, he would have been 85 now—perhaps a tired, infirm old man. Through death, he became eternally young, eternally vital and alive. I see him, and shall always see him, as I last saw him—at his desk, happy in his work, younger and stronger than I am now, and wiser and kinder than I shall ever be. And I am much happier in the recollection of him —of his unflinching eyes, his gentle smile, his whimsical way of reminding us of the eternal things—than I could be in any prospect of meeting him again as a disembodied spirit.

Every wise word he ever spoke, every kind act he ever did, is immortal. "I never knew your father," a woman remarked to me the other day, "but *my* father told me of so many fine things he did and said." Loving life, and free to go where he pleased, my father died at his post of duty. Thereby he added to the immortal tradition of courage and nobility.

At that time he was United States Consul at San Salvador. When we begged him to use steamship tickets bought for the vacation that was due him, but that he had put aside because yellow fever was decimating our colony, he answered, "I don't think any responsible officer should be away at a time like this. Our people are frightened and confused; some of them have been refused Christian burial. It's my job to stay here and look after them."

He did stay, frequently reading the funeral service over our countrymen who succumbed to the pestilence. "Have you no fear?" my mother asked. "None as great as the fear of not doing what I believe to be right," my father said. He contracted the fever that day. Because of his example, I resigned my position at 19 on a Washington newspaper when the editor insisted that I swell his advertising by writing what I didn't believe to be true, and, in consequence, nearly starved before I found work on a dock in New York. And because of my example my son may do the like when I am gone, and his son when he is gone. This seems to me the only kind of survival worth striving for. Certainly, it has accomplished more for heaven and earth than any bait of celestial compensation.

Hu Shih, father of the Chinese Renaissance, wrote: "As I reviewed the life of my dead mother, whose activities had never gone beyond the trivial details of the home but whose influence could be clearly seen on the faces of those men and women who came to mourn her death, and as I recalled the lasting effect of her life on myself, I came to the conviction that *everything* is immortal. Everything that we are, everything that we do, everything that we say is immortal in the sense that it has its effect somewhere in the world, and that effect in turn will have its results somewhere else, and the thing goes on in infinite time and space. A man is what he thinks and everyone who has influenced him —from Socrates, Plato, and Confucius down to his parish preacher and his nursery governess—lives in him."

We are not children who must be made to behave by the promise of candy; we are not weaklings who must be held up, instigated, consoled by glory to come. Eternal bliss may be grand in eternity; our present concern would seem to be intensified perception of the beauty about us, intensified progress toward justice, human love for humankind, and the by-no-means-trifling job of leaving the world, or some one of its population, a little better for our having been in it.

Civilization is a pyramid to which each man contributes a grain of sand—a pyramid whose broad base was laid on the Nile, and to which almost every successive generation has added something.

My heaven is everywhere about us. If you need to believe in the other kind, don't let me dissuade you. It isn't that I *don't* believe; only that, for me, that other heaven doesn't matter. Not now, anyway. I'm too busy. I want to go on with my work, and leave the outcome to God.

A Will of Your Own

By

JEROME BEATTY

MOST HUSBANDS, no matter how kind and considerate, punish their widows cruelly when they die. Fewer than four out of ten persons who own property have wills, and when men or women die without a will they usually leave a perfect hell to remember them by.

Go into a probate court, pick a case at random and this is about what you will find:

A man dies, leaving a widow, two young children and an estate of $8000—not including life insurance which, of course, is paid to the beneficiary, will or no will. He meant to leave everything to his widow. But because the nitwit had no will, the widow receives about $1866; otherwise she would have received about $5600. The poorer a man is, the more his widow needs all she can get, and the less likely he is to have a will.

There is nothing the matter with our laws. They take it for granted, when there is no will, that the children must be provided for. So automatically, in most states in such cases, two thirds of the estate goes to the children to be held in trust until they become of age. They *can't* give it to their mother; it can be touched only by court order and then only for small amounts for support and education. If there are no children, and the estate is more than $5000, part goes to the deceased's parents. If they are dead and the estate is more than $10,000, part goes to his brothers and sisters, or, if they are dead, to their children.

Usually the court and legal costs of administering an estate are about the same, will or no will. With bills due, installment payments, funeral expenses, court costs and lawyer's fees, estates of less than $2500 shrink from 40 to 70 percent. Those between $2500 and $10,000 shrink from 25 to 40 percent. So you don't make a will to save administrative costs. You make it to provide mercifully for those you leave behind and keep your property out of the hands of what the Germans call "the laughing heirs"—those who are delighted when you die.

350

It is not always the husband whose death brings disaster. The wife should have a will, whether she has extensive property of her own or only wants to make sure the second wife doesn't get her jewels and heirlooms. It is fair for her to assume that if she dies first, her husband may marry a woman who is not at all the sort she would choose as her successor—for that's what a lot of widowers do. She is in no way insulting her husband if she makes sure her property goes to her children. Both father and mother should protect the children from a grabby step-parent. Widowers have a tendency to marry young wives, to become more active socially and to turn over the family jewels to the bride, which instantly in most homes makes the children furious. A will helps to prevent such family discord.

Often the home and other property is in the wife's name, although probably it was paid for with the husband's money. If she dies intestate and there are no children, part may go to the wife's parents or to her brothers and sisters, or to her children by a previous marriage. To divide the property a quick and unprofitable sale may be necessary.

In one case, throughout the depression a formerly wealthy man had hung onto a house worth $60,-000. It was in his wife's name and was about all they owned. The wife was superstitious and didn't want to make a will. She was ten years younger than her husband and since presumably she would outlive him, he did not insist. They had no chil-

dren. Her parents were dead. When she died, a $25,000 share in the home, rightfully her husband's, went to her brother, a good-for-nothing who for years had been estranged from his sister.

How to make a will? The best way is for you and your wife to go to a lawyer after deciding as best you can the details of what you want. The lawyer probably will suggest ideas that you have overlooked. It is better to agree upon a fee before the consultation begins. It may be from $15 to $25 for a simple will, or up to almost any amount for a complicated one disposing of a large estate.

Husband and wife each should know the contents of the other's will, and the reasons for various restrictions and bequests. Many a widow has been puzzled and pained by discovering strange provisions in her husband's will which seemed to show that he did not trust her. When a wife dies, blunt statements in the will as to how her property shall be kept out of the hands of a second wife are distressing to the distraught husband who at that time is quite sure he never will marry again. If the two make their wills at the same time, the reasons for the provisions are clear and the reading of the will after death brings no shock.

The lawyer will give you a carbon copy of each will to be kept for reference. The originals should be kept in one of three places: in the lawyer's safe, in a safe-deposit box, or in your local probate or surrogate's court where usually they can be filed for one dollar each.

In almost any other place they might be lost or destroyed. If your lawyer is familiar with your affairs, it is just as well to leave the wills with him, so that he can remind you when the wills should be changed.

In 19 states* and Alaska a will entirely in your own handwriting, signed and dated but not witnessed, is good enough if your wishes, in the court's opinion, are stated clearly. Men have written merely, "I want my wife to have everything," and the will has been as good as if it were filled with legal phrases.

On the other hand, wills have been broken on trivial technicalities. In Georgia a man lay dying on a hospital bed in the middle of a room. He prepared his will, and witnesses were called. The most convenient place for the witnesses to write was on a chest of drawers against the wall, six feet back of the head of the bed. They all went around there and signed. The court ruled that because the head of the bed concealed them from the sight of the dying man, they were not actually in his presence as required by law. The will was thrown out.

In Kansas, under almost identical circumstances, the witnesses went outside the room and signed on a table in the hall. The court held

*Arizona, Arkansas, California, Idaho, Kentucky, Louisiana, Mississippi, Montana, Nevada, North Carolina, North Dakota, Oklahoma, South Dakota, Tennessee, Texas, Utah, Virginia, West Virginia and Wyoming.

the will had been properly executed because the testator could have turned his head, and seen the witnesses, if he had so desired.

It is all such a goofy state of affairs, with laws varying in different states, that it's best to be sure your will will stand up in any court. Today you may scoff at a suggestion that anybody would sue to break your will. But no person is more bitter than he who, expecting a bequest as his family right, is scorned in the will. Particularly is there danger that married children will be influenced by their husbands and wives, when all the estate goes to the mother. And badly drawn wills tempt shyster lawyers to urge the disinherited into suits they may know can't be won, but which they hope will be compromised out of court.

Even when a will is legally drawn, it may not dispose of property exactly as the testator intended. Two sisters owned a good deal of property, left them by their mother. They had quarreled with their father and, determined that he should have none of the property, had made their own wills, properly witnessed, each leaving all to the other sister. Then each had attached a note saying that if both died, the fortune should go to a woman friend. The sisters died simultaneously in an automobile accident. The wills were good but the notes, not witnessed, were thrown out. All the property went to the father.

There are hundreds of cases like this: A husband died leaving a will that he prepared himself, which gave everything to his widow. When he made it, he had no children, and he did not know enough to make a new one when, later, a boy was born. As a result of his ignorance his widow got only one third of the estate, the other two thirds going into a trust for his son.

Some states recognize common property that can't be taken away from the surviving spouse. In most states, the widow has the lifetime use of one third of the real estate, no matter what the will says, no matter what documents she may have signed.

Under ordinary circumstances children can be disinherited, but if you feel that way about your children and your estate is large, get a lawyer to tell you how to do it. All they have to do is to break the will on any point whatsoever and they automatically collect two thirds of the estate. Better explain why your children are getting no part of your millions and your lawyer will shape your language so the children won't be able to point to it and prove that you were of unsound mind when you wrote it. Stick to simple and necessary facts, or your preachment and withering indictment may be judged to be only the ravings of a senile old fool.

You may be as well off without a will—*if you take the proper precautions*. If *all* your property is in real estate and in banks, put it in the name of "John Jones or Mary Jones (his wife) or survivor." If you want to leave money to individuals, put it in a savings bank, held by "John Jones in trust for

So-and-So." You may draw from that account while you live, but upon your death it becomes the property of "So-and-So." The court procedure is simplified, there is no estate to administer.

You can buy a printed form for a will, but there seems to be a temptation to change it, to get witnesses' signatures in the wrong place, and generally to fix up the document with your own ideas. For that reason, form wills are often broken in court.

Nor is it always wise to ask your bank to help you, for when banks make wills or recommend lawyers, you probably will find the bank named as executor and trustee. This may be perfectly proper, but there may also be a clause absolving the bank from all responsibility if it makes mistakes. And banks do make mistakes.

Now, lawyers and judges agree that complicated legal language is not often necessary. But they add: "You never can tell when you'll get before a finicky judge, and it's best to make the will absolutely tight."

Suppose you want to leave all to your wife. Take a sheet of paper and write in your own handwriting:

I, John Jones, of the City of———, do make, publish and declare this to be my last will and testament.
I give to my wife, Mary, all property of whatsoever kind and nature, whether real or personal, of which I may die possessed. I hereby appoint my said wife as executor without bond, with full power to sell, convey, rent, mortgage, transfer and assign

any or all of my said property upon such terms and conditions as she may deem to be to the best interests of my estate.

(Signature)————— (SEAL)
(Date)——————

In some states, as noted, that's a perfectly good will—unless children are born after it is made.

But *don't* stop there. In some states it's worthless. Make it good in every state. Don't sign it yet. Add, on the same page, this conglomeration of funny, but important, phrases:

Subscribed, sealed, published and declared by the said John Jones, the above-named testator, as and for his last will in our presence, who at his request, and in his presence and in the presence of each other have subscribed our names as witnesses thereto this — day of ——, A. D. 19—, in the City of——————.

Now you come to the situation in which most mistakes are made. When a will is thrown out, usually it is because it was not properly witnessed. Two witnesses are enough in some states, but some require three, so get three adults, none of whom has any interest in the estate, together in one room. You show them the document— they don't need to know what is in it—and announce so they understand perfectly, "This is my last will and testament. Please sign as witnesses." You sign in their presence, and at the end of your signature write, "(SEAL)," for some states require that. Nobody seems to know why, but they do. Your witnesses sign at the end of the will. All four of you must be "in the presence of each other" during that ceremony.

That's all there is to it except that you and the witnesses will stand around and talk about it and each of the witnesses will say, "I think it's a fine thing to have a will. I must get one some day." But probably they never will. Time will prove that you were the only wise man in the bunch.

It is best to select witnesses who are your close friends, so they can easily be found, and those who are younger than you, so they will be likely to survive you. However, even though witnesses may die, the will can be probated when proof is given that the signatures are genuine.

This rigmarole about the witnesses is necessary because, when the witnesses are called into court, their testimony must prove conclusively that this *is* your will, that there was no forgery, no substitution.

Many wills are thrown out because witnesses testify:

"He didn't say it was his will."

"Yes, he said it was his will and I signed it. Then he took it into the boss's office and I suppose the boss signed it in there."

"We were all together when we signed it. He told me he was making me his executor, but I didn't know that disqualified me as a witness."

If at any time you want to change the will—and you should check it every time a child is born or when the children become of age—you may prepare a codicil, which must be witnessed. But best tear up the old will and make a new one. Don't try to save time and expense by writing alterations on the original document, for a touch of the pen, adding or eliminating, kills it instantly.

What if you and your wife die in the same motorcar or airplane accident? If there are no wills, your children get two thirds of the estate and the remainder goes to the relatives of the spouse who died last. If there are no children, those relatives get it all.

In accidents of this sort, will or no will, the families of the husband and wife may go to court, each attempting to prove that their blood relative died last. To block this, the wills may carry a "common disaster" clause stipulating how the estate is to be divided in the event that husband and wife die within 30 days of each other.

Some parents may want to name a guardian, in case a common disaster makes orphans of the children. Lawyers usually advise against it. In administration of the will, the court must appoint a totally disinterested guardian, usually a lawyer, to see that the heirs' rights are properly handled. This protects children and others and is a wise safeguard. Although there have been cases in which courts have erred in appointing guardians, they usually do an excellent job in selecting them—probably better than you and your wife can do through your wills, for the documents you draw today may not become effective for many years and conditions and personalities may change.

Forget the guardian and do this: state in your will that in case your husband (or wife) shall predecease you, a trust shall be provided for your children if they are too young to handle the estate, placing the trust, usually, in the hands of a near relative *and* a trust company, one to check the other. Don't choose Uncle John and the Farmer's Trust Company merely because Uncle John is a nice man and you've heard the Farmer's Trust is all right. Consider whether you'd want Uncle John to handle your money today. If you decide he's all right, be sure he will be willing to serve. Ask a lot of questions about the men behind the Farmer's Trust. Too many trust companies have been known to be less than conscientious in handling estates. If you're careless in establishing your trust, your children may reach maturity with no inheritance except a lot of pretty but not-so-valuable bonds.

Your trustees will have the authority to sell or rent your property, for the best interests of the children. If the income is not sufficient for their care and education, the court may give permission to use some of the principal, even though you have made no such provision.

Don't say, "To my brother William I leave $5000." When you make your will you may be worth $50,000. When you die your estate may be so small that Brother William will get all of it. Instead, leave him one tenth of the residue, "which sum in no event however shall exceed $5000." Qualify all bequests in this manner and protect your principal heirs.

You may feel your estate is so small that no court proceedings will be necessary—that your wife and children will settle everything amicably. Probably they'd be willing, and in a few states under certain circumstances this is possible. But in most, the notice of death must be published and banks check these and, awaiting court orders, immediately seal safe-deposit boxes and refuse to pay checks drawn on accounts, even though they are in the names of husband and wife.

But if you just never someway got around to making a will, didn't think enough of your wife to take the trouble, the court awards her only one third of your estate. The remainder must be held in trust for the children.

So, wondering why you did all this to her, your widow must find often-reluctant relatives who will help care for her, or wearily start looking for a job. While you rest in peace under a tombstone which tells what a great fellow you were.

This Age of Ingenuity

AMONG the many sensational uses claimed for Polaroid, the recently announced invention of Edward H. Land, Boston scientist, elimination of headlight glare has the most appeal. Polaroid, which looks like ordinary glass, combs out the tangled masses of light rays that cause glare. A pair of blinding headlights, when fitted up with sheets of Polaroid and viewed through a Polaroid windshield, look like dull glowing spots, but intervening objects are brilliantly illuminated. It is stated that, on road tests at night, the whole of an approaching car could be seen, even objects around and behind the headlights—license plate, radiator, and exhaust fumes from the rear —and because there was no glare in the driver's eyes, he enjoyed a feeling of daytime security.

PANEL HEATING, the most radical departure in heating methods since the central heating plant came into use, is now widely employed in England. Hot water is circulated through coils of steel pipe concealed in the ceiling, from which heat rays are sprayed downward. Unlike all other methods, by which the air itself must be heated to around 72° for comfort, panel heating produces the same pleasant sensation of warmth as the sun, at an air temperature of 65° or lower. Because the warmth of the invisible rays is retained longer by the skin and clothes, windows can be opened oftener to dispel any discomfort or dryness. Cost of installation is high, but operating costs show savings as high as 25 percent.

—*Architectural Forum*

Combatting Early Syphilis

By

JOHN H. STOKES, M.D.

FOREWORD BY
DR. THOMAS PARRAN
Surgeon-General U. S. Public Health Service

Control and ultimate extermination of syphilis is the frank objective of the war now being waged by the U. S. Public Health Service and other health authorities throughout the nation. This difficult goal can be attained only by the co-operation of an informed public, alive to the menace of this devastating, highly-prevalent disease. In the following article Dr. John H. Stokes of the University of Pennsylvania, one of the leading syphilologists in the United States, and for many years a consultant of the U. S. Public Health Service, describes the standard medical procedure in the diagnosis and treatment of early syphilis. Dr. Stokes' contribution contains information that is absolutely essential to the success of our campaign; a thoughtful reading of the article should enable the layman to understand what can and must be done by the private physician and his patient in controlling the disease.

SYPHILIS, the wrecker and disabler, ranks high if not actually *first* among the causes of death. Untreated or insufficiently treated, it invades heart and brain, may ravage the nervous system and lay waste the mechanisms of sight and locomotion. It is the great ventriloquist among diseases; in its final stages it may speak from any organ or tissue of the body. And yet this pitiless killer can be brought to heel by modern treatment. Indeed the most encouraging aspect of the stern campaign now being waged against syphilis is the fact that if physician and patient wisely perform their respective functions, cure is all but inevitable.

Quick recognition of *early* syphilis is the hope of the afflicted and the test of the physician's skill. The first sign of the disease is usually an unobtrusive, often painless, moist spot or sore appearing on the genitals or lips, or in the mouth or throat, from 10 to 30 days after exposure. This initial lesion, or chancre, is rarely conspicuous; sometimes it does not appear at all, and in women may be totally out of sight. Fortunate indeed is the patient whose primary warning is so obvious that competent advice is sought at once. Early identification not only makes it possible to stop transmission, but every hour counts toward a cure.

The very moment a person suspects he has syphilis he should go, he *must* go, to a competent doctor. If he knows no such doctor, let him call the Board of Health, the city or county medical society, or a local hospital, and be told where to find help. Under no circumstances should he apply the salve or take the medicine recommended by a drug clerk or friend; an untreated sore is essential to quick recognition. And lastly, he must not kiss or have sex relations with anyone until he is instructed by his doctor, for in its first stage syphilis is terribly contagious.

A competent physician painstakingly scrutinizes the patient's entire body in a good light, looks in his mouth. Then he asks questions: what, how long, the circumstances? Patient, be truthful here, for your life may depend on it! Tell what you can, for your cure and the safety of others often hinge on this first frank talk. No decent physician will betray you. Trust us.

Putting on rubber gloves the doctor now gets a few drops of serum from the early sore and either sends it to a laboratory or examines it himself if he has a "darkfield" microscope. The spiral germ of syphilis can be seen in a darkfield examination, alive and moving, as dust motes are visible in a sunbeam. The spotting of this corkscrew-shaped organism is the first step in diagnosis, for if the germ can be discovered by darkfield before the blood test becomes positive (of which more presently) infectiousness and transmission can be shut off within a few hours, and cure is a matter of nearly 100 percent certainty.

But even expert examination may not find the syphilis germ the first time; possibly several attempts must be made. Perhaps if examination is delayed the sore disappears. If this occurs, do not be lulled into a feeling of false security, for trifling beginnings in syphilis often have the gravest consequences. Other signs must be looked for, other tests made —prime among which is a blood examination, usually a Wassermann test, based on the fact that a syphilitic infection is accompanied by changes in the blood serum which identify (within very narrow limits of error) the presence of the disease.* Such a test must be taken repeatedly during the early days or weeks before the patient is dismissed.

So useful is this Wassermann test that it has tended to become the first, and too often the only resort of the doctor in identifying syphilis. Enormously valuable though it is, this test fails us just at the critical time for securing the highest percentage of cures. For a Wassermann test does not "come positive" as we say, until the 10th to 12th day after the first sore, and when it *does* become positive, the chance of cure has already been diminished. Lucky is the person who, though proved to have the germ by darkfield, still has a "negative" blood. For he, the sero-negative primary case, has 86 to 90 chances of cure,

*The Kahn and Kline tests are simplifications of the original Wassermann procedure, and detect the presence of syphilitic changes in the blood and spinal fluid by producing a precipitate that is visible to the eye or microscope.

while a later case has only from 60 to 80 percent.

When the laboratory reports come in, the patient asks inevitably, "Doctor, can I be cured?" An honest answer is, "Yes, up to 80 or 90 percent certainty, if you have the determination to play the game according to the rules." *First rule:* put treatment before every other obligation; stick; be regular, no excuses, no letdown, no crying off. *Second,* expect to see the thing through on faith, for so quickly do signs and symptoms vanish that you will soon be inclined to think that you are out of danger. But remember this: syphilis is the greatest relapser of all diseases! Treatment to prevent relapse is carried through on a schedule based on enormous medical experience, sifted to the bottom in the last 10 years, so do not constitute yourself as a judge of your own cure. Only your doctor has the knowledge and the right to tell you when your treatments may stop.

If you are a woman you have a better chance for a mild course of the disease than a man. Syphilis is chivalrous, but left-handedly so, for it may strike at you through your unborn child, which is brought into intimate contact with the infection. But we can control your infectiousness, if you will let us treat you through your pregnancy. Conceive only when we say you may; treat moderately for the disease as soon as you know you are pregnant, or at least before the fifth month— and you have a 90 percent chance, plus, of having a well baby. Have a blood test, whether your doctor or anyone else thinks you need it or not! Don't hunt up an abortionist if, having syphilis, you find you are pregnant. Pregnancy makes syphilis milder, is actually treatment for it; and the child, if you are treated even a little, may be born healthy, 70 to 90 chances in a hundred. Even if it has the disease it can be successfully treated.

Now you have the facts from your doctor. You find, heaving a deep breath, that you are not in Hell's caldron after all, but still a hopeful, aspiring being, rallying to the determination to get well. What is ahead of you, and what principles shall guide you?

Early syphilis should be treated on one of two definite schedules, known as the American "continuous" and the Danish-British "intermittent," each of which specifies the dosage of the essential drugs, and the times to give them, together with the necessary tests, all with the accuracy of a pilot's chart. These schedules are the result of a world-wide survey by a League of Nations Commission, and the United States Public Health Service coöperating with a group of American clinics and authorities. In the United States, the American continuous treatment has the weight of a large body of evidence in its favor, so let us confine our discussion to this system, which goes on week after week for approximately 65 weeks and gives top-notch curative results.

In treating early syphilis today two drugs, arsphenamine and bismuth, are used in alternation. The arsphenamines are yellowish powders which must be dissolved in specially purified water, and then injected *very slowly* into a vein, usually in the bend of the arm. An injection hurts little or not at all. The drug circulates to various organs which change it into compounds that destroy the spiral germs of syphilis outright and with astonishing rapidity. This yellow liquid which goes so painlessly into your vein is a refinement of Paul Ehrlich's "606," an arsenical compound introduced in 1910 that brought new hope, meaning and method into the treatment of syphilis. Today the arsphenamines will control your infectiousness, bring about your cure, and *nothing else but arsphenamine and its derivatives will do it*. In an early case usually 30 to 40 of these treatments are required, given in courses which alternate without lapses or rests with those of bismuth. The old days of treating syphilis with mercury pills and other medicines by mouth are gone for good.

Bismuth, the second drug used in the treatment of syphilis, has largely displaced the comparatively poisonous mercury, with less relapse and more cure, and less trouble from complications, especially of the kidney. Bismuth today is safely and effectively given in only one way— in a suspension or solution injected through a 2½-inch needle into the muscle of the buttocks. It is given once every five or seven days, alternating with the arsphenamine injections in the arm; in the average case the schedule calls for 60 of these bismuth "hip" treatments.

Don't be thrown into a panic over any of this treatment, or even by an uncomfortable reaction—a little nausea or headache. Real drugs must cause some flurry if they are to work, and an experienced physician can find a way around every complication. Composure on your part helps, directly and powerfully. The first four hip treatments may make you a little stiff, but if your doctor will take time to massage, deeply and firmly, for two or three minutes over the spot, the treatment is not even a nuisance.

Sometime between the sixth and 12th month of treatment, a spinal fluid examination should be made, because only in this way can the great group of nervous diseases, including locomotor ataxia and general paralysis, be recognized and cured or arrested before they have established themselves in the nervous tissues. If the fluid that surrounds the brain and spinal cord is examined thus early, it is solemn truth that much blindness, chairbound crippling, and practically all insanity due to the disease could be utterly stamped out. Here again, the procedure in competent hands is safe, the reactions are few and insignificant. But the information gained from the standard tests on spinal fluid by a competent laboratory is absolutely priceless; if the result is negative, or normal, it is a legitimate excuse for the most heartfelt "Thank God!" the doctor and patient ever uttered. Consoling, too, is the fact that a negative spinal fluid, after standard early treatment, almost never becomes positive or abnormal.

The worst that can happen after a spinal fluid examination is a one in 10 chance of a headache that may make you lie down (it stops at once on doing so) for a few hours.

You may have unconsciously exposed other persons before you knew you had the disease. The wise course here is to insist upon a full investigation of everyone involved, and this means blood tests, at least. If possible, bring to the doctor for treatment the person who gave it to you. Sweat your memory until it yields all the facts; you will be protected and so will he or she. We want to stop this disease, not punish or pass moral judgments.

For yourself, remember that time and treatment control infectiousness, and *nothing else does*. After 20 treatments in the arm and 20 in the hip, rarely is there relapse or infectiousness—after 18 months' treatment, almost none at all, if treatment has been steady, regular, uneventful. You are entitled to know that you may hope to marry, but hardly within two years, better after three or four, and always under direction of your doctor, with fair play to the partner as to knowledge of the facts, and with control of pregnancy.

What of the patient who cannot afford the services of a private physician? Shall he be barred from the possibilities of a cure? If a patient is honestly unable to pay for private treatment, he can secure skillful medical attention from the clinics operated by his community or attached to his local hospital. If possible, he pays a small fee; if he is wholly without money, drugs and medical service cost him nothing. Even under our present system of public clinics, admittedly inadequate and destined for complete reorganization in the near future, no citizen can plead poverty as an excuse for avoiding the personal and social responsibility of "taking the cure."

In the general testing of bloods by an aroused public and medical profession in the days to come, a vast number of persons will be found to have an infection of which they were never aware. For these, and for all others who innocently or through their own action may contract syphilis, I have nothing but reassurance if they will seek out a trustworthy physician. When I say that the modern treatment of syphilis does not fail beyond the inevitable small expectance of mischance in all human affairs, I mean it, man to man and eye to eye. But I must also add that the cure of syphilis and the unclenching of its throttle-grasp on human life and happiness demands from the infected person a fine and enduring exercise of courage and coöperation. From the physician it requires an outgoing humanity and sympathy, and a determination to keep up with the racing special knowledge in this field of medicine. With patient and doctor working shoulder to shoulder, failure is impossible, and syphilis will, we confidently believe, cease to plague the earth.

Syphilis Can Be Stamped Out

By

THOMAS PARRAN, M.D.

SYPHILIS, our most menacing health problem and No. 1 American killer, can be controlled as effectively as smallpox and more cheaply than tuberculosis! There is not even serious difference among authorities as to methods of combatting it. Yet in no other national welfare situation is the lag so great between the much we know and the little we do. Other countries have shown that syphilis can be mastered: in England the number of new cases has been cut in half since 1920; in the Scandinavian countries syphilis has become a rare disease. Our problem here is this: to teach 130 million citizens that by the coöperation of private and official agencies, and a reasonable expenditure of money, they can buy safety against this virulent and highly communicable disease.

At the recent Washington Conference on Venereal Disease, 900 physicians and educators, state and city health officers, were asked to recommend a nation-wide campaign. It was agreed that syphilis can be controlled by a three-part attack:

First, every early case must be located, reported, its source ascertained, and all contacts followed up to find possible infection; *second,* enough money, drugs and doctors must be secured to make treatment possible for all cases; *third,* private physicians and public health officials must be re-educated to form a united front and to use scientific methods in the fight against syphilis; in addition, the public must be informed as to methods required for its protection.

1. *Locate syphilis.* In 1935, 518,-000 new cases came to light. An equal number probably were unrecognized or treated only by patent medicines or quacks. In many cases early symptoms are so slight—a sore, a rash, sometimes a fever—that a person may be honestly ignorant he has the disease until it passes through the latent period and appears, often after years, in the varied and ghastly forms of its less curable stages. Doctors frequently do not see these unfortunates until they appear with serious diseases of the heart and blood vessels, or when they bring in a wizened syphilitic

baby for treatment, or manifest symptoms of approaching insanity, paralysis, deafness or blindness.

The danger to one's self and others of harboring syphilis could be averted if everyone would submit voluntarily to a Wassermann or other blood test, but since there is no mortal chance of this, the next best thing is to make such blood tests routine wherever possible. Many hospitals make the Wassermann test a regular procedure with all patients. This practice should be extended to all hospitals. Every pregnancy should mean a Wassermann test; treatment of the mother, begun early in pregnancy, will prevent congenital syphilis in the child. Life insurance companies might profitably make such a test in every medical examination; at least one large company takes a Wassermann on all applicants for policies of $20,000 or more. Twenty-five states forbid marriage when either person is infected with a venereal disease; these statutes should be stiffened and extended to all states.

Sound policy suggests that all applicants for positions in the public service, from policemen to postmasters and commissioners, should be examined for possible infection. A few large industries, notably the Du Ponts, are examining their employes and requiring treatment when needed. This type of personnel work in all industries would pay for itself many times over, both in greater efficiency of the worker and in lesser amounts paid out for employes' compensation. Except in rare cases it is not desirable or necessary that persons having syphilis be discharged or refused employment.

After syphilis has been diagnosed it should be reported to the health department, like smallpox, typhoid or diphtheria. The ancient and desirable doctor-patient relationship of absolute secrecy need be disturbed very little. The actual *name* of the patient need not be reported; his initials, his date of birth or a number are sufficient for purposes of record. But if, while still dangerous to others, he fails to continue his treatments or to coöperate with his doctor in tracing the source of his infection, he should lose the privilege of privacy. It is urgently necessary for all states to adopt a uniform case-reporting system which will end the present confusion and duplication of records in some sections, and the complete lack of them in others.

When a patient presents himself for treatment either at the office of a private physician or at the clinic, two problems immediately arise. First, he must be rendered noninfectious; and, if possible, cured. One of the most encouraging factors in the drive is that after a few injections of arsphenamine the patient ceases to spread the disease. (He is not cured, and if he ceases treatment before he is cured, he is apt to relapse into an infectious condition.) From the public health standpoint this is important, since it means one link in the chain of the infection has been broken. The second problem is equally important—to discover the source of the patient's infection. It is the duty of the physician, usually acting through the health officer, to make sure that the source of infection does not give rise to more new cases. One encouraging factor in syphilis control is that infections always come singly. There is no mass epidemic.

The task of tracing infection has frightened off many who were honestly eager to help. Investigators must be specially trained, and scrupulously careful to protect the patient. When patients understand that the purpose is not punishment but help, a surprising number do everything they can to bring under treatment both the source of their own infection and their own possibly infected contacts. Recent proof of this is found in the test investigations reported by Doctor George H. Ramsey of the New York State Department of Health, and in routine experiences reported from the University of Pennsylvania clinic.

The expense of effective clinic treatment for a new case of syphilis is relatively small. Dr. J. E. Moore, chief of the Johns Hopkins clinic, estimates that in his clinic $50 is sufficient to treat a patient with standard drugs for a period of 18 months, the usual time required for a cure. Figures for other clinics range between $30 and $150.

Any person who can afford it naturally prefers the personal service of a skilled and interested private physician. Such service is cheap at any price, compared with the utter ruin of untreated syphilis. But thousands of sufferers can pay nothing at all for treatment. Other thousands can pay only a little. Yet in the public interest *all* must be treated, for all are a menace in the infectious stage of the disease, and most of them become a burden if allowed to progress to the later stages. Which brings us directly to the second step:

2. *Adequate treatment must be assured for all infected persons.* At present most states are spending less than one cent annually per capita to control syphilis. Some states actually spend only one tenth of a cent. Last year Delaware led the venereal fight with an outlay of three cents per person. Clearly, we must make more than a gesture if we are to root out syphilis. Yet the taxpayer need not shudder at the cost, for if we spend more for prevention, the present cost for institutional and other relief of uncured late syphilis can be enormously reduced.

This year, the National Conference on Venereal Disease asked Congress to appropriate $25,000,-000* for syphilis control, or about 11 cents per capita of federal funds, to be matched by states and localities. Backward states would be required to meet minimum standards of personnel and service before receiving federal grants. In each case responsibility for the work rests with the state. Since syphilis recognizes no state boundaries and every effective campaign must have a GHQ, responsibility rests with the

*Compare this sum with the $246,000,-000 of state and federal funds used for bovine tuberculosis since 1917.

Public Health Service for integration of local and national programs.

Public health is purchasable, as has been proved in the past when aroused public interest has stamped out plagues which once ravaged the population. But before syphilis can be brought under control, facilities to treat it must be improved almost everywhere; must be built from the ground up in many places. Venereal clinics are, on the whole, undermanned and poorly organized. A recent survey showed them capable of effective work for less than 25 percent of the present case-load and less than 10 percent of the potential case-load. If free drugs and reliable laboratory service were available to private physicians, many marginal patients able to pay only small amounts for treatment could be served by the personal physician instead of being shifted to the impersonal public clinic.

Reconstruction of clinical facilities will require time, coöperation and shrewd expenditure of all available funds. Specifically, the following steps must be taken: *First*, a trained, full-time health officer with an adequate staff should be placed in charge of the venereal division of every large city and state department of health. *Second*, all states must be frankly liberal with antisyphilitic drugs and laboratory services. *Third*, communities must greatly increase the number of free and part-pay clinics, and adopt reasonable standards of efficiency. These include privacy for the coöperative patient, active follow-up, a uniform system of case reporting with a central clearinghouse, and a trained personnel.

3. *Education of the private physician and general public*. Sufficient stress cannot be laid upon the importance of the private physician in the control of syphilis, but the average medical practitioner must frankly ask himself: "Am I qualified to diagnose and treat syphilis? Have I adequate knowledge of the accepted drugs and techniques employed against it?" Fifty-five percent of the doctors in the United States do not treat syphilis, but every doctor should at least be able to diagnose it. For the re-education of doctors, postgraduate medical courses in syphilology are being instituted at leading universities, and the curriculum of medical schools is being reorganized to treat syphilis not as a skin disease but as a malady which cuts across all medical specialties and may affect every organ of the body.

Lastly, a tremendous amount of popular education is needed to remove all stigma of shame and turpitude from the syphilitic sufferer. Not until we have stripped the disease of its traditional moral implications can we make headway against it. We must think of syphilis scientifically as a dangerous disease, which it is, rather than moralistically as a punishment for sin, which it often is not. All of us together—physician, public official and private citizen—must learn that this is everybody's business, that everybody is endangered, that everybody pays for it, whether afflicted by the disease or not, and that no single agency is big enough or clever enough to do everyone's job alone.

And finally we must be realistic. Forget the humanitarian appeal of lives saved, suffering lessened, homes unbroken. The job of stamping out syphilis will pay for itself and pay dividends. Our economic stresses are difficult enough without the extra load of a syphilis-ridden population. Syphilis cannot be downed in a year, or a decade, but we have already dragged the specter of the spiral death into the light, seen it to be conquerable, and it will be strange indeed if we do not prevail against it.

There Must Be Some Mistake

In 1907 the United States Mint coined eagles and double eagles fatter in the middle than at the rim, with the result that they would not stack and had to be withdrawn.

Keeping up with the World

Excerpt from a regular department in Collier's

Freling Foster

Under Paris lies the most famous mushroom-producing center in the world. It is a complete subterranean city, with a perfect ventilating system and eight miles of illuminated streets lined with mushroom beds and the homes of people who cultivate and ship them.

Building a Personality

Condensed from Physical Culture

HARRY EMERSON FOSDICK, D.D.

A CONSULTING psychologist told me recently that most cases of emotional maladjustment are due to the fact that people will not accept themselves. They resent their limitations. They want to be someone else. They keep daydreaming about what they would do if they had another's chance. And so, disregarding their own possibilities, they never make anything worth while out of themselves.

Well, anybody can find sufficient cause to dislike his own lot. William Wilberforce did not like himself. Diminutive edition of a man, Boswell went to hear him speak once and said afterward, "I saw what seemed a mere shrimp mounted upon the table; but, as I listened, he grew and grew, until the shrimp became a whale." That shrimp of a man never had good health. For 20 years, on doctor's orders, he took opium to keep body and soul together and had courage never to increase the dose. But more than any other Englishman, he stopped the British slave trade; and as one stands in Westminster Abbey beside the grave of "The Attorney General of the unprotected and the friendless," one sees that that sensitive, suffering life translated itself into a persistent, unconquerable sympathy for down-trodden people that a lusty hulk of a man in perfect health probably never would have felt.

The most stimulating successes in history have come from persons who, facing some kind of limitations and handicaps, took them as part of life's game and played splendidly in spite of them. Once when Ole Bull, the great violinist, was giving a concert in Paris, his A string snapped and he transposed the composition and finished it on three strings. That is life—to have your A string snap and finish on three strings.

As soon as a man begins to accept this positive technique for handling his handicaps, they present themselves to him as opportunities always challenging, sometimes fascinating. Rebellion against your handicaps gets you nowhere. Self-pity gets you nowhere. One must have the adventurous daring

367

to accept oneself as a bundle of possibilities and undertake the most interesting game in the world—making the most of one's best.

In a battle with the Saracens in Spain, so the story runs, the Scots threw the heart of Robert the Bruce ahead of them and then with all their might fought toward it. That is the method of procedure. Take charge of your life, hurl some ideal and hope ahead and then fight toward it; organize your living around a purpose. Many folk fail to become personalities because they think that life is something we *find* instead of something we *create*. The fact is that existence is what we find. The big business of being a person is to take existence and so organize it around our plans and purposes that it becomes a life.

A friend of mine landed in Boston a half century and more ago. His old Scotch father had told him that he was of less than average ability. He began his life in America as a foundryman and he roomed over a saloon. Such was his existence to start with. What he made of it, however, was a great life, for he turned out to be George A. Gordon, one of the best scholars Harvard ever graduated; for over 40 years in the Old South Church in Boston, his pastorate was one of the most notable for intellectual quality and spiritual influence in the annals of American churches. His existence was what he found; his life was what he created. Often the best friend a man has is not comfort, but the challenge of antagonistic environment to awaken his slumbering soul.

At least three factors enter into the achievement of this sort of personality. First, imagination. Great living starts with a picture, held in some person's imagination, of what he would like some day to do or be. Florence Nightingale dreamed of being a nurse, Edison pictured himself an inventor; all such characters escaped the mere shove of circumstance by imagining a future so vividly that they headed for it.

Look at John Keats: orphaned in early boyhood, pressed by poverty, lacerated by the cruelty of his literary critics, disappointed in love, stricken by tuberculosis, and finally shoved off the scene by death at 26. But with all his ill fortune, Keats' life was not driven by circumstance. From that day when, a youth, he picked up a copy of Spenser's *Faërie Queene* and knew beyond doubt that he too was born to be a poet, Keats' life was drawn by a masterful purpose which gave him a lasting place among the world's renowned. "I think," he said once, "that I shall be among the English poets after my death." He got that picture in his imagination, and to him it was like the heart of Robert the Bruce to the fighting Scots.

Hold a picture of yourself long and steadily enough in your mind's eye and you will be drawn toward it. Picture yourself vividly as defeated and that alone will make victory impossible. Picture yourself vividly as winning, and that alone will contribute immeasurably to success. Do not picture yourself as anything and you will drift like a derelict.

Second, common sense. There is no use in a round peg's imagining itself fitted in a square hole. As a matter of fact, many people flounder around pitifully before they discover the true direction of their lives. Whistler, the artist, started out to be a general and was dropped from West Point because he could not pass in chemistry. "If silicon had been a gas," he said, "I should have been a major general." Sir Walter Scott wanted to be a poet and turned to novel writing only when Byron outshone him in his chosen field. Phillips Brooks failed as a teacher before he turned to preaching. Study yourself and use your head in picturing your goal. But whether with wisdom or without, pick a goal; don't drift.

Third, courage. Real personalities always have the kind of faith that produces courage. When his generation was against him, Richard Wag-

ner had faith in his music, and it overcame the world. After centuries had borne unimpeachable testimony to the devastating virulence of yellow fever, a little group of American medical men in Cuba had faith that it could be conquered, and it was. Charles Darwin worked for 20 years in a little English garden succeeding and failing, trying and keeping on because he had faith that he had found a clue, and he conquered. Faith is not credulity. It is creative power. It is vision plus valor.

Imagination, common sense and courage—even a moderate exercise of these will produce remarkable results. If a man is primarily after wealth, the world can whip him; if he is primarily after pleasure, the world can beat him; but if a man is primarily growing a personality, then he can capitalize anything that life does to him.

Keeping up with the World
Excerpts from a regular department in Collier's
Freling Foster

AT LEAST HALF of the marriages taking place throughout the world today are not preceded by courtship or inspired by mutual love. They are family alliances arranged by parents.

ONE OF the greatest acts of courtesy in history took place at the Battle of Fontenoy in 1745. As the armies met, the English invited the French to fire first. The French refused and asked the English to begin, which they did—killing 50 officers and 760 men with the first volley.

THE LARGEST mass wedding in history took place in 324 B.C. at Susa, Persia, when Alexander the Great had 10,000 of his Macedonian soldiers married to Persian women at one time.

THE MOST stupendous death warrant in all history was signed by King Philip of Spain in February, 1568. It sentenced to death as heretics the whole 3,000,000 people of the Netherlands.

Labrador Crusader

Condensed from Review of Reviews

DONALD CULROSS PEATTIE

A<small>NCIENT</small> and leaky, ice-battered, indomitable, 1000 fishing schooners every year used to put out of the harbors of Newfoundland and southern Labrador, as soon as the ice left them, for six months of fishing "on the Labrador," famous for fogs, gales, and icebergs. To these craft some 30,000 fishermen and their families trusted their lives. Birth, sickness, and death took place at sea, or on deserted shores. Superannuated ships commonly sprang leaks and sank in a few minutes. Every year many died of gangrene from accidents that could not be treated. A toothache went on until it got better—or ended in necrosis of the jaw. Rickety children were allowed helplessly to pass the incurable point. Only frames of iron escaped beriberi, scurvy, pneumonia, and tuberculosis.

On August 4, 1892, the fleet, lying in Domino Run, ran up greeting flags as a little ketch-rigged British hospital ship, the first ever to visit this floating city of hoping and suffering humanity, sped in on a fair breeze. There were cheers and salutes, visits and explanations. When the courtesies were over, to the hospital ship's one medicine man, Wilfred Thomason Grenfell, came a hail from a miserable little tub.

"Be you a real doctor?"

"That's what I call myself."

"Us hasn't got no money," fenced the helmsman, "but there's a very sick man ashore, if so be you'd come and see him."

Dr. Grenfell went ashore on his first case in the New World. In a hovel he found a tubercular man in the last stages of pneumonia, six neglected children huddled in a corner, with only a future of starvation before them.

Few in Labrador and northern Newfoundland ever sought medical aid (when any was available) until the situation was practically hopeless. Before health could become anything like as prevalent as disease and maimed limbs and early death, a population scattered over a thousand miles of dangerous coast would have to be educated in hygiene and child care, would have to unlearn age-old superstitions.

370

The whole economic life would have to be reconstructed.

In that enlightened year, 1892, there was nobody in the region who had the vision and the will to alter a whole country, from its monetary system to its spiritual outlook, except Wilfred Grenfell, 27 years old.

Grenfell was born on the Sands of Dee in Cheshire, England. As a child on that treacherous estuary he had known fishing ships fail to come back after great storms. Though he was the son of a Church of England clergyman, the blood of old sea fighters was in his veins. He traces descent from Sir Richard Grenville who sailed out (1591) in the little *Revenge* and gave battle to 53 gigantic Spanish galleons, whipped, shamed, and sank them by the score, and died on his own quarter-deck.

The schooling of Wilfred Grenfell was the accepted type of the day in England. Even a second-grade medical college today would look with scorn on the best training a physician could then obtain. Doctors operated in bloodstained frock coats, carrying gangrene from patient to patient, talking about "laudable pus." For the young medical students wenching, drinking, non-attendance on classes or rowdy behavior during lectures were all too often considered normal behavior. But from the rowdier student life, fastidious young Wilfred held himself aloof. Believing firmly in the bodily and spiritual prophylaxis of sport, he organized rowing, swimming, cricket, football and tennis among his fellow students, and among the tough boys of East End London, where his hospital was situated. He saw plenty of the effects of drunkenness. Women who had gashed each other's scalps open with broken bottles, men with delirium tremens, seduced and diseased girls, children hopelessly warped from sheer starvation by the rule of the bottle in the home, made him early an implacable foe of alcohol.

Returning one night from an outpatient case, he stepped into a big tent where Moody and Sankey were holding a revival meeting. A tedious prayer-bore was maundering on, and Grenfell got up to leave. The watchful Dwight Moody saw him and called out, "Let us sing a hymn while our brother finishes his prayer." This brought the young doctor back to his seat, in admiration of the leader's "practical Christianity." "When I left," says Grenfell, "it was with the determination to make religion a real effort or frankly to abandon it. That could have but one issue while I lived with a mother like mine." All his life his Christianity has been vigorously active. In a grog shop he knocked out a blasphemer. When he put to sea to do duty on a hospital ship with the North Sea fishing fleet, it was with the resolve to be a fighting Christian, who began the betterment of his fellow man by patching up his body. But he wanted to go on, providing decent resthouses for sailors on shore, entertainment to vie with that of the bar and the brothel, and economic self-respect.

These were the principles Grenfell brought to Labrador and to that frost-bitten, barren peninsula of Newfoundland that points with a granite finger at the arctic seas. At sea or ashore, starvation threatened. An icy climate grips a barren soil where grew no cereals and few vegetables or cultivated fruits. When sheep or cows were first brought to this grim land they were slain by the fierce sledge-dogs. At sea the power-driven boats of "Southern" companies were sweeping the seals into oblivion, slaughtering the young that could not swim. In the forested hinterland the ancient fur trade was dwindling. And for centuries the Hudson's Bay Company had held the trappers in its economic control; it never paid cash for furs; payment was either in kind or in "counters," good only at Company stores.

There were then no agencies of mercy on the Labrador, except the Moravian Brethren and a few clergy, their influence weakened by inter-denominational rivalry. What was needed was a permanent Red Cross, a Salvation Army, circulation of free money, and a few cool millions in capital to start lumbering and quarrying industries to alternate with fish and fur, a chain of hospitals, orphanages, and non-denominational schools, and a whole corps of doctors and nurses. What came was Wilfred Grenfell.

After two years of lonely battling, the fame of this young man, working against the suspicion and calumny of old or vested interests, was spreading through Newfoundland and Canada. In a few years more the United States was aroused. Nurses and young doctors went north for the short sub-arctic summer. Boats for hospital duty, for traveling library duty, were donated. And boys from Harvard, Yale, Princeton, Brown, and Johns Hopkins, looking for adventure in their vacations, put heart and muscle into the Sisyphus task. Presently Grenfell had a chain of small hospitals, covering nearly a thousand miles of coastline, connected by hospital ship. Modern surgeons proudly gave their services to Grenfell's fishermen and half-breed Eskimos and Indians.

All the time Grenfell never lost himself in executive red tape. Though he was the responsible head of half a dozen ventures, institutions, and industries, he was still personally on call at any instant to attend to anybody's needs, from a young man with love troubles to burying an unmarried ship's drudge who had died at sea of a premature birth. Over her grave he placed a cross on which was carved: *Jesus said, "Neither do I condemn thee."*

Racing across a frozen bay to save a boy's life, the Labrador Doctor found that his dogs were carrying him over "sish" ice, a treacherous, crackled and rotting crust over deathy waters. As they sank through, he sprang off his sledge and let the dogs fight their way to the biggest pan of ice he could see, dragging him through the water by the traces tied to his wrists. Coatless, hatless, and bootless he lived the night through by killing three of his dogs for the warmth of their skins. When morning broke he was drifting rapidly to sea where ice pans were grinding up and down and crushing each other to bits. Making a flag of his last remaining garment, his shirt, he waved for hours at the receding cliffs, but no one seemed to see him. Actually, on shore, the whole village was wringing its hands for its Guardian Angel. At last, in such an ice-covered sea as not even these modern Vikings had ever before attempted, his rescuers, speechless with emotion, grasped his hands. On that shore still stands a bronze tablet that Grenfell erected "To the memory of three noble dogs, Moody, Watch, and Spy, whose lives were given for mine on the ice, April 21st, 1908."

Next summer Grenfell went back to England and brought his mother over for a visit to the New World. Even on the old *Mauretania*, queen of the seas, Mrs. Grenfell suffered from seasickness, and this left her son a free hand with a beautiful young passenger. With New York drawing ever nearer Grenfell proposed to the girl, not even knowing her name.

This was Miss Anne Elizabeth Caldwell MacClanahan of Lake Forest, Illinois. That November they were married. It was in a subzero, death-white January that Grenfell's bride first saw Newfoundland, her lifelong home. By her husband's side Lady Grenfell has worked for 28 years. The three Grenfell children were all born in Newfoundland. Wilfred Jr., 26 years old,

teaches at St. Mark's School for boys. Two years younger, Kinloch Pascoe is an engineer for the General Electric Company, and 20-year-old Rosamond is a student at McGill University.

Grenfell's work has required financial as well as physical and moral courage. To break the vise-grip of the trading companies, he induced the fishermen to start their own stores, purchasing and selling collectively. At the first meeting called to discuss the project, the old traders, bitterly antagonistic, packed the meeting, took up every moment of discussion with denunciations. Outside, the fishermen decided that there must be something in these "copper stores" if the traders were so afraid of them. But Grenfell found that he had to lend his friends the capital ($10,000) with which to start.

With time, a chain of small cooperatives was doing business along the coast. Not all were honestly or wisely run. One day the St. John's merchants from whom the supplies were purchased came down on the Labrador Doctor for $25,000 unpaid bills. Legally, it appeared, Grenfell was solely responsible. A beautiful new schooner, his personal property, had just arrived. He sold her as she dropped anchor, and threw in every scrap of personal property. The remaining and reorganized cooperatives are now owned by the fishermen themselves and have paid as high as 10 percent dividends to their shareholders.

On the day that George V was crowned, he pressed a button and laid the cornerstone of the "King George V Seamen's Institute," built by Sir Wilfred through the generous help of many friends, in St. John's (Newfoundland's capital), for fishermen and for their daughters who come to the city. When in 1927 the main hospital at St. Anthony was rebuilt in fireproof construction, crowning a lifetime's achievement, George V knighted the Labrador Doctor, and he became Sir Wilfred Grenfell, Knight Commander of St. Michael and St. George; and the Lake Forest girl, Lady Grenfell.

Among Sir Wilfred's successes have been the flourishing vegetable gardens, the introduction of cows and sheep, the lumber mill, and above all the orphanages. Grenfell found that it took years of explaining, of exhausting lecture tours, to get people to see that orphans will shout spontaneous hymns of gratitude to their Maker if you so improve their economic status that they can get jobs and support themselves. Nothing has paid such sound return as the orphans. Years ago Grenfell found himself with one abandoned baby. He had to bring it back to the orphanage on a hospital ship manned only by sailors. The baby got into everything. In a terrible sea it wriggled out of the swinging cot into which it had been lashed and was found in the scuppers playing peek-a-boo with the raging Atlantic. This dauntless foundling was one of the pioneers of the St. Anthony orphanage. Today the brightest children are sent to the States or Canada for a higher education and come back as nurses, teachers, electrical engineers, carpenters, to labor among their own people. Most have paid back to the Grenfell Association dividends in human service for what it cost to shelter and educate them.

The biggest business men of New York, Boston, Ottawa and London act as trustees for the financial help that, in Grenfell's name, flows northward to Labrador and northern Newfoundland; they quit their affairs to attend annual meetings in New York. Young men and women who give strength and intellect and heart are proud to say they served with Grenfell in the North. The Grenfell Association of America, with offices at 156 Fifth Avenue, New York, manages the cause in the States.

The Grenfell personality has been, undoubtedly, the most valuable asset in the mighty business that his practical Christianity has become. Sheer bonniness has disarmed enemies who met him. His winning smile, his flashing sense of humor, his memory packed to the doors with a lifetime of episodes hazardous, funny, or heartbreaking, charm from hard-headed business men the needed river of gold to flow northward.

Teetotaler, Bible scholar, sports organizer, the Labrador Doctor has all the old-fashioned virtues, and plenty of peccadilloes to salt them. He is at times excruciatingly absent-minded, and considers precise punctuality a bore. Manlike, he never reads novels; he admires the "Men of Action" series. For music he has no ear. His wife tells of him that when the church organ rolled "All People that on Earth Do Dwell," he stood up loyally to what he supposed was "God Save the King."

How, in the lonely years, did this man fight the battle of civilization itself against a backward wilderness, against reactionary influences? It wasn't will alone, though it couldn't have been done without an optimism that no discouragement could crush out. It has been an insatiable zest for life, for the sheer adventure of the conflict, that made Grenfell accomplish more than any one man who had no state treasury, no guns, and only the sketchiest official authority at his back. He says, "Life is short. Things have to be crowded into it."

An iron constitution saw Sir Wilfred through the worst, a constitution that sleepless nights and grinding days could not wear down. When a man came in with his hands blown off and Grenfell had bonegrafted him two "flippers," he took strips of his own flesh to cover the improvised "hands." As a good English Public School boy should, he has made sport out of his work and treated play as if it called for heroics. When a thing was known

to be impossible, when wiseacres shook their heads, when common sense urged retreat, Sir Wilfred "saw it through."

Also, Sir Wilfred Grenfell, like Clara Barton and unlike many saintly people, has always had a bubbling sense of humor. He has laughed his way through many an ugly predicament. On the subject of missions, this practical Christian is outspoken. He says that missionary money and effort are often wasted by red tape. He sees no sense in praying the Lord to do something when we could do it ourselves if we wanted to take the trouble. To make the world a better place to live in, Sir Wilfred does not believe that you have to overturn governments. He believes, and has gone far to prove, that you can actually make a people and a land over, from obstetrics to the salvation of the soul, within established law and order. At heart he is a rugged individualist: "Has one man more than another the right to be called 'missionary,' for of what use is any man in the world if he has no mission in it? Christ's life is one long emphasis on the point that in the last analysis, when something has to be done, it is the individual who has to do it."

Table Talk

A VERY unpalatable delicacy at a Chinese bridal feast sometimes consists of preserved eggs. These eggs are said to be planted in a field in rows, much like potatoes. Each row is dated, and after several years have elapsed the eggs are dug up.

SIGN on a Long Island farmer's gate: Eggs laid while you wait.
—*The New Yorker*

The Case for Chastity

By

MARGARET CULKIN BANNING

In preparation for over a year, the following article is based on extended research and interviews and on data supplied by doctors, psychologists and others who deal daily with difficulties arising from sex conduct. It may be said, therefore, to represent not only the author's own considered opinion, but also the best informed opinion of the day. Mrs. Banning, mother of four children, is widely known for her numerous articles on problems of youth, marriage and the family.

IF THERE IS a case for chastity, it should be stated. Religion and obedience to moral codes still settle the question for many. But the increasing secularization of thought and the frequent denial that any moral issue is involved in sex conduct leaves uncounted thousands of young people today supposedly free to "make up their own minds," if such a phrase can be used concerning conduct which is nearly always the result of runaway emotion.

They make up their minds with insufficient knowledge and without hearing the full argument. They are told that "everyone does it" and that unchastity or even promiscuity "doesn't make any difference any more." Thus misled, they may proceed to action which will almost surely have a permanent effect on the life of any girl involved and which in most cases alters her psychology as well as her physiology.

There are parked and lightless cars on side roads everywhere. There is a "couple trade" at tourist cabins which cater to a few hours of intimate occupancy. The dean of a coeducational university said to me that almost every hotel in the city adjoining the campus was open to boys who wanted to take girls to them for the night. From 1100 questionnaires sent to college students, 200 to post-college students, and from 300 interviews, it seems plainly apparent that there remain few taboos about sex in the college groups, and that while some girls prefer to wait until marriage, they are not shocked by the sex experiences of their friends. And we know that there are 50,000 unmarried mothers registered yearly in the United States; that through wealth and influence many unmarried mothers are not registered; that many couples marry after pregnancy is discovered; and that birth control and abortions prevent motherhood in most illicit affairs.

Nevertheless, we must remember that unchastity, common though it may be, is not the norm. That still is chastity. Society does not approve nor is it set up for the general practice of unchastity. Every adult must know, as I do, many young girls who are not troubled by this problem, and others whose lives offer no opportunity for it. They keep regular hours. They are preoccupied with study, sports, domestic tasks and wholesome social activities.

Yet they cannot but hear, and hence we adults cannot ignore, the widespread whispering campaign that is now condoning unchastity and even advocating premarital relations. So there is sound reason for going right after the facts and unveiling a few that may still be shrouded even in a period of frankness. Some parents believe that the subject should not be given publicity, lest argument increase undue curiosity or foster morbid interests. But it is secret rather than open discussion which creates morbidity; and, what is more, young people are increasingly frank among themselves, and adult silence only serves further to separate generations which are already quite far enough apart in matters of advice and sympathy.

Boys urging sex experience often say, "Why not?" and treat it as a matter of light concern. But it is revealing that no reputable physician who has handled thousands of cases and thousands of confidences is equally casual. No psychologist who has seriously investi-

gated the problems of sexual relations outside of marriage treats them as trivial. That conscience and emotion will make the final decision in each case is obvious. But the personal and social consequences of unchastity, as they are apparent to those in a position to know, ought to be matters of public information.

First of all, there are the facts about venereal disease and abortion. The American Social Hygiene Association estimates that five percent of the American people have syphilis and ten percent have gonorrhea. The highest attack rate for syphilis occurs during the early adult years, 16 to 30. If venereal disease is ultimately stamped out, one risk of unchastity will be destroyed. But we are a long way from that yet. In the meantime, there is a serious and constant danger of disease in premarital relations because a girl does not go freely to her doctor for advice.

Some information comes her way —a great deal of it wrong. She is apt to believe she is safe from conception because of certain contraceptives. Here is a comment on that by Dr. Hannah Stone, Medical Director of Margaret Sanger's birth control clinic in New York:

The best concerns offer absolutely unreliable contraceptives. A firm enjoying the respect of the medical profession advertises a vaginal jelly that is only about 60 percent safe. Suppositories on the market are between 40 and 50 percent safe. The strongest douche is successful about 10 percent of the time. The situation is further complicated by the fact that different women are susceptible to different contraceptives.

This is borne out by Dr. Maurice Bigelow, director of the Institute of Practical Science Research. His institute tested hundreds of rubber condoms bought from a reliable manufacturer and discarded 25 out of every 100 as being imperfect. The equipments involving chemicals lose their effectiveness unless perfectly fresh. In other words, "You're perfectly safe" is not only an ugly and abnormal statement but it happens to be untrue. The conditions commonly surrounding acts of unchastity make it doubly untrue.

Figures show beyond a doubt that a tremendous number of unmarried young women go to abortionists. No doubt many of them have heard the current claptrap about an abortion being nothing at all to endure. Let them also hear this: Ten thousand girls and women lose their lives each year at the hands of abortionists. Dr. Frederick J. Taussig says:

The risk of infection is approximately ten times greater than at ordinary childbirth for the reason that the uterine cavity must be invaded, while in childbirth this is rarely the case. Also, for every woman who dies as a result of abortion, several women are disabled, sometimes permanently, or rendered sterile, or, at a subsequent pregnancy, suffer from the aftereffects of the abortion.

The medical point of view is not the only aspect to consider. The psychological effects of abortion are equally serious. Girls often suffer horror for the rest of their lives, as well as increasing grief for the lost child. An abortion may injure not only the woman's health but also her emotional outlook. In hours of childbirth a woman often resents the results of her sex experience. But later she has the child to make up for the pain, and she has the protection of her husband and the respect of the community. The unmarried girl who goes to an abortionist has the resentment but neither the child nor a husband's protection to balance what may easily grow into hate of a man she loved, or perhaps dread of sex relations in a subsequent marriage.

These dangers—disease, abortion, emotional disasters, and even death —surround every premarital relation. But many people run the risks and escape. If the girl does escape, is there still no case for chastity? The argument for it certainly is not sound or effective if it rests only upon the fear of consequences. Dr. Thomas Parran, Surgeon General of the United States, says, "I have always hoped that we could divest our social hygiene program from the fear motive. If gonorrhea and syphilis were unknown diseases, the ideal of monogamous sex relationship should, and I believe would, still stand upon its own intrinsic merits."

What, then, are these intrinsic values that make the case for chastity? Here is the conclusion of one young woman who went through an extra-marital experience:

Much is talked of the evils of frustration in the case of the woman who denies herself the physical expression of love. In my opinion that vague and generally periodic torment is as nothing compared to the frustration suffered by the woman who seeks happiness in love outside of marriage. With all the latent instincts of her sex released and intensified by the mating experience, awake for the first time in her life to the full design of married love, she realizes with a sense of dumb defeat that for her the fulfillment of that design must remain, perhaps forever, an unaccomplished thing. It is a trapped, blind-alley feeling that only one who has experienced it can appreciate. The conflict set up as a result casts its dark shadow over an experience which one had expected to be all light and freedom.

There is far more to be said. Early and casual sex experience often inhibits and spoils mature experience. "Coming too soon," writes L. S. Hollingsworth in his *Psychology of the Adolescent*, "it may block maturity by putting the emphasis on physical release"—as against the mature satisfaction which includes mental and esthetic elements. There are plenty of girls who pride themselves on never "going any farther than petting" without any idea of how disastrously far they have already gone. The dean of a woman's college, after considerable research, states that petting is apt to create habits which give a semblance of satisfaction without intercourse and so unsuit a girl emotionally for marriage. One authority has declared flatly that petting is far more dangerous than the complete sex act, for it can ruin normal sex experience. Following many consultations, a psychologist of the Y.W.C.A. says that substitute satisfactions tend to make intercourse an anti-climax. Over-stimulated and wrongly stimulated, girls who have indulged in petting find it difficult to respond to normal sex relations, and their chances of satisfaction and compatibility in marriage are very poor indeed.

The question of where to stop is not easy to answer. But any girl can differentiate between the romantic embrace which is a natural expression of young love and experiments in sexual sensation. She can differentiate, that is, as long as she is reacting normally, and here one cannot possibly ignore the influence of drinking. Alcohol inflames the senses, is an acknowledged aphrodisiac in most cases. A girl who has been drinking, and especially the girl who is not used to drinking, cannot possibly stand guard over her judgment or her conduct. And even if she keeps command of herself and "knows what she is doing," I doubt if she knows that doctors and psychologists think that by petting she may be doing herself a possibly permanent injury.

And if the girl goes, as they say, "all the way," what does she confront? Each girl's chastity is the interweaving of her moral code, her nervous system, her physical being, and her mind. Does she realize how profoundly that interwoven fabric may be altered in a few yielding moments?

In the breaking down of chastity, her moral code is often violated.

True, she may think she has none. Yet the great weight of tradition and poetry and romance is pressing on her, even if she is without a belief in orthodox religion. Hence many girls cannot but carry with them into early sexual experience a sense of sin which they never lose. This "guilt sense" is spoken of by almost all the doctors who have investigated such things. Even without a sense of actual sin against religion, the "guilt sense" persists in a large majority of cases.

The girl who thus feels that she is doing wrong suffers shockingly. The wound in her conscience may heal and harden and make her into a liar, or it may never heal so that she will go about with an actual fear of punishment and retribution. Often she confuses her sexual disappointments with the punishment due to sin.

On the other hand, there are girls who have really cast off conventions—who feel no spiritual or moral connection with their sex conduct. How do they come out? Usually they are deserted. If a woman has this point of view, she almost always believes—and says so once too often —that she can look out for herself. In many cases that is what her lover ultimately allows her to do. And then she becomes an outlaw. Society provides no protection for her. She may have the bravado of the outlaw, but she also has his loneliness.

One authority points out that there is growing up a large body of women who, because they were deserted by their first lover, or have found emotional release without the responsibility of marriage, are remaining unmarried and childless. This group is not only dangerous to other marriages but tragic in itself. Many are intellectual, healthy people who should be reproducing themselves instead of leading one-sided, uncreative lives.

So though people may say that morality is no longer involved in this question, I think they talk nonsense. Unchastity does affect the moral system, if only to set a girl's hand against society. Many girls fancy themselves in that rôle, rebels against a social system they consider stuffy, and religions they consider obsolete. But these girls do not know what they combat, what protections they will strip from their future life, and what a weight of experience and history is against them.

The effect of unchastity on the nervous system is as serious. Being clandestine, it is rarely either well housed or comfortable. It lodges but does not live. Think of the wayside cabins, the cheap hotels, the back seats of cars, as an environment for what we call love. Hurried, watchful, fearful of interruption or discovery—these are inevitable descriptions of unchastity.

On this point it is hard to find any more competent conclusions than those of Dr. Oliver M. Butterfield, director of the Family Guidance Service in New York:

The sexual adjustment is not a simple thing to make under the best of conditions and when hampered by guilt and apprehension it is almost impossible. At a time when man and woman may need expert advice they are forced to hide their relationship. Because of this secrecy many things are likely to happen. If the woman is a virgin she may need medical attention before she can have intercourse. The sex act is not instinctive. Premarital relationships can build up, through ignorance, incorrect, unsatisfying behavior that must be painfully unlearned after marriage.

The ordinary situation of unchastity is the case, then, of an apprehensive pair of people, in an uncongenial or uncomfortable environment, wondering if anyone has seen them. What harm such experiences do to the nervous systems of young girls, who are at such times under the added strain of great excitement, cannot be measured.

It is generally agreed that repressions are bad for almost everyone, and that argument is often given for indulgence in unchastity. But it works the other way too. Loudly as it may boast of its freedom, unchastity carries repression right along with it. There are places where it cannot go. The unchaste girl often lacks escort and open companionship. There are times when she may not speak to the one person she cares about. As long as passionate love or even excitement is growing and deeply shared, this may not matter. Secrecy is then a delicious privacy. But every recorded experience shows that such secrecy has the seeds of bitterness in it. The girl usually becomes resentful, hating to be hidden and unacknowledged, and yet more fearful of the discovery of her relation.

Of course, the couple may marry. But they still are cheating themselves. They enter on the responsibilities and adjustments of living together, take up the hard work that marriage is, without the delights and fresh discoveries which make those responsibilities pleasurable and easy. Even with its natural rewards and emotional impetus, marriage is difficult enough. But if the end of romance has already been reached before a couple marry, they face its problems without the natural compensation for them. They are apt to be jealous, for each knows the other as an experimenter.

On the other hand, the relationship is more than likely to be broken off. Remember, it is with the immature that we are chiefly concerned—the young people who are thinking only of an immediate pleasure, an adventure. They have heard that youthful sex experiments may be casual, carefree and harmless. But have the girls who act on this heard also what the best medical and psychological authority has to say—that a first sex adventure can rarely be either casual or carefree to any normal girl? That it will not satisfy the mating instinct, but will only arouse it more powerfully, and fix it upon one individual? Most girls feel that there is a tie-up between sexual and spiritual experience, and associate sexual experience closely with the identity of the lover. But if the adventure is, as it very well may be, casual in fact to the boy in the case, who passes on to other conquests, the consequences to the girl can only be torments of jealousy, frustration and despair.

Such breaks and the resultant sense of inferiority and pain often make a women promiscuous. Not a voice of the slightest authority is raised for promiscuity. Doctors may and do differ in their vehemence as to what harm the premarital relation does, but as far as the harm of promiscuity is concerned, for either a woman or a man, they are completely agreed.

The promiscuous woman is usually in doubt of her own attractiveness and is seeking reassurance by repeated and varied experience with men. The fact of inferiority is also true of promiscuous men, who in such ways prove a virility which they secretly doubt. It is bad for a man who ultimately wants a happy home relation because he soon becomes neither romantic nor patient enough to give his wife satisfaction. Also, the promiscuous man or woman finds adjustment to monogamy almost impossible. An unchaste past is intrusive and a troublemaker. Sex loses charm, but the craving for satisfaction and the nervous search for it goes on. Promiscuity makes people lose the greatest experience in life—love.

It is all very well to say, "People look at these things differently today." They may look at them differently, but they feel about the same.

Jealousy, for example, is still very much alive. It is true that reason is having a quieting effect among well-bred people. But, on the other hand, it is reason itself which often argues with a man that if his wife was un-chaste before marriage, she has already destroyed certain inhibitions, which makes her more apt to be unfaithful. Psychologists say, too, that the promiscuous woman often suffers the most of all from jealousy.

Again, we cannot ignore man's preference for a virgin as wife. As to this we have the testimony of those who have built up records from cases. The preference is both modern and historic truth. Westermarck's *History of Marriage* bears testimony to that. Though boys of today may talk big and pretend to indifference, they still don't want the girl they love to have had previous possessors. So it is as true now as ever that in sacrificing chastity a girl may be gambling away her later chances of lifelong married happiness.

As a matter of fact, we have not so much that is new to add to what history teaches about sex. It is incorrect to say that we are reverting to savagery when sex conduct becomes lax. Among savage tribes, sex behavior was always subject to rules, though they were not like our own. What history very clearly reveals is that there have always been laws governing chastity. These are often the oldest primary laws, and infringement of them was subject to grave punishment because it presented complications of life and excited angers and conflicts which were bitter.

Unless sexual relations are to become disintegrating, there is always a necessity of trust between the individuals concerned. Such trust is usually not sustained after the first height of passion has been reached and passed, unless it is connected with the religion or the philosophy of man or woman—whatever ties the person up to life itself. It is not sentimental but hard fact that sex relationship either has to be connected with a moral code which is self-sustaining (and this is very rare indeed), or it has to be based on a belief that sexual relations involve a duty to the race as well as to the individual. Olga Knopf puts the case plainly when she says that "sexual relations are not private affairs alone. They are the concern of the whole of society."

That is what young people, those who are still only curious and those who are already on the defensive, should be helped to understand. Without scolding, or without minimizing the rights of individual love, it ought to be shown that though the laws involving marriage may be evaded and broken, they do exist and penalties are still exacted for their infraction.

Now if you could make the young couple in the back of the car or in the tourist cabin believe this in advance, nothing would be better. But how? The boy and girl are young, eager, and together. They have to be shown first of all that those who wish to control the mating instinct are by no means plotting against their attraction for each other, but against the influences that will do violence to their love—or what might in the end become love.

The thing to do is to help these young couples out, and, if their attraction is not casual, to encourage their marriage. As the authorities who were interviewed on this subject of chastity made their comments, the statement came again and again with repeated emphasis that the best solution was early marriage. This is not by any means synonymous with hasty marriage. But if a boy and a girl felt that they did not have to face an indefinite postponement of sex relations, their attitude would change. It is the hopelessness cast in their faces, the long gap between the awakening of their passion and its decently authorized expression which makes for rebellion against conventions and accepted rules.

We hear on all sides that economic conditions make early marriage difficult now. But it has never been very easy for young people to marry. Throughout history we see that parents have always had to help them out at the start. And modern parents, say those who know best, should be ready to do likewise; should encourage early marriage. But they should also frankly state the case for premarital chastity.

For there is, as we have seen, such a case. Men have devised no way of protecting the unchaste woman, except in some cases from childbearing and disease. She is in danger of moral and psychological breakdown. Unchastity gives the richest experience in life the poorest and most ignoble surroundings. It checks and stunts the development of love. It breeds lonely women and selfish men.

Finally, normal young men and women do not want unchastity. They are searching for an ethic to guide them. College investigations show that students believe in fidelity, want marriage. They want an emotional life with vitality in it, one that will wear. The case for chastity does not need much pleading before young people thus disposed. Given proper ideals, decent upbringing, half a chance, it is what girls and boys want.

Experts, doctors, psychologists and friends may advise. But they do not decide in the end. This is one of the social problems which is broken up into individual cases for decision. Out of this tangle of impulses, some of them inherited and some the product of immediate environment, the burden of the race as well as individual happiness is laid upon each boy and girl. The attitude toward chastity is as important a matter as may come to each one of them in a whole lifetime. That means that the effort of their elders should be to keep plainly before them all these scientific, spiritual and historical arguments for chastity which will strengthen their own normal resistance to the laxness they are aware of around them.

This Age of Ingenuity

HIGHWAYS of salt are now being built as the result of experiments by the International Salt Company of Ithaca, N. Y. The salt is either mixed with or inserted between layers of the road material and rolled to a firm surface. It draws moisture from the air and at the same time reduces the film of moisture around each particle of clay, so that the clay packs down harder. Once the salt has crystallized on the surface, the road sheds water during a rain and does not become slippery or muddy. It resists traffic abrasion to a marked degree. Salt roads can be built for around $450 a mile, whereas $1500 is the minimum cost for a mile of asphalt road. A highly successful one, connecting Ithaca with its new airport, has been in use for the past two years.—*Science News Letter*

FIREPROOF wood has been developed by a New Jersey manufacturer who impregnated red oak and maple in pressure tanks with ammonium salts which, when hot, release combustion-smothering gases. The treated wood is almost as easily tooled as ordinary wood, and takes varnish well. Testers from the National Board of Fire Underwriters created conflagration conditions in large chambers fired by gas nozzles. Although untreated walls went up in flames, the treated wood did not burn at all. When exposed to intense heat for long periods, it charred deeply, but did not produce appreciable flame or aid the spread of combustion.—*Time*

A Professor Quits the Communist Party

Condensed from Harper's Magazine

STUART BROWNE

As I look back on it now, I feel sure that when I joined the Communist Party, I believed myself a martyr in a noble cause. On our campus, salaries had been cut 35 percent, class hours increased—and even worse, we were subjected to vicious propaganda against professors in certain newspapers. We believed that the president of our university was secretly aiding the attack on our intellectual freedom. Faculty liberals organized to meet these conditions, and in one of the discussion groups I met a Communist leader. Through him I was led to speak at labor union meetings; gradually I talked myself into the Party.

When I joined, it seemed clear to me that united action by all liberal groups, under the leadership of the Communists, was needed lest Fascism sweep the country and university professors find themselves muzzled in America as effectively as they are in some European countries. I joined the Party because I believed it would foster and protect that precious freedom which we

Americans believe in. My Communist friend made me feel that I had at last become a man and not a cloistered parasite.

At the first meeting I found two other faculty men and their wives and eight other professional workers. We were classed as a professional unit, attached to a larger section made up of industrial workers. The Organizer explained to us how the United States was divided into 12 regions each ruled by a District Organizer, or D.O.; and each region divided into sections, with a Section Organizer and an Agitprop.

"What is an Agitprop?" I asked.

"He is the Comrade in charge of Agitation and Propaganda," said the Organizer. "He examines you in theory, indicates what you should read, takes care of your intellectual development."

"I am the Agitprop," said a little man with a hairline mustache.

I recognized him as a bookkeeper in a downtown furniture store. This bookkeeper, whose intellect had never impressed me when I made my monthly furniture payments,

385

would now have charge of my mental development.

Next came introductions by our new Party names (no Party member who wishes to be protected uses his real name). Everyone used the prefix Comrade. After that I was given my Party Book, and the Agitprop showed me how to figure my dues from a table in the back. My yearly salary was $3600. The scale of dues ranged from two cents a week for unemployed members, to $3.50 a week for me. To this was added extra levies for the International and for the American Party Convention. Then there were books, pamphlets, magazines and newspapers to buy, and once each year we contributed a day's salary to the *Daily Worker* drive.

In all, my financial obligation to the Party amounted to approximately $900 in two and one-half years. After I had been in the Party for a year I was forced to give up my usual two weeks' vacation trip. I discontinued membership in two historical associations, I stopped subscriptions to three magazines, I stopped buying books in my field.

Unit meetings were held in the homes of members, except where the wives were not Comrades. Every meeting had a conspiratorial undertone. Fascists were lurking in every corner of the city. If someone in the excitement of a discussion should raise his voice he was immediately hushed. If some innocent caller rang the doorbell a dead silence fell. I went through the first year without letting my wife know

I was a member. I had to lie about my absences from home. After I got well into the routine I was fortunate if I had two nights a week free to devote to my family.

I returned home at three o'clock one morning to find my wife sitting by the fire, crying.

"Please come here and talk to me," she said. "What is wrong? I have waited a long time for you to explain, until now I am desperate." After a brief pause she said softly, "Do you love someone else?"

Like a fool, I had never thought she would doubt my love. I told her I had joined the Party. We talked till dawn. I shall never forget the joy of the next few days as I moved free from the endless lies.

A week later my wife said, "If the Party is good enough for you it's good enough for me. If we have to lie and deceive, let's do it together." The Party accepted her, somewhat doubtful of her "political maturity," but the Agitprop promised to give her some special education.

At one of her first unit meetings she made some light, joking reference to Stalin's mustache. This remark produced a profound silence. She found that only Hitler, Roosevelt, and such people were subjects for jokes. "This is war, class war," said our Organizer, "and if we don't defend the Soviet Union we are traitors to the working-class movement."

That night, after I thought she was asleep, my wife suddenly burst into a fit of laughter. When I asked her what was so funny she answered, "Stalin's mustache. It's part of the working-class movement."

After my wife had been in the Party a month we were given a joint assignment. My wife's father owns a small factory employing nonunion labor. We were asked to get him to tell us what plans were being made by the executives in his factory to oppose unionization. Would the officers put up a fight? Whom were they planning to fire? These things we were to worm out of him while we sat as guests at his dinner table.

One day the Section Organizer came to my house asking me to contribute $20 to an emergency fund. A crisis had arisen. (Crises arise frequently in the Party.) I said I didn't have $20, very foolishly explaining: "This afternoon an old friend, whose wife is expecting a baby, asked me to loan him $50."

The Organizer's face grew red, "You gave him $50 and you deny $20 to the Party. That is not Bolshevist behavior."

"But he told me his wife's condition was critical and that she must be delivered in a hospital."

"I suppose," the Organizer said, "we can't expect middle-class ideology to adjust itself to the higher loyalty of the Party. I'd cheat my grandmother if it would further the cause of the revolution."

One of the "concentration tasks" of our unit was to raise money. At every meeting we discussed the names of well-to-do people who might be made to contribute to organizations existing only in the minds of Party members. We were asked to sponsor dinners, picnics, and excursions in the interests of workers and get people to contribute to these affairs. We were requested to have parties in our homes, charge our friends admission, and then turn the money over to the Party. In addition to exploiting our middle-class friends, we were to recruit Party members from the faculty. We did not have much luck. When I entered the unit there were 13 members. When I withdrew there were 16. We had recruited six and lost three.

The meetings droned on endlessly with rules, regulations and plans interspersed with laudatory testimonials of Party achievements in the past. I remember a typical meeting. We listened to a poorly written paper on Volume I of Webbs' *Soviet Communism*. We heard reports on the activities of the various Comrades, how one had gone to a Socialist meeting but had not seen fit to move anything; how another had attended a public meeting of the Women's Republican Club. This Comrade gave a long account of what the speaker had said. The report was as monotonous as it was painstakingly accurate (the speech had been expertly reported in the daily press three days before). So we went round the circle.

Tiresome as the average politician may be, he is a wonder of ingenious perspicacity when contrasted to the Communist Party leader. The Communist leaders fit a pattern more perfectly than any other human beings I have ever known. They are all dogmatic, and move in an atmosphere of humorless sanctity. If a Comrade disagrees with a D.O. he is told about his error and the "true line" is explained to him. If he still persists in opposition he is assigned to a study unit where he is instructed in Marx and Lenin. No evangelist ever pointed with greater pride to a Bible text than do the Party leaders to the text of Marx as amended by Lenin and practiced by Stalin.

In their last campaign for Browder, the Party leaders devoted their whole energy to defeating Landon. This was following the Party line as laid down by Comrade Dimitroff. But one man persisted in saying that if the Party wanted Roosevelt elected, why didn't they say so, instead of beating about the bush. He was summoned to a hearing, in which the judges did all the talking. The man stuck to his point. "Furthermore," he said, "I am going to vote for Roosevelt."

A hushed silence fell over the group. I felt as though we were in Moscow and this man a wrecker and a spy whose doom would be execution. At last the D.O. spoke. "Turn in your book. From now on you are no longer a member of the Party." I wiped my brow and went over to the window. The sun was shining on a familiar American city. At that moment I admitted to myself for the first time that I wished I were out of the Party.

Our withdrawal was a little sad, a sort of weary cessation of useless activity. When I notified our Unit Organizer he looked disturbed, then asked me to come to the unit meeting and explain. I replied that I didn't think he would want me to tell the group what my objections were.

I outlined them to him: "The rigorous routine, the stifling of individual initiative, the inevitable deception which forces one to live in two worlds, disturb my peace of mind. I have lost contact with my old friends, and those in the Party have no time for friendship. I have no time to read the books and magazines that are nonpartisan, that give joy and adventure to reading. My intellectual life has become dull. The solemnity with which the Party treats every problem weighs upon my spirit. I cannot believe that the revolution is imminent. Yet every unit meeting is as serious as though it were held in a cellar in Madrid. The interference with my personal liberty is no longer endurable to me. I used to enjoy the feeling, when I entered a voting booth, that no one, in spirit or in fact, went with me. As a Communist I have had to vote according to the *line* laid down for me and all Communists by the Seventh World Congress in Moscow. These are a few of the reasons why I must withdraw."

In the silence that followed I could not help wondering why I had stayed in the Party so long. I suppose I was ashamed to admit defeat; I did not want to be a quitter. For a long time I tried to believe that the Party could organize an effective protest against the worst aspects of labor exploitation. As time passed, I felt certain that the Party leaders aimed at creating a strike situation for its own sake, and not primarily in order to gain advantages for the workers. The Party wins, according to its theory, even though the individual worker may lose, because strikes and more strikes bring the day of revolution nearer. The idea of all workers united in a common cause had appealed to me; but when I realized that my activities were furthering a dictatorship, with the name of democracy used as bait for the un-wary, the one hope that had supported me was lost.

My friend sat staring out the window. It was a long time before he answered.

"Did you bring your book?"

"Yes, and I also brought my wife's. You don't want me to come to the unit meeting, then?"

"No, I think it best to accept your books today."

I joined the Communist Party in the interests of freedom, and I withdrew in order to be once more free.

Honorable Mention

PEOPLE WITH A PURPOSE

U. S. HIGHWAY 1, which carries the bulk of the auto traffic to Florida from the North, also carries large numbers of thumb-and-foot travelers, most of whom are honest and industrious but down on their luck. Young Bradley King, whose father's farm is on U. S. 1 near Wise, North Carolina, sought a way to help these transients. Nine years ago he built two cabins which cost, in addition to his own labor, and materials which were available on the farm, $1.75, not including furnishings. Each cabin contains a bunk, a homemade dresser, a stove, a lamp and a chair; bedding is changed and the cabin disinfected after each guest. It is beyond King's means to furnish food or loans except in the most extreme cases, but down-and-out travelers can always count on a night's rest and a shave. A reporter's reference to his roadside shelter as "Hobo's Haven" once brought a sharp rebuke from King. His guests are not hoboes by choice, he says, but are victims of circumstance.

WILLIE LEE BUFFINGTON, a white millworker of Edgefield, South Carolina, had a capital of only ten cents, but he wanted to found a library for his negro friends. With the ten cents he purchased five two-cent stamps, and wrote to five local people he didn't know, asking for books. If they couldn't furnish books, said his letter, would they please refund a stamp, so he could write to somebody else? One of his letters brought a thousand books, and with these as an incentive, Buffington and his friends built a log-cabin library. In the backwoods, there is more lumber than anything else, and as more books came in, more cabins were built to house them. Today there are four Buffington log-cabin libraries, all of them doing a thriving business with a negro clientele.

The Man Who Did Something About It

By

WILLIAM SEABROOK

HE'S A SANDY, ordinary-looking little man, in every respect, except for a round bump in the middle of his forehead —as if God had tagged him with a humorous outstretched finger and said, "You're It."

His papa tried to make a concert violinist of him, but he could never "get hot" on the violin. He "got hot" later, however, on something else, and has been burning for 20 years with one of the strangest self-imposed jobs in the world. He stops people from stuttering. He is Dr. James Sonnett Greene of the National Hospital for Speech Disorders at 126 East 30th Street, New York; and when Lucius N. Littauer gave him a quarter of a million to enlarge his clinic, I went to see him.

He was busy, so I wandered into a hall in the basement where two children were playing. Fatty, in knickers and polo shirt, was an explosive stutterer. Skinny, in overalls, was an outboard or machine-gun stutterer. Later Dr. Greene sauntered in, stuck his hands in his pockets and glared at his two Huckleberry Finns. "Hi, Doc!" said Skinny by way of a polite good morning, and dragged Fatty off for a game of checkers.

I had never seen Dr. Greene before, but he treated me as if I had merely come back from a stroll round the block. He is a dynamic man, with a mind hard as nails and a heart as soft as a kitten. He takes everything tremendously seriously, but laughs a thousand times a day. The force of his personality is terrific, yet he has no more dignity than a puppy.

I said, "Doc, how'd you ever come to specialize in stutterers?" He told me. His father, a well-to-do merchant, finally decided that the boy was no musician and sent him to Cornell to study medicine.

"So about 30 years ago," he continued, "a young doctor hung out his shingle in New York. I began to wonder how I'd pay the rent, when finally my first patient came— an unhappy young man who wanted to be cured of *stuttering!* I had never heard of stutterers being treated by doctors. A stutterer just kept on stuttering or 'grew out of it.'"

The young man was desperate, wanted to be operated on. Dr.

Greene sent him away, and began to read everything he could find about speech disorders—which wasn't much. He wrote the young man, and a few days later a little old lady, in mourning, came to tell him it was too late. Her son was dead. He had "fallen" off a roof.

"That was my first patient," said Dr. Greene, "and you can imagine how it ate into me. I moped, worried, studied, pondered. I learned that there were more than a million stutterers in the United States, many of them unhappy and a burden because they couldn't hold their jobs. I thought, 'Somebody ought to do something about it.'

"Of course, it never occurred to me that I might be 'somebody,' but when I went to Jena and Berlin for graduate study I worked with Dr. Gutzmann, who had a speech disorder clinic. I learned that stuttering was not basically a speech defect, but a nervous maladjustment of the whole personality. Your stutterer hasn't really got a twisted tongue; he's worried about something—often unconsciously, of course. He suffers from an anxiety neurosis.

"Well, I came back to America still thinking that somebody ought to do something about it. And one day the notion occurred to me that I might be that somebody. I had no funds, my father had done all he could, and I went to see an old friend, the late Dr. George Parker."

Dr. Parker gave him a check for $1000, and on that gambled shoestring Dr. Greene opened the first free clinic for speech disorders in New York. It was small, and patients were poor. He had set-backs, heartbreaks, failures—but he began to stop people from stuttering.

In 1920 he cured the late Albert Bigelow Paine, Mark Twain's biographer, who had stuttered so badly he had been forced to move because he could never ask for a railroad ticket to his home in Mamaroneck.

Mr. Paine, already famous as an author, blossomed out as a speaker, told people and organizations about the little miracle man. That same year he and Dr. Greene founded *Talk*, the first monthly magazine for stutterers, and through it awakened public interest. Dr. Greene's is still the only clinic in New York and one of the few in the country where stutterers can get free treatment, but schools, universities and practitioners are now treating speech disorders, and the American Speech Correction Association is broadening its work each year.

Dr. Greene has had other famous patients but he still gets his biggest kick out of curing patients who have lost their jobs because they stutter, and who can't pay him anything. He helps get jobs for them, treats them at the same time, and finally sends them out under their own steam. At his large but still too small clinic, there are as many as 200 patients a day, 1000 applicants a week.

I visited a class of a dozen grown-up stutterers, three of them young ladies. A big motto on the wall said, "SLOW, EASY," and the teacher kept telling them to speak slowly, calmly, rhythmically. "We'll hear from the Kingfish now," said the teacher, and a grinning young North Carolina farmer, actually in overalls, drawled:

"Ah think ah want to talk to you this morning about—porpoises." The teacher, the whole class and Dr. Greene broke into laughter. The Kingfish stood grinning, took his time and told us about porpoises. He stuttered in spots, but not much. Once his cheeks began to swell out as he was trying to say "porpoise" and Dr. Greene said, "Hey, Kingfish, are you blowing a trumpet?"

The boy laughed, relaxed, and finished his talk. "Why, in God's name," I whispered, "did he pick porpoises?"

"He has trouble with his p's," said Dr. Greene. "We don't encourage them to invent difficulties, but we let them, if they wish."

Dr. Greene writes solemn pieces for medical journals, in which he says that stuttering is an affliction, and that you don't laugh at cripples, but an outstanding characteristic of the clinic and of Dr. Greene himself is an amiable, ever-present sense of humor. One way of relieving tension is to break it with something that brings a smile.

In spite of the casual air Dr. Greene's personality lends, all this is part of the carefully practiced method of therapy which he has worked out in 20 years treating thousands of stutterers. At the outset a phonograph record is made of the new patient's speech. (Later, when he is discharged, a similar record is made of his new voice on the reverse side.) A physician examines the patient and he has every attention which might improve the physical basis for clear speech.

Surgical measures are rarely necessary. Manipulation, massage, and electrical treatment are at times employed—as, for example, in treating falsetto voices—but for the most part defective speech is treated as a symptom which will disappear when the underlying anxiety is removed. Physical obstructions to speech are reduced chiefly by teaching the student to relax and coördinate, to bring his emotions under the command of intelligence. The whole personality of the stutterer is reorganized.

Private consultations are available, but much of the work is done in groups. The stutterers are much more at ease, and hence learn better, when in a group of others similarly afflicted, than when tensely alone with a teacher. In one room, a class of grown-ups reads with the teacher in unison; in other rooms they hold group conversations, put on impromptu plays and do choral singing. There are classes also in calisthenic exercises to music, since stutterers frequently stutter in other ways besides speech.

In another part of the building there is a speech kindergarten—a room with fairyland decorations on the wall, filled with toys and sand boxes with happy or earnest little faces bending over them. Teachers are gay as well as patient, and the tots are having fun while undergoing treatment.

That night I went to the general meeting in the auditorium. The place was crowded. A piano sounded opening chords, and the congregation sang *Sweet and Low*. The presiding stutterer called on stutterers in the audience to come up on the platform and do their stuff.

A patient who had quit high school because he couldn't recite in classes and who was now back in high school, told about a recent boat ride to Bear Mountain. When he told about the light that came through the trees and of "basking in its seductive shimmer," his audience applauded and roared.

With us at this riot was a Yale psychiatrist, Dr. Ernest G. Lion, who was studying methods in connection with a clinic his department plans. When we got out I said, "What did you think of it?" and he said, "Marvelous."

I've been asking myself the effect of all this in the light of the now universal agreement that stuttering is a manifestation of emotional disorder, involving fear. (The use of the right hand by a naturally left-handed person may have a bearing on individual cases, but the idea that it might be a key to the whole problem is now exploded.)

The objections to any "cure" which does not completely eradicate the neurosis are that stuttering may return later, or that the neurosis may shift to some even more harmful field. But apparently Dr. Greene feels that a stutterer who has been stopped from stuttering is more likely to conquer his neurosis than if he went on spluttering until some psychoanalyst told him it was safe to stop.

Dr. Greene is as proud of his pupils as a missionary who has converted savages. And patients talked to me as if they had gone through a deep religious experience. One, a stuttering machinist 15 years ago, was not only cured, but turned into a minister. He says, "It completely changed my life."

Dr. Greene, besides being a pioneer, has been stopping more stutterers than any other doctor or hospital to which patients may go for free treatment. Last year he treated more than 2200 cases of speech disorder and is said to have rehabilitated more than 24,000 sufferers in all. He is helping people, and getting a deep joy out of it. He has a lot of fun, but it goes deeper than that with him. He is not a religious man in any orthodox sense, and yet he is one of the most deeply religious men I have ever known.

Table Talk

IF YOU have never tried applesauce and apple pie made with maple, or part maple, sugar, you had better get busy.

BONELESS frog legs ready to fry are being packed in cans.

—Printers' Ink

What Every Citizen Should Know

Condensed from a Columbia Broadcast

THOMAS E. DEWEY

IT HAS BEEN said that crime in this country costs more than the annual federal budget. Something has happened which is in desperate need of earnest public attention.

Thirty years ago, business was just growing into large organizations. Now with big industries, increasing attention is given to the regulation of banking, corporate business and the sale of securities. Workmen's Compensation was unknown 30 years ago. Unemployment insurance, Old Age Relief and many other progressive measures are recognized as necessary in a country which has become highly organized.

Unfortunately, however, the regulation of modern crime has been given little attention indeed! Thirty years ago there was no organized crime. The American criminal was a free lance. He was a small-time burglar or pickpocket. True, once in a long time some robber or band of robbers became famous. There were even small-time gangs in some of our large cities. They shook down pushcart merchants and neighborhood shops and they were known as toughs. But their organization was loose—the leader was just the toughest man in the gang.

In these 30 years crime too has grown into a national industry. Today we have criminal syndicate; with interests in many cities. They are rich and powerful, and have brains even more than brawn. There are few illegal enterprises which have not become a part of the empire of organized crime.

It is just as foolish to think only about the man who commits the act of violence as it is to regard the left end of a football team as the whole team. Every large criminal organization which my office has prosecuted has been set up like an industrial enterprise, with department heads and a strong-arm squad and lawyers who advise in every act. Each department has its own job. One without the other would not be successful.

There is, of course, the president of the organization, otherwise known as a "big shot" gangster. He

394

lives in the best hotels, conferring with subordinates. He would not think of doing a criminal job himself. Quite frequently he is married and has children who play with your children in the parks. One important gangster whom I prosecuted had two sons in good private schools.

When our present methods of prosecution were developed, it was the accepted idea that to catch the criminal and imprison him served the dual purpose of warning others and of punishing the guilty man. That is still true of the criminal who operates alone. It is the furthest thing from the truth when you are dealing with any kind of organized crime. The arrest and conviction of the dope peddler may be inconvenient, and it costs the syndicate money. But unless the whole gang who imported those narcotics is caught, the flow of drugs into this country is not for one moment interfered with. More than that, the arrest and conviction of that dope peddler conveys the general impression that law enforcement is effective, giving a false feeling of security to the public.

In any racket, we may find the man who threw the stink bomb or the man who made the threat or the man who took the money on the extortion. We may even catch the murderer. And what have we got when he is caught? In every case it has been my experience that we have only the front man, a salaried worker in the vineyard of crime. His arrest and conviction may cost his bosses a little money to provide lawyers and appeals. It will cost them something for his pin money while he is in jail. It will not stop the racket.

Worse than that, the continued support and help of the gang for the man who is caught may actually encourage others to go into crime when they see that the bosses go free and will help their hired men when they are caught.

It is important enough to catch the burglar who robs your home, but if we stop there, others will take his place because the receiver of the stolen goods—the "fence"—is the backbone of the business. So long as the "fence" is in business, there are plenty of recruits to continue to steal and sell their stolen goods to him for a fraction of their value.

It is clear, therefore, that we can no longer be satisfied with the conviction of the man who committed the crime. In many cases he is young, and if he can be forced to break with his old habits, he can be reformed and made into a useful citizen. Thousands of petty offenders can be imprisoned and the total result may be that men who could have been reformed are made into confirmed criminals. A completely new emphasis and purpose of law enforcement must be achieved. There is only one way to stamp out crime. Every case must be the steppingstone to get at the real man behind the scenes. The little fellow should be urged to testify against his master and, of course, he must then be protected and helped. For this there are two major reasons: First, it accomplishes the real result of getting the important men. Second, once a criminal has been persuaded in his own self-interest to take the side of society, experience shows that he is unlikely to return to crime. More than that, he becomes an outcast from the criminal underworld. Thus, not only is a petty criminal removed from the service of his masters but he is also likely to find that he must turn to making an honest living whether he wants to or not.

The time has come when citizens must insist upon a thorough revision of the machinery of law enforcement. You can quickly recognize the new approach when it appears. No longer will you be told of the number of petty criminals who have been marched into jails and then out again, the worse for the experience. You will hear then that those minor criminals who have in the past been regarded as the final objective of law enforcement have become of real help to the community. You will hear that they are put on probation and given the aid of society in reward for their services, and you may also hear of their ultimate rehabilitation in society. You will no longer hear of special drives on a particular type of crime. Instead you will hear of petty criminals regularly turning state's evidence and coming over to the side of the people; of the arrest and indictment of their masters, and of the use of the accumulated information by prosecuting officers to wipe out whole combines of crime. When these things happen you will know that your homes and your children are safer and that real progress is being made in combating our criminal problem.

Honorable Mention

PEOPLE WITH A PURPOSE

THE FACT that Hawaii is well populated with brilliantly plumaged songbirds is due, not to accident, but to Hui Manu, an organization formed six years ago by Mrs. F. J. Lowrey. When Mrs. Lowrey first undertook her work, the rare tropic birds which were once indigenous only to Hawaii had almost entirely disappeared. Hui Manu went about its work quietly, studying the song, plumage and habits of birds which were candidates for importation, and ruling out any which were likely to become destructive pests. From the mainland have come Kentucky cardinals, southern mockingbirds, indigo and nonpareil buntings, Brazilian cardinals, Japanese bluebirds and many other attractive varieties. They have been liberated in the districts most suited to them, and all have thrived in the natural bird paradise of Hawaii. The work is financed by bimonthly tourists trips to private gardens in Honolulu.

A Way to Chastity:

A LETTER FROM DONALD CULROSS PEATTIE

October 18, 1937

SIRS: The whole country has been talking about "The Case For Chastity," the article written by my friend and neighbor, Margaret Banning, which appeared in the August issue of The Reader's Digest. It is heartening to have someone argue this case, above all a woman known for her good works and her high ideals.

But it strikes me that Mrs. Banning's article is composed of exactly the same old don'ts that have been used on young people since the time of Solomon, with what degree of success I leave her own appalling figures on venereal disease and illegitimacy to speak. At best she seems to say that chastity pays, in dividends of health and respectability.

In college I knew a few friends who confessed to a regular and unrepentant looseness of living. But any one of them could offer practical suggestions that would take the thunder out of our threats. The prophylaxis of disease and the prevention of pregnancy, while not absolutely sure, are, in the hands of the skillful, a great deal surer than crossing the street in traffic. So that of the pursuing Furies there remains nothing for the expert sinner but social censure. A frail gesture! When I was a boy a divorced woman, even from a drunken husband, was an object of suspicion. Behold the change in a score of years! Social censure has never trampled on a young man's wild oats. Now we seem to be coming to tolerate it when a girl casts a little of this cereal about her, provided she reaps the crop deftly.

But Mrs. Banning would not be so exercised about chastity if it were anything less than a principle at stake. Chastity *is* important, because it is right. And because it is beautiful, and something in which to take a pride such as nothing else can give you.

Yes, I hear the jeers: "Try to tell that to young people nowadays!" But that is just the thing I *have* told them on occasion. And the response would astound the cynics.

For if you catch them young enough, young people are longing to be told that to be good is worth it. They only ask you to give them a retort to the whispers of the cynical that because ideals hang high they are sour grapes. They are grateful to you when you tell them, honestly, something out of your best experience. Secretly youngsters hunger after plain old-fashioned advice, palatably served. They are too busy living, with pounding pulses and flying hair, to be quite sure of themselves.

Early they meet forks in the road; swiftly they make their choice. If you don't like the choice, you will blame everybody—except yourself for having kept quiet when you might have spoken out. But you were shy; you didn't think they would listen; they talked so knowingly that you thought they knew more than you! So the brave, the unashamed, the beautiful thing, died.

To fight against the temptations of sexual wrongdoing, youth must be armed with something stronger than fear; Mrs. Banning has shown that this is not enough. I do not mean that I would hide any of her facts. They ought to be discussed and expounded to youth, coolly and impersonally. But not in the same breath with love.

Yes, love. This is the thing that is stronger than fear, stronger than shame. This is the thing we ought to talk about. Anybody who is here beginning to be embarrassed for me, may go off and blush in the corner.

How easy it is to lead youth to die for an ideal upon the advice of their elders, the cemeteries in France declare. It should not be more difficult to persuade a young man that chastity is an experience he owes himself, as well as owing some of its spiritual and bodily integrity to his bride and his babies. There are of course some boys, never trained to any sort of self-discipline, from whom it is already too late to expect any response to these ideas. And some girls also. There have always been such, and the blame for them can be laid squarely at the parental door. But are you going to hold up for the rest nothing in chastity to admire and desire? Are you going to do no better than threaten them with the awful consequences of getting caught? Are you going to fail, because you didn't even try, because "you can't tell that to young people nowadays?"

I have three sons, and I suppose it will only be known twenty years from now whether I am teaching them wisely. I shall tell them all the accepted "facts of life" as a matter of routine. But I shall consider that my job in their amatory training has not even begun at that stage.

My ideal is to make my sons good lovers, for love and chastity are facets of the same stone. And that is something that needs to be said all the time, particularly in an age when cynics are proclaiming that there is no such thing as romantic love and that it is only a silly Victorian gloss spread over a purely glandular urge. And purely a personal affair, in no way concerning society or (so maintain the worldly wise) involving responsibility.

But to a young lover, such a philosophy is beyond redemption. For the young lover, of either sex, understands that chastity is his personal Constitution, his covenant with love itself.

I have said that I want my sons to be good lovers, because the lover is, voluntarily and naturally, chaste. It is a corollary, of course, to this proposition, that I want my sons to be chaste because I want them to be good lovers. For I honestly believe that chastity on both sides before marriage is worth far more than any advantages possessed by the previously experienced lover.

When I say I want my sons to be good lovers I do not mean skillful seducers, or perennial ladies' men. By good lovers I mean good husbands. And something better than settled, faithful, and patient husbands. Someone, in short, who can make love well enough to get his wife to feeling like the Duchess of Windsor just when she knows she must be looking like the Witch of Endor. Somebody who slips a loving hand just under the weight of her heart, and so makes it perpetually feel a little lighter than it really is.

The father of my young boys is busy, even now, in showing them, directly and indirectly, that he thinks womankind is sacred. Their mother is teaching them how not to be led around on a string by some snippy little chit. Blending humor and boldness with sincerity, we parents hope to train these three so that they will instinctively search

out the best, and never be content with anything less. Chastity, in this quest of the best, is no galling yoke and will never, in our home, be presented as such; it is in itself, rather, a Christian grace and source of manly pride, a feather in the cap of him who wears it.

I hope that my boys fall genuinely in love early, and stay in love —the best protection for their chastity. I shall not pretend that it is an easy thing to keep. Few of the best things in life are come by easily. Most take years of self-discipline and application. It is precisely the element of the difficult about chastity that puts the high value on it, and I am counting on my children's understanding this, because they are not moral softies who give up if a thing requires any exertion. They are learning right now that the rights of others have to be considered, that deprivations have to be borne uncomplainingly, and that every privilege carries responsibility with it. So that I shall not be springing on them, in mid-adolescence, a self-discipline for which they have never been prepared.

But they shall be armed with something less negative than admonitions to refrain, with something prouder than mere caution for their health and reputations.

First I am going to present the sheerly biological case for chastity —by itself a good one. In plain language, which youngsters prefer, sexual intercourse is every time and always an act of mating. With intent of children or without, with ring and book or without, it still is the same final act. It always implies some choice of a sexual partner; preceded by love-making, it is followed by deep inner consequences in the souls and bodies of both communicants.

I am not passing any superior moral judgments on the lovers who, now and in past ages, have dispensed with bells and rice. But I am talking about the great sex instinct, with which we are all born. Instincts are divine commands of the race to the individual. The self-preservation instinct says: Thou shalt not let thyself die, neither starve, nor fall off things, nor contract diseases. The maternal instinct commands the mother to think first of her children. The sex instinct propels us to seek a mate; mating is its only aim, and everything connected with sex has no other meaning.

But man, I am going to go on to say to my sons, is not a thoughtless beast. Man stands up and directs his destiny. He cannot permanently deny the sexual instinct, nor should he, but he can pick his time and his partner. And if he cannot even perform so agreeable a task as this decently, he has every reason to be ashamed of himself. For life, I am going to repeat often to my sons, is holy ground, and we should all walk here with some reverence, grateful for the short time that we are allotted to till that ground and, mastering it, make it bear us fruit.

And that fruit is our children. So that it matters to a man not only out of whose womb they are going to be born, but also what sort of a father gives his blood to their blood. It is hardly reasonable of a man who "tore around" nightly for 10 or 15 years before he settled down to marriage with a decent girl, to be astounded if he should have a daughter with morals no better than his own. It need not surprise him, if he once succumbed to a wishy-washy girl and had to marry her, if she gives him wishy-washy sons. Such sons and daughters come by their qualities quite honestly, and their parents cannot reproach them.

I shall remind my sons that each one of them is the converging point of a vast number of hereditary lines. When they choose a girl they choose more than an armful of sweetness. They choose her family, living and all the way back.

And they are making this fateful choice, for all they know, when they are not proposing marriage at all but just trying a little experiment. Almost parenthetically, because I expect my children to be as sensible and decent as most young people, I shall remark that it is playing with fire to start intimacies; for after a certain point there is no turning back, and that point is reached far sooner than expected due to the fact that in sex pleasure-hunting one has always to go a little farther than the last time to revive the original thrill. I shall point out that the "easy girl" has lost the habit of faithfulness and never acquired the habits of wifely love. And the young man who doffs his chastity with a scornful laugh for it may not find that light and shining garment again.

I do not mean that one misstep must damn soul or body; I would certainly not want my boys to think that their parents would not forgive anything and try to understand. But missteps in love are steps going down, and everybody knows it in his heart. They lead down into bitter regrets that don't mend the situation, into shuddering revulsion that the chaste lover never has to know, into a hardening of the spiritual arteries, a relentless soul-coarsening.

It is possible, for a very strong and determined spirit, to climb back up those steps again and scrape himself clean. But strong and determined souls are not, usually, the ones who can be persuaded to descend in the first place. They are the ones who have generally kept their chastity. And while it is kept, the rapture and the pride of sex remain enthroned.

Cordially yours,
DONALD CULROSS PEATTIE

How Doyousayit?

I WAS STARTLED recently when my little granddaughter demanded insolently "*Whose* bookisthis?" The child is not an insolent baggage, and I stared at her in amazement. Then it came to me that what she really wanted to say was "Whose *book* is this?" or perhaps "Whose book *is* this?"

The style of asking a question with the accent entirely on the first word of a sentence seems to be growing. To an old-fashioned person like myself it is strangely offensive to have a question fired point-blank: "*What* isyourname? *Where* doyoulive? *What* wereyoudoing?" And one would shudder to think that Juliet, leaning on the balcony, might have murmured, "*What's* inaname?"

The accenting of words in a sentence is a much more difficult affair than the accenting of syllables in a word; yet a carelessly accented sentence will go as far toward branding you illiterate and uncultured as a badly accented word. It is a matter that receives far too little attention in American speech.—*Atlantic Monthly*

Take Your Profits from Defeat

Condensed from The Forum

WILLIAM MOULTON MARSTON

IF THERE IS any single factor that makes for success in living, it is the ability to draw dividends from defeat. Every success I know has been reached because the person was able to analyze defeat and actually profit by it in his next undertaking. If you confuse defeat with failure, then you are doomed indeed to failure. For it isn't defeat that makes you fail; it is your own refusal to see in defeat the guide and incentive to success.

Defeats are nothing to be ashamed of. They are routine incidents in the life of every man who achieves. But defeat is a dead loss unless you do face it without humiliation, analyze it and learn why you failed to make your objective. If you look upon defeat in the light of a friendly tipster, it ceases to be mortifying, and the task of analyzing its causes within yourself becomes both interesting and profitable.

Defeat, in other words, can help to cure its own cause. Hiram Kimball, a middle-aged New Englander, inherited his uncle's bookshop, which had been modestly success-

ful for more than 20 years. Fired with ambition to modernize and expand the business, Hiram leased a new corner, put in a larger stock, advertised extensively and doubled his overhead. A couple of years later he was bankrupt.

Defeat left Kimball with the firsthand experience he had previously lacked and a lot of secondhand books the receivers had been unable to sell. He put defeat to work. He built a shack with his own hands on a much-traveled highway and spread his old books all over the place invitingly. Results came with surprising promptness. Secondhand books, as Hiram well knew, are gateways to mental adventure which few passers-by can refrain from exploring. In three seasons he made twice the money he had lost. His defeat equipped him for a satisfying and original success.

Not only does defeat prepare us for success, but nothing can arouse within us such a compelling desire to succeed. The desire to dominate is the first of four primary emotions to appear. If you let a baby grasp a rod and try to pull it away he will cling more and more tightly until his whole weight is suspended. It is this same reaction which should give you new and greater strength every time you are defeated. If you exploit the power which defeat gives, you can accomplish with it far more than you are capable of when all is serene.

John Paul Jones stood on the shot-torn deck of the *Bon Homme Richard*. The *Alliance* had deserted him. He was raked fore and aft by cruel fire from British men-o'-war. The *Richard* began to sink. John Paul was a beaten man. But when the British commander asked Jones to surrender, a fighting fury of defeat suddenly boiled over in the American. Said he, "I have not yet begun to fight." He rammed his waterlogged ship against the nearest British vessel, grappled and boarded her, and in no time at all the fight was over. From the bitterness of defeat, John Paul Jones drew a conqueror's spirit which assured him victory.

Heroes are often made in moments of defeat. Theodore Roosevelt, who insisted on finishing a political speech after a would-be assassin had pumped a revolver bullet into his breast, got that way by virtue of a good licking he took as a terrified boy. T. R. made up his exceedingly dominant mind that he would learn to box, to shoot, to play tough games with the best of them and to give more than he received. He carried out his resolution because he had the impetus of defeat behind him.

Once you have analyzed defeat, you perceive a specific obstacle to climb over instead of a vague, terrifying bogeyman of imagined inferiority which is likely to leap upon you at every step of your next effort.

I know a man who suffered very unpleasant consequences from a love affair. The experience conditioned his whole life; it induced in him a fear of women which expresses itself in running away or turning in upon himself when they are present. To everybody but himself this fellow's phobia is amusing. But for him it is real and painful. Instead of facing his love defeat, analyzing its real causes and taking profits in future relationships, he is beaten by one reverse.

It will pay you to search your own behavior for stupidities of this type and get rid of them. There are people who have lost their jobs who are afraid to ask for work; people rebuffed when they sought a raise who are afraid now to speak to the boss; mothers whose children almost drowned who will not permit them to go into the water to learn to swim. Any fear of defeat which you do not possess will impress you as ridiculous. But the chances are you have a pet defeat of your own from which you run away with equal unreasonableness.

People try in many ways to disguise the fact that they are running away. The simplest trick is to tell yourself that you are not defeated, that you are making satisfactory progress when, as a matter of fact, you are completely blocked. I know a man who tries to keep his self-confidence by continually telling himself and his friends that he is about to get a promotion. His underconsciousness isn't fooled; he knows well enough that he long ago reached the limit of advancement in his present position. Actually he is losing confidence in himself with every pathetic attempt to cover up defeat.

Another trick some people play on themselves is to "forget" their defeats. There might be merit in this method if it were psychologically possible to amputate unpleasant memories. But it isn't. All you can do is repress them. Experiences thus buried throw off emotional poisons, fears, depressions, hatreds, antisocial feelings. They cause not only mental disorders but physical sicknesses. And instead of bolstering up your self-confidence, such a complex will in time destroy it completely.

If the shock of an imagined failure has numbed you for the moment so that you cannot think clearly, go out on a party, chop down a tree, punch a heavy bag; do something violent and unusual. Then sleep for a while. When you wake up you will find that your brain is thinking hard and fast. Now is the time to spot your profits and make your comeback. Note particularly the false values, the silly, futile desires which this temporary setback has stripped away. Then set your fundamental desires to work, free from the encumbrances which defeat has revealed to you. For this profit alone, defeat is worth while. Put all your resentment into a thrust toward your goal. If defeat releases inside of you an unbeatable dominance, nothing can keep you from success on your next attempt.

Models of Brevity

An Englishman told his son at school that he was too busy to read long letters and requested him to be brief. The boy replied: "S.O.S., £.s.d., R.S.V.P."—Dean Inge,
Lay Thoughts of a Dean (Putnam)

Representative Maury Maverick replied to a five-page attack by a constituent: "Dear Sir: Ph-f-f-ft.
"Yours very truly."
—*The Forum*

Sir Herbert Beerbohm Tree, to a would-be dramatist: "My dear Sir: I have read your play. Oh, my dear Sir!
"Yours faithfully."
—*The Albatross Book of English Letters*

Bernard Shaw one day received an invitation from a celebrity hunter: "Lady X will be at home Thursday between four and six."
The author returned the card; underneath he had written: "Mr. Bernard Shaw likewise."—*Neues Wiener Tagblatt*

One Way Out of Our Tax Troubles

Condensed from Fortune

WHEN the average American can talks of reducing taxes he usually means reducing federal taxes. In so doing he is barking up the wrong tree. For barely over eight percent of his income goes to federal taxes, while he pays some 12 percent to a confused agglomeration of state and local governments—chiefly to counties, cities, townships, school districts, all the way down to mosquito-abatement districts. The number of these overlapping taxing units the country over amounts to the incredible sum of 175,000!

And anyone who wants to find waste and inefficiency on a grand scale should look at these jigsaw puzzles of government by which local affairs are run. He should watch the states fight among themselves over sources of revenue—at the taxpayer's expense. For not only is the bulk of the U. S. tax burden imposed by the states and their little subdivisions; also most of the *unnecessary* part of that burden—from the standpoint of a reasonable price for services performed—can be laid to the states and the localities.

Moreover, though many costly services that used to be handled by states and localities are now being taken over by the federal government, local taxes have not decreased. Unemployment relief used to be handled locally. Road building, once a chief reason for local taxes, is receiving more and more federal funds. There are other "public works"—buildings, sewers, parks— which used to be paid for out of local taxes and to which the U. S. Treasury now contributes a larger and larger share. Yet local taxes have not gone down.

For a miniature of local taxation, look at Brighton School District No. 1, in Monroe County, N. Y. Within that single school district there are over 60 taxing authorities ranging from 21 pavement districts and 11 lighting districts through many garbage, ash and hydrant districts. These overlap in such a way as to create 114 different tax zones —each zone paying to a different combination of districts.

Illinois contains more taxing units

than any other state: 17,336. But Missouri has 11,626; New York, 11,184; Michigan, 8905—and so on all over the country.

It is easy to see that this duplication of government services and officials means waste to the taxpayer. For instance, Macon County, Ill., saved $800,000 in 15 years merely by abolishing its superfluous township tax collectors.

The simple answer to the problem of our wasteful tax structure is centralization of taxes. For instance, each state could collect all property taxes within its borders, so that property would be taxed just once at a uniform rate—instead of several times, as now, at varying rates by different districts. States could be sensibly split into non-overlapping cities and counties. Enough money could be turned over by the state to each city and county to take care of the government services best handled locally. The local tax mess would disappear; the cost of local government, stripped of wasteful duplications, would go down; taxes would not only become simpler but immeasurably lower.

Mincing steps toward centralization have been taken by a few states—notably Wisconsin, Kentucky and North Carolina. But the big barrier to centralization is the tenacity of local political jobholders, who well know that the savings of centralization would be at their expense.

Overlapping of federal with state taxation lays another unfair burden on the taxpayer. Of the nine chief sources of state revenue—taxes on gasoline, liquor, tobacco, death bequests, personal income, corporate income, automobile licenses, general sales and property—the first six are also used by the federal government. On them the taxpayer pays twice.

Moreover, state tax rates present a disorderly lack of uniformity, and uniformity is probably the best single test of whether taxes are "fair." Take for example the gasoline tax, the biggest single source of state funds. In Florida and Tennessee the state rate is seven cents a gallon. But in parts of Florida there is a one-cent city tax. In parts of Alabama, where the state rate is six cents, there is a three-cent county tax and a two-cent city tax, making a total of 11 cents a gallon exclusive of the federal tax. At the other end of the scale is Missouri, with only a two-cent state tax.

Another flaw in our confused tax structure is interstate rivalry over tax revenue. Newspaper readers may notice when William Randolph Hearst threatens to move out of California to escape its high tax on personal incomes. Or when corporations threaten to move out of Wisconsin because its corporate-income tax rate is higher than that in surrounding states. Or when Pennsylvania and New Jersey carry to the Supreme Court their battle over the right to tax the estate of Dr. John Thompson Dorrance, late Campbell Soup king.

But newspaper readers get no inkling of the tens of thousands of such disputes that do not get to court at all. And it is the rare newspaper reader who contemplates the problem raised when a man living in state A receives income from a trust set up in state B and managed by a trustee who lives in state C, the income being in the form of dividends of a corporation that is incorporated in state D, with its main office in state E and its business extending throughout states F to X. Any or all of these states may want to tax all or part of the income.

These examples could be multiplied throughout countless situations involving almost every one of the important state taxes.

The solution of this state-federal tax mess is again centralization of taxes. For example, the federal government could increase its personal and corporate income tax rates, and this additional revenue could be considered as having been collected *for* the states. Washington could then offer to each state its share of that extra money *provided* that state collected no income tax itself—an offer that any state would find it hard to refuse for long. The same plan could be used for all important sources of revenue wherein the states conflict with the federal government—death taxes, liquor, tobacco, and gasoline taxes.

Such a scheme would make all these taxes absolutely uniform throughout the 48 states. It would mean immense savings in the cost of collecting taxes, with one collector taking the place of 49. And it would mean immense savings to taxpayers, especially large corporations, in the cost of computing and paying taxes.

Such centralization would not seriously infringe on state powers. The states' share of the tax money would come back to the states. Moreover, legalistically speaking, the states would surrender no powers; they would keep them but fail to exercise them. Any state *could* spurn the federal offer at any time and collect its own taxes instead. Further, state revenue would not be limited to the funds distributed by the federal government. For that biggest single source of tax revenue, the property tax, would remain in state hands—the Constitution forbidding the federal government to collect property taxes.

Under this plan the present haphazard potpourri of federal, state and local taxes might be linked into a purposeful and co-ordinated chain.

This centralization program could not be put into effect overnight. It is not a program to please local politicians. But our present U. S. tax system is the most complicated and disorderly tax system in the world. If U. S. taxpayers become sufficiently indignant, here is a way by which its wastefulness can be eliminated.

"*Why Do They Let Us Run It?*"

A PRIMER IN GOOD GOVERNMENT

By

FRANK R. KENT

WHY DO YOU suppose they let us run it?" That question, in a tone of amused contempt, was asked of the writer a number of years ago by a sly, cynical subordinate in the old and extremely unsavory Brennan machine of Chicago, now expanded into the equally unsavory but even more powerful Kelly-Nash machine through which in the past few years many millions of federal funds have filtered and to which have fallen slices of federal patronage, huge and juicy beyond all previous political dreams.

In that question "*Why do they let us run it?*" is involved the whole story of the dangers that lurk in our democratic system. It pierces deeply our national Achilles heel and its answer is a devastating indictment of the people as a whole. Because, as sure as fate, unless some day they substitute for their political lethargy and ignorance an informed, alert and ceaselessly vigilant political activity, they will vindicate—clear to the hilt—those prophets who have scoffed at the notion that

a people are fit to govern themselves, and who predict an ultimate period of chaos brought about by the dead, mushy weight of popular incompetency.

It is, of course, old stuff to point out that great machines such as the Kelly-Nash in Chicago, the Pendergast machine in Kansas City, the Frank Hague machine in New Jersey, the Earle-Guffey machine in Pennsylvania, what was the former Huey Long machine in Louisiana, Tammany in New York, and the numerous smaller ones in less populous towns are nourished at the public expense, and exact a cash contribution from every citizen, rich and poor, male and female. It is perhaps trite, but it is none the less necessary to repeat that the waste and graft ("cakes" they call the latter in Chicago) of local government force the people to pay not only much more in direct taxes, but immensely more in indirect taxes, reflected in higher cost of rent, clothes, food and everything else. The basic fact is that these grafting parasites, who are gradually sapping the security of the country, could not exist but for the absurd inertia of honest citizens. They could be thrown out with a little intelligent effort. No wonder that cunning old Brennanite asked "Why do you suppose they let us run it?"

Two incidental points should be emphasized. First, despite its many flaws and manifold faults, our system is the best ever devised by man for the general welfare of a people. Of course it worked better—as every governmental process must—before the country grew to such vast proportions. But even now, even with the sex and illiteracy bars down, with voting practically unrestricted and the field open for every demagogue to plow, still it remains the most desirable.

Second, the yardstick by which to measure its life line is the character and intelligence of the people. If it survives, it will be because, alarmed by what they see and stirred by appeals, the American people stop being saps, take their politics seriously and insist vehemently upon competency and economy in county, city, state and federal governments. If they can be stirred, or prodded, or scared into that state of mind, the system can be salvaged. If not, then we will bumblepuppy along for an indefinite number of years until the accumulated and intolerable burdens of debt, taxes and bureaucracy will break the communal back.

What can be done to check the present downward trend of democracy? We must come out of the fog in which we live politically and get

down to brass tacks. For example, one of the worst popular misconceptions is that national government and politics are more important than local government and politics. They are not. It is just the reverse. Local politics is not only more vital but it is basic. It is the foundation upon which the whole structure rests—and if it is not sound, then nothing built on it is sound. The whole business starts in the precinct and to confine our interest to the top and ignore the bottom is simply stupid.

Yet a great many supposedly smart men, who pride themselves on their political knowledge, are concerned exclusively with national affairs. Contemptuously, they leave local politics to the local machines, though any politician could tell them that the basis of political power is local and that Presidents, as well as Senators and Representatives, depend upon the local units for their political survival and support. The best way to have influence in national politics is to have influence in local politics.

A second misconception, closely related to the first but even more paralyzing to political competency is the widely cherished belief that the general election is more important than the primary election; that while it is a duty to vote in the general, the primaries can well be left to the politicians. That is the average voter's idea. And it is wickedly and dangerously untrue. The truth is that the primaries are infinitely more vital than the general election. The truth is that the primaries are the key to all politics. The truth is that, in general, the possession of that key gives to an individual or an organization a power such as no individual or organization ought to have in a country such as this; a power which makes a joke of majority rule; a power which is always and inevitably abused. It is held by the professional leaders of the political machines, and held not because they have won it or earned it, but solely because the great masses of the voters do not participate in the primaries. It is largely acquired by default, the result of popular ignorance. That's what my political acquaintance meant when he said, "Why do you suppose they let us run it?"

That slick fellow knew that indifference to the primaries was equivalent to handing the country over to the politicians to run—not only locally but nationally. Presidents are nominated in conventions made up by delegates chosen in primaries—and if the primaries are controlled by the machine bosses, the machine bosses can pick the President. Any national convention of either party can be controlled by less than 50 men. There is no way for candidates of either of the two great parties to get on the general election ballot except through the primaries.

Let that fact sink in and the logic of the rest is irresistible. Primaries are the exclusive gate through which all party candidates must pass. Control of that gate in any community clearly means control of the political situation in that community. It

ought then to be plain that so long as the machine controls the primaries it has the power to limit the choice of the voters in the general election to its choice in the primaries.

That is the second fact to let sink in. It is the real secret of machine power. Defeating its candidate in the general election not only does not break its grip; it often does not make a dent in it. It continues to function as a political machine after a general election defeat just as it did before—chagrined, perhaps, and perhaps a little chastened, but not really hurt.

The only place a machine can be beaten is in the primaries. All over the country, in 99 percent of all elections, the choice of the voters in the general election is limited to the choice of the voters in the primary elections.

When, as happens, the vote in the primaries is sometimes as low as a fortieth of the general election vote, often less than a tenth, rarely more than a third, it is easy to understand how the politicians with their organized jobholders, machine dependents and precinct workers can control. It is, as I have said, largely a matter of default, and on general election day the voters have to choose between candidates selected for them by the two party machines. Clearly, this is a state of affairs which breeds waste and graft, fills public offices, high and low, with incompetents, frauds and fakirs. Unchecked, it is a mere matter of time until the collapse comes.

What can be done about it? Perhaps "the people" are not sufficiently alert or intelligent to do anything about it. Perhaps we will continue to wobble dumbly along, bleating like sheep and letting the politicians "run it," until we all land in the well-known ditch. However, I do not believe that. I very firmly believe that there is enough intelligence in this country, if only it can be concentrated and energized and unified in thought on this subject, to provide the leadership for the great confused and strangely mingled mass of voters needed to restore health to politics. But to do that it is essential for the great number of informed and capable individuals, groups, agencies, societies and organizations in this country, who really want decent government, who believe in our system and want it to last, to cast aside inertia and impress certain facts upon the people of our country as a whole:

First, that local politics is very much more important than national politics.

Second, that the primary is more important than the general election.

Third, that these two things are basic and controlling, and not to appreciate this fact makes us a nation of political suckers, who soon or late will come to grief.

If, through persistent and continuous educational campaigns, these facts can be drilled into the great, soggy, collective mind, eventually sentiment can be aroused. That is the main thing—sentiment and understanding. And, of course, there are three concrete things for which intelligent leadership should ceaselessly fight:

First, simpler and shorter ballots.

Second, fewer elections.

Third, honesty in count.

As much as anything else, the unnecessarily numerous city and state elections and the outrageously complicated and bewildering ballots discourage the people from participation in their local affairs and play into the hands of the politicians.

The picture is by no means hopeless. This country is so rich and so tough that even fools could not wreck it if once the people became sensibly vibrant about politics. But wreck it they can and will unless we make it impossible for cynical politicians to ask, "Why do they let us run it?"

Table Talk

The X-ray has found its way into the food field. It is used in inspecting canned products to detect any foreign substance. In other fields internal bruises in hams can be detected; internal decay in pineapples and other fruits can be seen.—*Food Industries*

Crippled

Condensed from The Atlantic Monthly

RUTH SAWYER

Across the narrow stretch of hospital room lies my John Paul, whimpering. For 20 days he has been whimpering. It has taken an amazing lot of drugs to keep under so small a boy. At rare intervals words break through his stupor, like embedded needles working their way to the surface. "Mummy, I want to get up. Please, Mummy!"

John Paul is four years old. He will never get up again—that is, never as a whole, free, exultant little boy. He will never drop like a plummet on our bed, stomach down, shouting, "Here I come—Daddy and Mum—Daddy and Mum! It's time to get up—up—up!"

Sometimes John Paul plucks at his chest with his uninjured hand and says: "Take it off, please, Mummy. It's so heavy." He is in a plaster cast from his throat to his thighs; there are casts on his legs, and one arm. There is a metal contrivance around his neck to support his head. He looks like a tiny bird trussed up with a steel girder. Take from a bird all power to fly—would

he still be a bird? Likewise all childhood has ended for John Paul.

Many letters have come to me here which have meant to be kind. They have succeeded in being ghastly for they have bidden me think that God has shown me a special mercy because John Paul is going to live. I wish they could hear him whimpering now.

Throughout these 20 sullen days the doctors and nurses have done superb watching and working—the X-ray man, the surgeon, a bone specialist, two nurses, all trying to compensate for what a boy in one instant did because he was late for his date with a girl. Inch by inch they have beaten death back—while I have prayed the victory would not be to them. They didn't expect John Paul to live through that first night. After that they shook their heads, said they did not know; then they talked about hope. Today they said: "He will live!"

Those words have stayed imprisoned in the room all today. Tonight they are beating back at me like devil drums: "He will live—live—

412

live!" No one who has not prayed that death might come to a beloved, one can understand. I feel ground under those same wheels which went over John Paul. Every night, drugs have snuffed out my consciousness for a few merciful hours; I have gone to sleep praying, "Please, God, let John Paul go before another day." Now I must face life; I must face all its implications and fears for the three of us.

No one must know that we are not glad our child is to live. Big Paul and I must face a lie—and live it, convincingly, cheerfully. All our lives we must act as if we thanked God that we have in our keeping this small crushed body, somehow held together, that it may live in torment.

I wonder if we shall have the courage and wisdom to outstride the years that stretch ahead of us. For the present, John Paul will do his living on a wheeled stretcher—that much the doctors know. After that a wheel chair, perhaps.

There will be winters when we three will watch other boys buckling on their skis, slinging skates over hockey sticks and taking the road to the pond. There will be summers with bicycles and tennis rackets, and the lake to swim in. Can we by grit and prayer help John Paul perform that miracle of freeing his spirit, sending it forth to skim ice, top snowbound hills, follow the trail with the strong, free bodies of other boys?

But for this I can be honestly thankful: John Paul can never drive a car at 50 miles an hour around a corner and, by so doing, cage another's spirit in a helpless body.

We have known two boys who have grown up in wheel chairs. Their limitations have bitten into them deep—like an acid; they are lonely and rebellious souls, their spirits bitter as gall. One has scored his parents throughout a lifetime for not letting him die. How are we going to keep John Paul from becoming as one of these?

We are very young, untempered. I am 23. Big Paul is, at 27, a university instructor; his salary is small. Now we are facing an enormous expense. John Paul must have everything that money can buy to make him less helpless, less set apart from normal childhood, that he may not be warped in anything but body. If we allow ourselves only enough to cover the bare bones of living, we shall still be always in debt.

Can we keep the burden of this debt from settling somehow on John Paul's shoulders? If he continues to love us, will he not grow disturbed, because of what we carry? Can his father and I so detach ourselves from debt-consciousness that even the shadow of it will not rest over our life for our son to mark? It must be so—but how?

In the past, we have made much of little happinesses, picnics, holidays and friendships; these we have shared almost equally, the three of us. Winters we skated, with John Paul buckled into his sled; in summer we played tennis, and he ran for the balls that went over the backstops. Now, for a time at least, this togetherness cannot go on. Big Paul must take his recreation, and I what I need for a sound, refreshed mind, apart.

I am writing things as I think them out—groping along a blind path. I must learn to be all things to John Paul; I must renew a glad spirit within me. Right now I must know what to say to him when there are no longer drugs to dull his consciousness and he plucks at his plaster cast and begs, "Mummy, take it off. It's so heavy—please, Mummy!" Can I help him bear that weight—help him lie still and not let his spirit corrode in the interminable months ahead of us?

That night nurse has been to see if I was asleep. I heard her coming and hid my writing, feigned slumber. She eased John Paul to his pillows, gave him a drink through his tube, then stood and looked down at him so long I wanted to scream. What was she thinking? Perhaps she, too, thinks that surgery, that skilled care, are not always merciful.

She's gone, and I go over again and again that afternoon. I was sitting on the porch, sewing. John Paul was running his scooter down the sidewalk, the gray kitten at his heels. The kitten made a swift dart toward the center of the street. John Paul sprang after the kitten. He was off the curb before I could call.

The boy in the car stopped and came back. He said straightforwardly to the police: "I was going 50—late for a date." He doesn't know what he has done. He has come often to the hospital to ask after John Paul; and this afternoon when he heard what the doctors had said, he was relieved of all responsibility. "Gee, I'm glad. If he'd died now I'd have felt awful." There is no case against him; he has no money to lose. He is probably thanking his stars tonight that he got out of it so easily.

I am not writing just as John Paul's mother; I am writing for all people who have had to suffer for this irresponsible crippling of someone dear to them, who have had to rebuild lives as I shall have to.

Is there no one to speak for the 50,000 crippled each year by someone's negligence? Is there no way of arousing the conscience of the drivers of this nation? It is too late for my John Paul, but not for other childhood, as yet whole, able, free.

This Age of Ingenuity

SPURRED ON by bridge-expert Ely Culbertson, the plastics industry has produced playing cards made of Lumarith, a cellulose acetate material. The new cards look exactly like any other cards, but they are indestructible. They will not crack when bent, stain, nick, or mark, and are moisture-proof and washable. One deck, used for 15,000 deals, showed not a sign of wear.—*Modern Plastics*

Death Has No Terrors

By

LESTER HOWARD PERRY

SOME DAY you are going to die and, if you're like most of us, you are probably afraid to die; you believe that death will be unpleasant. In that you are wrong.

It is not unpleasant to die. The dying person slips drowsily away much as we all, hundreds of times, have drifted into sleep. At the last there is no pain. Doctors say so. Those who come close to death say so. With their last words, those who die say so. And those who return from death (some do!) say so.

This is not to ignore the suffering that may precede death. But the slow suffocation of pneumonia, the jerky strangles of the drowning— all the pain of fatal illness or injury —these are a part of life, not death. While the body still fights for survival, there may be great suffering. But that familiar and sinister phrase, "a man in his death agony," has frightened many of us into a false belief that our very last moments, as we relinquish this life forever, must also be horrible.

Let us hear the testimony of Sir James F. Goodhart, eminent Eng-

lish physician, who, when a resident in Guy's Hospital, arranged to be present at the bedside of every dying patient. He reached the conclusion that "there is nothing terrible to the dying person in death itself. The veil between the two worlds is but a cloud, and one passes through it imperceptibly."

This opinion has been corroborated by other distinguished physicians—by Sir Benjamin C. Brodie, for instance, and by Sir William Osler. "Dying," says Dr. Alfred Worcester, former Professor of Hygiene at Harvard, "is always easy at the last." In its final stages, cancer is usually one of the most painful diseases; yet Dr. J. Shelton Horsley, well-known cancer specialist of Richmond, Virginia, is authority for the statement that "the actual process of dying is apparently not accompanied by pain or by any marked conscious discomfort."

One of the truly comforting facts of life is this: those experiences which we fear most as we anticipate them nearly always lose much of their terror when actually encountered. That is true of death. When it comes close, it is friendly.

About 15 years ago, a big jovial fellow on a lecture tour lay stricken in a Boston hotel. Suffering from an internal hemorrhage, he was told his chances were slim. "At last I knew that I was very near the borderline between life and death," Irvin S. Cobb recalls. "I began to sink. It was a physical feeling. I was sinking, gently, slowly and easily, into a darkness which rose to meet me. There was something soothing, almost alluring, about this darkness. I knew that if I completely surrendered myself to it I should rest. I accepted the prospect of impending death as most of us accept the prospect of continued life—as a matter of course.

"The blackness had almost completely enveloped me before a force within me asserted, 'If I quit now, I'm yellow. I'm leaving things undone.' Slowly, wearily, I dragged myself up. I fought to live.

"Some may look upon death with a shrinking dread in their souls. To all such, I who have skirted the Valley of the Shadow say that we will face it without fear and without bitterness, without reluctance and without repining, without suffering, whether physical or mental; we shall find it, at the last, but a peaceful transition, an eternal change mercifully accomplished."

Bruce Barton tells of a similar drama. In a hospital room a cultured middle-aged man lay dying of pneumonia. The crisis came. Neither the doctor nor the nurse, who held his hand as if to keep him from slipping away, could be sure whether their patient was alive or dead. Then the moment passed; the man lived.

"The doctor says you were almost over the threshold," Bruce Barton said to the patient some time later. "What did you think or feel?"

He answered: "Nothing! I had no interest whether I lived or died. I was just terribly tired, and I thought, 'Now I can sleep.'"

These patients lived to tell their stories—what about those who don't? A careful analysis of the recorded "last words" of 1229 distinguished individuals has been made: at the most, one statement in 60 might be interpreted as intimating some sensation of fear or pain; the experience of the other 59 ranges from indifference to ecstasy.

An unusual study of the sensations of dying is reported by Dr. Edward Hammond Clarke in his book entitled *Visions*. One of Dr. Clarke's patients agreed to report his feelings as he sank into the unconsciousness of death. A system of signals by finger movements was arranged so that the patient could answer questions when no longer able to speak or shake his head. To the very last, after he had apparently lost consciousness, he wiggled *no* in answer to Dr. Clarke's oft-repeated question: "Are you suffering?"

Thousands now living have been dead—actually, legally, biologically dead! So says Dr. Alexis Carrel—

Nobel Prize winner, biologist, surgeon, author of *Man, the Unknown*.

Death, says Dr. Carrel, is not instantaneous. There are two stages: general death or the death of the individual, and local death or the death of the organs. General death takes place with the last pulsation of the heart, for then all vital functions cease and personality vanishes. But each organ dies at its own rate. The brain dies in a matter of minutes; the kidneys can live for more than an hour.

Dr. Carrel calls the first stage "reversible death" because life can be restored by immediate first-aid measures if the vital organs are not diseased. The second stage is "irreversible death." A swimmer is dragged to the shore unconscious; a motorist is found slumped over the steering wheel of his car, the garage doors shut and the engine running. The doctor can feel no pulse, sense no respiration. He orders a pulmotor. Minutes speed by. Occasionally life returns.

Yet, according to Dr. Carrel, the victim had been dead—as dead as he will ever be insofar as his bodily totality, including his consciousness, is concerned. Persons who respond to the pulmotor differ from those who remain dead in only one respect—their vital organs have not been destroyed.

What do those who have been revived from death by drowning tell us? They almost always say that they experienced no suffering whatever after the initial struggle. The original distress gives way to a feeling of drowsy comfort. Thus one of them, Grant Allen, distinguished British author, wrote:

"The knowledge that I have experienced death has had a great deal to do with my utter physical indifference to it. Dying is as painless as falling asleep. It was only the previous struggle, the sense of its approach, that was at all uncomfortable, but even that was not half so bad as breaking an arm or having a tooth drawn. There was a total absence of craven shrinking."

Sound scientific reason explains our attitude toward death as the hour approaches. The simple process of physiologic degeneration is responsible. Each succeeding beat of the heart pumps the blood with a little less force than the one before. As the blood pressure sinks to ever lower levels, the brain is soothed by the gentle anesthesia of receding vitality. The turbulent tidal wave of individual vitality ebbs back toward the sea of universal life whence it came, a recessional undercurrent, flowing on and on into the quiet deepness far below the surging surface. We relax, and in our relaxation we face life's greatest adventure with serenity—

"Like one who wraps the drapery of
    his couch
About him, and lies down to pleasant
    dreams."

The Lord Helps Those . . .

Condensed from Survey Graphic

BERTRAM B. FOWLER

IN THE fishing villages, the agricultural communities, and the coal mines of Eastern Nova Scotia you hear the name of "Father Jimmy" Tompkins spoken with respectful affection. And among sociologists all over America you hear increasingly about the work being done by Dr. J. J. Tompkins and St. Francis Xavier University, a small Catholic college located in the little town of Antigonish.

In the years following the war, Father Tompkins was vice-president of St. Francis Xavier University. Like other colleges it offered the usual courses for those who could afford to attend. Such a program was not enough for Doctor Tompkins. He believed that the University should not merely keep its doors open for the favored few, but should go out to the people and help solve the economic problems that were crushing them.

But he was talking ahead of his time. Before he could initiate such

From *The Lord Helps Those*, by Bertram B. Fowler, published by The Vanguard Press.

a program, he was assigned in 1923 to the parish of Canso on the eastern shore of the Province. Along that barren coast the fishermen lived in abject poverty. The lobster canneries gave them three cents a pound for their small lobsters. Larger ones brought five cents; other fish similar returns. No one in Little Dover, a village of 300, owned either horse or cow. There was no milk supply for the semistarved children. Illiteracy was appallingly prevalent. The people were sunk spiritually and economically. Practically all of them were on either government or private relief.

Father Jimmy accepted this bleak post as an opportunity to prove some of the things about which he had been preaching.

Investigators who had gone to Little Dover declared that nothing could be done for these people where they were. They must be resettled in some more favorable location. Father Jimmy refused to accept such a dictum. He believed in the ability of the common people to remake their own surroundings. For years he fought illiteracy and sullen apathy. Slowly he won converts, started them studying their own plight. He taught the illiterate to read and write. In the tumble-down, one-room schoolhouse he formed study clubs of men and women who had known and accepted poverty so long that any sort of prosperity was but a legend.

The rebirth of Little Dover began in 1931 when the fishermen put into practice some of the ideas learned in the study clubs. They shouldered axes and cut timber to build a coöperative lobster cannery. Having no horses they dragged the lumber, and stone for the foundation, out by hand. When the cannery was finished the banks refused them a loan for canning machinery, but they found a friendly source from which they borrowed $1000. The first year's operation brought a profit of $4000 —enough to pay off the whole loan and award themselves an extra cent a pound for their catch.

In swift succession they built a fish-processing plant, set up a consumer coöperative and bought a herd of goats to supply milk for the children. Their coöperative store saved them as much as $4 on a fishnet, five cents a pound on rope, four cents a pound on nails; small items, but in those savings and the higher prices obtained for their catch lay the difference between poverty and prosperity.

When Father Jimmy went to Little Dover there was one underpaid teacher in the unlovely, one-room school, teaching the few ill-fed children who had sufficient clothes to permit their attendance. Today there are two full-time teachers; every child in the village goes to school, and all are well fed and clothed.

Relief disappeared from Little Dover years ago. Today a self-reliant group of people run their own economic affairs, plan cultural improvements and execute those plans with their own funds.

All along that section of the coast, people began to demand similar action based on what Father Jimmy had proved could be done. Responding, St. Francis Xavier University set up an extension department with a simple plan of action: First, groups meet in the evenings to study the problem of credit. Out of the study clubs comes the credit union, or coöperative bank in which the nickels and dimes of the members are collected. The credit union wipes out the basic evil of chronic debt. This done, the groups go on to the next community problem. If it is a problem of selling, then a lobster factory, a fish plant or a farm-marketing organization is developed.

Thus, the men of Larry's River built their own wharf, lobster factory, fish-processing plant. They opened their store. They didn't ask the government for help. They built their own sawmill which brought the price of their lumber down from $37 to $7 a thousand. They built a four-department school employing four teachers. For the first time the children of Larry's

River were able to get a high-school education.

All along the coast the fishermen took the marketing of their lobsters out of the hands of dealers and began to ship direct to Boston through their own coöperatives. Last summer, lobsters that a few years ago brought them five cents a pound netted them 20 cents.

In the farming communities poultry pools were formed, chickens and turkeys graded and shipped to market. In three years the quality of poultry shipped had risen from last place in the Province to first. Coöperative groups banded together to make further savings. They chartered a ship to bring flour through from the Great Lakes, saving $8000 a year. They pooled their orders for fertilizer and saved $75,000 in three seasons.

In the coal-mining areas around Sydney, Cape Breton, the miners are studying coöperative housing. Already one group has purchased a tract of land and planned a community, with tennis courts and a playground for children. The houses will be held individually. Probably the most significant feature is the community barn and henhouse to supply the members with fresh milk and eggs, which, with the individual gardens, will give these miners the backlog of subsistence farming that will be of far greater importance than a wage rise.

In eastern Nova Scotia today, after only eight years, 108 credit unions and 26 coöperative stores are in operation. Fourteen other groups are applying for charters. The fishermen own 17 lobster canneries and five fish-processing plants. Experiments in coöperative hospitalization are under way. The women are reviving forgotten handicrafts and increasing their profits on wool by sending it to market as tweeds and knit goods.

The idea is spreading. Two years ago the movement was launched on Prince Edward Island. In neighboring New Brunswick, groups have set up the same program. In Newfoundland the government has organized an education division to stimulate the idea in the fishing and farming villages.

One significant result of the movement in Nova Scotia is the closeness with which religious groups are now working together. In the past, religious lines were pretty sharply drawn. But, while this program has come from a Catholic university, Protestant clergymen are as active as Catholic priests in pushing it in their communities. Everyone accepts the truth of Father Jimmy's statement: "There is no Methodist or Catholic way of cutting coal or marketing fish."

The St. Francis Xavier extension program is the outstanding work of rehabilitation going on in America today. Men who a few years ago knew nothing of economics now run lobster factories and stores, and operate credit unions in such a way that many of them have become the real banks of the communities.

With the economic advances go new concepts of community responsibility. There are many cases like that of Roddy MacIsaac, who had a few hundred dollars and a chance for a small contract on a new road that was being built. He borrowed $500 from his credit union to buy a truck. Shortly after he had put the truck in operation Roddy was taken to the hospital. Ordinarily he would have lost his truck to his creditors and come out of the hospital with a burden of debt. But the credit union directors hired a man to run the truck. After the wages of the driver had been paid there was enough to keep up the credit union payments and return a substantial sum to Roddy's family. Therefore, when Roddy went back to work he was out of debt. Such cases are not rare.

Last winter throughout the Maritime Provinces hundreds of men and women met in schoolrooms, in kitchens and parish halls to discuss plans for still more credit unions, coöperative stores and factories. Behind these men and women stands the frail figure of Father Jimmy, with white hair and eyes of unquenchable youth—a flaming evangelist with a fixed idea: the belief that within the people themselves lies dormant all that is necessary for building a way of life founded on justice, equity and practical Christianity.

Keeping up with the World

Excerpts from a regular department in Collier's

Freling Foster

THE Fingerprint Bureau of the New York City Police Department maintains a "Reincarnation File" in which a considerable number of persons have recorded their fingerprints so they will be able to prove their identity upon returning to earth.

UP TO 1840, American hotel registers sometimes competed in interest with the publications of their day. Guests not only entered their names and addresses but also their business, merits of their product, their choice for President, reason for leaving their wives at home—and puns, poems and indecent stories. After their departure the proprietor entered his opinion of them with phrases such as "constantly drunk," "fat but pretty," and "forgot to settle."

Try Giving Yourself Away

Condensed from Forbes

ANONYMOUS

L IKE MOST people, I was brought up to look upon life as a process of getting. The idea of giving myself away came somewhat by accident. One night, lying awake in my berth on the Twentieth Century Limited en route to New York, I fell to wondering just where the Centuries passed each other in the night. "That would make a good subject for one of the New York Central's advertisements," I thought to myself— "Where the Centuries Pass." Next morning I wrote the New York Central System, outlining the idea and adding, "no strings attached." I received a courteous acknowledgment, and the information that the Centuries passed near Athol Springs, N. Y., nine miles west of Buffalo.

Some months later I received a second letter informing me that my idea was to be the subject of the New York Central calendar for the new year. You may recall it: a night picture of the oncoming locomotive of one Century and the observation platform of the other, a scene rich in color and railroad romance.

That summer I traveled a good deal, and in almost every railroad station and hotel lobby and travel office I entered, even in Europe, hung *my* calendar. It never failed to give me a glow of pleasure.

It was then that I made the important discovery that anything that makes one glow with pleasure is beyond money calculation in this world where there is altogether too much grubbing and too little glowing.

I began to experiment with giving-away and discovered it to be a lot of fun. If an idea for improving the window display of a neighborhood store flashes to me, I step in and make the suggestion to the proprietor. If an incident occurs, the story of which I think the local Catholic priest could use, I call him up and tell him about it, though I am not a Catholic myself. If I run across an article some Senator might want to read, I mail it to him.

It has come to a point where I sometimes send books to virtual strangers when I feel sure they would be interested in some "find"

I have made. Several fine friendships have been started in that way.

Successful giving-away has to be cultivated, just as does successful getting. Opportunities are as fleeting as opportunities for earning quick profits. But you will find that ideas in giving are like some varieties of flowers—the more you pick them, the more they bloom. And giving-away makes life so much more exciting that I strongly recommend it as a hobby. You need not worry if you lack money. Of all things a person may give away, money is the least permanent in the pleasure it produces and the most likely to backfire on the giver. Emerson was wise and practical when he wrote, "The only gift is a portion of thyself."

People have different things to give. Some have time, energy, skill, ideas. Others have some special talent. All of us can give away appreciation, interest, understanding, encouragement—which require no money expenditure unless for a postage stamp or a telephone call.

The giver-away should "major" in the items in which he is "long," and fill in with the rest. Having no special talent myself, I specialize in ideas and appreciation and assorted surprises. If I am buying popcorn at a popcorn wagon and a couple of urchins are watching longingly, without looking at the children I order three bags, pay for them, hand the urchins their two bags and walk away without a word. It never fails to make the world more exciting for three people.

Of course you will be tempted to backslide. An idea popped into my head one day which I thought some department store might be able to use profitably. "Now *this* idea is worth money," I said to myself. "I'll try to sell it."

"You'll do nothing of the kind," said my wiser self. "You'll not spend your time peddling an idea; you'll give it away and get it out of your system."

So I wrote a letter to one of the world's most famous department stores, outlining the idea. It was immediately adopted with appreciation, and now I have a big department store as a friend.

I have made several discoveries about giving-away. The first is that to be successful at it one must act fast, while the impulse is fresh. Another is that little gifts are as potent as big ones in producing surprise and inducing a glow of pleasure. Simple appreciation, for example, is one of the most acceptable forms of giving-away. I have found that authors, actors, musicians, editors, lecturers, playwrights, public servants—even the biggest of them—are hungry for genuine expressions of approval. We think of them as being smothered with appreciation, whereas all too often they live on crumbs. The manufactured publicity that is created to promote them does not warm their hearts. What they crave is the spontaneous, human, friendly appreciation of the people they are trying to serve.

The other noon I was in a hotel dining room where an orchestra was playing. It was a good orchestra, offering well-chosen selections, well played. On the way out impulse prompted me to stop and say, "Gentlemen, I have thoroughly enjoyed your playing." For a second they looked almost startled. Then all of their faces broke into smiles and I left them beaming over their instruments. My own afternoon went off better for it, too.

Another discovery I have made is that it is almost impossible to give away anything in this world without getting something back—provided you are not trying to get something. Usually the return comes in some utterly unexpected form, and it is likely to be months or years later.

For example, one Sunday morning the local post office delivered an important special delivery letter to my home, though it was addressed to me at my office, and the post office had discharged its obligation by attempting to deliver it there. I wrote the postmaster a note of appreciation. More than a year later I needed a post-office box for a new business I was starting. I was told at the window that there were no boxes left, that my name would have to go on a long waiting list. As I was about to leave, the postmaster appeared in the doorway. He had overheard our conversation.

"Wasn't it you who wrote us that letter a year ago about delivering a special delivery to your home?"

I said it was.

"Well, you certainly are going to have a box in this post office if we have to make one for you. You don't know what a letter like that means to us. We usually get nothing but kicks."

I had a box within the hour. Bread upon the waters!

After years of experience, this is how I have come to feel about my hobby: I have a job which pays me a living, so why should I try to drive a sharp bargain with the world for the extra ideas and impulses that come to me? I say let the world have them if they are of any value. I get my compensation out of feeling that I am a part of the life of my times, doing what I can to make things more interesting and exciting for other people. And that makes life more interesting and exciting for me, and keeps my mind keener.

As if this were not enough, I find that friends multiply and good things come to me from every direction. I've decided that the world insists on balancing accounts with givers-away—provided their hands aren't outstretched for return favors.

Twelve Good Men—Untrue!

Condensed from The Christian Science Monitor

UPTON CLOSE

FOR THE first time we have an official "low-down" on the American jury. The Ruth Commission of Pennsylvania, armed by the legislature with authority to subpoena, has put scores of ex-jurors on the stand and made them tell what really happens behind locked jury-room doors.

One result of the Commission's first year of work is that 117 individuals in Pennsylvania, ranging from professional criminals to court employes, lawyers and politicians, are under indictment by Judge Curtis Bok's special "blue ribbon" grand jury. But punishment of offenders is incidental. Of first importance to every American who wants justice is the Commission's factual survey of shocking practices existing all over the United States.

The Commission's report, going to press as this is written, and previewed only by this writer, was very nearly smothered by the bosses in Pennsylvania, who cut off funds with the hope that the findings could not be published. We shall have the report only because the

fearless young director of the Commission, Chet Keyes, put aside each month a sum now sufficient to publish the book.

It all began with a series of newspaper articles by Dave Wittals in the Philadelphia *Record*, exposing the probation racket in that city. The legislature took notice, and Governor Earle appointed as chairman of an investigating commission State Senator Frank W. Ruth, pastor of a small-town Dutch Reformed Church.

Most common of the sins of juries, says the Ruth report, is their tendency to regard lightly misconduct in office: a mayor sharing the proceeds of prostitution, a police chief collecting from illicit liquor dealers, political bosses conspiring to deprive the American citizen of his right to vote freely seem to arouse jurors so little that they are willing to determine the verdict by the flip of a coin.

One such case, for instance—and it is only slightly more outrageous than others brought out in the Ruth report—concerned the foreman of a jury at Easton.

"Let's get this over with!" he urged his fellows as soon as the bailiff had locked them in. "It's all very confusing—none of us really knows whether to acquit or convict. Why not leave it to Lady Luck? I'll toss for each of you. If it's heads you're for acquittal; tails you're for conviction—okay?" All 11 agreed. The foreman tossed for each of his fellow jurors, one at a time. All 11 came up heads. That decided the verdict. Some of the jurors had misgivings, but didn't like to accuse the foreman of cheating. They didn't know then that he was a political henchman of the accused.

Jurors in one instance confessed to agreement in order to get to a lodge dance on time, in another instance to see a ball game. The ease with which one or two determined jurors can swing the remainder was evidenced by testimony after testimony. The ordinary juror seems to assume that one or two of his fellows who take definite stands know more about the case than he.

In one prominent case, a jury of conservative citizens received evidence, including a confession, of an assault followed by death, committed by a young lady defendant. But the extraneous introduction of testimony which, in the minds of the jurors, offended the religious faith in which the defendant was reared made them decide to overlook the killing, although forgiveness was no part of their prerogative. Later, when the Commission subpoenaed the jurors in this case to find out why they had disregarded legal fact, it got such explanations as these: "There was a lot of argument—I did not know what it was all about." "I not understand English." "How do I know what happened, I wasn't there—see?" "The foreman was very stubborn."

And here is the foreman's logic: "We are not going to convict of murder! . . . If we let her go free she will worry more about her wicked act and really suffer more than if she served a few years' imprisonment."

Is this typical of what goes on in a murder trial jury? The Commission's work shows that such warping of logic and placing of prejudice above duty is all too common.

Justice suffers, too, because courts forget the surprising ignorance of many jurors in such fundamental matters as court language and procedure. Ex-jurors in whose hands had lain the disposition of men's liberty and property admitted under oath that they had reached verdicts without knowing who was the plaintiff and who the defendant, never having absorbed the meaning of the words during trial.

Often the juror is asked to perform unreasonable feats of memory. In one case a jury was asked to bring in verdicts against 53 defendants, of varying degrees of guilt, without so much as a written note on the evidence produced or the impressions made by the defendants at the trial. The baffled jurors couldn't remember them apart! Who could?

In some states (Kansas for one)

jurors are provided, when they go into closet, with all trial exhibits and a transcript of the testimony to refer to. In many states, however, a juror must rely on his confused remembrance of what witnesses, lawyers and court said throughout the trial, which may have lasted many days.

How much justification exists for the tradition (rather than law) that jurors may not take notes or carry memoranda into the jury room? There is, of course, the danger that memoranda may be partial, or "loaded" from the outside. Yet judges when serving in the function of the jury work from copious notes. The unfortunate juror, however, is required to recall from memory the gist of 50 contradictory statements! And though he may not have notes, he may have the newspapers, screaming sensational guesses.

The Commission found that only the barest start has been made in rendering simple instruction to jurors. The judges of Northampton County, Pennsylvania, have prepared vest-pocket printed booklets for jurors. In some western states mimeographed instructions are provided. The Commission urges the improvement and standardization of such instructions.

Damaging to justice as ignorance may be, actual corruption is less forgivable. The Commission found it to be a custom in some counties for a defendant to look up prospective jurors directly or otherwise. Amazing industry was shown by one embezzler-suspect. His first

trial brought conviction, but he won retrial on a technicality. By direct visit or through intermediaries he got pretty well around to the members of two complete panels of 90 each. Trial Two resulted in a hung jury. Trial Three in acquittal!

The Commission found the most startling and widespread jury malpractice to be service under false name. This is prevalent in large cities, and our "best citizens" are collaborators. A busy man or woman receives a summons to jury duty and goes to a "friend with influence" to get him out of it. What happens is that a henchman of the local boss turns up for jury duty, answers to the name of the impaneled citizen, and serves throughout the life of the panel for his three or five dollars a day—meanwhile being in a perfect position to "throw" cases damaging to his political machine.

In Philadelphia and several lesser Pennsylvania cities, juror-substitution has become common practice. And it has a charity angle. A ward boss tries to have on hand a few "jury tours" for faithful unemployed voters who appreciate the addition of jurors' fees to their relief dole.

In a sardonic case reported from Oregon the defendant's wife was on the jury—unknown to all save the defendant and his attorney. But when certain secrets the defendant had hidden from his spouse came out in court, the poor fellow rushed to his lawyer with the demand that he "get that woman off the jury at once!" She was in a fine position to revenge a wife's wounded pride.

The Commission received another shock when it subpoenaed jurors who had brought in a verdict of acquittal in a flagrant larceny case. Jurors testified that they followed the foreman, who blithely admitted that he had once served four years for larceny and shied away from causing similar distress to a fellow being.

This case pointed up an evil existing in many states: the foreman is designated at the start of trial, making him a marked man to those seeking to influence the verdict. In Kansas, for opposite instance, the jury chooses its foreman after it receives commitment of the case.

Legal qualification requirements for juries, varying in the 48 states, add up to a huge joke at the expense of society. Twenty-four states require the juror to possess "good moral character"—or "one or more of the qualities of good moral character"! Thirty states, that the juror be "generally reputed to be intelligent." Eighteen states ask no positive qualities at all, but specify, more or less, against a person with a criminal record. Some say that he must be "not an idiot." Men of the learned professions—doctors, lawyers and teachers—are usually exempt by statute or get off by custom. No wonder the report says: "By the time the higher type get excused, one out of three or four capable jurors remains. Our methods of selection blow away the wheat and save the chaff."

The panels from which juries are chosen are commonly made up of names drawn by lot from voters' registration lists, tax books, or even telephone directories. This proceeding is designed to insure impartiality of choice, but it offers no guarantee of fitness to serve. In some instances politics enters into the selections, as in Berks County, Pennsylvania, where the panel is "nominated" by the big party bosses: one Republican, one Democrat.

The Commission believes that a fundamental reform—procuring of good jury timber—can be brought about by pre-examination of names for fitness by a semijudicial, semicitizens' board. In Los Angeles such a board has been established.

After that comes reform of the business of challenging prospective jurors. Attorneys have a certain number of peremptory challenges—varying in the various states—whereby they can dismiss jurors without revealing any reason. Aside from this, they can ask the judge to dismiss any prospective juror whom they can cajole or bluff into admitting that he has set ideas about the case in hand. The inevitable result is a battle between contending attorneys, each trying to seat jurors susceptible to his own argument. Actual fitness to serve becomes a secondary consideration.

Instead of this scandalous lawyers' game, the Commission would have the judge provided with a brief on each summoned citizen, procured by investigators who cannot know on what case he will serve. Secondly, it would have the reasonableness of all challenges ruled on by the judge. The right of peremptory challenge would be eliminated.

After an improved method of selecting juries, two final reforms are recommended. Bewildered by the inconsistency and even brutality of the law in fixing punishments, jurors frequently return arbitrary verdicts of not guilty or guilty in lesser degree than charged. If all states had the indeterminate sentence law now being tried by California, without minimum and maximum, leaving length of punishment to decision of an expert penal board according to merit, juries would bring in more honest convictions.

The last reform—which had wide discussion prior to the Ruth Commission's work—would authorize a "majority verdict" of ten or nine jurors. This is being tried now in a few places, in civil cases. It saves many hung juries and consequent retrial costs and time. It enables the thoughtful members of a jury to get past one or two stubborn members, and makes "fixing" harder, since at least three jurors instead of one must be reached.

We Americans are not purposely careless about a matter which touches us so closely as the administration of justice. But we have been at a loss to know how reforms can be achieved. The Ruth Commission's report gives a layman's-language picture of the abuses that exist, and suggests common-sense ways to correct them.

Americana

Excerpts from The American Mercury

Massachusetts: Convincing bit of medico-theological dogma, as offered in the correspondence columns of the Christian Science Sentinel:

I HAVE FOUND Christian Science as effective with animals as with people. While aboard ship a cat appeared to have what would generally be called a fit. It acted as if blind, and ran around crying and bumping into things. I took it into my quarters and read from *Science and Health,* just as if I were reading to a person, and in a few minutes it quieted down and went to sleep. In a couple of hours it awakened and was all right. After that it kept close to me whenever possible.

Nevada: An enterprising citizen gets in a publicity plug for his home town, as reported in the letter columns of the Nevada State Journal:

"IT MIGHT interest you to know that I have written a letter to the Duke of Windsor. Here's a copy of it:

DEAR SIR: The world admires your courage in choosing a charming and beautiful life mate. . . . If by chance the marriage is not successful, Reno, the world's divorce capital, will welcome you.
—FRED PHILLIPS"

So You're Going to Stop Smoking?

Condensed from Your Life

HENRY C. LINK, Ph.D.

SOONER OR LATER, nearly every cigarette smoker discovers that he is not smoking by choice but by habit, and that the habit is probably harmful. So he tries to break free from it, but finds that he doesn't know how. Sometimes half-heartedly, sometimes earnestly, he wrestles with his addiction—but in vain. His self-control has been perilously undermined by a mere mechanism of habit.

For years he has been practicing daily that mechanism, without realizing that it was becoming automatic, that he was perfecting a whole chain of habitual motions, an irresistible nervous-muscular process. It begins with lifting the pack, extracting a cigarette, tamping one end, placing it between the lips, striking a match, inhaling the first gulp of smoke, and so forth, until the stub reaches the ash tray. Every cigarette consumed involves the same chain of actions and reactions, which seem to set themselves in motion and go on automatically to the end. Often the smoker is not even aware of them.

Like an old-fashioned clock wound up to strike, he is set to go and set to finish, dozens of times a day. Like a robot, he moves at the command of an invisible master.

Is there anything he can do about it?

Behind that question lies an important lesson in psychology. For the habit of cigarette smoking is only a familiar instance of the psychology of all habit forming and habit breaking.

During the last decade the consumption of cigarettes in the United States has increased from 106 billion to 162 billion a year. Today about 60 percent of the men and nearly 25 percent of the women are consistent cigarette smokers. The average consumption for men is 20 cigarettes a day, and for women, 11 a day, with each smoker drifting helplessly toward a still larger quota. This habit of smoking, although it appears to many to be a trivial part of living, may be viewed as symbolic of a fundamental trend in modern civilization. That trend is the increasing fre-

430

quency with which individuals permit themselves to become the *creatures* of their habits rather than the *creators* of their environment.

To find out what factors enter into this deep-rooted problem of character weakness, the Psychological Corporation has recently completed a sample study of 1000 men who were or had been inveterate smokers. Of this group, 145 had stopped smoking. Of the remaining 855, nearly half had stopped at one time or another but had been unable to give up the habit permanently. While some had by now abandoned hope of success, 28 percent still wanted to stop. *But they could not.*

The reasons they gave were generally as follows:

"I haven't the necessary will power."

"Can't do without them."

"I'm too weak."

"I stopped once, but I can't any more."

"Why can't I? That's what I'd like to know."

Verily, here is a sad commentary on a large portion of our adult population. From the recent studies of Dr. Raymond Pearl at Johns Hopkins, we know that tobacco smokers do not live as long as nonsmokers. Yet, despite the fact that millions of persons comprehend the harmful effects of smoking, they confess their inability to conquer this purely mechanical habit.

The majority of the 145 men who had succeeded in stopping permanently, and many of those who had stopped temporarily, were quick to announce their satisfaction.

"I slept more soundly and didn't cough."

"Better taste in my mouth."

"My sense of smell returned acutely."

"Had more pep and a better appetite."

Even more enthusiastic were comments such as these:

"I can't say how, but I feel better all over."

"Got a tremendous kick out of being able to stop, finally."

"Gave my entire morale a great boost."

Here we have the antithesis of the statements from men who could not stop. Note how the triumph over a confirmed habit gave to many persons a sense of well-being and of strengthened character.

I know something of this feeling personally. For 23 years I had smoked cigarettes incessantly, sometimes 60 a day. In earlier years I had been able to stop for a week or two, but more recently I had never succeeded in stopping for more than a day. After many failures I decided that my studies of this habit-problem had been too superficial. Therefore, before trying again, I decided to write out a plan for breaking the habit.

Herewith is an abstract of that statement, written eight months before I stopped.

The strength of the smoking habit lies in the neuro-muscular chain of acts which is so easily set off. The whole body is involved. When not in motion, the chain sets up a craving until started, and when started, it has to go to the end. Therefore, instead of trying to stop it, I will interrupt this routine. When I reach for a cigarette I will put it down and wait. This will break the routine. Occasionally I will light up, but before taking a good puff, will put out the cigarette and wait a few minutes.

At home in the evening, I shall place the pack on the mantel and schedule my smokes. Before the time is up, I may want to smoke, but to do so I shall have to walk to the mantel. By that act the routine cycle will have been broken and at times I shall be able to postpone the smoke. In this way the number of cigarettes per day will be reduced.

In short, I shall contrive frequent interruptions, frictions, delays, in the smooth-flowing chain of habitual action. I shall do this for six months, so as gradually to break down the mechanism I have spent years in perfecting. I should be able to stop, in time, for a day or two without much difficulty; then maybe for a week, and ultimately altogether. I will set no definite date, but feel my way.

I formulated this plan in June, 1937. By January, 1938, I was stopping a day or two at a time. Since February first, I have not taken a puff.

Is this method one which smokers in general might try? Psychologists will agree that no single formula is applicable to every situation. Most of them will also agree that the formula laid down by William James, the great student of habit, is basically sound. His principles may be summarized as follows:

Make a strong resolution and base it on as many sound reasons as you can muster.

Never permit an exception until the new habit is firmly fixed.

Reaffirm your resolution from time to time, marshaling new reasons in support of it.

In our survey of the 145 men who had stopped smoking permanently and of the 366 who had stopped temporarily, we found that they had relied on three major methods. The most common was the method James advocated—to give up smoking at once and completely, with no concessions. The second method relies on substitutes, *i.e.*, a pipe, cigars, gum or candy. The third method is the well-known one of cutting down on cigarettes gradually.

Although the *abrupt* method was more widely used by the men we studied than the *gradual* method, we discovered that the percentage of those who succeeded in stopping permanently was considerably higher among those using the gradual method. My method of *interruptions* is a gradual method, with this important difference: it systematically practices smoking in ways which will disrupt the smooth flow of the habit chain. It breaks a monotonous series of automatic activities into single, unusual acts, each of which serves as a warning signal to the mind.

All such successful experiments are in sharp contrast to the expressed despair of the many who now consider themselves helpless victims of the cigarette. The control of this specific habit may not seem to be of any considerable social importance. But a defeatist attitude toward any of the habits of living is actually of vital concern—to parents, to children, and to society at large. It is this attitude which leads individuals to consider themselves victims of circumstances —victims of the depression, victims of politics, victims of miseducation, victims of an indulgent family, victims of unhappy experience.

The person who admits, openly or tacitly, his slavery to habit mechanisms, has lost the sense of self-mastery, and by the same token has become a less responsible and effective member of the community.

When I attended school our physiology textbook contained warnings against tobacco and alcoholism. However, I am unaware of any lessons in the grade schools which teach children even the simplest elements of forming habits and breaking them. Whether smoking is desirable or not, children have a right to be taught the mechanics of the habit *before they have acquired it.* The same is true of many other habits. Our educational system has concentrated on mental development and has failed to give any understanding of the way emotional and personality habits are acquired or corrected.

The student who emerges from grade school, high school or college without the intelligent conviction that he is the creator of his habits, rather than their victim, is educated for defeat rather than power, for slavery rather than for freedom.

Table Talk

ARE YOU WATCHING the color of your food, or don't you give it a thought? Perhaps it is sheer ignorance in you that you sit down to a meal improperly contrasted, a meal of all sickly yellows, say, such as chicken soup, calf's liver, squash, sauternes, cornbread and butter, fig pudding, and yellow chartreuse. Not a green anywhere, nor a red, nor even a dirty orange. Well, probably you haven't studied the recent findings of the Kellogg scientists, makers of All-American All-Bran. It seems that the latest way to a balanced diet is through color. Bring the red stewed tomatoe next to the yellow potato chip; bring the mauve eggplant next to the green broccoli. Then you will grow sturdy and carbohydrated, and the sparkle will come back in your eye. It is quite revealing to learn that certain people whose stomach trouble we had supposed to be attributable to some chemical maladroitness are in fact deficient not calorifically but esthetically.—*The New Yorker*

THE AVERAGE American would not care for an Eskimo's diet. The writer has more than once observed one devouring a can of lard.
—*Review of Reviews*

Nerves and Indigestion

Condensed from Hygeia

WALTER C. ALVAREZ, M.D.

WHEN A MAN or woman begins to suffer with indigestion, what is its most likely cause? Will an examination show disease, or will physicians blame nerves, worry or eating too fast? Actually, much depends on age and sex. Young people, particularly young women, are more likely to suffer with nervous indigestion than old people; but persons past middle age who only recently have begun to have abdominal distress, are probably suffering with organic disease.

Particularly alarming is the indigestion that comes suddenly to the older person who has always boasted of a "cast-iron stomach." Obviously something has gone wrong: perhaps a tumor has begun to grow, or a gallstone, or the heart has begun to fail. Every person past middle age who, after years of good health, begins to suffer with indigestion or abdominal pain should hasten to have a careful examination, including an X-ray study of stomach and bowel.

The digestive tract is supplied richly with nerves which connect one part with another, and with the brain. This connection with the brain, once useful, is now largely a nuisance. When a man's life depended on his ability to beat a tiger to a tree, his nerves helped him by shutting off all unnecessary activity in the digestive tract, and by pouring into his blood powerful drugs (such as adrenalin) which helped him to run or fight. Today when a man fights for his life in our economic jungle the old nervous processes still stop his digestion; the powerful chemicals still pour into his blood. But since he doesn't use them up in muscular action they remain to irritate his colon and to make him feel sick.

It is this nervous interference with the normal processes of digestion that causes numberless persons to complain of "stomach trouble." And even in the cases of organic disease, a doctor may have to combat psychological influences if the patient is to be helped.

For instance, a man gets a pain in the pit of his stomach at 11 in the morning and five in the afternoon, a pain which he can relieve by a little food or an alkaline tablet. He probably has a duodenal ulcer, an organic disease. But the chances are that every acute flare-up of the trouble is the direct result of worry or unhappiness. In prescribing treatment, the physician insists upon three things: rest; the avoidance of psychic upsets; and the taking of some easily digestible food every two hours. The average ulcer can be healed by this treatment, but a new one commonly forms if the patient does not find mental and emotional peace.

Inflammation of the gall bladder usually causes gassy indigestion with occasional attacks of agonizing colicky pain. Although the disease is organic, many of the colics follow emotional excesses and fits of temper, which probably cause spasm in the ducts that carry the bile to the bowel. Although some gallstone sufferers can be helped by diet, many must be operated on sooner or later. There is no way of dissolving the stones, and their presence always constitutes a menace.

Another organic cause of indigestion is *cancer of the stomach*. The symptoms vary, but whenever a person, healthy for 50 years, begins to suffer with indigestion and to lose weight and strength, a careful examination should immediately be made, because cancer can often be cured when treated early enough. Unfortunately the average person waits too long.

Organic causes for indigestion often lie *outside* the digestive tract.

Here, for instance, is a man in his 50's who, after a large meal, cannot walk half a block without getting a cramping pain under the left breast. Sure it is due to indigestion, he goes to a stomach specialist, but he really should consult a cardiologist because his pain is due to a narrowing of the coronary arteries which supply the heart muscle with blood.

In 50 percent of indigestion cases, the specialist can discover nothing wrong with the digestive tract. He is faced here by the functional type of indigestion, in which a seriously upset nervous system causes untold misery. The commonest causes of nervous indigestion are fatigue, worry, hypersensitiveness and insomnia. *Functional indigestion is common, nothing can be found to explain the symptoms, and the patient never comes to any bad end.* When nervous invalids learn these important facts they will save themselves an untold amount of suffering and expense. They must learn to believe a good clinician when, after a careful examination, he assures them that there is nothing seriously wrong.

When a worrisome woman is told that she hasn't a gallstone, she commonly refuses to believe that her suffering could be without organic cause. Usually she cannot bear to think of the months of self-discipline against worry necessary to peace and health.

I do not wish to imply that the nervous patient is *imagining* her distress. No, it is very real, and probably more trying than the pain of ulcer. I often think of two women who came into my office together. The mother, a gentle old lady with a cancer of the stomach, maintained that she was not suffering and that she needed no treatment. But she was concerned about her daughter who for three weeks had been vomiting everything she had eaten. What was the matter? Nothing but fear. She became ill the minute she heard of the mother's trouble. Here, then, was one woman with the worst form of organic disease and no complaint to make, and another with no organic disease, but a painful illness requiring hospitalization.

Many persons who can understand how acute fear may upset the digestive function fail to understand how chronic anxiety often explains their ill health. Fretting over a sickly child, grieving for a wayward husband or constant worrying about an insolvent business—all may seriously affect digestion. As the great psychiatrist Maudsley used to say, "The sorrow which has no vent in tears may make other organs weep."

Financial worry ranks as a chief cause of nervous indigestion. Every day I see patients who need no other medicine than a little more money to free them from miserable situations. How fruitless to prescribe diet or sedatives for them! Unless they can get the needed dollars which would solve their financial problems, they are often doomed to a life of racking headaches and other violent forms of nervous indigestion.

The weak nerves that cause stomach derangements may be inherited as well as acquired. Often, mentally unbalanced, alcoholic or misfit ancestors hand down an instability of the nervous system sufficient to cause most of the handicaps which hound millions of nervous, sickly and unemployable persons in this country today.

This miserable inheritance accounts for much of what we physicians call "constitutional inadequacy" or an inability to stand up to the strains of life. Such inadequacy, unfortunate enough when the victim is rich, is doubly tragic in the shop girl, the schoolteacher, or the stenographer who has to keep working or starve. These patients, facing a lifetime of discomfort and frustration, often desperately beg surgeons to "operate for something." Unfortunately, what they want is impossible—an operation that would make a new personality.

But the situation of these inadequate persons is not hopeless. Charles Darwin, for example, was so frail that he could never work more than three hours a day. Any small excitement, such as a visit with friends, sent him to bed with a shivering fit and nervous vomiting. His life demonstrates that by accepting one's handicap, and by working within one's limit of strength, the constitutionally inadequate person can round out a happy and useful life.

Many sufferers with functional indigestion can get well if they will bravely face the fact that they cannot do all the things their stronger fellows do. First they must stop looking for a quick way out via surgery. Many must settle down to a long course of self-discipline. If for years they have overdrawn on the bank of strength, staying up late and frittering away energies, they must begin to live so quietly that each day they can put back something of what they have borrowed and spent.

Men who have gotten jittery from overwork can "come back" if they will only get away for a month of complete rest, and then return to work for half days until their old energies return. Women could often cure themselves of functional indigestion if they would only spend mornings quietly in bed for a few weeks. With rest and relaxation would come lowered irritability and less trouble from jangling nerves. Often when I tell a patient this, she replies, "Rest! I've done nothing else for months and I'm no better!" Usually she is wrong: she may not have been working but she wasn't resting. All day and part of the night her mind was racing painfully from one fear to another: fear that the real disease hasn't yet been found, fear of cancer, or that her husband—a few minutes late for dinner—has had an accident.

Most of the fears that bring on nervous indigestion are silly, and the good patient knows it. At first it is hard to fight them but gradually they can be conquered, and health regained. During this period of re-education, patients can profit much from the help of a kindly, sensible physician, but ultimate success depends on the determination with which the individual sets out to re-make himself.

New York Newsreel

CELEBRITY SERVICE, recently organized in New York City by Earl Blackwell and Ted Strong, will, for a fee, send their subscribers daily bulletins on the goings and comings of the people with important names—thus enabling them to lunch at "21" at the same time as Gloria Swanson, or attend the same theater as Marlene Dietrich, Robert Taylor or other stars. "We are able to do this because we have the full coöperation of press agents, movie studios, theaters, broadcasting companies, and air and travel lines," says Mr. Blackwell. "We have more than 300 contacts."

Already Celebrity Service has several hundred "social" subscriptions—people in café society who, if staging a night-club dinner, like to know what important people they will see. Also on the list are resident manufacturers who want to give the visiting buyers a thrill.—N. Y. *World-Telegram*

Einstein, a Study in Simplicity

Condensed from The Nation

EDWIN MULLER

PRINCETON people no longer stare at Einstein; they have become subconsciously aware of him as a massive reality in the background, like Nassau Hall or the football stadium. Einstein may be the "greatest thinker of the age" but he has none of the grand manner.

They found that out upon the Herr Doktor's arrival five years ago. At that time public curiosity boiled. Even the senior faculty members turned to gaze, as he took his first walk. Others shamelessly followed the great man, wondering what profound thoughts seethed behind that vast forehead. Where was he going and what would he do?

If Einstein was aware of all this he gave no sign of it. Finally he turned meditatively into a drugstore. Some of the bolder spirits pressed right up to the window where they could see the great man —eating an ice cream cone.

Einstein lives in a frame house in a quiet back street. The room in which he works is a small chamber, one end of which is almost filled by a big window that looks out upon a garden. He greets you wearing a loose coat, a zipper shirt open at the neck. The mane of fine white hair trembles a little in the breeze. The great eyes under the bushy brows are deeper and softer than any of his pictures can indicate. With a gentle smile of apology he asks for a moment at his table, as he pens a few final sentences of tiny, neat script and mathematical symbols.

His life has been spent in covering thousands of these blank sheets, most of which have gone into the wastebasket. He gropes intuitively, his pen driving on hour after hour. Coming to a blank wall, he plays the piano or violin or goes for a walk. But, consciously or unconsciously, his mind is still on the problem. Essential parts of his theory of relativity occurred to him while wheeling his son in a baby carriage, and during a solitary ramble in Prague.

As you study Einstein's face, you are struck with the look of a man at

438

peace with himself, who has found the way to supreme happiness—a discovery at least comparable to that of relativity.

Is he happy because he has won a renown that seems secure for the ages? His theory of relativity has completely changed the conception of the universe. It has been called the greatest single stride that science has ever made. The 12-page leaflet in which it was presented is, perhaps, the most important document of the century. Within 15 years of its publication 3775 books and pamphlets have been written about it.

More surprising is his reputation with the general public. His face is as widely known as any movie star's. Something about him commands instant response and deference. On a battlefield tour after the war he was lunching at Rheims. A few tables away sat two French officers of high rank and a distinguished lady. They had quickly recognized Einstein. When he got up to leave, all three rose without a word and bowed low and respectfully to the great physicist.

Fame, however, has not made him happy. On the contrary, he literally runs from reporters, photographers and all the hangers-on of glory. When he travels, every day is a struggle between his violent desire to keep curiosity seekers at arm's length and his inability to hurt anybody's feelings.

Part of Einstein's serenity, no doubt, comes from his having had immense potentialities for work. But, equally or more, it is because he has remained a simple, human being with a love for his fellow man.

In all his habits his bent is for simplification. He uses the same soap to wash and to shave with because he doesn't see the need of complicating life by keeping two kinds. In warm weather socks seem superfluous, so at home he doesn't wear them. He throws away letters that don't interest him, no matter how important the people from whom they come. He is sublimely indifferent to money. Once for several weeks he used for a bookmark a $1500 check from the Rockefeller Foundation. Then he lost the book.

His pleasures too are of the simpler sort: walking, sailing a boat. When he sails he sometimes wears a towel draped around his head, making him look like a benevolent pirate. He doesn't believe in wasting mental energy on such games as bridge and chess. He likes to write doggerel, to play parlor games—though only the easier kinds. No alcohol. Smoking is a permitted luxury—three pipes a day. He's not much of a reader. "Reading," he says, "after a certain age diverts the mind too much from its creative pursuits. Any man who reads too much and uses his own brain too little falls into lazy habits of thinking."

He has never had an intellectual's disdain for service to others. When he won the Nobel Prize, he gave the entire $25,000 to charity, though he could ill afford to do it. He is an active champion of causes he believes in.

Once a liner on which he was a passenger stopped over in New York for five days. Greatly in need of rest, he laid down the law: no interviews, no photographs, no public appearances.

But therein he reckoned without himself. The first reporter found the vulnerable spot. "You ought to give us the interview, Dr. Einstein, because it would help the cause of Zionism." Before the ship left Quarantine he had promised to address a public luncheon, a dinner, to broadcast. The whole five days became a turmoil of activity—for Zionism.

That Einstein has a wholesome disregard for the tyranny of custom was shown when, as the guest of honor at a dinner given by the president of Swarthmore, he was called on for a speech. "Ladies and gentlemen," he said, "I am sorry but I have nothing to say—" and sat down. Then he arose and added, "In case I do have something to say, I'll come back." Six months later he wired the president, "Now I have something to say." Another dinner was held, and Einstein made his speech.

Einstein's earliest years were spent in Munich, where his father conducted an unsuccessful electrical business. It never occurred to young Einstein that he was a Jew until one day his teacher showed the class a nail from the True Cross, one that the Jews had driven into the feet of Christ. Pupils turned to stare at Einstein. After that he knew what it was to be a Jew.

In those days too he got his bias toward pacifism. In the 1880's the streets of Munich were full of steel helmets. The little boy conceived a horror of drums and marching soldiers that has lasted all his life.

The course of his early life impelled him to internationalism. While he was still in his teens his family moved to Italy, where he spent some of his happiest days. Then he went to Switzerland to school. He was not a brilliant pupil. He failed completely on his first entrance examination to the school at Zurich. His mind was not responsive to the organized teaching and discipline of schools. The greater part of what he has learned he taught himself. At 14, Kant was his favorite philosopher.

In later years he was a professor in Austria-Hungary, then in Germany. He has been a citizen of many lands and an ardent patriot of none. He yearns for the good of the human race, not to push forward any section of it at the expense of others.

"Nationalism," he says, "is an infantile disease. It is the measles of mankind."

When he was 26 he published his first work on relativity. Then for 10 years he built it patiently, stone by stone. At last, in 1915, the structure was complete.

He had started with the daring assumption that there could be no such thing as absolute time, that two events that are simultaneous to one observer may not be simultaneous to another. That led to the conception of time as a fourth dimension. Every body in the universe, moving relatively to every other body, has its own length, breadth and thickness—and its own time specification.

When Hitler came into power, Einstein shook the dust of Germany from his feet. The Nazis made characteristic gestures of farewell to their greatest scientist—turned him out of the Academy of Sciences, seized his sailboat and other personal property, confiscated his bank account. As a crowning irony they solemnly searched his house for arms.

A woman once asked Einstein if he was convinced that his theory was true.

"I believe it to be true," he answered. "But it will only be proved for certain in the year 1981, when I am dead."

"What will happen then?"

"Well, if I am right the Germans will say I was a German and the French will say I was a Jew; if I am wrong the Germans will say I was a Jew and the French will say I was a German."

In Princeton Einstein has made himself at home again. He works harder than ever. But he remains a simple, emotional, very human being. Before you meet Einstein, you look forward to the experience of talking with a great man. But afterward you realize that you have had a more moving experience—you have seen and talked with a good man.

*A*mericana

Excerpt from The American Mercury

Kentucky: Important civic spectacle is staged by the burghers of Maysville, according to the Portsmouth (Ohio) Times:

E. L. WEAVER walked off with the championship of Mason County in long-distance tobacco spitting. The Orangeburg man nosed out a Mayslick expectorator by a mere one inch when a Weaver stream—propelled from a steady between-the-fingers stance—splashed 17 feet 6 inches away from the line. A crowd of 200 men looked on while the 38 contestants arched their shots eastward on Market Street. Four were disqualified—three for blowing.

We Are Not Poor

Condensed from The American Mercury

ETHEL AMBLER HUNTER

IN A COUNTRY where the doleful refrain of "hard times" still echoes, it might be well to look our poverty in the face and see of what it is made.

Nothing is more demoralizing to the character of a nation or an individual than self-pity; and right now this country seems to be drenched in self-pity. The fact, however, that a large part of our population is considerably better off than the entire populations of other countries seems to suggest that perhaps we are not so unfortunate as we think. At least it is true that we have no need for many of the things we crave—some of them are actually bad for us—and, in comparison with other peoples and other times, the great majority of our 130,000,000 are not poor—not in the true sense of the word, which is destitution.

We *are* poor in the sense of want —we want everything the other fellow has, and if we cannot have it we cry poverty. Poverty is the prevailing excuse for every evasion of debt and duty, used when hard, unpleasant work is offered or when the time comes to contribute to funds for churches, community chests and hospitals.

For example, let me present a young couple in our neighborhood —and to be found in almost any neighborhood—who consider themselves among the so-called poor. The husband has had no luck as a salesman and the young wife supports them, for the most part, by secretarial work. They owe nearly everyone in town. Yet they have a car (a good one), send their boy to a summer camp, take trips during the wife's vacation, and dress well. Mary says it costs her eight dollars a month to keep her hair decent. She forgets that generations of women with handsome hair relied on soap and water and a clean hairbrush instead of a beauty parlor. Certainly they are not poor, and had they belonged to the "poor" of 20 or 30 years ago they would have gone without the things I have mentioned rather than owe money.

On Saturday afternoons in our town, Scout leaders find it impos-

442

sible to organize country hikes, despite their educational and healthful features, and even with refreshments offered free; for Saturday is Movie Day for the children, and this includes the children of those on relief. Out-of-work adults, bitter and discouraged, may need the anodyne of the movies, as social workers say, but why spend money to stupefy children with such unrewarding excitements?

The truth of the matter is that the movies are just another of the extravagances stimulated by contemporary high-pressure salesmanship, which is also responsible for the great demand for glossy new cars, elegant refrigerators, abundant cosmetics and similar luxuries-not-necessities. Since 1932 the American public has decreased its gifts for support of churches by 30 percent, for general benevolences 29 percent, for community chests 24 percent and colleges 18 percent. At the same time, however, expenditures for the luxuries mentioned above, and for theaters, cigarettes, automobiles, liquor, jewelry, radios and other dispensables, have soared by 25 percent to as much as 317 percent.

Years ago, when Americans had fewer luxuries and often ran short of necessities, we were not, strange to say, nearly so self-conscious about poverty. When I was a child few of our neighbors thought they were poor, although today everyone in that neighborhood—my own family among them—would be so labeled. We had no electric or gas lights and no refrigerator. Perish-

ables were kept in the cellar or down the well. Clothes were washed on Monday in two wooden tubs; then the tubs were put away until Saturday, when they were used for the weekly bath. (We had no bathroom.) We had, at most, two pairs of shoes, a best pair and an everyday pair. We had a coat; not a raincoat or a sport coat or a fur coat—just a coat.

Work at the shoe factory where my father was employed was more seasonal than in factories of today, and sometimes he was laid off for months at a time. There was coal to buy, and food and taxes and interest on the mortgage and sometimes a doctor's bill. Yet we never felt poor. We expected to get along and did. Paying the bills was planned far ahead, and paid they were. Nothing was bought that we were not sure we could pay for, and consequently merchants trusted us.

One thing which, I believe, made us happier was that almost forgotten commodity, "elbow grease." After doing a good job we could look anyone in the eye with pride, or face any situation with interest and courage.

Using oil lamps isn't being poor, nor is going without white coats or cars or permanents. Living in a cellar is, and so is insufficient milk for the baby, or the responsibility for sick, indigent parents. The greatest calamity, however, is *feeling* poor— the beaten spirit, the petty stinginess to keep up an outside show.

A sturdy sense of well-being *can* be cultivated and the will-to-do restored, if only we will find another god than the "good car"; other happiness than that found in costly and exhausting amusements and expensive (or expensive-looking) clothes. There are still sunshine and fresh air, soap and water, books, friends, fields to walk in, streams to fish in, woods to roam.

If we can't go back to something simpler and more wholesome, or forward to something finer, then the whole race of Americans as the world thinks of them—the American of robust humor, courage and the ability to turn in casually a tremendous amount of excellent work —will have vanished from the earth. Then, indeed, we shall be poor.

Greenbelt Goes Completely Coöperative

THOSE who lament that America's last frontier is gone should visit Greenbelt, Md., the little resettlement town founded by the New Deal. Here, in a new outpost in the wilderness of economics, a band of men and women, in homes flung in crescent pattern among the trees, have voluntarily decided to try something never tried before in a modern American community. They are about to buy, and operate for themselves, all the stores which serve their town.

Ownership will be acquired through the sale of stock. Each share will cost $10. Half of Greenbelt's families must invest to make the coöperative effective under the charter granted the town by the government. One family may buy as many shares as it likes, but, no matter how many, it gets only one vote in the management. Each share-holder becomes a part owner of everything in town: The food store, the drugstore, the gas station, the motion picture theater which will open soon, etc.

Belief in the coöperative idea is exhibited in unmistakable ways. For example, salaries in Greenbelt run from $22 to $45 a week, mostly in the lower brackets. Anyone earning more may not remain a resident of Greenbelt. The Greenbelt health association guarantees for its members medical care, preventive and remedial, at a cost of a $5 membership fee and weekly payments ranging from $1.50 for an unmarried person to $2.25 for a man, wife and four children.

There are 698 families now living in Greenbelt. The Resettlement Administration spent more than $14,000,000, and employed 3000 WPA workers to provide sewage and garbage disposal, to put modern plumbing and electricity (including electric stoves) in every home, to build modern schools.

Greenbelt critics ask whether it was worth so much of the taxpayers' money to try to prove the worth of resettlement. The people of Greenbelt answer that "a couple of Greenbelts could be built for the cost of one battleship," and besides, the government expects to get its money back in rents over 60 years.

© *1938, AP; N. Y. Herald Tribune (August 7, '38)*
230 W. 41 St., N. Y. C.

The Personal Touch

Condensed from Forbes

FRANK J. TAYLOR

"DON'T LET your employes tell you how to run your business," was the advice older business men gave young W. A. Patterson when he was tossed unexpectedly into the presidency of United Air Lines.

But he does. He spends a full third of his time talking with pilots, radio men, hostesses, dispatchers, watchmen and clerks. He chats with every one of United's 2000 employes at least once a year. They tell him what they think he ought to do. And he does it.

Here are some of their suggestions: Flight control from the ground; high level flights; the flying laboratory to study storms and static; free trips for wives, to overcome women's prejudice against air travel. Every one of these innovations was adopted. And more than half of the progressive steps United has taken under Patterson grew out of talks with employes.

Patterson believes in the personal touch. "When I look at my job coldly," he explains, "I realize that I am merely the fellow who moti-vates policies; their success depends upon many people, and I know I can't get results without their enthusiasm."

He wasn't always that way. New in his job in 1933 and full of the spirit of "I'll run my own business," he met the threat of a pilots' strike with plans to use strike breakers. Still, when three veteran pilots asked him to come to the Newark airport one night and hear their side of the story, he went.

An all-night powwow ensued. The pilots told how they had risked their lives to help build the air mail service through its hectic, dangerous infancy. They told how they lived, how they had been treated by the nonfliers who gave them their orders. They aired their pet grievances and argued their need for better pay. Most of the things they asked were so reasonable that along about sunrise Patterson exclaimed: "I've learned something tonight. I think you fellows are about 90 percent right and the company is 90 percent wrong. Let's submit our wage and hour differ-

445

ences to an arbitrator. Meantime, I'll go over the whole line and settle every pilot's individual grievance personally."

The strike order was canceled and the new president packed his bags. He spent all of the next two months out along the main line. He listened to pilots and co-pilots hour after hour, encouraging them to tell him how to run the company.

Patterson returned to his office full of new ideas. Schemes for getting more business. Ways to save time and reduce hazards. In fact, the two months proved so fruitful that he spent five additional months that year soliciting suggestions from every man and woman working for the concern. At each airport he gathered the staff around a table and began, "I've come out here to talk some company problems over with you, but first let's take up your own. They're just as important."

Discussing company problems, he gave frank, open answers to anything any employe wanted to know about the concern. Patterson holds that any employe is entitled to know how much money the company has in the bank, how much the executives are paid, who owns stock, what costs are, or anything else. Every employe feels that United is his company; every United man or woman is a public relations assistant able and eager to answer questions the public asks.

On the president's desk each morning is a report telling him the condition of every employe who has been ill over a week. Likewise, every birth or death in any United

worker's family. If anyone working for the company is in financial straits, and a superintendent finds out about it, this is reported, too. Shop men or ticket agents or stewardesses wonder how in the world their chief knows about them, when he greets them along the line. The answer is, he makes it a major part of his job to know.

He analyzes living costs monthly in every city in which the company has employes. If living costs in Cheyenne jump, Patterson wants to know it before the employes in United's huge overhaul shop there feel the pinch, so that he can adjust the payroll to offset it.

Each December, the president visits every division center and shop. From the payroll list every employe's name is read, after which his immediate superior has to answer these questions:

How long has this man been with the company? When was his last raise? Is he entitled to an increase? Why not? Does he know what's the matter? Why not? Six months later, the president checks to see if John Jones has made an improvement.

A few years ago, union agents undertook to organize United's Cheyenne shops but the shop men soon objected to paying dues in order to get a square deal when they didn't have to go to that expense. The only employes of United Air Lines who belong to a union today are the pilots, and their minimum guarantee is above the A. F. of L. scale.

Every three months each pilot and co-pilot must take rigid examinations to prove that he has kept pace with the amazing progress of air navigation. As the older men fall by the wayside, making way for the younger men highly trained in technical schools, the company tries to find posts for them on ground jobs.

Soon after United Air Lines absorbed Varney Air Lines, a superintendent handed in a list of Varney employes he did not think were needed.

"Wait a minute," Patterson exploded. "The personnel is three quarters of an air line's assets and these people must be worth something or they wouldn't have built Varney up to be worth the $2,000,-000 we paid for the line." Jobs were found for most of them, to the company's advantage as well as the men's.

Pilots once had to cancel trips in questionable weather at their own expense because under the union wage agreement they were paid by the mile. When his talks with pilots brought this to light, Patterson guaranteed them their monthly minimum of $650 through the winter, thus eliminating the premium on taking chances.

He discovered a practice of docking men when they were ill. When he ordered full-time pay for sick leave, other executives protested that it would cost the company $10,000 a month. "All right, it's worth it," he argued. Actually it has cost only $1800 a month. The good will it developed was worth many times the added expense.

Last winter two pilots came unannounced to say that they wanted to discuss wages. (Any employe who wants to see him takes precedence over anyone else.) The president settled back and prepared for the worst.

"Pat," began one of them, "we know the recession has hit the business. So we've taken it upon ourselves to sound out sentiment along the line, and everybody we've talked to is willing to take a voluntary 10 percent cut to help you pull through."

Patterson recovered from his astonishment, and voiced his gratitude, but added that cutting wages was the last thing he intended to do to reduce expenses. "A 10 percent wage cut would save about $300,-000 a year," he said. "I bet we could save that much by eliminating waste."

"All right," proposed one pilot. "Let's see how many economies we can effect."

The two fliers organized a drive against the little losses in human effort and materials. They quickly passed the word along the 5000-mile air line that the boss had refused their offer to cut wages, and urged every employe to help make up the deficit by more efficient operating. In the eight months since, Patterson estimates that the voluntary war on waste saved the company at least $185,000. Which is one more reason why the president's door is always open to anyone in United's rank and file who wants to talk things over.

Toward a More Picturesque Speech

How Else Would You Say It?

¶Let your speech be always with grace,
seasoned with salt. — Colossians IV:6

HE'S a very small patch on the seat of government.[1] . . . He knows so little and knows it so fluently.[2] . . . A dogma-in-the-manger attitude, discouraging argument.[3]

HIS BREAKFAST is an affair of a hand groping out from behind a paper.[4] . . . The noise from good toast should reverberate in the head like the thunder of July.[5] . . . Wherever he sat was the head of the table.[6]

THE COOL kindliness of sheets, that soon smooth away trouble.[7]

SHE ENTERED as quietly as a sunbeam.[8] . . . We met and she thought I was a pane of glass.[9] . . . Across the floor they sailed, a coquettish yacht convoyed by a stately cruiser.[10] . . . Inseparable as a pair of pants.[11] . . . An appendix girl, the kind that gets taken out.[12]

HE WAS savaging the end of a cigar.[13]

SHE FELT as if her mind had a temperature.[14] . . . A mental toothache.[1] . . . Her heart stuttered.[15]

SHE WAS built in terraces.[16] . . . Already a second edition of his chin had been published.[17] . . . His Adam's apple slipped a cog.[17] . . . A fat hand corseted with rings.[18] . . . Hair blacker than a yard up a chimney.[19] . . . Sexless as a nut.[20] . . . A handlebar mustache.[21]

CLOUDS: the traveling mountains of the sky.[22] . . . The cat poured itself through the fence.[23]

SHE WAS regarded less as a woman than as a memorable occasion.[2] . . . A golden character, his entire fortune.[11] . . . A little nosegay of an old lady.[24] . . . A scorpion of a woman, stinging her way through life.[25] . . . She sputtered like a string of firecrackers.[26] . . . Always acting as if she were playing the title rôle at a funeral.[27] . . . She does a good deal of her thinking in quotation marks.[28]

1. Mary Roberts Rinehart. 2. Ellen Glasgow. 3. Weare Holbrook. 4. Helen Hull. 5. E. V. Lucas. 6. "Gentleman With a Duster." 7. Rupert Brooke. 8. William Makepeace Thackeray. 9. Clemence Dane and Helen Simpson. 10. O. Henry. 11. Mark Twain. 12. Graeme and Sarah Lorimer. 13. David Frome. 14. Sylvia Thompson. 15. Robert Smith. 16. Dorothy Parker. 17. P. G. Wodehouse. 18. Edith Wharton. 19. Damon Runyon. 20. Henry Seidel Canby. 21. Norman Klein. 22. Robert Louis Stevenson. 23. Anne Parrish. 24. Rebecca West. 25. Dale Collins. 26. Katherine Haviland-Taylor. 27. Ring Lardner. 28. Eleanor Mercein.

Address Unknown

Condensed from Story

KRESSMANN TAYLOR

Schulse-Eisenstein Galleries
San Francisco, California
November 12, 1932

Herrn Martin Schulse
Schloss Rantzenburg
Munich, Germany

MY DEAR MARTIN:

Back in Germany! How I envy you! Although I have not seen it since my school days, the spell of *Unter den Linden* is still strong upon me—the discussions, the music, the lighthearted comradeship. And now the old Junker spirit, the Prussian arrogance and militarism are gone. You go to a democratic Germany.

Of course you are right to go. You never became American despite your success here, and now that the business is so well established you and Elsa must take your boys back to the homeland to be educated.

The business continues to go well. Mrs. Levine has bought the small Picasso at our price, for which I congratulate myself, and I have old Mrs. Fleshman playing with the notion of buying that hideous Madonna.

A delightful letter came yesterday from Griselle. She writes that she is about to make me proud of my little sister. She has the lead in a new play in Vienna and the notices are excellent. Poor child, it has not been easy for her, but she has never complained. She asked about you, Martin, in a very friendly way. Bitterness passes quickly when one is as young as she is. Of course neither of you was to be blamed. Those things are like quick storms, for a moment you are drenched and blasted, then it passes, and although you have neither quite forgotten, there remains only gentleness and no sorrow.

I have not yet written her that you are in Europe but I know she would be glad to feel that friends are not far away.

With the most affectionate remembrances to Elsa and the boys,

MAX

Schloss Rantzenburg
Munich, Germany
December 10, 1932

Mr. Max Eistenstein
Schulse-Eisenstein Galleries
San Francisco, California

MAX, DEAR OLD FELLOW:

The check and accounts came through promptly, for which my thanks. Here at Munich we are established, but what a turmoil! The house I got at an amazing bargain. Thirty rooms and about ten acres of park, you would never believe it. But then, you could not appreciate how poor is now this sad land of mine. To Elsa's family we seem millionaires, for our American income places us among the wealthy here. The better foods are high in price and there is much political unrest even now under the presidency of Hindenburg, a fine liberal whom I much admire.

You write of Griselle. So she wins her success, the lovely one! I rejoice with you, although even now I resent it that she must struggle to win her way alone. Although you were silent during our stormy affair, you know that our decision was not easy. For Griselle I keep a tenderness that will last long after she has married someone else.

You must urge her to make contact with us. Elsa will welcome your sister, as she would welcome you. Give her our most warm congratulations for her success.

MARTIN

San Francisco
January 21, 1933

MY DEAR MARTIN:

I was glad to forward your address to Griselle. What jollification there will be when she sees you all! And I too shall be with you in spirit.

The oils you sent for the gallery are excellent, and the prices amazing. I shall dispose of them at an appalling profit almost at once. And the ugly Madonna is gone! Yes, to old Mrs. Fleshman. How I exulted as she bore the horror off, you alone will know.

Who is this Adolf Hitler who seems rising toward power in Germany? I do not like what I read of him.

Your ever affectionate
MAX

Munich
March 25, 1933

DEAR OLD MAX:

You have heard of course of the new events in Germany. I tell you truly, Max, I think in many ways Hitler is good for Germany, but I am not sure. The man is like an electric shock, strong as only a great orator and a zealot can be. But I ask myself, is he quite sane? His brown-shirt troops are of the rabble. They pillage and have started a bad Jew-baiting. But these may be minor things, the little surface scum when a big movement boils up. For I tell you, my friend, there is a surge—a surge. The people everywhere have had a quickening. The old despair has been thrown aside like a forgotten coat. A leader is found! Yet cautiously to myself I ask, a leader to where?

Publicly, as is natural, I express no doubt. I am now an official and a worker in the new regime and I exult very loud indeed.

So much for politics. Ourselves, we delight in our new home and have done much entertaining. Tonight the mayor is our guest, at a dinner for 28. We spread ourselves a little, maybe, but that is to be forgiven.

Meanwhile, our hearts go out to you across the wide sea, and when the glasses are filled we toast "Uncle Max."

Yours in affectionate regard,

MARTIN

Eisenstein Galleries
San Francisco
May 18, 1933

DEAR MARTIN:

I am in distress at the reports that come pouring in to us from the Fatherland, picturing a terrible pogrom, and I turn to you for light. I know that from you I can have the truth. These things may be, as you have said, but the brutal surface froth of revolution. But to us Jews it is almost unbelievable that the old familiar martyrdom must be endured in a civilized nation today. Write me, my friend, and set my mind at ease.

Griselle's play will close in June after a great success. She has a very fine offer in Berlin for the autumn, but I have written her to wait until the anti-Jewish feeling has abated.

Forgive me for so distrait a letter but I cannot rest until you have reassured me.

MAX

Deutsch-Voelkische Bank und
Handelsgeselschaft, München
July 9, 1933

DEAR MAX:

You see that I write upon the stationery of my bank. This is necessary because I have a request to make and I wish to avoid the new censorship which is most strict. We must for the present discontinue writing. If a communication becomes necessary you must enclose it with the bank draft and not write to me at my house.

As for the stern measures that so distress you, I myself did not like them at first, but I have come to see their painful necessity. The Jewish race is a sore spot to any nation that harbors it. I have never hated the individual Jew—yourself I have always cherished as a friend, but in all honesty I have loved you, not because of your race but in spite of it.

But this Jew trouble is only an incident. Something bigger is happening. If I could show you, if I could make you see—the rebirth of this new Germany under our Gentle Leader! In defeat for 14 years we bowed our heads in shame and poverty. But now we are free men. We purge our bloodstream of its baser elements, rise in our might and hold our heads up before the nations.

But no. I am sure you will not

see how necessary is all this for Germany. You will not see that a few must suffer for the millions to be saved. You will be a Jew first and wail for your people. This is the Semitic character. You lament but you are never brave enough to fight back. That is why there are pogroms.

I regret our correspondence must close this way, Max.

Perhaps we can someday meet again on a field of better understanding.

As ever your
MARTIN SCHULSE

San Francisco
September 5, 1933

DEAR MARTIN:

Enclosed are your draft and the month's accounts. It is of necessity that I send a brief message. Griselle has gone to Berlin. She is too daring. But she has waited so long for success, and she laughs at my fears. She will be at the König Theater.

You are an official. For old friendship's sake, I beg of you watch over her. Go to Berlin if you can and see whether she is in danger.

Your new attitude I cannot discuss. But understand me. I did not expect you would take up arms for my people because they are my people, but because you were a man who loved justice.

I commend my rash Griselle to you. The child does not realize what a risk she is taking. I shall not write again.

Good-bye, my friend.
MAX

San Francisco
November 5, 1933

MARTIN:

I write again because I must. A black foreboding possesses me. I wrote Griselle in Berlin and she answered briefly. Rehearsals were going brilliantly; the play would open shortly. My second letter has been returned to me, marked only *Adressant Unbekannt*. Addressee unknown—what a darkness those words carry! How can she be unknown? It is surely a message that she has come to harm. They know what has happened to her, those stamped letters say, but I am not to know. This they tell me in two words, *Adressant Unbekannt.*

Martin, need I ask you to find her? Do not attempt to write to me. I know I need not even ask you to aid. It is enough to tell you that she must be in danger.

I leave her in your hands, for I am helpless.

MAX

San Francisco
November 23, 1933

MARTIN:

I turn to you in despair. For two months there has been only silence from Griselle, and now dread rumors begin to come. She appeared in the Berlin play for a week. Then she was jeered from the audience as a Jewess. She is so headstrong, she threw the word back in their teeth. She told them proudly that she *was* a Jewess.

Some of the audience started after her, but she escaped and took refuge with a Jewish family. After several days, she changed her appearance as much as she could and started south, hoping to walk back to Vienna. She did not dare try the railroads. She told those she left that she would be safe if she could reach friends in Munich. That is my hope, that she has gone to you, for she has never reached Vienna. God grant you can send me a word of relief!

MAX

Deutsch-Voelkische Bank und Handelsgeselschaft, München December 8, 1933

DEAR MAX:

Heil Hitler! I much regret that I have bad news for you. Your sister is dead.

Unfortunately she was, as you have said, very much a fool. Not quite a week ago she came here, with a bunch of storm troopers almost right behind her. By luck I answer the door. At first I think it is an old woman and then I see the face, and then I see the storm troopers have turned in the park gates. Can I hide her? It is one chance in thousands.

Can I risk being arrested for harboring a Jew and lose all I have built up here?

"You will destroy us all, Griselle," I tell her. "You must run back further in the park." She looks at me and smiles (she was always a brave girl) and makes her own choice.

"I would not bring you harm, Martin," she says, and she runs toward the trees. But she must be tired. She does not run very fast and the storm troopers catch her. I am helpless. I go in the house and in a few minutes she stops screaming, and in the morning I have the body sent away for burial. She was a fool to come to Germany. Poor little Griselle.

I grieve with you, but as you see, I was helpless to aid her.

I must now demand you do not write again. I cannot tell how soon they may start to open the mail to the bank. It is not so good for me that a Jewess came here for refuge, and no further association can be tolerated.

A new Germany is being shaped here. We will soon show the world great things under our Glorious Leader.

MARTIN

Cablegram

MARTIN SCHULSE
MUNICH JANUARY 2, 1934
YOUR TERMS ACCEPTED PAN EXHIBITION MAY FIRST PREPARE LEAVE FOR MOSCOW IF MARKET OPENS UNEXPECTEDLY FINANCIAL INSTRUCTIONS MAILED YOUR NEW ADDRESS
EISENSTEIN

San Francisco January 3, 1934

Herrn Martin Schulse
Schloss Rantzenburg
Munich, Germany
OUR DEAR MARTIN:

Don't forget grandma's birthday. She will be 64 on the 8th. American contributors will furnish 1000 brushes for your German Young Painters' League. Mandelberg has joined in supporting the League. You must send 11 Picasso reproductions, 20 by 90, to branch galleries on the 25th, no sooner. Reds and blues must predominate. We can allow you $8000 on this transaction.

Our prayers follow you daily, dear brother.

EISENSTEIN

San Francisco
January 17, 1934

MARTIN, DEAR BROTHER:

Good news! The Fleishmans have advanced another $10,000. This will fill your Young Painters' League quota for a month but let us know if opportunities increase. Swiss miniatures are having a vogue. You must watch the market and plan to be in Zurich after May first.

Uncle Solomon will be very glad to see you and I know that you can rely heavily on his judgment.

Our hopes will follow your new efforts.

Success to you!

EISENSTEIN

Munich
February 12, 1934

MAX, MY OLD FRIEND:

My God, Max, do you know what you do? I shall try to smuggle this letter out with an American. I write in appeal from a despair you cannot imagine. This crazy cable!

These letters you have sent. I am called in to account for them and they demand I give them the code. A code? How can you, a friend of long years, do this to me?

Already the results of your madness are terrible. I am bluntly told I must resign my office.

Yes, yes, I know why you do it —but do you not understand I could do nothing? What could I have done? I did not dare to try. I beg of you, not for myself, but for Elsa and the boys—think what it means to them if I am taken away and they do not know if I live or die.

Do you know what it is to be taken to a concentration camp? I beg of you, stop. I am in fear for my life—for my life, Max!

I have loved you like a brother, my old Maxel. My God, have you no mercy? I beg you, Max, no more, no more! Stop while I can be saved. From a heart filled with old affection I ask it.

MARTIN

San Francisco
March 3, 1934

OUR DEAR MARTIN:

A shipment of 1500 brushes should reach the Berlin branch for your painters by this week-end. This will allow time for practice before the big exhibition. American patrons will help with all the supplies.

Young Blum left last Friday with the Picasso specifications. He will leave oils in Hamburg and Leipzig and will then place himself at your disposal. We leave all final plans to your discretion but urge an early date for wholly successful exhibit.

The God of Moses be at your right hand.

EISENSTEIN

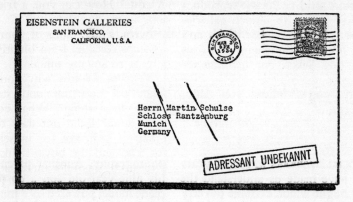

EISENSTEIN GALLERIES
SAN FRANCISCO,
CALIFORNIA, U.S.A.

Herrn Martin Schulse
Schloss Rantzenburg
Munich
Germany

ADRESSANT UNBEKANNT

Keeping up with the World

Excerpts from a regular department in Collier's

Froling Foster

LIVE premature births have taken place as early as 215 days, or more than nine weeks before the normal duration of 280 days, and post-mature births have occurred as late as 330 days, or a little over seven weeks after the full term, a total difference of nearly four months.

HEALTHY BABIES have been born to mothers as young as seven years of age and as old as 62 years.

The youngest paternity case known to medical science is that of a boy who was only 13 years of age, while the oldest is that of a man who was more than 100.

Our Overprivileged Children

Adapted from Your Life Magazine

ROSE G. ANDERSON, Ph.D.

SOCIAL WORKERS in recent years have made us understand the blight which extreme poverty visits upon underprivileged children. Yet intimate contact with homes in many parts of the United States convinces me that all too often parents in better circumstances impose equally severe handicaps upon their children by giving them too *many* privileges. They surround them with possessions which they themselves were denied in their own youth. They pamper them, satisfy their every desire, and think that thus they are giving their youngsters advantages. Actually, in the case of thousands of boys and girls, normal childhood is blighted by such "advantages."

No one denies that children should be warmly clothed and supplied with proper play equipment. But the damage is done when parents *anticipate* the child's every wish. One father I know presented his ten-year-old boy with an expensive movie camera before the child had expressed any desire for it, or had mastered the elements of photography. Another parent gave his nine-year-old son a costly airplane model powered by a miniature gas engine. On its first flight the machine was wrecked. How much better if the father had first let the boy build his own model from ten-cent store material.

By such extravagant indulgences as these, parents deny their children one of the most precious experiences in life—the opportunity to *yearn* for something. Only by yearning is the child challenged to work and plan and save for his objective. Remove this incentive, and you destroy a tremendous stimulus to growth.

Fond mothers, straining to hurl their small daughters over social hurdles, go to preposterous lengths. It is not uncommon to see 10-year-olds at a children's party with marcelled hair and fashionable evening frocks. The warping effect of such nonsense upon grade-school children is more than the strongest character can stand.

No wonder these children grow up with a distorted sense of values,

456

and without regard for property that they never wanted in the first place. I know a 12-year-old girl who left a pair of riding boots and a hand-knitted sweater in her locker at the end of the school year. When her teacher asked what to do about them, the girl replied, "Throw them away. I never liked them anyway." At another school, despite every effort to return unclaimed articles, there remained at the end of the year 19 pairs of gloves, 17 hats, six sweaters, many pairs of rubbers and sneakers, and miscellaneous articles including bracelets, fountain pens and manicure kits. Either the children did not recognize their property or were too indifferent to claim it!

What a commentary upon parental training! When a child makes no effort to locate lost possessions it means that the parents were indifferent to the loss, or that they were so complacent about spending money to replace it that the loss made no impression on the child. Obviously those parents are neglecting an important opportunity for habit-training.

It is only a step from disregard of one's own property to disregard for the property of others. Teachers tell me that children from such homes are carelessly destructive of school and playground property; even that common honesty is not a major concern with them. They pick up fountain pens or sporting equipment wherever they find them.

A 12-year-old girl in a fashionable New York school handed her teacher a ten-cent tip for picking up her coat from the floor. Her twisted little mind led her to believe that money was a valid substitute for ordinary politeness. Unmannerly conduct, bordering on insolence toward parents, teachers and servants, is a characteristic of the overprivileged but underbred child. This is not primarily the child's fault; the blame must be borne by parents who are either animated by false ideals, or are too "busy" with social and financial strivings to instruct their children in the rudiments of courtesy.

Parents frequently complain that the school "doesn't teach my son work-habits." But the school is not to blame for your son's failure to see a task through. Instead of grounding him from early childhood in habits of self-reliance and application, you have given him money that he should have earned himself, permitted him to grow up without discipline or the need for ambitious self-direction. And now you are angry because he is failing at school! Even yet, perhaps, you haven't begun to realize that these failures in school will be followed by similar, graver failures in later life.

If one of the main objects of education is to prepare your child for adult life, then he muust be taught the importance of work and the thrill of accomplishment in a job well done. In too many of America's comfortable homes, children absorb the idea that physical work is "menial," degrading. Nothing could be more hurtful to the formation of character. From early years, they should be given regular household tasks and required to carry them through.

The value of money can be tied up with the importance of work. It is ridiculous to keep a child's little pocketbook stuffed with money far beyond his needs. Let him first learn how to manage a few pennies, how to spend some and save the rest. If this allowance is gradually increased, the child will develop a proper regard for the value of money, and what it can—and cannot—buy.

Lastly I would say to parents, "Give more of your own time and interest to your children's affairs." They are quick to appreciate the difference between lavish gifts—hollow things at best—and your companionship, your comradely concern with their pleasures and work. Spend yourself on your children—the dividends in family enjoyment and mental health, in juvenile character and adult integration will be more lasting and valuable than any material riches you can shower upon them.

Keeping up with the World

Excerpts from a regular department in Collier's
Freling Foster

A LARGE American company, which manufactures all kinds of crooked gambling devices, makes 62 different decks of marked cards that virtually defy disclosure and 73 kinds and combinations of transparent dice so cleverly loaded that they can be cut, burned, weighed or measured with calipers without detection.

ONE OF the cleverest card-cheating tricks ever devised is now being used by professional gamblers. The cards are marked with a certain ink that is visible only through the special dark glasses worn by the head of the gang, who keeps his confederates informed about each deal.

AT LEAST one man—a chemistry professor at Harvard—kept his promise to "eat his shirt" when he was proved to be wrong. He dissolved the shirt in acid, neutralized the acid with a base, filtered out the precipitated material, spread it on a slice of bread and ate it.

THE HATRED of Empress Anne of Russia for a certain bridal couple attached to her court resulted, in 1740, in one of history's most singular honeymoons. She made them spend it in a large house built of ice and equipped with ice furniture—which she had constructed in the center of a frozen lake.

PLAYING classical music on the piano requires faster thinking than any other activity. Notes and fingering, accidentals, interpretations, pauses, phrasing, pedaling, meter and rhythm of some pieces demand 60 mental operations a second.

Tim's a Capitalist Now

Condensed from Survey Graphic

WILLIAM F. McDERMOTT

TIM IS a warehouse truckman. For 19 years he has worked in the Chicago factory of the Joslyn Manufacturing & Supply Company, makers of electric light and power line equipment. Tim is on the threshold of 60 and is counting the days until he can spend all his time on his three-acre "patch" beyond the city limits.

"I'm a capitalist, now," he says.

Tim started on his way up by tucking away $1.50 weekly for 50 weeks each year, telling the company to take it out of his $30 pay envelope. For the first 11 years, the company's profit-sharing plan matched Tim's dollar four to one. The slump reduced the company's contribution for a time, but even so, with compound interest, Tim now has a credit of $15,200. That's about $11 for every $1 he has put in. He can invest it, if he wishes, in preferred stock of his company, or he can take the principal in monthly payments, with interest on the balance. Or he can collect a lump sum.

Another employe who this year reached 60 died a few weeks ago; his widow got one of the company's profit-sharing checks for $17,700. A machinist has paid in $97 a year since 1923. His contributions of $1452 in a little over 15 years have produced for him a credit of $11,200. A foreman soon to "check out" will receive $29,106, and another executive $36,278.

The Joslyn Company had its plan in operation for 18 years before the public found out about it. Then a financial editor who chanced in at a stockholders' meeting printed the story. Since then 6000 corporations and individuals have asked for details. A group of industrial relations experts recently pronounced it among the best of 165 profit-sharing and pension systems minutely studied—the 165 being chosen out of 4000 now in operation.

Employes "chip in" five percent of their wages; the company appropriates 10 percent of its net profits to the fund. It is controlled by a board of three officers and two elected employes. Factory workers number 85 percent of the members. When an employe reaches 60 or is disabled by accident or ill health, he receives the entire amount to his credit. A worker may retire at 50 or 55 if his health is not good. He will be regarded as disabled and receive the full amount. If he quits his job, he receives all that he paid in with half of what the company deposited to his credit and compound interest on both. The other half of the company contribution reverts to the fund.

At the end of three years' service, an employe must join the plan or resign. The company frankly says, "If a man can't see the advantage for him in this plan, he isn't the kind of man we want working for us."

On the other hand, a board of three executives and two employes governs labor relations and a man cannot be discharged without approval of one of the labor votes.

When M. L. Joslyn was graduated from Harvard Law School in 1896, he received a present of $5000 with which to tour Europe. He was gone three months, spent $1600. The $3400 he had left is the only capital he ever had.

The practice of law did not appeal to him. He took charge of a tottering concern, made it pay, became a "business doctor," and within a year after graduation, he was in 11 different kinds of business, including the ownership and operation of a telephone exchange. He bought a factory to manufacture equipment to extend his telephone system. When power lines began to develop, he expanded again, organized the present company in 1902.

In the meantime, the young industrialist was trying to work out his profit-sharing ideas, on the theory that you must get people to work *with* you, not *for* you. He held that if you want workers to defend capitalism, you must make capitalists out of them. He believed the easiest pushover for the political crackpot—they had plenty of them in those days, too—is the toiler who looks forward to a penniless old age.

Joslyn evolved a business philosophy: "Pay capital enough to keep it interested and pay management ability enough to keep it functioning, then give the rest of the profits to the workers."

So for 20 years, Joslyn tried one plan after another. He gave workmen stock certificates which brought generous dividends at the end of the year. He found that not one in ten had a nickel of the extra money left in 60 days. The bonus system was next, but its benefits were transitory. He figured the average pension system was but "a crust thrown to an old dog in the corner." He decided then on a profit-sharing plan which should be cumulative, so that a man would think seriously before throwing up his job, and so remunerative that an employe would be relieved of all worries about the future, thus releasing energies for more efficient work.

The Joslyn plan was launched January 1, 1919, when all industry was suffering from the postwar turnover of labor. At first it met suspicion that it was designed to offset low wages.

"We promptly announced that as in the past, our wages would be as high always as those paid by our leading competitors," said Mr. Joslyn. "The plan would be a sham otherwise. At the end of three years, all abnormal labor turnover was ended and every foreman reported that increased efficiency more than offset the cost of the plan. This has been true ever since, so capital has been satisfied. The plan has satisfied the public; we have produced better material at lower cost. Our executives have been satisfied; we have not lost a manager, salesman or office man of any standing in the 19 years. And we never have had one moment of labor trouble."

Joslyn lists other things the plan has achieved: High morale and loy-

alty; capital and labor antagonism eliminated by making workers capitalists; better production, because employes work for themselves as well as for the company; no loss of trained men to competitors.

The firm has averaged 13.3 percent net profit for 19 years. Yet the company is in a highly competitive field and enjoys no patent monopoly or other special privilege. Mr. Joslyn credits these results to efficient production.

He believes that any profit-sharing scheme superimposed on labor without effort on its part is worthless. He thinks it is a partnership enterprise—not a matter of beneficence, but of engineering, requiring good technique as well as good intentions if it is to succeed.

Nineteen years of successful operation during which the plan has survived a major boom and a major depression seem to prove the point.

$\mathcal{A}$mericana

Excerpts from The American Mercury

The Uplift invades the Windy City's twilight zone, according to the Chicago Tribune:

GAMBLING HOUSES, disorderly houses, and similar places are being visited by 150 federal agents who have been assigned to collect the Social Security tax.

The Chicago Tribune reports also a confusing sign on display in Jackson Park Hospital—in the Obstetrical Ward:

NO CHILDREN ALLOWED

Try Everything Once

Condensed from The Rotarian

WILLIAM MOULTON MARSTON

THE HAPPIEST people are those who touch life at the greatest number of points. People who suffer are those who have only one interest of which fate robs them."

If you ever saw a blind man recover his sight, the vital truth of those words of Colonel Theodore Roosevelt will strike you instantly. I remember a victim of brain tumor who had the growth removed after 15 years of darkness. I shall never forget the transfigured expression on that man's face when his dark glasses were taken off and he rediscovered the colorful world of vision. He had begun to touch life again at a whole mind-full of new points.

Hundreds of people who came to consult me about getting more happiness out of life are just as blind as the man with the tumor. They concentrate all their attention fiercely upon a single source of happiness. They need a psychological operation to open their mental and emotional eyes so that they can see all around them activities which would furnish new reasons for living.

With too many of us, growing up is a matter of narrowing down interests. Children at first are interested in everything. As their ability to concentrate develops they begin to eliminate those parts of the world which do not serve their immediate purpose. Unless carefully directed they soon form stupid habits of rejection and suffer loss of enjoyments accordingly. They may concentrate upon activities called "play" and reject everything called "work," forming a mental habit which blinds them for years, perhaps for life, to the joys of constructive endeavor.

Maturity usually means the adoption of new rejection habits. To concentrate on money-making and reject love, laughter and social life is the rule rather than the exception among many men. And to concentrate upon routine home duties to the exclusion of love, gaiety and broader mental interests is the rule among many women.

If a person has narrowed his

world constantly from childhood, the only way he can retrieve his lost liberty of living is to adopt and follow persistently the precept: try everything once—everything, that is, which adapts itself reasonably to human use. He must form a new, positive habit which will counteract the inertia created by his old one, which will pull him out of his easy chair and make him manipulate unknown objects.

People complain that they haven't money to see the pyramids, or time to study music or spend the winter in Florida. What they fail to realize is that one person's routine is another's high adventure. If you list the normal activities a dozen of your friends enjoy you will be surprised at the number of everyday experiences you yourself have never tried. Dealing with Arabian thieves and reading Egyptian hieroglyphics would certainly be novelties in my life but they are familiar routine to a man I know who conducts archeological expeditions. This same chap, however, recently visited the Bronx Zoo for the first time and read his first mystery novel, two quite ordinary acts in the lives of many, but new and adventurous to the archeologist.

Here are some of the things I recently suggested to a housewife for her first experiment: try skating with your children; try needlepoint—stores give free lessons; try reading Dickens; try listening to good music—buy some new records; try meeting your husband in town every Friday night and seeing a show—I've heard him suggest that;

try creating a new dish each week, without a recipe. I suggested ten things to try; she liked seven of the new experiences so much that she is keeping on with them. To touch life at seven new points is to be happier.

"I haven't time for anything but my present occupation," you rationalize. If that is true, you are in a dangerous spot. You are putting all your emotional eggs into one basket. The chances are a hundred to one that your basket will be lost, stolen or accidentally destroyed. And where are you then? Sunk, deprived at one blow of all your driving energy, of all your purpose and vital interest. Mothers whose children are their whole lives find themselves emotionally occupationless when the youngsters leave home. Some men, retiring from business, literally pine away. I cannot think of a single case where complete concentration of emotional interest brought happiness. And I can cite hundreds where it led the single-track individual to a dead-end crash.

Our habit of time-beating often shuts us off from entertaining and amusing objects and episodes along our way as effectively as an eye bandage. It concentrates the time-beater's attention on his watch, his schedule, and obstacles which may delay him. I know dozens of people who would pay a quarter to see a newsreel of the Stock Exchange but who hurry by the latter dozens of times every week, bent for nowhere, without even thinking of getting a visitor's pass. The chances are you've never gone inside interesting buildings and monuments which lie along your daily rush course. Yet it takes little effort to walk up steps and open doors, and the few minutes you lose is *always* a good investment in richening experience.

To cultivate variety, you need not abandon your principal line of concentration—only broaden it. There are plenty of experiences and subsidiary interests within your own chosen limits of specialization to keep you sane, healthy and growing. Go on concentrating, but freshen your abilities and energies by trying once everything that contains new fuel for your engine.

Tolerance of things, like tolerance of people, is gained only by trying them out. If you are accustomed to travel in Pullmans, try a daycoach or a bus. You'll find the experience amusing and it will open new channels of interest. If you travel habitually in daycoaches, save a few pennies and treat yourself to a Pullman—it works the same way. Mrs. Roosevelt recently advised a group of conventional girls: "Go out as discoverers in your own country. Be real voyagers even in a circumscribed area." Good advice —try everything from headcheese to flying in a snowstorm (if the company will let you) and you'll soon realize that you've been missing far more than you guessed.

This system of trying everything once, carried on over a period of years, gives you a vast amount of useful material for everyday living, new points of sympathetic contact with friends, with business acquaintances. It gives you something to talk about with Tom, Dick, and Maude.

I cannot see how any rational person, knowing the possibilities of expanding his life and the penalties of cramping it, can fail to decide upon expansion. But merely because you realize that you should try everything once does not mean that you will do so. There exists, unfortunately, a psychological gap between thinking about doing a thing and doing it.

The way to bridge this gap is to walk across it without pausing to think. A young schoolteacher I know had always wanted to go to Bermuda, but she kept putting off doing anything about it. I made occasion to stroll with her one day past a travel bureau. On the pretext of getting a steamship folder I walked in with her. At the counter I switched the conversation to Bermuda trips, and almost before she knew it she had made her reservation. She had moved toward her objective without thinking at all about the process.

A wholesome sampling of variety is the best safeguard against indiscriminate pleasure-seeking. Without the spirit of adventure, living is a pretty burdensome job from which we are prone to seek quick occasional relief, accepting Aldous Huxley's dictum that the normal rhythm of life is routine punctuated by orgies. If we allow our interests to remain narrow and limited, only flagrant excitement will divert us. How much better it is if we ardently cultivate chosen experiences instead of plunging into the first that offers itself. The person who is alert daily to the fascination of the world about him has a guarantee against boredom as well as against the fitful and spasmodic efforts to escape it.

Table Talk

FOR THE busy man who hates wasting his time at meals New York snack bars offer a machine which crushes up raw spinach, carrots, watercress, potatoes, apples and oranges, and extracts their juice. From its spigot runs apple-green liquid, a pint of which is guaranteed to be a full-size vegetarian meal complete with vitamins and mineral salts. The meal takes half a minute to consume.

A DAIRY in Long Beach, Cal., declaring that the world's greatest beauties have used milk as a beautifying medium, have made a complexion cream of 100 percent pure dairy cream with other ingredients. It serves as a cleanser, tissue builder, and powder base. Beauty Creme of Milk is being distributed by the milkmen along with the daily deliveries of Grades A and B.—*Food Field Reporter*

Bad Boys and Good Neighbors

Condensed from The Kiwanis Magazine

KARL DETZER

A DULL, 15-year-old girl fidgeted in a chair across the desk from young Judge Hatfield. Beside her sat the matron from the Berrien County Detention Home. The Judge tipped back his chair informally and studied some papers. The room was informal, too, with shelves full of shabby books, a bust of Lincoln in one corner, photographs of men and dogs everywhere. Outside an endless line of trucks rumbled toward Chicago, for this lake-shore town of St. Joseph, Mich. (pop. 8500), is the center of the greatest fruit-growing region in the Middle West.

It all looked very casual—but court was in session, just the same. The Judge was studying a police report.

"This girl frequents beer joints," it read. "Out nights with men. Uncle and teachers claim she is unruly."

"See me tomorrow," Hatfield bade. When matron and girl had left he drove to Blankville, the girl's home town. There he dropped in on a preacher, a grocer, a garage man and a country doctor, neighbors of delinquent Mary.

"Know anything about her?" he asked each in turn.

They knew a great deal, and told it. Not evidence which could be admitted in court, no scientific caseworker's notebook data. Just facts and opinions from four plain citizens to whom Mary and her Uncle Jake with whom she lived were neighbors and human beings.

"Jake's a skunk," the grocer said. "Works the kid to the bone. Whales her." "He starves her," the garage man added. "Dresses her in rags. He's mean and lazy." The preacher said Mary never attended Sunday school, took part in no group activity.

"Jake's house is a pigpen," the doctor grumbled. "Funny, too, him coming from good folks. His sister's a decent woman, teaching school near Watervliet. Can't see why she didn't get Mary when her folks died, instead of Jake."

Next day Jake and his sister sat in the courtroom, hearing Hatfield's plan. The sister would take Mary,

466

offer her a fresh start in new surroundings.

"See that she meets some young people," Hatfield counseled. "Take her to church and the movies. Help her with her school work. Get her a pretty dress."

That was six months ago. Mary is doing well, so far, in her new home, thanks to Hatfield's idea that one good neighbor is worth many scientific case records.

More than 2000 such neighbors in Berrien County serve as unofficial, unpaid friends of Hatfield's court. These volunteers represent all creeds and racial groups, speak a dozen languages. Hatfield picks them carefully, either from his own wide acquaintance, or from among the leaders in church, education or community betterment groups. They must be decent, stable, sensible folk, warm-hearted and square-shooting. The young Judge never picks an adviser quickly.

The county budget allows Judge Hatfield only one paid investigator to work in this community of 100,-000. So for six years he has depended upon the opinions and advice of plain citizens.

"Common sense and common helpfulness make pretty good law," he contends, and the state supreme court has backed up this opinion in all 15 appeals from his court.

Slight, intense, with a soft voice, eager gray eyes and a movie star's profile, Malcolm Hatfield looks younger than his 38 years. His father was a Hoosier village harnessmaker, broken in health by service in the Spanish-American War.

Plagued by illness and poverty, the family moved from Indiana to Colorado to Michigan and back to Indiana.

It may be the memory of these migrations which causes Hatfield to remove troublesome children promptly from homes where there is no stability, settle them with families which have deep roots.

Hatfield was earning 50¢ each ten-hour day in the onion fields when he was eight years old. He put himself through school. At 16 he enlisted in the army for the World War, was summarily discharged when officers discovered he had falsified his age. A year later he re-enlisted. Following the war he worked nights shoveling coal, by day attending the University of Notre Dame.

Completing a course in journalism, he decided he did not want to be an editor after all, and while studying for his master's degree, took a teaching job in the Niles, Mich., public schools, within easy commuting distance of his classes.

That year, 1933, all Michigan heard about him when, at a state teachers' convention, he angrily asserted, "If children play truant, it's because they dislike you teachers, and they don't dislike you unless you have given them good reason."

After that outburst the governor appointed him to the state council on delinquency.

In Michigan, children's courts are presided over by county probate judges. Unable to find a lawyer willing to be a candidate against the popular incumbent judge, politicians drafted the young school-master. To the amusement of old-timers, Hatfield built up his own "machine" among parent-teacher clubs, Ladies' Aid, church groups —and won, hands down. Twice since then voters have returned him to office on the Democratic ticket, in a county overwhelmingly Re-publican.

Last year he found that most of the children brought to his court came from families on relief. Par-ents got $2.50 a week for food, plus 50 cents for each child. So his wife and he emptied their cupboards, settled down on a relief subsistence allowance.

"Corn mush, potatoes and oat-meal!" he cries. "Day after day! You get so you can't eat. You'd beg, steal, do anything for a good steak or a glass of orange juice. We stuck it out two weeks. Now when a child from a home on relief is brought in for stealing, I always think back over those two weeks before I make a decision."

Hatfield does not claim that his is the only method of handling juvenile offenders, or even the best.

"Trained field staffs and well-equipped research bureaus and daily psychiatric clinics are splendid if you can get them," he says. "But remember that not more than 200 of America's 3000 counties can af-ford them. The rest of us have to get along as best we can with the brains God gave us."

Hatfield lectures to educational groups, church clubs, civic bodies, always for a fee. Much of the money is spent on his charges—for movie

tickets, dues to young people's so-cieties, summer outings, Boy Scout uniforms. With some of it he once purchased a pig.

A teacher had telephoned: "You must do something about Ralph P——. He runs away, hates his teachers, is a dangerous influence."

"I'll look into it," Hatfield prom-ised. He discovered that when Ralph played hookey he always headed for farm country. So he sent for the boy, suggested a walk together.

"Ralph got excited whenever we passed a herd of cattle or a team of horses," he explained. "But pigs were his passion. The rest was easy. His father, a poor man, agreed to move to the country."

The day after the family moved, the pig arrived. That was two years ago. Last fall the boy won a prize with his fattened hog at the county fair, he has several litters growing into bacon, belongs to the 4-H Club, makes good marks in school, never plays hookey, is saving his money to buy a farm.

Another time a tall 17-year-old Negro, ragged, underfed, sullen, faced the court on his third larceny charge in two years.

"Why do you keep on stealing, Charley?" Hatfield asked.

"Only way to get anything I know of," the boy replied. The Judge glanced at his record. Char-ley was right. In his miserable world, stealing was probably the only way. Kindness, self-respect, common decency, were outside his personal experience.

Hatfield telephoned to his wife.

"Bring me a complete change of clothes, quick," he requested.

"Lucky we wear the same size," he remarked. "I've got a job in mind for you, and I want you to look your best when you go after it."

One of Hatfield's good neighbors gave Charley part-time work. That was three years ago. Charley still holds the job, is finishing high school, plans to enter the State University next fall, later to study medicine.

Getting such results is often hard on Hatfield's wife and friends. One day last winter a relief agency petitioned that a family of six children be taken away from their parents, who could not or would not provide a home. The jobless father, without a roof, a stick of furniture, a scrap of food or a penny, had lost hope.

The Judge found a small house to rent for $5 a month. He hired a truck, sent it to the homes of friends to pick up such bedding, furniture, clothes and food as they could spare. He told his wife: "A man's coming round for the kitchen table and chairs in a few minutes—and a mattress, too."

"But what will *we* do without them?" she asked.

"We'll get along," he answered quietly. "The Lord's been good to us and we might as well pass along our blessings."

Each week he shares his ideas with several million readers of village newspapers and church journals. His column, "Children in Court," he distributes free to any editor who asks for it, and so many have asked that it costs him hundreds of dollars a year for printing and mailing.

This column, in one-syllable words, discusses "The Old-Fashioned Home," "Vulgar Language," "Hitch-Hiking," "The Air-Gun Evil," the responsibility of parents, the school and the church toward youth.

Children need not live in Berrien County to get his aid. Last fall a friend in Detroit, 150 miles away, telephoned to him about a young girl in poor surroundings who was "going to the dogs."

"Put her on the next bus," Hatfield directed. "We'll meet her." He hung up and turned to his wife. "We're going to have company for a couple of weeks," he announced, and a youngster from across the state did not "go to the dogs."

Young Judge Hatfield is salvaging many boys and girls. His tools are kindness, hope, common sense and human understanding. His helpers are 2000 good neighbors.

Table Talk

"CUP O' TEA, weak," said a customer at a London coffee stall. When the decoction was brought to him he eyed it critically.

"Well, what's wrong with it? You said weak, didn't you?"

"Weak, yes," was the reply, "but not 'elpless."—*Tit-Bits*

The Ingenious Eskimo

Condensed from Natural History

EDWARD WEYER, Ph.D.

Some wit once called the Eskimos "God's frozen people." The appellation is applicable, to some extent, to the barren northern wastes in which they live, but is far from the mark when one considers their clever ingenuity, an ingenuity at which I never ceased to wonder during several years spent in studying Eskimos both in Alaska and in faraway North Greenland.

Take the Eskimo's most annoying enemy, the wolf, which preys on the caribou or wild reindeer that he needs for food. Because of its sharp eyesight and keen intelligence, it is extremely difficult to approach in hunting. Yet the Eskimo kills it with nothing more formidable than a piece of flexible whalebone.

He sharpens the strip of whalebone at both ends and doubles it back, tying it with sinew. Then he covers it with a lump of fat, allows it to freeze, and throws it out where the wolf will get it. Swallowed at a gulp, the frozen dainty melts in the wolf's stomach. The sharp whalebone springs open, piercing the wolf internally and killing it.

Another vigilant animal is the seal, which provides not only food and clothing, but light and heat. It basks at the edge of open water, sliding off and disappearing in a split second. White men find it difficult to approach within 150 feet. But an Eskimo, inching along on his belly, fools his prey with seal-like movements and with an implement that has claws attached to imitate the sound a seal makes when scratching the ice. An expert Eskimo can crawl close enough to grab a flipper with one hand and drive his knife home with the other.

When the Eskimo gets a walrus weighing more than a ton on the end of a harpoon line, he is faced with a major engineering problem: how to get it from the water onto the ice. Mechanical contrivances belong to a world in whose development the Eskimo has had no part. No implement ever devised by him has had a wheel in it. Yet this does not prevent him from improvising a block-and-tackle that works with-

470

out a pulley. He cuts holes in the hide of the walrus, and a U-shaped hole in the ice some distance away. Through these holes he threads a slippery rawhide line, once over and once again. He doesn't know the mechanical theory of the double pulley, but he does know that if he hauls at one end of the line he will drag the walrus out of the water, onto the ice.

On the water the Eskimo sits in a one-man boat of seal hide stretched over a light framework fashioned from driftwood or sapling. The hide completely decks the top of the boat except for the hole into which he sticks his legs; and once in the boat he ties his waterproof jacket securely around the hole, making the boat so virtually part of his body that he becomes a water animal. When an overwhelming roller curls down upon him he voluntarily capsizes, receiving the blow on the bottom of his kayak, and righting himself when the deluge is past.

Though he rejoices in the impossible, even the Eskimo must have thought twice before settling on barren King Island, in Bering Sea. Marooned there, seemingly he would face starvation, for precipitous cliffs and a raging surf cut him off from the seal and walrus in the sea below.

But even on this bleak rock the Eskimo has established a flourishing village, from which he puts to sea even in the most forbidding weather. We think of the catapult method for launching airplanes as a last word in our mechanical age, but the Eskimo has used this principle for generations. On the land the paddler sits in his kayak or in his larger boat, the umiak, while companions on either side lift him, boat and all. Swinging him like a pendulum, they let fly at a given signal, and the fisherman and his boat are thrown clear of the breaking waves.

The Eskimo's inventiveness is the more remarkable when we realize the sparsity of his population. All the Eskimos in the world could be seated in the Yale Bowl without filling half the seats. Further, they are scattered east and west over a distance 800 miles greater than that from New York to San Francisco, and north and south over a distance greater than that from Maine to Florida.

The Eskimo has no technical school, no library to help solve his problems. What he knows he has learned in the school of experience. As example, let us follow Okluk on a three-day trip north to visit his cousins' camp for the yearly festival. First of all he must have a sledge. But there is not enough driftwood to build one and, like most of his people, he lives beyond the timber line.

So Okluk soaks broad strips of walrus hide in water and rolls them up with salmon inside, laid lengthwise. Then he sets the bundles outside to freeze solid. Soon he has enough solid pieces to lash together to make a walrus-skin sledge. This will carry him, and his baggage, as long as cold weather lasts.

He travels light, though he will

pass no settlement on the way. He does take fresh straw for his boots; he knows, though many a white man hasn't believed it and has suffered frozen toes as a consequence, that the straw in the boots should be changed daily if it is to continue to insulate against the cold. He takes food for his dogs, but little for himself. He takes seal oil to light and heat the overnight huts he will build. That is practically all. Yet he contemplates a trip that will be pleasant in every way.

At night in short order he builds a snow house in which he is soon too warm for comfort. He takes off most of his clothing, but continues to perspire though nothing separates him from 40 degrees below zero except a shell of snow. The source of this heat is his seal-oil lamp, whose long, low wick of moss gives a flame eight inches or more in length, which sends its cheerful glow through an ingenious window of clear ice onto the windy world of ice and snow.

Since Okluk possesses no matches, he produces a light for his lamp by friction. He spins rapidly a piece of dried wood, one of whose ends is in a socket held in his teeth while the other end turns in a socket pressed against the ground, in which there is a cotton-like substance for tinder.

Why does his snow house not melt? Okluk has never studied thermostatics, and can't count above six; but he knows that though the air in his hut is warm, the intense cold outside will neutralize this and keep the wall from melting.

Okluk has no gun or bow-and-arrow, yet he would like to breakfast on one of the birds flying about in the early morning. He enlarges the ventilating hole of his snow hut, sprinkles bits of meat near it, and quietly awaits a flutter of wings. When a bird swoops down to snatch a morsel, Okluk snatches first and has it by the legs.

At night Okluk hears wolves howling. He doesn't like wolves. But how can he kill a wolf without gun or trap or even his whalebone?

He smears his knife with blood and buries it in the snow with only the blade protruding. From the door of his hut he sees the wolf approaching, drawn to the blade by the scent. The wolf licks the blade, cutting his tongue. Excited by the taste and smell, he gourmandizes, literally whetting his own appetite. Okluk sees him drop from weakness, bleeding to death while gorged with his own lifeblood. Okluk has a fine pelt to take to the festival.

His hut is warm and dry, his belly is full of meat, but there is one thing that bothers him as he tries to sleep. He has to scratch too much. Calmly he unpacks a strip of bear fur with a string tied to each end. This he places under his clothing. When he pulls it out the unwelcome guests are found to have gone into the bear skin because of its thick fur.

The next day the snow is so dazzling that Okluk will soon be snow-blind and unable to pick his way to shelter. So he puts on his shatterproof goggles. He has never seen a piece of smoked glass, but his eyeshades of walrus ivory or wood, with fine slits in place of lenses, serve the purpose as well.

When he reaches his destination, Okluk uses his sledge for food. He feeds the thawed walrus skin to his dogs, and stuffs himself on the salmon that was rolled up inside.

Keeping up with the World

Excerpts from a regular department in Collier's

Freling Foster

MORE than 70% of all the fish consumed throughout Great Britain today is bought already cooked at its 30,000 hot-fish shops.

IN ENGLAND today more than 20,000 babies of wealthy families do not live at home but in fashionable "baby hotels" where they are taken at birth. Many remain until old enough for preparatory school.

ENGLAND has a unique organization called the "Voluntary Aunts," whose members, without compensation, gladly spend an afternoon or evening looking after children or invalids, so that relatives may leave their cares for a few hours' recreation.

Married Love

By

ALEXIS CARREL, M.D.

LOVE IS a mysterious thing. Invisible, immaterial, yet as real as steel. As elusive as smoke in the wind—and stronger than death. From wild passion, it may grow into this selfless, indissoluble affection, whose presence in the house even a stranger can easily detect. If carefully nurtured, it will, in spite of the progress of age and the extinction of reproductive life, continue to expand with the full strength of its beauty.

The origin of love is both organic and mental. The substances set free in the blood stream by the testicle or the ovary have a powerful influence on affective and intellectual activities. They permeate the whole organism with sexual desire. They inspire selfless love and dedication. They illuminate the world of lovers with the eternal joy of spring. In other terms, they supply the physiological requisites for the loftiest activities of the mind. Whether conscious or unconscious, the reproductive urge is the source of love. Man is unity and multiplicity. He has to create, love, and pray with all his organs.

Today, as in the remotest past, youth entertains the charming and dangerous illusion of its innate ability at love-making. In consequence, love-making, especially in marriage, is frequently not an enduring success. For married love is no easy enterprise. Unfortunately, the science of marriage has remained rudimentary, although its development is essential both to the happiness of man and to the greatness of civilization.

The immediate purpose of marriage is the gratification of the sexual urge, and fecundation. This urge is an inexorable law of nature. And it is more than a romantic glow. It is the biologic source of aspiration and achievement. It *can* be kept fresh and vital if intelligence and imagination are given creative scope. Such richly shared sex life is a cornerstone of marital stability and happiness.

Married love is a creative enterprise. It is not achieved by accident or instinct. Perfunctory coitus is a confession of lack of intelligence and character. There is profound beauty and even holiness in the act

474

of fecundation. We should not forget that the Church blesses the sexual union of man and woman by a sacrament. Mothers sometimes inflict grave injury by instilling in their daughters contempt of sex. "You will have to tolerate sex. Often you can escape by pleading tiredness." All the resources of science and technique must be used in order to make of marital relations an ever-flowing source of *mutual* joy.

The problem of marriage is to transform mating into an enduring union. Male and female are attracted by their opposite characteristics. The more masculine the man, the more feminine the woman, the more passionate the mating. But sexuality permeates both mind and body. Man and woman are profoundly different. While intimately united, they are separated by an abyss.

An enduring union is thus rendered difficult by the physiological and mental disparities that are the essence of femaleness and maleness. Man is active, hard, logical. Woman, passive, sentimental, and intuitive. Her nervous system, her temperament, prepare her for maternity. Marriage is an association of two different but complementary individuals. These characteristics of the partners are responsible for both the efficiency and the difficulties of the association.

Not only are husband and wife separated by organic and mental differences, but these differences vary from week to week, according to sexual rhythms. Sexual rhythms are incomparably more marked in woman than in man. During the whole menstrual cycle, fluctuations take place in activity, courage, temper, sex desire. Man also manifests oscillations of temper and activity. This knowledge should allow mutual understanding of various moods, and may prevent tragedies.

Success in marriage requires continence as well as potency. In other words, character is indispensable in well-ordered sexual life. Certain periods, including illness and pregnancy, impose continence. To refrain from sexual intercourse during married life demands nervous equilibrium and moral strength. For many individuals, it is true heroism. Before marriage, the ideal state is chastity. Chastity requires early moral training. It is the highest expression of self-discipline. Voluntary restraint from the sex act during youth, more than any other moral and physical effort, enhances the quality of life. The use of prostitutes is injurious. For paid lovemaking is a degradation of the real sex act. It lacks the essential quality of profound mutuality. It is without the benison of beauty.

Even true love may not protect husband and wife against certain dangers of sexual relations. Early excesses prevent the full development of body and mind. Late excesses accelerate the rate of aging and decay. When exhausted or worried, the husband should not be induced by an oversexed wife to perform the sex act. Reciprocally, the untimely ardor of an ignorant husband may tire or exasperate his undersexed wife. Love is incompatible with ignorance and selfishness. Also with disease. Since chastity in girls, as well as in boys, is far from being the habitual rule, lovers must ascertain before marriage whether they are free of gonorrhea and syphilis.

There is no apparent natural rule for sexual relations. The frequency of the sex act varies widely. There are sexual athletes as well as weaklings. Copulation can be performed at any time, while in other mammals it takes place only during the heat period. Therefore, intelligence and self-control must replace instinct in the management of sexual life. The enormous variations in individual constitution have rendered impossible the elaboration of precise rules. Each couple must take into consideration their physical and mental peculiarities. For the failure of married life often comes from technical ignorance.

Lovers are seldom perfectly mated. Often the husband has a stronger sexual appetite than the wife. Sex indifference may be induced by the ignorance or brutality of the husband. As in the animal kingdom, the female has to be enticed by the male.

In married life, sexual intercourse has a tendency to become a monotonous performance. On the contrary, it must retain its profound meaning. All senses, especially the sense of beauty, should participate in it. It is the capacity, through mind and spirit, to exalt the symbolism of the act that differentiates man from the animals. Affection must bestow a benediction upon emotional manifestations.

There are abundant resources in the field of sensory and psychologic stimulation. All the little arts of love-making should be brought into play. The expected, taken-for-granted attitude is to be avoided by both partners. An infinite variety of expressions can be given to sex love.

Small attentions kindle conjugal affection. Endearing words and expressions of appreciation should be liberally mingled with everyday matters not necessarily connected with sex. How can a woman accept the love addresses of a man who at all other times ignores or criticizes her? In the actual love-making ritual, words are as desirable as caresses.

In woman, sexual excitation rises slowly. She needs to be prepared for the act. Generally, the masculine orgasm occurs before her senses are totally roused. Thus, she is left unsatisfied, nervous, perhaps disgusted. In order that she may really consummate the sex act, her husband must learn self-control and enlightened technique. It will augur well for the future of the race when women demand a higher intelligence quotient of men as lovers.

Marriage should provide a proper environment for the offspring. The slow development of children, the necessity of their organic and spiritual formation, require permanency in human mating. In other terms, monogamy and indissolubility of marriage. Since the quality of the children depends on the hereditary endowment of the parents, the wise selection of a mate is of the utmost importance. Only in this manner can eugenics be realized.

Between husband and wife, intellectual union is highly desirable. Feminine intelligence, although differing from masculine intelligence, is not inferior to it. Girls should receive as advanced an intellectual education as boys do. In order to play their specific part in life, they need extensive knowledge. It is folly to confine their interests to the details of housekeeping, or to the so-called duties of society. Love becomes anemic if not helped by intellectual activity. Both the happiness of married life and the future of society depend on intelligence in love. The main enemy of love is the innate selfishness that modern education develops to its maximum in each boy and girl.

The sex act has been deprived of its natural consequences by the technical progress of contraception. However, the biological law of reproduction remains imperative. And transgressors are punished in a subtle manner. It is a disastrous mistake to believe we can live according to our fancy. Being parts of nature, we are submitted to its inexorable laws. Sterile love may sink into monotonous dreariness or selfish folly. Generally, the old age of those without children resembles a barren desert.

Insufficient fecundity is also dangerous. For the only child is deprived of the companionship, formative influence, and help that his potential brothers and sisters would have given him. In large families, there is more cheerfulness and mutual aid than in small ones. It is probable that three children are the indispensable minimum for the harmony of the family and the survival of the race. The true social unit is not the isolated individual, but the functional group constituted by husband, wife, and offspring. Curiously enough, democracy gives more importance to the individual than to the family.

We have not yet fully understood that love is a necessity, not a luxury. It is the only ingredient capable of welding together husband, wife and children. The only cement strong enough to unite into a nation the poor and rich, the strong and the weak, the employer and the employe. If we do not have love within the home, we shall not have it elsewhere. Love is as essential as intelligence, thyroid secretion, or gastric juice. No human relationships will ever be satisfying if not inspired by love. The moral command, "Love one another," is probably a fundamental law of nature, a law as inexorable as the first law of thermodynamics.

Those who achieve greatness in business, in art, in science, are strongly sexed. There are no sexual weaklings among the heroes, the conquerors, the truly great leaders of nations. But sublimated love does not need material consummation. Inspiration may come from the repression of sexual appetite. "If Beatrice had been the mistress of Dante, there would be perhaps no *Divine Comedy*."

To conclude: Man and woman have no innate knowledge of the physical, mental, and social requisites of married love. But they are capable of learning the indispensable principles and technique of this complex relation. Prospective husbands and wives will be wise in applying their sense of material and spiritual values to the selection of a mate, and to preparation for the great adventure. Those who are married, and perhaps already disappointed, should realize that failure is avoidable, that success can still be achieved. For intelligence, which has given man mastery over the material world, also possesses the power to usher him into the realm of love.

Echoes of Will Rogers

As LONG AGO as 1920 Rogers went up in a studio plane in California with a former army ace. The pilot did some fancy turns and rolls. Rogers just looked over the edge and chewed his gum a little faster. When they came down, he shifted his gum, and remarked drily, "I'll try anything once. Try some things oftener. When you goin' again?"—Willis Thornton in Vancouver *Sun*

The American Destiny

Condensed from Life

WALTER LIPPMANN

HERE IN America are the things which elsewhere in the world the nations stand in arms to conquer or to defend. A people with a long habit of freedom holds securely the space to live, a fertile soil, invested wealth, technical arts, everything a nation could need. Yet something is wanting. And for want of it the American people are profoundly troubled.

The American spirit is troubled not by the dangers, and not by the difficulties of the age, but by lack of clear purpose and a confident will. Considering the resources with which nature and the accumulated achievements of the past have endowed America, there ought to be no question in anyone's mind about the American future. Yet the American people have no vision of their own future. They are oppressed by doubt. They are living anxiously from day to day, feeling that the strength within them is being suffocated. Far from being inspired by America's riches, they at this moment recoil from those very constituents of greatness which vigorous peoples have hitherto everywhere struggled to obtain. It is as if this continent had raised up something too great for little men to deal with.

In this moment of bewildered indecision, the American people are acting on the assumption that their incomparable assets are their most dangerous liabilities. Whereas the problems of other nations are the problems of insufficiency, our problems are the problems of superfluity. In every field of activity we have come to think that there is a surplus to be gotten rid of: We seem to have too much land. The land seems to be too fertile. We have taken elaborate measures to reduce the yield, and we do not know how to dispose of the surplus. We seem to have too many factories, and the machinery seems to be too efficient, and we seem to have too much labor. We rack our brains to devise schemes for limiting the output and reducing the work done by the worker. We seem to have too much capital, and we worry about how to reduce our savings and how not to invest them where they will produce too many goods. We seem to have too much gold, and we bury it in Kentucky. We seem to have too much international power, and, in our foreign policy, we try to neutralize the fact that America has decisive influence in the affairs of the world.

The total effect is that the American people face the world, not with their old confidence and courage, but in a mood of withdrawal, defeat, and of wishing to escape from their opportunities and their responsibilities. This must be a transient mood, the mood of a people whose minds and spirits are not yet adjusted to a radically new situation. For in the long run a nation cannot grow rich by not producing, by not working, by not saving, by not being enterprising, by seeking only security and protection from risks, by trying to be small and unimportant.

This cannot be the permanent attitude of the nation. For here is this continent, lying between two great oceans; the heart of it is invulnerable and the nation can never be conquered. Upon this continent, or within easy and friendly reach of it, there is every material resource. The people who inhabit this continent selected themselves as colonists out of the civilized nations of Europe; they are adventurous, enterprising, and brave with high faith. They inherit a prodigious equipment of capital and technical wealth. They have political institutions, which, with all their faults, are one of the wonders of the world; nowhere else and never before has so large a population lived in one union on so vast a territory with such security and in such freedom. Nothing that a people could want, nothing that nations fight to obtain, nothing that men die to achieve is lacking, nothing except a clear purpose and the confident will to make the most of all these things.

And why are they lacking now? This country has passed through many trying days. But never before, even in the bleak winter of Valley Forge or on the field of Gettysburg, has it lacked confidence in its destiny.

The cause of our present lack of confidence is, I believe, the accumulated disappointments of the postwar era. Three times in these 20 years the American people have had a great hope and three times they have been greatly disappointed. They believed with Wilson that they could help to make a world that was safe for free men living in peace under just laws. They believed with Coolidge and Hoover that they had arrived at a New Era of certain prosperity. They believed with Roosevelt that they were organizing securely an abundant life for all the people. In each movement they began with enthusiasm and have ended in disillusionment. For the moment they think they were deluded under Wilson, under Coolidge, under Roosevelt, and now they believe nothing in particular.

But the American people were not deluded in what they undertook to do in the postwar era.

These were the things that still have to be done. They did not succeed on the first attempts because they had not yet acquired the training or the experience that were needed in order to succeed. They were right under Wilson when they recognized that as a result of the war the power and influence of America had grown so great in the world that on paramount issues the position of the United States, whatever it did or refused to do, was decisive. The insight was true, the execution gravely defective. The conduct of the foreign policy of a great power requires experienced men. That experience cannot be gotten in a few months or even in a few years.

The American people were right under Coolidge when they recognized that as a result of the war they had become the strongest creditor power, and that this gave them a clear obligation to take a leading part in the economic reconstruction of the world. But the American bankers, legislators, and business men of the Twenties had had almost no experience in such affairs.

And under Roosevelt the American people were right when they recognized that the time had come when the nation must organize itself to control the violence of booms and depressions, must take measures to preserve its agriculture and to conserve natural resources, must guarantee to all men an opportunity to work, must provide security for the old, the sick and the handicapped. But the wisdom to do all

these things was not equal to the need for doing them. Mr. Roosevelt's New Dealers were as untrained and ill-equipped to design and administer these reforms as had been Mr. Wilson's diplomats and Mr. Coolidge's financiers.

For the moment, therefore, a large part of the people have concluded that in each of these three undertakings of the postwar era the objective was wrong. They look upon the tragic consequences of Versailles as proof that it was a mistake to attempt to organize the world for peace under the reign of law. They look upon the crash of 1929 and the defaulted bonds and wasted savings as proof that it is a mistake for the world's creditor to extend credit. They look now with dismay upon the unending deficits and the millions of unemployed and the stagnation of business. These failures and disappointments have for the time being turned a substantial majority against domestic reforms, against general reconstruction, and against organized peace. They have produced the thoroughly disillusioned American of the present day who wants to withdraw within the three-mile limit, wants to bury the gold, and wants to suspend the reforms.

No doubt this reaction is human enough. But the more we have refused to go on with the things we undertook to do, and failed to achieve, the more compelling and urgent do these tasks become. Twenty years ago Congress refused to proceed with the work of organizing the world for peace. The refusal has not settled the issue. It is more acute today than ever before, and never in time of peace has the United States had to arm on such a scale as it is arming today. Ten years ago we refused to go on with the task of reconstructing the shattered economy of the world. The refusal has aggravated the difficulty of reconstructing our own domestic economy. Now a considerable number of the voters think they would like to put an end to social reforms. If these views prevail, we shall find that discontent makes necessary even more drastic social reforms.

We are finding that when a nation refuses to do the great things which it has to do, it is unable to do the littler things that it wishes to do. Men who will not face the big things become nervous and fearful in all things.

That is what ails us today. In the lifetime of our generation there has occurred one of the greatest events in the history of mankind. The controlling power in western civilization has crossed the Atlantic. America, which was once a colony on the frontiers of Europe, is now, and will in the next generations become even more certainly, the geographic, economic, and political center of the Occident. What Rome was to the ancient world, what Great Britain has been to the modern world, America is to be to the world of tomorrow. We might wish it otherwise. I do. Every man who was young in the easier America of the prewar world must long for it at times. But our personal preferences count for little in the great movements of history, and when the destiny of a nation is revealed to it, there is no choice but to accept that destiny.

The indecision which paralyzes us today will not be ended by reassuring statements from the White House, or by little changes in this or that policy, or by a change of party control. The indecision which pervades the American spirit, and manifests itself in the policies of plowing under, not producing, not saving, not investing, has its root in the refusal by the American people to see themselves as they are, as a very great nation, and to act accordingly. We are undecided and nervous because we are confronting the problems of the 20th century with minds formed in the 19th century, and attached to the smaller duties of a simpler past. We are afraid of the fertility of the American earth, afraid of the productiveness of American capital and American labor, afraid of American influence in the family of nations, because we still cling to the mentality of a little nation on the frontiers of the civilized world, though we have the opportunity, the power, and the responsibilities of a very great nation at the center of the civilized world.

The American people will move forward again, and feel once more the exhilaration and the confidence that have made them what they are, when they allow themselves to become conscious of their greatness, conscious not only of their incomparable inheritance but of the splendor of their destiny. Then the things that seem difficult will seem easy, and the willingness to be equal to their mission will restore their confidence and make whole their will.

Six Man Football

A NEW KIND of football—fast, high scoring, full of spectacular passing and open field running—is being played this year by 2000 high schools. It's six-man football. Invented in 1934 by Stephen Epler, coach of a small Nebraska school, the six-man game has swept like wildfire through the smaller high schools. Big schools and even varsities also are taking it up.

Spectators love it because there's action all over the field, every minute—and the crowds can follow it clearly; the reverses and trick plays the game encourages aren't screened by a converging jumble of 22 men.

The players, too, have a grand time. The fun of football is in running, kicking, and passing, not in the drudgery of the linesmen's job. The six-man team consists of a center, two ends and three backs, and any one of them may pass or receive a pass, make a sensational run or score a touchdown. The back who first receives the ball must pass it immediately. This rule prevents bone-cracking power drives into the line. In fact, the new game opens up so fast there's no line to plunge into. In one popular play, all six men handle the ball. There's plenty of kicking; rules put a premium on field goals, minimizing the danger of injuries in desperate goal-line defense. There's plenty of blocking and tackling, but no dangerous piling on.

The best part of it all is that nobody gets hurt! Eleven-man football is dangerous for small schools with their inadequate coaching staffs, poor equipment and small squads which they have to piece out with young boys. Records of 17,000 high school players in 1935 showed boys of 14 and 15 were only seven percent of the group, but suffered 24 percent of the injuries. Small schools have the worst record. There were no deaths from college football last year. But there were 13 in high schools. In a five-year period, 44 percent of all football deaths were among high school players. Six-man football spares the community the possible tragedy of crippling injuries or deaths in the name of sport.

From all over the country come reports of six-man football teams playing a whole season with no greater casualty than one sprained ankle or a broken collarbone. Leg injuries, often from cleated shoes, account for half of the total casualties in 11-man football; the six-man teams wear rubber-soled shoes.

Safe, inexpensive, exciting to spectator and player, six-man football should answer the need of 10,000 American high schools now without football teams. Many other small schools, now risking the lives of students with the 11-man game, might well adopt Mr. Epler's invention.

The Doctor of Lennox

By

A. J. CRONIN

THE MOST unforgettable character I ever met? To my surprise I find myself thinking, not of some famous statesman, soldier or tycoon, but of a simple soul who had no wish to dominate an empire, but set out instead to conquer circumstance—and himself.

I first knew him as a boy, small, insignificant and poor, who hung on to us, so to speak, by the skin of his teeth—barely accepted by the select band of adventurous youths of which I was one in my native Scottish town of Levenford.

If he were in any way remarkable, it was through his defects. He was quite comically lame, one leg being so much shorter than the other that he was obliged to wear a boot with a sole six inches thick. To see him run, saving his bad leg, his undersized form tense and limping, the sweat breaking out on his eager face, well—Chisholm, the minister's son, acknowledged wit of our band, hit the nail on the head when he dubbed him Dot-and-Carry. It was shortened subse-quently to Carry. "Look out," someone would shout, "here comes Carry. Let's get away before he tags on to us." And off we would dart, to the swimming pool or the woods, with Carry, dotting along, cheerful and unprotesting, in our wake.

That was his quality, a shy, a smiling cheerfulness—and how we mocked it! To us, Carry was an oddity. His clothes, though carefully patched and mended, were terrible. Socially he was almost beyond the pale. His mother, a gaunt little widow of a drunken loafer, supported herself and her son by scrubbing out sundry shops. Again Chisholm epitomized the jest with his classic epigram, "Carry's mother takes in stairs to wash."

Carry supplemented the family income by rising at five o'clock every morning to deliver milk. This long milk round sometimes made him late for school. Glancing down the arches of the years, I can still see a small lame boy, hot and trembling, in the middle of the classroom floor, while the master, a

484

sadistic brute, drew titters with his shafts.

"Well, well . . . can it be possible ye're late again?"

"Y-y-yes, sir."

"And where has your lordship been? Taking breakfast with the provost no doubt?"

"N-n-n-n-"

At such moments of crisis Carry had a stammer which rose and tortured him. He could not articulate another syllable. And the class, reading permission in the master's grim smile, dissolved in roars of mirth.

If Carry had been clever, all might have been well for him. In Scotland everything is forgiven the brilliant "lad o' pairts." But though Carry did well enough at his books, oral examinations were to him the crack of doom.

There was heartburning in this fact for Carry's mother. She longed for her son to excel, and to excel in one especial field. Poor, humble, despised, she nourished in her fiercely religious soul a fervent ambition. She desired to see her son an ordained minister of the Church of Scotland. Sublime folly! But Carry's mother had sworn to achieve the miracle or die!

Carry much preferred the open countryside to a stuffy prayer meeting. He loved the woods and moors and the wild things that lived there —was never happier than when tending some sick or maimed creature picked up on his wanderings. He had a most uncanny knack of healing. In fact, Carry had a tremendous longing to be a doctor.

But obedience was inherent in his gentle nature, and when he left school it was to enter college as a student of divinity. Heaven knows how they managed. His mother scrimped and saved, her figure grew more gaunt, but in her deep-set eye there glowed unquenchable fire. Carry himself, though his heart was not in what he did, worked like a hero.

And so it happened, quicker than might have been imagined, that Carry was duly licensed at the age of 24 in the cure of souls according to the Kirk of Scotland. Locally there was great interest in the prodigy of the scrubwoman's son turned parson. He was proposed for the parish church assistantship and named to preach a trial sermon.

A full congregation assembled to see "what was in the young meenister." And Carry, who for weeks past had rehearsed his sermon, ascended the pulpit feeling himself word-perfect. He began to speak in an earnest voice and for a few moments he went well enough. Then all at once he became conscious of those rows and rows of upturned faces, of his mother dressed in her best in a front pew, her eyes fixed rapturously upon him. A paralyzing shiver of self-distrust swept over him. He hesitated, lost the thread of his ideas and began to stammer. Once that frightful impotence of speech had gripped him he was lost. He labored on pitifully, but while he struggled for the words he saw the restlessness, the significant smiles; heard even a faint titter. And then again he saw his mother's face, and broke down completely. There was a long and awful pause, then falteringly Carry drew the service to a close by announcing the hymn.

Within the hour, when Carry's mother reached home, she was mercifully taken by an apoplectic seizure. She never spoke again.

The funeral over, Carry disappeared from Levenford. No one knew or cared where he went. He was stigmatized, branded contemptuously for life, a failure. When some years later news reached me that he was teaching in a wretched school in a mining district, I thought of him for a moment, with a kind of shamefaced sorrow, as a despairing soul, a man predestined for disaster. But I soon forgot him.

I was working in Edinburgh when Chisholm, now first assistant to the Regius Professor of Anatomy there, dropped into my rooms one evening. "You'll never guess," he grinned, "who's dissecting in my department. None other than our boyhood friend, Dot-and-Carry."

Carry it was. Carry, at nearly 30 years of age, starting out to be a doctor! A strange figure he made, with his shabby suit, his limp and stoop, among the gay young bucks who where his fellow students. No one ever spoke to him. He occupied a room in a poor district, cooked his own meals, husbanded the slender savings from his teacher's pittance. I saw something of his struggle for the next two years. His age, appearance, and traitorous stammer hampered him. But he went plodding indefatigably on, refusing to admit defeat, the old dogged cheerfulness and hopeful courage still in his eyes.

Time marched on. Five years and more. I found myself in London, and had long since again lost touch with Carry. But I saw much of Chisholm, whose good looks and glib tongue had destined him for political honors. He was now indeed a Member of Parliament and a junior minister into the bargain. In May of 1934 I went with him for a fishing holiday at Lennox in the Highlands. The food at our inn was vile and the landlady a scrawny shrew. It was something of a satisfaction when, two days after our arrival, she slipped on the taproom floor and damaged her knee-cap. Perfunctorily, we two renegades from the healing art offered our assistance. But the dame would have none of us. No one would suit but her own village doctor, of whose canny skill and notable achievements she drew an enthusiastic picture that made Chisholm glance at me and smile.

An hour later the practitioner arrived, black bag in hand, with all the quick assurance of a busy man. In no time he had silenced the patient with a reassuring word and reduced the dislocation with a sure, deft touch. Only then did he turn toward us.

"My God!" exclaimed Chisholm, under his breath. "Carry!"

Yes, Carry it was. But not the shy, shabby, stammering Carry of old. He had the quietly confident air of a man established and secure.

In a flash of recognition he greeted us warmly, and pressed us to come to supper at his home. Meanwhile, he had an urgent case to attend.

It was with an odd expectancy, half excitement and half lingering misgiving, that we entered the village doctor's house that evening. What a shock to find that Carry had a wife! Yet it was so. She welcomed us, fresh and pretty as her own countryside. Since the doctor (she gave the title with a naïve reverence) was still engaged in his surgery, she took us upstairs to see the children. Two red-cheeked girls and a little boy, already asleep. Surprise made us mute.

Downstairs, Carry joined us with two other guests. Now, at his own table, he was a man poised and serene, holding his place as host with quiet dignity. His friends, both men of substance, treated him with deference. Less from what he said than what was said by others we gathered the facts. His practice was wide and scattered. His patients were country folk, canny, silent, hard to know. Yet somehow he had won them. Now as he went through a village the women would run to him, babe in arms, to consult him in the roadway. Such times he never bothered about fees. More than enough came his way, and at New Year there was always a string of presents on his doorstep, a brace of ducks, a goose, a clutch of new-laid eggs, in handsome settlement for some quite forgotten service.

But there were other tales—of midnight vigils when in some humble home the battle for a human life was waged: a child, choking with diphtheria, a plowman stricken with pneumonia, a shepherd's wife in painful labor, all to be sustained, comforted, exhorted, brought back haltingly, their hands in his, from the shadows.

The doctor was a force now, permeating the whole countryside, wise and gentle, blending the best of science and nature, unsparing, undemanding, loving this work he had been born to do, conscious of the place that he had won in the affections of the people, a man who had refused defeat and won through to victory at last.

Late that night as we left the doctor's house and trudged through the darkness, silence fell between Chisholm and myself. Then, as with an effort, he declared:

"It looks as though the little man has found himself at last."

Something patronizing in the remark jarred me. I could not resist a quick reply.

"Which would you rather be, Chisholm—yourself, or the doctor of Lennox?"

"Confound you," he muttered. "Don't you know?"

Birth Control: The Case of the State

Condensed from The Atlantic Monthly

DON WHARTON

No spot in all North Carolina is more than 50 miles from a state-sponsored birth-control clinic. First to promote birth control officially, the state is going at the job in earnest.

North Carolina is pioneering because it has a public-health officer who for 25 years was a country doctor. He knows why his state has virtually the nation's worst record on all matters connected with births. Ignorance, poverty, poor sanitation, inadequate hospital facilities, little if any prenatal care—all these contribute to appalling infant and maternal mortality rates.

The chances that a North Carolina baby will die in its first year are 66 in 1000, compared with Connecticut's infant mortality rate of 40 and the nation's 54. Thousands of North Carolina mothers are attended by midwives, most of them untrained and ignorant of asepsis. Abortions are rife, especially among Negroes, and infanticide is still practiced. If the nation bred at the

North Carolina rate, it would have 700,000 more babies a year. That might be wholly desirable—but not if the extra babies are born into indigent, dirty homes where their chances of survival are poor.

To improve conditions so that dirt, poverty, and disease will disappear is the ideal solution. But that will take time. Birth control offers immediate help. Its advocates point out that the family without much to eat ought to have the choice as to whether it wants to bring another high-chair to the table. Birth control, they say, can help to stop the infant and maternal carnage and build a healthier and perhaps even a larger population.

So, too, believed Dr. George M. Cooper, to whom the appalling statistics represent people he knows. A native of the Tarheel State, he had, during his years of practice, listened, observed, and sympathized. He knew many a girl-wife living in a two-room mountain shack with six children and a tuberculous husband. He had seen many families like the hard-working but desperately poor Negro couple who had been married 17 years and produced 20 children—12 of them to die in infancy. He had heard many women tearfully beg, "Isn't there something we can do?"

When he became director of preventive medicine of the State Board of Health, Dr. Cooper preached to fellow physicians and laymen alike that North Carolina could not climb far toward better health without birth control for the poor. But his hands were tied by the federal law against spreading birth-control information—the Comstock law, dating from 1873—which frightened every physician in the country into silence. But in 1936 the federal courts ruled the law could not prevent physicians from prescribing contraceptives "for the purpose of saving life or promoting the well-being of their patients." Even then there were no funds for birth-control clinics, and Dr. Cooper knew the futility of taking a contraceptive promotion program before a state legislature. The situation seemed hopeless as ever.

Thereupon Fate stepped in—in the person of Dr. Clarence J. Gamble, philanthropic heir to a soap fortune. Dr. Gamble had long been interested in birth control and was financing an experimental program on the densely populated island of Bocagrande, off the Florida Everglades. Hearing of the North Carolina problem, Dr. Gamble offered Dr. Cooper sufficient funds for a three months' experimental program. Dr. Cooper looked the gift horse straight in the mouth. He

said he would accept a year's financing—not three months'—if no strings were attached. Dr. Gamble finally agreed and in March 1937 sent a check for $2250 as a starter.

When the plan was launched there were only three birth-control clinics in North Carolina. By the end of 1938 the state had created 56. It now has 62; only New York has more. Strategically located in 58 of the state's 100 counties, they provide a state-wide coverage. The counties participating had 50,565 births in 1937—a figure topped by only 18 entire states.

The spread of the program has gone ahead quietly, without ballyhoo. Dr. Cooper has never tried to force birth control upon any county. The Gamble funds were used to buy contraceptive supplies and to provide a consultant nurse, Miss Roberta Pratt, who had been in charge of Bocagrande work. The state made these supplies and services available to any county health officer who wished to set up a contraceptive clinic as a part of his existing county health unit. County health officers were asked to get the opinions of local physicians—individually rather than at meetings, which might lead to unmanageable debates. Particular caution was used to prevent public controversy.

Each health officer is free to run his clinic as he wishes, to use the simple technique which the state advises for the poor or to lean more heavily upon surer but more expensive individual examinations. In some counties the nurses carry information into the homes, while in others they bring the mothers to the county health office. Some clinics have secured appropriations for materials from the county commissioners; others depend upon donations from individuals and socially-minded organizations. In Winston-Salem, where young socialites have assumed financial responsibility, a pamphlet giving dates for clinics goes out with every birth certificate. Some counties make their funds go further by getting patients to pay anything they can —even as little as ten cents.

At the end of the second year of state contraception the clinics had provided instruction and materials for 2000 women. The present year may see this figure doubled. Of course, that is only scratching the surface; one nurse told me her center alone would have 1200 clients if funds were available. But Dr. Cooper's idea has been to build firmly and then expand. The clients are women who cannot pay for medical care, a fact certified in each case by a welfare officer or a private physician. And to these women pregnancy would be actually, or nearly, a tragedy.

Already the state has files of letters which comprise a social Magna Charta. Naïve, honest letters of thanks or pleas for information, most of them written in pencil on the rough, ruled paper sold in country stores. Chief beneficiaries of state birth control are the mountaineers, the textile and tobacco workers in the industrial section, and Negro tenant farmers.

In a cotton county, 50 Negro women appeared at the clinic the morning it was opened. One woman of 39, married 19 years, had ten children; her husband didn't make enough to support the family, so she took in laundry.

A cotton farm tenant's wife, 25, married at 16, had six children in seven years, all delivered by midwives in a small, unscreened shack. Water supply, questionable; sanitary facilities, none. After her fifth pregnancy this woman asked, "Isn't there something you can do?" And the county nurse—this was before state contraception—had to admit there wasn't. A few months later the nurse found the woman in tears —she was pregnant again; but at about that time the county set up a birth-control clinic, and there have been no more after the sixth child.

Here are my notes on one case in an industrial town of the Piedmont: Husband 40, wife 38. Husband has heart trouble—unable to work. In 1936, receiving fuel, groceries, and clothing from local charity; the wife had her eleventh child. At the time, she had factory work at seven dollars a week, but was laid off just before New Year, 1937; that year received food orders, did piecework at home along with children, and had twelfth child. Continued to receive cash, shoes for children, and then had thirteenth child, a seven-months baby who died after one month.

Most of the Piedmont cases are whites who came to the mills from the red-clay farms. In one cotton-mill center is a mother, 41, married 24 years, who has had 11 children;

when she came to the clinic her husband had lost his job and she was unable to get work. A few houses away is a woman who in 16 years of married life has had 10 children; her husband was on WPA when a welfare officer sent her to the clinic. There are no statistics to show what percentage of patients are on relief, but I rarely turned over three cards without seeing one marked WPA.

In the mountains, the nurses start on their rounds at 8:30 each morning, pushing back into the hills and hollows and up the forks of the creeks to cabins where human life has never been highly valued. But the women now are eager for birth-control information. A nurse went to a schoolhouse to give instructions on making a sickbed; she found 15 women there in bonnets and faded calico dresses—all wanting to know about birth control.

In one mountain section, I saw a sick husband and an overworked wife huddled with their five little children in two filthy rooms with but two beds; and a 29-year-old mother, married 12 years, with nine children, who was in such physical and mental condition that another pregnancy would endanger not only her life but the lives of her children.

Stimulated by the state program, two of North Carolina's largest manufacturing plants have set up birth-control clinics for their employes. One placed printed slips in pay envelopes telling employes that the firm's physicians and nurses might be consulted. The program has also had its effect on private physicians, previously fearful of being caught on some legal technicality; and druggists report that more and more women are bringing in prescriptions from their family doctors. Important research, using county clinic cases, is being conducted at Duke University.

South Carolina, after watching its sister state for two years, recently launched a parallel program. Georgia, spurred by resolutions of both its State Medical Society and its Conference of Social Work, is about to make a decision. Arizona has shown lively interest. National welfare and public-health organizations are asking for information and sending observers to North Carolina. Inquiries pour in from all quarters. Important as are the results of the program to North Carolina itself, the greatest importance may be the example set for others to follow.

Table Talk

BANANA POWDER, reducing the 80% water content of the fruit to 5%, has been approved by government specialists. A taste test shows that it appeals to many persons who do not eat bananas. The cost and difficulties involved in shipping bananas, which are very sensitive to weather, may be eliminated by processing them in tropical countries where they are grown.—U. S. News

The Faith That Is America

Condensed from The North American Review

WENDELL L. WILLKIE

FOR CENTURIES my ancestors lived in Central Europe. Some of them were peasants, some were artisans, others were landed proprietors; but all of them through those centuries had been restricted in their opportunities to the group in which they were born, and no one of them had ever known the true meaning of liberty. Those who did not observe the restrictions under which they were forced to live got into trouble: one had to flee his native land because he adopted the religion of his choice; another was ostracized because he believed in the principles of the French Revolution; and still another was jailed for expressing his own opinions. In 1848, my father and my grandparents came to America to escape this repression of individual liberties.

They were led to these shores, as were millions before and after them, by a special reputation that the United States has had among nations. This reputation is founded upon one simple fact: in the United States the plain man has always had a chance.

My father and mother were the first generation in their families to grow up in America. My mother became a lawyer. My father was also a lawyer. Of course, in Europe my mother would have found it impossible to practice a profession; and my father would have found it difficult to get out of the groove worn by his ancestors. Furthermore, it would have been utterly impossible for them to have given their six children the education which we received in America. We went to high school and college.

And with schooling finished, there were no doors closed to their children just because they came from a plain family in a small town. No class distinction, no law interfered with their effort to earn a living in the occupation of their choice, or to express their opinions as they pleased.

In all the long history of their family, these six children were the first to know, from the time they were born, the blessings of freedom. I don't want them to be the last.

This family record is the record of any number of American families. For us the value of freedom has had a practical demonstration. Free-

492

dom means for us not only a theoretical ideal, but definite practical rights. Freedom means, for example, that if you run a store, you can sell your products to anybody without a government official telling you what the prices must be; if you are a professor in a university, you don't have to alter science or delete history as a bureaucrat prescribes. If you own a newspaper you don't limit your editorial opinions to what an official censor approves. If you are a laborer, you can leave your job when you feel like it for any other job you prefer; you and your fellow workers can bargain collectively concerning the conditions of your work. If you think taxes are too high, you can vote against those officials you think responsible. And there is no limitation upon your inherent American right to criticize anybody, anywhere, at any time.

These are practical applications of this thing called freedom. In this country we take them for granted —perhaps too much for granted. But in more than half the world freedom does not exist. The present conflict in Europe is perilous to this freedom because in a modern war people destroy the very things they say they are fighting for. It is because we wish to preserve our free democratic system that we must remain at peace. But we cannot remain *carelessly* at peace. If the price of democracy in ordinary times is eternal vigilance, in a war period that vigilance must be doubled.

We must be careful that, under the guise of "emergency," the powers of government are not so extended as to impair the vitality of free enterprise and choke off free expression of thought. Already we hear of the need for the government to control prices, to license American business, to regiment American employes and employers, to censor the radio. In a critical time there is always a temptation to surrender the responsibilities of a free citizen, to say to the government: "During this emergency, you take charge. You tell us what to do, what to think."

If we should yield to this temptation, the end of our free democratic system might come as readily in peace as in war. Once these responsibilities of citizenship are given up, they are not readily returned. Government, in its practical working, consists only of aggregations of men; and men, having tasted power, do not easily surrender power. We must not be misled because suggested restrictions are for humanitarian purposes, for, as ex-Justice Louis D. Brandeis recently said:

Experience should teach us to be more on our guard to protect our liberties when the government's purposes are beneficent. . . . The greatest dangers to liberty lurk in insidious encroachment by men of zeal, well-meaning but without understanding.

The war has not changed the grave domestic questions confronting America; it has just temporarily diverted our minds from them. For ten years we have been haunted by our unemployment problem. Yet its solution has been in our hands for some time. During the depression decade, American industry accumulated an enormous deficiency in plants and modern machinery. To remedy this, industry will need even more than the present number of unemployed. Industry will also need a great deal of additional capital, and there should be no difficulty in getting this, as soon as the millions of American investors are reassured as to the future of free private enterprise.

The lack of confidence within industry is partly a result of industry's own defects in the period of overexpansion which ended in 1929. But since then we have had several years of reform; and some of these reforms have gone so far as to impair the efficiency and morale of business. In promoting recovery, the chief emphasis has been placed upon what the *government* should do: we have had colossal expenditures for "priming the pump," and a colossal tax program to pay for these expenditures. Here is just the point where our free democracy is threatened. We are not in immediate danger of losing our freedom of speech, or of press, or of worship. The greatest threat to the American system today comes from the effort to restrict free competitive enterprise. And such enterprise alone can make economic recovery possible.

We have been told that the frontiers are gone, that our established industries are slowing down, and that there is little to be expected in the way of new inventions. We have even been informed that the very basis of the American

dream is no longer true: that the plain man no longer has much of a chance. But such a philosophy is as false as it is cowardly. True, we no longer have new geographical frontiers; but other frontiers remain for searching and adventurous minds. Our people, comprising only seven percent of the world's population, still control more than 45 percent of the world's wealth. And we enjoy the highest real wages, the shortest working hours, and the greatest percentage of home ownership on earth.

The great days of America are by no means done. We have only touched the border of our achievement. If I did not believe this, I would not believe in America. Because that faith *is* America.

So my creed, if I were asked to define it, would run something like this:

I believe in America because in it we are free—free to choose our government, to speak our minds, to observe our different religions;

Because we are generous with our freedom—we share our rights with those who disagree with us;

Because we hate no people and covet no people's land;

Because we are blessed with a natural and varied abundance;

Because we set no limit to a man's achievement: in mine, factory, field, or service in business or the arts, an able man, regardless of class or creed, can realize his ambition;

Because we have great dreams—and because we have the opportunity to make those dreams come true.

When the German Fleet Sank Itself

Condensed from This Week Magazine

Tom Mahoney

FOOTNOTE TO HISTORY

WHEN, after the Armistice, the German fleet of about 70 warships lay interned at Scapa Flow while their fate was debated by the Allies at Versailles, Rear Admiral von Reuter laid plans to sink the ships rather than surrender them. As a first step, the crews were reduced to a handful of loyal officers and men. On June 17, 1919, he dispatched to his officers this secret order: *Make preparations for the immediate scuttling of all ships (1) if the British attempt to seize them by surprise, or (2) upon receipt of the code signal "Paragraph 11—Acknowledge!"*

On June 21, British Admiral Sydney Freemantle took his fleet to sea for torpedo practice. Only seven trawlers and two destroyers were left to guard the German fleet that morning when Von Reuter received news that the Versailles conference had rejected Germany's proposals. "Make the signal!" he ordered his chief of staff. "Paragraph 11—Acknowledge!"

Bright pennants fluttered in the sunshine, and immediately on each of the ships, officers opened sea cocks and began to abandon ship. Unaware of what was taking place, a party of school children watched the activity from a nearby excursion steamer. A London artist on a guarding trawler was the first to give the alarm. It was almost noon when he noticed that the *Kaiser Friedrich der Grosse*, which he was sketching, was settling in the water, her boats were being lowered, and she had raised a "ready for battle" pennant.

Frantic radio messages were flashed to the British fleet. Men on the trawlers attempted to make the unwilling German sailors go back and close the valves. Rifle shots rang out; 13 Germans were killed and a score wounded. The British managed to beach several destroyers but could do little with the big ships.

Shortly after midday the *Kaiser Friedrich der Grosse* turned over and sank; 15 more had gone by the time Admiral Freemantle's ships returned at 2:30. The British, working feverishly, could beach only four of the remaining ships. By the end of the afternoon the German High Seas Fleet, built at a cost of $300,000,000 to rival England's, lay at the bottom of Scapa Flow.

In 1924 a London scrap-metal firm began to salvage the German vessels. By 1926 all the destroyers had been raised. Year by year bigger boats have been brought up, and now only eight great ships remain at the bottom.

Scrap from the German fleet went into the *Queen Mary* and her sister ship, to be christened *Queen Elizabeth*. Much also has gone into Britain's rearmament program, and before the home demand became so great, some metal was even shipped to Germany.

Copyright 1939, New York Tribune, Inc., 230 W. 41 St., N. Y. C.

(This Week Magazine, June 4, '39)